THE LAW
OF WORK

THE LAW
OF WORK

ROSEMARY OWENS AND JOELLEN RILEY

OXFORD
UNIVERSITY PRESS

OXFORD
UNIVERSITY PRESS

253 Normanby Road, South Melbourne, Victoria 3205, Australia

Oxford University Press is a department of the University of Oxford. It furthers the University's objective of excellence in research, scholarship, and education by publishing worldwide in

Oxford New York

Auckland CapeTown Dar es Salaam Hong Kong Karachi
Kuala Lumpur Madrid Melbourne Mexico City Nairobi
New Delhi Shanghai Taipei Toronto

With offices in

Argentina Austria Brazil Chile Czech Republic France Greece
Guatemala Hungary Italy Japan Poland Portugal Singapore
South Korea Switzerland Thailand Turkey Ukraine Vietnam

OXFORD is a trade mark of Oxford University Press in the UK
and in certain other countries

National Library of Australia Cataloguing-in-Publication data:

Owens, Rosemary J.
The law of work.

Bibliography.
Includes index.
For tertiary students.
ISBN 9780195512229.

ISBN 0 19 551222 7.

1. Labor laws and legislation—Textbooks. I. Riley, Joellen, 1957–. II. Title.

344.01

Edited by Valina Rainer and Tony Rainer

Text design by Leigh Ashforth @ watershed art & design

Cover design by Linda Hamley

Typeset by Leigh Ashforth @ watershed art & design

Proofread by Angela Damis

Indexed by Puddingburn Publishing Services

Printed in Hong Kong by Sheck Wah Tong Printing Press Ltd.

Contents

Preface

In writing *The Law of Work* we set out to examine the ways in which the world of work is changing under the pressures of globalisation, and the role law plays both in constructing and responding to those changes.

Ever since the early 1990s, a fundamental shift in the nature of the law regulating work has been observable in Australia. The unique system of industrial awards, the product of a centralised system of conciliation and arbitration, has progressively been abandoned in favour of greater regulation through enterprise bargaining. An important dimension of this development has been the individualisation of bargaining, which has called into question traditional assumptions regarding the collective nature of the participants within the regulatory scheme and, indeed, of the scheme itself. Thus there has been a conceptual movement in labour and industrial relations regulation away from a public law focus to one based on contractual principles more readily identifiable with private law notions. Commensurate with this, recent common law cases pertaining to work relations have demonstrated a growing judicial appreciation of the significance of the changing world of work. At the same time, there has been an emphasis on work rights as human rights, and there has been a growing understanding of the importance of the discrimination statutes to the world of work.

In this context, *The Law of Work* aims to refocus the subject matter of the Australian law of workplace relations according to some fundamental concepts and principles. By identifying its subject matter as *The Law of Work*, we intended to signal that the book's concerns are somewhat broader than those traditionally encompassed in employment, labour and industrial relations law. The major themes of contract and cooperation, equality and diversity, and freedom of association provide the foundation for the coherent analysis and critique of the cases and legislation that together comprise the law of work.

Our objective has been to mainstream some of the issues that have conventionally been treated as peripheral, such as those at the interface of work/family/life, and in the process to rethink the nature and importance of the traditional subject matter. This book also reflects our conviction that context is of critical importance to an understanding of the law. Our hope is that this book will provide a firm foundation for a more principled understanding of the law governing work.

The Law of Work has been a long time in gestation. As our project was nearing completion in its first phase, the Howard Liberal Coalition Government indicated its intention to use its historic majority in both Houses of Parliament to rewrite the laws governing workplace relations in Australia. The stated policy aim was to provide

Australia with a regulatory system that would secure Australia's strong position in the new economy. In consultation with OUP, we decided it was prudent to refrain from publication at that point in time, and to revise the manuscript after the passage of the new legislation.

The *Workplace Relations Amendment (Work Choices) Act 1996* (Cth) received Royal Assent in mid-December 2005, and at that time we set about revising the manuscript to incorporate an account of the new regime. This decision changed in a number of ways the nature of the project as originally planned. Invariably it meant, for instance, that the book incorporated more matters of legislative detail than had been envisaged at the outset. Nonetheless, such was the magnitude of the changes, it seemed to us that there was a real need carefully to examine this new regime while placing it in the wider context of the issues relating to law and work that we had already identified as fundamental in the global era. We hope that in this process we have not compromised our initial goals.

Of course, there is no end point to the development of the law. There is as yet little case law explicating the new system. Even as we were writing in the first half of 2006 the constitutionality of the *Work Choices* legislation was challenged before the High Court. Argument in the case was heard in early May 2006, and a decision is now expected towards the end of 2006. Further legislative developments are also in the wings. The Employment, Workplace Relations and Education Legislation Committee of the Senate has just completed its inquiry into the *Independent Contractors Bill 2006* (Cth), which is currently before the Parliament. We have made every effort to ensure that the law is correctly stated as at 30 June 2006, and we have noted more recent developments at proof stage.

This book would not have been possible without the support of a number of people. The initial ideas for a project that focused on some of the fundamental legal issues in the changing world of work were developed in conversations between Rosemary Owens and Therese MacDermott, who at the time was a member of the Faculty of Law at the University of Sydney. Shortly afterwards Therese withdrew from this project and temporarily left academic life in order to better balance the demands of a very young family. We acknowledge with gratitude Therese's vision in conceiving this project and the role she played in early discussions about its direction. Although in the detail and emphasis much about the project has changed since those first conversations, the overarching themes identified at the outset remain.

We are fortunate to be part of a vibrant community of academic labour lawyers both in Australia and around the world. Were it not for the fine scholarly work of our many colleagues, this book would never have been possible.

In Australia, the intellectual leadership of Ron McCallum and Richard Mitchell has been inspirational and particularly important to both of us, and we are deeply grateful to them. We also thank Lee Adams, Chris Arup, Anna Chapman, Sean Cooney, Colin Fenwick, Bill Ford, Anthony Forsyth, John Howe, Richard Johstone, Shae McCrystal, Jill Murray, Anthony O'Donnell, Marilyn Pittard, Belinda Smith, Andrew Stewart, Joo-Cheong Tham and Karen Wheelwright for their support through intellectual companionship and a constant desire to challenge the boundaries of our discipline. We also acknowledge Breen Creighton, whose academic writings first made us aware of the significance of situating the law of work in Australia in the international context. We were saddened when one of our colleagues, Phillipa Weeks, passed away shortly after we finished writing this book. We are indebted to her for many things, especially her words of encouragement and her extensive comments on an earlier draft of this work.

A number of other academic and professional colleagues in Australia have enriched our understanding of the law of work—Ron Baragry, Sandra Dann, Kaz Eaton, Suzanne Franzway, Barbara Pocock, Lance Wright (President of the Industrial Relations Commission of New South Wales), and many members of the professional staff at Harmers Workplace Lawyers.

Beyond these shores, the opportunity to participate in INTELL, a network of labour law scholars committed to developing a transformative labour law that delivers fairness and justice has led us to a greater appreciation of the impacts of globalisation on the law of work. We are particularly grateful to the INTELL co-secretaries, Joanne Conaghan, Michael Fischl, Karl Klare, Kerry Rittich and Lucy Williams, for their role in facilitating a deeper scholarly engagement amongst academic labour lawyers and practitioners at the global level. Our thanks too, to Lizzie Barmes, Keith Ewing, Judy Fudge, Harry Glasbeek, Claire Kilpatrick and Katherine Stone.

Our respective institutions and our colleagues have supported our work in a variety of ways. We thank especially Adrian Bradbrook, Judith Gardam, Kathleen McEvoy, Ngaire Naffine and John Williams at the University of Adelaide, and, at the University of Sydney, Mary Crock, Jennifer Hill, Patrick Parkinson, Elisabeth Peden, David Rolph and Brett Williams. We would also like to acknowledge our many students, both undergraduate and graduate, for their contributions to our thinking about law and work. Their questions and responses to ideas have been provocative, challenging, and constantly invigorating. At different times during this project some have assisted further with their excellent research skills and we thank Alexander Giudice, Wing Hsieh, Alison Lloyd-Wright, Michael Rawling, Troy Sarina, Shane Stewart and David Sulan for that.

The staff at Oxford University Press embraced this project enthusiastically from the outset. Katie Ridsdale has been a constant source of encouragement throughout, and in bringing the project to fruition we would also like to thank Tim Campbell and the editorial team.

Last, we thank our families—Lew, Nicholas, Alex, Cecilia Owens and Peter Landers, and John Munton, Alexandra and Philippa—for their immense patience when our absorption in this project entailed a lack of balance between work and family life, for their ongoing moral support for our work, and for their unconditional love.

Rosemary Owens   Joellen Riley

Law School   Faculty of Law

The University of Adelaide University of New South Wales

31 August 2006

Acknowledgment

Some of the material contained in Chapter 7 is a development of an article by Rosemary Owens called 'Working Precariously: The Safety Net after Work Choices', previously published in the *Australian Journal of Labour Law*, 2006, volume 19, number 2, by LexisNexis Butterworths, Australia.

Table of Cases

Table of Statutes

AUSTRALIAN CAPITAL TERRITORY

NORTHERN TERRITORY

QUEENSLAND

SOUTH AUSTRALIA

TASMANIA

VICTORIA

NEW ZEALAND

UNITED KINGDOM

part

Work, Law and Context

The Law of Work

Work, context and law

The significance of work

In contemporary society, work has assumed an extraordinary significance. It is largely through work that we become who we are: work is central to personhood, to identity. And because work is intricately entwined in the creation of our sense of self, it has an infinitely complex meaning for us as human beings. Work is intimately linked with human dignity. Work is the primary means by which most people secure their own livelihood and very often that of their families too. The income derived from their work provides access to food, shelter and the other goods and services necessary for the sustenance and enjoyment of life. However, work also often provides much more than the satisfaction of the material fundamentals of life. Human beings commonly invest in their work much of the purpose and meaning of their lives. At work people grow in a very personal way by expressing themselves, developing new skills, gaining new knowledge and contributing to their community. Work is practical and productive; it involves doing, making things, imparting information and knowledge, and serving others. Through work human beings cooperate and connect with others. The social networks established through work often extend beyond it. Indeed, because the social status of individuals is frequently determined very largely by the work they do, work tends to mediate all social relations.

Work also plays a critical role in the very constitution of society: the interdependence of people through work relations is one of the most important structural bonds of any community. The significance of work is thus much larger than simply its meaning to the individual person. Through their productive labour individuals contribute economically, socially and culturally to make their communities. Without the labour of workers, enterprises could not grow to become part of an expanding economy and contribute to the wider material well-being of the community. This productive labour is also sustained by reproductive labour: the unpaid work that produces, maintains,

3

and enables others to labour productively. Through their work, individuals in a community care for one another. Through work, communities do more than survive; they can flourish.

The global context

There are enormous differences in the meaning and significance of work both across communities at various times and within any given community over time.[1] The meaning of work is always dependent on the wider context, be it political, social, economic or cultural, in which it is performed.

We now inhabit a global era. The industrial era is rapidly becoming a thing of the past. The context within which work takes on meaning has thus changed dramatically in recent times and the pace of that change is unlikely to abate for some time. The emergence of this global era has been facilitated by computer-based and digital technologies, which have revolutionised communications and the provision of information, methods of production, and indeed most aspects of daily life.[2] These technologies have simultaneously shrunk the world and destroyed many of its pre-existing internal borders. 'Boundary-less' has become a commonly used epithet to connote this principal change in many of the features of life in this 'new' era.[3] Technological developments make real the possibility of a global community. In the face of these developments the 'old' world is rendered impotent to resist it. Isolation from the 'new' world of the global era really is not an option. However, how we go about creating and ordering our human relations, including our work relations, in this global era is.

The global era is itself most frequently characterised or referred to simply as the 'new economy'. The use of the terminology 'new economy' usually does more than refer to the contrast between the 'old' national economies, which were 'closed' or surrounded and protected by customs barriers and featured strong control of currency and financial regimes, and the 'new' global or 'open' marketplace. When used as a synonym for 'globalisation', this expression 'new economy' encapsulates the dominance of the marketplace in the global era. The 'new economy' is bolstered by the new technologies, which carry its message in the form of insistent and ever-present mass advertising across the globe, altering perceptions of need and material satisfaction and influencing economic behaviour: the global society is a consumer society. The marketplace and its messages often can appear to be all-encompassing and indeed somewhat overwhelming. However, the adoption of the expression 'new economy' also carries with it the promise of a better future. Its claim is that the economic context is of first importance and is the medium through which will be delivered a wider range of social benefits. The rhetoric of the 'new economy' has thus come to incorporate theoretical and normative dimensions that have not only dominated understandings of globalisation but have forged its form and direction.[4] It is

---

1   See R Castel 'Work and Usefulness to the World' (1996) 135 *Int Lab Rev* 615; D Méda 'New Perspectives on Work as Value' (1996) 135 *Int Lab Rev* 633; and C Fox *Working Australia* (1999).

2   See further Chapter 2.

3   See K Stone *From Widgets to Digits, Employment Regulation for the Changing Workplace* (2004).

4   J Conaghan 'Labour Law and The "New Economy" Discourse' (2003) 16 *AJLL* 1.

thus important to remind ourselves that there are no immutable or natural features to the process of globalisation or the 'new economy' and just as much as any other phenomenon it is also subject to contest, challenge, change and development.

No less dramatic than these changes directly associated with the advent of the global era have been some of the other social developments that have occurred over recent decades. Many of the once familiar norms governing social arrangements now appear to be disintegrating. The nuclear family, comprising heterosexual married parents with children, is giving way to a diversity of familial arrangements. As different types of living arrangements proliferate, the family is being redefined: adults without children, single parent families, grandparents caring for children, gay and lesbian couple families, heterosexual couples and others living in various types of relations based on friendship, all challenge traditional understandings of the family. And for many people, perhaps especially those living alone or belonging to a traditional but geographically dispersed family, friendship rather than family is the basis of their closest and most important social relations.

Further significant demographic changes are underway. As 'baby boomers' grow old and as fertility rates decline, the population as a whole is ageing at an unprecedented rate issuing the prospect of all sorts of new pressures on aspirations for economic growth and the use of social resources.[5] The transformation in the social role of women over the last half century—in turn influenced by such things as access to effective contraception, the more ready availability of no-fault divorce, better educational opportunities, and changing social attitudes—has also been important. All these social changes are part of the context that informs our understandings of the world of work.

A new world of work

The transition from the industrial era to the global era has brought massive changes to the world of work. The removal of protective tariff barriers entailed by the opening of national economies to wider markets, the uncertainties attendant upon global competition, and the pressures on enterprises to meet these challenges have brought increased precariousness to many people's working lives and unsettled the organisational patterns around which work relations were structured in the past.

Productivity and flexibility have become the new watchwords of industry as businesses seek to adapt successfully to the new global world they now inhabit. Many enterprises have submitted themselves to a more or less constant process of restructuring, often in opposing directions with large organisations disintegrating and smaller organisations integrating. These organisational consequences for enterprises have presented a profound, normative challenge to the way in which work is organised.[6] Mass collections of workers, employed in a tightly integrated process of production for a single enterprise, are becoming more and more a thing of the past. Trade union membership has declined. Work issues are less often defined in

---

5   Productivity Commission *Economic Implications of an Ageing Australia* (2005).
6   H Collins 'Independent Contractors and the Challenge of Vertical Disintegration to Employment Protection Laws' (1990) 10 *OJLS* 353.

terms of their collective dimensions but are addressed from the perspective of the individual.

The standards that so often governed daily work in the factory are gradually being eroded and taking on new forms. For instance, the working-time norms of the old industrial era, which set the length of the working day at around eight hours, confined a working week between Monday and Friday, and assumed a 'lifetime' of continuous work with the same employer from the end of schooldays until retirement in old age, have all but been destroyed and are now replaced by a myriad of new and different working-time patterns. Of course those old working-time standards could always have been criticised as inaccurate because they only applied in a very partial way: after all, they were derived from a very gendered conception of work and traditional working-time patterns of women's work were quite different. But the impact of the global era on working-time norms seems to be that, for more workers than ever before, their time is 'spent' at work, leaving them little opportunity to 'pass' time, little 'time to dream'.[7] Disappearing too are the values of the workplace inculcated by the old world of more secure lifetime employment. Loyalty, reliability, and commitment are now replaced by independence, flexibility and autonomy, and the effects of this are carried over into personal lives.[8] In the global era, working life has seemingly become far more precarious and fragmented, threatening the realisation of many of the traditional aspirations linked to work.[9]

In this new world of work, the standard worker of the industrial era—the male breadwinner, with a dependent spouse and children, who worked 'fulltime', for a 'lifetime' with the same enterprise—is an endangered species. The new worker in the global era is just as likely to be a casual, a part-timer, an agency worker, a home-based worker. More and more workers are cast as independent entrepreneurs, 'enterprise workers'. They very often work through and assume the legal form of an incorporated business and yet all too often the reality of their work relations appears to be little different from that of traditional dependent labourers. The forms of work that could have been labelled 'atypical' or 'non-standard' in the industrial era are rapidly becoming the norm in the global era.

The structure of the labour market has also changed dramatically in recent years, especially as a result of the increased participation of women. This has had a profound impact on the structuring of what has traditionally been seen as women's work in the private or domestic sphere, especially as the shrinking state has implemented policies of de-institutionalising care of the aged, sick and disabled. While some of women's traditional work has been reabsorbed into the market—that is, many people have 'outsourced' the cooking, the cleaning, and care work to the market—the bigger issues arising from the conflict between work and family and care remain largely unresolved but in the foreground in a way not evident in the industrial era.[10]

---

7   J Conaghan 'Time to Dream? Flexibility, Families, and the Regulation of Working Time' in J Fudge and R Owens (eds) *Precarious Work, Women, and the New Economy: The Challenge to Legal Norms* (2006).

8   R Sennett *The Corrosion of Character: The Personal Consequences of Work in the New Capitalism* (1998).

9   See I Watson et al *Fragmented Futures: New Challenges in Working Life* (2003); and Fudge and Owens (eds), above n 7.

10   B Pocock *The Work/Life Collision* (2003).

It is, of course, simplistic to paint any picture of the real world, including the world of work, as if it can be neatly divided into different categories or eras and to suggest that the transitions between them are sharp and precisely defined and linear or even that the differences between them are absolute. The previous industrial era spanned more than two centuries and during that time the development of accurate methods of measuring time, the invention of electricity, the transport revolution in railways and shipping, and improvements in heavy machinery were some of the technological developments upon which the large manufacturing factories that characterised the era were founded. This industrial era differed in many senses from earlier agrarian times with more 'domestic' work arrangements. But that is not to say that primary industries, whether based on the farm or the mine, did not continue to be of economic and social importance. Likewise service industries, including education, finance and banking and clerical and office work, increased in importance during the industrial era. Workers in the industrial era no doubt were in reality also a diverse lot. They were not only factory workers but also agricultural labourers, domestic workers, office workers, members of the professions and much more besides. Nor were they all were male breadwinners. The real world is always infinitely more complex than anything that can be captured through broad classifications. However, broad classifications (and the assumptions inevitably implicit in those classifications) are analytical tools that form an inevitable part of the process of any human interactions with the world, including with economy, society and work. Of those human interactions, few are more important than law.

Law and work in context

Law has always played, and continues to play, a major role in constituting work as a primary signifier of a person's identity and their place in a community. Law does not simply explain the economic, social or cultural meaning of work, it also produces it. Law is a political, social, cultural and economic actor. This is usually obvious and well understood in the case of statutes, which are a direct expression or embodiment of government policies. But not always so readily acknowledged are the normative assumptions about work, work relations and their place in the world that are imbedded within statutes and other legal and regulatory forms such as international conventions, principles, the common law, industrial awards and agreements and employer policies. The law of work is not, therefore, simply the application of a set of rules, principles or norms to an already existing world of work. Rather, law also produces and gives shape to the world in which it operates, which includes work and work relations. In turn, law is influenced and shaped by the world it inhabits, including work and work relations.

The law of work in the global era

Traditionally scholars in Australia have referred to the regulation of work relations as employment, labour and industrial relations law. This subject area did not always pretend to be absolutely comprehensive, and it was always quite common for reference to the law regulating workers' compensation and rehabilitation and the wider subject of occupational health and safety law to be dealt with quite separately. Employment law was often regarded as the law governing the individual relationship of employees and employers, while labour and industrial relations law addressed the aspects of the law relating to the regulation of labour collectively. However, there was no rigid adherence to these divisions.[11]

How is this field of law faring in the new global era? As noted above, many aspects of the world of work that characterised the industrial era—large manufacturing factories, fulltime ongoing employment, large groups of workers with strong trade union representation—are now disappearing, along with the traditional structure of families and the pre-eminence of the nation state. Yet these formed part of the fabric from which were derived assumptions that underpinned the 'old' employment, labour and industrial relations law. Their disappearance could be expected to challenge the old law.[12] Certainly, law makers have seen the need to reshape the law governing work as they anticipate globalisation.

The changing law of work in Australia

In Australia the imperative for reform of labour law in the face of the challenges posed by globalisation has perhaps been perceived to be more urgent than it has elsewhere. In large part this is because the 'new economy' purports to recognise only a very limited role for the state, and in Australia the state, especially through the industrial tribunals set up more than a century ago, has played a much more obvious role in regulating work than it has in most other comparable jurisdictions.

The early federal response (from the Hancock Committee[13] set up in the early 1980s) to the challenges globalisation posed to Australia's system of labour law essentially endorsed, albeit with some suggestions for minor modifications, the maintenance of the conciliation and arbitration system, which had been the mainstay of Australian labour regulation in the industrial era. However, the impetus for more thorough change was not resisted for long at the political level. From the late 1980s, the law governing work in Australia was harnessed to the cause of the new economy.

Over the course of the next two decades, successive federal governments embraced a neo-liberal reform agenda more strongly and transformed Australia's traditional labour law. A stronger individual rights focus was adopted early on in an effort to implement international labour conventions and simultaneously wrest from the States more of the

---

11 See the first editions of some of the main Australian texts: EI Sykes and HJ Glasbeek *Labour Law in Australia* (1972); JJ Macken, G McGarry and C Sappideen *The Law of Employment* (1978); WB Creighton, WJ Ford and RJ Mitchell *Labour Law: Materials and Commentary* (1983); RC McCallum, MJ Pittard and CK Smith *Australian Labour Law: Cases and Materials* (1990); and B Creighton and A Stewart *Labour Law: An Introduction* (1990).

12 RJ Owens 'The Traditional Labour Law Framework: A Critical Evaluation' in R Mitchell (ed) *Redefining Labour Law: New Perspectives on Teaching and Research* (1995), 3–12; and J Fudge and R Owens 'Precarious Work, Women, and the New Economy: The Challenge to Legal Norms' in Fudge and Owens (eds), above n 7.

13 See K Hancock *Report of the Committee of Review on Australian Industrial Relations Law and Systems* vols 1–3 (1985).

terrain of work relations. For the most part, the federal legislative developments gradually implementing a new policy approach to labour law were ostensibly 'de-regulatory' in character. They emphasised bargaining at the workplace rather than industry-based standards established through conciliation and arbitration under the auspices of state tribunals; and they aimed to diminish the influence of trade unions and the values of collectivism, and placed greater emphasis on the individualisation of work relations.[14] Thus there was a fundamental shift in the nature of legal regulation of work in Australia. Many changes, such as the individualisation of labour relations, reflected trends elsewhere.[15] These changes also represented a conceptual movement in the regulation of work away from public law and towards private law based on contractual principles. At the same time, other statutory regimes such as those governing discrimination in the workplace, which when first established remained quite separate from labour and industrial regimes, became in many respects more strongly integrated within them.

At the federal level, the enactment of the *Workplace Relations Amendment (Work Choices) Act 2005* (Cth) (*Work Choices Act*) represents the latest of these regulatory responses to globalisation. This legislation effects the most thorough change in the law governing work relations in Australia in over one hundred years. It has been widely remarked that law, of all the disciplines, is likely to be the most profoundly disrupted by the phenomenon of globalisation, because imbedded deep within law are a set of assumptions relating to the existence, structure and nature of the nation state, and the nation state is itself threatened by globalisation.[16] But the *Workplace Relations Act 1996* (Cth) (*Workplace Relations Act*), as amended by the *Work Choices Act*, and the accompanying *Workplace Relations Regulations 2006* (Cth) together are a salutary reminder that in many senses globalisation and the new economy still depend on the nation state. Ironically, the 'freeing up' of the Australian labour market is achieved through very detailed provisions that seek to govern every aspect of work relations including the bargaining of workplace participants. Nonetheless, this legislation encapsulates an agenda that is clearly a very significant part of shifting Australia out of the old industrial era and into the new global era.

The end of labour law?

The *Workplace Relations Act* and the regime it establishes to regulate work look very different from that which operated a century ago. This legislation seeks to attain very different purposes from the old labour law and it is operating in a very different world. The enactment of the *Work Choices Act* provoked widespread and passionate debates and discussion, especially about its effects on workers, their standards of living and

---

14 The transformation of Australian labour law from the industrial to the global era is dealt with in Chapter 3.

15 S Deery and R Mitchell (eds) *Employment Relations: Individualisation and Union Exclusion—An International Study* (1999).

16 See H Arthurs 'Labour Law without the State' (1996) 46 *UTLJ* 1; H Arthurs 'Reinventing Labour Law for the Global Economy: The Benjamin Aaron Lecture' (2001) 22 *Berkley Comp JLEL* 271; and R Owens 'The Future of the Law of Work' (2002) 23 *Adel LR* 345, 347.

indeed the quality of their lives. Most other industrialised market economies have their own version of these conversations.

Little wonder then that it has been said for some time now that labour law is at the cross-roads or, worse still, that it is a discipline in crisis and one whose future might well be in doubt.[17] Indeed, the changes that are occurring in the world of work and law have provoked a widespread recognition that the old labour law paradigm is under pressure and that a new response is needed. The questions that are now being asked are whether the old legal framework for understanding work can adjust to meet the challenges posed by globalisation and the recent developments in economy and society, and in turn whether those challenges and that world are at the same time constructed by law and so could be reconfigured through law.

Prior to the enactment of the *Work Choices* amendments, State governments in Australia had begun legislative reform in the face of the pressures of globalisation and the changing regulatory agenda at the federal level. Several States conducted major reviews of their own industrial relations systems. These reviews were often intent on securing the protection of those workers who are likely to be the most vulnerable in the new economy, while simultaneously recognising the imperatives of developing their economies to be productive, competitive, efficient and flexible for the future.[18] The reviews also drew attention to the policy tensions, and duplication and gaps in a federal system where the regulation of work was shared amongst different jurisdictions.

Indeed, policy makers everywhere have become apprised of the urgent need to reappraise traditional approaches to the regulation of work. In Europe, the influential report presented to the European Commission in the late 1990s by a group of experts in the field is testament to the extent of these issues.[19] This 'Supiot Report' noted the growing diversity in the types of contracts covering work relations and explored the impact of globalisation on the nature of work and its place in society through five major issues—work and private power, work and membership of the labour force, work and time, work and collective organisations, and work and public authorities—and effectively called for the adoption of a new paradigm through which to regulate work.

The idea that there might be a paradigm shift in law's understanding of work relations is not historically novel. The transformation of Western societies from agrarian to industrial economies was wrought, at least in part, through a shift from status to contract in the legal conceptualisation of work relations. Now the transition from the

---

17 Eg B Hepple 'The Future of Labour Law' (1995) 24 *ILJ* 303; JR Bellace and MG Rood (eds) *Labour Law at the Crossroads: Changing Employment Relationships* (1997); M D'Amatona 'Labour Law at the Century's End: An Identity Crisis?' in J Conaghan, RM Fischl and K Klare (eds) *Labour Law in an Era of Globalization: Transformative Practices and Possibilities* (2002); and M Vranken 'Labour Law as an Academic Discipline: Can there be a Future?' (2003) 16 *AJLL* 381.

18 See eg RC McCallum, Chair, *Independent Report Prepared for the Victorian Industrial Relations Taskforce* (2000); G Stevens *Report of the Review of the South Australian Industrial Relations System* (2002); and WJ Ford *An Independent Review of the Amendments to the Industrial Relations Act 1979 made by the Labour Relations Reform Act 2002* (2004).

19 This report is published in English—see A Supiot *Beyond Employment: Changes in Work and the Future of Labour Law in Europe* (2001).

industrial era to the global era may be exposing inadequacies in one of labour law's fundamental constructs, the contract of employment, from the industrial era. Academic writing has recognised this for some time and wondered whether labour law can respond to the challenges of the new world of work in 'a positive and effective manner'.[20]

At the same time, scholars have been alert to the dangers inherent in making large generalisations, categorisations and assertions about law, just as similar dangers were noted above in relation to context. Legal concepts cannot always be packaged neatly into discrete and separately labelled bundles that are applicable at some periods and then not at others. Thus it seems better to acknowledge, for example, that the contract of employment is something that has evolved over time and has been heavily influenced by a range of other regulatory forms rather than something that emerged full-blown in the nineteenth century. Indeed, scholars elsewhere have argued that the contract of employment as a legal construct did not really become dominant until well into the middle of the twentieth century.[21] And even then its so-called dominance really depended on ignoring those many work relationships that never fitted its assumptions. Likewise there are even some connections that can be found between regulatory regimes as different as the federal *Workplace Relations Act* and the *Commonwealth Conciliation and Arbitration Act 1904* (Cth): an emphasis on bargaining is one, albeit within a very different context.[22]

Therefore, imagining the death of labour law (as we have known it) to be an event that will occur (or perhaps has already occurred) at a precisely defined time and place is really destined to be nothing but a theoretical exercise. Even after a so-called paradigm shift, traces of earlier and displaced concepts frequently remain embedded in the new. Aspects of the pre-industrial master and servant law, especially notions of the subservience of the worker, have thus continued as part of the law of the contract of employment.[23] In the real world, then, talk of a paradigm shift is really a dramatic way of making us think harder and more critically about the basic concepts underpinning law, work and society.

The more challenging aspect of the observation that we are in the midst of a paradigm shift is to begin to chart the structure of a new law of work. To this end, scholars from many parts of the globe have already set about the task of 'redefining' or 'reinventing' labour law. This project has taken a variety of forms. It involves critically evaluating labour law's traditional framework by bringing to the centre critiques and perspectives that have formerly been consigned to the periphery of the subject, by spelling out the limits of analyses that are confined within the discipline of law narrowly understood and exclude perspectives from other disciplines, and by pointing to the importance of examining approaches to the regulation of work in other jurisdictions.[24]

---

20 WB Creighton, WJ Ford and RJ Mitchell *Labour Law: Text and Materials* 2nd edn (1993), 31.
21 See eg S Deakin and F Wilkinson *The Law of the Labour Market: Industrialization, Employment and Legal Evolution* (2005).
22 B Creighton 'One Hundred Years of the Conciliation and Arbitration Power: A Province Lost?' (2004) 24 *MULR* 839.
23 See further Chapters 5 and 6.
24 See Mitchell (ed), above n 12.

The transformative possibilities engendered through a more explicit focus on the intersection of labour law with other areas of law, like social security law or immigration law, have also been advocated, and in the process the conventionally accepted notions of work, workplaces and workers have been disrupted.[25] The interface between work, family and care is being used to redraw the map of labour law, as what was once a women's issue is increasingly recognised 'as central to the regulatory challenges of the new economy'.[26] Other scholars have looked beyond the confines of employment relations to suggest that regulatory studies are (and perhaps have always been) a better conceptual focus for the organisation of the discipline.[27] The diversity of legal and regulatory mechanisms and their different functions in the construction of labour markets, some of which (like those made up by volunteers or unauthorised workers) are rarely examined in conventional labour law texts, have provided even further insights into the great range of regulatory mechanisms governing work.[28]

The Law of Work

The title of this book, *The Law of Work*, is intended to signal again that this juncture of the industrial and the global era is a critical point in the development of the law governing work. It takes the view that employment, labour and industrial relations law is moving beyond its traditional paradigm. However, it also acknowledges that changes in the law and work are complex, often partial, and always incomplete. New developments may expose internal contradictions in the law and provide few certainties. *The Law of Work* accepts the need to examine critically the paradigm in which law frames economy, society and work especially with a view to understanding the impact of law on working people's lives and the community in which they live. It notes that the worker in the global era is for the most part a very different being from the male breadwinner factory worker assumed to be the subject of labour law in the industrial era. The structures of work, or the ways in which work is organised, are also very different. It observes that this is often the result of a double action whereby the world of work sometimes seeks to escape law, just as law simultaneously seeks to shape the world of work. Thus, rather than simply assimilate the new forms of work and the new structures in which work is organised to the old legal forms, this volume moves to problematise those legal forms through examining their operation in the new world of work.

The Law of Work therefore focuses on the core of the discipline as it has been understood to date and examines the ways in which it is developing. Any study of the law of work is bound to be partial and incomplete. There are many important scholarly developments in the area that this book does not pursue or incorporate. In most cases this is not because they are deemed to be unimportant or insignificant. In fact often

---

25 See Conaghan, Fischl and Klare (eds), above n 17.
26 See J Conaghan and K Rittich (eds) *Labour Law, Work and Family: Critical and Comparative Perspectives* (2005), 3; and J Murray (ed) *Work, Family and the Law* (2005).
27 H Collins, P Davies and R Rideout (eds) *Legal Regulation of the Employment Relation* (2000); and R Johnstone and R Mitchell 'Regulating Work' in C Parker et al (eds) *Regulating Law* (2004).
28 C Arup et al (eds) *Labour Law and Labour Market Regulation* (2006).

the opposite is the case. They are so important and significant that justice could not be done to the issues they raise in this volume. The possibilities for tackling a topic such as the law of work are always bounded. This volume does seek to incorporate throughout its pages a discussion of the impact of the *Work Choices Act* because this legislation is without a doubt the most significant regulatory development in this area in Australia in recent years.

Two critical issues relating to the scope of the law of work are at the forefront of our thinking in writing this book.

The first of these may be posed as a question thus: 'how does the law of work differ from ordinary commercial law?' This question focuses on the fact that there is increasing pressure to abandon labour law to contract law. It is this pressure that suggests that the traditional terrain of labour law should reduce in scope as strong and successful work relations take on an entrepreneurial character. What distinguishes the worker who is an employee, as traditionally understood, from others who contract for services in the new economy? The counter side of this issue is the pressure to merge the law regulating those who are portrayed as weak or vulnerable in their work relations with welfare law. It raises the question of why workers who are vulnerable should be treated any differently from others in the community who are vulnerable, and whether responsibility in relation to that vulnerability lies with the state or the market.

The second issue arises from the intersection of public and productive work lives with private and reproductive work lives. While traditionally these domains have been constructed as separate in labour law, 'work and family' (as the issue is usually designated in Australia, although 'work and care' is a more inclusive and therefore often a more appropriate label) is increasingly forcing its way onto the main agenda. Like the commercial law/labour law/welfare law interface, work and family raises questions about the role of the state and the market in working lives and the intersection of all these things. Work and family also force us to confront the gendering of work and law, and its working out in the future is likely to be one of the most significant matters affecting the quality of individual and community life.

Because these issues are integral to this book it is appropriate to say a little more at this point about some of the concepts raised by them.

The person and work

In Australian law contract remains one of the fundamental conceptual tools for understanding and organising work. Contract in turn makes certain assumptions about the nature of persons, their relations with others and with their work. A helpful way to explore the adequacy of contract to deal with work relations is through a consideration of the principle that 'labour is not a commodity'. This principle is a central motif in modern labour law.[29] It is also a foundation principle of the International Labour Organization (ILO), as expressed in the *Philadelphia Declaration* appended

---

29 See H Collins *Employment Law* (2003), Ch 1.

to its *Constitution* in 1944.[30] This principle embodies the idea that the relation of persons to their labour is not the same as to other tradeable material items. It suggests an intimate connection between human persons and their work. At common law it could be said that the principle 'labour is not a commodity' captures not only the antithesis of law to extreme forms of slavery—whether the slavery of colonial times or the more recent international trafficking of sex slaves—but also the idea that workers are not mere chattels at the disposal of another for whom they may work.[31] That is, the legal understanding is that workers are not the property of those for whom they work. Workers are autonomous beings, they are persons not property.[32]

But what assumptions does law incorporate about these persons? One account portrays the individual as an independent, autonomous and pre-social being, in control of his own world through the exercise of choice. This is the person of liberal theory, as exemplified in the writings of the seventeenth-century political philosopher, John Locke. Locke understood labour as 'proper' to the person: that is, the individual by his very nature is the owner of his labour.[33] According to Locke, it is also through his labour that the individual creates private property. By working the individual can appropriate to himself the world that was originally (that is, in the state of nature) held in common by all. The creation of a private property in food and other necessaries Locke saw as the means to survival, but he also wrote that industrious individuals could create property surplus to their own survival needs, which then becomes the basis for commercial exchange. For Locke, work is thus structurally integrated into the third of liberal theory's trilogy of fundamental rights, 'life, liberty and property' and is part of the foundation of the market, the core of civil society.

A modern version of liberal theory, neo-liberalism, is very much part of contemporary law and also dominates thought in the global era. It helps to explain why autonomy and its associated values (like freedom and choice) have become increasingly the hallmark of the modern worker in law.[34] The explanation in liberal theory of the significance of work to the individual and the market assists in understanding the way legal concepts of contract are applied in relation to work. While work might often be treated by the market as just another cost in the production of commodities, there remains, perhaps paradoxically in these times of economic rationalism, a pervasive sense that work has a peculiar significance to us as human beings. Human labour is no mere 'thing' or object separable from the self.

The principle that 'labour is not a commodity' can also import into the law the sense that the worker must be respected as a human being who is constituted within a particular social setting. This necessarily brings a certain moral or ethical dimension

---

30 *ILO Constitution*. All information (including legal documents) relating to the International Labour Organization is available at <www.ilo.org>. See further, Chapter 2.

31 See *Somersett's Case* (1772) 20 St Tr 1; and *Nokes v Doncaster Collieries* [1940] AC 1014.

32 For a wider discussion of related issues see M Davies and N Naffine *Are Persons Property? Legal Debates about Property and Personality* (2001).

33 See J Locke *Two Treatises of Government* (1689). For an analysis of the importance to law of Locke's theory of work see RJ Owens 'Working in the Sex Market' in N Naffine and RJ Owens (eds) *Sexing the Subject of Law* (1997).

34 See also RJ Steinfeld *The Invention of Free Labour* (1991).

to work relations that demands decent conditions for workers and fair pay or just rewards to provide a decent standard of living. The operation of the principle in this sense has been claimed to be an Irish contribution to labour law dating back to the nineteenth century, albeit it is acknowledged that it also resonates with even earlier political and philosophical writings as diverse as those of Karl Marx and the papal encyclical of 1891, *Rerum Novarum*.[35] It is in Australia that one of the earliest judicial decisions giving it content can be found. The idea that the law should ensure that workers are treated in a way that regards them as human beings in a civilised society has never been far from the centre of the Australian law of work.[36] The way workers are treated is usually taken as an important indicator of the state of development of a society. A critical issue is whether this will remain so during the global era.

Law and the organisation of enterprise

The issue of power at work has traditionally been approached in law through an examination of individual and collective relations in the workplace. In the new global era, the contest over the structuring of work relations, whether on an individual or collective basis, is most keen in the area of freedom of association. There is, however, another important dimension to the individual/collective dichotomy in the regulation of work apparent in the corporate form. While the increasing individualisation of work relations has often resulted in the exclusion of trade unions from the workplace,[37] the 'collective' structure of the corporation has remained unchallenged. The corporation is conceived as a unitary being, a 'person', in law. As such, it is a player that can easily comply with the rules of the marketplace—it is made for competition, it is not inherently anti-competitive—whereas increasingly trade unions have been portrayed as exercising a power antithetical to the norms of the marketplace. The potential for the corporate form to mask issues of power in work relations is one of the central themes examined in this book.

The role of the state—regulation and de-regulation

The neo-liberal idea that there is something natural about contractual relations and the market as the sum of those relations is now quite pervasive. There is little recognition that contract law is as much the product of the state as other forms of regulatory control. The rhetoric accompanying the push for the 'de-regulation' of labour markets suggests that any regulation by states interferes with and impedes the new global order.

The assumptions in the 'de-regulatory' agenda have been uncovered by many scholars and are too well known to be rehearsed here. It is clear that the real issues are not whether or not to have regulation, or even more or less regulation, but what kind of regulation to have, what assumptions it contains, who or what does it privilege, and who or what does it neglect. Traditionally there have been multiple regulatory

---

35 See P O'Higgins '"Labour is Not a Commodity"—An Irish Contribution to International Labour Law' (1997) 26 *ILJ* 225.

36 Ibid. See *Ex parte HV McKay* ('*Harvester Case*') (1907) 2 CAR 1.

37 See Deery and Mitchell (eds), above n 15.

layers governing work in Australia and the significant role of the state in the past has been generally acknowledged. In this country there never was an 'abstentionist' approach to labour regulation, as there was in systems that placed greater emphasis on collective bargaining, although the differences from other jurisdictions can also sometimes be overstated.[38] While there may be assertions to the contrary, it is obvious from an examination of the federal *Workplace Relations Act* that there is no such thing as a market that exists outside of or prior to society and law. Rather, even in the global era, the state through law continues to play a critical role in creating and shaping labour markets.[39]

Law and productive and reproductive work

The primary concern of law has always been paid work, productive work in the marketplace. Reproductive labour has been ignored by law. There have been several effects of this. First, the worker in law has traditionally been assumed to be male. For a long time women were noticeably absent, not only in the pages of law reports and tribunal decisions, but also from traditional labour law scholarship.[40] In more recent times there has been a more conscious effort by scholars to redress this.[41] However, it is generally the case that women are still more or less confined to special areas. While it has been noted, for instance, that women predominate in areas of precarious employment, simultaneously this is treated as peripheral and hardly disrupts the more traditional concern of the text with the normative worker, a breadwinner in fulltime, lifetime employment. Thus women tend to get a mention but the subject of labour law has not yet been subverted in ways that really respond to the realities of the new workplace of the global era.

Secondly, in more recent developments the significance of the intersection of unpaid and paid labour has become more apparent as women have entered the workforce in unprecedented numbers. This has forced some reassessment of the intersection of paid and unpaid work, productive labour and reproductive labour, as a subject of labour law—recognising the importance of 'workers with family responsibilities' as an issue. However, the larger question about the dependence of the market on reproductive labour continues to be ignored. Yet this is an issue that has become especially important in the era of the 'shrinking state', for as government has withdrawn from providing many care services, women's work is being reconstituted in new and different forms. At the same time, much of the reproductive labour of women is being allocated to the market. The gendering of the construction of work in law is thus an issue that has been more fully integrated into this book.

---

38 See Johnston and Mitchell, above n 27; and K Ewing 'Australian and British Labour Law: Differences of Form or Substance' (1998) 11 *AJLL* 44.

39 C Shearing 'A Constitutive Conception of Regulation' in P Grabosky and J Braithwaite (eds) *Business Regulation and Australia's Future* (1993).

40 J Conaghan 'The Invisibility of Women in Labour Law: Gender-neutrality in Model Building' (1986) 14 *Int J Soc L* 377; R Hunter 'Representing Gender in Legal Analysis: A Case/Book Study in Labour Law' (1991) 18 *MULR* 305; and Owens, above n 12.

41 See eg B Creighton and A Stewart *Labour Law* 4th edn (2005), esp Ch 1; and MJ Pittard and RB Naughton *Australian Labour Law: Cases and Materials* 4th edn (2003).

Thirdly, equality and discrimination issues (which are often treated as a subset of issues arising from women's participation in the labour market but clearly have a much wider relevance than that) have either been ignored or acknowledged in only a minor way.[42] Even more problematically, the conceptual integration of discrimination matters into traditional labour law has often been quite awkward and has not acknowledged the importance of equality in the workplace.[43]

The purposes of the law of work

At times of revolutionary change there can be an instinct for idealising the past as a golden age, often forgetting that much about it was also 'ungolden'.[44] Thus there is sometimes a tendency to view the old employment, labour and industrial relations policies and the law that regulated work in the industrial era as embodying a set of principles and values that have been corrupted and destroyed by the new policies governing the law of work in the global era. Whether or not such an evaluation is correct, there will be no return to a past (either golden or ungolden) age of employment, labour and industrial relations law.

However, this is not to accept that the recent changes in the world of work or the law are inevitable or natural. The shape of work and work relations can be encouraged, resisted, or redirected by law. As Karl Klare has observed, 'a legal discourse is a medium or location of ideological encounter and conflict'.[45] This book in exploring the law of work in the global era seeks out spaces for change, and is inspired by the possibilities for the 'emancipatory' or 'transformative' potential of developments in the law of work in the global era. While the common law has generally been characterised as an inadequate basis for, and even hostile to, the protection of workers against the superior power of, and therefore potential exploitation by, capital, it is possible to reread the common law in a way that will promote fair dealing in the workplace.[46] Recent developments in the doctrine of mutual trust and confidence, for instance, suggest the possibility for the further development of a duty to accommodate better the needs of workers with family responsibilities.[47] While there may be serious practical limitations to relying on the common law as an adequate safeguard in the first instance for individuals (for a start the issue of costs and access to justice in the ordinary court system is a real problem for individuals), nonetheless the development of principles in even a few test cases can have a dramatic impact on workplace culture and practices.

---

42 This has been true in all jurisdictions: see K Ewing *Working Life New Perspectives on Labour Law* 1996; H Collins, K Ewing and A McColgan *Labour Law Text and Materials* (2001); and Collins, Davies and Rideout (eds), above n 27.

43 Eg Creighton and Stewart, above n 41, categorises discrimination simply as an unfair employment practice.

44 Cf K Hancock 'Work in an Ungolden Age' in R Callus and R Lansbury (eds) *Working Futures: The Changing Nature of Work and Employment Relations in Australia* (2002).

45 K Klare 'The Horizons of Transformative Labour and Employment Law' in Conaghan, Fischl and Klare (eds), above n 17, 3.

46 J Riley *Employee Protection at Common Law* (2005).

47 See also B Smith and J Riley 'Family-friendly Work Practices and the Law' (2004) 26 *Syd LR* 395.

In order to understand the transformation of the old employment, labour and industrial relations law into a new law of work and to see transformative possibilities for it there must be close attention to the purposes of the law. The purposes of the law of work determine its scope as well as express its values, and in the global era none is immune from contest.

The protection of workers

One of the most significant of the traditional functions for law is the protection of the worker. Although modern law's conceptualisation of work relations as contractual purports to incorporate assumptions about the equality of the parties in a work relation, it has always been obvious that this does not necessarily accord with the reality of these relations. The resources and comparative size of business enterprises, the often limited availability of work in a particular area, and the incapacity of most workers to withhold or withdraw labour, are all factors indicating that in usual circumstances workers do not enjoy equality of bargaining power with business. A central task of labour law in the past has thus been to distinguish those workers who are vulnerable (or subordinate or dependent) in their contractual dealings with business from those who are not. The members of the latter group are then of no special interest to the law *as workers*: law treats their work relations as no different from other commercial dealings. The protective function of law in relation to work has thus tended to mark the separation of labour law and commercial law.

In seeking to protect vulnerable workers, law's focus is on the power exercised by capital over labour, with law serving to counter and eliminate any exploitation. This remedial function has usually been performed in one of two different, though not necessarily mutually inconsistent, ways. First, the law may directly establish certain standards to govern the work relation that will override any inferior terms of the contractual bargain that business may seek to impose. These standards represent a claim by the state that it has a legitimate role in overseeing the substantive work conditions. Secondly, the law may establish mechanisms that enable workers to join together to bargain with business, and thereby through collective action overcome their individual lack of power. The role of the state here is to facilitate and enforce fair bargaining between parties by establishing procedural standards, such as freedom of association, that secure this. In both situations the law is conceptualised as intervening in the work relationship to prevent the abuse of power.

A central issue for the law of work in pursuing a protective function is the adequacy of its conceptual tools to identify, determine or define relevant vulnerability. In the global era pressure to abandon the protective goals of a law of work comes from two different directions. Protecting the vulnerable (whether they be workers or not) is pressed as a function of welfare law. Law's concern with abuse of power in the work relation is thus deflected because it is portrayed as potentially diverting the state from its more appropriate function of applying an even-handed response to all of its vulnerable citizens whether they be workers or not. Secondly, the law's concern with abuse of power in bargaining is often turned back against workers when the state provides support to them to act collectively, for the market demands an explanation as to why work contracts should be exempted from the normal rules governing 'trade practices' in the marketplace. In this debate the collective nature of capital in the corporation is rarely noted.

Redistributive justice

Despite some of its assumptions about formal equality in contract, also underpinning the law's recognition of the need to protect vulnerable workers is some understanding that work relations are comprised of two discrete groups, capital and labour, whose interests are often (some might say always) different and conflicting: capital looks to maximise its profits, which can be to the detriment of workers' interests, and workers intent on attaining better pay and working conditions can diminish the profits available to the business and to shareholders. An aspect of protecting vulnerable workers through regulatory mechanisms that oversee and set wages reveals a further goal of redistributive justice for the law of work. Wage setting may be governed by various parameters, usually involving some attention to standards of living, notions of the just rewards for the exercise of skill, as well as business interests. Other factors, such as the impact on the access of outsiders (for instance, the unemployed) to the benefits of work, are increasingly pressed as elements to be weighed by the law governing work and this shifts the redistributive focus of the law of work towards other purposes such as labour market participation. In addition, in so far as law may have a redistributive goal relevant to work, it is now more likely to be suggested now that taxation rather than wage setting laws are a more appropriate vehicle for its attainment.

Fostering social cohesion

The protective function of law, especially as implemented through general standards established by the state or where mechanisms for collective bargaining are extended beyond a particular enterprise, may also express a concern for the wider social goal that all workers are treated fairly not simply in relation to those for whom they work but when considered vis-à-vis other workers. Fairness suggests that, even beyond redistributive purposes, there is a just return for labour, which can only be judged in a particular social context. This arises from the acknowledgement that labour is not simply a commodity to be exchanged according to the dictates of the market, but must provide a decent standard of living. The concept of fairness arising from broad substantive standards can also reflect a commitment to the value of equality, that all workers ought to be able to enjoy decent work standards regardless of the enterprise for which they work. Fairness, equality and a commitment to a decent life for all workers build a social cohesion that extends far beyond the limits of any single enterprise.

Work as an expression of social citizenship

The broader articulation of the protective purpose of labour law as providing for fairness and decency fixes attention on workers not as isolated, pre-social individuals, nor simply in their relation with capital, but as persons within the wider social context. The purposes of law can therefore also reinforce the social utility of work. Some scholars have utilised the concept of social citizenship to capture this. Ron McCallum has pointed out that social citizenship is a complex concept capable of being deployed in a variety of ways.[48] When TH Marshall first espoused the concept of social and economic rights, they were expressed as derivative of political and civil rights and to be valued because they transferred the same kind of political and civil rights into the workplace, the one reinforcing the other. Freedom of association, for instance, was to be protected because it enabled workers to have a voice in the workplace that complemented and reinforced the wider political rights of workers as citizens to exercise a democratic vote.[49] This instrumental approach has been refined by later scholars to emphasise the constitutive function of social and economic rights.[50] Still more recently, the extension of civil liberties and social rights, such as the right to privacy, freedom of expression, health and safety, into the workplace is seen as a critical part of their maintenance in civil society.[51]

Social inclusion and participation

In more recent times the importance of, and therefore the encouragement of, work as a form of engagement or inclusion or participation in society has come to be articulated as a significant object of the law governing work. Work, especially paid work, is seen as one of the most critical ways in which citizens are integrated into society. In Australia rates of workforce participation have remained lower than those in comparable industrialised market economies and a clear modern policy objective is to increase the participation rate. The construction of labour markets—and especially the regulation of unemployment and the monitoring of those who are dependent upon social welfare—thus becomes a concern of the law of work.[52] It can also extend the scope of the law of work to such matters as education and training.

While one version of the idea of social citizenship as social inclusion emphasises the 'rights' of individuals, for example, the right to work, a more commonly adopted iteration now insists on a reciprocity between the citizen and the state. The citizen thus has a duty or responsibility to society to participate in work.[53] This is not an historically recent aim of the law of work, but it is underlined most clearly now in the conditions

48 See R McCallum 'Justice at Work: Citizenship and the Corporatisation of Australian Law', Kingsley Laffer Memorial Lecture (2006) 48 *JIR* 131; and R McCallum in 'The New Millennium and the Higgins Heritage: Industrial Relations in the Twenty-first Century' (1996) 38 *JIR* 294, 307–9.

49 TH Marshall *Citizenship and Social Class* (1950).

50 See eg KD Ewing 'Social Rights and Constitutional Law' [1999] *Public Law* 104.

51 Collins, above n 29, Pt IV 'Citizenship'.

52 See C Arup et al 'Employment Protection and Employment Promotion: The Contested Terrain of Australian Labour Law' in M Biagi (ed) *Job Creation and Labour Law* (2000); and J Howe 'The Job Creation Function of the State: A New Subject for Labour Law' (2001) 14 *AJLL* 242.

53 See Collins, above n 29, Pt IV 'Citizenship'; and Deakin and Wilkinson, above n 21, Pt 3 'The Duty to Work'.

attached to welfare payments and the nature of the links between the rewards that will be guaranteed to those who work and the rewards accorded to those who do not. Thus the recent emphasis on 'work-fare' schemes is an expression of this more complex citizenship.[54] According to this view it is work, the productive engagement of the individual, which activates the enjoyment of the decent life. The purpose of law is to ensure that all who can, do engage in productive work. It is thus no surprise that at the same time the *Work Choices* legislation was enacted the *Welfare to Work* laws were also amended.[55]

While such a view extends the traditional 'liberal' emphasis of rights talk, the person assumed by the law that embodies these purposes has many of the same characteristics of the individual in liberal theory. This person is self-reliant and able to survive by his or her own efforts. Above all this individual is independent, and does not depend upon the state. Economic dependence, on welfare payments, for example, comes to represent a failure of citizenship, or membership of the community. Paid work is linked with activity and contribution and contrasted with inactivity and dependency. The law's purposes in identifying work as a signifier of meaningful participation and inclusion in the community, and encouraging participation in the workforce thus risk suggesting simultaneously that those who do not participate in paid work in the marketplace are not worthy members of the community—they are outsiders.[56]

Work and the protection of human rights

A 'human rights' approach to the purposes of labour law is somewhat different from that articulated through the concept of social citizenship. The latter is more akin to the traditional protective purposes of labour law.[57] However, when workplace rights are conceived as human rights they can be seen more easily as extending to *all* workers and are not restricted to the class of workers identified as in a subordinate relation to capital. As the range of work relationships has diversified in the global era, this approach carries clear advantages in securing rights for all workers.[58] The implied universality of such rights also has other advantages. In a global era when capital often adopts a transnational form, the extraction of workplace rights from a particular locality or social context can be important. While an older conception of human rights may have emphasised only the responsibility of state actors to secure them, there is now a much wider acceptance of the responsibility of all social actors, including corporations, to ensure these rights are respected. Concern and awareness about the importance of human rights has had an impact on all areas of law, especially since the middle of the twentieth century.

---

54 See Commonwealth Department of Family and Community Services Consultation Paper 'Building a Simpler System to Help Jobless Families and Individuals' 12 December 2002 (available at <www.facs.gov. au/welfare_reform>) issued as part of the Howard Government's reform program *Australians Working Together*. See also J Shklar *American Citizenship: The Quest for Inclusion*, (1991), 63–101 exploring the role of earning in the validation of an individual's full membership of the community.

55 See R Owens 'Reproducing Law's Worker: Regulatory Tensions in the Pursuit of "Population, Participation and Productivity"' in Arup et al (eds), above n 28.

56 L Williams 'Beyond Labour Law's Parochialism: A Re-envisioning of the Discourse of Redistribution' in Conaghan, Fischl and Klare (eds), above n 17.

57 Hepple, above n 17, 317.

58 P Alston (ed) *Labour Rights as Human Rights* (2005).

Although the recognition of fundamental or human rights—such as freedom from slavery, freedom from the worst forms of child labour, equality, and freedom of association—is now widespread, there remains contest over their meaning. It can be seen, for instance, that to acknowledge these labour rights as human rights is to individualise them and thereby erase some of their importance to the collectivity of workers. Labour rights as human rights can also work to understate the importance of social context in the constitution of the worker; to deflect attention away from the causes of the abuse or exploitation of workers; and to deny the political element in law's construction of work and its values.

Fostering competition in the marketplace

An alternative goal of the law is to regulate work in a way that fosters competitive market relations. While most other purposes of law place primary attention on the worker, law here focuses on ensuring that work relations are conducted in ways that are efficient and flexible so as to foster the success of enterprises in the competitive marketplace of the new economy. The success of business is then assumed to overflow and provide better conditions in a way that meets the diverse needs of individual workers. In most contemporary industrialised market economies, including Australia, this has become a dominant objective of the law of work, supplanting the protective approach more typically a feature of the industrial era.

The goal of assisting business success in the new economy incorporates assumptions that the contracting parties are joined in a mutual enterprise. Rather than antagonism and conflict embedded in work arrangements, these relationships are conceived as based on mutual interest in cooperation. Flexibility, for instance, serves both the interests of the enterprise by enabling it to respond effectively to market demands and the interests of workers who will be able to accommodate more readily the other demands of their lives alongside those of work. According to this market view the parties are best placed to give effect to their own needs and desires. Through their own private agreement the parties have an incentive to arrange their affairs to suit their individual goals. The market approach to the regulation of work is reluctant to admit of any inequality of bargaining power between the parties in work relations. It assumes that the operation of a labour market means that workers will refuse to work for enterprises that would exploit them or offer them inferior conditions. Market forces are thus assumed to force all players to lift standards in a benchmarking exercise. Contract is the ideal regulatory form to further the goals appropriate to the competitive market. There is little or no place for the state to intervene explicitly in these contractual relations (except as a very final last resort of enforcement).

Multiple objectives

In examining the various goals and objectives above it is apparent that they are not necessarily mutually exclusive. At any one time policy and law may, and indeed generally do, incorporate a range of objectives and seek to attain complex social and economic outcomes. Some purposes may take precedence over others, and at times some may not be evident at all. These objectives and the interplay between them may also operate in ways that are unintended by policy makers and law makers. The contest over the meaning of law and its interpretation in tribunals and courts adds yet another layer of complexity. Provisions setting standards for wages or conditions, for instance, will vary depending on the desired policy mix. Thus even if it is conceded that the law should offer protection to vulnerable employees a very different approach will be taken depending upon whether the function of the protection is to achieve only an increased measure of redistributive justice between capital and labour, or to ensure that basic standards of decency are adhered to by all employers, or to do either of those things while at the same time encouraging greater labour market participation. It is not incompatible to maintain that the encouragement of the market economy must be the primary aim of the system of labour law, while at the same time adhering to the belief that workers also have human rights that cannot be abrogated under any circumstances. Likewise it may be a policy objective to ensure that all who are able to work have an opportunity to work, and thus regulate work in a way that does not establish conditions that preclude employment growth, while at the same time adhering to the view that decent work conditions must be accorded to all workers.

The structure of this book

This book is divided into four parts. Part 1 is concerned with 'Work, Law and Context'. Chapter 2 situates the law of work in the global context, providing an account of the globalisation process and its impact on the world of work, and examines legal developments at the global level for regulating work. While attention is paid to the ILO as the most important international institution regulating work in the global era, and the way in which it has responded to the challenges of globalisation, this chapter also provides an account of various other public and private regulatory mechanisms and the intersection between them. The transition of Australian labour law from the industrial era to the global era is the subject of Chapter 3. This chapter provides an overview of the development of labour law in Australia, highlighting the most significant features of its regulatory landscape. It provides an introduction to the *Work Choices* legislation and outlines its provisions governing the transition between the old and the new regulatory regimes. Chapter 4 then asks 'Who is the subject of the law of work?' in the global era. It explores the broad range of working arrangements found in the workplace of the twenty-first century. Equally importantly this chapter investigates the nature of the corporation and the identity of business enterprises as employers.

Part 2 focuses on contract, which has become the privileged regulatory form of the global era. Chapter 5 examines the theoretical underpinnings of classical contract law and interrogates their adequacy when applied to work arrangements. The chapter also outlines other regulatory interventions and influences on 'self-regulation' by contract, including equitable doctrines and statutory influences. In Chapter 6 there is a detailed examination of the rights and responsibilities imposed on workplace participants by contract law.

In Part 3, attention moves to an examination of those matters that can be described as the terms and conditions that are fundamental to ensuring that the law provides for decent work. These fundamentals are often said to make up a safety net of minimum standards and have traditionally been seen as a counterbalance to contract. Chapter 7 examines basic work standards, including the new Australian Fair Pay and Conditions Standard (AFPCS) and the Australian Pay and Classification Scales (APCSs) established by the *Work Choices Act*. Equality, which is considered in Chapter 8, and security, which is the subject of Chapter 9, are the two other fundamentals dealt with in this section of the book, and both are revealed to have a changing meaning and operation in the law of work in the twenty-first century.

The final section of the book, Part 4, takes freedom of association as its theme. In Chapter 10 the modern statutory protection of freedom of association is examined against a backdrop of the theoretical dimensions of this concept and its interpretation in the jurisprudence of the ILO. Freedom of association is then the point of departure for a consideration of the various types of bargaining under the *Workplace Relations Act* in Chapter 11. The final chapter in the book examines conflict in the workplace and the paths to its resolution that the law provides.

This book is about the law of work in Australia, and its focus throughout is primarily on federal regulation as it applies in the marketplace. There is virtually no attention paid either to the specific regulatory instruments relevant to employment in the government or public sector or to State-based laws governing work, though it is acknowledged that these continue to be of importance for some workers even after the introduction of the *Work Choices Act*. Throughout this book we have made every effort to take a broad and principled approach to the regulation of work; however, with the enactment of the *Work Choices* legislation in the middle of this project, this has been modified somewhat and the volume also endeavours to provide readers with a clear account of the amendments made by the *Work Choices Act* to the *Workplace Relations Act*.

The Law of Work
in the Global Era

Introduction

The international context has always been significant in understanding the law of work. The European imperial expansion beginning in the seventeenth century was accomplished in large part through the appropriation of colonised labour. Notoriously the transportation of slave-workers from Africa supported colonial expansion in North America. Only around the time of the American War of Independence did the common law reject slavery as part of the law of England and proclaim its allegiance to the worker as a free individual.[1] The white settlement of Australia after 1788 was facilitated first by the toil of a convict class and then by 'coloured labour' from other parts of the British Empire and, especially, from Asia and the Pacific Islands.

The law of work in Australia has always been influenced by legal developments elsewhere.[2] However, its 'internationalisation' is a more recent phenomenon, gaining impetus in the second half of the twentieth century from the proliferation of international human rights conventions. Important as these developments have been, the old order in which international law depends upon statutory incorporation in national law has come increasingly under challenge with the emergence of the global community. The time has now come to place the development of the Australian law of work in the context of globalisation.[3]

The impact upon the law of work of the transition from an international to a global order is the subject of this chapter. In the first section there is an examination of the International Labour Organization (ILO), the pre-eminent international institution responsible for the oversight of work since 1919. Secondly, the chapter considers the nature of globalisation, the changes it has wrought in the world of work, and the challenges it presents nationally and internationally to the regulation of work. In the final section the emerging new global law of work is discussed. Attention is devoted

---

1   See *Somersett's Case* (1772) 20 St Tr 1.
2   R McCallum 'The New Work Choices Laws: Once Again Australia Borrows Foreign Labour Law Concepts' (2006) 19 *AJLL* 98.
3   B Creighton 'The Internationalisation of Labour Law' in R Mitchell (ed) *Redefining Labour Law: New Perspectives on the Future of Teaching and Research* (1995), 115–16.

to the new 'public' law mechanisms for regulating work through labour clauses in trade treaties and the more recent reforms of the ILO, as well as to 'private' regulatory mechanisms such as codes of conduct and social labelling, and to the intersection between these public and private systems. Finally, this chapter examines the implications of conceptualising labour rights as human rights.

Regulating work under the 'old' international legal order—the International Labour Organization

The foundation of the International Labour Organization

The ILO has long been the pre-eminent international institution with oversight of work.[4] It was first established as an arm of the League of Nations, with its *Constitution* originally Pt XIII of the *Versailles Treaty*, which concluded World War I.[5] However, its genesis may be traced back even earlier, to the ideas of two nineteenth-century industrialists, Robert Owen and Daniel Le Grand, and the founding of the International Association of Labour Legislation in Basel in 1901. Since 1946 the ILO has been one of the specialised agencies of the United Nations. By the end of 2005 it comprised 178 member states.

The foundation of the ILO in 1919 was premised upon the conviction that universal and lasting peace could only be established and maintained if it were based on social justice and improved working conditions. The aims of the ILO, as broadly expressed in its constituent document, are to establish and achieve the application of global standards of social justice in respect to work, and thereby to ensure that some workers are not placed in a position of competitive advantage or disadvantage vis-à-vis others.

The original *ILO Constitution* identified the following general principles as being of 'special and urgent importance':

- The guiding principle that labour should not to be regarded merely as a commodity or article of commerce.
- The right of association for all lawful purposes by the employed as well as the employers.
- The payment to the employed of a wage adequate to maintain a reasonable standard of life as this is understood in their time and country.
- The adoption of an eight hours day or a forty-eight hours week as the standard to be aimed at where it has not already been attained.
- The adoption of a weekly rest of at least twenty-four hours, which should include Sunday wherever practicable.
- The abolition of child labour and the imposition of such limitations on the labour of young persons as shall permit the continuation of their education and assure their proper physical development.
- The principle that men and women should receive equal remuneration for work of equal value.

---

4   See J-M Servais *International Labour Law* (2005). The ILO website is at <www.ilo.org>.
5   *Treaty of Peace between the Allied and Associated Powers and Germany* (Pt XIII Labour)[1920] ATS 1 (*Versailles Treaty*). All revised constituent documents of the ILO are available at <www.ilo.org>.

- The standard set by law in each country with respect to the conditions of labour should have regard to the equitable economic treatment of all workers lawfully resident therein.
- Each State should make provision for a system of inspection in which women should take part, in order to ensure the enforcement of the laws and regulation for the protection of the employed.[6]

The preamble to the *ILO Constitution* was revised by the 1944 *Declaration concerning the aims and purpose of the International Labour Organization* (*Declaration of Philadelphia*), which reaffirmed these fundamental principles of the ILO.

The *Declaration of Philadelphia* also espoused antidiscrimination principles as well as affirming the right of everyone to pursue both 'their material well being and their spiritual development in conditions of freedom and dignity, of economic security and equal opportunity'. It encouraged international and national policy to have as a central aim the attainment of the conditions necessary to achieve these objectives. Specifically, the *Declaration of Philadelphia* professed the ILO's commitment to programs that would achieve full employment and improved living standards, provide opportunities for workers to contribute to the common good through the use of their skills, and ensure workers enjoyed a just share in material progress, through appropriate hours and conditions of work. It advocated the protection of a minimum wage and, where necessary, social security so that all would live in dignity. Equality in education and vocational opportunities, the provision of child welfare and maternity services, adequate nutrition, housing and facilities for recreation and culture, were also incorporated within its goals. The aspirations of the *Declaration of Philadelphia* were thus not at all narrow, and placed work in a broad social and economic context.

The structure of the International Labour Organization

Of all the United Nations organisations, the ILO has a unique tripartite composition. It includes the representatives not only of the governments of its various member states, but also of workers and trade unions and employers and their organisations. This tripartite structure is incorporated within the ILO's three principal bodies—the International Labour Conference, the Governing Body and the International Labour Office—that carry out its work.

The International Labour Conference, sometimes referred to as the international parliament of labour, is the ILO's central deliberative forum meeting once a year. At the Conference each member state contributes four delegates, two from government and one each from worker and employer groups, all of whom vote individually on all issues. The Conference discusses a broad range of social and labour issues, with much preparatory work done through the subcommittees reporting to it. The most important work of the Conference, however, is the adoption of conventions and recommendations and it also has ultimate supervision of their application at the national level through the receipt of reports from member states. Every three years, the Conference elects the Governing Body.

---

6   *Versailles Treaty*, Pt XIII, Section II 'General Principles'.

The Governing Body is the executive of the ILO, usually meeting three times a year to formulate the policy and programs of the Organization. It is composed of fifty-six regular members: twenty-eight represent member states including ten appointed from those of 'chief industrial importance' (Brazil, China, France, Germany, India, Italy, Japan, Russia, the United Kingdom, and the USA), and fourteen each representing employers and workers. Proposals, in 1986 and 1995, to reform the Governing Body did not gain the necessary support and its composition has remained the same since 1919. The Governing Body also has a range of committees, including the important Committee on Freedom of Association (CFA).

The permanent secretariat of the ILO, the International Labour Office, operates under the supervision of the Director-General, who is appointed for five years by the Governing Body. The International Labour Office works from the ILO headquarters in Geneva and from various regional and national offices around the world. The *Constitution* of the ILO provides that its staff shall be of different nationalities and include a certain, though unspecified, number of women.[7] The work of the International Labour Office includes research and the collection and distribution of information relating to conditions of industrial life and labour, especially for the preparation of conventions. It also produces publications, provides technical support to member states, and offers training to employer and worker organisations.

The *International Labour Code*

The conventions and recommendations of the ILO are often referred to collectively as the *International Labour Code*. By the end of 2005, this Code comprised 185 conventions and 195 recommendations.

The process leading to the adoption of a convention by the annual International Labour Conference is a lengthy one. Initially there are consultations with representatives from the member states and the ILO undertakes an extensive review of existing law and practice in member states. The subject matter of a proposed new convention is discussed at two successive sessions of the Conference and only adopted where supported by a two-thirds majority.[8] After adoption, a convention is open to ratification; a process whereby a nation agrees to be bound by *all* its provisions, for it is not possible to ratify ILO conventions subject to conditions. A convention becomes binding a year after ratification.

The ILO has no simple process for the 'repeal' of outmoded conventions. However, a convention may be closed to ratification if superseded, and therefore effectively amended, by a later revised convention.[9] Ratification of a revised convention can also be expressed to be tantamount to denunciation of the earlier outmoded convention. Otherwise, the process for denunciation of a convention is cumbersome and inflexible, because a signatory nation can only extricate itself

---

7   *ILO Constitution*, Art 9(3).
8   *ILO Constitution*, Art 19(2).
9   See eg *Maternity Protection Convention, 2000 (ILO C 183)*; *Maternity Protection (Revised) (1952) (ILO C 103)*; and *Maternity Protection Convention, 1919 (ILO C 3)*. See J Murray 'The International Regulation of Maternity: Still Waiting for the Reconciliation of Work and Family Life' (2001) 17 *Int J Comp LLIR* 25.

from its obligations in the year following every tenth anniversary of a convention's coming into force.[10]

The legal status of recommendations is quite different from that of conventions. They are not available for ratification and create no formally binding legal obligations on member states. Recommendations are intended to provide guidance in relation to national policy, legislation and practice. They often contain principles that complement convention obligations but do not have the required level of support for incorporation in a convention. Sometimes they provide more detailed elaboration of convention principles, and in some instances they include provisions that are inappropriate for inclusion in conventions.

The development of the *International Labour Code* charts the changing focus of international standards on work. The early ILO conventions tended to enunciate more detailed standards. Prior to World War II, the stress was on securing basic conditions at work, such as hours of work, or establishing the processes for securing a minimum wage or income maintenance through social security.[11] The ILO also sought to protect workers who were especially vulnerable, such as women and young workers or those in particular industries, like the agricultural industry, by formulating conventions and principles designed specifically for them.[12] After World War II there was a stronger emphasis on general standards applicable to all workers, such as freedom of association, equality, and the abolition of forced labour.[13] Some of these issues had been addressed in earlier conventions, but after World War II they were articulated in a more forceful fashion with an emphasis on the basic principles, consonant with the development of international law of human rights in the same period.[14]

The ILO committee structure and its supervision of convention compliance

All member states of the ILO are required to bring new conventions and recommendations to the attention of the appropriate national authorities with a view to ensuring their implementation at the national level.[15] Effective implementation and enforcement of norms of international law are recognised as notoriously difficult, and the ILO has developed a variety of approaches and mechanisms to assist with implementation, and

---

10 See also B Creighton and A Stewart *Labour Law* (2005), 68–9.

11 See eg *Hours of Work (Industry) Convention, 1919 (ILO C 1)*; *Unemployment Convention, 1919 (ILO C 2)*; *Minimum Wage-Fixing Machinery Convention, 1928 (ILO C 26)*; *Hours of Work (Commerce and Offices) Convention, 1930 (ILO C 30)*; and *Forty Hour Week Convention, 1935 (ILO C 47)*.

12 See eg *Maternity Protection Convention, 1919 (ILO C 3)*; *Night Work Women Convention, 1919 (ILO No 4)*; *Minimum Age (Industry) Convention, 1919 (ILO C 5)*; *Night Work of Young Persons (Industry) Convention, 1919 (ILO C 6)*; *Minimum Age (Sea) Convention, 1920 (ILO C 7)*; and *Minimum Age (Agriculture) Convention, 1921 (ILO C 10)*.

13 See *Freedom of Association and Protection of the Right to Organise Convention, 1948 (ILO C 87)*; *Right to Organise and Collective Bargaining Convention, 1949 (ILO C 98)*; *Equal Remuneration Convention, 1951 (ILO C 100)*; *Abolition of Forced Labour Convention, 1957 (ILO C 105)*; *Discrimination (Employment and Occupation) Convention, 1958 (ILO C 111)*; *Minimum Age Convention, 1973 (ILO C 138)*. Australia has ratified all these conventions with the exception of *ILO C 138*.

14 On human rights law, see below pp 73ff.

15 *ILO Constitution*, Art 19(5)–(7).

monitor and ensure ongoing compliance.[16] It convenes seminars to assist in institution building, trains social partners, and provides advisory councils, in-country services or direct contact missions to deal with technical and other issues. Advice is available in relation to everything from legislative drafting, methods of administration and inspection, and training in the prevention of accidents. All these measures are, naturally, dependent upon the cooperation of member states.

The ILO also has a range of institutional mechanisms to respond to instances of non-compliance with the *International Labour Code*. The International Court of Justice is the body reposed with responsibility for the authoritative interpretation of the *ILO Constitution* and the *International Labour Code*. However, in reality several key ILO committees are more significant and their decisions effectively make up a body of practical jurisprudence on the interpretation of the *International Labour Code*.

The implementation of ratified conventions is monitored through the Committee of Experts on the Application of Conventions and Recommendations (CEACR), which reports to the annual Conference. The CEACR comprises twenty eminent and independent persons with specialist expertise in labour matters, who are appointed on the recommendation of the Director-General on a renewable three-year basis. Under Article 22 of the *ILO Constitution* member states have to report annually to the CEACR on the measures taken to ensure compliance with their obligations under the *International Labour Code*. Where it appears there is non-compliance, the CEACR may make a 'direct request' to a member state. If the response from the government of the member state is inadequate, as a next step the CEACR may publish an 'observation' in its annual report, which is presented to a special tripartite Conference Committee on the Application of Standards, which in turn reports to the Conference in plenary session. This process involves public review and debate and is usually followed by discussion with the relevant government and, if appropriate, the provision of technical assistance. The CEACR's attention may also be drawn to cases heard by other ILO committees, such as the Committee on Freedom of Association, to enable further follow-up if necessary. In the past the CEACR has also carried out a 'General Survey' based upon reports from member states examining the implementation of, and compliance with, specific conventions (and recommendations) in all member states.[17]

The ILO committee system also has complaint-handling procedures. Any member state of the ILO has the right to file a 'complaint' against another member state not observing a convention that both have ratified.[18] Upon receipt of the complaint the Governing Body may set up an independent Commission of Inquiry to deal with it. However, this complaint procedure is not often used and a more commonly initiated procedure involves 'representations' made by organisations of employers or workers to a Committee of the Governing Body.[19]

---

16 See generally L Swepston 'Supervision of ILO Standards' (1997) 13 *Int J Comp LLIR* 327, 334 ff. See also ILO *Your Voice at Work, Pt II* (2000).
17 *ILO Constitution*, Art 19(5)(e).
18 *ILO Constitution*, Art 26.
19 *ILO Constitution*, Art 24.

Because of the importance the ILO has traditionally placed on the principle of freedom of association the Governing Body has established a Committee on Freedom of Association (CFA) to deal with representations or complaints regarding the infringement of the two main conventions, *Freedom of Association and Protection of the Right to Organise Convention, 1948* (ILO C 87) and *Right to Organise and Collective Bargaining Convention, 1949* (ILO C 98), which enshrine this principle. The CFA was established in 1951 and consists of nine members of the Governing Body with an independent Chair appointed from outside the Governing Body. The procedure devised to handle complaints is one of written pleadings and responses, which are considered at a meeting of the CFA. The CFA always sits prior to the Governing Body's meetings, reporting to that body its findings including any recommendations about matters that need to be drawn to the attention of the government of the relevant member state.[20]

The ILO and the law of work in Australia

Australia has been a member of the ILO since its establishment. The *ILO Constitution* as amended has been legislatively approved by enactment of the *International Labour Organisation Act 1947* (Cth) and *International Labour Organisation Act 1973* (Cth). In the mid-1990s the Liberal Coalition Government led by John Howard downgraded Australia's role at the ILO by removing its special adviser from Geneva, refraining from seeking re-election to the ILO's Governing Body and reducing the size of its delegation to the International Labour Conference.[21] In 2005, however, this approach was reversed. For the years 2005–08 the Australian government is once again sitting on the ILO's Governing Body, as well as Peter Anderson, from the Australian Chamber of Commerce and Industry (ACCI) representing Australian business, and Sharan Burrow, the Australian Council of Trade Unions (ACTU) President, representing Australian workers.

Ratification and implementation of the International Labour Code in Australia

By mid-2006 of the 185 ILO conventions Australia had ratified 54 (but denounced 8 of them). This is more than most nations in the developing world including some of Australia's important trading partners in the Asian region [for example, China (24 ratifications), Indonesia (17), Japan (47), Malaysia (15), Singapore (24), Thailand (14) and Vietnam (16)]. By contrast Western European nations have ratified many more ILO conventions than Australia [for example, France (127) and the United Kingdom (85)], while in North America the number is much smaller [Canada (30) and the USA (14)].

Although there has never been any legal impediment to Australia ratifying and legislatively implementing ILO conventions, up until the end of World War II it had only ratified 12 conventions. Breen Creighton has identified a number of, mainly political,

---

20 On the procedure of the CFA see KP McEvoy and RJ Owens 'On a Wing and a Prayer: The Pilot's Dispute in the International Context' (1993) 6 *AJLL* 1, 3–5.

21 Australia, *Parliamentary Debates*, House of Representatives, 2 May 1996, 277–78 (Hon Peter Reith). See also A Kent 'Australia and the International Human Rights Regime' in J Cotton and J Ravenhill (eds) *The National Interest in a Global Era: Australia in World Affairs 1996–2000* (2001), 267.

reasons for this.[22] These include Australia's ambivalent international standing before it achieved full independence from Great Britain, and a belief that Australia's work standards were either superior to those enunciated by the ILO or that its system of conciliation and arbitration rendered them irrelevant. In addition, the Australian practice of ratifying a convention only with the agreement of all its States and when existing law was already in conformity with it inhibited the rate of ratification.[23] However, in the 1970s the changed political environment, both nationally and internationally, brought equally dramatic change in Australia's policy on ratification with 30 ILO conventions ratified since 1970.

Australia now follows a procedure whereby there is parliamentary scrutiny before it commits to final ratification of international conventions. Because Australian law incorporates the dualist theory of a separation between the international and national legal systems, legislative enactment is necessary before Australia's obligations at international law are incorporated into domestic law in a way that can create new, or modify existing, public or private rights or obligations.[24] The incorporation into Australian law of the principles and standards contained in ILO (and other international) conventions is thus dependent on national will and initiative. Although since the 1970s discrimination legislation applying to work has been enacted to implement Australia's international obligations under a range of UN conventions, only with the passage of the *Industrial Relations Reform Act 1993* (Cth) was there any incorporation of ILO standards into the mainstream of Australian labour law by relying upon the external affairs power, s 51(xxix) of the *Australian Constitution*. Termination of employment, parental leave, limited immunity from liability for certain strike action, and a legislative framework for ensuring minimum wages and equal pay for work of equal value were all provided for in that legislation.[25] However, since 1993 reliance on the external affairs power has diminished in mainstream labour legislation regulating work, especially after the turn towards the corporations power, s 51(xx) of the *Australian Constitution*, in the *Workplace Relations Act 1996* (Cth), a move confirmed by the enactment of the *Workplace Relations Amendment (Work Choices) Act 2005* (Cth).[26] However, in other areas, reference to

---

22 B Creighton 'The ILO and the Protection of Human Rights in Australia' (1998) 22 *MULR* 239, 254–61.

23 Two notable departures from this practice occurred when Australia ratified the *Workers with Family Responsibilities Convention, 1981 (ILO C 156)* in 1990, and *Termination of Employment Convention, 1982 (ILO C 158)* in 1993.

24 See *Walker v Baird* [1892] AC 491. See JG Starke 'The High Court of Australia and the Rule in *Walker v Baird* [1892] AC 491' (1974) 48 *ALJ* 368; and GPJ McGinley 'The Status of Treaties in Australian Municipal Law: The Principle in *Walker v Baird*' (1990) 12 *Adel LR* 367.

25 The relevant legislative provisions drew on the following ILO conventions: *Minimum Wage Fixing Convention 1970 (ILO C 131); Discrimination (Employment and Occupation) Convention, 1958 (ILO C 111)* and *Discrimination Employment and Occupation Recommendation,* 1958 *(ILO R 111); Equal Remuneration Convention, 1951 (ILO C 100)* and *Equal Remuneration Recommendation, 1951 (ILO R 90); Termination of Employment Convention, 1982 (ILO C 158)* and *Termination of Employment Recommendation, 1982 (ILO R 166); Workers with Family Responsibilities Convention, 1981 (ILO C 156)* and *Workers with Family Responsibilities Recommendation* 1981 *(ILO R 165); Freedom of Association and Protection of the Right to Organise Convention, 1948 (ILO C 87);* and *Right to Organise and to Collective Bargaining Convention, 1949 (ILO C 98).* Other provisions drew support from UN conventions, including the *International Covenant on Economic, Social and Cultural Rights,* and the *Convention on the Elimination of All Forms of Discrimination against Women.* See also R McCallum 'The Internationalisation of Australian Industrial Law: The *Industrial Relations Reform Act 1993*' (1994) 15 *Syd L R* 122.

26 See further Chapter 3.

international and ILO conventions continues. The amendments to the *Criminal Code* concerning slavery or forced labour provide one recent example.[27]

Compliance with the International Labour Code by Australia

The significance of the operation of the ILO committee processes in maintaining a general oversight of compliance with the *International Labour Code* is amply demonstrated in decisions relating to Australia.[28] The CEACR has made numerous 'direct requests' to Australia, inviting explanation of its law and seeking assurance of compliance with the *International Labour Code*. These 'direct requests' have touched upon many aspects of Australian law including provisions dealing with discrimination in employment and equality of opportunity, the regulation of essential services, the capacity of public servants to take industrial action, and the encouragement of individual over collective bargaining.[29]

Australia's compliance with the principles of freedom of association has been the subject of many 'direct requests'. In times past, Australia's traditional system of regulating industrial disputation through compulsory arbitration as an alternative to collective bargaining and a right to strike raised questions regarding compliance with the principles of freedom of association as understood in the jurisprudence of the ILO. Australia's laws in relation to demarcation disputes, the right to strike (including sympathy strikes), and secondary boycotts have all been the subjects of numerous 'direct requests' to Australia by the CEACR, which has condemned on more than one occasion both Australian common law and statute law.[30] The prohibitions that have been in place since 1996 under the *Workplace Relations Act 1996* (Cth) regarding strikes in relation to multiple employers and sympathy action and pay during strikes, and the capacity to render illegal a wide range of strike action that may cause damage to the Australian economy, all have been areas of concern for the CEACR, as has the prohibition of a wide range secondary boycotts under s 45D of the *Trade Practices Act 1974* (Cth). The CEACR continues to request that Australia amend its legislation to conform to the principles of the *International Labour Code*.[31]

The Australian government's response to 'direct requests' has on some occasions satisfied the CEACR. At other times Australia either has been unable to provide enough information to allay all the concerns of the CEACR, or it has re-asserted

---

27 *Criminal Code Amendment (Slavery and Sexual Servitude) Act 1999* (Cth); and *Criminal Code Amendment (Trafficking in Persons Offences) Act 2005* (Cth).

28 Recent decisions of ILO committees concerning member states' compliance with the *International Labour Code* are available on a country-by-country basis on the ILO website.

29 See Creighton, above n 22, 261–78 regarding the ILO's monitoring of Australia's compliance with the *International Labour Code*.

30 See eg *Direct Request relating to Convention No 87 from the Committee of Experts to the Australian Government* (1989); *Direct Request relating to Convention No 87 from the Committee of Experts to the Australian Government* (1991) following *Case No 1511* (Australia). See also CEACR *Individual Observation concerning Convention No 87, Freedom of Association and Protection of the Right to Organise, 1948 (Australia)* (ratification: 1973) (2001).

31 See eg CEACR *Individual Observation concerning Convention No 87 Freedom of Association and Protection of the Right to Organise, 1948 Australia (ratification: 1973)* (2004); and CEACR *Individual Observation concerning Convention No 98 Right to Organise and Collective Bargaining, 1949 Australia (ratification: 1973)* (2005).

claims that its practices and law are in compliance with its obligations, or it has presented a justification or excuse for its inability to comply. Where the response has not been entirely satisfactory, the CEACR has published an 'individual observation' on Australia, requesting further information or restating the need for compliance with ratified conventions at all levels of law and government. Between 1988 and 2005, there were thirty-nine 'individual observations' in relation to Australia. In recent years, for instance, Australia has been asked to continue to provide information on the measures taken to promote equal access to education and training and employment for Indigenous Australians,[32] and, again, to amend its laws that infringe the principle of freedom of association.[33]

The breadth of the ILO's concern to ensure compliance with its conventions can be seen by the CEACR's superintendence over the use of prison labour in Australia's private prisons.[34] In the 1990s, prison management in some Australian states was privatised, as part of a larger trend whereby many government services were either outsourced or sold to private business ostensibly to lower costs and increase efficiency. In 1998 a 'direct request' was made to Australia seeking assurances that labour in these private prisons was not being appropriated by private individuals or corporations, or if that were the case, prisoners could freely consent to such work so that their conditions of labour 'approximated' to conditions in the open market. Although *Forced Labour Convention, 1930 (ILO C 29)* was initially intended to deal mainly with the use of 'native' slave labour by colonial governments, the CEACR stressed that it must be adaptable to new phenomena and that, in any event, the drafters had also noted the problem of the exploitation of penal labour and therefore the convention was not to be interpreted in a narrow fashion. The ILO also emphasised the place of the *Forced Labour Convention, 1930* alongside other international human rights instruments so that a cohesive body of international jurisprudence on the topic was developed.[35]

The Australian government provided an extensive report in response to the initial request from the CEACR, but was asked to supply further information.[36] In the years following, Australia continued to assert it was not in breach of the *Forced Labour Convention, 1930*. It argued that its private prisons remained ultimately under public control, that the terms of work were the same in its public and private prisons, and that the regulation of prisons was the responsibility of the States rather than the Commonwealth and therefore the issue was difficult for the Australian government to resolve any further. The issue was ultimately reported to the International Conference by the CEACR as a serious matter. While the process did not lead to any change in Australian law or practice, the expectation was that there would be ongoing dialogue

---

32 CEACR *Individual Observation concerning Convention No 111, Discrimination (Employment and Occupation) 1958 Australia (ratification: 1973)* (2004).

33 See above n 31.

34 See also C Fenwick 'Regulating Prisoner's Labour in Australia: A Preliminary View' (2003) 16 *AJLL* 284.

35 See ILCCR *Examination of Individual Case concerning Convention No 29, Forced Labour, 1930 Australia (ratification: 1932)* (1999).

36 See CEACR *Individual Observation concerning Convention No 29, Forced Labour, 1930 Australia (ratification: 1932)* (2004, 2002 and 1999).

between the ILO and Australia, with the ILO expressing the hope that Australia would take into account the best practice of ILO member states in its regulation of prison labour. The process thus involved a thorough examination of Australia's law and practice in this area, prompted a serious response by government, and involved high-level international discussion and the prospect of ongoing scrutiny. However, as in all other cases the ultimate effectiveness of the ILO's superintendence of the issue depends heavily on the response of the national government and what, if any, remedial action it is prepared to take.

A number of complaints have been made to the CFA against Australia and in several of these cases Australian law has been held to be inconsistent with its international obligations.[37] In the most notorious of these cases, the 1989–90 pilots' dispute, although the CFA condemned Australia's common law in relation to strikes and the provisions in the *Trade Practices Act 1974* (Cth) concerning secondary boycotts, Australia did not change its law in response to this.[38] However, after *Case No 1559* concerning a complaint about restrictions on the number of members necessary to register a trade union in Australia, the Parliament amended its legislation in 1993 to comply with the *International Labour Code*.[39]

These cases serve to remind us that ultimately the enforcement of the *International Labour Code* requires cooperation and action by member states. While adverse findings by the ILO in relation to the compliance of domestic law cause international embarrassment and perhaps even shame, the response of the Australian government has varied. Sometimes criticism from the ILO has prompted legislative amendment and compliance. In other instances there has been a defiant assertion of the correctness of the Australian position and a stubborn determination to ignore international condemnation. The effectiveness of the international legal order is thus always mediated by response and action at the national level. Globalisation, by potentially diminishing the significance of the nation, poses a quite different challenge.

Globalisation and its challenges

The emergence of a global community

Globalisation refers to the complex set of phenomena transforming the world from an international to a global community.[40] In large part globalisation has been facilitated by the technological revolution and the emergence of the information age. With modern computer-based communications systems, the limitations of geography can be

---

37 See further Chapter 10.

38 *Case No 1511*, 277th Report of the Committee of Freedom of Association, 1991, Geneva, paras 151–246. See also McEvoy and Owens, above n 20.

39 See *Complaint against the Government of Australia Presented by the Confederation of Australian Industry (CAI) and the International Organisation of Employers (IOE) Report Nos 281 and 284 (Case No 1559)*; and CEACR *Individual Observation concerning Convention No 87 Freedom of Association and Protection of the Right to Organise, 1948 Australia (ratification: 1973)* (1995).

40 See J Fudge and R Owens 'Precarious Work, Women, and the New Economy: The Challenge to Legal Norms' in J Fudge and R Owens (eds) *Precarious Work, Women, and the New Economy: The Challenge to Legal Norms* (2006), 4–15.

transcended and in the process the boundaries of place are rendered far less constraining and less significant than ever before. Simultaneously a vast range of new possibilities for human interactions and relations has opened up so that globalisation has come to embrace every dimension of human life. In politics, the fall of the Berlin Wall in 1989 was a dramatic symbol of the crumbling of the old world order. A global 'new economy' has begun to emerge, facilitated by the opening up of national economies, primarily through the 'deregulation' of their trading and financial institutions and their integration into world markets. The gradual transformation of China into a market economy and its entry to the World Trade Organisation signals the strength of this movement. The new global era is dominated by, and given form through, the restructuring of capital: with cross-border flows of goods and services and the increase of foreign direct investment, the transnational corporation is displacing the nation state as the locus of economic, and therefore political, power.

Globalisation is a movement that is by no means complete: its outcomes are not fixed or defined; its end point is by no means inevitable. The new global terrain is one that is deeply contested. To begin with, the effects of globalisation are not homogenous; it is not simply that the entire world is now encompassed within one new and monolithic order. The formation of regional groupings, in the form of trading blocs, strategic alliances or political organisations, is an important element of wider global transitions. The social division between rich and poor is forging new political alignments, expressed in a regrouping of nations: the destruction of the old 'East'/'West' political divide has erased neither the division between the industrialised market economies of the 'North' and the developing economies of the 'South' nor the cultural and religious differences between a different 'East' and 'West'. All of these divisions form part of the new global politics. The primacy of the nation is certainly challenged by globalisation, but the national and the local still remain important sites of power. As individuals and peoples negotiate this new world, their cultural, racial, religious, and sexual as well as their national identities constitute new affiliations and allegiances. All intersect in a multiplicity of ways and as part of the process of globalisation destabilise old alliances and offer transformative opportunities.

The impact of globalisation on work

Most striking of all are the social effects of globalisation. In few areas of human relations is the impact of globalisation more marked than in the world of work. Here it is not simply that globalisation has been accompanied by, or given a fillip to, many new industries devoted to the production of new goods and new services that are marketed at the global level. Nor that many workers are finding that their way of working has changed, and continues to change, with a rapidity that can scarce be comprehended as the pace of technological development continues unabated. The real significance of globalisation is of a deeper and structural nature.

With the expansion of international trade, the revolution in communications and the diminution of transportation costs, work can often now be performed easily and economically in one continent for a business situated in another. Capital, especially through transnational corporations, has reorganised and restructured itself in a way that can exploit this to its advantage. In an effort to maintain their competitiveness in the global economy, transnational corporations employ workers in different parts of the globe to work on the various components of a particular product. The characteristics of the 'world car' now apply to many goods. It is not uncommon, for instance, for a garment to be designed in one country, cut in another, assembled in yet another, finished elsewhere and then marketed and sold in numerous countries. The transnational corporation will typically have its headquarters in one country, even though much of the work of its head office, such as its data and accounts processing, will be performed elsewhere and linked to it through 'Internet' technology.

However, the transnational corporation is not the only manifestation of the re-organisation and restructuring of global business. Large and small businesses are now often linked in complex webs of interaction through franchising arrangements and joint ventures.[41] The co-dependence of many businesses in production chains is emphasised by 'just in time' production as businesses attempt to respond more flexibly to market pressures. The opening-up and dominance of global markets impacts in many ways upon the organisation of work so that today the decision of any business as to where to situate its workplace(s) is likely to be determined by a range of factors, but significant among them will be the cost, skills and stability of the labour force and the nature of any regulation applicable to that labour force. A global labour market is more and more a reality.

For some workers, globalisation presents exciting new prospects. It offers opportunities to gain wide experience and new skills and places a premium on knowledge and creativity. The possibility that the work of an individual can create an impact on a global scale is seductive and empowering. A promise of a new status, of 'global citizenship', is the reward offered to many workers who traverse the world even if this is often more in a virtual rather than a real sense. The new 'knowledge workers' are highly skilled and are engaged in a process of continual education to develop their 'human capital'. They are fashioned as the new capitalists, as 'enterprise workers' who own the means of production, a description that suggests a blurring of the division between capital and labour in the new economy. Skilled knowledge workers are also often enticed to move about the world in pursuit of work or are relocated around the globe on a temporary basis by their transnational employer. For these knowledge workers such migrations lead to greater wealth. Their skills, their own intellectual capital and the networks they create with other similarly situated workers give them a power capable of inverting the traditional relations of dependency between workers and the businesses for which they may work. The knowledge workers of Silicon Valley are the archetype of this worker.[42]

---

41 See M Castells *The Rise of the Network Society* (1996).

42 See A Hyde 'A Closer Look at the Emerging Employment Law of Silicon Valley's High Velocity Labour Market' in J Conaghan, RM Fischl and K Klare (eds) *Labour Law in an Era of Globalization: Transformative Practices and Possibilities* (2002).

However, for many other workers, globalisation has thus far been a negative experience, bringing more threats than opportunities. For these workers the pace of change in the world of work has been, and continues to be, accompanied by increased inequality and insecurity. Many workers in industrialised nations previously sheltered by protectionist barriers must now compete for work with those from developing countries who have much lower pay and poorer conditions of work. Consequently many have seen their once secure positions disappear altogether or become replaced by precarious forms of employment. The demands of business for flexibility to respond to the pressures of the marketplace of the new economy have changed patterns of work so that jobs once designated as 'non-standard' or 'atypical' have now come to represent the norm. For the vast majority of workers the old 'Fordist' paradigm, of the worker as breadwinner with security of employment for a lifetime who performs a standard set of skills in large-scale production enterprises, is rapidly becoming a thing of the past. At the same time it has often become difficult to distinguish many work relations from commercial relations as a result of the increased utilisation of new forms and patterns of contracting for services even though the income from such arrangements often falls far short of that required to support the worker.[43] More and more workers have become marginalised as the gap between rich and poor increases.[44] A wave of poor and unskilled immigrant workers in search of better opportunities is now a phenomenon observed in many parts of the globe. However, the work that is available for them at their destination is too often low skilled, temporary or seasonal, and low paid. They often become a 'guest worker' in an alien nation, seeking to fulfil their economic needs in a new environment while their families and others with whom they have a primary social attachment remain far away in their country of origin. The growing use of women from developing nations as domestic labour in industrialised economies is but one example of this. The seasonal fruit picker is another. The 'global citizenship' of many of these transnational workers is often insecure and at best second-class. These trends are observable and of growing importance in Australia.[45]

Globalisation and the legal order

Since the 1990s it has became increasingly apparent that globalisation has the potential to challenge, even to the point of destruction, what may be termed the 'old' international legal order. This appears odd at first blush, for ordinarily it might be thought that globalisation would mean an increasing importance of all things international. But the old international legal order was based upon the primacy of the nation state. As the nomenclature indicates, it was *inter-national*: its structure and its very existence depended upon and comprised links *between nations*. For at least the last two centuries the concept of law has been

---

43 J Fudge 'Self Employment, Women and Precarious Work: The Scope of Labour Protection' in Fudge and Owens (eds), above n 40.

44 ILO, Working Party on the Social Dimensions of the Liberalization of International Trade *Final Report on the Impact of Globalisation* (1999).

45 ABS *Australia's Most Recent Immigrants*, Cat No 2053.0, 2004; and Senate Employment, Workplace Relations and Education Committee, Parliament of Australia, *Inquiry into Pacific Region Seasonal Contract Labour* (2006).

inextricably linked to that of the *nation* state.[46] Constitutions are the fundamental law of national legal systems and the source of the validity of all other legal norms within the nation. In legal terms the nation is a bounded entity presided over by a sovereign with a power to maintain its borders against the outside world and to control all within those borders. But the nation and law are now confronted by and must operate within a radically different context: one in which the global transcends the national and the international.

National legal systems, and therefore the old international legal system, are profoundly challenged by the new economy of the global market because national sovereignty is potentially less effective in this context.[47] Law is based upon a territorial conception of (political) power. But economic power is mapped differently in the global era, erasing national borders, evading the disciplinary potential of local national law.

Nothing illustrates this more strikingly than the relation of the transnational corporation and the nation state. Transnational corporations, the most powerful players in the global market, exist beyond the limits of the nation state. While it is true that they continue to depend on national legal systems, if only as the source of their legal status, transnational corporations can operate outside the effective control of the nation state. They have a vast economic power that can be turned against a host state. Through threats to relocate their operations elsewhere they can dictate the terms of their participation in a local or national economy. These threats may result in these corporations becoming beneficiaries of the largesse of the state, often through the receipt of tax concessions, but invariably such 'corporate welfare' is effective only in the short term and any inability on the part of the state to continue or increase payments fails to prevent the corporation's departure. Corporate welfare inverts traditional meanings and marks the dependency not of the recipient corporation but of the donor state.

There are also other ways in which the power of transnational players can subvert the law of nation states, with flow-on effects for the organisation and regulation of other market players, including workers, within the nation state. In some countries special export zones are established, which are cocooned from national regulation, leaving workers often unprotected. The threat to relocate is also effective against other workers whose protection might be the intention of any regulatory system erected by the nation state. The power a locally based trade union or group of workers might exercise under laws promoting freedom of association or collective bargaining can be diminished dramatically in the face of the threat to relocate to another jurisdiction where there is no such protection.[48] For those workers who are trapped by geography a job at any cost can appear to be better than no job at all.

Neo-liberal theory

The challenge to the law of work posed by the new economy is particularly complex because globalisation is a process dominated, controlled and shaped by neo-liberal

---

46 See H Arthurs 'Labour Law without the State' (1996) 46 *UTLJ* 1, 45; and R Owens 'The Future of the Law of Work' (2002) 23 *Adel LR* 345, 347–9.

47 See S Picciotto and R Mayne (eds) *Regulating International Business: Beyond Liberalisation* (1999).

48 See ILO, above n 16, Ch 1, para 20.

ideology. In the global era prime emphasis is placed on the restructuring of the economic order along market lines and this is represented as a natural and, therefore, inevitable process. Under neo-liberal theory 'deregulation' and 'privatisation' have become the primary mechanisms to effect the transformation of political, social and legal institutions, including the law of work, into the new world order. As rhetorical devices they have constructed regulation (especially statutory law) and the state as antithetical to the new economy, and deny that the legal doctrines of contract and property that shape the marketplace are equally the product of the state and its (judicial) institutions.

Contract

Neo-liberal theory has a conception of the individual as a pre-social being, someone whose existence and most important relations exist prior to the state. In the marketplace the most significant issue for these individual actors is their ability to deal freely with each other. Accordingly the law of the global market is a 'private' law; that is, a law determined by individual actors (whether natural persons or corporate entities). Contract is the mechanism through which their market deals or relations are organised, for only contract is expressive of, and responsive to, the needs of individual players. In contract the autonomy of the individual actor is respected: parties to a contract make their own relations, or so the theory goes. Contract is thus seen as the spontaneous and organic form of the marketplace. In order to function, the marketplace also respects the private property of its individual players for their primary goal is its accumulation through contractual deals. The economic rationalism of neo-liberal theory claims that the underlying structure of the market values the efficiency of competitiveness above all else and, therefore, demands freedom and absolute flexibility for its players to maximise production and amass profits. Contract as it has been developed by the courts is perceived to be the perfect vehicle to secure these goals.

Deregulation

Just as contract is constructed as integral to the market and the new economy, so too is 'deregulation'. Exogenous intervention by the state or other non-market players is portrayed as anathema to neo-liberal conceptions about the organisation of market relations. The role of 'external' parties is cast as an artificial intervention in the market introducing inefficiencies. Competition between individual players is considered the natural, efficient and, therefore, best regulatory mechanism. Thus the only 'standards' that are relevant are the ones that emerge through the 'best practice' of the market participants. In this market there is no place for 'public' law.

Privatisation

The dominance of the market, its congruence with economics, and the assertion of the norms of its practices as expressed in the contracts between its players, all depend on the denial of the relevance or importance of the state or a wider 'public' or community interest. The market is constructed on the assumption that it can best flourish where it is free of political interference from the state. The articulation by the 'external' state of overarching commonalities is anathema in this context. Likewise the participation of the state in the market is deemed to be inappropriate because it is assumed to subsidise its own operations and not subject itself to the same risks as other market players and thus to be inefficient. In the new economy many functions of the state have thus been privatised; either outsourced through contractual arrangements or transferred by sale to the private sector.

The labour market

The dogmas associated with contractualism, deregulation and privatisation now influence everywhere the development of the law of work. In neo-liberal theory a free or 'deregulated' labour market is an integral part of the wider global market. Any regulatory interference with the labour market is said to introduce inefficient distortions and additional costs: that is, regulation of the labour market, either directly in the form of protections and stipulation of work standards or indirectly through, say, social security measures, is claimed to increase costs or cause unemployment by removing those to whom the market would otherwise offer employment. Deregulation of the labour market is taken to be a *sine qua non* of progress. Competition is revered as the only incentive necessary to provide workers with good conditions and safe workplaces, because neo-liberal theory posits that a failure to do so will result in an exodus of workers to businesses that meet the market's own 'best practice' standards. The resultant loss of skills and expertise from, and lack of stability in, their workforce will make it impossible for industries and workplaces that do not conform to these best practice standards to survive. The global market is thus predicted to produce a 'race to the top' with transnational corporations and other market players providing ever better wages and conditions of work: best practice, so it goes, will produce a 'ratchetting up' effect.[49]

The global market is thus presented as a positive environment for all players (corporations and individuals, capital and labour) who are assumed to be equal. The market is portrayed as the facilitator of economic growth, necessary for the generation of the wealth that will be available ultimately to be shared equally by all. There is an implicit assertion that everyone will be able to access equally the benefits of globalisation. Any appearance of inequality is dismissed as a temporary aberration as nations go through a process of adjustment and evolution. Interference by the state to ameliorate interim inequalities is discouraged as threatening the disruption of the market as a whole and its long-term benefits.

The development of the global market in neo-liberal theory has thus been based on the assumption that there is an internal logic to the market order that is properly anterior to the attainment of social goals. State interference in the market through regulation introduces inefficiencies and distortions hindering the attainment of its natural, and hence good and equitable, consequences. Growth in global trade is an important part of modern market theory: larger markets enable more competition, create greater efficiencies, and hence work better. In neo-liberal theory, the economics of the marketplace inevitably

---

49 See eg A Fung, D O'Rourke and C Sabel *Ratcheting Labour Standards: Regulation for Continuous Improvement in the Global Workplace* (2000).

brings in its train better social consequences.[50] Opening up economies, whether local, national or regional, to the global market has become the primary goal in the new global agenda. The market economy, rather than its effects, is the focus of attention. The flourishing of global trade is posited in neo-liberal theory to be crucially a matter of economics requiring an absence of exogenous constraints. The assertion of the primacy of the economic sphere, and its implied separation from social and political spheres, may not be entirely new but from the 1980s it was promoted with vigour and achieved an unprecedented dominance in all discussions concerning globalisation. This has impacted on the development of the law of work in the global era.

In the context of neo-liberal philosophy the assertion of the inevitability of the globalisation movement is the denial that political or social action can hold any sway over the economic. However, it seems no longer adequate simply to assert that the opening up of markets will produce greater wealth. The critical question is the distribution of that wealth. While the globalisation process is often argued to be one of wealth creation, the reality is more complex. Although some may no longer accept that there is a straightforward inequality in the distribution of the fruits of the globalisation movement, with the poor getting poorer and the rich richer, the complexities of the economic consequences of the entire process continue to require careful monitoring and analysis.[51] This issue remains one that is keenly contested between the proponents and opponents of globalisation. Although there are debates among economists as to the accuracy of the global picture, what can be clearly asserted is that at present the social benefits of globalisation are at best mixed. While globalisation may have the capacity to bring a range of benefits to many around the world and improve their standard of living and the quality of life, the gains are still unevenly distributed.

Together the changing nature of employment patterns and the global economy has brought both prosperity and inequalities, and together they demand attention and test the limits of global collective responsibility. As the ILO has noted:

> The simultaneous inclusion and exclusion of people, regions and economic sectors is a significant characteristic of globalisation and presents some of its greatest challenges.[52]

The mounting evidence of the present circumstances of the lives, including the working lives, of many has forced a political analysis of the social consequences of the economics of the globalisation movement. There is growing support for the view that the market should only be allowed to operate within a set of constraints that are alive to the social impact that accompanies the globalisation process. Otherwise, it is argued, trade liberalisation will simply induce a 'race to the bottom' as nations cast aside social protections in order to encourage foreign investment and international trade. In recent years there appears to

---

50 D Ben-David, H Nordstrom and LA Winters, WTO Special Studies 5 *Trade, Income Disparity and Poverty* (1999).

51 Joint Standing Committee on Treaties, Australian Parliament '*Who's Afraid of the WTO? Australia and the World Trade Organisation*' (2001) Recommendation 1; and UNDP *Human Development Report* (1999). Cf P Collier and D Dollar *Globalization, Growth and Poverty: Building an Inclusive World Economy* (2001).

52 ILO, above n 16, Ch 1, para 17.

have been some turning around from the harshness of the neo-liberalism so dominant in the 1980s and 1990s to emphasise not the dismantling of public institutions but the importance of adapting them to ensure their ongoing relevance.[53]

The ILO and the challenges of globalisation

The challenge of globalisation to the old international legal order and its institutions like the ILO became apparent by the end of the 1980s. The neo-liberal values of the global marketplace that focus strongly on individualism contrast with many of the values, like protection of workers and collectivism, traditionally embraced by the ILO. The ILO, it was said, had become a prisoner of history 'locked into certain perspectives and processes that are, in the current international political economy, no longer appropriate'.[54] In the global era the very features of the ILO that were once lauded as its greatest strength threatened to hinder its effectiveness.

The International Labour Organization—too bureaucratic?

The ILO was designed to enable broad participation, guarantee accountability and fair treatment, and ensure that large-scale projects could be planned, managed and achieved. Its structure as a very large, hierarchical and formalised bureaucracy was intended to facilitate those purposes. But such an organisation can come to demand more and more resources for its own internal arrangements and gradually cease to serve its own constituents effectively. One criticism of the ILO is that it fell into this trap.[55] Its bureaucratised procedures had become cumbersome, time consuming and inflexible. In monitoring conventions, for example, the ILO placed uniformly onerous demands on all countries for reporting regardless of their resources to respond. These institutional characteristics contrasted dramatically with the less formalised, more flexible methods of operating favoured in the marketplace. The bureaucratic structure of the ILO thus appeared to be at odds with the dominant values of the new world order.

Structural issues at the International Labour Organization

Although the ILO was created as an international body, from the outset it had been strongly influenced by its Western European foundations. The ideal animating the United Nations' organisations, like the ILO, is of equality between all member states. However, at the ILO the ideal had never been translated into reality. For the first half of the twentieth century it operated as 'a club of like minded states' from Western Europe.[56] After World War II it was influenced most strongly by the nations referred to as the 'states of chief industrial importance'. The two-thirds majority vote required by the *ILO Constitution* for determining issues at the International Labour Conference

---

53 World Bank *World Development Report: The State in a Changing World* (1997), 75.

54 S Cooney 'Testing Times for the ILO: Institutional Reform for the New Political Economy' (1999) 20 *Comp Lab L & Pol'y J* 365, 367.

55 Ibid 373 ff, and Creighton, above n 3, 106–7.

56 J Braithwaite and P Drahos *Global Business Regulation* (2000), 234.

appeared to ensure that its decisions were truly representative; but in practice whole regions of the world could be effectively excluded. The influence of the major players was exerted in a myriad of subtle ways. The arguably 'Western' bias of the organisation affected everything, and even seemed inappropriate to nations like Australia that had a very different regulatory system and traditions from those of the European model.[57] But by the end of the twentieth century the evolution of the European Common Market into the European Union weakened the affiliation to the ILO of many nations that had formerly been amongst its strongest supporters. At the same time there was little effective representation from Asian, African or Islamic nations. This was patently not appropriate[58] and globalisation made it unsustainable.

The tripartite structure of the ILO, long considered its defining and strongest feature, was also placed under increasing pressure in the new economy. The unique representation of government, business and worker interests previously gave a peculiar legitimacy to the *International Labour Code*. Now the marketplace did not adhere to the view that the state, employer and worker organisations were equally important players in the world of work.

Furthermore, there were significant changes in each of the ILO's constituent groups. As nations became more and more animated by a desire to become part of the new economy they became less concerned to participate in the ILO. The interests of many businesses and workers were also no longer effectively represented at the ILO. In the global era, business increasingly defied any attempt to assign to it a single focus or unanimity of interests making its representation through peak employer bodies at the ILO a contentious issue.

A problem also emerged regarding the representation of workers. Trade unions, the traditional organisations of workers, held a privileged position at the ILO as the official voice of workers. However, in developing economies, trade unions were often weak, especially when compared with their traditionally strong base in the manufacturing industries of industrialised market economies. And everywhere fewer workers were joining trade unions.[59] With a declining membership the legitimacy of trade unions as the voice of workers began to be questioned. Trade unions struggled to adapt to the new realities of the global economy as it became steadily apparent that the issues of significance to many workers were very different from the concerns of the standard worker of the old economy. Those who were most marginal, least powerful and most vulnerable to the impact of globalisation were also less likely to be members of a trade union. There thus developed a 'representation gap' in the world of work, and at the ILO.[60] Equally problematic, precariousness of employment was forcing many workers to adopt the guise of business, whether operating as lone independent contractors or through a family business or as the franchisees of transnational corporations, and this challenged the distinction between business and worker. As was the case elsewhere,

---

57 See eg Creighton, above n 3.
58 See Cooney, above n 54.
59 ILO *World Labour Report 1997–98* (1997).
60 ILO, above n 16, 12.

NGOs emerged as having the potential and the capacity to give voice at least to some of those who were particularly vulnerable to the forces of globalisation. But the processes of the ILO were not well equipped to receive their representations. Therefore, despite the ILO's ostensibly strong representative structure, the voices of many of its constituents were gradually being erased.

The role of the *International Labour Code* in the global era

Although it might have been expected that the globalisation movement would accord increasing importance to the *International Labour Code*, in the final two decades of the twentieth century the number of ratifications of ILO conventions steadily declined and this most basic function of the ILO was placed under intense scrutiny.

Several explanations have been given for the decline in adherence to the *International Labour Code*.[61] First, the appropriateness of applying universal standards to different social and economic contexts has always been recognised as a difficult and important issue by the ILO. Article 19(3) of the *ILO Constitution* specifically envisages that modifications to convention standards may be necessary to take account of particular conditions, and most ILO conventions include flexibility clauses. However, by the late 1980s, the possibility of devising meaningful standards, acceptable to countries as diverse as the industrialised market economies of nations of 'the North' and the struggling 'underdeveloped' economies of 'the South', was seen as diminishing. Critics were of the view that it was unrealistic for developing nations to sign up even to aspirational conventions let alone those with specific detailed standards. They also observed that there was an overproduction of labour standards because the adoption of a convention placed reporting burdens on member states, whether or not they ratified it.[62]

Secondly, with the emergence of regional trade blocks the attention of many of those states traditionally amongst the strongest supporters of ILO standards was now diverted towards ensuring compliance with the norms established by the other economic and political organisations to which they now belonged. Often the supranational norms of these regional groupings of nations had a higher status than those of the ILO, sometimes directly binding in a way that ILO norms were not. Even their very existence introduced further complexity into ILO negotiations.[63]

Thirdly, the problem of outdated conventions was perceived to be acute as the number of ratifications of ILO conventions dropped markedly. Finally, and perhaps most significantly, the international context in which the ILO was conceived and operated for the most part of the twentieth century had now changed. As Breen Creighton observed, the individualism of the global marketplace threatened not only the legitimacy of the ILO to set global standards but also had a deeper impact threatening ILO values. ILO standards, especially those that were prescriptive, were increasingly perceived to be an

---

61 Creighton, above n 3, 100–5. See also B Creighton 'The Future of Labour Law: Is there a Role for International Standards?' in C Barnard, S Deakin and GS Morris (eds) *The Future of Labour Law: Liber Amicorum Bob Hepple* QC (2004).

62 E Cordova 'Some Reflections on the Overproduction of International Labour Standards' (1993) 14 *CLL* 161; and Cooney, above n 54, 373 ff.

63 J Murray *Transnational Labour Regulation: The ILO and EC Compared* (2001).

unwarranted intervention into the free ordering of work relations through contract, the imposition of uniform rules or standards sitting uncomfortably with the dominant philosophies of an era of 'deregulation'. The challenge for the ILO was how to remain relevant in a global world.

The emergence of a new global law of work

Trade agreements and a 'labour clause'

Trade liberalisation and the separation of the economic and social spheres

The most influential forces shaping the global market have come from outside the United Nations and its affiliated bodies like the ILO. Since World War II the norms governing global economic policies, especially those concerning growth and development, have been dominated by two institutions: the International Monetary Fund (the IMF) and the International Bank for Reconstruction and Development (the World Bank).[64] The establishment of these 'Bretton Woods Institutions', so labelled because their foundation in 1944 followed a meeting in the US town of the same name, aimed to secure global peace and financial stability by ensuring the application of sound economic principles and the provision of access to reputable finance for economic development. They are dominated by the rich, developed nations of the world, for unlike the United Nations where, at least in theory, each member state has an equal voice, it is wealth that determines the share of voting power in these institutions. Since the 1980s, the assistance provided by these institutions to developing countries has often been conditional upon acceptance of a fairly uniform model of structural adjustment, incorporating principles of privatisation and labour market flexibility to achieve debt reduction.[65] In the 1980s and 1990s their requirements often in effect conflicted with, and therefore prevented, the adoption of the *International Labour Code* in many developing economies.

After World War II global trade was to be the province of a third Bretton Woods institution, the International Trade Organization (ITO). Efforts to establish an international trading order were slow, mainly because of the reticence of the United States in signing up to the 1948 *Havana Charter* for the ITO. The *General Agreement on Tariffs and Trade* (GATT), established in 1947, was always intended as an interim arrangement. However, until the formation of the World Trade Organisation (WTO) by the *Marrakesh Agreement* of 1995, the global trade market was facilitated under the auspices of the GATT, which established trade rules aimed at lowering tariffs and also dealt with trade disputes.[66]

The foundation of the GATT and then the WTO challenged the traditional relation in international law between the economic and the political, between the

---

64 *Articles of Agreement of the International Monetary Fund* [1947] ATS 11; and *Articles of Agreement of the International Bank for Reconstruction and Development* [1947] ATS 15.

65 See K Rittich *Recharacterizing Restructuring: Law, Distribution and Gender in Market Reform* (2002) for an analysis and critique of this strategy.

66 *General Agreement on Tariffs and Trade (GATT)* [1948] ATS 23; and *Marrakesh Agreement Establishing the World Trade Organization (WTO Agreement)* [1995] ATS 8.

private sphere of the market and the public sphere of the state, because the GATT/ WTO agreements were conceived as more akin to commercial contracts rather than political agreements between states. This in turn reinforced the idea of the autonomy of the market. The WTO, which comprised 149 member states by the end of 2005, is now the legal and organisational foundation of the multinational trading system.[67] The Ministerial Conference is the WTO's highest authority and it meets at least once every two years. The administration of the WTO is conducted through a General Council and its subsidiary bodies. The WTO operates as a forum to facilitate trade negotiations, to administer multilateral trade agreements, and to monitor national trade policies. It also settles trade disputes for which it has established a legal regime that comprises four stages of consultation, panel adjudication, appeal and adoption and implementation.

The Bretton Woods institutions and the WTO continue to be powerful institutions influencing the direction of global economic development and trade law. The primary aim of the WTO is to promote the opening of markets worldwide and to create a truly global market. In this its focus is, in practice, narrowly economic. The social effects of trade liberalisation are ignored by the WTO. Article VII of the *Havana Charter* exhorted members to eliminate 'unfair labour conditions' and the GATT constituent documents included the explicit goal of 'ensur[ing] full employment and raising the standard of living', but these provisions never figured prominently in the operation of GATT multilateral trade. Nor do they in the interpretation of WTO agreements, although some commentators argue that a different interpretative approach is possible.[68] In any event over the last decade the often negative impacts of the opening up of markets forced the issue of social protection and labour rights back onto the agenda, where it first crystallised around the idea of the inclusion of a 'labour clause' in trade agreements.

The labour clause debate

The debate about the connection between economic and social issues is not new.[69] However, in the late 1990s, the inclusion of a labour clause in major trade agreements was identified as one of the major challenges facing the world.[70] A labour clause in trade agreements means that failure to adhere to identified labour standards may ultimately justify the imposition of some form of trade sanction or penalty. Labour clauses thus have

---

67 Information about the WTO, including all relevant legal documents, can be found at <www.wto.org>.

68 See E Alben 'GATT and the Fair Wage: A Historical Perspective on the Labour–Trade Link' in (2001) 101 *Col L R* 1410; and A Blackett 'Whither the Social Clause: Human Rights, Trade Theory and Treaty Interpretation' (1999) 31 *Col HRLR* 1.

69 See S Charnovitz 'The Influence of International Labour Standards on the World Trading Regime: A Historical Overview' (1987) 126 *Int Lab Rev* 565; E de Wet 'Labour Standards in the Globalized Economy: The Inclusion of a Social Clause in the General Agreement on Tariff and Trade/World Trade Organisation?' (1995) 17 *Hum Rts Q* 443; OECD *Trade Employment and Labour Standards—A Study of Core Workers' Rights and International Trade* (1996) 169; and V Leary 'Workers' Rights and International Trade: The Social Clause' in J Bhagwati and RE Hudec (eds) *Fair Trade and Harmonization: Prerequisites for Free Trade* (1996).

70 See DK Brown 'International Trade and Core Labour Standards: A Survey of the Recent Literature' in *Labour Market and Social Policy—Occasional Papers No 43* (2000); D Chin, *A Social Clause for Labour's Cause: Global Trade and Labour Standards—A Challenge for the New Millennium* (1998); and E Lee 'Globalisation and Labour Standards: A Review of the Issues' (1997) 136 *Int Lab Rev* 173.

the potential to be an effective enforcement mechanism for labour standards, although their application can also raise difficult issues regarding the connection between the violation of the labour standard and the relevant trade, the level of violation, and the proportionality of sanctions to be imposed.

The use of a labour clause as a mechanism for securing adherence to labour standards has long been controversial. The argument for a labour clause has been most strongly supported by some of the industrialised market economies of the 'North', and especially European nations, where it is feared that trade liberalisation will induce a 'race to the bottom'. Trade unions have also added their voice to the call for a labour clause.[71] However, the debate has not been conducted along lines replicating a strict 'North'/'South' or labour/capital divide. Australia, for instance, has argued against the inclusion of a labour clause in trade agreements. Even within national governments, different departments may place different emphasis on the most appropriate approach to adopt depending on their differing perceptions of shifting international alliances, the changing significance of trading partners and political ideology.[72]

The proponents of a labour clause claim that the market must be underpinned by a floor of social rights including labour rights, to counteract 'social dumping' from unacceptably low labour conditions. In economic terms that amounts to an advantage unrelated to productivity and thus distorts competition.[73] But there has been a sustained resistance to the linkage of trade and labour standards especially from developing economies of the 'South', which have generally considered that labour clauses in international trade agreements amount to little more than a thinly disguised protective ploy by wealthier countries of the 'North' to deny them one of the few competitive advantages, that is, cheap labour, that they possess in the global marketplace.

These arguments for and against the inclusion of a labour clause in trade agreements replicate many of the arguments for the adoption of labour standards more broadly. Rarely do these arguments challenge either what Sean Cooney calls 'stale binary logic'[74] or the dominant neo-liberal theoretical framework. On one side, interference in the market is rejected as introducing distortions. Cheap labour, on this view, is simply a competitive advantage. Competition is advocated as the best, and an appropriate, regulatory mechanism to deal with labour issues. The market, it is asserted, will thus generate its own upward pressure to deliver labour rights. On the other side, it is argued that addressing the problem of labour rights through a labour clause will establish the level playing field upon which fair competition within the market can then take place: free trade is not necessarily fair trade. Labour rights and economic efficiency can and do go together, with proponents pointing to evidence that adherence to labour

71 ACTU *Submission on Australia's Position for the November 2001 WTO Ministerial Meeting* (2001).
72 See C Nyland and R Castle 'The ILO and the Australian Contribution to the International Labour Standards Debate' (1999) 41 *JIR* 355.
73 Cf S Deakin and F Wilkinson 'Rights vs Efficiency? The Economic Case for Transnational Labour Standards' (1994) 23 *ILJ* 289.
74 S Cooney 'Labour Law and the World Trade Organization: Towards a Reconstruction of the Linkage Discourse' (2005) 10 *Deakin LR* 83.

standards can and does lead to economic development.[75] The market, it is asserted, must be underpinned by some consensus as to broad standards that are agreed upon to preserve respect for human rights. Economic expansion must therefore be paralleled by social protection.

The WTO and rejection of a labour clause

The history of efforts to include the social effects of trade liberalisation on the agenda of the WTO charts the progress of the labour clause debate. The first Ministerial Conference of the WTO in Singapore in 1996 rejected proposals for the inclusion of a labour clause in multilateral trade agreements, but declared:

> We renew our commitment to the observance of internationally recognised core labour standards. The International Labour Organization (the ILO) is the competent body to set and deal with these standards, and we affirm our support for its work in promoting them. We believe that economic growth and development fostered by increased trade and further trade liberalization contribute to the promotion of these standards. We reject the use of labour standards for protectionist purposes, and agree that the comparative advantage of countries, particularly low-wage countries, must in no way be put into question. In this regard we note that the WTO and ILO secretariats will continue their existing collaboration.[76]

While this *Singapore Declaration* was the first recognition in a WTO document of labour issues, the separation of the economic and social spheres and the institutions establishing the norms governing them was simultaneously reasserted. However, the labour clause issue did not go away. Public protests took place at the WTO Ministerial Conference in Geneva in 1998 and intensified at the Third Ministerial Conference held in Seattle in 1999, where a broad alliance of disparate groups, including trade unions, NGOs, and environmentalists, mobilised to demonstrate the power of civil society. They demanded that account be taken of human rights in the expansion of the global market. Many of these groups had observer status at the WTO,[77] and the power of their protest was enhanced spectacularly by the Internet.

At Seattle the linkage of labour standards to trade agreements was again rejected. The 'Costa Rica Document', which outlined a strategy to continue discussions on trade, development, globalisation and labour standards between the WTO, the ILO, the World Bank and the United Nations Conference on Trade and Development (UNCTAD) established in 1994, was not adopted before the Third Ministerial Conference was finally suspended. At Seattle the only statement on labour issued by the WTO welcomed the then recent establishment by the ILO of a Working Party on the Social Dimension of the Liberalization of International Trade.

---

75 See OECD, above n 69. See also KV Champion, 'Comment, Who Pays for Free Trade? The Dilemma of Free Trade and International Labour Standards' (1996) 22 *NCJ International and Commercial Regulation* 181; and S Charnovitz 'Trade Employment and Labour Standards: The OECD Study and Recent Developments in the Trade and Labour Standards Debate' (1997) 11 *Temple Int'l & Comp LJ* 131. Cf D Kucera *The Effect of Core Worker's Rights on Labour Costs and Foreign Direct Investment: Evaluating the Conventional Wisdom* (2001).

76 *Singapore Ministerial Declaration*, para 4, WTO Doc WT/MIN(96)/DEC/W (13 December, 1996) reprinted in 36 ILM 218, 221.

77 The number of NGOs entitled to attend WTO meetings increased dramatically from 108 at Singapore in 1996 to over 1000 at Hong Kong in 2005.

Criticism of the WTO continued. Before the Fourth Ministerial Conference in Doha, Qatar, in November 2001, the Australian Council of Trade Unions condemned the WTO for simply advancing the economic agenda of business and argued that it needed to focus on trade 'in the context of civil society and working families'.[78] However, again in Doha little attention was paid to the issue of labour standards, and the *Doha Declaration* simply reaffirmed the *Singapore Declaration* and again noted the work of the ILO on the social dimension of globalisation. By the time of the next Ministerial meetings in Cancún, Mexico, in 2003 and Hong Kong in 2005 attention did not focus at all on the labour issue. There now seems little prospect of including a labour clause in WTO agreements, with the WTO firmly placing the responsibility for consideration of the social dimensions of trade liberalisation, especially the effects on work, with other international institutions and especially the ILO. This is an approach that Australia supported.[79]

The inclusion of a labour clause in regional and bilateral free trade agreements

The difficulties besetting the negotiation of a multilateral world trade agreement under the auspices of the WTO since the failure of the Seattle Ministerial Conference were evident again at WTO meetings in Cancún (2003), Geneva (2004) and Hong Kong (2005). This has resulted in nations devoting increased attention to regional and bilateral trade agreements, which often prove (politically) easier to negotiate. There are a number of regional trading blocs around the globe including the European Union, Asia Pacific Economic Co-operation, the Caribbean Common Market, and Mercado Común del Sur/Mercado Commum do Sul (MERCOSUR) in South America.

Progress towards Australia's inclusion in a future Association of South East Asian Nations (ASEAN) Free Trade Agreement was initially slow, but moved forward with more alacrity after the ASEAN–Australia and New Zealand Commemorative Summit in Vientiane, in November 2004, where agreement was reached to negotiate an Australia–ASEAN–New Zealand free trade agreement within two years. Australia's signature of ASEAN's core *Treaty of Amity and Co-operation* in 2005 further signals the potential for Australia's inclusion in any future ASEAN Economic Community or perhaps East Asian Economic Community.

Australia has already established a number of important bilateral free trade agreements, including with Singapore, Thailand and the United States of America, as well as an agreement with New Zealand on Closer Economic Relations. At the end of 2005 it was pursuing the possibility of free trade agreements with China, Japan, Malaysia and the United Arab Emirates. It also has concluded an agreement with Indonesia to develop a comprehensive economic framework, which is the likely precursor of a free trade agreement. Bilateral free trade negotiations and agreements have thus flourished in recent years.[80]

---

78 ACTU, above n 71.
79 Joint Standing Committee on Treaties, Parliament of Australia, *Report 42: Who's Afraid of the WTO? Australia and the World Trade Organisation* (2001), Recommendation 21.
80 Information on Australia's trade policy and free trade agreements can be found at <www.dfat.gov.au/trade>.

The inclusion of labour clauses in regional and bilateral trade agreements is still a hotly contested issue. However, several regional trade agreements, including that of the European Union, include some form of labour clause. The conclusion of a number of bilateral free trade agreements containing labour clauses, including between countries with market industrialised economies and with developing economies, also indicates a continuing preparedness in some areas to link free trade agreements with labour standards.[81]

There are a number of different models for labour clauses in trade agreements.[82] The formalised political and economic alliances known as the European Union offer what Katherine Stone has called an 'integrative' model whereby a relatively uniform set of standards applies across its different nation members. In the European Union the binding constitutive legislation or treaty between the member nations ensures uniformity on the fundamentals, with matters of detail governed by 'directives' stating more precisely minimum standards. These directives encourage harmonisation as they must be picked up and translated into each member state's particular national legal system. With the passage of time, the expectation is that the integrative impetus will become stronger leading to greater uniformity in each of the constituent member states.

Contrasted with 'integrative' models are those labelled by Stone as 'interpenetrative', whereby through an international agreement there is an overarching cross-monitoring by each of the parties of the laws of the other, such as the cross-border monitoring and enforcement, which occurs in relation to the North America Free Trade Agreement (NAFTA). Labour clauses may also be directly incorporated into a trade agreement or they may be adopted as an additional agreement running parallel to a trade agreement. The North American Agreement on Labour Cooperation (NAALC) is a supplementary agreement to NAFTA.[83] This labour side agreement does not seek to change the labour laws of the participating nations. It purports to promote a set of fundamental principles such as freedom of association, non-discrimination, the prohibition of child labour, minimum wages, and occupational health and safety, which parties are encouraged to promote and to implement through their own labour laws, and it allows a monitoring of the enforcement of those national laws. In the NAALC there is a mechanism whereby complaints concerning labour conditions and laws can be brought to a Commission for Labour Co-operation, which attempts to resolve them in the first instance by consultation and cooperation.

Australia has traditionally been opposed to trade–labour linkage, and labour clauses are not included in its free trade agreements with Singapore or Thailand. However, the Australia–United States Free Trade Agreement (AUSFTA) concluded in 2004 has a labour clause in which both parties have agreed to enforce their own labour laws and to ensure that those laws do not derogate from internationally recognised principles and rights. These are defined as:

---

81 G Griffin, C Nyland and A O'Rourke 'Trade Promotion Authority and Core Labour Standards: Implications for Australia' (2004) 17 *AJLL* 35, 51–6.

82 See K van Wezel Stone 'Labour and the Global Economy: Four Approaches to Transnational Labour Regulation' (1995) 16 *Mich J Int L* L987; and E Cappuyns 'Linking Labour Standards and Trade Sanctions: An Analysis of their Current Relationship' (1998) *Col J T L* 658.

83 NAFTA, 17 December 1992, Can-Mex-US, 32 ILM 289 (entered into force 1 January 1994).

- the right of association;
- the right to organise and bargain collectively;
- a prohibition on the use of any form of forced or compulsory labour;
- labour protections for children and young people, including a minimum age for the employment of children and elimination of the worst forms of child labour; and
- acceptable conditions of work with respect to minimum wages, hours of work, and occupational health and safety.[84]

This complements the reaffirmation of commitment by the parties to their obligations as members of the ILO and to the *ILO Declaration on Fundamental Principles and Rights at Work*,[85] but also goes somewhat further in its commitment to guarantee minimum standards relating to wages, working time and occupational health and safety.

The AUSFTA is particularly important because Australia's resistance to the inclusion of a labour clause in free trade agreements was overcome by the USA's insistence that the clause be included. Indeed it is somewhat telling that the United States, which has generally been considered in the past to have work conditions and protections inferior to those offered by Australian law, should have been so insistent on the inclusion of a labour clause in its free trade arrangements.[86] Thus the AUSFTA establishes an important precedent, reference to which can be made to resist assertions by Australia that labour clauses should not be included in future free trade agreements.

However, the AUSFTA is also likely to reveal the frailty of protections in labour clauses. There is no clear indication of how the clause will be interpreted if compliance with it is challenged. In a number of respects, compliance of Australian law with principles contained in the AUSFTA, such as freedom of association, has already been found wanting by the ILO, yet no remedial action has been taken.[87] The AUSFTA itself notes that Australia does not enshrine in national law a minimum age below which children cannot work, but this was obviously not problematic in concluding the agreement. The AUSFTA labour clause also recognises a wide area of discretion reposed in the respective national government parties in enforcing their labour laws and it resiles from questioning the decisions of national courts applying national law.

As to enforcement, the AUSFTA provides for a process of consultation and ultimately reference of problems to a Joint Committee, but like many trade agreements the procedures for ensuring compliance are ultimately not particularly strong. It is not at all evident that the AUSFTA labour clause and penalty provisions will operate in a way that gives greater legal effect to the labour principles that it enshrines. Nonetheless, the importance of the inclusion of the labour clause in the AUSFTA should not be dismissed too lightly for its political effect may prove stronger than its legal impact.

Evaluating the potential for labour clauses to secure decent conditions of work is difficult given the variety of forms such clauses can take. However, the inability to secure a more widespread adoption of labour clauses in trade agreements is less likely

---

84 AUSFTA, Arts 18.2 and 18.7 (full text of the AUSFTA is available at <www.dfat.gov.au>).
85 AUSFTA, Art 18.1. On the *ILO Declaration on Fundamental Principles and Rights at Work* see below pp 54–57.
86 See Griffin, Nyland and O'Rourke, above n 81.
87 See above pp 33–35 and Chapter 10.

now than in the past to be seen as a failure. Increasingly, the effectiveness of labour clauses is doubted. The NAFTA side agreement, for instance, once seen as one of the most ambitious trade and labour linkages, has been criticised for its timid use by the parties and its lack of an independent and effective enforcement mechanism: according to the NGO Human Rights Watch it represents an 'unfulfilled promise'.[88]

Questions have now also been raised as to whether the international trade arena is the best place to tackle labour issues. Whereas arguments about a labour clause were in the past usually couched in terms of a market-based rationale, in more recent years there has been an attempt to move the debate on to what is seen as a more neutral terrain. Increasingly workers rights are now discussed using the language of human rights[89] and as such they seem too important simply to attach as an adjunct to commercial agreements. In striking contrast to the history and background of the WTO, that of the ILO suggests the potential for a less compromising approach to labour issues and one more commensurate with the traditional conception of human rights. At the very least, labour clauses in free trade agreements do fulfil an important symbolic function as a reminder of the interconnection between the economic and the social spheres as markets expand. However, characterising labour rights as human rights tends to avoid the most critical issue concerning the intersection of trade and labour issues—that is, the political dimension of the ordering of the market and the distribution of its goods. Thus what is needed is, as Sundhya Pahuja has put it, 'some form of disruptive reconceptualisation', the opening of a 'new space' in which the separation of international trade law and human rights law can be reconfigured.[90]

Transforming the old international legal order—the response of the ILO to the challenges of globalisation

The ILO has not ignored the challenges threatening its once pre-eminent position of influence. Faced with the realities of the new international order, on its seventy-fifth anniversary in 1994 the International Labour Conference resolved to review its structures in order to remain relevant in the changing global environment. A lengthy course of action was initiated, in which the ILO aims to reposition itself in order to face the future and respond proactively to the changes occurring in the world of work. Juan Somavia, who is the first Director-General of the International Labour Office from the 'South', promised to work towards a reconciliation of international labour standards and the market. Recognising the reality of globalisation, the ILO has announced itself in favour of the new world order: '[t]he ILO is for open economies and open societies'.[91] The caveat imposed by the ILO is that they must work for all. Ever since its foundation the ILO has recognised the intersection of political, economic and social issues. The challenge in the global era is how to reassert and secure a wide adherence to its values.

---

88 Human Rights Watch *Trading Away Rights: The Unfulfilled Promise of NAFTA's Labour Side Agreement* (2001), available at <www.hrwatch.org>.
89 See Blackett, above n 68, 26 ff. See also the discussion below, pp 73–76.
90 S Pahuja 'Trading Spaces: Locating Sites for Challenge within International Trade Law' (2000) 14 *A Fem LJ* 38, 41.
91 Statement of the Director-General to the Working Party on Social Dimensions of the Liberalisation of International Trade, March 2000.

Work standards for the global era: *Declaration on Fundamental Principles and Rights at Work*

Since the inception of the ILO, setting international labour standards has been its most important function. For the first half century there was a period in which there was a remarkable degree of agreement, at least in the West, about work standards and ILO conventions were assumed to be effective through national adoption and implementation. However, by the 1990s it was obvious that the ILO faced a crisis in the relevance of its standards. Recognising the onerous administrative burdens it imposed, as a first attempt to deal with these problems the ILO changed the requirements for reporting on ratified conventions in 1993.[92] A year later, in 1994, the ILO established various committees, including a Working Party on Policy regarding Revision of Standards, with one of the primary tasks being the identification of those standards that were obsolete and required revision. A proposal before the 1997 ILO Conference, to authorise that body to abrogate conventions considered obsolete, was not accepted. But acting on the Working Party's recommendations the ILO has now effectively 'shelved' more than twenty-five conventions and no longer requires nations to report on them. The process of updating conventions has since commenced, with the Committee on Legal Issues and International Standards recommending in 2000 a wholesale comprehensive review of ILO standards.[93] However, most significant of all for the conduct of its normative activities were three major reports produced by the ILO in the 1990s,[94] which called for a new approach emphasising fundamental principles and rights.

In June 1998 the International Labour Conference adopted, with the support of the vast majority of delegates, the *Declaration on Fundamental Principles and Rights at Work*.[95] A long conversation with other institutions also preceded the *Declaration*. The United Nations convened a World Summit for Social Development in Copenhagen in 1995 at which it was agreed that it would promote respect for ILO conventions,[96] and the ILO launched its campaign in May 1995 identifying its fundamental conventions.

The *Declaration on Fundamental Principles and Rights at Work* is a social and political statement representing a new, more targeted approach aimed at ensuring widespread adherence to labour standards. The ILO presented the *Declaration* in terms that were commensurate with the global market order, assuring that its adoption will not only eliminate unfair competition but also encourage the goals of the market. Thus it argued that social dialogue through freedom of association would lead to greater worker commitment and better productivity and enable a better balance between flexibility and security, and that equal opportunity workplaces tend to be more productive. However, more significantly the ILO made it clear that the *Declaration* also represented a move to reorient the debate on labour standards in the global era away from a 'social dumping' versus 'protectionism' focus and towards a recognition of labour rights as

---

92 See ILO GB 258/6/19, paras 1–40.

93 See ILO GB 277/LILS/2 (2002).

94 Reports of the Director-General of the ILO *Defending Values, Promoting Change—Social Justice in a Global Economy: An ILO Agenda* (1994); *Standard Setting and Globalisation* (1997); and *Decent Work* (1999).

95 International Labour Conference, 86th Session, Geneva, June 1998: 273 voting in favour and 43 abstentions.

96 See UN Report of the Summit for Social Development, Copenhagen, doc A/Conf 166/9, 19 April 1995.

human rights, and the need for all in the global community to respect some common norms and values.

The *Declaration* entails no new obligations for members of the ILO but reaffirms the constitutional values of the ILO. It identifies, in Article 2, four fundamental principles and rights at work, each of which is expressed in ILO conventions:

- freedom of association and the effective recognition of the right to collective bargaining (*ILO C 87* and *ILO C 98*);
- the elimination of all forms of compulsory labour (*ILO C 29* and *ILO C 105*);
- the effective abolition of child labour (*ILO C 138* and *ILO C 182*); and
- the elimination of discrimination in respect of employment and occupation (*ILO C 100* and *ILO C 111*).

The *Declaration* is primarily promotional, with the ILO committed to encouraging all nations and other organisations to support its principles. Although it has been suggested that the *Declaration* is binding by virtue of membership of the ILO, this is not in line with the *Vienna Convention on the Law of Treaties 1969*, which requires ratification before a treaty is binding. Australia has ratified all but two of the conventions (*ILO C 138* and *ILO C 182*) in which the core principles and rights at work are elaborated.

In association with the *Declaration* the ILO also announced there are a number of other 'priority conventions',[97] and other conventions are grouped together in subject categories: basic human rights, employment, social policy, conditions of work, social security, employment of women, employment of children and young persons, migrant workers, indigenous and tribal peoples, indigenous workers in non-metropolitan territories, and other special categories such as seafarers and nursing personnel. The *Declaration* thus sits within the context of the *International Labour Code* and does not seek to negate the importance of all international labour standards. Nonetheless, there seems to be also an increasing acceptance that in the future, international standards will more likely be restricted to principles and guidelines, which will need to be adapted to particular local contexts.

The *Declaration*, it has been said, represents 'a middle way'.[98] The ILO's requirement on member states to report compliance with conventions changed following the adoption of the *Declaration*, with annual reports now only required in relation to the fundamental principles and rights and the priority conventions, while reports on compliance with other conventions are required to be submitted only every four to five years. The *Declaration* utilises a promotional follow up procedure: the annual reports from member states are used to chart progress on actions to implement conventions not yet ratified. A 'Global Report' from the Director-General to the International Labour Conference provides a more comprehensive review of one of the fundamental principles and rights every four years.[99] These global reports

---

97 *Tripartite Consultation (International Labour Standards) Convention 1976* (*ILO No 144*); *Labour Inspection Convention 1947* (*ILO C 81*); *Labour Inspection (Agriculture) Convention 1969* (*ILO C 129*); and *Employment Policy Convention 1964* (*ILO C 122*).

98 A Frazer and C Nyland 'In Search of the Middle Way: The ILO and Standard Setting' (1997) 10 *AJLL* 280.

99 See ILO *Your Voice at Work* (2000); ILO *Stopping Forced Labour* (2001); ILO *A Future without Child Labour* (2002); ILO *Time for Equality at Work* (2003); ILO *Organising for Social Justice* (2004); and ILO *A Global Alliance against Forced Labour* (2005).

enable the initiation of action plans for technical cooperation. Sanctions are not anticipated as part of the *Declaration's* enforcement structure. The *Declaration* is in this sense a restatement of the ILO's favoured approach to enforcement: the voluntary assumption of obligation by nations is the most appropriate, and ultimately the most effective, way to implement labour standards. It is an endogenous rather than a punitive approach, with the primary role of the ILO one of providing the technical backup to aid institution building. The significance of the *Declaration* is thus in reaffirming the universality of the principles and rights and reorienting the priorities of the ILO by following the issues identified in the 'Global Reports'. It is presented by the ILO as a high road enabling economic progress to be matched with social progress through the attainment of decent work for all.

There has been considerable support for the *Declaration on Fundamental Principles and Rights at Work* among academic commentators. Sean Cooney finds the move from aspirational statements to fundamental principles and rights a welcome one.[100] According to John Braithwaite and Peter Drahos, the strengthening of emphasis on the offering of technical assistance as the primary follow-up enforcement mechanism to the global reports is a form of 'reintegrative shaming' and likely to be far more effective than stigmatisation or, even worse, misplaced tolerance.[101] Certainly there has been a rapid increase in the number of ratifications to the core conventions since 1998. In addition there have been frequent references to the 1998 *Declaration* in other regional and framework agreements as well as in private initiatives.

However, the adoption of the *Declaration on Fundamental Principles and Rights at Work* has not been without criticism. In a powerful critique Philip Alston has argued that the *Declaration* downgrades the rights contained in ILO conventions. There is no philosophical coherence, according to Alston, in the reference to 'principles' and 'rights' in the *Declaration* and, in any event, the former are weaker than rights. He thus sees the *Declaration* as a backwards move to a 'softer' form of regulation with the emphasis totally on voluntarism, which, he concludes, is not adequate to protect labour rights as human rights. Furthermore, Alston questions the content of the *Declaration*, observing that it seeks to protect only procedural rights and includes none of the substantive measures needed for the attainment of decent work and a decent standard of living.[102] There has been a long debate over what it is that makes some principles and rights 'fundamental' and others not. The *Minimum Wage Fixing Convention 1970* (ILO C 131) is an obvious candidate for consideration containing matters that are arguably at least as fundamental as any included in the *Declaration*.[103]

The rejoinders to Alston have been equally vigorous in defending the *Declaration*. Brian Langille relies on the writings of Amartya Sen to suggest that the *Declaration* should

100 Cooney, above n 54, 374.
101 Braithwaite and Drahos, above n 56, 239.
102 P Alston '"Core Labour Standards" and the Transformation of the International Labour Rights Regime' (2004) 15 *EJIL* 457.
103 See B Hepple 'New Approaches to International Labour Regulation' (1997) 26 *ILJ* 353.

be understood as a way of enhancing the freedom of individuals to lead lives they value and that in this way the distinction between substance and procedure is dissolved.[104] The vigorous ongoing debate about the best way for the ILO to develop, and indeed the best way to regulate labour in the global era, indicates both the complexity and the significance of these issues.[105]

The ILO's relations with international institutions

The *Declaration on Fundamental Principles and Rights at Work* also signals a new way for the ILO to engage with other global institutions. In the past the effectiveness of the ILO in meeting the challenges posed by globalisation appeared to be compromised by the existence of a plethora of other institutions and agencies that also operated at the international level. The ILO Governing Body made a significant move to grapple with these issues when it established the Working Party on the Social Dimensions of the Liberalization of International Trade in 1994. The purpose of the working party was to address the problem of the equitable sharing of the benefits of economic progress. The most important goal of the Working Party was to try to initiate an integrated approach at the global level to the intersection of economic and social issues accompanying globalisation. The rejection of the linkage of labour standards and trade agreements in the WTO's *Singapore Declaration* sounded as a warning about the still precarious status of this project. As the designated institution with ongoing responsibility for labour standards, the ILO recognised the need to adopt a broader approach than it had in the past. The ILO understood that it cannot operate in a vacuum and that its relations with various other international institutions had to be restructured. The Working Party's reports ensured the ILO was informed on what other key international institutional players were doing.[106]

In the decade following the establishment of the Working Party, dialogue between the major international players has greatly increased. The ILO has now been granted observer status on the policy committees of both the World Bank and the IMF. Charting the impact of these arrangements on international players, such as the World Bank and the IMF, is an imprecise task. Criticisms of those institutions are still prevalent, along with criticism that the ILO has in turn also become more captive of their philosophies.[107] By the end of the 1990s certainly the rhetoric of those institutions incorporated poverty reduction as a more central concern along with a recognition that labour is often the only asset of the poor. Thus the World Bank concluded in the *World Development Report 2000*: 'inequality is back on the agenda'.[108] The ILO is also developing closer links with other United Nations agencies, by participating in major international meetings such

---

104 BA Langille 'Core Labour Rights—The True Story (Reply to Alston)' (2005) 16 *EJIL* 409, 412. See also F Maupin 'Revitalization Not Retreat: The Real Potential of the 1998 ILO Declaration for the Universal Protection of Workers' Rights' (2005) 16 *EJIL* 439. Cf P Alston 'Facing Up to the Complexities of the ILO's Core Labour Standards Agenda' (2005) 16 *EJIL* 467.

105 See also B Hepple *Labour Law and Global Trade* (2005).

106 See eg ILO, Report of Working Party on the Social Dimensions of Liberalization of International Trade *Overview of Developments in other International Organizations and Bodies Relevant to the Work of the Working Party* (2000).

107 See K Rittich 'Rights, Risk and Reward: Governance Norms in the International Order and the Problem of Precarious Work' in Fudge and Owens (eds), above n 40.

108 World Bank *World Development Report 2000/01: Attacking Poverty* (2000), 33.

as the United Nations Conference on Trade and Development and through the United Nation's *Global Compact*.

Decent work

The context in which the *Declaration on Fundamental Principles and Rights at Work* was made is one of wider changes in the ILO. In response to globalisation the ILO redefined its policy aims, announcing a new agenda to embrace the aspirations and needs of all, both in the developed and the developing world. Globalisation, the ILO acknowledged, has been accompanied by increased inequality and in many instances its social impact has been nothing short of catastrophic. While the ILO concedes that developments in technology, and the communication and information revolution may be irreversible, it refuses to accept that social inequality is an inevitable aspect of globalisation. A 'fairer globalisation' in which opportunities are created for all is its goal.[109]

In order to forge for itself a new role in the global era the ILO has outlined an ambitious program in which it aims to create a sense of common purpose and global collective responsibility. In order to achieve this the ILO is now focusing on four strategic objectives: fundamental principles and rights at work; employment; social protection; and social dialogue. For the ILO all these issues converge around the concept of decent work.

> Decent work means productive work in which rights are protected, which generates an adequate income, with adequate social protection. It also means sufficient work, in the sense that all should have access to income-earning opportunities. It marks the high road to economic and social development, a road in which employment, income and social protection can be achieved without compromising worker's rights and social standards.[110]

Work that is decent is identified as work in conditions of freedom, equity, and security thus enabling human dignity.

The ILO and the worker in the new economy

In its analysis of globalisation the ILO has been forced to re-examine its understandings of the worker and it has come to recognise that its previous conceptions are outmoded. The young, the old, the unemployed, the non-standard worker, and the immigrant worker are all now within a more central focus at the ILO as it seeks to respond to the needs of *all* workers in the new economy. This is difficult because recognising and extending regulation to these formerly marginalised groups entails, in many instances, legitimising the practices that have produced them. Devising protective standards for non-standard workers has been one of the most significant aspects of the ILO's response to globalisation. Several new conventions evidence this.[111] However, the ILO has also found it exceedingly difficult to break away from traditional understandings in responding to the needs of these workers.

---

109 See World Commission on the Social Dimension of Globalization *A Fairer Globalization: Creating Opportunities for All* (2004).
110 ILO *Decent Work*, above n 94, 11.
111 *Part-time Work Convention 1994* (ILO C 175); *Home Work Convention 1996* (ILO C 177); and *Private Employment Agencies Convention 1997* (ILO C 181).

The ILO's approach to the issue of agency or labour-hire work is a case in point.[112] These triangular work relations caused the ILO to re-evaluate the meaning of one of its foundation values: that labour is not a commodity. The ILO's former prohibition on the practice of labour hiring through employment agencies was overturned with the adoption of the *Private Employment Agencies Convention 1997 (ILO C 181)* revising the earlier *Fee-Charging Employment Agencies Convention 1949 (ILO C 96)*. The new convention attempts to protect agency workers by envisaging that responsibilities are owed to them by both employment agencies and the businesses in which they work. However, it makes no attempt to stipulate how the responsibilities are to be allocated and sets in place no particular standards with which there must be compliance. The new convention recognises the triangular work relationship but does not develop a new classification for conceptualising this type of work relationship. Rather, agency relationships are assimilated into the employer/employee dichotomy.

Likewise there were significant difficulties in extending protection to home-based workers. At the ILO debate over the definition of the home-worker to be inserted in the new *Home Work Convention 1996 (ILO C 177)* was fierce. The final approach adopted by the ILO was far from revolutionary, reflecting negotiation and compromise. However, ultimately the convention included in the definition of employer not only those who parcel work out to home-based workers directly but also those who do so indirectly through an intermediary. This was an important step in the extension of concern by the ILO to those workers who were most marginalised. However, resistance from the employers' group in the negotiations leading up to the adoption of the convention meant it included little detail and no specific binding provisions that member states were obligated to implement. Rather, the specific provisions were included only in *Homework Recommendation 1996 (ILO R 184)*.

Attempts to develop a new convention on contract labour were also initiated in the 1990s but again resistance was encountered, as business and some member states perceived the ILO to be straying from a concern with work to interfering in commerce.[113] Since then the focus has moved to 'workers in situations needing protection', which includes dependent contractors, triangular employment relationships and self-employment in conditions of dependency. However, a new convention has been slow to materialise, reflecting in large part the difficulty of resolving differences between the various constituencies represented at the ILO.[114]

The adoption of the *Part-time Work Convention 1994 (ILO C 175)* is a salutary reminder of how difficult the process can be. Proposals for a convention covering part-time workers were first put forward in the mid-1970s but were resisted for almost twenty years on the basis that regulation would destroy the flexibility advantages that

---

112 See LF Vosko 'Legitimising the Triangular Employment Relationship: Emerging International Labour Standards from a Comparative Perspective' (1997) 19 *CLL* 43; LF Vosko *Temporary Work: The Gendered Rise of the Precarious Employment Relationship* (2000), 200–29; and LF Vosko 'Gender, Precarious Work, and the International Labour Code: The Ghost in the ILO Closet' in Fudge and Owens (eds), above n 40.

113 J Fudge 'Self-Employment, Women and Precarious Work: The Scope of Labour Protection' in Fudge and Owens (eds), above n 40.

114 LF Vosko 'Decent Work: The Shifting Role of the ILO and the Struggle for Global Social Justice' (2002) *Global Social Policy* 19, 36–8.

part-time work presented and hinder the further creation of part-time work. To gain support for the convention a comprehensive survey of part-time work internationally was conducted,[115] and worker representatives had ultimately to convince the other members at the ILO that a convention would likely increase the number and the flexibility of part-time workers. When the convention was finally formulated it was a less adequate response to this form of precarious work than it ought to have been.[116] It allowed for certain categories of workers and businesses to be excluded from its protections, guaranteed equality on a pro-rata basis only for minimum pay, and its rights and protections remained dependent on a comparison of part-time and fulltime work.

The structure of the ILO determines in large part its ability to respond to those in precarious non-standard work, including those in the informal sector of the economy, and to formulate new standards that are relevant to their needs.[117] The ILO remains convinced that its tripartite structure still positions it well to deal with these issues and in this sense the *Decent Work* agenda is more reformist than radical. The success of the ILO's response to the changing worker in the global economy is thus linked in large measure to the parallel adjustments of its constituents.

In most other global public forums, representatives of civil society in the form of non-government organisations (NGOs) exert pressure on international institutions and national governments to include those who are marginalised within their vision. A commitment to the alleviation of social and economic oppression is the hallmark of these NGOs. The possibility for other organisations within civil society, such as NGOs, to argue for the needs of those excluded from traditional representation and most marginalised by globalisation is also now acknowledged by the ILO.[118] Although the adequacy of the ILO's reception of information from NGOs could be enhanced by the adoption of some minor procedural reforms and policies to facilitate the ability of NGOs to speak for the marginalised, a start has been made.[119]

Enlarging the world of work

An important part of the ILO's strategy to ensure that decent work is accessible and available for all involves a commitment to enlarging the world of work. There are two critical elements to this: the relation between employment and unemployment and the relation between paid and unpaid work.

Exclusion from paid work

The transformation of the world of (paid) work in the new economy has rendered many vulnerable to being removed altogether from it. Contemporary work patterns in many countries, including Australia, reveal that some have no work, some have

---

115 ILO *Conditions of Work Digest: Part-time Work* (1989).

116 J Murray 'Social Justice for Women? The ILO's Convention on Part-time Work' (1999) 15 *Int J Comp LLIR* 3.

117 See E Prügel 'What is a Worker? Gender, Global Restucturing and the ILO Convention on Homework' in MK Meyer and E Prügel (eds) *Gender Politics in Global Governance* (1999).

118 L Baccaro *Civil Society, NGOs and Decent Work Policies: Sorting out the Issues* (2001).

119 Cooney, above n 54, 390; and V Leary 'Human Rights at the ILO: Reflections on Making the ILO More User Friendly' in P Nikken and A Cancado-Trinidade (eds) *The Modern World of Human Rights: Essays in Honours of Thomas Buergenthal* (1996).

not enough work and some are overworked. Those who work in the informal economy or in non-standard forms of work often inhabit both realms of paid work and non-paid work, although their hold on the former can be precarious. By highlighting the importance of the unemployed and the underemployed, the ILO has questioned the traditional divide between work and non-work, between work and welfare, and made explicit the way in which one side of this divide also constructs the other.

Implicit in the concept of decent work is an affirmation of the dignity of work for the individual and a recognition of its function in securing a decent standard of living in a community.[120] The connection between work and social protection follows from this. The ILO is committed to the view that everybody, regardless of where they live, needs a minimum level of social protection and income security defined according to their society's capacity and level of development. The ILO's approach to decent work is to link labour market and employment policies with social protection through the concept of 'social inclusion'. Many nations are now adopting a similar approach. The policy goal of Australia's system of social security, which imposes 'mutual obligations' on welfare recipients to do some paid work, or search for work, or complete training programs, is to reintegrate them into the labour market rather than encourage welfare dependency. Essential to this endeavour is the elimination of poverty and unemployment traps when people fall between the two systems. However, although acknowledging the intersection of labour and social security policy and law is important, it also risks compromising the aim of enlarging the world of work by valorising paid (or productive) labour over unpaid (or reproductive) labour and fails to problematise the concepts of 'independence' and 'dependence'.[121]

Mediating the relation between paid and unpaid work—the ILO and women workers

Globalisation has in many instances exacerbated the problems of women workers, who have been more vulnerable to its negative impacts.[122] Occupational segregation, a major factor internationally in confining women to low-paid work, has increased. Very few women hold higher paid or senior managerial positions in the workforce, and fewer still in the powerful global corporations. Women continue to predominate in non-standard work and in the proliferating informal economy. The active participation of women in trade unions continues to be low. Across the globe women have a disproportionate share of poverty.

Since its inception the ILO has acknowledged the economic rights of women, although its early agenda was, unsurprisingly, a fairly limited one. The ILO early understood that its mission in relation to women's participation in the paid workforce was to protect their role in the home. By the middle of the twentieth century it focused more on the need to treat men and women the same in paid work. It was

---

120 See ILO *Decent Work*, above n 94, 25–7.
121 See L Williams 'Beyond Labour Law's Parochialism: A Revisioning of the Discourse of Redistribution' in Conaghan, Fischl and Klare (eds), above n 42.
122 ILO *Gender: A Partnership of Equals* (2000); and ILO *Global Employment Trends for Women 2004* (2004).

otherwise unconcerned with unpaid or reproductive labour, except to assume that this was women's realm.

The adoption of the *Workers with Family Responsibilities Convention 1981 (ILO C 156)* heralded a broader approach. The convention, formulated in gender-neutral terms, emphasised the responsibility of *all* workers, not just women, for *all* care work, not just for the care of young babies. This represented an important change from the *Employment (Women with Family Responsibilities) Recommendation 1965 (ILO R 123)*. Importantly the 1981 convention emphasised the right to paid work of everyone with caring responsibilities. From the early 1990s the ILO also paid more attention to the need to denounce some of the early protective conventions and revise them in the light of current notions of women's equality. The ILO has now resolved to articulate a 'gender perspective of the world of work' developed through 'mainstreaming' gender issues into ILO policies, programs and activities.[123] A commitment to substantive, real equality is promised.

In order to attain these goals, the ILO has acknowledged that it is imperative that women's voice is heard within the organisation. Despite Article 9 of the *ILO Constitution* emphasising the participation of women in the staff of the International Labour Office, the reality is far from this. Like other United Nations organisations the ILO has had a masculinist culture.[124] Gender sensitive training is now being implemented in the hope of assisting in the transformation of the whole bureaucracy. The Bureau for Gender Equality, replacing the Office of Special Advisor on Women Worker's Questions, and reporting directly to the Director-General, is intended to make the gender focus of the organisation more evident.[125] It is even more critical to provide an effective way of representing women's interests, for the ILO's treatment of women workers tends naturally to reflect the interests and priorities of its own constituents. In the past agenda of government, business and trade unions, women's interests were at best marginalised and at worst ignored. The ILO has called for a greater representation of women by its constituent groups, but this is a matter that remains largely outside its control and thus the translation of rhetoric into reality is far from assured.

Despite the apparently revolutionary assessment of its own shortcomings, the ILO's approach to gender and work in *Decent Work* nonetheless remains firmly within the traditional paradigm. The ILO purports to embrace all productive activity, including unpaid work, but the task of formulating this in a new manner is far from easy. The ILO's attitude to women's responsibility for caring work illustrates this. Observing that caring work is part of a growing area of voluntary (and often informal) community work, the ILO notes that it is nonetheless real work meriting recognition and deserving compensation. How care work is treated, it adds, has a direct bearing on the position of women in society. The immediate challenge for social and labour market policy, and one deserving a higher priority than it has had for the past century,

---

123 ILO *Decent Work*, above n 94, 9.
124 H Charlesworth 'Transforming the United Men's Club: Feminist Futures for the United Nations' (1994) 4 *Transnat'l L & Contemp Probs* 421.
125 ILO Director-General 'Decent Work for Women: ILO's Contribution to Women 2000' (2000).

is to avoid exploitation while at the same time providing care work that is beneficial for those requiring care and those providing it.[126] But, at this point, the ILO observes rather than challenges the relation between paid and unpaid work: 'we must ensure that the basic values of solidarity, family responsibility and friendship are not eroded by a purely commercial view of the problem'.[127] Thus while the placement of the issue of reproductive work and unpaid care work on the agenda for examination represents some kind of achievement, it is not easy to see progress beyond this point without a real challenge to the structure of the systems that lead to the privatisation of care work.

The difficulties experienced by the ILO in embracing all work, paid and unpaid, are clearly demonstrated by its most recent efforts to revise the conventions concerning maternity protection. A new convention was adopted in 2000 providing for a fourteen-week period of leave (six weeks of which is compulsory), and incorporating the principle that it should be paid at not less than two-thirds income, with the exception that in nations that are insufficiently developed this may be lowered to the level of benefits paid in the case of sickness or temporary disability. It also provides for breaks for breastfeeding.[128] As such the convention is not radically different from the two earlier conventions it revised. The only really new element is protection against dismissal on the ground of pregnancy and the extension of protection to *all* employed women including those in non-standard forms of employment.

Like other recent conventions covering women's work, this convention allows for exemptions to be granted to specific groups of workers if this is needed for reasons of flexibility. This has the potential to weaken considerably the effectiveness of its protections. Furthermore, as Jill Murray has pointed out, even though worker's rights in respect of other areas of leave, such as annual leave, have expanded and developed both in detail and underlying rationale, there was no comparable development here.[129] Assessing the *Maternity Protection Convention 2000* against the trends that the ILO is trying to develop, Murray shows it to be wanting: the convention integrates work and care in a very limited way, incorporating traditional assumptions of a dichotomy between the public and private spheres, between paid work, care work and leisure. In Murray's view the ILO failed to grasp the opportunity to put in place a more radical conception of care work when in 2000 its Conference rejected the incorporation into this convention of aspirational statements regarding a fairer division of work between men and women. Rather, the old world view of women's exclusion from paid work and their primary responsibility for unpaid work still resonates in the new *Maternity Protection Convention 2000* and it remains within the discrimination mould carrying with it all the baggage regarding comparisons between men and women. The debate on the *Maternity Protection Convention 2000* saw the triumph of economic arguments over social values, but as Murray comments:

---

126 ILO *Decent Work*, above n 94, 27.
127 Ibid.
128 *Maternity Protection Convention 2000 (ILO C 183)*, Arts 5–6.
129 J Murray 'The International Regulation of Maternity: Still Waiting for the Reconciliation of Work and Family Life' (2001) 17 *Int J Comp LLIR* 25.

> The cost of doing nothing to reconcile work and family life is not nothing—it is a tangible cost which is borne by those providing caring work for others, and a cost to the economic system through the loss of the integration of those people in the most appropriate way into the world of work.[130]

For women the convention disappoints in a double sense: it defers to the nation state's capacity to exclude limited categories of women workers where their protection would create difficulties and it steps back from the *Workers with Family Responsibilities Convention 1981 (ILO C 156)* by neither stressing the right of all to work nor placing maternity protection in the context that all workers have care responsibilities.

Privatising the regulation of work in the global era

The dominance of neo-liberal theory in the new economy and its championing of privatisation and deregulation has seen a growth in support for private regulation of work relations by the corporation or the firm. This repatriation of responsibility for protecting worker's rights away from the public sphere and into the private sphere has been described as 'the stirrings of a second human rights revolution'.[131] The new private regulatory forms may operate either in isolation from or in conjunction with more traditional forms of regulation. Corporate codes of conduct and social labelling are but two of the more prominent of these regulatory forms. Importantly these mechanisms highlight the complexity of power in social, and especially work, relations because to be effective, codes of conduct and social labelling depend on broad understandings that consumers and others have a social responsibility for the conduct of work relations.

Corporate codes of conduct

The adoption by business of voluntary codes of conduct is a comparatively recent, but now rapidly expanding, development in labour regulation. It has gained acceptance especially in developed economies, such as the USA and Australia. Some business organisations press this as the most appropriate form of regulation in the global era.[132] Initially, in the 1960s and 1970s, the inclusion of labour standards in codes of conduct was an exercise of 'self' regulation and tended to concern only the internal management practices in the main offices or headquarters of companies. Since that time it has become increasingly common for codes to expand in scope and they can cover the entire chain of business transactions involved in the production of goods.[133] To date it is mainly large enterprises involved in the manufacture and retail of goods in the international market that have shown the greatest interest in codes of conduct. Voluntary codes of conduct commit an enterprise to observe certain standards in the conduct of its

---

130 Ibid, 44.

131 D Cassel 'Corporate Initiatives: A Second Human Rights Revolution?' (1996) 19 *Fordham Int'l L J* 1963.

132 See eg Australian Mines and Metals Association (AMMA) *Beyond Enterprise Bargaining: The Case for Ongoing Reform of Workplace Relations in Australia* (1999); AMMA *A Model of Internal Regulation of Workplace Employee Relations: Discussion Paper* (2002); and see R Naughton 'Self Regulation of Australian Workplaces' (1999) 12 *AJLL* 131.

133 ILO *Private Initiatives and Labour Standards: A Global Study* (1998), examining 215 codes and 12 social labelling programs.

business. This form of self-regulation usually looks to the internal governance principles of the corporation itself, often including social principles in mission statements and requiring adherence to them in management practices. While codes of conduct are usually formulated by a particular business enterprise, their development can involve business associations, industry groups or employers' organisations. In some instances there may be also consultation with others, such as NGOs or trade unions.

The most commonly expressed rationale underlying the adoption of codes of conduct is a commercial or market-oriented one: a commitment to guaranteeing minimum labour standards extends beyond the immediate benefit to workers to other things like higher quality work, a lower rate of accidents, the retention of workers, and ultimately to increased economic benefits for the business itself. Corporate codes of conduct can induce, so it is said, a 'race to the top'.[134] Because self-regulation is said to generate high standards of managerial systems and leadership, and relations of mutual trust between management and workers, it is often also envisaged that codes of conduct will supplant much state legislation and operate without external intervention.[135]

But the emphasis nowadays is not solely on the economic implications for business. Notions of good corporate citizenship are also at the centre of the commitment to self-regulation. The increasing interest in socially sustainable, responsible, and ethical investment[136] is indicative of a growing societal belief that the social and other consequences of business's economic activity cannot be ignored. However, the idea that a corporation bears a responsibility to articulate and impose upon itself minimum labour standards does not necessarily sit well with traditional legal understandings of the corporation and directors' duties. At law, workers are not an internal part of the structure of the corporation. The prime duty of directors in law is to act in the best interests of the company, which translates as the economic interests of shareholders.[137] In this traditional view, the responsibility for securing matters relating to the public good, such as the protection of workers, is more the duty of government not private corporations.[138]

The notion that corporate responsibility for social matters, such as labour standards, can transform corporate law is arguably some distance away. However, since the 1965 'Delhi Declaration', establishing what has now become known internationally as 'stakeholder theory',[139] communities and other groups, such as consumers, are more aware of the complex networks of power that can be wielded and used to influence corporate governance. The prominent campaigns that have been waged against transnational

134 B Hepple 'A Race to the Top? International Investment Guidelines and Corporate Codes of Conduct' (1999) 20 *Comp Lab L & Pol'y Jl* 347, 355 ff.

135 See AMMA *Discussion Paper 2000*, above n 132.

136 See the Dow Jones Sustainability Indexes <www.sustainability-indexes.com>; the Domini 400 Social Index at <www.domini.com/dsi400>; and the *Global Reporting Initiative* at <www.globalreporting.org>.

137 See *Corporations Act* Pt 2F 1A. See also JD Heydon 'Directors' Duties and the Company's Interests' in P Finn (ed) *Equity and Commercial Relationships* (1987).

138 M Friedman 'The Social Responsibility of Business to Increase Profits' *New York Times* (Magazine) 13 September 1970, 32; and M Friedman 'The Social Responsibility of Business is to Increase Profits' in WM Hoffman and JM Moore (eds) *Business Ethics: Readings and Cases in Corporate Morality* (1984).

139 This theory was developed at an international seminar in India on 'Social Responsibility of Business'—see the ILO *Report of the Working Party on the Social Dimensions of the Liberalization of International Trade* (1998).

corporations accused of exploiting workers have demonstrated the power of critics in an era of global communication. Globally, there is increasing public pressure demanding that business and corporations be accountable for the 'triple bottom line', that is, for economic results and the social/labour and environmental effects of their activities. Parallel to this, theories of corporate social responsibility have also now developed considerably.[140] Thus alongside their annual reports to shareholders some corporations now also issue corporate social responsibility reports in an effort to be more open and accountable to their stakeholders. The nature of corporate social responsibility continues to be vigorously contested in the political arena. Australia earlier rejected the stakeholder model as a basis for the development of its corporate law, but the issue continues to be debated.[141] In the meantime, many corporations are coming to accept more responsibility for the effects of their business practices on workers, even if primarily because this might also enhance their financial performance.

However, as a mechanism for securing labour standards for workers, codes of conduct are not without serious deficiencies. The problem of monitoring and enforcement remains at the core of doubts raised about the potential for self-regulation to play a strong role in promoting labour standards. The possible conflicts involved undoubtedly compromise this as an ultimate form of labour standard setting. Codes of conduct are often akin to a statement of ethics or values. Generally their implementation procedures are vague and leave matters to internal or self-assessment rather than any external judgment, though it has been said that both are useful, the former for securing a change of culture in a business organisation and the latter for assessing its reality.[142] In determining the effectiveness of codes of conduct, much can depend on the size of the corporation, the industry in which it operates, and the labour principle or right sought to be protected. Codes of conduct are probably more effective in securing protection against child labour in manufacturing industries than in securing freedom of association for those working in the service industries.[143] The proponents of codes of conduct argue that as ideas of corporate social responsibility gain a practical hold the pressures exerted in the marketplace will become even more forceful than the more formalised enforcement of the public legal system. It can also be noted that the intersection of corporate codes with conventional legal regulation can increase their effectiveness.

The other major problem of voluntary codes is the *ad hoc* nature of their content. Those drawing up the code usually determine this content, sometimes but not always with reference to international standards.[144] Workers who are most affected by such codes usually have no input into their formation. Voluntary codes tend to be highly

140 T Donaldson and TW Dunfee 'Toward a Unified Conception of Business Ethics: Integrative Social Contract Theory' (1994) 19 *Acad Mgmt Rev* 252.

141 See Senate Standing Committee on Legal and Constitutional Affairs, Parliament of Australia, *Company Director's Duties* (1989) Ch 6; and Parliamentary Joint Committee on Corporations and Financial Services, Parliament of Australia, *Inquiry into Social Responsibility and Triple Bottom Line Reporting*, 2005–06.

142 ILO, above n 133, Pt II Section 6, paras 63–6.

143 A Owens 'Testing the Racheting Labour Standards Proposal: Indonesia and the Shangri-La Workers' (2004) 5 *MJIL* 169.

144 The UK-based Ethical Trading Initiative was drawn up by government and makes reference to the ILO's fundamental principles and rights at work: <www.ethicaltrade.org>.

selective in the labour issues they address.[145] While occupational health and safety, discrimination, child labour and forced labour are commonly addressed in codes of conduct, freedom of association and the right to bargain collectively are matters seldom considered. In the AMMA proposal, [146] there was a statement of commitment to adhere to a range of minimum standards: a state set minimum wage, four weeks' annual leave, thirteen weeks' long service leave after fifteen years' service, personal carer's leave including sick leave, fifty-two weeks' parental/adoption leave, equal pay for work of equal value, and fair treatment procedures for dealing with complaints. No mention was made of collective bargaining, although the freedom of association provisions in the *Workplace Relations Act 1996* (Cth) were assumed to remain applicable. Codes of conduct thus tend to promote an individualised rather than collective conception of work relations. Furthermore, codes of conduct can contain quite idiosyncratic definitions of the standards or values they incorporate. Inconsistencies that develop between the codes and legal standards can be problematical. Certainly, the comprehensiveness of the labour protections offered by these self-imposed codes of conduct is generally more limited than that encouraged by public agencies such as the ILO.

The coverage of these private regulatory forms is also often limited. Codes of conduct often tend to be applicable in particular locations or in relation to the production of particular products. Codes governing the practices of corporations within developed countries of the 'North' often do not extended to govern behaviour where the corporation also operates in the less developed 'South'. The Australian 'Fairwear Campaign', for instance, has endorsed a code of conduct that is restricted to goods produced within Australia.[147] Thus while a certain amount of moral and ethical leadership can be important, in practice the tangible benefits guaranteed to workers by such codes have to date been less than considerable. Not surprisingly then, codes of conduct have been strongly criticised.[148]

Social labelling

Social labelling, whereby a label is attached to goods as a trademark of labour standards, is another mechanism that has gained support as a way of ensuring global pressure is brought to bear on manufacturers wherever situated. The 'RUGMARK' label that guarantees rugs are not produced by child labour is widely known.[149] The concept behind social labelling is not really new.[150] It is now often adopted by trade union or other organisations, such as NGOs, as a promotional strategy to extend protections to workers in the informal economy where conditions of work are more difficult to monitor by the formal public enforcement processes. Social labelling depends on harnessing consumer power in the marketplace and encouraging a broader view of

---

145 ILO, above n 133, Pt III, Section 5; and Hepple, above n 134, 357.
146 Above n 132.
147 The Fairwear campaign website is <www.fairwear.org.au>.
148 JF Perez-Lopez 'Promoting International Respect for Worker Rights through Business Codes of Conduct' (1993) 17 *Fordham Int LJ* 1.
149 See <www.rugmark.org>.
150 See *Federated Clothing Trades v Archer* (1919) 27 CLR 207.

responsibility for ensuring that workers are treated with dignity. To be most effective social labels must be able to guarantee precisely defined conditions of labour used in the production of goods. The label and what it stands for must have a high recognition rate, and therefore its proponents need to use the media to communicate its message. Once well known, a label can stimulate concern for a particular issue or issues among the public at large.

Like codes of conduct, social labelling has limitations as an instrument for the upholding of labour standards. Social labelling tends to revolve around the promotion of a single issue. However, its scope need not necessarily be limited in this way: for instance, the general conditions of outworkers have also been the target of social labelling campaigns. In Australia, the ACTU has embraced the 'Fairwear' campaign initiated by the Textiles Clothing and Footwear Union Australia (TCFUA) to encourage businesses to sign up to a *Homeworkers Code of Practice* for the garment industry, which seeks to ensure compliance with labour standards by requiring assurances to this effect at every level of contract in relation to the goods from suppliers, through subcontractors and retailers, to customers. Legislation has also been enacted to link this essentially private regulatory mechanism to the *Clothing Trades Award 1982* of the public regulatory system.[151] Codes of conduct and social labelling should not be rejected out of hand as of no use at all. They can be a significant part of a multifaceted approach to ensure that decent work is delivered to all workers.

Linking the public and private regulation of work in the global era

The Fairwear Campaign is an example of public and private regulatory mechanisms operating in conjunction to secure decent work standards. Because one of the problems with self-regulation is related to standards and credentials, the participation of public institutions in private ordering seems an obvious development. There have already been moves by regional and national governments to promote adherence to labour standards. In Australia an attempt to require by legislation corporations to comply with fundamental rights and principles at work failed.[152] Encouraging the adoption of codes of conduct embodying international labour standards is another way of doing this. There has been a push at the global level to increase adhesion to labour standards by public institutions endorsing private regulation. That is, 'public' international institutions are now seeking to play a role in relation to what were formerly purely 'private' codes of practice.

It is envisaged that the conjunction of public and private can overcome some of the disadvantages of self-regulatory codes of conduct. Publicly endorsed codes of conduct are usually more comprehensive than their traditional private counterparts, recognising

---

151 See eg *Industrial Relations (Ethical Clothing Trades) Act 2001* (NSW) and the mandatory code of practice attached to it, the *Ethical Clothing Trades—Extended Responsibility Scheme*, which regulates those who fail to sign and comply with the voluntary *Homeworkers Code of Practice*, aimed at ensuring compliance with the relevant industrial award; and *Outworkers (Improved Protection) Act 2003* (Vic). See also C Fenwick 'Protecting Victoria's Vulnerable Workers: New Legislative Developments' (2003) 16 *AJLL* 198.

152 *Corporate Code of Conduct Bill 2000* (Cth), which was a private, not a government-sponsored, Bill.

and adopting standards set in the public arena where there are broader participation processes. Public international agencies have begun to promote these essentially private mechanisms as an additional form of 'soft law' to encourage and promote the adoption of fundamental principles and rights at work. Adopting the language of the marketplace, the international public agencies can operate as a standardising body for codes of conduct.

The reason for the enthusiasm of public international agencies to embrace this approach is not difficult to discern. Globalisation, in privileging the private law of contract over traditional public law forms of regulation, has simultaneously also threatened to marginalise the public institutions of international government. By encouraging self-regulation, public institutions connect private or market purposes to their own goals in a pragmatic strategy alive to the fact that if nation states become less effective in controlling transnational corporations then other avenues need to be explored. Harnessing business in the adoption and enforcement of shared values and labour standards is also recognition of the major shift in international power from the nation state to the transnational corporation. One of the other important advantages of linking public and private regulation is that instruments like codes of conduct can be shaped and revised far more quickly than international conventions, and thus they enable agencies to be more immediately responsive to changing circumstances.

Voluntary codes of conduct have been recognised as part of the international regulatory schema since the 1970s. Amongst the earliest were the OECD *Guidelines for Multinational Enterprises* (1976) and the ILO *Tripartite Declaration of Principles Concerning Multinational Enterprises and Social Policy* (1977, and with 1987 addendum). Although these early efforts of international governmental agencies to regulate transnational enterprises did not progress far,[153] they have recently been reinvigorated and, in addition, the United Nations has also entered the field with its *Global Compact*.

The *Tripartite Declaration of Principles concerning Multinational Enterprises and Social Policy*

The ILO has long recognised that the control of transnational corporations or multinational enterprises is problematic. However, its first attempt to deal with the matter was not particularly successful. In 1977 the *Tripartite Declaration of Principles concerning Multinational Enterprises and Social Policy*, which was addressed not only to the ILO's immediate constituents of national governments, employers and workers, but also to multinational corporations, could not get sufficient support to become a convention.[154] For many years it was the only international statement on the social responsibility of transnational corporations.

---

153 RR Blanpain 'The Kenneth M Piper Lecture: Transnational Regulation of the Labour Relations of Mutinational Enterprises' (1982) 58 *Chi-K LR* 909.

154 H Günter 'The Tripartite Declaration of Principles on Multinational Enterprises and Social Policy' in R Blanpain (ed) *International Encyclopaedia for Labour and Industrial Relations* (1992); and B Brett *International Labour in the Twenty-first Century: The ILO—Monument to the Past or a Beacon for the Future* (1994).

The *1977 Tripartite Declaration* covered matters of concern to individual workers, including employment promotion, equality of opportunity and treatment, security of employment, training, conditions of work and life, safety and health. It also included other provisions that had an industrial relations focus, such as freedom of association and the right to bargain, collective bargaining, consultation and grievance procedures. The *1977 Tripartite Declaration* listed conventions relevant to its contents, and this was revised in 1987. Thereafter the ILO periodically monitored the *1977 Tripartite Declaration* and reported on it to its Governing Body.[155] The ILO also established a procedure, overseen by its Multi-National Enterprises Branch, through which an authoritative interpretation of the *1977 Tripartite Declaration* can be granted on request. The *1977 Tripartite Declaration* itself also contains a procedure for the resolution of disputes that arise under it. However, it was always intended only as a guide to multinational enterprises, and to be adopted by them on a voluntary basis. With no mechanisms for sanctions or other form of enforcement, the *1977 Tripartite Declaration* remained ineffectual and almost forgotten for two decades.

However, in the 1990s the ILO once again began seriously exploring private, self-regulatory mechanisms as part of the redefinition of its role in the global era.[156] To this end it has gathered together a collection of model codes of conduct and the *1977 Tripartite Declaration* has been revamped.[157]

The regulatory approach in the *Tripartite Declaration* is pragmatic. The ILO's renewed interest in it signals an acknowledgment that the state and trade unions have had a diminishing influence in the global marketplace where capital is highly mobile and frequently operates beyond the boundaries of any one state. Like other international agencies, the ILO has come to the view that adopting a diverse range of regulatory approaches is the most effective strategy to achieve compliance with labour standards. If in the global world, achieving the fundamental principles and rights at work will take the cooperation of all players, the strategy of the ILO is to use codes of conduct for its own purposes, acknowledging that these may not necessarily be identical to those of business.

The *OECD Guidelines for Multinational Enterprises*

The Organisation for Economic Co-operation and Development (OECD) is not usually thought of as an organisation concerned with labour standards. However, in 1976, as part of its *Declaration on International Investment and Multinational Enterprises*, it first set down *The OECD Guidelines for Multinational Enterprises*, which have since have been amended a number of times.[158] The latest revision, in 2000, was approved at an OECD Ministerial meeting with the theme 'Shaping Globalism'. The 2000 amendment refers to the ILO's fundamental principles and rights, and followed the OECD's own

---

155 ILO *The ILO Tripartite Declaration of Principles concerning Multi National Enterprises and Social Policy—Ten Years After* (1988).

156 ILO, above n 133.

157 See ILO, Seventh Survey on the effect given to the *1977 Tripartite Declaration* (2001).

158 For an online copy of the OECD Guidelines see <www.oecd.org//daf/investment/guidelines/mnetext.htm>.

study of ninety-one countries, which found labour standards did not impact negatively on market competitiveness.[159] There was extensive input into the amendment process from the OECD's own affiliates, such as the Trade Union Advisory Committee (TUAC), a freestanding organisation with links to the trade unions in OECD member countries, and the likewise constituted Business Industry Advisory Committee (BIAC), as well as external organisations, such as the ILO. Comments were even invited via the Internet, in anticipation that the transparency of the process could only add to its legitimacy.

In comparison with other international instruments such as conventions, it was the speed with which the *Guidelines* were remodelled and accepted that caused the OECD to predict that such instruments would become more significant in the future. The new version of the *Guidelines* is presented as part of a proactive agenda of the OECD, to assist positively the development process throughout the world. The OECD *Guidelines* are firmly grounded within the neo-liberal values of the global market, and are expressed as aiming at creating a 'level playing field' for the conduct of global trade and investment, while at the same time reaffirming that they are not to be used in a protective fashion. It is also a matter of frequent emphasis that the OECD *Guidelines* are not a replacement for, and certainly are not to conflict with, national law. The *Guidelines* also stress that the primary responsibility for human rights belongs with governments, though the role of business in respecting social values in undertaking economic activity is accepted. The *Guidelines* take the form of recommendations by government to business operating in and from signatory nations. They are government-backed standards available for voluntary adoption by all business enterprises but not legally binding. By the end of 2005 the *Guidelines* had been adopted by thirty members of the OECD, including Australia, and nine non-member countries—Argentina, Brazil, Chile, Estonia, Israel, Latvia, Lithuania, Romania and Slovenia—have also declared their adherence to them.

The *OECD Guidelines for Multinational Enterprises* include a general statement of principles, values and general policy. Chapter IV concerns 'Employment and Industrial Relations' and commences with a clause that in effect reinforces the fundamental principles and rights set out in the ILO's 1998 *Declaration*. The OECD *Guidelines* encourage enterprises to observe standards and conditions of work not less favourable than those of comparable employers in the host country. Encouragement of the use of, and the development of skills in, the local workforce is also a part of the OECD *Guidelines*.

In line with the principle of voluntarism, the OECD *Guidelines* have no enforce-ment provisions as such. Rather they incorporate an implementation, follow-up and monitoring process, which is overseen by the Committee for International Investment and Multinational Enterprises (CIME). The main task of CIME is to clarify the *Guidelines* and report to Council. It does not adjudicate or determine issues regarding the conduct of individual enterprises. Arguably the more significant role in practical terms is that envisaged for the National Contact Points (NCPs), usually a government-appointed officer, whose duty it is to host discussions at the national

---

159 OECD, above n 69.

level to resolve issues arising under the *Guidelines* with the aim of getting agreed resolution. Where no such agreement is reached the NCPs may issue a statement. NCPs report annually to CIME.

The OECD *Guidelines for Multinational Enterprises* can be easily criticised: most of the principles they contain have been set out better and more fully elsewhere; they are directed to enterprises operating in the richest countries, which generally have a better record in relation to labour rights; where enterprises operate in a developing economy they contain no direction to engage in conduct that would in a meaningful way raise the living standards of workers; and there is nothing that amounts to an enforcement regime. While it can be conceded that the OECD has played an important part in assisting the ILO to define its 'core' conventions and that the *Guidelines* now play a role in promoting them,[160] such a derivative function is far smaller and less significant than what might have been achieved. Nonetheless, members of the OECD are far more likely than other countries to be the home to the powerful transnational enterprises, and the *Guidelines* therefore offer another way of bringing labour rights to their attention. The hope has been expressed that the *Guidelines* will be a useful tool in achieving stronger adherence to fundamental rights at work.[161]

The UN and the *Global Compact*

Among the publicly supported private codes of conduct, perhaps the most ambitious program in scope is the United Nations' sponsored 'global compact'. The *Global Compact*, initiated at the Davos World Economic Forum in 1999 and launched the following year, aims to harness the assistance of the world's business community in the implementation and adoption of universal values in the areas of international human rights, labour rights and environmental rights.[162] The *Global Compact* is part of the United Nations' effort to involve all relevant social actors, and especially business, in the task of ensuring that the social consequences accompanying global economic activity are not ignored.[163]

The *Global Compact* comprises nine principles covering human rights, labour and the environment, to which has also been added a tenth covering anti-corruption. In relation to work, the *Global Compact* requires committed businesses to uphold the following:
- Principle 3: freedom of association and the effective recognition of the right to collective bargaining;
- Principle 4: the elimination of all forms of forced or compulsory labour;
- Principle 5: the effective abolition of child labour; and
- Principle 6: the elimination of discrimination in respect of employment and occupation.

---

160 J Salzman 'Labour Rights, Globalisation and Institutions: The Roles and Influence of the Organization for Economic Cooperation and Development' (2000) 21 *Mich J Int'l L* 769.
161 J Murray 'A New Phase in the Regulation of Multinational Enterprises: The Role of the OECD' (2001) 30 *ILJ* 255.
162 The *Global Compact* website is at <www.globalcompact.org>.
163 AM Taylor 'The UN and the Global Compact' (2001) 17 *NYL Sch J Hum Rts* 975, 980–1.

These four principles were adopted at the World Summit for Social Development, in Copenhagen in 1995, and are now incorporated in the ILO's 1998 *Declaration*. The *Global Compact* is intended to complement but not replace corporate codes of conduct and action by national governments in compliance with the ILO's 1998 *Declaration*.

The efficacy of the *Global Compact*, which has both some of the advantages and the disadvantages of 'soft law', remains to be demonstrated. It is a voluntary initiative, intended to mainstream certain values, and to goad to action corporations through making their commitment to these values transparent and thus increasing their public accountability. It is designed as a framework of reference in which to encourage 'best practice' around universally accepted values that corporations will include in their mission statements and give effect to through management practices. Those who sign on to the *Global Compact* are expected to become advocates for its principles, posting on the *Global Compact* website examples of the particular steps they have taken to implement the principles of the *Compact* and to publish in or alongside their annual report the ways in which they are promoting those principles. It is envisaged that the scrutiny by NGOs of these 'good global citizens' will provide the incentive for compliance. There is also a certain legitimacy coming from participation in a '*Compact*' sponsored by the Secretary-General of the United Nations that is attractive to global corporations.

The International Organisation of Employers (IOE) and the International Confederation of Free Trade Unions (ICFTU) have given their support to this initiative, along with other peak labour organisations, NGOs and more than 1500 transnational corporations. But the support has not always been unqualified. Human Rights Watch has criticised the *Global Compact's* lack of enforceable standards.[164] The Secretary-General of the International Chamber of Commerce cautioned that the first responsibilities of business are to shareholders, customers and employees, not ensuring the general enforcement of the law or determining the appropriate distribution of goods.[165] The United Nations' role in the *Global Compact* has also been criticised as running the risk of allowing big business and those who promote globalisation to gain too powerful a foothold in the United Nations and thereby compromise its strong reputation for humanitarianism and the protection of rights.

Work rights as human rights

The twentieth century witnessed a transformation in the subject matter of public international law. No longer is it concerned only with the 'external' relations between nation states. Through an embrace of human rights, public international law has come to encompass many issues that were once considered to be within the sovereign control of the nation state. The focus of public international law is now as much the individual person as it is the nation state.[166] An emphasis on human rights has also become more

---

164 Human Rights Watch *Corporate Social Responsibility: Letter to the United Nations* <www.hrw.org/press/2000/07/hrw-ltr-july.htm>.

165 ML Cattui, Letters to the Editor, *Financial Times*, 24 March 1999 cited in Taylor, above n 163, 982.

166 See HJ Steiner and P Alston *International Human Rights in Context* (2000); and H Charlesworth and C Chinkin *The Boundaries of International Law: A Feminist Analysis* (2000), Ch 7.

prominent at the regional level, and, with the notable exception of Australia, most industrialised nations also have a constitutional 'bill of rights'.

However, the law of work has for the most part been a somewhat neglected area of mainstream public international law, constitutional law and human rights discourse.[167] This is despite the recognition of the importance of social and economic rights, including rights in relation to work, in such instruments as the *Universal Declaration of Human Rights,* the *International Covenant on Economic, Social and Cultural Rights* (*ICESCR*), the *Convention on the Elimination of All Forms of Racial Discrimination* (*CERD*), and the *Convention on the Elimination of All Forms of Discrimination against Women* (*CEDAW*). These instruments protect a range of work-related rights including those arising from principles of equality and non-discrimination; the rights of association including the right to join trade unions and right to bargain collectively; the right to strike; the right to social security; the right to work in a profession of one's choosing and in just and favourable conditions with protection against unemployment; the right to fair and just remuneration; the right to an adequate standard of living; prohibition on slavery; and the right to fair working conditions. There are also other international conventions that protect other specific groups of people in relation to work. The *United Nations Convention on the Rights of the Child,* for instance, seeks to protect children from economic exploitation and emphasises the child's right to education.

The omission of work-related rights from human rights discourse may be explained in part by the fact that the ILO has always been organisationally separate from the mainstream of the United Nations to which it belongs. The reluctance to acknowledge labour rights as human rights a half century after the *Universal Declaration of Human Rights*[168] may also derive from the 'generational' development of human rights. Seventeenth- and eighteenth-century liberal philosophical thought informs the modern understanding of 'rights' in Western jurisprudence. Civil and political rights are conceived as restraining the state from interfering with the freedom of the individual who is a naturally free and autonomous being. Because all individuals are equal in the state of nature, these rights are also held to be universal. In seeming contrast to the 'first generation' of civil and political rights, 'second generation' social and economic rights can only be understood by reference to the society in which the individual lives. Further, their realisation requires governmental action rather than mere restraint from action. Social and economic rights are thus regarded as positive rights, to be contrasted with the negative civil and political rights. However, because the state in liberal theory has discretion in its determination of scarce resources, judicial enforcement of an individual's social and economic rights is difficult to theorise.

The apparent differences between the foundation of these different categories of rights and the chronology of their emergence in Western political and legal thought buttressed the concept of a hierarchical arrangement between them: civil and political rights comprising a first tier of 'real' human rights, with a second tier of social and

---

167 T MacDermott 'Labour Law and Human Rights' in D Kinley (ed) *Human Rights in Australian Law* (1998).
168 See N Valticos 'International Labour Standards and Human Rights: Approaching the Year 2000' (1998) 137 *Int Lab Rev* 135.

economic rights whose status was more controversial. In the mid-twentieth century the adoption of two separate international covenants, the *International Covenant on Civil and Political Rights* and the *International Covenant on Economic, Social and Cultural Rights*, to embody the principles in the *Universal Declaration of Human Rights* appeared to reaffirm this hierarchical separation.

Gradually, however, the idea of work 'rights' has taken hold.[169] This is no doubt because there has been much work done to secure the wider recognition of social and economic rights as real rights. The 'constitutionalisation' of some regional arrangements, for example, the European Union, has also played a part. However, the idea of work rights as human rights first gained wider global support as a way out of the 'free trade' versus 'protectionism' debate over work standards in the global marketplace. Not surprisingly then support was at first garnered through an economic argument: that is, work rights can be instrumental in achieving a stronger market-competitive position. The liberal foundation of 'rights' resonated with the neo-liberal foundation of the new economy, thus also serving to give the idea of work rights greater purchase in the global marketplace. There has since been a growing responsiveness to the idea of work rights as human rights by transnational corporations and others in the business sector keen to establish credibility in the human rights arena. The overlap of human rights objectives with corporate goals points to what David Kinley has referred to as the 'privatisation of human rights'.[170] The rhetorical integration of human rights and neo-liberal market based rationales for the protection of labour rights is captured in the observation of Mary Robinson, the United Nations High Commissioner for Human Rights, that 'human rights is a key performance indicator for corporations all over the world'.[171]

One of the most important advantages of the application of rights discourse to the law of work is the implicit assertion it contains of an overarching notion of law as justice from which there can be no derogation. In this way rights talk also reinforces an ideal of the potential unity of the global community. Nonetheless there remain important questions when the law of work is conceptualised in terms of rights. Social and economic rights must necessarily be realised in a particular social context that is situated both in time and place. Their formulation in legal instruments can be difficult. The right to work for just remuneration, for instance, is framed in Article 23(2) of the *United Nations Declaration of Human Rights* in terms of the worker as breadwinner 'ensuring for himself and his family an existence worthy of dignity' and thus in a way that is somewhat out of step with current understandings. As work rights have been appropriated to the purposes of the market in more recent times there is ongoing contestation over their content. In neo-liberal theory the

---

169 See Steiner and Alston, above n 166, Ch 4 'Economic and Social Rights'; B Hepple (ed) *Social and Labour Rights in a Global Context: International and Comparative Perspectives* (2002); and P Alston (ed) *Labour Rights as Human Rights* (2005).

170 D Kinley 'Human Rights as Legally Binding or Merely Relevant?' in S Bottomley and D Kinley (eds) *Commercial Law and Human Rights* (2002).

171 M Robinson *Business and Human Rights: A Progress Report* (2000) available at <www.unhcr.ch/business. html>.

holder of work rights is a certain kind of worker, an autonomous individual who is free to contract for his or her labour: this being is likely to be an individual who values a right to privacy or to whom the right of association means more a freedom to dissociate rather than a right to associate with others by joining trade unions and bargaining collectively.

The success of the ILO in promoting its *1998 Declaration* has been an important counterbalance to a neo-liberal interpretation of work rights (although the *Declaration* can also be interpreted in a way that supports neo-liberal theory[172]). Even though the ILO has adopted a pragmatic approach that acknowledges that fundamental principles and rights are of instrumental value in the new economy, it also espouses the centrality of work to human dignity and human flourishing through its core value that labour is not a commodity. However, the formulation of the *1998 Declaration* in also referring to fundamental *principles* as well as rights at work has been seen by some as diluting its value as a human rights instrument.[173]

Australia's record of compliance with the ILO's fundamental principles and rights at work has been relatively good.[174] And there are some recent legislative enactments that seek to provide protection against the worst forms of abuse of workers.[175] But in Australia there has been more generally a certain reluctance about rights, not just those relevant to work.[176] Paradoxically this is expressed as an assertion of national sovereignty, standing alongside an assertion of the importance of Australia's participation in and integration into the global marketplace. The social and economic continue to be separated as the politics of neo-liberalism remains dominant.

Judicial interpretation may aid the neo-liberal agenda. In the *Industrial Relations Act Case* there was a suggestion that some aspirational international conventions may not enliven the external affairs power, s 51(xxix), of the *Australian Constitution*.[177] The implications of this may prove very significant. International law increasingly tends to state aspirational goals and to promote the broad principles through which these goals might be achieved and refrains from designating any particular, specified or detailed means for fulfilling obligations. Social and economic rights are often expressed in aspirational terms. The *ICESCR*, for instance, provides that governments must use 'all appropriate means' to achieve the goals contained within it. 'Soft law' embodying broad principles in non-binding instruments is also more common now and the ILO's *1998 Declaration* is one such example. It would be tragic if Australia were excluded from the global community because of a constitutional incapacity.

---

172 Langille, above n 104.
173 Alston, above n 102.
174 Creighton, above n 22.
175 See above n 27.
176 See H Charlesworth 'The Australian Reluctance about Rights' (1993) 31 *OHLJ* 195; and H Charlesworth, M Chiam, D Hovell and G Williams, 'Deep Anxieties: Australia and the International Legal Order' (2003) 25 *Syd L R* 423.
177 *Victoria v The Commonwealth (Industrial Relations Act Case)* (1996) 187 CLR 416, 486.

Globalisation and the future of the law of work

The emerging law of global relations has been, in large part, a captive of neo-liberal theory through the dominance of contract and the emphasis on deregulation and privatisation. In the international legal arena this has led to the promotion of 'private' ordering or work relations over 'public' forms of regulation. After an initial retreat by the old public international order, reform followed. In the global legal order there is now a wide variety of regulatory forms, often intersecting in their operation. The emergence of the 'new' global law of work still carries traces of the 'old'. Although it is too drastic and simplistic to present the 'old' and the 'new' as a strict or rigid dichotomy, this nomenclature is useful as a reminder of the magnitude of the transformations taking place.

The changes in the global law of work should not be interpreted as meaning that national law is no longer important. It is national law that immediately regulates working lives. But the development of national law occurs in the global context and is influenced most strongly by the response at national level to that context. In the new economy it can be expected that some previously little utilised aspects of domestic law may be relied upon more frequently. Thus, for instance, the more liberal approach recently adopted by Australian courts to the doctrine of *forum non conveniens* may see an increase in litigation under the rules of private international law.[178] The extraterritorial application of national laws can also be utilised to control from within the nation the behaviour of global actors elsewhere. This was the intent of The *Corporate Code of Conduct Bill 2000* (Cth), which sought to require transnational corporations to abide by ILO conventions when operating in other countries as a precondition to any operation within Australia.[179] But in the end the emergence of the new global law of work will shape developments in national regulation. The bounds of what is legally possible in the global era are not the primary determinants of national legal regulation, but political judgement about the practical implications of national regulation in the new economy. Political reluctance to insulate the nation from the new economy is a recognition of the impracticality of such an action in the global era. The development of a new law of work for the global era depends crucially on developments at both the global and the national level and, in particular, on the political purposes behind it.

---

178 See *CSR Ltd v Cigna Insurance Australia Ltd* (1997) 189 CLR 345. See also RC McCallum 'Conflicts of Laws and Labour Law in the New Economy' (2003) 16 *AJLL* 50.

179 See also S Cooney 'A Broader Role for the Commonwealth in Eradicating Foreign Sweatshops?' (2004) 28 *MULR* 290.

3 Australian Law of Work in Transition

Introduction

The *Workplace Relations Amendment (Work Choices) Act 2005* (Cth) (*Work Choices Act*) was introduced into the Australian Parliament with a stated primary goal to

> simplify the complexity inherent in the existence of six workplace relations jurisdictions in Australia by creating a national workplace relations system based on the corporations power that will apply to the majority of Australia's employers and employees.[1]

The historic rarity of an Australian Government with a majority in both Houses of Parliament enabled the passage of this legislation, which not only incorporated many changes that had been foreshadowed in previously unsuccessful Bills but also enabled the Commonwealth to implement much more comprehensive changes. The *Work Choices Act* has all but completely dismantled the traditional Australian labour law system, with the Commonwealth Parliament abandoning (for the most part) its century-long reliance on the conciliation and arbitration power (*Australian Constitution*, s 51(xxxv)) and turning instead to the corporations power (s 51(xx)) as the new foundation for regulating the work of employers and employees in the global era. 'Regulating for competitiveness' sums up the policy agenda that directs this legislation.[2] The *Work Choices Act* represents the most radical rewrite of the Australian law governing work in over a century.

Shortly after the people of the Australian colonies joined in a federal Commonwealth, the *Commonwealth Conciliation and Arbitration Act 1904* (Cth) was enacted. It established the legal framework that was to govern work in Australia during the industrial era, structuring Australian labour law in a way that was distinctly different from that in most other industrialised economies. The labour law model developed elsewhere came to be characterised as one of 'collective laissez-faire' in which the state adopted an 'abstentionist' role.[3] But this was not an apt description of the Australian system. Central to

---

1   Parliament of the Commonwealth of Australia, House of Representatives, *Workplace Relations Amendment (Work Choices) Bill 2005, Explanatory Memorandum* (circulated by the Hon K Andrews, Minister for Employment and Workplace Relations).

2   Compare H Collins 'Regulating the Employment Relation for Competitiveness' (2001) 30 *ILJ* 17.

3   P Davies and M Freedland (eds) *Kahn-Freund's Labour and the Law* (1983), 18.

the Australian approach to regulating work in the twentieth century was a statutorily established system of conciliation and arbitration for the prevention and settlement of industrial disputation. The foundations of this public and compulsory system derived from ideas about the arbitration of work matters in nineteenth-century Britain, Europe and North America, as well as drawing on the English tradition of regulating labour and wages by statute that dated back to medieval times.[4] But whatever its origins, the antipodean system of regulating industrial relations by conciliation and arbitration developed in a way that was quite unique.

At the dawn of the twentieth century, the Australian political, economic, and social context presented a confluence of circumstances peculiarly receptive to the growing role of the state in the regulation of work. With the development of parliamentary democracy and the extension of the franchise, a broader range of social classes was participating in government, influencing its directions and demanding changes. Geographic isolation also dictated that the state take a more prominent role. Nineteenth-century Australian statutes, such as the Masters and Servants legislation and the Factory Acts, were often more interventionist than their British counterparts.[5] Prior to Federation, wages boards or conciliation and arbitration systems to regulate wages were already established in some colonies. In this context, the establishment after federation of an Australian system of compulsory conciliation and arbitration for the prevention and settlement of industrial disputation was not out of place.

The conciliation and arbitration system along with 'White Australia' immigration controls and tariff protection constituted the 'three pillars' of Australian economic and social policy for much of the twentieth century.[6] The edifice erected around them distributed the benefits of work in the industrial era primarily to white males and their families.[7] Because work is integral to the identity of a community, to its survival and flourishing, controls over the entry and exit of workers are not uncommon. Even in mediaeval times in England the *Ordinance of Labourers* (1349) and the *Statute of Labourers* (1350) performed (at least in part) this function. The nature of Australian colonial expansion meant that immigration and labour market supply issues were inextricably linked. This continued to be the case in the twentieth century. The *Immigration Restriction Act 1901* (Cth) imposed strict (and racially based) controls on entry into the country, and hence the performance of work by 'outsiders'. Internally, 'white Australian' identity was reinforced by the exclusion of Indigenous Australians from both political and industrial citizenship: they were excluded from the vote and

---

4   R Mitchell 'State Systems of Conciliation and Arbitration: The Legal Origins of the Australasian Model' in S Macintyre and R Mitchell (eds) *Foundations of Arbitration: The Origins and Effects of State Compulsory Arbitration 1890–1914* (1989); and R Johnstone and R Mitchell 'Regulating Work' in C Parker et al (eds) *Regulating Law* (2004).

5   M Quinlan '"Pre-arbitral" Labour Legislation in Australia and Its Implications for the Introduction of Compulsory Arbitration' in Macintyre and Mitchell, ibid, 312; and A Merritt 'The Historical Role of Law in the Regulation of Employment—Abstentionist or Interventionist?' (1982) 1 *Aust JL & Soc* 56.

6   B Creighton 'One Hundred Years of the Conciliation and Arbitration Power: A Province Lost?' (2000) 24 *MULR* 839. See also J Isaac and S Macintyre (eds) The *New Province of Law and Order: 100 Years of Australian Industrial Conciliation and Arbitration* (2004).

7   G Whitehouse 'Justice and Equity: Women and Indigenous Workers' in Isaac and Macintyre (eds), ibid.

other forms of participation in public life by the Commonwealth *Franchise Act 1901* (Cth), and they were also in practice to be deprived of the benefits of the conciliation and arbitration system.

In colonial Australia the economy was largely dependent on rural industries. It remained so well into the twentieth century, whereas by that time the industrial revolution had taken a firmer hold and already changed the economic and social landscape in the 'mother country' Britain. The transformation of Australia into a more industrialised economy in the twentieth century was actively fostered by a strong tariff protection policy. The *Harvester Case*, which first established the federal basic wage for a male breadwinner, was a decision under the *Excise Tariff Act 1906* (Cth), which exempted from excise duty the goods of manufacturers who remunerated labour according to a 'fair and reasonable' standard.[8] Thereafter this basic wage was under the custodianship of the conciliation and arbitration system and the gendering of its protective standards became a hallmark of the traditional labour law framework.[9]

The advent of the global era has seen radical adjustments in the form of the 'three pillars'. Immigration policy is now focused on responding to, accommodating, and positioning the nation as part of the global labour market. New issues, such as greater provision for short-term immigration of both high-skilled knowledge workers and lower-skilled seasonal workers, now dominate policy debates.[10] Tariff protection steadily decreased over the last two decades of the twentieth century as Australia progressively opened its economy to global markets and pursued free trade agreements.

In the global context of the twenty-first century vigorous contest and debate continues in many areas of law over the shape of labour markets, the direction of the regulation of work, and the construction of its beneficiaries.[11] While it is impossible to understand the law of work in any complete way without paying attention to the diversity of labour markets and the multiplicity of laws that construct and regulate them, this chapter focuses attention on the arena of traditional labour law. It traces the evolution of the old conciliation and arbitration system, which resolved industrial disputes through awards applying to workers collectively, into a system that embodies the neo-liberal values dominant in the global era and is focused on the individual employment relationship and workplace bargaining.

This chapter sketches the major aspects of the system as it operated in the industrial era from 1904 until the late 1980s. It then examines the transition from the old to the new regulatory system that occurred between 1988 and 2005. During that period the conciliation and arbitration system underwent major reforms as a system of bargaining at the enterprise and workplace level was grafted onto the old award system, and

---

8   *Ex parte HV McKay* (*Harvester Case*) (1907) 2 CAR 1.

9   RJ Owens 'The Traditional Labour Law Framework: A Critical Evaluation' in R Mitchell (ed) *Redefining Labour Law: New Perspectives on the Future of Teaching and Research* (1995).

10 See eg Senate Employment, Workplace Relations and Education Committee, Parliament of Australia, *Inquiry into Pacific Region Seasonal Contract Labour* (2006). See also M Crock and K Lyon (eds) *Nation Skilling: Migration, Labour and Law in Australia, Canada, New Zealand and the United States* (2002); and A O'Donnell and R Mitchell 'Immigrant Labour in Australia: The Regulatory Framework' (2001) 14 *AJLL* 269.

11 See C Arup et al (eds) *Labour Law and Labour Market Regulation* (2006).

the award system itself was transformed into a safety net of minimum entitlements. The final section of the chapter discusses the regulation of work in Australia under the *Workplace Relations Act 1996* (Cth) (*Workplace Relations Act*) after amendment by the *Work Choices Act*.

The conciliation and arbitration system in the industrial era

Foundations

The Commonwealth Parliament does not have any single power that enables it to regulate work in a comprehensive manner. Historically, the power with respect to 'conciliation and arbitration for the prevention and settlement of industrial disputes extending beyond the limits of any one State' (*Australian Constitution*, s 51(xxxv)) has been dominant. The debates at the constitutional conventions of the 1890s reveal considerable hesitancy when this power was first proposed for the new Parliament, but it was finally supported at the last session held in Melbourne in 1898.[12] Coincidentally the prolonged industrial action of the 1890s in Australia's then most significant industries—the shearing, mining and maritime industries—had already demonstrated the need for the new Australian Parliament to have power to manage effectively any widespread industrial disputation that would impact at the national level.

The enactment of the first piece of legislation under the conciliation and arbitration power was no less politically controversial, with several governments falling during the period between the introduction of the first Bill and the final passage of the *Commonwealth Conciliation and Arbitration Act 1904* (Cth).[13] The conciliation and arbitration system that this legislation established was envisaged as providing, in the words of one of its founders, Henry Bournes Higgins, 'a new province for law and order' and an alternative to the 'rude and barbarous' method of the strike that was an inevitable part of any system of collective bargaining.[14] In the strikes of the 1890s the main issue had been the workers' claim to a right to join together in trade unions to negotiate collectively with their employers who were insisting on 'freedom of contract' to agree to terms and conditions of employment with workers on an individual basis. Coinciding with a period of economic recession, the workers' resistance was not successful and the dislocation and harm caused to the economy and to society at large during this period made a deep impression.

The founders of the federal conciliation and arbitration system, all men of liberal politics, were animated by the idea of restoring harmony to class relations.[15] When

---

12 See *Official Record of the Debates of the Australasian Federal Convention* (1891), 688–9 and 780–5; (1897), 782–93; and (1898), 180–215.

13 After numerous amendments and several changes of name, the current successor of the original 1904 Act is the *Workplace Relations Act 1996* (Cth). On the history of the legislation see generally Isaac and Macintyre (eds), above n 6; and The Hon Justice M Kirby 'Industrial Conciliation and Arbitration in Australia—A Centenary Reflection' (2004) 17 *AJLL* 229.

14 HB Higgins 'A New Province For Law and Order' (1915) 29 *Harv LR* 13.

15 S Macintyre 'Neither Capital nor Labour: The Politics of the Establishment of Arbitration' in MacIntyre and Mitchell (eds), above n 4.

Prime Minister Deakin presented the *Commonwealth Conciliation and Arbitration Bill* to Parliament in 1903 he expressed their hopes thus:

> No measures ever submitted to any legislature offer greater prospects of the establishment of social justice and the removal of inequalities than do those which are based upon the principle of conciliation and arbitration.[16]

Awards made to prevent and settle industrial disputes would thereafter often establish the same terms and conditions for all employees across an industry, thus fostering equality and a sense of social cohesion, and many (although by no means all) of the disruptions of industrial action were avoided through the establishment of a public and fair system for resolving disputes between capital and labour.

The Australian conciliation and arbitration system

The structure of the Australian system of labour law was determined in large part by the nature of the constitutional power underpinning the *Commonwealth Conciliation and Arbitration Act 1904* (Cth). The Act established a Commonwealth tribunal—variously named over the course of the next 100 years as the Commonwealth Court of Conciliation and Arbitration, then the Conciliation and Arbitration Commission, later the Australian Conciliation and Arbitration Commission, and finally the Australian Industrial Relations Commission (AIRC). For the first nine decades of its existence this tribunal exercised powers of conciliation and arbitration to resolve industrial disputation extending beyond the limits of any one State. During this period important legal developments impacted upon the way the tribunal functioned. Not the least of these was the articulation in the mid-1950s of the constitutional doctrine of the separation of powers in the *Boilermakers' Case*.[17] This case made it clear that the tribunal could not exercise both arbitral power *and* powers of enforcement, and from that time forward the formal judicial enforcement of federal awards or orders made by the tribunal was reposed in a federal court.

Even though the conciliation and arbitration system underwent a more or less constant evolutionary change during the industrial era, including as a result of judicial interpretation of the constitutional and statutory provisions defining the jurisdiction of the tribunal, there was remarkable stability in the system. Its most distinctive features were the special role of the tribunal; regulation on an industrywide basis; a recognised role for trade unions; and the importance of the public interest.

The role of the tribunal
Conciliation and arbitration
The role played by the tribunal in the prevention and settlement of industrial disputation was the most striking characteristic of the traditional Australian labour law system. The tribunal's arbitral powers were quasi-legislative and quasi-judicial in character, enabling it to declare for the future the rights and obligations of the

---

16 Commonwealth, *Parliamentary Debates*, House of Representatives, 30 July 1903, 2868.
17 *R v Kirby; Ex parte the Boilermakers' Society of Australia (Boilermakers' Case)* (1956) 94 CLR 254; (1957) 95 CLR 529.

parties to an industrial dispute.[18] However, the central focus of the system was for the most part on conciliation: 'the coming together of parties with a view to amicable settlement' of their differences.[19] In conciliation the role of the tribunal was to facilitate the resolution of disputation by assisting the parties to reach agreement. As conciliator the tribunal could suggest ways for parties to resolve their differences, stopping short of imposing a solution. Over the years, the majority of industrial disputes brought before the tribunal were resolved through the conciliation process. Only where parties could not reach agreement did it intervene to arbitrate and impose a resolution upon them. Importantly, however, the tribunal was always able to exercise its powers on a compulsory basis: whether acting on its own motion to investigate industrial disputation or dealing with industrial disputes notified to it, parties could be required to submit to its jurisdiction and could not escape its oversight.

'Equity, good conscience and the substantial merits of the case'

Ever since the enactment of the *Commonwealth Conciliation and Arbitration Act 1904* (Cth) the tribunal was directed to determine matters before it according to 'equity, good conscience and the substantial merits of the case' without the constraints of other technicalities or legal forms.[20] To facilitate this, the tribunal enjoyed a wide discretion in determining its own procedure, including the method it employed to investigate issues and the process it adopted to hear and determine a matter.[21] It was not restricted by the rules of evidence in the same way as a court exercising judicial power. However, the tribunal had a duty to accord natural justice to the parties to an industrial dispute.[22] They were notified of, and invited to participate in, the various conferences and hearings constituting the processes leading to the making of an award. It was the role of parties that imparted to the federal conciliation or arbitral processes a quasi-judicial character.

Binding parties to industrial disputation

Powers of conciliation and arbitration are by their very nature exercised vis-à-vis particular parties who are in dispute. Thus constitutional limitations meant that the awards or orders of the tribunal, given legal effect by the statute, could bind only the parties to the industrial dispute and those who brought themselves into the arena of the dispute and whom it was necessary to bind in order to secure its effective ongoing settlement.[23]

Federal industrial awards could not operate as a common rule, binding generally those who had no connection to the industrial dispute. As early as 1910 in *Whybrow's*

---

18 *Waterside Workers' Federation of Australia v JW Alexander* (1918) 25 CLR 434.
19 *Re Bain; Ex parte Cadbury Schweppes Australia Ltd* (1984) 159 CLR 163.
20 *Commonwealth Conciliation and Arbitration Act 1904* (Cth) s 25; and see *Workplace Relations Act*, former s 110(2)(c).
21 See *Workplace Relations Act*, former s 110.
22 *R v Commonwealth Conciliation and Arbitration Commission; Ex parte Angliss Group* (1969) 122 CLR 546. See R Naughton 'Natural Justice in the Australian Industrial Relations Commission' (1993) 35 *JIR* 3.
23 *George Hudson Ltd v The Australian Timber Workers Union* (1923) 32 CLR 413. See *Commonwealth Conciliation and Arbitration Act 1904* (Cth), s 29; and *Workplace Relations Act*, former s 149.

Case the High Court invalidated an attempt by Parliament to vest power in the Conciliation and Arbitration Court to establish minimum standards at a general industry level.[24] Nor was it possible under the conciliation and arbitration power to provide for the resolution of industrial disputation by, say, a committee comprised of general representatives of capital and labour who had no specific connection to the disputation.[25] Likewise industrial players could not approach the tribunal and request that it determine the terms and conditions to apply to them simply according to what the tribunal considered appropriate. The parties themselves had to be in real dispute over such matters.[26]

The tribunal therefore never had any general regulatory powers, although in practice 'test cases' and national wage cases often led to the establishment of standards that were then adopted widely across different industries through a 'flow-on' process involving variation of awards.[27] However, the authority of the tribunal, including as arbitrator, was never at large but was always constrained by the doctrine of ambit, which ensured that its power was exercised only to resolve the industrial dispute between the parties.[28] The doctrine of ambit governed the relationship of the award to the dispute, and set the boundaries within which the award could be later varied.

Industrywide regulation
Industrial disputation
Regulation under the Australian conciliation and arbitration system was for the most part industrywide, because the jurisdiction of the tribunal was constitutionally confined to exercising powers of conciliation and arbitration for the prevention and settlement of 'industrial disputes'.

In the mid-1980s the High Court in a unanimous decision in the *Social Welfare* case ruled that the constitutional expression 'industrial disputes' was not 'a technical or legal' one. Rather the words were to be given 'their popular meaning'.[29] The *Social Welfare* case harkened back to the broad interpretation that had been endorsed early, in the *Jumbunna* case,[30] but later abandoned. So ended many decades when the emphasis had been on whether or not the dispute concerned employees 'in an industry'. 'Industry' had been confined quite narrowly in the *Municipalities* case to mean 'productive' industries involving 'organised business carried on for a profit'.[31] For a long period after, the system was effectively restricted to dealing predominantly with disputes involving blue collar workers in primary and secondary industries in the private sector. While the banking

---

24 *The Australian Boot Trade Employees' Federation v Whybrow & Co (Whybrow's Case)* (1910) 11 CLR 311. Where the legislation was constitutionally supported by other powers, eg the Territories power (*Australian Constitution*, s 122), there was no such constraint.
25 See *Australian Railways Union v The Victorian Railways Commissioner* (1930) 44 CLR 319.
26 *Re State Public Services Federation; Ex parte Attorney General (WA)* (1993) 178 CLR 249.
27 See below, pp 90–93.
28 See *Workplace Relations Act*, former s 120, and *R v Holmes; Ex parte Victorian Employees Federation* (1980) 145 CLR 68, 76.
29 *R v Coldham; Ex parte The Australian Social Welfare Union (Social Welfare)* (1983) 153 CLR 297, 313.
30 *Jumbunna Coal Mine, No Liability v Victorian Coal Miners Association (Jumbunna)* (1908) 6 CLR 309.
31 *The Federated Municipal and Shire Council Employees' Union v Melbourne Corporation (Municipalities)* (1919) 26 CLR 508.

and finance industries were early encompassed within the tribunal's jurisdiction by virtue of being characterised as 'incidental' to industry,[32] the industrial character of many disputes, including those involving schoolteachers, firefighters, clerical assistants, public sector clerical staff and university staff, was denied for much of the twentieth century and hence for many years treated as beyond the scope of the federal tribunal's jurisdiction.[33]

Real industrial disputes

Although the jurisdiction of the federal tribunal was enlivened only by a real industrial dispute, that did not necessitate strike action, lockout or other industrial dislocation. In law, 'disagreement, difference or dissidence' was the essence of disputation.[34] Thus a genuine 'paper dispute', in which a 'log of claims' was issued by a trade union in writing to employers and employer organisations across an industry and then was rejected, sufficed. Mildly extravagant claims did not negate the genuineness of a dispute: by broadening the ambit of a dispute they ensured that its eventual settlement would be effective over time allowing workers' terms and conditions to be maintained in the context of other developments in the industrial arena including changes in the cost of living.[35] On some occasions demands were more fanciful than genuine and failed to activate the jurisdiction of the tribunal.[36] Paper disputes also had the advantage of making it relatively easy to 'rope in' to a dispute at a later stage any new business or employer in the industry, thus ensuring that awards continued to provide fairly comprehensive coverage across an industry.

Disputes extending beyond the limits of any one State

Paper disputes also facilitated the fulfilment of constitutional and statutory requirements that industrial disputation 'extend beyond the limits of any one State'. The operation of trade unions at national level with members in every State also aided this, especially as it was not necessary in a dispute to have an even distribution of members across various States.[37] However, the interstate requirement was not satisfied merely by a series of similar disputes in different States: the dispute itself had to extend beyond the limits of a State.[38] By the end of the twentieth century it was accepted that this meant showing the disputants in more than one State were joined in a 'community of interest' and

32 *Australian Insurance Staffs' Federation v Accident Underwriters' Association and The Bank Officials' Association v The Bank of Australasia & Ors* (1923) 33 CLR 517.

33 See *Federated State School Teachers' Association of Australia v Victoria* (1929) 41 CLR 569; *Pitfield v Franki* (1970) 123 CLR 448; *R v Marshall; Ex parte The Federated Clerks' Union of Australia* (1975) 132 CLR 595; *R v Holmes; Ex parte the Public Service Association of New South Wales* (1977) 140 CLR 63; and *R v McMahon; Ex parte Darvall* (1982) 151 CLR 57. Cf *R v President of the Commonwealth Conciliation and Arbitration Commission; Ex parte Professional Engineers Association* (1959) 107 CLR 208.

34 *Metal Trades Employees Association v Amalgamated Engineering Union (Metal Trades)*(1935) 54 CLR 387, 429.

35 See *Re Printing and Kindred Industries Union; Ex parte Vista Paper Products Pty Ltd* (1993) 113 ALR 421. See also *Attorney-General (Qld) v Riordan* (1997) 192 CLR 1.

36 Eg *Re State Public Services Federation; Ex parte Attorney-General (WA) (SPSF)*(1993) 178 CLR 249.

37 *R v Blakely; Ex parte the Association of Architects, Engineers, Surveyors and Draughtsmen of Australia* (1950) 82 CLR 54; *R v Portus; Ex parte Federated Clerks' Union of Australia* (1949) 79 CLR 428. Cf *R v Gough; Ex parte BP Refinery (Westernport) Pty Ltd* (1966) 114 CLR 385.

38 *R v Commonwealth Conciliation and Arbitration Commission; Ex parte The Australian Workers Union* (1957) 99 CLR 505.

this, in turn, could be evidenced by economic, industrial or financial considerations. The presence of employers in a common industry or with a commercial nexus between them, or common demands put to employers, or an economic connection between the employment conditions of employees, or the similarity of the work performed by or the calling of the participants in the dispute, were all factors relevant to establishing the existence of a 'community of interest'.[39]

Disputes about matters pertaining to the employment relationship

The *Social Welfare* case made it clear that the scope of the constitutional expression 'industrial disputes' was limited only by its understanding in the wider community. Some years earlier Justice Murphy had foreshadowed the potential breadth of these words, by suggesting that even if industry was no longer conducted through employment relations, the conciliation and arbitration power in the *Constitution* would not cease to be relevant. In his view, the expression could readily apply to disputation between, say, independent contractors and business.[40]

However, the jurisdiction of the tribunal was always more limited. Under the statutory definition, an industrial dispute was confined to 'industrial matters' or 'matters pertaining to the relationship between employers and employees'.[41] Indeed one of the reasons behind the narrow interpretation of the statutory expression 'industrial dispute' in some twentieth-century cases was that the newer concept of 'employee' was not always sharply differentiated from the older one of 'servant' in judicial understandings. This meant that those engaged in non-manual, professional work or working outside the factory gate were sometimes assumed to be independent contractors.[42]

The expression 'industrial matters' was initially interpreted broadly. A dispute over employees wearing a badge at work to signify their trade union membership, for instance, was early held to be covered by it.[43] However, later interpretations were more constrained, extending only to those disputes about matters 'directly affecting' the relation between employers and employees and not to those impacting upon that relationship in an 'indirect, consequential and remote' way.[44] In some cases this distinction was used to contrast industrial matters with, say, political or social matters,[45] or matters within management's prerogative.[46] However, over time the notion of mutual exclusivity between certain subject matters was downplayed and emphasis was placed

39 *Re Australasian Meat Industry Employees Union; Ex parte Aberdeen Beef Co Pty Ltd* (1993) 176 CLR 155; *SPSF*, above n 36; and *Re Australian Education Union; Ex Parte Victoria (AEU Case)* (1995) 184 CLR 188.

40 *R v Coldham; Ex parte Fitzsimmons* (1976) 137 CLR 153, 174–5. On the distinction between employees and independent contractors see Chapter 4.

41 *Commonwealth Conciliation And Arbitration Act 1904* (Cth), s 4; and *Workplace Relations Act*, former s 4.

42 Eg *R v Commonwealth Industrial Court Judges; Ex parte Cocks (Cocks)* (1968) 121 CLR 313.

43 *The Australian Tramways Employees Association v The Prahran and Malvern Tramways Trust* (1913) 17 CLR 680.

44 See eg *R v Findlay; Ex parte The Commonwealth Steamship Owners' Association & Ors* (1954) 90 CLR 621, 630.

45 *R v Portus; Ex parte ANZ Banking Group Ltd* (1972) 127 CLR 353, 371. See also R Doyle 'The Industrial/ Political Dichotomy: The Impact on the Freedom of Communication Cases on Industrial Law' (1995) 8 *AJLL* 91.

46 Eg *R v Commonwealth Conciliation and Arbitration Commission; Ex parte The Melbourne and Metropolitan Tramways Board* (1965) 113 CLR 228.

more strongly on whether the demands were addressed to 'the employer in their capacity as an employer' and concerned 'the employee in their capacity as an employee'.[47]

To the lay observer (and some lawyers) there was a degree of artificiality in this. The distinction between two types of demands concerning payments to a third party provides an example. A demand that employers contribute to a pension or superannuation trust fund on behalf of their employees was eventually held to be one regarding a well-accepted benefit attaching to employment and as such an industrial matter, overriding earlier reasoning that focused on the receipt of the benefit in the post-employment period.[48] It was even accepted later that employers could be required to use their 'best endeavours' to influence the decision-making of trustees of a superannuation trust for the benefit of employees.[49] By contrast a demand that employers deduct trade union dues from the employee's wages and pay them directly to the trade union on behalf of the employee was always treated as being a matter concerning employees not 'as employees' but as 'debtors' to their trade union.[50]

Although it was recognised towards the end of the twentieth century that demands should not be treated in an overly legalistic way, nonetheless the formulation of a demand could be significant. Where the motivation behind a dispute was, for instance, a desire to protect the terms and conditions (and ultimately the jobs) of employees covered by an award from being undercut by independent contractors working on lower terms and conditions, a demand might be shaped in one of several different ways. A demand that business refrain from engaging independent contractors was likely to be characterised as instigating a dispute about a matter directly affecting the freedom of business to arrange its contractual affairs and only indirectly concerning employees. On the other hand, a demand that any independent contractors engaged by the employing business be accorded the same terms and conditions as employees was more likely to be seen as one directly affecting the employment relation.[51]

Likewise a demand that employers restrict the opening and closing hours of shops was seen as a matter only indirectly affecting the employees' hours of work but directly pertaining to the conduct of commerce and the relation between businesses and their customers. On the other hand, demands that sought to restrict the hours that employees worked clearly raised an industrial matter.[52] Disputes over staffing levels when formulated in terms of, say, concern for passenger safety rather than the employees' conditions of work also risked being characterised as intruding on the relation between the business and its customer rather than being industrial in character.[53] Not

---

47 Eg *R v Portus; Ex parte ANZ Banking Group* (1972) 127 CLR 353; and *Re Alcan Australia Ltd; Ex parte Federation of Industrial and Manufacturing Engineering Employees* (1994) 181 CLR 96.

48 *Re Manufacturing Grocers' Employees Federation of Australia; Ex parte Australian Chamber of Manufacturers* (1986) 160 CLR 341. Cf *R v Hamilton Knight; Ex parte The Commonwealth Steamship Owners' Association* (1952) 86 CLR 283.

49 *Re Amalgamated Metal Workers Union of Australia; Ex parte Shell Co of Australia Ltd* (1992) 174 CLR 345.

50 See cases cited above n 47.

51 *Cocks*, above n 42. Cf *Federated Clothing Trades v Archer* (1919) 27 CLR 207; and *R v Moore; Ex parte Federated Miscellaneous Workers Union of Australia* (1978) 140 CLR 470.

52 *Clancy v Butchers Shop Employees' Union* (1904) 1 CLR 181 (a decision concerning NSW legislation). Cf *R v Kelly; Ex parte Victoria* (1950) 81 CLR 64.

53 *Australian Federation of Airpilots v The Flight Crew Officers Industrial Tribunal* (1968) 119 CLR 16.

surprisingly, the distinction between matters directly affecting employees and those with only an indirect, consequential or remote effect on them sometimes seemed to represent the triumph of form over substance.

The distinction between matters with direct or an indirect effect on the employment relationship often marked a boundary between 'industrial' and 'commercial' issues. The latter were the province of capital, controlled by management, and excluded from the regulatory gaze of the tribunal. The positioning of this industrial/commercial divide was challenged in the second half of the twentieth century by the movement for industrial democracy. In Justice Murphy's words, industrial democracy represented a demand by workers 'to be emancipated from industrial serfdom, which will otherwise be produced by the domination of corporations; [it was] a demand to be treated with respect and dignity'.[54] By the 1970s and 1980s a range of matters that had previously been assumed to be within management's exclusive control—including the mode of recruiting staff, staffing levels, promotion, the integration of seniority lists across different parts of an organisation, and retrenchment—was acknowledged as potentially raising issues directly pertaining to the relationship between employers and employees.[55] Managerial prerogative was 'in retreat', and although the law initially expressed some wariness about the tribunal dealing with issues that had traditionally been for management alone, by the late 1980s the growing emphasis in human resource management on cooperation and the sharing of responsibilities in the workplace led to its continuing demise.[56] Despite this the law never abandoned its understanding that capital and labour had quite distinct roles in the business enterprise: although the conciliation and arbitration system might insist that workers be consulted about the way in which management's decisions were put into effect, it never challenged the right of capital to determine the direction of the business.

The role of trade unions

In the conciliation and arbitration system industrial disputation was understood to be collective in nature, and did not encompass a dispute between an individual worker and an employer unless it could be shown to have a collective dimension. In an industrial dispute a 'number of employees' made 'common cause'.[57] Concerned only with industrial disputation about matters pertaining to the relationship between employers and employees, the focus of the system was always on securing terms and conditions for labour collectively.

Because the processes of conciliation and arbitration directly involved parties to industrial disputation, effective representation of collective interests was essential.

---

54 See *Federated Clerks' Union of Australia & Anor v Victorian Employers Federation* (1984) 154 CLR 472, 494.

55 See eg *R v Coldham; Ex parte Fitzsimmons* (1976) 137 CLR 153; *Federated Clerks' Union of Australia v Victorian Employers Federation* (1984) 154 CLR 472 (a decision concerning Victorian legislation); and *Re Cram; Ex parte New South Wales Colliery Proprietors' Association* (1987) 163 CLR 117.

56 See A Stewart 'The Federated Clerks' Case: Managerial Prerogative in Retreat?' (1985) 59 *ALJ* 717; A Stewart 'Federal Jurisdiction over Industrial Management Matters: The Demise of Managerial Prerogative' (1988) 1 *AJLL* 70; and Hon Mr Justice JT Ludeke 'Whatever Happened to Managerial Prerogative?' (1992) 66 *ALJ* 11.

57 *Jumbunna*, above n 30, 332.

The system was premised upon the organisation of capital and labour into groups.[58] The organisation of labour was critical to the working of the conciliation and arbitration system. While workers could engage in industrial disputation as a loose collection of individuals, this was rarely practicable.[59]

Thus from the outset the statutory scheme provided a mechanism for registering those trade unions that complied with stipulated conditions regarding their organisation and the conduct of their affairs. This arrangement was held in *Jumbunna* to be constitutionally valid as incidental to the conciliation and arbitration power.[60] Registration accorded the trade union corporate status, though of a peculiar kind with powers confined to the purposes of the Act.[61] As a corporate entity the trade union was endowed with a legal personality, it could hold property and it could sue and be sued. Most significantly as a legal 'person' the trade union was able to function as a party principal in industrial disputation. It did not act merely as an agent for its present membership. Consequently a registered trade union could initiate an industrial dispute with employers, including those who did not employ any trade union labour at the time, over the terms and conditions of their present and future trade union employees.[62]

In order to protect fully the interests of their members, trade unions usually demanded that employers accord the same terms and conditions to both union and non-union labour, and the law recognised their ability to do so.[63] Superior workplace rights for trade unionists would have risked providing an incentive to employers to hire non-union labour on terms and conditions undercutting award conditions and thus leading ultimately to a loss of jobs for trade unionists. Trade unions thus played a pivotal role in the regulation of the working conditions of *all* workers, both unionist and non-unionist alike, under the conciliation and arbitration system. In addition, because of their role in drawing up the logs of claims to initiate industrial disputation, trade unions exercised significant direction over the issues that became prominent in the system. In the conciliation and arbitration system, trade unions became the authorised voice of labour.

The conciliation and arbitration system never gave legal sanction to compulsory unionism. However, it did allow the inclusion of 'preference' provisions in awards. Trade unionists could be given preference in relation to a full range of workplace entitlements, whether at the point of entry to the workplace, or in promotion, or the allocation and the timing of holidays, to give just a few examples. At every level the system incorporated a strong systemic advantage to those who belonged to trade unions.[64] Under this regime trade unionism flourished. However, participation in the conciliation and arbitration system entailed trade-offs for trade unions. Under the system they formally gave up any claim to a right to strike and accepted the channelling of industrial disputation through

---

58 *Australian Tramway Employees Association v Prahran and Malvern Tramways Trust* (1913) 17 CLR 680.

59 Cf *R v Portus; Ex parte McNeil* (1961) 105 CLR 537.

60 See *Jumbunna*, above n 30.

61 Ibid, 355.

62 *Burwood Cinema Ltd v Australian Theatrical and Amusement Employees' Association* (1925) 35 CLR 528.

63 *Metal Trades*, above n 34.

64 For an excellent account of the operation of the system in relation to trade unions see P Weeks *Trade Union Security Law: A Study of Preference and Compulsory Unionism* (1995).

the processes of the tribunal towards a resolution that ultimately could be imposed upon them if agreement was not reached with employers. Non-compliance with the norms and rules of the system could result in deregistration and ultimately exclusion from the protection of the system.[65]

The public interest

Ever since the introduction of the *Commonwealth Conciliation and Arbitration Act* in 1904 one of the chief duties of the tribunal when exercising its powers to regulate the relations between capital and labour was to take account of the public interest.[66] Thus while the role of parties was integral to federal award-making, it was never an essentially private process restricted to a consideration and assessment of their immediate interests. The system of conciliation and arbitration was established with an expectation by its founders that it would bring great benefits not only to industrial parties but also to the community at large. The assumption underpinning the system was that the regulation of work impacted on the wider public good.

The breadth of the expression 'the public interest', as the High Court has noted, meant it 'often depend[ed] on balancing interests, including competing public interests, and [was] very much a question of fact and degree'.[67] The statute, its subject matter, scope and objects, provided the only constraint upon the broad range of matters that were considered under the rubric of the 'public interest'.[68]

Over the course of the twentieth century the public interest was a central feature of the system. It was the significance of its 'public interest' mandate that explains why the tribunal evolved into a major player, especially in the 1970s and 1980s, in determining macroeconomic policy, through what became a centralised wage fixing system. Later in the 1980s and into the 1990s it proved equally adept, through processes of award restructuring and the introduction of trade-offs for demonstrated changes in structural efficiency of businesses, at instituting microeconomic reform.

Test cases

The tribunal always exercised its powers with an eye to the impact on the particular parties and according to the precepts of 'fairness and equity', but because of its duty to take account of the public interest, the tribunal was not constrained by the submissions and views of the parties to the industrial dispute. Indeed in making or varying an award clause it could override their agreement. In the *Basic Wage and Standard Hours Inquiry 1952–53*[69] the then Commonwealth Court of Conciliation and Arbitration removed an award clause for macroeconomic reasons, contrary to the wishes of the parties. There was an unsuccessful challenge to this in *R v Kelly; Ex parte Australian*

---

65 See KP McEvoy and RJ Owens 'The Flight of Icarus: Legal Aspects of the Pilot's Dispute' (1990) 3 *AJLL* 87.

66 *Commonwealth Conciliation and Arbitration Act 1904* (Cth), s 16.

67 *Re Queensland Electricity Commission; Ex parte Electrical Trades Union of Australia* (1987) 72 ALR 1, 5.

68 *Comalco Aluminium (Bell Bay) Ltd v O'Connor* (1995) 131 ALR 657, 681. See also *O'Sullivan v Farrer* (1989) 168 CLR 210, 216 citing *Water Conservation and Irrigation Commission (NSW) v Browning* (1947) 74 CLR 492, 505.

69 (1953) 77 CAR 477.

Railways Union.[70] In that case the High Court also upheld the test case 'flow-on' process of proceeding from dispute to dispute and applying a commonly worded clause on each occasion, declaring it was not equivalent to a legislative process.[71] As long as the clause was within the ambit of the dispute then changing economic circumstances, among other things, could necessitate an award variation to maintain an effective settlement of the dispute even against the wishes of the parties. At the same time the High Court emphasised that the Conciliation and Arbitration Court did not have any *general* control or direction of industrial, social or economic policies. Later in *R v Moore; Ex parte Australian Telephone and Phonogram Officers' Association* the High Court unanimously held that a single commissioner did not fetter his own discretion in considering himself bound by general principles where the power to enunciate those principles was expressly given to the Full Bench by the statute.[72]

Test cases were usually initiated, at least towards the end of the industrial era, by the Australian Council of Trade Unions (ACTU), which worked with particular trade unions to identify and select appropriate industries and suitable awards in which to 'test' a claim for a new work standard that could apply across a broad range of industries. The test case process was in many senses absolutely conventional, initiated by a log of claims issued to employers or their organisations. Often conducted over quite an extensive period, all participants prepared their case, set out their contentions or the basic principles that structured their arguments, and presented wide-ranging evidence in support of their positions. As was the usual procedure for dealing with an industrial dispute, there were conciliation meetings to find common ground on which the parties agreed, prior to the tribunal arbitrating when agreement could not be reached. The test case standard was then available for insertion into other awards.

In the later test cases the Commission (as it became after the mid-1950s) often received evidence and submissions from a wide cross-section of the community regarding the impact of industrial standards. It had broad power to grant applications to intervene, and the Minister had a right to intervene in relation to the public interest in matters before the Full Bench.[73] The participation of third party interveners was particularly important in 'test cases'. As well as hearing from the peak organisations of trade unions (the ACTU) and of employers and business, such as the Confederation of Australian Industry (CAI), the Business Council of Australia (BCA) and the Australian Industry Group (AIG), the Commonwealth and often State governments would also usually make submissions in test cases.

In addition there would generally be a wide range of representations from various interest groups. Typically these might include other government agencies such as the Human Rights and Equal Opportunity Commission (HREOC); NGOs such as Parents Without Partners or Women's Electoral Lobby; and church groups and charitable organisations such as St Vincent de Paul, the Salvation Army charities, or

---

70 (1953) 89 CLR 461.
71 Ibid, 474–5.
72 (1982) 148 CLR 600.
73 *Workplace Relations Act*, former ss 43(1) and 44.

the Brotherhood of Saint Lawrence. Particular social groups were also often represented especially where they felt vulnerable and not represented by any of the major players. Indigenous Australians, rural groups, or carers' associations, for instance, have at times presented submissions to the tribunal.

The submissions of parties and interveners usually addressed the wider economic and social impacts of test case standards, as well as providing information about standards both internationally and in Australia.

Economics was central to the Commission's expertise and thinking. The consideration of detailed economic evidence and information was critical in the earlier *National Wage Cases* and the later *Safety Net Wage Reviews* of the 1990s. The risks and implications of the Commission's decisions were examined in terms of their impact both at the micro-economic level, including on individual wage earners, and at the macro level, and involved deliberation about international trends, the impact on foreign debt, and the general state of the economy especially whether it was and was likely to be buoyant or in recession.

The Commission also assessed the social impact of any new test case standards. It was not uncommon for reference to be made to statistical information from the Australian Bureau of Statistics or research especially commissioned by the parties. The significance of the social context in which awards operated was frequently explicit in the reasoning of the Commission. For instance, the changed social (and economic) role of women in relation to work and its impact on families was regularly noted in the last quarter of the twentieth century.[74] It included information about changes in the workforce participation of married women, the diversity of family types, and community attitudes to gender roles.

The interaction between social context and award standards was complex. Quite often the decisions of the Commission merely validated existing social practices. In the 1994 *Family Leave Test Case*, for instance, the standard adopted simply reflected the evidence that workers were *already* using their own sick leave entitlements when they needed to care for others: a de facto situation was made lawful.[75] However, award standards could also be intended to alter or construct new social roles. In the *Parental Leave Test Case* the Commission observed that the existing regulatory system reinforced the traditional role of women as carers for young children by denying to fathers a right to take paternity leave. In handing down its decision it expressed the hope that the provision of parental leave would in fact encourage fathers to take greater responsibility for the primary care of their children.[76]

In test cases too the Commission was alert to other existing rules and norms. International standards were often influential. Conventions and Recommendations of

---

74 See the following important test cases: *Maternity Leave Test Case* (1979) 218 CAR 120; *Adoption Leave Test Case* (1985) 298 CAR 321; *Parental Leave Case* (1990) 36 IR 1; *Family Leave Test Case* (1994) 57 IR 121; and *Personal/Carer's Leave Test* (1995) 62 IR 48. See further Chapter 7.

75 *Family Leave Test Case*, ibid.

76 *Parental Leave Case*, above n 74.

the ILO were particularly important, and other major United Nations conventions, such as the *International Covenant on Economic, Social and Cultural Rights* and the *Convention on the Elimination of All Forms of Discrimination against Women*, were also often cited. Later these conventions also had an indirect impact because they underpinned the discrimination statutes to which the AIRC also had to have regard.[77]

The regulatory practices and standards of other countries were also frequently remarked upon before the Commission, with parties often comparing Australia's regulatory standards with those of other comparable countries such as the members of the OECD.[78] This reinforced the significance of the international context. On the other hand the Commission sometimes also pointed out that the Australian historical or legal context was different from that of other countries and therefore lessened the persuasive value of reference to the regulatory practices adopted elsewhere.[79]

In test cases the Commission would also usually assess the potential impact of any new award standard in the context of existing Australian regulation. Sometimes examples drawn from existing regulation formed cogent evidence that the requested standard was workable and not likely to have negative consequences. In the *Maternity Leave Test Case* in 1979, for instance, it was pointed out that maternity leave was already established in the public sector and in some parts of private industry without damaging effect.[80] In creating a new test case standard, the Commission would also consider how a proposed standard would relate to other award provisions. Thus in the *Working Hours Test Case* in 2002 the AIRC indicated that, in assessing arguments about the impact of working time on work/family balance, other award clauses such as those providing for leave to attend to care responsibilities ought not to be forgotten.[81]

From the industrial to the global era
The pressure for reform

From the mid-1980s Australia began to confront the challenges of the global era. The floating of the Australian dollar in 1983, the subsequent deregulation of its banking and finance systems, the gradual reduction in tariff barriers and the opening of borders to increased competition and eventually the negotiation of 'free trade' agreements, all signalled Australia's integration into the new economy.

In the early 1980s the Commonwealth Parliament established a Committee of Review chaired by Professor Keith Hancock to examine the operation of the conciliation and arbitration system and advise whether changes were required to enable it to adjust to this new environment. The resultant *Hancock Report* was wide-ranging.[82] However,

---

77 See *Workplace Relations Act*, former ss 93 and 93A.

78 Eg J Murray *International Legal Trends in the Reconciliation of Work and Family Life*, a report prepared for the ACTU's submission in the *Family Provisions Test Case* (2004).

79 Eg the *Working Hours Test Case* (2002) 114 IR 390, 452–3. Cf O Kahn-Freund 'On Uses and Abuses of Comparative Law' (1974) 37 *Mod LR* 1.

80 Above n 74.

81 Above n 79, 437.

82 K Hancock *Report of the Committee of Review on Australian Industrial Relations Law and Systems*, vols 1–3 (1985).

while it recommended among other things a need for a greater focus on bargaining in the workplace and more attention to the growing problem of 'quasi-employees', the *Hancock Report* was ultimately more reformist than radical. It took the view that any major reform of the system would not be supported by the major industrial players, and that in any event federal/state intersections in the system would make any fundamental change so complex as to be unviable. It found no compelling evidence that the conciliation and arbitration system had negative effects on microeconomic reform, and further concluded that it offered some positive advantages in the macroeconomic realm. The findings of the *Hancock Report* were bolstered over the next couple of years by the conclusion of an Accord between the federal Labor Government and the trade union movement on matters of economic policy concerning prices and incomes including the boundaries governing industrial demands for wage rises.[83]

However, the Accord served simply to make even clearer to opponents of the conciliation and arbitration system that it was held 'in contempt'.[84] Criticisms of the system continued, but politically the initiative for change was taken up by the States. In particular, the New South Wales government commissioned a report from Professor John Niland, which led to reforms incorporating a more market-oriented model of industrial regulation in the *Industrial Relations Act 1991* (NSW).[85]

In the two decades following the *Hancock Report* pressure to reform and 'deregulate' the labour market intensified. Award regulation on an industrywide basis was criticised as restrictive and inhibiting the structural reform necessary to take Australia into the global era. By the end of the industrial era awards had become very large documents itemising many matters of detail regarding work practices. They often contained numerous different classifications, each strictly marking out a separate territory of work to be performed and the skill required to do it. This system of award classifications was criticised as functionally inflexible, and there were calls for a reduction in the number of classifications and for workers to be 'multiskilled'.

Regulation centred on the enterprise or the workplace was also argued to be more appropriate for businesses operating in a competitive market economy. In addition, there were persistent criticisms that the necessity of 'manufacturing' an industrial dispute to activate the jurisdiction of the Commission fostered adversarial relations between capital and labour that were antithetical to the values of mutual cooperation and shared goals said to be appropriate to the new workplace. Localised bargaining at the enterprise or workplace was also said to have the advantage of making parties directly responsible for the conduct of their relations. Increasingly the role of the Commission was subjected to the criticism that it was inappropriate for a 'third party' to intrude into the essentially 'private' relations between a business and its workers.

---

83 ACTU *Statement of Accord by the Australian Labor Party and the Australian Council of Trade Unions Regarding Economic Policy* (1983).

84 HR Nicholls Society *Arbitration in Contempt* (1986).

85 J Niland *Transforming Industrial Relations in New South Wales: A Green Paper* (1989). See also Business Council of Australia *Enterprise-based Bargaining Units: A Better Way of Working* (1989); and J Niland and O Clarke *Agenda for Change: An International Analysis of Industrial Relations in Transition* (1991).

For similar reasons trade unions were also criticised as third party interlopers. This view gained potency because trade unions could draw employers into an industrial dispute even when they did not employ trade unionists. This also led to trade unions being criticised for having no connection with the workers at the 'grass roots' level. On the other hand, because trade unions still often tended to be organised along the lines of different trades, demarcation disputes could arise between them as to who should represent the workers doing a particular job in the workplace. Business also complained about inefficiencies caused by having to deal with multiple trade unions operating in a single enterprise. The trade union movement noted these criticisms—not the least because its membership was declining—and it sought to develop strategies to confront them, especially through the amalgamation of unions.[86]

From the mid-1980s there were also massive changes in the composition of the labour force and the organisation of work. With women's employment growing by 33.4 per cent between 1983 and 1989, the 'feminisation' of the labour force was the most marked of these changes. 'Non-standard' forms of employment became more common, as firms sought to achieve numerical flexibility and contain costs by reducing the number of core workers employed on a fulltime ongoing basis and entitled to award conditions. These developments converged notably in the growing service sector of the economy and in the working lives of women.[87] The 'privatisation' and 'corporatisation' of businesses previously conducted under the auspices of government also made their mark in Australia as they did elsewhere.[88] At the same time, seeking to avoid many of the costs of, and the constraints imposed by, award regulation businesses were restructuring. Work was increasingly outsourced, often with former employees bidding to do the same work only now as independent contractors.

These changes placed enormous pressure on the conciliation and arbitration system, which did not always prove adept at responding quickly to the challenges they posed. A growing number of workers were unprotected by the system. Many of the new non-standard workers, such as casuals, were often not unionised and though they might be profoundly affected by the terms of settlement of an industrial dispute their voice was frequently not heard in the Commission.[89] These difficulties were exacerbated by the initial inability, and sometimes resistance, of trade unions to represent the needs of the fast growing group of non-standard workers, who were often women.[90] For many, the traditional system of conciliation and arbitration was ceasing to deliver on its promise of social justice and the removal of inequalities.

In the contest over the reform of the regulatory system that ensued in the two decades following the mid-1980s the central ideals of the conciliation and arbitration

---

86 See ACTU *Future Strategies for the Trade Union Movement* (1987); and Evatt Foundation *Unions 2001: A Blueprint for Trade Union Activism* (1995).

87 See R Hunter 'The Production of Precarious Work' in J Fudge and R Owens (eds) *Precarious Work, Women and the New Economy: The Challenge to Legal Norms* (2006).

88 P Fairbrother, M Paddon and J Teicher (eds) *Privatisation, Globalisation and Labour: Studies from Australia* (2002).

89 Eg *Re Media, Arts and Entertainment Alliance; Ex parte ARNEL* (1994) 179 CLR 84.

90 B Pocock (ed) *Strife: Sex and Politics in Labour Unions* (1997).

system in the industrial era, including the 'public' nature of the regulation of work, collectivism, and emphasis on fairness for all workers, were pitted against the values lauded in the marketplace, including the 'private' contract model as a regulatory ideal, individualism and freedom from the intrusion of all others including the state and trade unions. Although concerns about productivity had always been evident in the conciliation and arbitration system,[91] they were portrayed as subordinated for the most part to the function of protecting workers. Neo-liberal philosophy inverted this relationship. It did not embrace the concept of work as primarily a means to social citizenship. Its focus was more firmly on the economic well-being of business and its need to thrive in a competitive market environment, assuming social benefits would flow from this. Out of this contest the main features of the regulatory system were substantially redrawn over the next two decades.

Reforming the conciliation and arbitration system: 1988–2005

The principal objects of the system

The broad direction of the changes to the conciliation and arbitration system between 1988 and 2005 was indicated by Parliament's restatement of the principal purposes of its legislation. The 'chief objects' of the original *Commonwealth Conciliation and Arbitration Act 1904* (Cth) were preventing strikes and lockouts, preventing and settling industrial disputation primarily by conciliation but in default of amicable agreement by arbitrated award, and facilitating the organisation of employers and of employees.[92] Thereafter variations in these objects in the industrial era were relatively minor. In 1930 the prohibition on strikes and lockouts was repealed and the aim 'to promote goodwill in industry by conciliation and arbitration' was elevated to a position of greater prominence.[93] For a short period after World War II there was a refocusing of attention on conciliation in the legislative objects.[94]

In 1998 the *Conciliation and Arbitration Act 1904* (Cth) was amended and renamed the *Industrial Relations Act 1988* (Cth). While the objectives of the Act were revised the long-standing goals of the system continued with only a slight change of emphasis. The first listed goal focused on the promotion of industrial harmony and cooperation amongst industrial parties, but otherwise there was a restatement of the traditional purposes of the conciliation and arbitration system.[95]

The first really major revamp of the legislation came with the enactment of the *Industrial Relations Reform Act 1993* (Cth).[96] In proclaiming that its principal object was 'to provide a framework for the prevention and settlement of industrial disputes that promotes the economic prosperity and the welfare of the people of Australia' there was nothing particularly startling. But it was the enunciation of the means to achieve

---

91 Eg *Amalgamated Engineering Union v J Alderdice & Co Pty Ltd (The 44-Hour Case)* (1927) 24 CAR 755.
92 *Commonwealth Conciliation and Arbitration Act 1904* (Cth), s 2 i–vii.
93 *Commonwealth Conciliation and Arbitration Act 1930* (Cth), s 2.
94 *Commonwealth Conciliation and Arbitration Act 1947* (Cth), s 5(2)(a)–(g).
95 *Industrial Relations Act 1988* (Cth), s 3(a)–(h).
96 *Industrial Relations Reform Act 1993* (Cth), s 3(a)–(g).

this that indicated real change in the system. While there is no *legal* significance in the order that Parliament selects for legislative objects—that is, things appearing near the top of the list are not of greater *legal* significance than those further down the list—the ordering does indicate policy priorities. First among the seven listed goals in the 1993 Act was the encouragement and facilitation of agreement-making between parties involved in industrial relations 'particularly at the workplace or enterprise level'. The setting up of 'fair and effective' bargaining processes was third in the list of itemised regulatory goals. The objectives hinted at a new role for awards as the 'framework' for protecting wages and conditions of employment. Alongside award regulation, the legislation referred for the first time to the aim of ensuring that Australia complied with its international obligations in relation to labour standards. A new objective of ensuring that discrimination in the workplace was prevented and eliminated concluded the list.

In the mid-1990s the title of the legislation was again changed with the passage of the *Workplace Relations Act 1996* (Cth) and its purposes were once again redefined.[97] Reference to dispute settlement though conciliation and arbitration by the AIRC was now dropped altogether from the stated objects. Providing 'a framework of cooperative workplace relations' was the primary objective, with the Act stating its intention to implement this by:

> encouraging the pursuit of high employment, improved living standards, low inflation and international competitiveness through higher productivity and a flexible and fair labour market.

Like the 1993 reforms the encouragement of bargaining was high on the list of objects but this time the legislation made it quite explicit that 'primary responsibility' for determining industrial matters was to be with the employer and employee at the workplace or enterprise level. Following this was a stated intention that parties should be able 'to choose the most appropriate form of agreement for their particular circumstances, whether or not that form is provided for by this Act'. Awards were henceforth to provide only 'a foundation of minimum standards' and act as a 'safety net' underpinning bargaining. The power to arbitrate was to be exercised only 'where appropriate and within specified limits'. 'Freedom of association' was included for the first time in those terms in the list of objects, and although the objects initially also included an explicit reference to the role of trade unions in representing their members this was repealed a short time later in 1999. The importance of balancing work and family through what were described as 'mutually beneficial work practices with employers' was also introduced as a new goal for the system, and the discrimination objective also remained. Relegated to last in the 1996 list of objects was the aim of giving effect to Australia's international obligations. The objects as adopted in the 1996 Act thus differed quite markedly from those incorporated in previous versions of the legislation. In their expression and substance they indicated a decided shift in regulatory emphasis away from the kind of system that had operated in the industrial era.

---

97 *Workplace Relations Act*, former s 3(a)–(k).

The main features of the Australian system 1988–2005
Bargaining at the enterprise and workplace level

During the period 1988–2005 the regulatory emphasis shifted steadily away from industrywide awards (especially arbitrated awards), towards direct bargaining between the parties in the workplace or enterprise.[98] This cannot be viewed entirely as a new departure, because one of the 'chief objects' of the 1904 Act was 'to provide for the making and enforcement of industrial agreements between employers and employees in relation to industrial disputes'.[99] Indeed, up until 1928 the Conciliation and Arbitration Court could certify bargains without attention to the public interest. In an important re-evaluation of the traditional regulatory system, Breen Creighton has pointed out that the framers of the conciliation and arbitration system envisaged that collective bargaining would be the usual means of determining the terms and conditions of employees, and awards would be a support mechanism.[100] In the very early years of the system, agreements were more common than awards. And agreements continued to be a feature of industrial relations in Australia, whether as 'consent awards' or as 'over award' collective agreements.

The 1988 reforms continued to recognise 'consent awards' and, more importantly, vested power formally in the Commission (now renamed the AIRC) to certify enterprise agreements between (all or any of) the parties to an industrial dispute where it considered that the agreement was in their interest and was not contrary to the public interest.[101] The 1988 Act allowed these agreements to override awards and envisaged that in some cases they might not conform to Full Bench principles. The statutory bargaining provisions were amended again several times in the early 1990s. In 1992 more extended provision was made for trade unions to negotiate at the enterprise level and the discretion of the AIRC to refuse certification of the agreements was diminished.[102] The following year, the *Industrial Relations Reform Act 1993* (Cth) broke with the past in a number of important ways, most significantly by introducing 'enterprise flexibility agreements' in which unions had no involvement.[103]

In the *Workplace Relations Act 1996* (Cth) bargaining was consolidated as the primary mechanism for determining terms and conditions of employment.[104] This 1996 legislation established two main streams of collective bargaining—and again there was provision for collective agreements that did not involve trade unions. However, the really

---

98 See RC McCallum 'Enhancing Federal Enterprise Bargaining: The *Industrial Relations (Legislation Amendment) Act 1992* (Cth) (1993) 6 *AJLL* 63; R Naughton 'The New Bargaining Regime under the *Industrial Relations Reform Act*' (1994) 7 *AJLL* 147; A Coulthard 'Non-Union Bargaining: Enterprise Flexibility Agreements' (1996) 38 *JIR* 339; M Pittard 'Collective Employment Relationships: Reforms to Arbitrated Awards and Certified Agreements' (1997) 10 *AJLL* 62; and RC McCallum 'Australian Workplace Agreements—An Analysis' (1997) 10 *AJLL* 50.
99 *Commonwealth Conciliation and Arbitration Act 1904* (Cth), s 2vii.
100 *Commonwealth Conciliation and Arbitration Act 1904* (Cth), Pt VI. See Creighton, above n 6.
101 *Industrial Relations Act 1988* (Cth), ss 112 and 115–17.
102 *Industrial Relations Legislation Amendment Act 1992* (Cth), Pt VI Div 3A.
103 *Industrial Relations Reform Act 1993* (Cth), Pt VIB Div 2 (certified agreements) and Div 3 (enterprise flexibility agreements).
104 *Workplace Relations Act*, former Pt VIB Div 2 (agreements with constitutional corporations) and Div 3 (agreements about industrial disputes and industrial situations).

radical innovation of this *Workplace Relations Act* was the introduction of individual statutory agreements, called Australian Workplace Agreements (AWAs), which in some instances had the capacity to override collective agreements.[105]

Awards as a safety net

As bargaining became established as the dominant regulatory mechanism from 1993 onwards, awards were transformed into a diminished safety net underpinning the bargaining stream. The new 'safety net' character of the award was evident from the 1993 reforms, but it was the changes in 1996 that were really dramatic. Although there were few constraints on the content of agreements, which could incorporate terms and conditions as long as each pertained to the employment relation, the content of awards was circumscribed by the 1996 Act and restricted to minimum conditions, about twenty 'allowable matters' and associated incidental matters.[106] All other matters had to be dealt with in agreements made at the enterprise or workplace. Only in rare circumstances—where there were 'exceptional matters' and it was in the public interest that they be dealt with by order of the AIRC, or where it was necessary for the AIRC to terminate the bargaining of the parties because industrial action was endangering life, personal safety, health or welfare of the population or part of it or causing significant damage to the national economy—could orders or awards be made by the AIRC to deal with subjects or issues other than those listed amongst the twenty allowable matters.[107]

The no-disadvantage test

The no-disadvantage test, a form of which was first introduced by the 1992 Act, mediated the relationship between agreements and awards.[108] The no-disadvantage test was a very flexible 'safety net', one that did not guarantee specific minimum standards.[109] It required a comparison of the terms of an agreement considered as a whole with the terms of the relevant award considered as a whole.[110] As such it was always a very weak mechanism to preserve any notion that there were accepted community or minimum standards applicable to everyone at work, because no particular standard was ever really guaranteed, although that was the initial intent.[111] It was, in effect, possible to bargain away any award standard provided something else (perhaps increased wages) was given in return so that it could be said the worker was not disadvantaged, although over time the AIRC began to develop principles that limited or at least sought

105 *Workplace Relations Act*, former Pt VID.
106 *Workplace Relations Act*, former s 89A.
107 *Workplace Relations Act*, former ss 89A(7), 120 and 170MX(3).
108 *Industrial Relations Legislation Amendment Act 1992* (Cth), s 134E.
109 O Merlo 'Flexibility and Stretching Rights: The No Disadvantage Test in Enterprise Bargaining' (2000) 13 *AJLL* 207, 223.
110 *Workplace Relations Act*, former Pt VIE esp ss 170XA(1)–(2) and 170XE, s 170LT(2)–(3), and ss 170VPB, 170VPC and 170VPG(2)–(5).
111 See Commonwealth, *Parliamentary Debates*, Senate, 7 May 1992, 2519–20 (Minister for Industrial Relations); and Commonwealth, *Parliamentary Debates*, House of Representatives, 28 October 1993, 2777–89 (Minister for Industrial Relations). See also *The EFA Test Case* AIRC, Print M0464, 11 May 1995, 46; *The Tweed Valley Processors Enterprise Flexibility Agreement 1995* AIRC, Print M6526, 26 October 1995; and *The Lilianfels Blue Mountains Case* AIRC, Print L4744, 16 January 1995.

to set some limits on this.[112] The test was inherently problematic because invariably the required comparison of very different terms and conditions was difficult if not impossible.[113] The 1996 reforms weakened the earlier version of the no-disadvantage test as a protective mechanism even further, by diminishing the 'public interest' element of the test and thereby reducing the potential for the system to maintain any concept of community standards. The no-disadvantage test was at its weakest when applied to the new AWAs.[114]

The evolving role of the AIRC

The role of the AIRC in making and varying awards to prevent and settle industrial disputation continued under the legislation throughout the period from 1988 until 2005.[115] In performing its function in this arena it was directed by the statute to have regard to a broad range of issues. Under the 1996 Act these included ensuring the maintenance of wage relativities between awards based on 'skill, responsibility and the conditions under which the work is performed', as well as paying attention to the wage needs of trainees, young and disabled workers, and to principles of pay equity and antidiscrimination. The Commission took account of the public interest, the objects of the Act, the state of the national economy, and the impact of its awards and orders on employment and inflation. At the same time the 1996 Act also ensured that the role of the Commission was less interventionist in dealing with industrial disputation. Its powers of arbitration were to be exercised only as a matter of 'last resort', while its conciliation powers included a very wide discretion to do everything 'right and proper' to prevent and settle the disputes.

The new emphasis on the parties determining the terms and conditions of work through agreement at the workplace or enterprise entailed a major change in the role for the AIRC. Under the 1993 amendments the Commission was given power, in effect, to examine the substance of enterprise flexibility agreements and to exercise its discretion to refuse to certify them where they were judged not to be in the public interest.[116] After 1996 its role further evolved so that it played an important part in ensuring compliance with the bargaining process and that its outcomes were fair and equitable and the product of genuine negotiations.[117]

However, the diminished role of the Commission attendant upon the move to bargaining at the enterprise and workplace level was most apparent in relation to AWAs. Under the 1996 Act the primary regulatory oversight of these agreements was

---

112 See *Shop Distributive and Allied Employees Association v Bunnings Building Supplies* AIRC, P6024, 21 October 1997; *Australian Municipal, Administrative, Clerical Services Union re Clerks (Breweries) Consolidated Award, 1985* AIRC, C0024 Dec 591/00 M Print S6443 26 May 2000; and *Cobax Mining Services Pty Ltd, re Cobar Mining Services Certified Agreement 2002* (2002) 52 AILR ¶94–671(6).

113 See R Mitchell et al *Protecting The Worker's Interest in Enterprise Bargaining: The 'No Disadvantage' Test in the Australian Federal Industrial Jurisdiction* (2004). Cf *Re MSA Security Officers Certified Agreement 2003* AIRC, PR937654, 15 September 2003.

114 *Workplace Relations Act*, former ss 170VCA, 170VPA(2)–(5), 170VPB, 170VPC(2), 170VPG(2)–(5) and 170VPH(2)–(5).

115 From 1996 see *Workplace Relations Act*, former Pt VI Div 1 esp ss 88B(3), 90, 93, 93A and 100–4.

116 *Industrial Relations Act 1988* (Cth), s 170ND.

117 *Workplace Relations Act*, former Pt VIB, Div 4. See A Stewart 'The AIRC's Evolving Role in Policing Bargaining' (2004) 17 *AJLL* 245.

reposed in a new Office of the Employment Advocate.[118] Only where an AWA was forwarded to the AIRC by the Employment Advocate for non-compliance with the no-disadvantage test did the Commission have a role and then, as was the situation when the Employment Advocate itself dealt with AWAs, the processes of the Commission were private and not open to public scrutiny.

While the Commission's public arbitral functions were downplayed, there was a growth in its role as a private arbitrator. After 1988 it was possible to include provisions in statutory agreements empowering the AIRC to settle disputes arising under the agreement, and after 1996 the inclusion of a dispute resolution clause was required as a prerequisite to certification.[119] The private arbitration function of the AIRC grew steadily after 1996.[120]

The changing role of trade unions

The role of the trade unions within the system was transformed quite dramatically in the period between 1988 and 2005. Trade unions were no longer the exclusive voice of labour after the introduction of non-trade-union enterprise flexibility and certified agreements. While under the 1993 reforms trade unions were still able to participate in bargaining even where there were no trade union members in a particular enterprise, this was curtailed by the 1996 amendments.[121] Trade unions continued to be able to represent their members in all forms of collective bargaining; however, the caveat operating in situations where the firm was negotiating directly with employees was that the trade union had to have a member at the workplace. Importantly too in all cases of collective bargaining, there was a requirement that a 'valid majority' of employees directly approve any collective agreement, even if the trade union was the party to the agreement.[122] There was strong growth in the bargaining stream where employers negotiated directly with their employees.[123]

Even more significantly the *legal* role of the trade union was very different in relation to AWAs. Here the individual was the party to the agreement, and a trade union could at most act as their bargaining agent where requested. The capacity of the trade union to operate as a legally independent actor in the system was thus gradually being stripped away, and in any event the ideology of the trade union movement was against the individualisation of work relations, not to mention that in a practical sense its resources were inadequate to represent members in bargaining on an individual basis.

Under the conciliation and arbitration system in the industrial era the role of trade unions was one vis-à-vis collective labour. The system had been premised on the surrender by collective labour of any notion of a right to strike in return for the protection offered by the system. With agreements central to the system of regulating work, after 1993 the

---

118 See *Workplace Relations Act*, former Pt IVA.

119 *Industrial Relations Act 1988* (Cth), s 170MH, the constitutional validity of which was upheld in *Construction, Forestry, Mining and Energy Union v Australian Industrial Relations Commission (Private Arbitration Case)* (2001) 203 CLR 645; and *Workplace Relations Act*, former ss 170LT and 170LW.

120 C Sutherland 'By Invitation Only: The Role of the AIRC in Private Arbitration' (2005) 18 *AJLL* 53, 69.

121 *Industrial Relations Reform Act 1993* (Cth), s 170NB; and *Workplace Relations Act*, former ss 170LJ, 170LK and 170LL.

122 *Workplace Relations Act*, former ss 170LE and 170LR.

123 *Workplace Relations Act*, former s 170LK.

legislation for the first time in its history expressly provided immunity from prosecution for industrial action during a bargaining period. This 'right' (and the parallel 'right' of employers to lockout workers) was, however, closely circumscribed, exercisable only by those who were negotiating parties during a bargaining period and only in relation to those negotiations. Even more significantly the new era legislation constructed freedom of association as an individual rather than a collective concept: a right equally to not belong as to belong to a trade union.[124] Any form of preference to trade unions or their members was therefore prohibited by the 1996 Act.[125]

Changing values

During the years from 1988 to 2005 the transformation of the Australian system gave expression to the neo-liberal values that have come to dominate in the global era. In the old system the dominant values were public and collectivist. The importance of the role of the state was acknowledged, both as represented through the functions of the Commission per se as well as through its consideration of the public interest. In the marketplace of the global era the public is reconfigured as private: that is, the public interest is treated as identical to the agreed private interests of the parties at the enterprise and workplace level. The role of institutional players such as the AIRC was increasingly portrayed as an external interference in private affairs except where its function was derived from the private agreement of the parties. Regulatory forms became more diverse. The inclusion of facilitative clauses gave more scope to parties at the workplace to make adjustments to the operation of awards so as to suit their particular circumstances at the workplace within a framework of overarching provisions, putting the Commission at a further regulatory remove.

Individualism was in the ascendancy in the new system. In part this reflected the growing dominance of 'rights rhetoric' at the global level. The 1993 reforms had for the first time introduced a number of statutory rights that could be pursued by individual workers, initially before the Commission and ultimately in the courts. These included rights in relation to termination and redundancy, and rights to parental leave.[126] This was a marked change from the old conciliation and arbitration system, which had always focused on the collective interests of workers. Under that system a dispute over an issue concerning the industrial rights of a worker under, say, an award was beyond the jurisdiction of the tribunal. Only when its collective dimensions were articulated and a way of assuaging collective concerns about the way a similar problem would be dealt with in the future could the tribunal act in relation to an individual matter. It was this that largely explained why the tribunal for many years did not deal with issues relating to the termination of employment.[127] By providing individual access to workplace rights that were established by statute rather than industrial means where the role of

---

124 *Workplace Relations Act*, former Pt XA. See further Chapter 10.
125 *Workplace Relations Act*, former s 94.
126 *Industrial Relations Reform Act 1993* (Cth), Pt VIA Div 3 and Div 5.
127 *R v Gough; Ex parte Meat and Allied Trades Federation of Australia* (1969) 122 CLR 237; *R v Portus; Ex parte City of Perth* (1973) 129 CLR 312; *Re Ranger Uranium Mines Pty Ltd; Ex parte Federated Miscellaneous Worker's Union of Australia* (1987) 163 CLR 656; and *Re Federated Storemen and Packers Union of Australia; Ex parte Wooldumpers (Victoria) Ltd (Wooldumpers)* (1989) 166 CLR 311.

trade unions in protecting workers was more obvious, the potential for downgrading even further the values of collectivism in the system was revealed.

However, it was the introduction of AWAs under the 1996 amendments that really indicated the demise of collectivist values. The impracticability of trade unions acting as bargaining agents for their members, even if they were so inclined to do, served to emphasise the function of such agreements as hostile to collective interests. AWAs were the antithesis of industry-based regulation through awards. Though the take-up rate of AWAs remained low in the years following 1996, they were a potent symbol of the new individualisation of work relations.[128] The legislative provisions governing the process for making, approving and filing AWAs also made clear the new reverence in the system for the private. Unlike awards and collective agreements, there was no public access to, or scrutiny of, AWAs. Unless a party to an AWA revealed the content of the agreement to another person it remained strictly private.

Towards a national system of workplace relations

Federalism and Australian labour law

Despite legislative changes between 1988 and 2005, the Australian labour law system continued to be subjected to criticism. Calls for further reform stressed the ongoing need for higher productivity, greater flexibility, and a lowering of labour costs. The conciliation and arbitration power, which still underpinned much of the system, was blamed for perpetuating adversarial work relations, and for being too focused on disputation and not enough on cooperation. Demands for even greater 'deregulation' in favour of a simple, flexible, non-prescriptive system offering more freedom to parties to determine everything about their relations, from the style of bargaining (collective or individual) to the process for negotiating agreements and resolving grievances, did not cease. In short, it was argued that more responsibility and control over every aspect of work relations needed to be devolved to the parties at the workplace level. Some protagonists advocated an even more extreme form of de-regulation, in which externally imposed statutory requirements were minimised and 'best practice parties' were given the opportunity to opt out all together and self-regulate.[129]

While these criticisms were part of the ongoing neo-liberal critique of the regulation of work relations, much of the agitation for greater reform was also directed at the complexity in Australia's regulatory system. Much of this increased complexity over the previous decade was a result of additional layers of regulation in the form of the different types of statutory bargaining, the interaction of the different regulatory instruments (for example, the diverse ways agreements might refer to other agreements, awards, statutes and common law obligations), and the lack of clarity in the operation of the no-disadvantage test.[130] However, legislative drafting also contributed to this

---

128 S Deery and R Mitchell (eds) *Employment Relations: Individualism and Union Exclusion* (1999).

129 Eg ACCI *Modern Workplace: Modern Future—A Blueprint for the Australian Workplace Relations System 2002–2010* (2002).

130 J Fetter and R Mitchell 'The Legal Complexity of Workplace Regulation and Its Impact upon Functional Flexibility in Australian Workplaces' (2004) 17 *AJLL* 276.

complexity: Commonwealth statutory provisions became more and more detailed as Parliament attempted to ensure constitutional validity and control and constrain institutions such as the AIRC and trade unions, and respond to and correct the effects of judicial interpretation. Ironically as work relations were increasingly 'deregulated', the size of the statute continued to grow!

Politically even greater attention was focused on the complexity arising from federalism.[131] Up until 27 March 2006 (or the end of 1996 in the case of Victoria) State industrial systems operated in parallel to the federal system.[132] There were broad similarities between them. However, not limited by constitutional constraints State awards could, for example, operate as a common rule across an industry, or profession or calling. The States also regulated by statute a variety of other work-related matters like termination of employment in parallel with the Commonwealth.

Viewed from the perspective of business there was often a regulatory overlap. Within the one enterprise different employees could have different rights in relation to the same issue. All businesses, even those operating only within a single State, had to be aware of the multiple layers of regulation with which they must comply. For businesses operating at the national level, the complexities were multiplied. Compliance with various layers of regulation at both federal and State level was argued to result in additional costs and inefficiencies, and to inhibit Australian business from competing successfully in the global arena. In addition, pressure was applied by organisations, such as the IMF and the OECD, for Australia to simplify its industrial relations system.[133]

The Australian system was also criticised as offering little prospect of securing comprehensive and equal protection of what might be considered the most basic rights. The federal nature of the system also meant that State-conferred 'rights' were often precarious, in the sense of being open to disruption from overriding federal regulatory mechanisms. The consequent lack of certainty inhibited, at the very least, knowledge of rights and their practical utility. As the Hon Justice Giudice, President of the AIRC, pointed out, where a worker was dismissed there might be up to eight different ways of resolving the matter in as many different courts and tribunals. Not only did this create risks of additional costs if a litigant selected the 'wrong' jurisdiction in which to bring their case, but it also made it difficult to predict the outcome in a case and achieve consistency of treatment because there was no consistent theoretical dimension underpinning the different statutory contexts. The resultant variety of standards applicable to those in the Australian labour force, the President concluded, meant 'a lack of equality that

---

131 Ministerial Discussion Paper *Getting the Outsiders Inside—Towards a Rational Workplace Relations System in Australia* (1999); Department of Employment, Workplace Relations and Small Business *Breaking the Gridlock: Towards a Simpler National Workplace Relations System—Discussion Paper 1, The Case for Change* (2000).

132 See *Industrial Relations Act 1996* (NSW); *Industrial Relations Act 1999* (Qld); *Fair Work Act 1994* (SA); *Industrial Relations Act 1984* (Tas); and *Industrial Relations Act 1979* (WA).

133 IMF *Australia: Staff Report for the 2004 Article IV Consultation* (2004), 8 (available at <www.imf. org/external/pubs/cat/longres.cfm?sk=17830.0>); and OECD *Economic Survey of Australia 2004: Policies to Lower Unemployment and Raise Labour Force Participation* (2005).

undermines our society'. He thus added his voice to the call to rationalise industrial laws and the number of courts and tribunals exercising jurisdiction.[134] Indeed the calls for a unitary system of workplace relations in Australia even garnered support from '"neutral" observers' of the system, 'so obvious are the advantages in terms of cost savings and policy coherence'.[135]

The intersection of Commonwealth and State regulatory systems

When the *Australian Constitution* was drafted, industrial relations were recognised as a significant issue in the working out of the new Commonwealth–State relations. No doubt it was then anticipated that most matters relating to work would be regulated at the State level. The conciliation and arbitration power had an obviously federal element, enabling the Commonwealth to deal with industrial disputation with effects beyond a single State.

However, the federal arena had taken on a broader role by the end of the twentieth century. As the federal and State systems evolved over time the 'centralisation' of Australian industrial relations was in part an expression of the interaction between them at a *practical* level. State Commissions invariably adopted the major wage and test case decisions of the AIRC. In some instances they were required by statute to do so.[136] However, the relation was not always one way. Sometimes it was a State or States that would lead the way on an issue and influence decisions at the federal level. After 1988 there were greater efforts at cooperation between the two systems through dual appointments to federal and State Commissions, and at the practical level there were regular conferences and intersection of personnel.[137] At various times too some of the States made efforts to harmonise their system more closely with that operating at federal level, but such schemes were always likely to flounder with a change of government or even when amendments were later made in one polity but not picked up in the other.[138]

The *legal* dominance of the federal conciliation and arbitration system came about because, under s 109 of the *Australian Constitution*, inconsistencies between Commonwealth and State laws are resolved in favour of the former. The s 109 jurisprudence establishes that a Commonwealth law is inconsistent with, and therefore overrides, State law not only when there is a direct inconsistency between the two laws, such as when they establish inconsistent rights and duties, but also whenever the Commonwealth Parliament evinces an intention for its law to cover the field. From the earliest times there was a provision in the Commonwealth legislation declaring that awards override state laws.[139] On many occasions inconsistency was found to

---

134 The Hon Justice Giudice *Address to the Bar Association of Queensland Industrial and Employment Law Conference* (2001), and The Hon Justice Giudice *The Industrial Relations System in Victoria: A Unitary IR System?* (2002).

135 A Stewart 'Federal Labour Laws and New Uses for the Corporations Power' (2001) 14 *AJLL* 145, 167.

136 See eg *Industrial Relations Act 1996* (NSW), s 50. See also *Fair Work Act 1994* (SA), s 100.

137 Eg *Industrial Relations Act 1988* (Cth), ss 13–14 and 171–5.

138 Eg *Industrial and Employee Relations (Harmonisation) Amendment Act 1997* (SA).

139 See *Commonwealth Conciliation and Arbitration Act 1904* (Cth), s 30; and see also *Workplace Relations Act*, former s 152(1).

exist,[140] but the Commonwealth's industrial law also operated against the backdrop of general State legislation, such as discrimination legislation,[141] except where a direct inconsistency arose.

Because the Commonwealth controls the intended scope of its own legislation, it always has, constitutionally speaking, the upper hand and is able to determine to a large extent the way the federal and state industrial jurisdictions intersect. Indeed, it has been observed that the covering the field test enables the Commonwealth to 'manufacture' an inconsistency and thus ensure the superiority of its legislation (and hence its policies).[142] The Commonwealth cannot constrain the legislative power of the States to make laws in any area, because that would be counter to the constitutional doctrine of intergovernmental immunities,[143] but it can by expressing its intention to cover a field effectively exclude any State law from operating on that field.

Prior to 27 March 2006 the Commonwealth's legislation did not operate to exclude altogether State legislation from the industrial arena. The former provisions of the *Workplace Relations Act* explicitly acknowledged the various State industrial regimes and placed some emphasis on maintaining their integrity. They required the AIRC, subject to a public interest proviso, to cease dealing with an industrial dispute where it was satisfied that a State award or agreement governed the wages and conditions of the disputants.[144] This meant it was not possible, as it had been previously,[145] for parties who were disgruntled with State regulation to escape its strictures by seeking coverage under the federal award system. The same legislation also enabled parties covered by State awards to make federal statutory agreements. These agreements generally prevailed over other State laws, awards and agreements except laws governing such matters as occupational health and safety, workers' compensation and apprenticeships. The operation of State unfair termination provisions was also preserved where this was compatible with federal agreements.[146] Thus the former *Workplace Relations Act* deferred for some purposes to the State system of awards, but generally allowed federal agreements to trump the State systems thus enhancing the ability of parties to bargain. The legislation further supported bargaining through an express intention that Commonwealth awards were not to override State employment agreements or agreements approved under State legislation.[147]

---

140 Eg *Clyde Engineering Co Ltd v Cowburn* (1926) 37 CLR 466; and *Ex parte McLean* (1930) 43 CLR 472. See also G Williams *Labour Law and the Constitution* (1998), Ch 6.

141 *Ansett Transport Industries (Operations) Pty Ltd v Wardley* (1980) 142 CLR 237.

142 *West v Commissioner of Taxation* (NSW) (1937) 56 CLR 657, 707.

143 *Melbourne Corporation v Commonwealth* (1947) 74 CLR 31, 60–1 and 78–9; *Austin v Commonwealth* (2003) 215 CLR 185, 249, 282–3, and 301.

144 *Workplace Relations Act*, former ss 111(1)(g)(ii) and 111AAA. See also G Williams 'The Return of State Awards—Section 109 of the *Constitution* and the *Workplace Relations Act 1996* (Cth)' (1997) 10 *AJLL* 170.

145 See *R v Ludeke; Ex parte Queensland Electricity Commission* (1985) 159 CLR 178 and *AEU Case*, above n 39.

146 *Workplace Relations Act*, former ss 170GC, 170LZ and 170VR. *Workplace Relations Amendment (Termination of Employment) Bill 2002* unsuccessfully tried to reverse this. See G Williams 'The First Step to a National Industrial Relations Regime? Workplace Relations Amendment (Termination of Employment) Bill 2002' (2003) 16 *AJLL* 94.

147 *Workplace Relations Act*, former s 152.

Establishing a unitary system—constitutional limitations

Although the significance of each stage of the transformation of Australia's regulatory system since 1988 was symbolised by the changing title of the Commonwealth legislation—from the *Conciliation and Arbitration Act*, to the *Industrial Relations Act* and finally the *Workplace Relations Act*—it was changes in the underlying constitutional foundation of the legislation that most clearly indicated the nature of the revolution taking place.[148]

The Commonwealth Parliament has always relied on a range of constitutional powers to regulate work,[149] including the trade and commerce power (s 51(i)), the taxation power (s 51(ii)), the defence power (s 51(vi), the Territories power (s 122), and the power over matters relating to the Commonwealth public service (s 52(ii)). In addition, laws made under the immigration power (s 51(xxvii) and the pensions powers (s 51(xxiii) and (xxiiiA)) have played a significant role in constructing labour markets. This continues to be the case.[150]

However, instituting a national and uniform system in Australia has always been hindered constitutionally by the fact that the Commonwealth Parliament has no comprehensive legislative power to regulate work. Constitutional referenda were held in 1911, 1913, 1919, 1926, 1944 and 1946 to extend the Commonwealth Parliament's powers in the area, but all were unsuccessful.[151] Absent constitutional reform there is no ideal way to achieve a unitary system for the regulation of work in Australia. A number of powers present possibilities, but each has limitations.[152] The trade and commerce power has some real potential, especially if allowed to develop in line with more recent trends in constitutional interpretation.[153] The conciliation and arbitration power, the external affairs power, and the referral power have all attracted attention in recent years.

The conciliation and arbitration power

While the conciliation and arbitration power was increasingly criticised towards the end of the twentieth century as inappropriate to found a regulatory system governing work in the global era, the power was never utilised to its full extent. The statutory definition of an 'industrial dispute' was always more limited than the *Constitution* allows.[154] Greater recourse to the prevention aspect of the power could also have supported a wider role for the federal tribunal, perhaps even enabling it to make common rule awards or

---

148 See W Ford 'The Constitution and the Reform of Australian Industrial Relations' (1994) 7 *AJLL* 105; and W Ford 'Reconstructing Australian Labour Law: A Constitutional Perspective' (1997) 10 *AJLL* 1.

149 See N Gunningham, *Industrial Law and the Constitution* (1988), and its successor G Williams *Labour Law and the Constitution* (1998).

150 See Arup et al (eds), above n 11.

151 See T Blackshield and G Williams *Australian Constitutional Law and Theory: Commentary and Materials* 3rd edn (2002), 1303–8.

152 WJ Ford 'Politics, the Constitution and Australian Industrial Relations: Pursuing a Unified National System' (2005) 38 *Aust Econ Rev* 211.

153 *R v Wright; Ex parte Waterside Workers' Federation of Australia* (1955) 93 CLR 528 and *Seaman's Union of Australia v Utah Development Co* (1978) 144 CLR 120. See also D McCann 'First Head Revisited: A Single Industrial Relations System under the Trade and Commerce Power' (2004) 26 *Syd LR* 75.

154 *Social Welfare*, above n 29.

deal with sympathy disputes.[155] However early judicial interpretation declared that 'arbitration on the nebulous' was unimaginable.[156] Thereafter the prevention aspect of the conciliation and arbitration power remained effectively written out of the *Constitution*,[157] even though the later legislative definition of an 'industrial dispute' was framed widely to encompass a 'situation likely to give rise to … a threatened impending or probable industrial dispute'. Not until the late 1980s and 1990s was there a suggested reawakening of the prevention power to deal with localised disputes or situations that could be the harbinger of wider industrial disputation.[158]

The failure to rely on the prevention power earlier in the history of the conciliation and arbitration system can be explained by the fact that it was rarely seen as necessary. The formation of national trade unions, the conduct of business by many employers at a national level, and the recognition of paper disputes meant it was comparatively easy to activate a full-blown industrial dispute extending beyond the limits of a State that needed to be settled. Although, the prevention aspect of the power could well have offered greater scope to deal with issues at an enterprise level or workplace level, the conciliation and arbitration system came to be considered by its critics as generally inimicable to the neo-liberal values of the global era and too much associated with the very different regulatory agenda of the industrial era.

The external affairs power

Several of the changes introduced by the *Industrial Relations Reform Act 1993* (Cth) represented the first major break with the tradition of reliance on the conciliation and arbitration power. Its provisions concerning minimum wages, equal remuneration, termination of employment, and parental leave, were founded on the external affairs power, s 51(xxix) of the *Australian Constitution*. These provisions sought to implement into domestic law some of Australia's obligations under international law, including both UN Conventions and ILO Conventions and Recommendations.[159] The external affairs power already provided the constitutional foundation for the Commonwealth's discrimination legislation,[160] but this was the first time that it had been relied upon in mainstream 'labour law'.

The constitutional validity of these provisions was challenged in the *Industrial Relations Act Case*.[161] The High Court upheld the legislation for the most part, reaffirming

---

155 Cf *Whybrow*, above n 24; and *Caledonian Collieries Ltd v Australasian Coal and Shale Employees' Federation No (1)* (1930) 42 CLR 527.

156 *Merchant Service Guild of Australia v Newcastle and Hunter Steamship Co (No 1)* (1913) 16 CLR 591, 616. See also *Whybrow*, above n 24; and *R v Heagney; Ex parte ACT Employers Federation* (1976) 137 CLR 86, 90.

157 *R v Turbet and Metal Trades Industry Association and Another; Ex parte ABCE &BLF* (1980) 144 CLR 335, 353–6; and *R v Duncan; Ex parte Australian Iron and Steel Pty Ltd* (1983) 158 CLR 535.

158 See *Wooldumpers* above n 127, 320–1, 327–8; and *Attorney General (Qld) v Riordan* (1997) 192 CLR 1, 34 and 40; and *Re Printing and Kindred Industries Union; Ex parte Vista Paper Products Pty Ltd* (1993) 67 ALJR 604.

159 *Industrial Relations Reform Act 1993* (Cth), Pt VIA, and Schs 5–13, and 15–16.

160 *Racial Discrimination Act 1975* (Cth), *Sex Discrimination Act 1984* (Cth), and *Disability Discrimination Act 1992* (Cth). The *Age Discrimination Act 2004* (Cth) enacted later also relied largely on the external affairs power. See further Chapter 8.

161 *Victoria v The Commonwealth (Industrial Relations Act Case)* (1996) 187 CLR 416.

in a strong majority judgment the basic constitutional principle that a law that was reasonably capable of being seen to be 'appropriate and adapted' to implementing Australia's international obligations would be supported by the external affairs power. On this basis the provisions of the legislation concerning 'harsh, unjust or unfair' dismissals were invalidated because there was no reference to those concepts in the ILO convention or recommendation on termination of employment.[162]

Ominously, especially given the trend to 'soft law' and broadly stated principles in the international arena, the majority also hinted that perhaps not all international conventions enlivened the legislative power conferred by the external affairs power: an aspirational treaty, for instance, urging governments to promote full employment, which does not specify sufficiently precisely the means by which its goal is to be attained, was provided as an example. However, the judges also noted previous judicial statements observing that an absence of precision was not necessarily tantamount to an absence of obligation at international law.[163]

The use of the external affairs power to support major reforms introduced in the *Industrial Relations Reform Act 1993* (Cth) demonstrated its potential to facilitate uniform national legislation governing a whole variety of work issues. Resort to the external affairs power might be thought of as 'natural and inevitable' in the global era. However, as Ron McCallum has so perceptively noted, reliance on the external affairs power in 1993 had little to do with global issues and was more a response to a political contest between the Commonwealth and States over industrial relations.[164] Since 1993 there has been little political willingness to utilise more widely the external affairs power as the foundation of Australia's law of work, although after *Work Choices* the provisions in the *Workplace Relations Act* governing equal remuneration, unlawful termination of employment, and parental leave continue to be supported by it.[165]

Referral of power by the States to the Commonwealth

Within existing constitutional constraints the most effective way to implement a national system for the regulation of work relations is if the States agree to refer their power on the topic to the Commonwealth Parliament thus enabling it to legislate under s 51(xxxvii) of the *Australian Constitution*. In 1996 Victoria did this, and since then the Commonwealth's *Workplace Relations Act* has covered employment matters there in a relatively comprehensive fashion.[166] However, given the deep political divisions that exist between governments of different hues over many of the regulatory issues arising in respect to work, a wider agreement by all States to refer power in this area is primarily a matter of politics. From a legal perspective there is always an element of

---

162 Ibid, 517–18.
163 Ibid, 486–7.
164 See R McCallum 'The Internationalisation of Australian Labour Law' (1994) 16 *Syd L R* 112.
165 *Workplace Relations Act*, Pt 12, Div 3, Div 4, Subdiv C and Div 6.
166 See *Workplace Relations Act*, Pt 21 (and former Pt XV); *Commonwealth Powers (Industrial Relations) Act 1996* (Vic); *Workplace Relations and Other Legislation Amendment Act (No 2) 1996* (Cth); *Workplace Relations Amendment (Improved Protection for Victorian Workers) Act 2003* (Cth); and *Federal Award (Uniform System) Act 2003* (Vic). See also S Kollmorgen 'Towards a Unitary National System of Industrial Relations?' (1997) 10 *AJLL* 158.

uncertainty in such arrangements: such references are usually expressed to operate only for a limited period of time often necessitating further political negotiations at the end of the period, and in any event a reference may be revoked at any time.[167] However, a referral of power underpins the *Corporations Act* and there is a certain air of inevitability about a referral of power over industrial relations at some time in the future.

The corporations power

With the benefit of hindsight greater significance can be attributed to the legislative provisions in the reforms in the 1990s that depended upon the corporations power. Under s 51(xx) of the *Australian Constitution* the Commonwealth Parliament has power to make laws with respect to 'foreign corporations and trading and financial corporations formed within the limits of the Commonwealth', which are sometimes referred to collectively as 'constitutional corporations'. The corporations power was the foundation of federal provisions outlawing secondary boycotts introduced in 1977.[168] This power underpinned the insertion into the industrial legislation of unfair contracts provisions in 1992 and then the making of non-union enterprise flexibility agreements in 1993.[169] The *Workplace Relations Act 1996* (Cth) extended even further reliance on the corporations power, with its provisions concerning some collective agreements, AWAs, unfair dismissal, and freedom of association all supported primarily by s 51(xx).[170] Little surprise then that the federal Liberal Coalition Government indicated an interest in using the corporations power to underpin a national workplace relations system focused on bargaining.[171] This it did in December 2005 with the enactment of the *Work Choices Act*. Although some parts of the Act came into effect in December 2005, it was not until 27 March 2006 that its main provisions were proclaimed.

Australian labour law after the *Work Choices Act*

Constitutional foundations

When the Commonwealth Parliament enacted the *Work Choices Act* its intention was to institute within constitutional limits a national system to regulate the work relations of employers and employees. In constitutional terms the legislation is founded primarily upon the corporations power: s 51(xx). It also relies on other constitutional powers: the Territories power, s 122; Commonwealth public sector power, s 52(ii); and the trade

---

167   *R v Vehicle Licensing Appeal Tribunal (Tas); Ex parte Australian National Airways Pty Ltd* (1964) 113 CLR 207, 226. The *Fair Employment Bill 2000* (Vic) represented an attempt to revoke in part Victoria's referral following recommendations of the *Independent Report of the Victorian Industrial Relations Task Force: Pt I Report and Recommendations*, Melbourne, 2000. See SJ Zeitz 'The Industrial Relations Taskforce Report: A Phoenix from the Ashes' (2000) 14 *AJLL* 308.

168   *Trade Practices Act 1974* (Cth), ss 45D and 45E. The validity of these provisions was upheld in *Actors and Announcers Equity Association v Fontana Films Pty Ltd (Actors Equity)* (1982) 150 CLR 169.

169   *Industrial Relations Legislation Amendment Act 1992* (Cth), s 127A–C; and *Industrial Relations Reform Act 1993* (Cth), Pt VIB Div 3.

170   *Workplace Relations Act*, former Pt VIB Div 2, Pt VID and Pt XA.

171   Department of Employment, Workplace Relations and Small Business *Breaking the Gridlock: Towards a Simpler National Workplace Relations System—Discussion Paper II*, *A New Structure* and *Discussion Paper III*, *A Focus on Agreement Making* (2000).

and commerce power, s 51(i).[172] Because Victoria has referred its powers over industrial relations to the Commonwealth Parliament, the legislation also covers Victorian employers and employees by virtue of s 51(xxxvii). Some parts of the legislation, for example the provisions relating to parental leave and termination of employment, continue to depend on the external affairs power. The conciliation and arbitration power no longer underpins the legislation, except for some of the transitional provisions in Schedule 6.

At the time of the enactment of the *Work Choices* legislation there was some uncertainty as to the scope of the corporations power. In the *Industrial Relations Act Case* in 1996 the validity of the previous provisions regarding 'enterprise flexibility agreements' between corporations and their employees had simply been assumed because of a concession by the parties arguing that case.[173] Both before and after that decision there were dicta in High Court judgments suggesting that the scope of the corporations power was quite wide enough to support a comprehensive system of workplace regulation.[174] There were also a number of Federal Court cases in which the constitutional validity of provisions in the *Workplace Relations Act 1996* (Cth) was questioned, and in each the majority of judges rejected arguments that the corporations power should be narrowly construed.[175] However, very early interpretation of the corporations power had been quite narrow—indeed so narrow that the power had been virtually ignored until the 1970s[176]—and there were also some other quite recent dicta by the High Court suggesting that the power was limited to supporting laws where the *nature* of the constitutional corporation, as a *trading* or *financial* corporation, must be significant to the way it was regulated.[177] The issue thus remained unsettled. So politically controversial were the *Work Choices* amendments that their validity was tested in the High Court, not only on the question of the scope of the corporations power but also on other constitutional grounds, including constitutional limitations relating to federalism.[178]

The coverage of the Workplace Relations Act *after* Work Choices

Since the *Work Choices* amendments the *Workplace Relations Act* identifies its constitutional foundation primarily through the definition of 'employer', and the related definitions of 'employee' and 'employment': ss 5–7 (and s 858 in relation to Victorian

---

172 See *Workplace Relations Act*, ss 5–7.

173 *Industrial Relations Act Case*, above n 161, 539.

174 Eg *Actors Equity* above n 168, 195, 207, and 212; *Tasmania v Commonwealth (Tasmanian Dam Case)* (1983) 158 CLR 1, 148–53, 179, and 268; *Re Dingjan; Ex parte Wagner (Dingjan's Case)* (1995) 183 CLR 323, 333–4, 364–5, 352–3 and 369; and *Re Pacific Coal Pty Ltd; Ex parte Construction, Forestry, Mining and Energy Union (Award Simplification Case)* (2000) 203 CLR 346, 375.

175 *Quickenden v O'Connor* (2001) 109 FCR 243; *Rowe v Transport Workers Union of Australia* (1998) 90 FCR 95; and *Australian Workers Union v BHP Iron—Ore Pty Ltd* (2000) 106 FCR 482.

176 *Huddart, Parker and Co Pty Ltd v Moorehead* (1909) 8 CLR 330; overruled by *Strickland v Rocla Concrete Pipes Ltd* (1971) 124 CLR 468.

177 See eg *Actors Equity*, above n 168, 182; *Tasmanian Dam Case*, above n 174, 117, 202 and 316; and *Dingjan's Case*, above n 174, 346.

178 *New South Wales v Commonwealth (Workplace Relations Act Case)* [2006] HCATrans 215–18 and 233–5 (4–5 and 8–11 May 2006).

employers and employees). The majority of the substantive provisions of the Act operate by conferring privileges or imposing obligations on those who fall within the scope of the above definitions. In some parts of the legislation, including those dependent upon the external affairs power, 'employer' and 'employee' have their ordinary meaning: see Sch 2, cll 2–4. Thus the *Workplace Relations Act* regulates primarily:

- constitutional corporations and their employees;
- the Commonwealth and its public sector employees including those employed by Commonwealth authorities;
- flight crew officers, maritime employees and waterside workers employed by businesses operating in interstate and overseas trade and commerce; and
- all employers and employees in Victoria and in the Territories .

The coverage of the *Work Relations Act* is therefore quite extensive, although not comprehensive. It is estimated that up to 85 per cent of employees are governed by it. State public sector employment (where it has not been 'privatised' and 'corporatised') is the largest area to fall outside the legislation, and sole traders, partnerships, trusts, and any corporations that are not constitutional corporations, and their various employees are also not covered by the federal legislation (except in Victoria and the Territories).

Constitutional corporations

The identification of many of the employers and employees covered by the *Workplace Relations Act* is a relatively straightforward matter. However, an employer who is a foreign or trading or financial corporation must fit within the constitutional concept. The identification of these employers requires attention to constitutional jurisprudence.

From the words of the *Constitution* it is obvious that a foreign corporation is one that is not 'formed within the limits of the Commonwealth': the place of incorporation (ie outside Australia) is the key thing.[179] However, the constitutional understanding of a trading or financial corporation is more complex and it is one that has developed over time. In 1900 the character of a corporation was referable primarily by its purposes.[180] Trading and financial corporations were thus distinguished from corporations formed for different purposes, such as mining, manufacturing, religion or charity.[181] The focus on purposes was explicable by the fact that early in the twentieth century the memorandum and articles of association of a corporation itemised in some precise detail the limits of a corporation's powers. However, the constituent documents of corporations are now much more flexible. Not surprisingly then by the late 1970s the High Court by majority turned away from focusing on corporate purposes to place emphasis on a corporation's activities.[182]

---

179 *New South Wales v Commonwealth* (1990) 169 CLR 482, 498.
180 See eg J Quick and RR Garran, *The Annotated Constitution of the Australian Commonwealth* (1901), 606–7.
181 See *Huddart, Parker and Co Pty Ltd v Moorehead* (1909) 8 CLR 330, 393.
182 *R v Federal Court of Australia; Ex parte WA National Football League (Adamson's Case)* (1979) 143 CLR 190; *Re Kur-ing-gai Co-operative Building Society (No 12) Ltd* (1978) 22 ALR 621; and *State Superannuation Board of Victoria v Trade Practices Commission (State Superannuation Case)*(1982) 150 CLR 282. Cf *R v Trade Practices Tribunal; Ex parte St George County Council* (1974) 130 CLR 533.

The 'activities test' asks whether the relevant trading or financial activity of a corporation is a 'sufficiently significant', 'substantial' and 'not merely a peripheral' activity, regardless of whether it is incidental to other activities.[183] It is not necessary to identify the 'predominant and characteristic activity' of the corporation.[184] As the question is always whether a corporation can be described as a trading (or financial) corporation it is only sensible to make the judgment of the significance (or otherwise) of its trading (or financial) activities in the context of its own activities rather than as measured by some objective standard.[185] A corporation undertaking trading or financial activities, where these are a peripheral or not a significant part of its overall activities, does not fall within the constitutional concept of a trading or financial corporation.

Trading and financial activities are understood quite broadly. Trading involves business activities and exchange of either goods or services for revenue. In the marketplace, corporations that trade might usually be expected to return a profit, but profit is not an essential element of the constitutional conception. Financial activities encompass a broad range of commercial dealings.[186] A wide variety of different types of corporations have been held to be trading corporations. Corporations whose main purpose is the promotion of sporting activities or education have been found to be trading corporations.[187] Local councils, not-for-profit organisations, incorporated community organisations funded by government grants, and incorporated organisations devoted to serving the community, have all been held to be trading corporations.[188] A trading corporation has also been found where its revenue comprises primarily the reimbursement of its expenses by a joint venturer.[189] It is apparent too, applying the activities test, that many trade unions are trading or financial corporations.[190] The same will be true of some business organisations.

Because of the nature of the activities test as articulated by the courts, in any particular instance whether the activities of a corporation are enough to merit it a description of 'trading' or 'financial' will be a question of fact and degree. Immediately it can be seen that a potentially problematic issue is that a corporation might change its character from time to time as the overall mix of its activities changes.

The operation of the activities test is demonstrated by the approach of the Federal Court in *Quickenden v O'Connor*, where the University of Western Australia was found to be a trading corporation. The University was a statutory corporation established by the State. It engaged in a range of activities, including the running of festivals and sale of accommodation, computing equipment and publications, the income from which

---

183 *Adamson's Case*, ibid, 208, 233, and 239.

184 *Re Ku-ring-gai Co-operative Building Society (No 12) Ltd*, above n 182; and *State Superannuation Case*, above n 182.

185 Cf *Adamson's Case*, above n 182, 239; and *E v Australian Red Cross Society* (1991) 27 FCR 310.

186 *State Superannuation Case*, above n 182, 304.

187 *Adamson's Case*, above n 182; *Quickenden v O'Connor*, above n 175.

188 *Ian Todd v City of Armadale* (1998) 44 AILR 3–812; *Belcher v Aboriginal Rights League Incorporated* (1999) 45 AILR ¶4–045 where the corporation also derived a proportion of its income (15.39 per cent) from payments to it from the pensions of those resident in the hostel; *E v Australian Red Cross Society*, above n 185.

189 *CEPU v Ensham Resources Pty Ltd; re the Ensham Mine Employees' Enterprise Flexibility Agreement 1995* (1997) 43 AILR ¶3–564.

190 *Rowe v Transport Workers Union of Australia* (1998) 90 FCR 95.

amounted to about 18 per cent of its net operating revenue in a year. Because the University was also a substantial investor and lessor of lands as a means of managing its finances (including grants and bequests), some judges took the view that it was also a financial corporation.[191]

While in most instances it will be clear whether there is trading going on, sometimes even though there is an exchange of money for goods or services a question may still arise as to whether it amounts to 'trade' in the relevant sense. In *Quickenden v O'Connor* there was a difference of opinion as to whether student payments to the University under the Higher Education Contribution Scheme (HECS) amounted to a 'trading activity'. Under the *Higher Education Funding Act 1988* (Cth), students are liable to the University to pay the HEC or they can request a loan from the Commonwealth in order to do so. Justice Carr thought such payments constituted a trading activity, especially in the context of an environment where universities compete for students, but Chief Justice Black and Justice French doubted whether trading 'extends to the provision of services under a statutory obligation to fix a fee determined by law and the liability for which, on the part of the student, appears to be statutory'.[192]

Public and statutory corporations

The *Workplace Relations Act* after the *Work Choices* amendments does not regulate State public service employees. However, since the 1990s the States have 'corporatised' and privatised many of their functions. The *Tasmanian Dam Case* made it clear that corporations wholly owned by government and subject to ministerial direction may nonetheless also be trading or financial corporations.[193] Thus, many of the public corporations that have been set up to perform functions for State governments, such as operating hospitals or investing public servants' superannuation funds, are regulated by the *Workplace Relations Act*, which is expressed to bind the Crown in each of its capacities: s 10. Prior to the commencement of the *Work Choices* changes New South Wales legislated to transfer the employees of statutory corporations to the public service in order to avoid this.[194]

Constitutional implications drawn from the federal nature of the Australian community prohibit Commonwealth legislation from imposing 'special burdens' on the States or 'curtailing' their 'capacity' to function as governments.[195] For this reason in the *AEU Case* it was held that the Commonwealth could not regulate the terms and conditions of employment of senior State employees, the number of State employees, the number of employees the State could dismiss on redundancy grounds, and possibly issues relating to the promotion of State employees.[196] While the *AEU Case* concerned the State (rather than a State-owned corporation) as employer, nonetheless similar consideration may be relevant to State-owned corporations depending on Ministerial

191 Above n 175, 273, following *State Superannuation Case*, above n 182.
192 Ibid, 191–92.
193 *Tasmanian Dam Case*, above n 174, 293.
194 *Public Sector Employment Legislation Amendment Act 2006* (NSW).
195 See above n 143.
196 *AEU Case*, above n 39.

power in relation to them, and so the *Workplace Relations Act* as it applies to those corporations and their employees may need to be read down, to avoid contravening the *Constitution*.[197]

The regulatory regime under the Workplace Relations Act *after* Work Choices

The changes introduced into the *Workplace Relations Act* by the *Work Choices Act* represent a definitive and radical break from the historical tradition of Australian labour law. The amending legislation cemented in place a predominantly market-based orientation to the Australian system of labour law. Only a few minor remnants of the system of conciliation and arbitration established a century ago now remain. The old system focused on fair work conditions and placed the public interest at centre stage to be considered alongside the interests of the parties. Economic issues such as productivity and the well-being of businesses were never ignored in the old system, but they were not the only consideration. After *Work Choices* the public interest is implicitly redefined in terms of private economic interests. The protective function of the regulatory system has almost disappeared. The safety net has been reconfigured and lowered for the vast majority of workers. Better terms and conditions must be achieved by bargaining, which is assumed to deliver better outcomes for both capital and labour.

When the *Work Choices Bill* was first introduced into the Parliament it provoked widespread criticism.[198] Some scholars, such as Ron McCallum, have argued that reliance upon the corporations power is a one-sided approach to the regulation of work, which would inevitably set aside the democratic traditions present under the historic conciliation and arbitration system and under which workers would ultimately be seen 'as little more than actors in the economic enhancement of corporations'.[199] For McCallum the significance of the shift away from the conciliation and arbitration power and towards the corporations power is not only symbolic but real. The intensity of these reactions to the *Work Choices* changes indicated the radical nature of the changes that had occurred in the regulation of work relations in Australia.

The broad parameters of these changes are sketched here, but are discussed in greater detail throughout the remainder of this book.

The safety net—legislative standards and awards

The nature of the safety net was changed by *Work Choices*: legislated standards are more significant than ever before and the role of awards, although they still have a safety net function, is changed and diminished.

The *Workplace Relations Act* now incorporates a wider range of statutory entitlements for individual employees than before. *Work Choices* introduced a set of minimum

---

197 See *Industrial Relations Act* Case, above n 161, 503.

198 See especially Group of 151 Industrial Relations, Labour Market and Legal Academics, Australian Parliament, Submission to the Inquiry into the *Workplace Relations Amendment (Work Choices) Bill 2005*, Senate Employment, Workplace Relations and Education Legislation Committee, *Research Evidence about the Effects of the 'Work Choices' Bill* (2005).

199 R McCallum *Justice at Work: Industrial Citizenship and the Corporatisation of Australian Labour Law*, 2005 Kinsley Laffer Memorial Lecture (2006) 48 *JIR* 131.

statutory standards, which is collectively referred to as the Australian Fair Pay and Conditions Standard (AFPCS).[200] Each component of the AFPCS is in the form of a 'guarantee', emphasising that it cannot be undercut by other regulatory instruments including workplace agreements (although there is a degree of 'flexibility' in several of these standards allowing their variation by agreement). In addition, the Act now also contains new legislated standards on meal breaks and work on public holidays.[201] The previous provisions on equal remuneration and parental leave remain, as do statutory remedies for some employment terminations although these are more limited and access to them is more restricted than before.[202]

Awards continue to comprise minimum or safety net standards, but they are much diminished.[203] Wages and classification of employees are no longer award matters. From the commencement of the *Work Choices* changes, employees who were reliant previously on award wages now have their pay determined according to an Australian Pay and Classification Scale (APCS), to be controlled through the Australian Fair Pay Commission (AFPC).[204] The AFPC also makes any changes to the statutory federal minimum wage (FMW), initially set by the *Work Choices Act* at $12.75 per hour, and sets special FMWs for disabled, young or trainee workers. The content of awards is also further reduced because there is more extensive prescription of matters that are expressly excluded from them and there is a more limited range of 'allowable matters'.

More importantly, the function of awards has changed. Although the AIRC has the regulatory duty 'to ensure that minimum safety net entitlements are protected through a system of enforceable awards' (s 511), awards are no longer dispute resolution instruments. The AIRC no longer makes new awards and only has a very restricted power to vary or update existing awards. Some award terms are 'preserved' in a frozen form.

Under the new regime, awards are to undergo processes of simplification and rationalisation, transforming them into a smaller number of national broad-based work standards. However, the new system seems designed to render awards ultimately otiose: awards have little relevance once parties move to a workplace agreement, there is no longer a no-disadvantage test measuring workplace agreements against awards, and after workplace agreements are terminated parties do not return automatically to the award but only to 'protected award terms'.

Workplace agreements

Work Choices confirmed workplace agreements as the central regulatory mechanism in Australia's labour law regime and makes provision for five types of agreement.[205] The hierarchy amongst agreements is clearly established. AWAs are now able to undermine existing collective agreements, and so the function of these agreements as instruments to forward the interests of capital and diminish collective labour is more obvious than ever before.

---

200 *Workplace Relations Act*, Pt 7. See Chapter 7.
201 *Workplace Relations Act*, Pt 12, Divs 1–2. See Chapter 7.
202 *Workplace Relations Act*, Pt 12, Divs 3–4 and 6. See Chapters 8 and 9.
203 *Workplace Relations Act*, Pt 10. See Chapter 7.
204 *Workplace Relations Act*, Pt 2 and Pt 7 Div 2. See Chapter 7.
205 *Workplace Relations Act*, Pt 8. See Chapter 11.

In many senses after the *Work Choices* amendments the regulation of workplace agreements has a lighter touch, with lodgement procedures easier and more responsibility effectively devolved to the parties, especially employers who can self-regulate through compliance declarations. On the other hand, agreements are also more highly regulated than ever before, with the Executive Government able to declare their 'prohibited content' by regulation. The system thus provides for active governmental intervention in the direct regulation of workplace relations. Although this curtails the 'free' agreement of capital and labour, it was clearly intended on the introduction of the *Work Choices* system to consolidate and enhance capital's control of its workplace in the face of collective labour. Employers' bargaining power is also dramatically increased because once an agreement's expiry date is reached it can be unilaterally terminated and workers revert to only a few basic minimum statutory and some 'protected' award standards. For 'new projects' or 'new undertakings' an employer greenfields agreement gives capital unilateral power to determine the terms and conditions of employees.

Regulatory institutions

The *Work Choices* amendments altered the role of some of the existing regulatory institutions and also established some new ones.

The Office of the Employment Advocate (OEA)[206]

The chief functions of the Employment Advocate remain as previously, to promote agreement-making, to offer a wide range of advisory services to individuals and business, and to provide advice and information to the Minister. However, the Employment Advocate now has an expanded role and is responsible for the oversight of *all* agreements under the *Workplace Relations Act*, not just individual AWAs. *Work Choices* streamlines and simplifies agreement-making and because agreements come into operation at the time of their lodgement with the Office of the Employment Advocate (OEA), there is little prospect of active policing of compliance by the OEA, although the OEA also has power to work with the Workplace Inspectorate.

The AIRC[207]

It is the role of the AIRC that has changed most dramatically under the *Work Choices* amendments. Its powers in relation to award-making are now drastically reduced and altered. Its main role in relation to awards after *Work Choices* is to implement the award simplification and rationalisation processes. The AIRC can no longer make new awards except as part of the rationalisation process, although it does retain some powers to vary, albeit only in a minimal way, existing awards. Its functions in relation to pay and classifications under awards are now taken over by the AFPC.

One of the main functions of the AIRC is now dispute resolution under the legislature's model process.[208] Its jurisdiction here is dependent upon parties selecting the AIRC to resolve their disputes. From experience in the years immediately preceding

---

206 *Workplace Relations Act*, Pt 5.
207 *Workplace Relations Act*, Pt 3.
208 *Workplace Relations Act*, Pt 13, Div 2–3. See Chapter 12.

the *Work Choices* changes it is likely that many parties will continue to select the AIRC as the body to conduct a dispute resolution process where they cannot agree. However, there is no obligation on parties to choose the AIRC and there are private providers of such services who may be expected to compete increasingly for business in this area. The model dispute process applies to a wide range of disputes, including disputes over the application of the AFPCS, meal breaks, parental leave, and awards, as well as disputes in relation to workplace agreements that incorporate the model dispute resolution process. In this role the AIRC facilitates the parties resolving their own disputes, exercising mediation or conciliation powers, but it cannot arbitrate and impose solutions or orders upon them. The AIRC also continues to conciliate unfair and unlawful termination cases and may arbitrate where necessary if unfair termination cases are not conciliated.[209]

The other important area of dispute resolution relates to industrial action, and here the AIRC continues its previous role in relation to industrial action during bargaining periods.[210] Its power to suspend or terminate a bargaining period is also retained and where this is done in the public interest it has a power to make Workplace Determinations (the equivalent of s 170MX awards under the former provisions of the Act). The AIRC also polices the more stringent right of entry provisions that the *Work Choices* amendments established.[211]

The Australian Fair Pay Commission (AFPC)[212]

Work Choices established a new Australian Fair Pay Commission (AFPC), consisting of a Chair and four Commissioners appointed for terms of up to five and four years respectively. The Act requires that the Chair have 'high level skills and experience in business or economics'. Professor Ian Harper, an economist, has been appointed as the inaugural Chair. A wider range of fields of expertise and experience—including in the areas of community organisations or workplace relations, as well as business or economics—is included in the criteria for appointment of Commissioners. The main function of the AFPC is wage setting, including wage reviews. This means the AFPC has the power to set a federal minimum wage (FMW) including a special FMW for those who are a junior, in a trainee position or have a disability, and to set minimum wages, piece rates and casual loadings for different award classification levels through the Australian Pay and Classification Scales (APCS).

From 27 March 2006 the Act establishes a radically different approach to wage setting and wage review processes from that operating in the past. In carrying out its statutory obligations the AFPC is required to have regard to the recommendations of the Award Review Taskforce (ART), which the Government established to make recommendations about the rationalisation of award wage and classification structures as well as the rationalisation of federal awards.[213] However, the AFPC is not restricted, like the AIRC was previously, to exercising powers of conciliation and arbitration and it is

---

209 See Chapter 9.
210 *Workplace Relations Act*, Pt 9. See Chapter 12.
211 *Workplace Relations Act*, Pt 15, Div 9. See Chapter 10.
212 *Workplace Relations Act*, Pt 2. See Chapter 7.
213 See <www.awardreviewtaskforce.gov.au>. See Chapter 7.

able to determine its own procedures. In undertaking its wage setting functions the AFPC is directed to consider a more restricted range of factors and impacts than did the AIRC. Its focus is on the effect of wage levels on the unemployed and on 'employment and competitiveness' across the economy. The wider social impacts of wage levels, the public interest as broadly conceived, and a wider conception of fairness, alert to wage patterns generally prevailing in the labour market, are excluded from its regulatory gaze: s 23.

Workplace inspectors[214]

Enforcement has long been a complex issue in labour law. Because work relations are often ongoing, compliance with a regulatory system is best and most likely to be achieved when its goals are internalised by those who are governed by it. In large measure the function of the AIRC in the past has been one of engendering amongst parties a commitment to the regulatory system. There has been comparatively little use of punitive measures.[215] Nonetheless it is also clear from previous history that the monitoring of compliance and follow up enforcement has been weak, and there have been serious questions raised as to whether the system has always delivered on its promises to those participating in it.[216]

The *Work Choices* changes have promised a much enhanced role for the Office of Workplace Services (OWS) in monitoring general compliance with, and the enforcement of, the legislation. The compliance powers of the OEA have been shifted to the OWS so that there is a 'one-stop shop'. While the OWS is touted under the new provisions as providing a free and easily accessible service for workers to ensure their entitlements are respected, it is difficult to imagine that the reality of enforcement will be much different from the past. Despite the expansion in the inspectorate to more than 200 after *Work Choices*, it still remains comparatively small given the number of workers and workplaces in Australia.

The ongoing role of Government in workplace regulation

The workplace relations system established by the *Work Choices* legislation is characterised by extensive provisions for the Minister to intervene in, or direct, many of the processes conducted by the regulatory institutions established under the Act. Thus, for instance, the rationalisation of awards is a process to be undertaken by the AIRC, but only in accordance with a request from the Minister who may also set parameters for this exercise including as to the nature of and the future coverage of the relevant awards as well as the matters that they can include: s 534(2)–(3).

The *Work Choices Act* vested a wide power in the Governor-General to make regulations under the *Workplace Relations Act*: s 846. The *Workplace Relations Regulations 2006* (Cth) issued just prior to the commencement of the *Work Choices* changes in March 2006 are extensive and cover matters relating to almost every part of the Act. These regulations, for example in the requirements they impose for detailed record keeping by employers and in the stipulation of the 'prohibited content' of workplace agreements, demonstrate the

---

214 *Workplace Relations Act*, Pt 6.
215 B Creighton 'Enforcement in the Federal Industrial Relations System: An Australian Paradox' (1991) 4 *AJLL* 197.
216 L Bennett *Making Labour Law in Australia: Industrial Relations, Politics and Law* (1994), Chs 5–6.

way in which the *Work Choices* system establishes in many areas 'command and control' style regulation.[217] It is certainly not a model of 'de-regulation'.

The role of trade unions

The *Workplace Relations Act* after the *Work Choices* amendments intensifies the trend towards the individualisation of workplace relations and hence weakens further the position of trade unions. It achieves this by provisions operating at every level in the regulatory system.

Trade unions no longer have a role in securing basic workplace standards and terms and conditions for employees. In a system where the safety net is made up predominantly of legislative standards providing individual employment rights, trade unions have no formalised role in its enhancement. The system also prohibits the inclusion in awards or agreements of any provisions that facilitate trade union membership, including by attendance at trade union meetings or training, or the celebration of trade union achievements through picnic days. The rights of trade unions to enter workplaces and hence to advocate for their members are strictly controlled and quite restricted.[218]

The bargaining and agreement system also constrains trade unions more than before. Protected industrial action is more restricted, with the *Work Choices* legislation now necessitating the holding of a secret ballot unless such action is in response to a lockout. The system thus requires workers to turn their minds specifically to the issue, implying perhaps that trade union members have followed blindly their leadership in the past. Nonetheless the impact of the voting procedures will be no doubt that industrial action will become rarer. Pattern bargaining, through which a feeling of strength and solidarity between workers across different enterprises in an industry can be developed, is now also prohibited under the legislation. The legislation continues the individualisation of workplace relations by making it easier to use AWAs, especially in workplaces where there are also collective agreements.[219] Finally, the *Work Choices* amendments further enhance the individualised conception of freedom of association introduced by the 1996 legislation,[220] in particular, by removing access to some of the litigation mechanisms, such as the reversal of the onus of proof in application for interim injunctions, that trade unions have used successfully since 1996.

The establishment of a national system of labour law

The *Work Choices Act* moves towards the establishment of a national system for the regulation of the relations between employers and employees by incorporating a clear, general statement that it is the Commonwealth Parliament's intention to override other State or Territory laws operating in the same field so far as they apply to employers and employees as defined by the Act: ss 16. The main provisions effecting this are drawn

---

217 See S Cooney, J Howe, and J Murray 'Time and Money under Work Choices: Understanding the New Workplace Relations Act as a Scheme of Regulation' (2006) 29 *UNSWLJ* 215.

218 *Workplace Relations Act*, Pt 15. See Chapter 10.

219 *Workplace Relations Act*, Pt 8. See Chapter 11.

220 *Workplace Relations Act*, Pt 16. See Chapter 10.

very broadly and state an intention to exclude State or Territory industrial laws, which are defined as meaning specifically named statutes[221] and laws with purposes relating to a range of matters including the regulation of workplace relations, employment and industrial associations (ie, trade unions): ss 4 and 16. Also excluded are State or Territory laws that apply to employment generally and deal with leave other than long service leave, or provide for State courts or tribunals to deal with equal pay issues, or unfair contracts provisions, or regulate the entry of trade union representatives to workplaces: s 16(1)(b)–(e). Commonwealth awards and agreements are also stated as intended to prevail generally over State and Territory law, except in matters of workers' compensation, occupational health and safety, training arrangements and other matters that may be prescribed by regulation, such as child labour: s 17 and *Workplace Relations Regulations*, Ch 2, Pt 1, Div 2. While the general statements of Commonwealth intention are found in ss 16 and 17, the Act is also clear that further indications of intended inconsistency may be found elsewhere in the Act or in the instruments made under it: s 18.

It is trite law that it is the inconsistency between Commonwealth and State laws that attracts the operation of s 109. The Commonwealth has no power to preclude the States from legislating on a particular field. To do so would infringe the doctrine enunciated in the *Melbourne Corporation Case*, which prevents the Commonwealth imposing a 'special burden' or 'curtailment' on the 'capacity' of the 'states to function as governments'.[222] When the Commonwealth expresses an intention that its legislation is to be the only law on that area, the *Constitution* itself operates to invalidate (meaning render inoperable, rather than void altogether) the State law to the extent of any inconsistency.[223] The statements of intention in the *Work Choices Act* that it applies to the exclusion of certain State laws (including those that may be specified by regulation) are thus circumscribed in this way.

In the past Commonwealth awards have covered the field that they regulate, but industrial players have for the most part been able to choose whether they come under the Commonwealth or a State system. Since the *Work Choices* amendments that is no longer possible. The *Work Choices* legislation implemented the long-held policy aspiration of the Liberal Coalition Government that there would be 'a withering away of the States' in relation to workplace law.[224] Nonetheless, the field covered by the *Work Choices Act* is restricted to employment relations. Further legislation was, therefore, necessary to ensure that the States and Territories did not continue to regulate other workers, for example by deeming independent contractors to be employees under State industrial laws.[225]

With the coming into effect of the *Work Choices* amendments the jurisdiction of various State commissions and tribunals has been seriously curtailed. From the time the

---

221 The definition of 'State or Territory industrial law' in s 4 lists the *Industrial Relations Act 1996* (NSW); *Industrial Relations Act 1999* (Qld); *Industrial Relations Act 1979* (WA); *Fair Work Act 1994* (SA); and *Industrial Relations Act 1984* (Tas).

222 See above n 143.

223 *University of Wollongong v Metwally* (1984) 158 CLR 447.

224 Commonwealth of Australia, Parliamentary Debates, House of Representatives, 13 November 2002, 8853 (Hon Tony Abbott)—Second Reading Speech, *Workplace Relations Amendment (Termination of Employment) Bill 2002*. See also Williams, above n 146.

225 *Independent Contractors Bill 2006* (Cth).

Commonwealth Government indicated its intention to legislate for a national system, it has been clear that this would be contested. The Industrial Commission of New South Wales sitting in Court Session (a superior court of record) presaged this with several decisions prior to the commencement of the *Work Choices* regime asserting its jurisdiction to deal with industrial disputation even where it arose in relation to federal agreements. However, although the Commonwealth Parliament cannot directly interfere with or limit the jurisdiction of State courts or tribunals, it is equally clear that Commonwealth legislation may require certain matters to be dealt with only by its courts or tribunals.[226]

State laws governing employment after Work Choices

State laws governing work relations still govern those employers and employees not covered by the *Workplace Relations Act*.[227] However, the *Work Choices* amendments also indicate that there is no general intention to override State and Territory laws in certain defined areas. State law may thus continue to be applicable to those who are also governed by the *Workplace Relations Act* in these defined areas. These include discrimination and the promotion of equal employment opportunity (EEO) matters: s 16(2)(a). In addition, State and Territory laws dealing with any of the specifically listed 'non-excluded matters' are also still able to continue to operate in relation to employers and employees covered by the *Workplace Relations Act*: s 16(2)(c) and (3). These 'non-excluded matters' are:

- superannuation;
- workers' compensation;
- occupational health and safety (including entry of a representative of a trade union to premises for a purpose connected with occupational health and safety);
- matters relating to outworkers (including entry of a representative of a trade union to premises for a purpose connected with outworkers);
- child labour;
- long service leave;
- the observance of a public holiday except the rate of payment of an employee for the public holiday;
- the method of payment of wages or salaries;
- the frequency of payment of wages or salaries;
- deductions from wages or salaries;
- industrial action (within the ordinary meaning of the expression) affecting essential services;
- attendance for service on a jury;
- regulation of any of the following:
  - associations of employees;
  - associations of employers;
  - members of associations of employees or of associations of employers.

---

226 See *CFMEU v Newcrest Mining Limited* (2005) 139 IR 50; and *Re Inquiry into the Boeing Dispute at Williamstown* [2006] NSWIRComm 52. Cf *Boeing Australia Limited v Australian Workers' Union* AIRC, PR968945, 23 February 2006.

227 See above pp 111–12.

However, it must be remembered that a more specific intention expressed in an instrument made under the *Workplace Relations Act*, for instance in an award or workplace agreement, may still be able effectively to exclude such State laws: s 17(1). There is also a specific provision relating to the exclusion of certain Victorian laws: s 898.

In addition, after the *Work Choices* changes regulations may also specify other State or Territory laws that the Commonwealth's law either does not or does intend to override: s 16(2)(b) and (4). Initially, for instance, the *Workplace Relations Regulations 2006* have made it clear that State laws are not overridden with retrospective effect; that the remedies against unfair dismissal in Queensland's *Industrial Relations Act 1999* continue to be available for certain whistleblowers; but that the *Contracts Review Act 1980* (NSW) in so far as it deals with employment contracts between employees and employers is intended to be overridden by the *Workplace Relations Act*: rr 1.2–1.4.

The interaction of the Commonwealth and State systems is thus quite dynamic and changes in the regulations as well as the main statute need to be monitored closely.

Transitional arrangements after the Work Choices Act

The introduction of the *Work Choices* changes involves a major reorganisation of work relations. Complex transitional provisions are necessary to implement this new system. These include, for example, special transitional arrangements for trade unions previously registered under State law but now seeking transitional registration under the *Workplace Relations Act*.[228] Even in Victoria, which had previously referred its powers to the Commonwealth, transition provisions have had to be put in place.[229]

For some employers and employees the commencement of the main substantive provisions of the *Work Choices Act* on 27 March 2006 did not involve a change in the jurisdiction. Those who have previously had their affairs regulated under one of the State systems and who are not covered by the new federal regime are unaffected by the changes.

For all other employers and employees there is some kind of transitional arrangement. These may be grouped in the following way. First, many employers and employees will continue to have their work relations governed by the federal system as had been the case previously, albeit after 27 March 2006 under a radically changed regime. Transitional provisions stipulate the way pre–*Work Choices* federal industrial instruments operate. Secondly, for many others the commencement of the *Work Choices* amendments signalled a transfer of jurisdiction and transitional provisions also regulate them. This second group is further divided into two parts. After *Work Choices* some employers and their employees transferred into the federal arena from a State jurisdiction. However, some other 'excluded' employers and their employees, who had been previously covered by the federal system, no longer fall within its coverage after *Work Choices*. For this 'excluded' group, arrangements during a transition period allow them to remain temporarily in the federal system until they take some action to select participation under either the federal or state systems over the longer term.

---

228 *Workplace Relations Act*, Sch 10.
229 *Workplace Relations Act*, Sch 6 Pt 7.

Employers and employees remaining in the federal system

For the group of federal employers and their employees who were already regulated under the federal system prior to *Work Choices* and who are covered by the new regime there are some transition arrangements. Constitutional corporations and their employees with federal awards or agreements prior to *Work Choices* are members of this group.

Pre-reform awards

For this group the *Workplace Relations Act* makes it clear that existing federal awards continue to apply. This is because the definition of 'award' in the Act now includes not only new rationalised awards but also 'pre-reform' awards: s 4. Since 27 March 2006 all awards conform to the new more restrictive provisions regulating awards: Pt 10.[230]

Transitional arrangements for pre-reform federal agreements[231]

The transitional arrangements ensure that pre-reform federal agreements binding those who are federal employers and employees under ss 5 and 6 continue to operate under identified former provisions of the *Workplace Relations Act* until either they are replaced by new agreements or are terminated according to the former legislative provisions of the *Workplace Relations Act:* Sch 7, cl 2. It is possible for parties to make a new agreement at any time, even before the pre-reform agreement has reached its nominal expiry date. New agreements may include or 'call up' content from pre-reform agreements. The content of pre-reform agreements is largely unaffected by the *Work Choices* changes; however, the new provisions of the *Workplace Relations Act* do apply to these pre-reform agreements to make any anti-AWA terms that prevent an employer from making AWAs 'prohibited content': Sch 7, cl 8. A pre-reform certified agreement has no effect where an employee has an AWA: Sch 7, cl 3(2). Pre-reform agreements also nullify the effect of any previous State agreements or awards, and override awards: Sch 7, cl 5. Some former provisions of the *Workplace Relations Act* continue to apply to pre-reform agreements: Sch 7, cl 2.

Transitional treatment of State industrial instruments[232]

For those, such as constitutional corporations and their employees, who were formerly regulated by State industrial instruments, whether agreements or awards, but who 'moved' into the federal arena as a result of the *Work Choices* changes, the broad scheme of the transitional provisions is to assimilate them as far as possible to the position of their federally regulated counterparts. Thus the terms and conditions of employment that these employees enjoyed under State agreements or awards immediately prior to 27 March 2006 are generally preserved during the transition period, which for this group of employers, employees and organisations may extend up to three years.

Preserved State agreements(PSAs)[233]

State agreements binding those who after 27 March 2006 became covered by the federal legislation are known under the *Workplace Relations Act* as either 'preserved

---

230 See further Chapter 7.
231 *Workplace Relations Act*, Sch 7.
232 *Workplace Relations Act*, Sch 8.
233 *Workplace Relations Act*, Sch 8 Pt 2.

individual State agreements' or 'preserved collective State agreements'. These preserved State agreements (PSAs) bind the employers, employees and organisations, who were previously a party to, or bound by, the agreement under State law and also, in the case of preserved collective State agreements, any future employees whose employment would have been governed by the agreement: Sch 8, cls 4 and 11–12. Preserved State agreements operate for a limited period of either three years from 27 March 2006 or until their expiry date, whichever is the sooner: Sch 8, cls 6 and 14.

There are four components to the contents of PSAs. First, there are the terms of the original agreement in force immediately prior to 27 March 2006. Secondly, the PSA is also taken to include the terms of any other State industrial instruments, that is, awards and/or (in the case of a preserved individual State agreement) State collective agreements, which also determined the terms and conditions of the employee's employment at the time of the commencement of the *Work Choices* regime. Thirdly, State or Territory industrial laws governing 'preserved entitlements'—that is, annual, parental, personal/carer's, bereavement or ceremonial leave; notice of termination; redundancy pay; overtime or shift loadings; penalty rates; or rest breaks—and which also determined any of an employee's terms and conditions of employment immediately prior to 27 March 2006 are also taken to be included in their PSA: Sch 8 cls 5 and 13. Finally, all PSAs are taken to include a term requiring disputes about the application of the agreement to be resolved in accordance with the model dispute resolution process set out under the *Workplace Relations Act*: Sch 8 cls 8 and 15A.

However, to ensure that the regulation of these PSAs is in line with that of other federal agreements, they are void in so far as they contain 'prohibited content' as defined by regulation, and they may be altered by the Employment Advocate to reflect this: Sch 8, cls 9, 15B and 19. Awards, the AFPCS or the federal provisions in respect of public holidays have no effect in relation to an employee who is bound by a PSA: Sch 8 cls 15D–15F. Rather, there is now only one industrial instrument applicable to these employees and all the relevant terms and conditions of their employment are contained (or taken to be contained) in the PSA.

Since 27 March 2006 a PSA is enforceable only in the federal arena and in the same way as federal collective agreements. PSAs may be varied by the AIRC but only in limited circumstances such as when necessary to remove an ambiguity, or discrimination if an application has been made via the President of the Human Rights and Equal Opportunity Commission (HREOC) and the process under s 46PW of the *Human Rights and Equal Opportunity Commission Act* is activated: Sch 8 cl 18. As mentioned above, the Employment Advocate also has the power to remove prohibited content from PSAs: Sch 8 cl 19. During the period of operation of the PSA the assimilation of the position of those governed by the PSA to that of their federal counterparts means, for instance, that it is no longer lawful (even if formerly it was so under State law) to take part in any industrial action during the period of its operation: Sch 8, cls 23–4.

PSAs continue to operate until either they are terminated, and that can only be done in the same way that other federal collective agreements or AWAs are terminated, or until they are replaced by a new workplace agreement or a workplace determination: Sch 8 cl 15G and 21. Finally, if and when a new workplace agreement is negotiated to replace a PSA, any of the terms of the PSA that regulate 'protected preserved conditions' are taken to be included in the new workplace agreement unless those terms are expressly excluded. It should also be noted that provisions in PSAs protecting outworkers cannot be diminished or removed even by express terms. These 'protected preserved conditions' are broadly the same as 'protected allowable award matters' and cover such things as rest breaks; incentive-based payments and bonuses; annual leave loadings; State or Territory public holidays; monetary allowances for employment expenses, responsibilities or skills, or for any disability arising from working in particular conditions or locations; loadings for overtime or shift work; penalty rates; outworker conditions; or other matter specified by regulation: Sch 8 cl 25A.

These transitional provisions thus have the impact of immediately placing those employees whose terms and conditions were governed by a State agreement and perhaps also a State award and/or law immediately prior to 27 March 2006 in an analogous situation to those who are governed by a federal workplace agreement.

Notional agreements preserving State awards (NAPSAs)[234]

For those federal employees whose work was not covered by a State agreement but whose terms and conditions of employment were determined either wholly or partly by a State award and/or by a State or Territory industrial law immediately prior to the reform commencement, a 'notional agreement preserving State awards' came into effect from 27 March 2006: Sch 8 cl 31. That is, by the stroke of the legislative pen the form of regulation governing these employees has been transformed from one centred on an industry, a calling, or a wide range of employees across a State to one centred on the workplace.

The content of NAPSAs is taken to include the relevant State award provisions, as well as any terms and conditions concerning 'preserved entitlements' that derive from State or Territory industrial laws and that were applicable to the employee immediately prior to the reform commencement: Sch 8 cl 34. As with PSAs, NAPSAs are also considered to include a term incorporating the model dispute resolution process: Sch 8 cl 36. Likewise too, any provisions in the NAPSA dealing with prohibited content are void and may be removed by the Employment Advocate: Sch 8, cls 37 and 42.

A NAPSA ceases to operate after three years, or earlier if a workplace agreement or a federal award becomes binding on the employee in which case the NAPSA lapses so as never again to bind the employee: Sch 8 cl 38A. In order to ensure that a NAPSA does not undercut the AFPCS guarantees, its terms are unenforceable in so far as they purport to cover a matter also governed by the AFPCS: Sch 8 cl 44. However, if there are 'preserved notional terms' providing an employee with either an entitlement to annual, parental, or personal/carer's leave that is more generous than the AFPCS, or an entitlement to such leave that they do not enjoy under the AFPCS, it continues to have effect. Various other entitlements that are contained in the notional agreement—for

---

234 *Workplace Relations Act*, Sch 7, Pt 3.

example, long service leave, notice of termination, jury service, and superannuation—are also preserved and thus also continue to have effect: Sch 8 cls 44–9. Preserved notional terms are also taken to be incorporated in any federal award that becomes binding on an employer and employee already bound by a NAPSA: Sch 8 cl 50. The effect of these transition provisions is thus that any terms and conditions governing the employee in relation to annual, parental, personal/carer's leave must be at least as good as the AFPCS, and in so far as they are 'more generous' than the AFPCS they are also preserved. The meaning of 'more generous' is taken to have its 'ordinary meaning', and this is more fully elaborated in the regulations: Sch 8 cls 46–7; and Regs: Ch 5, Pt 3, Div 5, r 3.2.

As is the case with PSAs, NAPSAs are enforced after 27 March 2006 as if they are federal collective agreements: Sch 8 cl 43. While in operation NAPSAs may be varied by the AIRC only to remove ambiguity or uncertainty or on application of the President of HREOC to remove a discriminatory provision: Sch 8 cls 40–1. Any provisions that deal with prohibited content are void and therefore unenforceable and may be removed by the Employment Advocate: Sch 8 cls 37 and 42.

Where a new workplace agreement is put in place it is taken to include 'protected notional conditions', which are about the same kinds of matters covered by 'protected preserved conditions' in PSAs, unless they are expressly excluded, but as with PSAs protections for outworkers cannot be excluded or diminished.

'Excluded employers' in the federal system

The changes introduced by the *Work Choices Act* also mean that there are a number of employers, employees and organisations that were previously regulated under the federal system, but who are no longer covered by the new regulatory regime. This is the situation for most employing businesses that are not constitutional corporations. These 'excluded employers' include sole traders who are not incorporated, those employing businesses organised as partnerships or trusts, and corporations that do not satisfy the definition of a 'constitutional corporation'. Transitional arrangements, supported by the conciliation and arbitration power and operating over a period lasting up to five years, govern this group.[235]

Excluded employers and transitional federal awards

The *Work Choices* amendments continue in force the federal awards that existed prior to 27 March 2006. These transitional awards remain binding on excluded employers in respect of the employees they had at the time the *Work Choices* changes took effect. However, they no longer bind any excluded employers who are also already bound by a State agreement. In addition, where the excluded employers or employees are bound by the award only by virtue of their membership of an organisation, then cessation of their membership releases them from the award: Sch 6 cls 4–5. However, new employees taken on by these excluded employers after the introduction of the *Work Choices* regime are not covered by the federal system but by State law and/or industrial instruments. Excluded employers have a period of up to five years in which they can decide whether

---

235 *Workplace Relations Act*, Schs 6 and 7.

to take action, for example by incorporating, to bring themselves and their employees under the new federal regime, or they may transfer into the State system by making a State agreement with an employee: Sch 6 cl 57. Where excluded employers are unsuccessful in attempts to do the latter they may apply to the AIRC for an order releasing them from the transitional award: Sch 6 cl 58.

In terms of content the provisions of the legislation governing transitional awards generally replicate the main provisions on awards in the Act: Sch 6 Pt 3 Subdiv B–D. Thus transitional awards can only contain 'allowable transitional award matters' and 'preserved transitional award terms', which can include matters relating to long service leave, jury service, notice of termination, and superannuation, and clauses providing for redundancy pay are applicable only where the transitional employer has fifteen or more employees.

Transitional awards are prohibited from dealing with a range of matters that might constrain employers' flexibility in the organisation of their workforce or that involve entitlements relating to trade union membership. Thus clauses providing for conversion from casual employment, or restrictions on the number or terms of employment of labour hire workers or independent contractors are no longer allowed. Provisions governing the rights of a trade union to participate in dispute settling procedures are now subject to the employer or employee 'choosing' them as their representative. Transitional awards cannot contain terms providing for the entry of unions to workplaces or for any discrimination or preference for trade union members. Facilitative provisions can no longer contain any proviso requiring a majority vote.

The AIRC continues to have powers of conciliation and arbitration to prevent and settle industrial disputation in order to update the transitional awards but only so that access to minimum safety net payments (including rates of pay, incentive based payments, loadings, and allowances) is maintained. In exercising these powers the statute requires the AIRC to have regard to the desirability of ensuring there is consistency with the wage setting decisions of the AFPC. However, with the exception of this and a power to remove discriminatory provisions from transitional awards, the AIRC has otherwise no power to vary them nor can it make any new awards: Sch 6 Pts 2–3 cls 7–8 and 28–30. The powers and procedures of the AIRC to deal with industrial disputation during the transition period are set down in some detail: Sch 6 Pt 3.

Because, as noted above, the AIRC has only limited powers to vary or update transitional awards, the terms and conditions of any employees covered by transitional awards are therefore effectively frozen until an employer either corporatises and thus opts into the federal system for the longer term or opts to move back into the State system. If no such action is taken by the employer before the end of the five-year transition period, these excluded employers then simply cease to be bound by the transitional awards.

There are also provisions governing the situation of a transmission of business during the transmission period: Sch 6 Pt 6A. A new transitional employer who is the successor, transmittee or assignee of an existing or 'old' transitional employer will also be bound by the transitional award in relation to transferring transitional employees until any one of a number of things occur, including that the award is revoked; there are no more transferring transitional employees in relation to the transitional award; the transmission period (which is twelve months) ends; or the transitional period ends: Sch 6 Pt 6A, cl 72G(2).

Excluded employers and transitional Division 3 certified agreements[236]

As a transitional arrangement, special rules have also been put in place for Division 3 pre-reform certified agreements for excluded employers during the transitional period: Sch 7 Div 2. These agreements were made under former provisions of the *Workplace Relations Act* supported by the conciliation and arbitration power. Identified former sections of the Act continue to govern these agreements, which remain in place for the five-year transitional period or until they are terminated or are replaced after they expire by a State agreement.

The law of work in the States after Work Choices

Even though the majority of employers and employees have their work relations governed by the *Workplace Relations Act* after 27 March 2006, the State labour law systems still operate for excluded employers and their employees.[237] All State public sector workers, for instance, have their terms and conditions of work determined under State legislation, including the specific statutes applicable to those in the public sector.[238] In addition, where an employer is not a constitutional corporation and the terms and conditions of their employees were regulated under State industrial law or industrial instruments prior to the commencement of the *Work Choices* changes, that continues to be the case after 27 March 2006. Furthermore, the *Work Choices Act* for the most part regulates only the employment relation, and has virtually nothing to say with respect to other workers including independent contractors.[239] Finally, some employment matters—including the prescription of methods or frequency of payment of wages—remain issues that after *Work Choices* may be governed by the States.

In addition, although it aimed to establish a national system of workplace relations law for employers and employees, the *Work Choices Act* also made clear that State and Territory law could continue to regulate a large number of topics relating to work for all employers and employees. Indeed, a long list of matters is specifically precluded from the exclusive oversight of the Commonwealth, although the list is susceptible to alteration by regulation: s 16(3)–(4).[240]

The *Work Choices Act* also makes it clear that State laws regulating workers in the areas of rehabilitation and compensation, occupational health and safety, training

---

236 *Workplace Relations Act*, Sch 7, Div 2.
237 See in particular *Industrial Relations Act 1991* (NSW); *Industrial Relations Act 1999* (Qld); *Fair Work Act 1994* (SA); *Industrial Relations Act 1984* (Tas); and *Industrial Relations Act 1979* (WA).
238 *Public Sector Employment and Management Act 2002* (NSW); *Public Service Act 1996* (Qld); *Public Sector Management Act 1995* (SA); *State Service Act 2000* (Tas); *Public Sector Management and Employment Act 1998* (Vic); and *Public Sector Management Act 1994* (WA).
239 But note *Workplace Relations Act*, Pt 16 (freedom of association) and unfair contracts review provisions. See *Workplace Relations Legislations Amendment (Independent Contractors) Bill 2006* (Cth).
240 See above p 122.

arrangements, and discrimination and the promotion of equality in the workplace, will continue to operate and in relation to the first three of these topics State law overrides the terms of Commonwealth awards and agreements: s 17(2)–(3).

Conclusion

The passage of the *Work Choices Act* marked a point of radical departure from the historical direction of Australian labour law. For more than a decade before the *Work Choices* changes scholars were observing the slow demise of the old labour law model of the industrial era and wondering whether the conciliation and arbitration system would survive into the global era.[241]

The *Work Choices Act* establishes a new system for the global era. It also marks for Australia a new phase in the continuing contest over the purposes and function, and indeed the very definition, of labour law. The great labour lawyer Otto Kahn-Freund once declared: 'The main object of labour law has always been … to be a countervailing force to counteract the inequality of bargaining power which is inherent and must be inherent in the employment relationship.'[242] But the conciliation and arbitration system in Australia had always been more than that. It had recognised the broad interest of society in the way work was regulated. It had always understood that labour law regulation impacted on the construction of labour markets and the well-being of the economy. It had channelled and controlled the relations of labour and capital, and in doing so had been quite explicit about the public interest in the outcomes of those relations. The system was effective in large part because it was compulsory and there were, for instance, always potentially far more serious consequences, such as deregistration and attack through the common law, for parties like trade unions that opted to operate contrary to the system.

The legal regulation of labour relations in twentieth-century Australia differed markedly from that in the jurisdictions of other industrialised economies. The regulatory regime introduced by the *Work Choices* amendments has changed all that. Regulating for competitiveness, fostering productivity and encouraging flexibility are its guiding principles. For its supporters, this is a necessity given the global environment we inhabit. In terms of labour relations the *Work Choices* provisions assume that labour market participants will determine their relations primarily through bargaining, and that this is done best when there is no 'interference' from 'outsiders' like trade unions or governmental institutions. The neo-liberal agenda denies the role of the state, redefines the public interest in terms of the private interests of parties, and implicitly asserts the neutrality of the market. Of course the very size of the legislation makes it obvious that this is not an exercise in *de*-regulation.

The *Work Choices Act* places only a very small emphasis on the protection of workers. Its safety net of minimum conditions is very low. Indeed, the legislation assumes

---

241 See R Mitchell and R Naughton 'Australian Compulsory Arbitration: Will It Survive into the Twenty-First Century?' (1993) 31 *OHLJ* 265; and M Vranken 'Demise of the Australian Model of Labour Law in the 1990s' (1994) 16 *CLL* 1.

242 O Kahn-Freund *Labour and the Law* (1977), 6.

for the most part that protective provisions are an exclusionary tool that will work to keep others out of the labour market. Participation in the labour market is thus elevated above any more immediate concern for the quality of working lives once so central to the foundations of the former system in the *Harvester Case*. It is now left to the market, to bargaining, to produce decent work conditions. In so far as there is a social need for mechanisms that protect workers and ensure they can secure a decent life, neo-liberal policies suggest these mechanisms must be found in other areas of law: for instance, welfare law might subsidise the income of certain workers, and taxation law might be used to increase or decrease the rewards of work for others. However, the more labour law treats workplace relations as if they are simply a matter of agreement-making in relation to work and not about protecting the worker as a human person, the more difficult it is to distinguish agreements for work from agreements for any other commodity.

The critics of the *Work Choices* regime thus argue that labour law is becoming simply a part of commercial law. The corporations power is seen as a perfect and highly symbolic vehicle for this task. Ron McCallum has likened the use of the corporations power to regulate work to using a power about one sex to enact a traditional marriage law.[243] The point McCallum makes is that a law regulating work that is supported by the corporations power is bound to be one-sided. The *Work Choices* legislation certainly places fewer restrictions on managerial prerogative. Yet it is also not too difficult to think of ways the corporations power might be used differently. It could support an AFPCS that is much higher than the one in the current Act.

The *Work Choices* legislation was born out of a very particular political situation in which the Liberal Coalition Government controlled both Houses of the federal Parliament. It represents one moment in an ongoing contest over labour law, and it certainly is not the end of that contest. Almost immediately after its introduction to Parliament it was criticised as not delivering on a promise of a simpler system of labour law for Australia. The continuing complexity is in part a function of constitutional limitations, and in part a function of the size of the new legislation and the real problems that arise from trying to translate the old system into a new form. Nor does it, and nor could it, deal comprehensively with work relations. Just prior to the enactment of the *Work Choices Act* the Commonwealth Parliament also enacted specific legislation, the *Building and Construction Improvement Act 2005* (Cth), to regulate some aspects of the building and construction industry including by setting up an Australian Building and Construction Commissioner to regulate standards of conduct in that industry. So from the outset there was not the pretence for a new single comprehensive labour law model.

Although there are many negative aspects to regulatory systems that are overly complex, there are always in complexities openings for transformative possibilities and making law an instrument of justice not power. Law constitutes identities, relations and communities. Its workings are inevitably a complex set of intersections within

---

243 McCallum, above n 199.

any community and between the community and those whom it would declare to be outsiders. The theoretical, social and historical context within which law operates also shapes it. Law takes on meaning and content through politics. In Australia the perceived destabilising tendencies of federalism are also opportunities for multiple political activities that can produce openings that might become fertile sites of contestation and transformation.

As the policy agenda of the Liberal Coalition Government to adopt a regulatory system focused on competitiveness and the economy firmed in recent years, so too the States investigated more seriously the need and prospects for further protecting workers. They also seriously commenced to think about the diversity of labour markets, their interactions and the need to extend protections beyond traditional forms of work. Thus since the turn of the century a number of the States had instituted inquiries into the need for reform of the laws regulating work with a view to providing increased protection to the most vulnerable workers, while at the same time ensuring that the competitiveness of business was not compromised.[244]

Given the shape of the Commonwealth's new laws there will continue to be contest and resistance in the politics of workplace relations law. Soon after the enactment of the *Work Choices* legislation the NSW Government repatriated into the public sector all those who worked for government owned corporations in that State.[245] The enactment of the *Workplace Rights Advocate Act 2005* (Vic) is another example of the way transformative politics over labour law might take shape. The *Workplace Rights Advocate Act 2005* establishes an Office of the Workplace Rights Advocate to 'provide information about, and promote and monitor the development of, fair industrial relations practices in Victoria'.[246] The Office has a statutory brief to inform and educate those in the State of Victoria about workplace rights, to investigate unlawful behaviours and report to Parliament and advise Ministers. The legislation imposes penalties on anyone who victimises a worker for seeking assistance from the Workplace Rights Advocate (WRA). The Act thus presents an opportunity for focusing ongoing contest over the protection of employees and workers at the political level. The very naming of the Act and the Office allows a rhetorical play to invert the developments under the Commonwealth legislation—the Victorian WRA will comment on the effects of the Commonwealth *Workplace Relations Act*.

In the end perhaps the most powerful contest to the new *Work Choices* regime will come from the diversity of work arrangements. In a very significant way, the *Workplace Relations Act* after *Work Choices* remains an 'old economy' regime because it is concerned only with employment relations whereas, as we shall see in the next chapter, the nature of employment relations is also increasingly contested in the global era.

---

244 See RC McCallum, Chair *Independent Report Prepared for the Victorian Industrial Relations Taskforce*, (2000); G Stephens *Report of the Review of the South Australian Industrial Relations System* (2002); and WJ Ford *An Independent Review of the Amendments to the Industrial Relations Act 1979 Made by the Labour Relations Reform Act 2002*, A report to the Hon J Kobelke, MLA Minister for Consumer and Protection Law (2004).

245 *Public Sector Employment Legslation Amendment Act 2006* (NSW).

246 *Workplace Rights Advocate Act 2005* (Vic), s 1.

The Subject of the Law of Work

Who is the subject of the law of work?

A fundamental issue for the law of work is the identification of its subject. Who inhabits the world of work according to law? Who is included within its realm? And who is excluded? With the emergence of the new economy these questions demand especially close attention. The transformation of the world of work presents new challenges to the law. However, the law does not simply respond to and act upon a pre-existing subject in the social and economic environment. Law also actively constitutes its subject, classifies and categorises it, gives it a (legally) recognisable form and endows it with (legal) meaning.

In the feudal era the law of work was part of the law of domestic relations, and the legal incidents of work relations were determined according to the status of those within the household—the master, his wife and children, and his servants. By the end of the industrial era the law had come to conceptualise work relations as contractual, signalling the preoccupation of modern labour law with paid work in the marketplace.

The transition in the legal understanding of work relations from status to contract was complex, and one in which judicial conceptions of the worker protected by statute played an important part.[1] Loosening the influence of the old masters and servants legislation, inherited from the United Kingdom and still operating in Australia well into the twentieth century, was only a gradual process. The interpretation of the industrial relationship of employer and employee, as incorporated into twentieth-century statutes like the *Commonwealth Conciliation and Arbitration Act 1904* (Cth), was often infused with the old characteristics of the master and servant relationship. For much of the industrial era the law was familiar with the relations of master and servant, principal and independent contractor, employer and employee.

---

1   See A Merritt 'The Historical Role of Law in the Regulation of Employment—Abstentionism or Interventionist?' (1982) 1 *AJLS* 56; J Howe and R Mitchell 'The Evolution of the Contract of Employment in Australia: A Discussion' (1992) 12 *AJLL* 113; and B Creighton and R Mitchell 'The Contract of Employment in Australian Labour Law' in L Betten (ed) *The Employment Contract in Transforming Labour Relations* (1995). See also S Deakin 'The Evolution of the Contract of Employment 1900–1950' in N Whiteside and R Salais (eds) *Governance, Industry and Labour Markets in Britain and France* (1998).

Now law conventionally divides workers in the marketplace into two main types—independent contractors and employees. Independent contractors, operating in business on their own account and contracting their services in freely negotiated commercial agreements, are seldom the focus of labour law. Rather its central subjects are employees, those who are party to a 'personal' contract of employment in which they are subordinate to the one for whom they work.[2] It is these employees who for the most part have been the intended beneficiaries of any legal protections offered to workers.

The distinction between independent contractors and employees has been fundamental to labour law, as it has developed to date. As Otto Kahn-Freund once famously commented, the contract of employment is the 'cornerstone' of the edifice of labour law.[3] At common law this distinction between an independent contractor and an employee is drawn from cases concerning the vicarious liability of another for a worker's negligence.[4] Many statutes regulating work have adopted the common law's concept of 'employee' as the basis for defining their scope and coverage.[5]

In the global era the utility of the classification of workers as independent contractors and employees is increasingly being called into question.[6] The worker is less likely than ever before to be the employee of old who worked fulltime, for a lifetime, in an ongoing position with the same employer. Work is now organised in a myriad of new and different ways. There is an increasing emphasis on commercial contracting, franchising, consulting, working through an agency, casual work, and home-based work, to name but some. The capacity of the law to respond to the realities of these new work relations is vital, but not always made easy by the adoption of the independent contractor/employee divide.

There is widespread contest over the binary divide between independent contractors and employees.[7] This contest is informed by understandings of law's purposes. A central rationale of labour law since the nineteenth century has been to protect those who are vulnerable and powerless in the marketplace, the subordinate worker who is the archetypal employee. If new forms of work organisation mean that many such workers are no longer encompassed within law's recognised category of employee, the foundation of labour law will be gradually undermined. However, if law's purposes in governing work are different—say, intended primarily to facilitate market competitiveness—then the divide may not be thought so deficient.

---

2   M Freedland *The Personal Employment Contract* (2003).

3   O Kahn-Freund 'Blackstone's Neglected Child: The Contract of Employment' (1977) 93 *LQR* 508.

4   It is a long-standing principle that employers are vicariously liable for the negligence of their employees: *Hollis v Vabu Pty Ltd* (2001) 207 CLR 121. However, principals may also be liable for the negligence of independent contractors, especially if they create the risk and have some responsibility for coordinating the independent contractors working as part of it: *Northern Sandblasting Pty Ltd v Harris* (1997) 188 CLR 313, 366–7; *Sutherland Shire Council v Heyman* (1985) 157 CLR 242; *Stevens v Brodribb Sawmilling Company Proprietary Limited* (1986) 160 CLR 13, 45.

5   See eg *Workplace Relations Act 1996* (Cth).

6   Eg Freedland, above n 2, denies the unity of the categories either side of the dichotomy.

7   See ILO *The Employment Relationship* (2006); and J Fudge 'Self Employment, Women and Precarious Work: The Scope of Labour Protection' in J Fudge and R Owens (eds) *Precarious Work, Women and the New Economy: The Challenge to Legal Norms* (2006).

Work in the marketplace is legally ordered not only by the categorisation of workers, but also through the creation of the legal structures through which capital operates. At the centre of many of the changes in the world of work in the global era is the corporation. The corporation is the single most important legal construct impacting upon the world of work. It is thus a significant subject of the law of work for the rules defining the corporation determine the nature and structure of many work relations in the marketplace.

In focusing on work in the marketplace, modern law also draws a distinction between productive and reproductive labour, between the workplace and the home or domestic sphere, between work and familial relationships. More than that, it assumes for the most part that each side of this binary divide exists in a dichotomous relation, separate and independent from the other. Until quite recently the normative subject of labour law has been a male breadwinner, a being wholly committed to work in the marketplace and assumed to have no responsibility for work in the domestic sphere. Work in the home was organised according to a 'sexual contract', which is not acknowledged in law as a contract at all.[8] Labour law has thus ignored the (usually female) worker in the home, and denied the dependence of the marketplace on reproductive labour. The world of work according to law has thus been bifurcated between public and private, and the gendering of this division also influenced the approach of labour law to work in the marketplace.[9]

While law feigns a continued lack of interest in work in the private sphere, it has been unsettled by the feminisation of the labour market. The increased participation of women in paid employment has challenged traditional assumptions about the worker, and the relation of work in the private and public spheres. Simultaneously, the characterisation of some forms of 'non-standard' work as particularly suitable for women, because it enables the conflict between work in the market and in the home to be accommodated, reasserts labour law's normative worker as 'unencumbered' and endorses 'a new gender contract' between a fulltime male worker and a part-time female worker.[10]

This chapter examines the subject of the law of work and the role of the law in the construction of the worker. It first looks at the conventional legal division of those performing work for payment in the marketplace into employees and independent contractors, and notes some of the long-standing problems arising from this classification. It then examines the challenges that some of the new forms of

---

8   *Balfour v Balfour* [1919] 2 KB 571. See also R Graycar and J Morgan *The Hidden Gender of Law* 2nd edn (2002) Pt Two 'Women and Economic (In)dependence'; and C Pateman *The Sexual Contract* (1988).

9   R Hunter 'Representing Gender in Legal Analysis: A Case/Book Study in Labour Law' (1991) 18 *MULR* 305; RJ Owens 'Women, "Atypical" Work Relationships and the Law' (1993) 19 *MULR* 399; and RJ Owens 'The Traditional Labour Law Framework: A Critical Evaluation' in R Mitchell (ed) *Redefining Labour Law: New Perspectives on the Future of Teaching and Research* (1995).

10 See S Berns *Women Going Backwards: Law and Change in a Family Unfriendly Society* (2003); R Broomhill and R Sharp 'The Changing Male Breadwinner Model in Australia: A New Gender Order?' (2004) 15 *Lab Ind* 1; A Chapman 'Work/Family, Australian Labour Law, and the Normative Worker'; and J Fudge 'A New Gender Contract? Work/Life Balance and Working Time Flexibility' in J Conaghan and K Rittich (eds) *Labour Law, Work and Family: Critical and Comparative Perspectives* (2005).

work pose to law's classifications and its understanding of the worker, and the way the law is implicated in the production and classification of these new forms of work. Law's structuring of capital through the corporation, the role of the corporation in the creation of new forms of work, and the relation of the corporation with workers are also considered. Finally, the chapter evaluates some of law's responses to the new forms of work and its attempts to develop new approaches more attuned to the present realities of work. In particular it considers the limitations of conceptualising work relations as contractual and the significance of understanding the social and economic context of these relations.

Employees and independent contractors

Conventionally the subject of modern labour law is the employee. The law distinguishes employees who are engaged in a contract *of* service, from independent contractors who agree to work for a principal in a contract *for* services. The contract of service is a contract of a personal nature, and in law it still carries some of the traces of the old master and servant relationship. It incorporates the notion that the worker is a subordinate to the person or entity served. By contrast the person entering a contract for services is treated as an independent operator in the marketplace, at arm's length from the other contracting party receiving the benefit of those services. Contracts for services are considered by the law as essentially no different from other commercial deals in the marketplace.

The 'totality of the relationship'

At common law the distinction between an employee and an independent contractor is usually drawn in cases concerning the question of the vicarious liability for the negligent acts of the worker. In determining whether a worker is an employee or an independent contractor judges consider all the circumstances of the work relationship. These factors commonly include, but are not necessarily limited to:

- the degree of control exercised over the worker in the doing of the work;
- the obligation on the worker to do the work personally; or, to put it another way, their capacity to delegate the work to others;
- the freedom to work for others, including whether the worker advertise for, or seeks generally, work in the marketplace;
- the place of work;
- the mode of remuneration, especially whether the worker is paid for time spent doing the work or for the completion of tasks;
- responsibility for the provision and maintenance of assets and equipment used in the work and their cost;
- the creation of goodwill or saleable assets through the work and the ownership of these;
- the risks and responsibility for loss or profit;
- the degree of integration of the worker into the organisation of the other party;

- payments for sick leave, annual leave, and long service leave;
- the arrangements made in relation to payment of taxation, workers' compensation levies; and
- the parties' own characterisation of their relationship.

In considering these multiple indicia, no one factor is determinative; rather, all must be considered together. In most cases some factors may indicate that the worker is an employee, others point to the worker being an independent contractor, or increasingly likely many of the factors are consistent with either interpretation. In the end it is a question of taking account of them all. This approach was authoritatively established for Australia by the High Court in *Stevens v Brodribb Sawmilling Co Pty Ltd*, a case concerning liability for the negligence of a 'snigger' who was working with other truck drivers loading logs for the sawmilling operations of the defendant.[11] The High Court confirmed this approach to the classification of the worker in *Hollis v Vabu Pty Limited*, where there was a question as to a corporation's vicarious liability for the negligence of one of its bicycle couriers.[12]

Control

This 'multiple indicia test' incorporates a number of elements that have long been treated as significant by the law in the classification of workers. Foremost among these is the element of control. In feudal times control signified the subordination of the servant to the master. The master was recognised as a person in law, responsible for all the property in his household including his servants and his wife. In the transformation from feudal, to agrarian and then to industrial society, the law continued to see the degree of control exercised over the worker as the critical element in understanding the nature of work relations. The control of an employer over every aspect of the execution of work—over when, where and how the work was to be done—became in the law's eyes the defining characteristic of the employment relation.[13] By contrast where an agreement was essentially one in which the worker provided a result or an end product, as was often the case where the worker was skilled and worked without direction, the relation tended to be characterised as one between a principal and an independent contractor.

The assessment of the control exercised over a worker in modern work relations has long proved problematic. Control can be viewed in terms of commands given by one individual to another. But since the agrarian age this has not been an adequate conceptualisation for most work relations. Whether employees are labourers in the field, workers in the factory, clerks in the office, or attendants in shops, control over their work is as likely to be exercised through the hierarchical structure of the organisation for which they work as by immediate personal direction. Furthermore,

---

11 (1986) 160 CLR 16, 24 and 36–7.

12 Above n 4, 33 and 45.

13 See eg *Performing Rights Society Ltd v Mitchell & Brooker Ltd (Palais de Danse)* [1924] 1 KB 762; *Federal Commissioner of Taxation v J Walter Thompson (Australia) Pty Ltd* (1944) 69 CLR 227, 231; *Queensland Stations Pty Ltd v Federal Commissioner of Taxation* (1945) 70 CLR 539; and *Humberstone v Northern Timber Mills* (1949) 79 CLR 389.

the specialised skills of many workers means it is inconceivable that their employers would or could instruct them in any detailed way about how to do their job. Yet many of these skilled workers clearly do not function at arm's length from those for whom they work. As Otto Kahn-Freund noted in referring to the control test:

> It reflects a state of society in which the ownership of the means of production coincided with the possession of technical knowledge and skills and in which that knowledge and skill was largely acquired by being handed down from one generation to the next by oral tradition and not by being systematically imparted in institutions of learning from universities down to technical colleges.[14]

Once the social circumstances and the organisation of work changed it became increasingly difficult to justify control as the core definitional element of the employment relation. And in any event control can be seen to be an element in many contracts for the performance of work that clearly do not involve employees: that is, control no longer necessarily signifies subordination, and it is really the latter that indicates that a worker might need the protection of the law.[15] Despite its obvious inadequacies the courts showed, as Breen Creighton describes it, 'a dogged persistence in trying to adapt this pre-industrial concept of control to the circumstances of the late twentieth century'.[16]

The inadequacy of the control test did, however, prompt the law to change its focus away from the actual day-to-day exercise of control over the work to the notion of ultimate authority, or 'right to control'. Using this idea, the High Court was able to reason in *Zuijs v Wirth Bros Pty Ltd* that a circus acrobat was a subordinate worker not an independent contractor. But even in this case the right to control was not by itself adequate as an explanation. The Court further supported its decision by pointing out that the acrobat was employed on a weekly basis for an indefinite period, worked at the premises of the other party, and was required to participate in the circus's grand parade.[17] The right to control was thus a more or less residual conception indicating the employer's superintendence over a wide range of organisational arrangements that made up the context in which the work was performed.

Control is often a significant element in the multiple indicia test, and the legal understanding of it has become quite sophisticated. It can encompass, for instance, work situations where workers are required to follow closely manuals of instruction, even though there is little or no immediate face-to-face interaction between the workers and those for whom they work (like those who run meetings for Weight Watchers, or market researchers).[18] However, control is no longer a sole criterion for defining an employee, and in some cases it may not be very important at all in determining the category to which a worker belongs.

---

14 O Kahn-Freund 'Servants and Independent Contractors' (1951) 14 *Mod LR* 504, 505.

15 See A Merritt 'Control v Economic Reality: Defining the Contract of Employment' (1982) *ABLR* 105, 111.

16 B Creighton 'The Forgotten Workers: Employment Security of Casual Employees and Independent Contractors' in R McCallum, G McCarry and P Ronfeldt (eds) *Employment Security* (1994), 58.

17 *Zuijs v Wirth Bros Pty Ltd* (1955) 83 CLR 561, 571. See also *Federal Commissioner of Taxation V Barrett* (1973) 129 CLR 395, 402; and *Humberstone v Northern Timber Mills*, above n 13, 404.

18 *Narich Pty Ltd v Commissioner of Pay-roll Tax* (1983) 2 NSWLR 597; and *The Commissioner of State Taxation v The Roy Morgan Research Centre Pty Ltd* (2004) 57 ATR 148.

Integration into the business

Another significant element in classifying workers is the degree of their integration into the enterprise of the other contracting party who receives the benefit of their work. As a stand alone test this was never much relied upon in Australia, though it was elsewhere,[19] and it was criticised on the grounds that it was impossible to measure the 'economic reality' of the work relation by reference to it.[20] However, it had the advantage of capturing the idea that the distinction between an employer and an independent contractor is 'rooted fundamentally in the difference between a person who serves his employer in his, the employer's business, and a person who carries on a trade or business on his own'.[21] Expressing the distinction in this way provides an alternative conceptual formulation from that of subordination to contextualise work relations and evaluate other factors incorporated in the multiple indicia test.

The identification of workers with the business of another, for instance through a contractual requirement to wear its livery, can indicate that they are not operating in their own business but as employees. The uniform tells outsiders who the workers represent. Likewise the provision by workers of expensive equipment, such as a truck, may indicate a contract for services (or a contract for the provision of mechanical traction) by people who are working on their own account.[22] The ownership of assets used in the execution of the work and the assumption of the business risk are very often seen as indicating that the workers are operating in the marketplace on their own account rather than in the cause of another's enterprise. This is especially so if it can be seen that goodwill is acquired through the performance of the work.

Delegation of work

The ability of a worker to delegate work to another is an important classification factor. Where an agreement is essentially to produce an outcome or a product, the capacity to delegate the performance of the work may sometimes be inferred. Certainly for many who contract to do work and also operate their own business in which they employ others, the capacity to delegate (or subcontract) work is essential to their success. If a contract for work does not require the contracting party to render personal service this can be a strong 'almost conclusive' indicator that the worker is an independent contractor.[23] Indeed, it has been said that the capacity to delegate the performance of the work is now 'arguably the single most determinative factor' of an employment

---

19 *Stevens v Brodribb Sawmilling Co Pty Ltd*, above n 4, 27. See also *Stevenson Jordan & Harrison Ltd v McDonald & Evans* (1952) 1 TLR 101, 111; *Bank Voor Handel En Scheepvaart NV v Slatford* (1953) 1 QB 248, 295; and *Australian Timber Workers Union v Monaro Sawmills Pty Ltd* (1980) 29 ALR 322, 328–9.

20 CP Mills 'The Contract of Employment: Control is Economic Reality' (1982) 10 *ABLR* 270, 275–7. Cf Merritt, above n 15, 118.

21 *Marshall v Whittacker's Building Supply Co* (1963) 109 CLR 210, 217. See also *Market Investigations Ltd v Minister of Social Security* [1969] 2 WLR 1, 9; and *Hollis v Vabu Pty Ltd*, above n 4, 38–9.

22 *Ready Mixed Concrete (South East) Ltd v Minister of Pensions and National Insurance* [1968] 2 QB 497; *Humberstone v Northern Timber Mills*, above n 13, 404–5; and *Australian Air Express Pty Ltd v Langford* (2005) 147 IR 240.

23 *Australian Mutual Provident Society v Allan* (1978) 52 ALJR 407, 410; and *Stevens v Brodribb Sawmilling Co Pty Ltd*, above n 4, 26 and 38. Cf *Australian Air Express Pty Ltd v Langford*, above n 22, 254–56.

relationship.[24] However, cases where an employee has some capacity, albeit usually limited, to delegate the work to another are not unknown.[25]

The multiple indicia test at work

With the multiple indicia test there is no limit, beyond relevance to the nature of the work relation, on the matters to be considered in determining whether a worker is an employee or independent contractor. And all relevant matters must be considered. Because of this the multiple indicia test has drawn criticism. Classification made by applying the test is a matter of 'fact and degree', in respect of which views might legitimately differ.[26] Although there were some early indications of a lingering judicial emphasis on control as the 'surest guide to whether a person is contracting independently or serving as an employee' it has been made clear that the control test in its original form is no longer appropriate.[27] There is no judicial exegesis as to which factors are more important than others, because no one factor or even a group of factors is determinative. This can make it difficult to predict with certainty whether or not a particular worker is an employee or an independent contractor. Indeed Lord Wedderburn famously described the multiple indicia test as the '"elephant test", an animal too difficult to define, but easy to recognize it when you see it'.[28]

The difficulty in predicting the outcome of the test does not follow simply from the number of indicia that need to be considered, nor from the fact that in any case various factors may point in different directions, which then have to be weighed in the balance, nor even from the fact that some factors may point in different directions at once. Inherent in the multiple indicia test are some of the problems previously identified in earlier tests. There is the danger of circular logic in the application of the test, for some factors are as much a consequence as a determinant of the very thing that needs to be identified.[29] More tellingly others have criticised the test for downplaying critical issues such as the subordination and dependency of the worker and the superior bargaining strength of business.[30]

Dependent contractors

In some instances where workers have been categorised as independent contractors, they were working all of the time for one business rather than for a range of businesses, prompting the suggestion that this is a form of 'disguised employment' involving 'dependent' workers. Some of the cases concerning owner-drivers provide typical

---

24 A Stewart 'Redefining Employment? Meeting the Challenge of Contract and Agency Labour' (2002) 15 *AJLL* 235, 244.

25 *Sammartino v Mayne Nickless t/as Wards Skyroad* (2000) 98 IR 168.

26 See *Stevens v Brodribb Sawmilling Co Pty Ltd*, above n 4, 36 and 49; and *Roy Morgan Research Limited v Commissioner of State Revenue* (1997) 37 ATR 528, 533.

27 See *Stevens v Brodribb Sawmilling Co Pty Ltd*, above n 4, 24 and 36.

28 KW Wedderburn *The Worker and the Law* 3rd edn (1986), 116.

29 See A Brooks 'Myth and Muddle—An Examination of Contracts for the Performance of Work' (1988) 11 *UNSWLJ* 48, 52.

30 P Benjamin 'Who Needs Labour Law? Defining the Scope of Labour Protection' in J Conaghan, RM Fischl and K Klare (eds) *Labour Law in an Era of Globalization: Transformative Practices and Possibilities* (2002).

examples, the emblazoning upon the trucks of the name of the business for whom they deliver goods symbolising the point. In *Re Porter* Gray J observed that even where a worker supplies a substantial asset, such as a truck, as part of a work contract, it may be indicative of a high level of economic dependency upon the entity for whom they work rather than their independence in the marketplace.[31] The practical reality of the situation may be that unless the workers provide, for instance, their own vehicle (or computer or sewing machine) they will not get the offer of work in the first place. Ownership and contribution of assets to the performance of work for this reason should not per se, therefore, distinguish between independent contractors and employees. And yet the fact is that in many cases it continues to be treated as strongly determinative.[32] Dependency is particularly pertinent to the inquiry as to whether the worker is an employee or an independent contractor given the traditional purposes of labour law. Because it is relatively easy to ensure that a worker does not appear to be integrated into the business of the other entity, the protection of vulnerable workers can be easily subverted if that is a dominant focus.

The classification of couriers provides a neat illustration of the above issues arising out of the multiple indicia test. In *Hollis v Vabu Pty Limited* the High Court held that bicycle couriers were employees.[33] The facts revealed that the couriers provided their own bicycle, which they had to maintain in good order and Vabu provided numerous smaller articles of equipment including radios, which remained its property; Vabu set the couriers' rate of remuneration, with no scope for negotiation by individual cyclist couriers, and it deducted insurance money from the couriers' payments; Vabu allocated and controlled the delivery work on a daily basis and required the couriers to wear the 'Crisis Couriers' uniform it provided. The High Court's decision that the bicycle couriers were employees overturned that of the Supreme Court below, which held that couriers working for Vabu were independent contractors. The Supreme Court had considered itself bound by an earlier decision, *Vabu Pty Ltd v Federal Commissioner of Taxation*,[34] from which the High Court had refused leave to appeal, thus reinforcing the sense that it was correct.

What was the distinction to be drawn between the two cases? One difference was that the earlier case dealt with the classification of *all* the couriers working for Vabu, those who provided light commercial and domestic vehicles and motorcycles for delivery work as well as the bicyclists. The High Court hinted that had the courier who injured Hollis been driving a motor vehicle rather than a bicycle the outcome in the case may have been different.[35] But the distinction can hardly be just a matter of the value of the asset contributed by the worker (and anyway, what amount of money marks the dividing line?). The High Court also suggested another consideration was whether the vehicles were only used at work or whether they could also be used for private or

---

31 *Application by DJ Porter for an Inquiry into an Election in the Transport Workers' Union of Australia* (1989) 34 IR 179, 184–5.
32 See eg *Australian Air Express Pty Ltd v Langford*, above n 22.
33 Above n 4.
34 *Vabu Pty Ltd v Federal Commissioner of Taxation* (1996) 33 ATR 537.
35 *Hollis v Vabu Pty Ltd*, above n 4, 32 and 41.

domestic purposes. Again that line can be difficult to draw. Certainly the provision of a vehicle, especially one designed for commercial purposes, has generally been held to indicate the presence of a contract for services,[36] but not always.[37] Other distinctions could be made between the bicyclist and the other couriers. Could they be seen to be in business on their own account, building goodwill in their own business? The High Court thought not when it considered the situation of the bicycle couriers—but would the answer really have been any different in respect of the couriers who supplied a truck and worked for Vabu? Although this discussion shows that it is not hard to present the law's classification of workers as somewhat arbitrary, further analysis suggests this is not so.

The purposes of law and the classification of workers

It may be objected that comparison on the basis of one factor, or even several selected factors, is to miss the point of the multiple indicia test. This seems a weak objection here given that the couriers considered in the two cases all worked under similar terms for the same business. But it is a point that generally should not be overlooked.

More importantly, such comparisons do not take account of the legal purpose in distinguishing employees from independent contractors. This is all-important. In *Hollis v Vabu Pty Limited* the High Court had to determine whether Vabu Pty Ltd was vicariously liable for the negligent harm to Hollis caused by a cyclist courier who rode off after the accident and was never identified except as someone wearing Vabu's 'Crisis Couriers' uniform. Vabu sought, unsuccessfully, to defend the case by arguing that the bicycle courier was an independent contractor not its employee. In this context there is an important 'policy' aspect to the decision: Vabu made no effort to ensure that the bicyclists could be identified individually, and the consideration of deterrence of negligent behaviour while delivering goods indicated that Vabu, which knew of the dangers created by the demands of its delivery work, should assume liability for the work it directed.[38]

The majority judges in the High Court indicated this when they commented in *Hollis v Vabu Pty Limited* that the terms 'employee' and 'independent contractor' should be understood as *expressing* rather than *determining* the legal result in the case. They cautioned:

> Terms such as 'employee' and 'independent contractor', and the dichotomy which is seen as existing between them, do not necessarily display their legal content purely by virtue of their semantic meaning.[39]

Approaching the issue of the classification of the worker with this in mind it is clear that someone may be described as an employee for some legal purposes but not for others.

---

36 See *Ready Mixed Concrete (South East) Ltd v Minister of Pensions and National Insurance* [1968] 2 QB 497; *Humberstone v Northern Timber Mills*, above n 13; and *Stevens v Brodribb Sawmilling Co Pty Ltd*, above n 4.

37 *Sammartino v Mayne Nickless Express t/a Wards Skyroads* (2002) 98 IR 168; and *Application by DJ Porter for an Inquiry into an Election in the Transport Workers' Union of Australia* above n 31.

38 *Hollis v Vabu Pty Ltd*, above n 4, 42–5.

39 Ibid, 38.

In *Vabu Pty Ltd v Federal Commissioner of Taxation* the reason for classifying the couriers was the quite different one of determining whether the couriers working for Vabu were 'employees' under the *Superannuation Guarantee (Administration) Act 1992* (Cth). If employees Vabu would be obliged to make compulsory superannuation payments for them. The decision by the NSW Supreme Court was that it did not have to do so. The Act adopted the 'ordinary meaning' (that is, the common law meaning) of the term 'employee' but it also imported the additional gloss that where a person works 'under a contract that is wholly or principally for the labour of that person, the person is an employee of the other party'.[40]

Another factor that influenced the judges in *Vabu Pty Ltd v Federal Commissioner of Taxation* was that the contractual documentation between the parties anticipated that the couriers could operate through a business or corporate form, and the judges commented, 'A company does not usually have employee corporations.'[41] Indeed the conception of the contract of employment as a *personal* contract seems to support the conclusion that a corporation cannot be an employee because a corporation by definition cannot render *personal* service.[42] When a corporation contracts to perform work it must necessarily delegate the work task to a human person, for corporations can act only through human beings. (However the fact that an individual can now also have a corporate status is already blurring the distinctions here.[43])

By considering the purpose of the classification of the workers in these two cases involving Vabu, it can be seen that it is neither arbitrary nor contradictory to hold that Vabu has responsibility for the harm caused to the injured Hollis and at the same time is not obliged to make superannuation contributions for its couriers. The question in *Vabu Pty Ltd v Federal Commissioner of Taxation* was clearly not without difficulty and an argument can be made that the decision of the NSW Supreme Court was wrong.[44] The basis of such an argument must be that in reality these couriers were not the kind of workers who the statute intended should be responsible for making their own superannuation arrangements.

To the extent that the NSW Supreme Court's decision relied upon the contractual documentation, with its requirement that the couriers provide and maintain the delivery vehicle and its concession that the worker could incorporate and use a business name, it reveals the most difficult aspect of the classification of the worker in law—that is, the scope for the parties to determine by their own contract whether the worker is an employee or an independent contractor.

Contract, intention and the reality of the work relationship

The parties to a contract for the performance of work may, and often do, explicitly state that the worker is an 'independent contractor' or an 'employee'. However, the courts

---

40 *Superannuation Guarantee (Administration) Act 1992* (Cth), s 12(3); and Australian Taxation Office, *Superannuation Guarantee Ruling* SGR 2005/1.

41 *Vabu Pty Ltd v Federal Commissioner of Taxation*, above n 34, 539 and 542.

42 See *Australian Mutual Provident Society Ltd v Chaplin* (1978) 18 ALR 385, 391–2. Cf *Hartnett v Aardvark Security Services Pty Ltd* (1988) 85 IR 315.

43 See below p 146 for further discussion of this point.

44 See eg B Creighton and A Stewart *Labour Law* 4th edn (2005), 289–90.

have stressed on numerous occasions that the law's concern is with the reality of the work relation. Form cannot dominate substance. The parties cannot, with the strokes of a contractual pen, impose their own classification when it is contrary to the reality of their work relation. Or as Gray J so evocatively expressed it: the contracting parties cannot create something with all the features of a rooster and call it a duck![45] And there are many cases where the courts have in effect held this.[46]

However, the more difficult and fundamental issue is whether the indicia used to determine the classification of the worker can be manipulated. In addition to an express statement of the worker's legal classification, the contract between the parties may include express terms governing any number of other factors relevant to the classification of the worker. The contract may, for example, allow delegation of the work to another, or stipulate in quite precise terms the way the work is to be done, or provide that payment is to be made per item produced or delivery made rather than on the basis of the time worked.

To the law the parties' contractual expression of their relationship is always of significance. The important question is, 'can it be determinative?' The law is always reluctant to look behind the bargain made by the parties and question or interfere with their expressed intention. However, the reality is that most contracts for the performance of work are contracts of adhesion: that is, the terms are set by one of the parties and presented to the other on a 'take it or leave it' basis. This raises the possibility that the 'chosen' classification and contractual arrangements are simply imposed by the dominant, more powerful party for its own purposes and to the detriment of the other party (usually the worker). The incentive to do this is primarily economic: if the worker is taken on under a contract of employment the employer may incur the costs of complying with statutes and industrial instruments setting pay and conditions, and of paying levies arising under workers' rehabilitation and compensation legislation, payroll tax, and superannuation contributions. If the contract is one where an independent contractor is engaged, these costs are either avoided altogether or the risks they quantify are transferred from the one receiving the benefit of the labour to the one providing it or, in some instances, to society at large. Andrew Stewart believes that 'any competent lawyer knows how to "exploit" these indicia so as to arrive at the right result for their client.'[47] That is, the more powerful party can manipulate the indicia to ensure that enough of the criteria point away from the worker being an employee. And if the indicia are ambivalent, then the parties' expression of intention as to the classification of the worker becomes more significant.[48] The inequality of bargaining power also explains why there is a problem of circular logic in the application of the multiple indicia test—many of the factors are a consequence rather than the determinant of the nature of the unequal relation.

---

45 *Application by DJ Porter for an Inquiry into an Election in the Transport Workers' Union of Australia*, above n 31, 184.

46 See eg *Cam & Sons Pty Ltd v Sargent* (1940) 14 ALJ 162; *R v Foster; Ex parte Commonwealth Life (Amalgamated) Assurances Ltd* (1952) 85 CLR 138, 150–1; *Australian Mutual Provident Society v Allan* (1978) 52 ALJR 407, 409; *Narich Pty Ltd v Commissioner of Pay-roll Tax* (1983) 2 NSWLR 597, 607; and *Hollis v Vabu Pty Ltd*, above n 4, 45.

47 Stewart, above n 24, 244.

48 See eg *Building Workers' Industrial Union of Australia v Odco Pty Ltd (Troubleshooters)* (1991) 29 FCR 104; and *Forstaff Pty Ltd v The Chief Commissioner of State Revenue (Forstaff)* (2004) 144 IR 1, 26.

Law and the worker in the new economy

The utility of the dichotomy between employees and independent contractors is now under scrutiny as never before. The contract of employment—with its associations of subordination and integration into a business enterprise—is a construct that was more suited to the development of large integrated business organisations in the early twentieth century.[49] 'Taylorism', and the closely associated 'Fordist' model of production, emerged as styles of business organisation where production was managed by subordinating armies of workers with specialised job functions in production line processes. Every worker was a cog in a greater machine, with a central nervous system in its hierarchical management structure.[50] In the industrial era, it was typical for all aspects of production—supply of materials, labour, processing, packaging, sales and marketing—to be brought under the umbrella of the single integrated enterprise. Take, for instance, the typical news publishing house of the 1960s. The one corporation would employ writers and photographers, editors and subeditors, typesetters, printers, advertising sales staff, subscription sales staff, and drivers. All stages in the production of the newspaper, from news gathering to delivery of the papers to the newsagents, were integrated into a single corporate enterprise, controlled by a hierarchy of managers and line managers, ultimately answerable to a board of directors, who were in turn answerable to the shareholders of the company.

Throughout the 1980s and 1990s, however, this business organisation model underwent transformation. The increased competition attendant upon the opening up of economies created incentives for business to operate more efficiently and to respond more flexibly to the demands of the market. Under these challenges and aided by the technological revolution organisations rationalised. Why employ typesetters and printers, when these functions could be provided more cheaply by outside—often offshore—specialist typesetting and printing organisations? Why employ drivers, when small business contract drivers could perform the same functions, and in addition take over the costs of fleet ownership and maintenance? Many industries have thus witnessed what Hugh Collins describes as 'vertical disintegration'.[51] Returning to their 'core business', many larger enterprises have also carved off specialist functions into separate enterprises that contract with each other in business networks.

These organisational changes have simultaneously begun to challenge the centrality of the contract of employment in the legal regulation of work relationships. Work in the global era is increasingly organised in ways that are quite different from the employment relationships of the old industrial era.[52] No longer is the standard worker likely to

---

49 See A Supiot *Beyond Employment, Changes in Work and the Future of Labour Law in Europe* (2000), 3.

50 For a concise explanation of the 'scientific management' system instituted in US enterprises by Frederick Winslow Taylor at the turn of the twentieth century, and the production systems instituted by Henry Ford, see K van Wezel Stone 'The New Psychological Contract: Implications for the Changing Workplace for Labor and Employment Law' (2001) 48 *UCLA LR* 519, 529–39.

51 H Collins 'Independent Contractors and the Challenge of Vertical Disintegration to Employment Protection Laws' (1990) 10 *OJLS* 35.

52 See I Watson, J Buchanan, I Campbell and C Briggs *Fragmented Futures: New Challenges in Working Life* (2003); and B Pocock *The Work/Life Collision* (2003) for accounts of changing work patterns in Australia in the global era.

conform to the model of the employee, who works fulltime and for a lifetime often for the same employer. Instead the worker in the new economy is as likely to be a contractor or a franchisee, perhaps working on their own account, and sometimes acquiring some of the trappings of business such as an Australian Business Number (ABN) for taxation purposes, or assuming a corporate identity, or working in partnership or through a trust with others including family members; a worker engaged through a labour-hire agency; a worker on a limited-term contract, perhaps working on a particular project or task; someone who does not work at the factory or the office of an employer but from home; a part-time worker; or a casual worker.

These categories are not necessarily mutually exclusive: a home-based worker, for instance, might work part-time on a casual basis. Furthermore, an individual may have several different contracts all at the same time: working through an agency in one job, as a casual in another, and on a part-time limited-term contract elsewhere. These once 'atypical' or 'non-standard' work forms are steadily becoming the norm in the global era. They are characterised by precariousness or contingency when compared with the contract of employment in the industrial era in which security was very often the quid pro quo for managerial control.[53] The employee of old was usually assumed by the law to be, and indeed was very often in reality, a breadwinner who had no responsibility for work in the home. When the employee was not at work, he was assumed to devote himself to leisure. With women entering the workforce in unprecedented numbers over the last two decades, the image of the worker as the breadwinner has now shattered. In this context of changing work relations the distinction between independent contractor and employee as traditionally articulated in the law is less adept at fulfilling the traditional purposes of the law of work.

Outsourcing and contracting out

As business has restructured under the challenges of globalisation, work that was previously performed for a corporation by its employees is often outsourced to another business, perhaps a labour-hire firm, or directly to independent contractors specialising in the relevant type of work. A commercial agreement thus often replaces the employment contract. In many cases, the business entities that take over the outsourced work are sole shareholder/director companies incorporated by former employees in order to enter into contracts to provide the same or similar services that they once performed from within the employer corporation. Since July 1998, individuals have been able to incorporate under Australian corporations legislation. An Australian corporation, private or public, requires only one shareholder. Private (or 'proprietary limited') companies now require only one director.[54] Corporate law has thus facilitated the restructuring of work and its relabelling as a commercial arrangement, for once an individual has incorporated in this way and proceeds to work under contracts negotiated in the name of the corporation it becomes more difficult for the law to consider this a 'personal' employment contract.

---

53 S Deakin 'The Many Futures of the Contract of Employment' in Conaghan, Fischl, and Klare (eds), above n 30.

54 See *Corporations Act 2001* (Cth), ss 114 and 198E.

Not surprisingly the growth of self-employed contractors who are working on their own account has been remarkably strong in recent years. Indeed, self-employed contracting as a share of total employment is estimated to have grown by 15 per cent over the last two decades of the twentieth century. Tradespeople and related workers make up the largest group of self-employed contractors, followed by professionals. About one-third of these workers are to be found in the construction industry, with the next greatest concentrations in property and business services; transport and storage; and manufacturing.[55]

The evidence is also that the new 'entrepreneurial worker' is a gendered being: about two-thirds are men and only one-third women, although the proportions change slightly over the life-course with women more likely to run their own business when aged between thirty and fifty years than when they are older or younger, whereas the inverse is true for men. The patterns of work of this entrepreneurial class are also gendered. The majority of men running small businesses work fulltime, and often long hours, whereas women tend to work more often on a part-time basis. The majority (72.6 per cent in June 2004) of small businesses are single operators. And again there are gendered differences—women are more likely to be single operators, while men are more likely to employ others.[56]

There are alternative perspectives on the transformation in work arrangements. On one interpretation, workers have now emerged from subservient roles in large faceless corporations and become independent entrepreneurs, in control of their own working lives and contracting freely in the marketplace. On the darker side, these new small business entrepreneurs or 'enterprise workers' are now often doing the same work they once did as employees and shouldering greater risk and costs, but they lack the commercial muscle to set their own prices. Attempts by small business providers to join forces to negotiate terms face the threat of sanctions under competition laws with the laws regulating the commercial market operating to individualise work relations.[57]

However, not all outsourcing arrangements result in the work being transferred to independent contractors. In some outsourcing situations the work will be done in the future by employees who work for the business that won the contract for the performance of the work. Some of these may be former employees of the first business, who after losing their job now find themselves doing the same work again under the auspices of a labour-hire agency (and sometimes as an independent contractor in this role)[58] or by working for the new contractor having been 'transferred' as part of the outsourcing deal.[59] Although such an arrangement may in effect preserve the jobs of

---

55 ABS, *Forms of Employment* Cat no 6359.0, 2005; and M Waite and L Will *Self Employed Contractors in Australia: Incidence and Characteristics* (2001).

56 ABS, *Characteristics of Small Business Australia* Cat no 8127.0, 2005.

57 *Trade Practices Act 1974* (Cth), Pt IV regulates restrictive trade practices.

58 See *Damevski v Giudice* (2003) 133 FCR 438 for an example of an ineffectual attempt to create such an arrangement.

59 At common law a 'transfer' means that the contract of employment ends and the worker agrees to enter a new contract with the new employer. The 'transfer' cannot occur without the consent of the worker: see *McCluskey v Karagiozis* (2002) 120 IR 147. See *Workplace Relations Act 1996* (Cth), s 581 for the statutory definition of a 'transferring employee'.

these workers, this can sometimes be at the cost of the terms and conditions set by awards or workplace agreements with the previous employer. The precariousness of employment is thus likely to be amplified by outsourcing.

Where the outsourcing involves the transmission of a business or part of a business some protection may be available for employees at least for the statutory transmission period of twelve months.[60] The courts have interpreted 'transmission of business' and like phrases by focusing on a comparison of the two business entities, rather than by looking at whether there is an identity, or even a substantial identity, in the work that is done by the employees. In *Crosilla v Challenge Property Services (formerly Crothall & Co Pty Ltd)* a cleaner, whose employment was terminated when the motel for which she worked contracted out its cleaning requirements, began working for the contractor. The Court held that there was no relevant transmission of part of the business:

> In order to constitute a transmission of business, or part of the business, it must be shown that the business itself, or a severable part of the business itself had been transferred to the transmittee. It is not sufficient merely to show that, as a result of the contract entered into with the contractor, the contractor had been given a license to enter the principal's premises to perform certain functions, which are ancillary to the running of the business, by the principal.[61]

The legal approach to the issue of transmission of business between entities in the private sector was settled by the decision in *PP Consultants Pty Ltd v Finance Sector Union of Australia*.[62] The High Court held that there had been no transmission of business when a bank closed one of its local branches and made an agreement to continue some of its services through the agency of a pharmacist who in turn employed one of the bank's former employees to do this work. To establish that one business is the successor of another the two have to be compared to establish that they both have the same character, although the High Court intimated that the test may be somewhat different where the activities of a government agency are passed either to the private sector or another part of government. In the *PP Consultants Case* the pharmacy was not in the banking business though it performed some banking transactions.

However, it is also not enough merely to show an identity of activity between the two businesses as the *Gribbles Case* shows.[63] There must be a link—a transmission, succession, or assignment—between the businesses themselves. In the *Gribbles Case* a series of radiology practices performing the same activities had operated from the same premises in a medical clinic under licence from the company that ran the clinic. Under the licensing arrangement the company also supplied the radiology equipment. Radiographers were employed directly by the radiology practices, but in practice these workers stayed on working at the clinic when one radiology business left and another came. In the commercial context the 'business' of an employer, opined the majority judges, usually comprises the activities it pursues and the tangible and intangible assets

---

60 See *Workplace Relations Act 1996* (Cth), Pt 11.
61 (1982) 2 IR 448, 456–7.
62 (2000) 201 CLR 648.
63 *Minister for Employment and Workplace Relations v Gribbles Radiology Pty Ltd* (2005) 138 IR 252.

used in that pursuit.[64] Employees are not the property (assets) of a business,[65] and so could not provide the relevant link between the radiology businesses. There were no direct dealings between the radiology practices. Rather there was a series of (probably) identical licensing arrangements with another company. Thus the intercession of a third party through a quite commonplace commercial arrangement can easily result in the undermining of workers' terms and conditions of employment. Had there been some transfer of an intangible asset, like goodwill, between the radiology practices in the *Gribbles Case* the relevant link may have been established—but the reality was that it was co-location in the clinic with other medical practitioners that provided the customers, and little goodwill existed aside from that arising from the licensing arrangement.[66]

If the purpose of statutory intervention is to protect the terms and conditions of employment of employees, the transmission of business provisions as interpreted appear designed for a different era. They offer little protection to employees caught up in the kind of restructuring operations that are now commonplace, or where businesses come and go on a frequent basis. Thus labour law facilitates processes like outsourcing because it is often possible to get the same work done, and by the same people, but at a lower cost. There is therefore an economic incentive for business to reorganise in this way and in the process the law yields up its protective function for its subject.

Franchising

The commercialisation of work arrangements has come about not only through the transformation of the old employment arrangements through 'outsourcing' and 'contracting out' but because it is positively encouraged by the normative culture in the new economy, which valorises qualities of entrepreneurship and independence identified as integral to working in one's own business. This explains why working through business format franchising is now also one of the fastest areas of business growth in Australia. Its spread is also encouraged by other economic, demographic and social factors: workers who are no longer in, or are unable to get, employment but who have some investment capital realise they cannot stop working altogether and see more security in a franchising arrangement than establishing a business with little or no experience themselves.[67]

Franchising provides a structured induction for the uninitiated into the world of business. The business format franchise model imagines each franchisee as a small business entrepreneur, running his or her own business. The franchised business, however, is the clone of a model owned and strictly controlled by another organisation.[68] It thus provides a template, a complete set of comprehensive instructions, for individuals to establish their own business, thus removing some of the risks when an individual has no

---

64 Ibid, 262–63.
65 *Nokes v Doncaster Amalgamated Collieries* [1940] AC 1014.
66 Similar issues may arise where a franchise licence is extinguished and a new one issued: see *McDonald's Australia Holdings Ltd v Commissioner of State Revenue* [2004] 57 ATR 395.
67 I Bickerdyke, R Lattimore and A Madge, *Business Failure and Change: An Australian Perspective* (2000).
68 A Terry 'Business Format Franchising: The Cloning of Australian Business' in Franchisors Association of Australasia *Business Format Franchising in Australia* (1991).

previous experience in establishing and running a business. The small business franchisee pays for the right to operate a business under the name and according to the prescription of the original business franchisor. Often the franchisee is obliged to buy all supplies and services from the franchisor. The franchisee pays licence fees for the use of intellectual property (trade marks, designs, copyrights, patents) of the franchisor, and contributes to advertising and promotion budgets. Successful franchises typically depend on very strict operations manuals, which dictate the minutiae of daily business operation. There is ongoing monitoring of the arrangements by the franchisor for the period of their contractual arrangement. The control by the franchisor is just as absolute as that of the master or manager in an integrated business. And yet the form of the business structure precludes any finding of an employment relationship between franchisor and franchisee.[69] The control in the franchise arrangement is usually characterised as a quality control over the product or service rather than a control over work. Generally the franchisee adopts a corporate form—even where the franchisee will be working the business alone or in a partnership, without engaging any employees. While some larger franchised businesses—as typified by McDonald's or KFC or petrol distributors—appear to have all the trappings of commercial business operations, others are simply individuals working, perhaps as a cleaner (Bizzi Bees) or a gardener (Jim's Mowing) or a handy person (Hire-a-Hubby), often for relatively small financial returns.

Yet franchisees of whatever stripes are treated in law as a business and their work is regulated, if at all, as a purely commercial arrangement. The iron-fisted control of the franchisor over franchisees has given rise in some cases to abuses.[70] In Australia regulators have stepped in to attempt to control abuses by the promulgation of a *Franchising Code of Conduct* attached to the *Trade Practices Act 1974* (Cth). This is intended as a tool to ensure ethical standards in franchise contracts, mandating the disclosure of matters that identify business risks and costs, and allowing for cooling-off periods, dispute resolution mechanisms, and reasonable notice for termination. The code is enforceable, because non-compliance with an industry code is a matter that goes to whether conduct is unconscionable under s 51AC(4)(g) of the *Trade Practices Act 1974* (Cth).[71] So this method of regulation signals expected standards of behaviour, and provides an avenue for policing standards.

Triangular work relationships

In the industrial era work was usually structured as a bilateral arrangement, in law as a contract between two parties. However, it is possible to conceptualise many forms of work relations as trilateral or even multilateral. The indirect control of a franchisor over the work of employees of a franchisee provides one example, and the contractual chains organising outwork in the clothing industry are another.

---

69 P Rubin 'The Theory of the Firm and the Structure of the Franchise Contract' (1978) 21 *J L & Econ* 233; and G Hadfield 'Problematic Relations: Franchising and the Law of Incomplete Contracts' (1990) 42 *Stan LR* 927, 932.

70 *Australian Competition and Consumer Commission v Simply No-knead (Franchising) Pty Ltd* (2000) 104 FCR 253.

71 *Garry Rogers Motors (Australia) Pty Ltd v Subaru (Aust) Pty Ltd* [1999] ATPR ¶41–703.

The most common form of triangular work arrangement is that involving a labour-hire firm or agency. The pressure on large corporations to outsource services and the need of worker contractors for some kind of stability and continuity of work and incomes have created a niche for market intermediaries to provide broking services. Once these agencies supplied predominantly secretarial or nursing staff. However, in the new economy these trilateral work relations have proliferated and labour-hire firms now supply workers in the full range of occupations and industries. Communication services, manufacturing, property and business services are where labour-hire workers are most prevalent. People working through labour-hire firms are storepersons, forklift drivers, labourers, skilled tradespeople, seasonal fruit pickers, swimming pool attendants, information technologists, accountants, human resources practitioners and much more besides. While agency workers were once looked upon as a resource for a business to fill a short-term vacancy when one of its regular staff was absent or to respond flexibly to increased production demands over a short term, in the global era increasingly they are substituting on a more general basis for permanent employees.[72] Yet the conditions of work of the agency worker are likely to be far more precarious than those of traditional employees: whether filling a short-term need or occupying a position that is effectively ongoing, agency workers are usually engaged as casual employees or independent contractors.

Trilateral work relationships involving labour hire agencies can take a variety of forms. An agency may merely introduce workers to prospective employing businesses, sometimes acting as a 'head hunter' or at other times referring workers on its register to a business, and then leaving it to the business and the worker to determine their own future relationship.

In a second and more common arrangement, workers who are 'on the books' of the agency are offered work placements with the agency's business clients, but the agency maintains an ongoing role in the work relation. In this type of arrangement the business client usually agrees to pay the agency an amount that covers the cost of the work done by the worker placed with it and of the service provided by the agency. The worker is in turn paid by the agency. In this type of arrangement the agency may also be responsible for various other matters, such as the payment of workers' compensation levies.

In this type of agency arrangement the legal classification of the worker can be problematical. The worker may be an employee of the agency who is 'lent' or 'supplied' to the business client. The idea that an employee can be 'lent' by an employer to another business is well accepted in law. Law's caveat is that the worker must agree to the arrangement, for if it were otherwise the employee would be treated in effect as little more than a piece of the property, one of the material assets, of their employer.[73] Sometimes in these situations the workers wear the livery of the labour-hire agency and are thus identified as linked to it.[74] However, this is by no means always the case and often after being placed with the agency's business client the worker may have

---

72 See Australian Parliament *Making It Work: Inquiry into Independent Contracting and Labour-hire Arrangements* (2005); P Laplagne, M Glover and T Fry *The Growth of Labour Hire Employment in Australia* (2005); Parliament of Victoria *Enquiry into Labour Hire Employment in Victoria* (2005).

73 *Mersey Docks & Harbour Board v Coggins* [1947] AC 1.

74 *Forstaff*, above n 48.

little or no direct contact with the agency. Typically the agency is notified of the hours worked and it then ensures that appropriate payments are deposited electronically in the worker's bank account.

It seems counterintuitive to say that the worker is an employee of the agency, for there is no work performed for the agency. Indeed, the only relationship with the agency is that the worker has agreed to be hired out to the agency's business client. Little wonder that the International Labour Organization historically refused to acknowledge such arrangements considering that they contravened the principle that 'labour is not a commodity'.[75] In a real and practical sense the work relationship, as most would understand it, is between the worker and the business client who directs the worker and takes the immediate benefit of the work done. The fact that, to an outsider, the agency worker may be indistinguishable from those who are employed directly by the business simply reinforces this perception. Thus confusion can occur as to the nature of the legal relations established by such arrangements.

Initially perplexed because these triangular relationships do not neatly translate into the law's more familiar bilateral contractual arrangement, courts and tribunals sometimes declared that the worker was neither an employee nor an independent contractor but in a relationship that was *sui generis*.[76] Some were seen as working under a licensing arrangement.[77] Using the multiple indicia test in the *Family Day Care Workers Case*, the Australian Industrial Relations Commission (AIRC) found that although family day-care workers had to comply with strict requirements issued by local councils as part of the family day-care scheme these were not equivalent to an employer's control over the way they worked but were more in the nature of quality standards. In the circumstances the Commission considered that it was more likely that the parents of the children were the ones giving directions about the care of the children. The day-care workers were paid a fee directly by the parents, which was supplemented in certain circumstances by a government fee subsidy. The overall amount of the fees was set by the scheme. Thus the day-care workers were not, according to the AIRC, employees. But nor did they fit the conception of independent contractors, for there was little evidence that they were set up in business on their own account with the opportunity for profit or loss. Struggling with the tripartite nature of this work arrangement the AIRC resolved that the day-care workers operated as licensees under the scheme.

The problem with such a conclusion is that it places the worker beyond the protective reach of labour law. The potential for this was also dramatically realised in the *Troubleshooters Case*[78] where building workers supplied by a labour-hire firm to work for its builder clients were held to be neither the employees of the agency nor of its builder-clients. The building workers signed an agreement when they registered with

---

75 See also Chapter 2.

76 See eg *Construction Industry Training Board v Labour Force Ltd* [1970] 3 All ER 220. See also *Costain Building & Civil Engineering Ltd v Smith* [2000] ICR 215.

77 See eg *Cheng Yuen v Royal Hong Kong Golf Club* [1998] IR 131; and *Re Municipal Association of Victoria (Family Day Care Workers Case)* (1991) 4 CAR 35.

78 Above n 48. See also C Fenwick 'Shooting for Trouble? Contract Labour-hire in the Victorian Building Industry' (1992) 5 *AJLL* 237.

the agency that did not oblige them to accept any offer of work at a builder client of the agency. A contract for work was concluded only when a worker subsequently agreed to turn up at a particular site on a particular day. Applying the multiple indicia test, the court held that, there was no employment relation between the agency and the workers. Although the workers were paid by the agency, they did not work for the agency and the agency exercised no control over their work. Furthermore, the contractual documentation between the parties revealed, so the court found, an intention that the workers were to be regarded not as employees but as self-employed. The lack of provision for sick leave and annual leave and the failure to deduct income tax from payments made to the workers reinforced this. Nor were the workers the employees of the agency's builder-clients, for there was no wages-work bargain between them. Indeed, there was no contract at all between the workers and the builder-clients because there was no consideration from the builder-client. The only contractual obligation the builder-client had was to pay the agency. Although the workers worked under the direction of the builder-client at the building site, this control was not exercised in the course of an employment relationship. The workers were held ultimately to be independent contractors.

The arrangements in the *Troubleshooters Case* reveal how the various elements usually found in a bilateral contract of service can be effectively disaggregated and split between three parties through the use of a labour-hire firm. In this arrangement an employment relationship can be legally transformed into one where the workers are not entitled to the protections that the law provides to the employees alongside whom they work.

However, the law is not necessarily ineffectual in the face of such a trilateral relations work arrangements. Statutory protection can, and often is, expressed to extend to a wider range of workers than those who are employees. Thus in another case the same building workers were held to be the employees of Troubleshooters under the deeming provisions of accident insurance legislation.[79] The *Troubleshooters Case* may have been a hard case. Because of the nature of the industry in which they work, many building and construction workers do not have long-term employment relations with a particular business but work in a variety of different work relationships at different times on different sites. Sometimes they may be employed in the conventional way. At other times they offer their skills contracting for work as a principal, and quite often they operate in a partnership with other family members. However, it is difficult to consider that most of the builders' labourers who work like this are entrepreneurs, in business on their own account, in any real sense.

Since the *Troubleshooters Case* there have been numerous decisions regarding trilateral work arrangements involving labour-hire firms. In some cases the workers have been found to be self-employed, independent contractors,[80] in others they were employees of the labour-hire firm.[81] Only on rare occasions has it been decided that

---

79 *Accident Compensation Commission v Odco Pty Ltd* (1991) 29 FCR 104.

80 Eg *AMIEU v AICA and Sunnybrand Chickens* [2004] NSWIRComm 238.

81 Eg *Mason & Cox Pty Ltd v McCann* (1999) 74 SASR 438; *Swift Placements Pty Ltd v Workcover Authority of New South Wales (Inspector May)* (2000) 96 IR 69; *McMahon Services Pty Ltd v Cox* (2001) 78 SASR 540; *Drake Personnel Ltd v Commissioner of State Revenue* [2002] 2 VR 635; and *Forstaff*, above n 48.

the workers are employees of the business client of the agency, and these cases have all involved unusual circumstances: either where a worker approached the business client of the agency first, [82] or where a business failed to outsource effectively.[83] However, there is no reason why a worker introduced initially to a business client by an agency cannot become an employee of that business client, if the nature of the relationship changes and the worker subsequently makes an agreement directly with the business and abandons the relationship with the agency (although most labour-hire agreements either proscribe this or provide for additional payments to the agency should it occur).[84]

In the *Troubleshooters Case* it was observed that the elements of 'stability and continuity, which are a central part of every contract of service extending over a period of time, are not present'.[85] But this view of the employment relation is rooted in the past. In subsequent cases, courts and tribunals have been more willing to concede that simply because a trilateral arrangement does not have all the trappings of the old standard employment relation this does not necessarily negate the existence of an employment relationship. If labour-hire workers have no (legal) obligation to take up any offer of work and there are no guarantees that any work will be offered to them this is no different from being a 'casual'.

Elements of the multiple indicia test are often stretched to the limit when applied to trilateral work arrangements. The concept of control, for example, has been variously explained as of little importance in labour-hire cases,[86] or as referring to ultimate legal control rather than practical control,[87] although that distinction has also attracted critical comment.[88] Because of the contractual arrangements that are generally in place, courts have been consistently reluctant to rule that the labour-hire firm in paying the workers is acting as the agent of its business client.[89]

One very significant factor leading to the conclusion in the *Troubleshooters Case* that the workers were self-employed was the extensive contractual documentation between the labour-hire firm and the workers, stating an intention that there be no employment relation. In the face of a number of indicia that were inconclusive as to the nature of the relation, this was seen as a very clear factor pointing to the workers being independent contractors.[90] In other cases, the failure to make such a declaration has been treated as similarly significant and therefore pointing to an employment relationship.[91]

The documentation used by the Troubleshooters agency is easy to replicate. In *Country Metropolitan Agency Contracting Services Pty Ltd v Slater* a woman worked

---

82 See *Oanh Nguyen and A-N-T Contract Packers Pty Ltd, t/as A-N-T Personnel v Thiess Services Pty Ltd t/as Thiess Services* (2003) 128 IR 241.

83 *Damevski v Giudice*, above n 58.

84 See *Melbourne v JC Techforce Pty Ltd* (1998) 65 SAIR 372, 390–1.

85 *Troubleshooters*, above n 48, 124.

86 *Drake Personnel Ltd v Commissioner of State Revenue*, above n 81, 657.

87 *Humberstone v Northern Timber Mills*, above n 13, 404 for the distinction; and see *Mason & Cox Pty Ltd v McCann*, above n 81; and *Swift Placements Pty Ltd v Workcover Authority of New South Wales (Inspector May)* (2000) 96 IR 69.

88 *Damevski v Giudice*, above n 58, 451.

89 *Forstaff*, above n 48, 22. Cf *Damevski v Giudice*, above n 58.

90 See also *Personnel Contracting Pty Ltd t/as Tricord Personnel v Construction, Forestry, Mining and Energy Union of Workers* (2004) 141 IR 31.

91 *Forstaff*, above n 48.

through a labour-hire firm as a seasonal tomato picker under the very same contractual arrangements. She was an unskilled labourer supplying nothing but her labour and her gloves. The business client of the labour-hire firm supplied all the other equipment she used, such as a trolley and stanley knife, and directed her work. She had no capacity to delegate her work to another person and she worked in a way that was indistinguishable from the employees of the business, although she filled in a time book provided by the labour-hire firm. While there appeared little to distinguish this case from the *Troubleshooters Case*, here the court focused on 'subordination' and 'service' as the key issue and ruled that her hourly rate of $8.23, which amounted to less than the national award minimum wage, belied any assertion that she was operating as a business.[92] It held Ms Slater was covered by workers' rehabilitation and compensation legislation for the injury she received at work.

Slater is an important decision indicating that courts and tribunals can engage in a robust examination of the reality of work relations when the contractual agreement is a sham. As Justice Marshall commented in *Damevski v Giudice*:

> There is no legitimacy in arrangements which merely attempt to exploit difficult areas of law and create vehicles designed, *inter alia*, to enable employers to avoid their award and statutory obligations.[93]

Nonetheless the law's exposure of sham arrangements always reveals tension between the contractual foundation upon which the law's understanding of work relationships is based and the traditional purposes of labour law, and sometimes courts are still reluctant to allow concepts of subordination and dependency to displace express contractual provisions.

Joint employment

To assume, as most (including the ILO)[94] do, that trilateral work relations can be adequately conceptualised in terms of the conventional bilateral employment contract is to miss the challenge they pose to the law of work. In Australia sometimes legislatures reinforce this approach, requiring agencies to provide written documentation to the worker identifying their employer.[95] But this is of limited assistance when the parties assert there is no employer at all.

One alternative response to the challenge posed by triangular work relations is to use the concept of joint employment so that both the labour-hire firm and its business-client are treated as joint employers. This concept has developed in the USA in response to the use of labour-hire agencies and has been used where two parties who are separate businesses can be said to co-determine the work conditions and exercise control over the worker.[96] Although the concept has been referred to in a number of Australian cases

---

92 *Country Metropolitan Agency Contracting Services Pty Ltd v Slater* (2003) 124 IR 293, 312 and 315.
93 *Damevski v Giudice*, above n 58, 450.
94 See *Private Employment Agencies Convention 1997 (ILO No 181)* discussed in Chapter 2, p 59.
95 Eg *Employment Agents Registration Act 1993* (SA), s 20; *Employment Agents Act 1976* (WA), s 42; and *Agents Act 2003* (ACT).
96 See eg *Goodyear Tire* 312 NLRB 674 (1993). The concept has also been referred to in the United Kingdom: see eg *Brook Street Bureau (UK) Ltd v Dacas* [2004] EWCA Civ 217, [18]–[19].

it has not yet been applied here.[97] Certainly it can raise some difficulties, for instance as to responsibility for standard entitlements like annual leave or sick leave or payment of superannuation and workers' compensation levies. However, courts and tribunals have usually been more concerned by the inability to find a contract of employment between the worker and either of the parties, especially the business client of the labour-hire firm.[98] There may be greater openness to the concept of joint employment where related companies operate together in 'a firm' and the worker might reasonably be seen as employed jointly by the group.[99]

Working from home

Working from home—or, as it is sometimes referred to, outwork or home-based work—is not a new form of work arrangement, but it too is one that is flourishing anew in the new economy. By 2000 there was estimated to be almost a million home-based workers in Australia.[100] Much of the recent growth in home-based work has been facilitated by the technological and computer revolution.[101] Information technology enables a wide variety of professionals to work from home and deliver their labour to others anywhere around the globe. From medical diagnosis, to computer-assisted design work, to publishing, and all manner of accounting and clerical functions, technology has enabled the workplace to be transplanted into the home. The image of the new home-based worker, 'highly skilled' and reliant on the latest computer technology, contrasts with the more traditional image of the outworker in the clothing and textile industry, the 'unskilled' immigrant woman with minimal English language skills confined to the home by family responsibilities. The clothing and textile industry, known for its 'sweatshop' conditions since the nineteenth century, continues to operate under pressure in the new economy as tariff protection disappears and there is increased competition from goods produced more cheaply elsewhere. There are also many other poorly paid and 'unskilled' home-based workers in the new economy, performing tasks such as basic sorting, assembly and packaging work, who know they will be out of work when a machine is invented that can do their job more quickly. Others chop vegetables to deliver to local restaurants on a daily basis, already in competition with machines that can work faster but do not have the same ease of response to demand at the local level. Policies of privatisation and de-institutionalisation also mean that much care work,

---

97 *Morgan v Kittochside Nominees Pty Ltd* (2002) 117 IR 152; *Oanh Nguyen and A-N-T Contract Packers Pty Ltd, t/as A-N-T Personnel v Thiess Services Pty Ltd t/as Thiess Services* (2003) 128 IR 241; *AMWU v Waycon Services Pty Ltd* (2002) 120 IR 134; *National Union of Workers and George Weston Foods* AIRC, PR944285, 5 March 2004; *Staff Aid Services v Bianchi* AIRC, PR945924, 5 May 2004; *Personnel Contracting Pty Ltd t/as Tricord Personnel v The Construction Forestry Mining and Energy Union of Workers* (2004) 141 IR 31. See also *Oceanic Crest Shipping Company v Pilbara Harbour Services Pty Ltd* (1985) 160 CLR 626, 668; and R Cullen 'A Servant and Two Masters? The Doctrine of Joint Employment in Australia' (2003) 16 *AJLL* 359.

98 Eg *Costello v Allstaff Industrial Personnel (SA) Pty Ltd and Bridgestone TG Australia Pty Ltd* [2004] SAIRComm 13.

99 Ibid, [125]; and *Matthews v Cool-or-Cosy Pty Ltd* [2003] 136 IR 156 where the concept of joint employment was used with related companies—see further below p 173.

100 ABS *Australian Social Trends, Work—Paid Work: Working from Home*, (2002).

101 See M Pittard 'The Dispersing and Transformed Workplace: Labour Law and the Effect of Electronic Work' (2003) 16 *AJLL* 69.

previously delivered through hospitals, nursing homes or other similar institutions, has been transferred to the domestic sphere.[102]

Using the services of home-based workers offers to business many of the advantages of contracting out, from the provision of flexibility in responding to fluctuating production demands to the transferral to the worker of many costs associated with operating a factory or office. For governments, community services are much cheaper than providing full institutional support to those in need of care. From the worker's perspective, the reasons given for working from home include the need to catch up on work (15 per cent), flexible work arrangements (11 per cent), and conditions of employment (10 per cent). Although only 4 per cent of home workers give childcare or family responsibilities as the main reason for working from home, a higher proportion of women than men work from home and women working from home are more likely to have school age or younger children (42 per cent) than women who work in other locations (30 per cent).

Overwhelmingly, however, the most common reason (48 per cent) workers give for working from home is to operate a business.[103] More than two-thirds of small businesses are home-based, the majority (>65 per cent) operated by males.[104] Home-based work is certainly now rhetorically associated with freedom to organise working life in harmony with personal life and to enjoy independence in work. In short, working from home is usually described in ways that suggest it has all the advantages (and none of the disadvantages) of being an independent contractor when compared to an employee.[105]

However, the classification of home-based workers is more complex than this rhetoric suggests. Some highly skilled home-based workers may well work as independent contractors, perhaps operating as a consultant to a range of other businesses locally, nationally or internationally, in a highly successful and lucrative form of work. But in many of the other examples of home-based work there is little indication of entrepreneurial activity. Often the worker is tied to a particular enterprise, with no real capacity to decline work and few or no opportunities to work for others. These workers often provide their own equipment, such as a sewing machine or a computer or even a car, in order to obtain the work in the first place, and this underlines their economic dependence and vulnerability in the work relationship. Nor is it uncommon for a worker to be required to set up a corporate structure or submit a business number in order to get work through a complex arrangement involving a range of 'middle-men' and agents.[106]

Once the law simply assumed that home-based workers were independent contractors and not employees.[107] The origins of this assumption can be found in the nineteenth-century Factory Acts.[108] The impetus for this legislation was ostensibly to combat the evils of sweatshops. The Factory Acts restricted the employment of

---

102 See ABS *Australian Social Trends, Work: Community Service Workers* (2004).

103 ABS, above n 100.

104 ABS, above n 56.

105 ABS, above n 100, showed 42 per cent of those working from home are self-employed (compared with 13 per cent of all workers).

106 See C Stanworth 'Working at Home—A Study of Homeworking and Teleworking' (1996), 2–4.

107 *R v The Judges of the Industrial Court; Ex parte Cocks* (1968) 121 CLR 313.

108 See RJ Owens 'The Peripheral Worker: Women and the Legal Regulation of Outwork' in M Thornton (ed) *Public and Private: Feminist Legal Debates* (1995), 45.

women and children in all factories, defined as places where more than four or six people worked together. The effect of the factory legislation was also to reinforce the notion that a factory worker was a male breadwinner, for it required employers to allow women to have more breaks from work, and to provide them with special seating and to prohibit them working long hours, thus setting up economic disincentives to women's employment. Just as importantly, this legislation also confirmed for the industrial era a boundary between factory work, which was regulated by law, and home-based work, with which law was supposedly unconcerned. In the industrial era, labour law was often quite explicit about not intruding into domestic work, which was expressly excluded from the purview of the early conciliation and arbitration system, an exclusion that continues today in various statutes.[109]

Only a few Australian cases have directly raised the issue of the employment status of individual home-based workers. In *Filsell v Top Notch Fashion Pty Ltd*,[110] concerning the deduction of income tax from wages paid to women of non-English speaking background who worked in the textile industry sewing pre-cut fabric by following a template sample garment provided to them, the court held that, for the purposes of the relevant legislation, they were not employees and thus the tax did not have to be deducted from their wages. The court reasoned that there was an absence of any 'real or effective control … as to the manner in which they went about their work', they contracted to produce an outcome not a personal service because they could delegate work to others (and in fact most got assistance from family members)[111] and they could be required to redo unsatisfactory work, there was no legal obligation to take on work, and they used their own sewing machines and other assets. When they collected the materials upon which they worked from the city office of the alleged employer, a price was negotiated and a time frame set for the completion of the work. In order to meet the imposed schedule they would often rely on the assistance of other family members.

The *Top Notch Fashion* case shows how the location of work can impact on factors considered under the multiple indicia test. The transfer of work from the employer's premises to the worker's home has sometimes been enough to alter the classification of the worker from an employee to an independent contractor. In *McCoy v Glastonbury Children's Home*, for instance, when child-care workers previously employed at a children's home were contracted to perform the same work in their own homes, the control previously exercised by their employer was reconfigured as 'support' by the law and they became independent contractors.[112] In home-based work, control in so far as it exists is usually not exercised directly but is achieved nonetheless effectively through

---

109 Eg *Commonwealth Conciliation and Arbitration Act 1904* (Cth), s 4; *Sex Discrimination Act 1984* (Cth), s 14(3); *Equal Opportunity Act 1984* (SA), s 34(1); *Superannuation Guarantee (Administration) Act 1992* (Cth), s 12(11); *Industrial Relations Act 1996* (NSW), ss 5(1), 5(4) and 7; *Fair Work Act 1994* (SA), s 6; and *Industrial and Employee Relations Regulations 1994* (SA), r 5.

110 *Filsell v Top Notch Fashion Pty Ltd* (1994) 63 SASR 513.

111 Exploitative home-based work can raise serious issues regarding child labour—see B Creighton 'The ILO Convention No 138 and Australian Law and Practice Relating to Child Labour' (1996) 2 *AJHR* 293.

112 (1991) 33 AILR ¶19. Note also the classification difficulties in *The Family Day Care Workers Case*, above n 77. See L Bennett 'Women Exploitation and the Australian Child Care Industry: Breaking the Vicious Circle' (1991) 33 *JIR* 20.

indirect means such as the pressures imposed by a system of piece payments coupled with the threat of no payment for items that do not conform to a predefined standard, strict time schedules for the completion of the work, or the electronic monitoring of keystrokes at the computer. The fact that the work is performed in the home of the worker rather than at the premises of the business of the other contracting party has usually been considered of particular significance, and has lead many home-based work arrangements to be classified as not involving an employment relationship.[113]

The other concerns in the *Top Notch Fashion Case* related particularly to the question of 'mutuality of obligation', that is, whether the worker was under an obligation to take on work from the supplier of materials. In an earlier English case, *Nethermere (St Neots) Ltd v Taverna*, it was held that a very similar work arrangement to that in the *Top Notch Fashion Case* was in reality one of employment. The English court was prepared to find that there was an 'irreducible minimum of obligation on each side to create a contract of services' in an 'overall' or 'umbrella' contract obliging the company to continue to provide and pay for work and the workers to continue to accept and perform the work provided:

> I cannot see why well founded expectations of continuing homework should not be hardened or refined into enforceable contracts by regular giving and taking of work over periods of a year or more, and why outworkers should thereby become employees under contracts of service like those doing similar work at the same rate in the factory.[114]

The court found it 'wholly unrealistic' to think that a new contract was negotiated each time materials were collected, and so it assimilated the work relationship to that of a traditional ongoing employment contract. In English law, however, a lack of 'mutuality of obligation' usually means that the worker is not treated as an employee, whereas in Australia this is usually simply considered to be the nature of casual employment.[115]

The old assumption in Australian labour law that those working from home were independent contractors has had 'widespread material effects' especially for those in the clothing and textile industry.[116] For many years work in that industry has been part of a large unregulated 'informal economy', where vulnerable workers were paid trivial amounts for working long hours. However, by the mid-1980s, after much campaigning by trade unions and women's groups concerned at the increasing incidence of outwork, Australian labour law began to recognise that those working at home in the clothing and textile industries were employees deserving of the protection of the law.[117] To avoid any doubt over the classification of outworkers some statutes have incorporated definitions making it clear that outworkers are employees for the purposes of the legislation.[118] The definition in the *Industrial Relations Act 1999* (Qld) is typical where Sch 5 provides that:

---

113 See R Hunter 'The Regulation of Independent Contractors: A Feminist Perspective' (1992) 5 *CBLJ* 165.

114 [1984] ICR 612, 622 and 623. See also *Airfix Footwear Ltd v Cope* [1978] ICR 1210.

115 See below n 137.

116 Hunter, above n 9, 314.

117 See *Re Clothing Textile and Footwear Award 1982* (1987) 19 IR 416.

118 See eg *Industrial Relations Act 1996* (NSW), s 5(2)(d); *Industrial Relations Act 1999* (Qld), Sch 5; and *Fair Work Act 1994* (SA), s 5.

'outworker' means

a person engaged, for someone else's calling or business, in or about a private residence
or other premises that are not necessarily business or commercial premises, to

(a)   pack, process, or work on articles or material, or

(b)   carry out clerical work.

Some legislative interventions have been even bolder, extending the definition of employee
to those outworkers who work through a corporate entity, thus protecting those who are
forced to assume a business and corporate identity in order to get work.[119]

A problem with any such legislative 'deeming' definition is that it can be both
underinclusive and overinclusive. It is underinclusive because often it does not cover all
home-based workers. For instance, community service workers providing care to people
in their own homes would not be covered by the above definition. It is overinclusive in
so far as some home-based workers who are genuinely in business on their own account
nonetheless may fall within it.

By far the more difficult problem is ensuring that any regulatory protection is
effective. An early strategy was to incorporate a rebuttable presumption that workers
who undertook outwork were covered by the relevant regulation.[120] However, the
legacy of the practices of the informal economy was strongly entrenched and concerns
about exploitation persisted.[121] Because of the organisation of outwork through complex
contractual supply chains, to be effective regulation must often place legal responsibility
on a number of actors.

This requires a more sophisticated regulatory approach.[122] In the latest moves to
protect outworkers, legislation and awards incorporate a code of practice, either voluntary
or mandatory, which is coordinated on an industry basis and targets everyone in the
supply chain between the outworker and up to and including the retailer. The measures
include the statutory importation of contractual duties and use the power relations in
complex supply chains to ensure the protection of outworkers. The code of practice was
developed in the first instance by the Textile Clothing and Footwear Union of Australia,
and the regulatory strategy also seeks to raise public awareness about the conditions
associated with outwork. This comprehensive regulatory approach—integrating
commercial, consumer, industrial relations, workers' compensation and occupational
health and safety bodies of law—is aimed at ensuring decent pay and conditions, by

---

119 Eg *Fair Work Act 1994* (SA), s 5(1)(b).

120 *Re Clothing Textile and Footwear Award 1982* (1987) 19 IR 416.

121 See Textile Clothing and Footwear Union of Australia *The Hidden Cost of Fashion* (1995); Australian
Parliament, Senate Economics References Committee *Outworkers in the Garment Industry* (1996); New
South Wales Department of Industrial Relations Issues Paper *Behind the Label—The NSW Government
Clothing Outwork Strategy* (1999); and The State of Victoria *Independent Report of the Victorian Industrial
Relations Taskforce* (2000), Ch 8. See also the Fairwear website at <www.fairwear.org.au>.

122 See *Industrial Relations (Ethical Clothing Trades) Act 2001* (NSW) and the mandatory code of practice
attached to it, the *Ethical Clothing Trades—Extended Responsibility Scheme*, which regulates those who fail
to sign and comply with the voluntary *Homeworkers Code of Practice* aimed at ensuring compliance with
the relevant industrial award; and *Outworkers (Improved Protection) Act 2003* (Vic).

See also C Fenwick 'Protecting Victoria's Vulnerable Workers: New Legislative Developments' (2003)
16 *AJLL* 198; I Nossar, R Johnstone and M Quinlan 'Regulating Supply Chains to Address Occupational
Health and Safety Problems Associated with Precarious Employment: The Case of Home-based Clothing
Workers in Australia' (2004) 17 *AJLL* 137; and R Johnstone and T Wilson 'Take Me to Your Employer:
The Organisational Reach of Occupational Health and Safety Regulation' (2006) 19 *AJLL* 59.

ensuring conformity to minimum work standards and securing the occupational heath and safety of home-based workers that to date has proved an intractable problem. Because of the vulnerability of outworkers and some of the recent regulatory improvements initiated by the States to protect them, political pressure saw the final version of the *Work Choices* legislation preserve the power of the States to regulate outwork.[123]

Despite a concerted effort to draw some of those in traditional outwork into the fold of law's protection, there is also evidence of a disinclination to intercede in the protection of the new home-based worker of the global era. The *Workplace Relations Act 1996* (Cth) only permits the regulation of outworker conditions in federal awards where it is necessary to ensure that they are fair and reasonable when compared with those of workers who perform the same kind of work at the employer's business or commercial premises.[124] Thus basic award safety net minimum conditions cannot apply to home-based work in the new economy unless it is a substitute for work normally done in the factory or the office. Likewise many of these new workers do not come within the extended legislative definitions of 'outworker' in State legislation and so may have additional difficulties in proving they are employees, thus risking further their access to the basic legislative protections granted to other workers.

There also appears to be some reluctance on the part of some employers to allow employees to work from home. Paradoxically, then, just as organising home-based work is becoming easier from a technical perspective, employers are beginning to resist it: they are either unwilling to cede some of the control they have when the worker is at the office or apprehensive at their ability to fulfil some of the obligations, including those governing occupational health and safety, that exist in relation to employees working from home.[125] Certainly there is little evidence that employers are willing to grant their employees a 'right' to work from home, even when the flexibility this form of working offers would help resolve issues such as work/family conflict.[126] Working from home for employees thus remains tightly controlled through the managerial discretion of the employer and is very much a privilege accorded only to 'high trust' employees.[127] The willingness of business to contract with independent contractors working from home not only contrasts with the reluctance to allow employees to work from home—it also becomes another force ensuring that working from home becomes the domain of workers who by force of circumstances must try to work 'on their own account'.

The divide between 'work' and 'home' is becoming a more pressing challenge for labour law. As more women enter the paid workforce there is a growth in the 'outsourcing' of 'housework' so that workers in the paid labour market now do many domestic tasks.[128] When this work is done by an employee of a business operating in

---

123 *Workplace Relations Act 1996* (Cth), s 16(3)(d).

124 *Workplace Relations Act 1996* (Cth), s 513(1)(o).

125 See R Johnstone 'Paradigm Crossed? The Statutory Occupational Health and Safety Obligations of the Business Undertaking' (1999) 12 *AJLL* 73.

126 See *State of Victoria v Schou* [2004] 8 VR 120.

127 See Pittard, above n 101; and M Pittard 'Rethinking Place of Work: Federal Labour Law Framework for Contemporary Home-based Work and its Prospects in Australia' in J Murray (ed) *Work, Family and the Law* (2005).

128 Pocock, above n 52.

the marketplace they may be acknowledged and protected by the law. However, this is not usually the case if the worker is employed directly by the person wanting the 'housework' services. Like the servants of old, the domestic worker in the new economy is very often in a vulnerable position. Many statutes continue to exclude from protection those who are employed either by their own family members or by others to perform work for 'domestic purposes' in a private residence.[129] If these home-based workers are exploited it is often difficult to find an appropriate legal remedy for their situation. In one reported instance a young Indonesian woman, Ms Masri, was brought to Australia to act as a domestic servant, performing the full range of domestic duties, including cooking, cleaning, washing, gardening, tidying her employers' offices and taking care of the children.[130] For this work she was paid only $5000 over four years. Her employers argued that they merely facilitated her entry to Australia and only promised to help her to learn English so that she could marry an Australian. They said that she had agreed to work on a voluntary basis. However, the tribunal found that she was 'trapped' in this work relationship: she was poorly educated, brought into the country illegally and was told by the family not to speak about her work to anyone. In *Masri's Case* a remedy was provided under the New South Wales' unfair contracts jurisdiction and her employers were ordered to pay her $95 000, but such legal action even if available is rarely easily accessible by those such as Ms Masri who work in the 'informal economy'.[131]

Casual and part-time workers

The exponential growth of casual work has been the most striking characteristic of the Australian workforce in recent years. While it is difficult to calculate with exactitude the number of casual workers in Australia, it is estimated that approximately 28 per cent of the workforce is employed on a casual basis.[132] The rate of increase in casual employment was at its strongest in the 1980s and early 1990s, and although no longer growing with the same intensity it remains a strongly entrenched feature of the Australian labour market. Many labour-hire or home-based workers are also working as casuals. Casuals may also be employed directly by a business. There is an almost inexhaustible variety of casual work: it can be fulltime or part-time; it can range from a single engagement for a few hours to an ongoing relationship with the same employer over many years; and casuals are to be found doing everything from manual work, to service work, to professional work.

Defining a casual employee is not without difficulty because, as Anthony O'Donnell shows in a very careful analysis of the problem, the description 'casual' can have different legal meanings and these do not necessarily reproduce social meanings.[133] At common

---

129 See above n109.

130 *Masri v Nenny Santouso* (2004) 134 IR 184.

131 Cf *Workplace Relations Act 1996* (Cth), s 832, which does not cover contracts where work is performed for the 'private and domestic purposes of the other party to the contract'. See also G Orr 'Unauthorised Workers: Labouring beneath the Law?' in C Arup et al (eds) *Labour Law and Labour Market Regulation* (2006).

132 ABS, *Year Book Australia: Labour* 'Feature Article—Changes in Types of Employment', *Australian Labour Market Statistics* Cat no 6105.0, October 2004. See also *Australian Bulletin of Labour*, Special Issue on Casual Employment vol 27, no 2, 2000.

133 A O'Donnell '"Non-standard" Workers in Australia: Counts and Controversies' (2004) 17 *AJLL* 89. See also *CPSU v State of Victoria* (2000) 95 IR 54.

law there is no differentiation between casual and other employees. However, frequently it is necessary to identify a 'casual' as defined in a statute or award or workplace agreement. The problem for the law in understanding casual workers is that their patterns of work diverge from those of traditional employees in the industrial era. The contract of employment is a wages-work bargain in which the employee promises to work as directed by the employer: there must be between the parties a 'mutuality of obligation'.[134] However, casual work does not quite fit this picture even where the work relationship is a long-standing one. Although in practice, casuals who work for a particular employer may always accept an offer of work, knowing that a refusal will likely result in no further offers, they are generally under no legal obligation to do so. Courts have sometimes treated this as pointing away from the worker being an employee altogether.[135] The problem of mutuality of obligation and casual employment remains a difficult issue in English law.[136] In Australia there seems to be an acceptance that although there is no legal obligation on a casual to take work offered, this does not necessarily indicate that they are not an employee.[137] In terms of the conceptualising of casual work, the common law in Australia tends to understand that the work relation is formed anew, that is, through a new contract, every time the casual accepts a particular offer of work—say for a certain day, or for a particular shift.[138] This a rather inadequate understanding especially where the reality of a casual work relationship is that work is offered and accepted over the long term even if on an irregular basis.

The application to the casual worker of the indicia that law uses to distinguish employees from independent contractors may also present some difficulties. Casual employees are not integrated, at least not usually in any strong way, into the business for which they work; they often supply their own tools and assets, providing their own vehicle to deliver pizzas for example; they often work for a variety of businesses; they are sometimes paid for the completion of tasks, rather than the hours worked; they are not paid during absences for holidays or illness; and they bear many of the risks of the business operating in the marketplace. Casual work thus often has many of the indicia considered to be hallmarks of independent contracting.

The difficulty of distinguishing between independent contractors and casuals is illustrated by the work arrangements in an abattoir as revealed in *Macro Investments Pty Ltd v Amor*.[139] Here a group of boners, who had previously worked for another abattoir, approached the abattoir for work as independent contractors. The boners were part of the production process at the abattoir, where boning commenced at a fixed time every day. There was no fixed start time of work for any particular boner and no fixed

---

134 See above p 159. In *Dietrich v Dare* (1980) 30 ALR 407 a majority of the High Court held there was no 'mutuality of obligation' in an arrangement to pay a disabled person $2 per hour if he could paint a house, and hence he was neither an employee or an independent contractor.

135 Eg *Troubleshooters*, above n 48.

136 *Carmichael v National Power Plc* [1999] 1 WLR 2042, 2047; and *Brook Street Bureau (UK) Ltd v Daccas* [2004] EWCA Civ 217, [49]. See S Fredman 'Precarious Norms for Precarious Workers' in Fudge and Owens (eds), above n 7.

137 *Forstaff*, above n 48.

138 See eg *Troubleshooters*, above n 48, 126 and *Forstaff*, above n 48, 23.

139 [2004] SAIRComm 9.

finishing time. A certain number of carcasses had to be boned each day. Payment was on a per carcass basis, from which no income tax was deducted. These boners had no paid annual leave or sick leave; no superannuation was paid on their behalf; no workers' compensation levies were paid. The boners were free to work elsewhere; they provided their own tools; they each obtained an ABN when the Goods and Services Tax (GST) system was introduced; and although they wore the clothing provided by the abattoir, they paid for it to be laundered. The boners operated collectively for some matters, nominating one of their group to liaise with the abattoir. Although the abattoir had the right to say whether a particular worker was taken on for work, when a vacancy arose the boners nominated workers who might fill it; absences were reported to the group rather than to the abattoir and the group decided how many of them were required to work on any one day. Thus many of the indicia seemed equally consistent with the boners being independent contractors or casual employees. In the end the tribunal determined the boners were casuals, because it was difficult to say that these semi-skilled workers were carrying on a trade or business of their own in which they were building goodwill. As to the way in which their work was organised, the tribunal characterised the boners as operating in a 'self-directed work group' with the abattoir ultimately overseeing the quality of their work to ensure that it complied with health and export regulations.

The marginalisation of casual workers derives usually not so much from their lack of employment status, but from the inferior conditions they are accorded compared to those of the standard worker of old. From the beginning of the conciliation and arbitration system award entitlements constructed employment protection to reward length and stability of service in order to ensure a breadwinner worker was able to fulfil his familial obligations.[140] The legacy of this is that law often still excludes casuals from its benefits or interposes extra qualifying hurdles on them.

For the purposes of benefits available under awards and workplace agreements, the definition of 'casual' in those instruments is critical and it can be, and often is, different from other legal understandings. These instruments commonly define a casual as one 'who is engaged and paid as such'.[141] This means that the determination of the worker's status for the purposes of these industrial instruments is in the hands of the employing entity at the beginning of the relationship and takes no account of the fact that the work relationship may become an ongoing, long-term one. One of the most important consequences that flows from the different meanings given to 'casual' both in law and colloquially is that workers and employers can often believe, mistakenly, that a particular worker is a casual for all purposes. This can often lead to confusion as to legal entitlements, and at worst confusion facilitates exploitation.

The reasons for the strong growth of casual work in Australia are a matter of contest. Because the labour market is constructed through law, it is significant that historically the vast majority of awards in the conciliation and arbitration system made provision for casual employment. Casual work was first provided for in industries

140 See Owens 'Women, "Atypical" Work Relationships and the Law' above n 9, 410ff.
141 *The Award Simplification Decision* (1997) 75 IR 272.

where the work was intermittent, like loading and unloading ships, but eventually it extended to most other industries. However, as a potential threat to the concept of the worker as 'breadwinner', casual work was also carefully controlled with awards historically limiting both the numbers of casuals to a certain proportion of the employer's workforce and the length of their engagement. Furthermore, the casual loading was expected to function both as a wage supplement for the worker, who by virtue of the nature of the industry and work was unable to be a 'breadwinner', and as a deterrent lest that normative conception of the employee was challenged. In the industrial era few awards provided for part-time employment, but where they did, this work was usually restricted by reference to minimum and maximum hours (often equivalent to three to four days' work per week) and to a small proportion of the workforce. Only gradually did this change.[142]

From the mid-1990s award restrictions on casual and part-time employment were prohibited in some jurisdictions as part of the deregulation of the labour market.[143] The *Work Choices* amendments consolidate further this 'deregulation', prohibiting any award provisions that allow conversion from casual to ongoing employment or regulate the engagement and terms of work of other non-standard workers, such as labour-hire workers or independent contractors.[144] However, the huge growth in the numbers of casual workers in Australia had already occurred prior to 1996, and with the culture of utilising casuals well established, part-time work has continued to be offered usually on a casual basis.

Demand from business is plainly an important reason for the growth of casual work. There can be many advantages to firms employing casuals. Casuals enable the enterprise to respond to market fluctuations in demand for goods or services, without carrying the ongoing costs of maintaining a larger workforce during periods of lower demand. In many industries, time and task are now closely allied, with a small core of workers retained to perform the full range of duties and supplemented by a large number of casual workers at the periphery of the organisation. If there is an abundant supply of casual labour, skilled to the requisite level and readily available to respond to any call to work, production and service quality is not compromised. The additional cost of the casual loading is generally lower than the various costs of workplace benefits, including training, where workers are employed on an ongoing basis. Thus ultimately many of the risks and costs of operating in the marketplace are transferred from business to the worker through casual work.

Another common explanation for the growth of casual work is that it is a response to the demands of the unprecedented number of women who have entered the labour market in recent decades. The growth of casual employment and the feminisation of the labour market are related. The concentration of women in casual work has always been high. By the late 1980s nearly 30 per cent of all employed women worked on a casual basis. The proportion of women employed casually has not increased markedly in recent

---

142 See Owens, above n 9, 406ff.
143 See eg *Workplace Relations Act 1996* (Cth), former s 89A(4) and (5)(b).
144 *Workplace Relations Act 1996* (Cth), s 515(1)(b)–(h) and (2)–(3). See further, Chapter 7.

years. However, as casual employment has become more entrenched in the labour market its net has been cast wider: in the 1990s the proportion of men employed casually rose from 13 per cent to 22 per cent. There has been an increase too in the number of young people in casual work, and in the number of older casual workers. But the patterns of casual employment over a lifetime show a striking gendered pattern. Male employees tend to have casual jobs in their youth and towards the end of their working life, but nearly three-quarters of male employees still continue to occupy the traditional position of a fulltime worker with ongoing employment and that proportion is even higher (77 per cent) among those in the 25–34 years age range, and higher again (82 per cent) amongst those who are aged 35–54 years. On the other hand, the highest proportion of women working on a fulltime ongoing basis is only 58 per cent and is to be found only among those in the 25–34 years age group. Consistently across all age groups more than one-third of women work on a part-time basis and most of these are casuals.[145]

The explanation behind the statistics is often said to be that casual work provides workers with flexibility. It allows, for example, young people to earn income while studying. Equally, it is said, casual work enables women to fulfil their dual work responsibilities in the marketplace and the home because the flexibility it offers can better accommodate women's responsibility for social reproduction.[146] Certainly the reality is that regardless of their participation in the labour market, women continue to be primarily responsible for work in the home, especially the care of children, and policies of privatisation have also meant an increase in women's responsibilities for unpaid care work, particularly for elderly parents and family members with disabilities.[147] Casual work is thus said to be a matter of choice, and its flexibility claimed as a 'win–win' for business and worker alike.

Choice is, however, always bounded. Workers may 'choose' a non-standard work arrangement such as casual work for a variety of reasons: because of their family responsibilities, because they cannot afford to retrain after a career break, because they envisage too many difficulties in setting up their own business, or because they experience subtle discrimination based on age, race, gender or disability. But for most, and especially for women workers, there is little else but casual work available.[148] While the resolution of conflict between work and family may well be an important aspiration of many (especially women) workers, and while many other workers may wish to work flexibly for a wide range of reasons, it is difficult to conclude that workers choose the second-class conditions that attach to casual work (unless the rate of pay is so low that the promise of the casual loading proves irresistible). Most casuals are not entitled to basic employment benefits—like paid annual leave and paid sick leave. Casuals may lack the continuity of service to enable them to access unpaid parental leave or long service leave. They are often unable to seek redress when they are effectively dismissed or made redundant. They may work so few hours that they never earn enough to establish the

---

145 ABS, *Australian Social Trends—Work* Cat no 4102.0, 2000; and ABS, *Year Book Australia Labour Employed Persons* Cat no 1310.0, 2005.

146 Australian Government, *Work and Family: The Importance of Workplace Flexibility in Promoting Balance between Work and Family* (2005).

147 ABS, *Australian Social Trends—Work, Community Service Workers* (2004). See also RJ Owens 'Taking Leave: Work and Family in Australian Law and Policy' in Conaghan and Rittich (eds), above n 10.

148 See M Smith and P Ewer *Choice and Coercion: Women's Experience of Casual Employment* (1999).

threshold income that requires an employer to make superannuation contributions for them. While it is true that some 'long-term' casuals may have access to certain award-, agreement- or statutory-based workplace rights and benefits, this is usually only where they can establish work patterns that replicate those of the traditional employee, such as regular work for a specified qualifying period and an expectation of ongoing employment. Although many casuals can satisfy these criteria, they are easily manipulable by employers and in any event can be less easy to establish when the worker is employed through, for instance, a labour-hire firm. The distinction between 'true casuals' and 'long-term casuals' is thus a precarious one on which to base access to labour law's protections.

At the heart of the problem of the casualisation of the Australian workforce lies a lack of quality part-time work available in Australia.[149] However, while part-time work is a less marginalised form of non-standard work,[150] its gendered construction as 'women's work' still gives rise to some not so subtle forms of disadvantage ranging from assumptions about the commitment of part-time workers to the enterprise and beliefs about the underlying incompatibility of work and family responsibilities.

The firm and its employees

The configuration of 'the firm'

An examination of the subject of the law of work would be incomplete without some consideration of the nature of business enterprises, and the role of work and the workers within business organisations. After all, as Margaret Blair has identified: 'To a casual observer, the relationship between a firm and its employees would seem to be a central, perhaps defining, feature of the firm itself.'[151] And yet in the common law world, the law concerning business associations, and especially corporations, has often largely ignored the role of employees other than those who also perform the functions of directors. Traditionally, the fields of labour law and corporate law have been treated as mutually exclusive specialities.[152] In the twenty-first century, however, an understanding of the subject of the law of work requires an increasingly sophisticated understanding of corporations law, trade practices regulation and general commercial law.

The place of the employee in corporate law

Corporate law discourse tends to bifurcate the contributions of participants into the 'insiders' who provide equity—these investors are treated as the 'owners' of the company—and the 'outsiders' who provide resources under contract with the corporation.

---

149 See B Pocock, J Buchanan and I Campbell *Securing Decent Employment: Policy Options for Casual and Part-time Workers* (2003); and see *Lab Ind*, Special Issue on Part-time Work, vol 15, no 3, 2005. See further Chapter 7.

150 See B Creighton 'Employment Security and Atypical Work in Australia' (1995) 16 *Comp LLJ* 285, 300.

151 MM Blair 'Firm-specific Human Capital and Theories of the Firm' in MM Blair and MJ Roe (eds) *Employees & Corporate Governance* (1999), 58.

152 Recent scholarship is beginning to reddress this: see eg R Mitchell, A O'Donnell and I Ramsay 'Shareholder Value and Employee Interests: Intersections between Corporate Governance, Corporate Law and Labour Law' (2005).

The insiders include the shareholders who contribute capital (or in the case of unpaid shares, give a promise to contribute capital); the directors whom the shareholders appoint to manage the corporation's business enterprise and its relationships with outsiders; and of course the corporation itself, which upon registration becomes a legal person in its own right, separate from its shareholders and directors—even where there is but one shareholder and a single director. Financiers who lend money, trade suppliers who provide goods and services, and workers (whether employees or independent contractors) who provide labour, are all conceptualised as external creditors of the corporation.

According to this theory of the corporation, it is the shareholders who take the greatest risk in corporate enterprise. Shareholders rank last in the queue in a liquidation of corporate assets. Shareholders enjoy limited liability: that is, they are not obliged to contribute to meet the corporation's debts beyond their initial agreed investment, but they are at risk of losing all they have contributed to the enterprise. Other creditors, including employees, are entitled to claim payment for any debts owed to them out of the assets of the corporation before shareholders may have any return of capital. Because shareholders are seen as the 'risk takers', corporate law in the USA, the United Kingdom and Australia has traditionally focused on techniques to ensure the loyalty of company directors to these vulnerable owners of capital, who have entrusted their investment to the control of others. Contemplation of the role and responsibilities of workers within corporate enterprise rarely occupies much space in Australian, United States and English corporate law texts.[153]

Contemporary Australian corporate law reflects this dominant paradigm. The Corporate Law Economic Reform Program (CLERP) begun in the 1990s has been predicated on a shareholder-centred model of the corporation, where directors' accountability to investors in the company has been the principal concern. The adversarial, enterprise bargaining model of industrial relations supports this model of the corporation. The employer corporation, represented by its director agents, sits on the opposite side of the bargaining table from the worker representatives. The parties are locked in an inevitable struggle to further their own necessarily opposing interests in negotiation over wages and conditions.[154]

Increasingly, however, new theories of corporate governance are challenging this dominant paradigm.[155] These theories propose a concept of corporate responsibility and accountability to a broader range of stakeholders in the corporate enterprise, including the social welfare of the community generally, consumer interests, environmental concerns, and workers' interests in health and safety and security. This contest is not entirely new. It reinvigorates a debate from the 1930s. In the wake of the Great Depression,

---

153 See K Greenfield 'The Place of Workers in Corporate Law' (1998) 39 *Bost CLR* 283. One exception is JE Parkinson *Corporate Power and Responsibility: Issues in the Theory of Company Law* (1993).

154 J Hill 'At the Frontiers of Labour Law and Corporate Law: Enterprise Bargaining, Corporations and Employees' (1995) 23 *Fed LR* 204.

155 See eg L Johnson 'New Approaches to Corporate Law' (1993) 50 *Wash LLR* 1713; K van Wezel Stone 'Labour and Corporate Structure: Changing Conceptions and Emerging Possibilities' (1988) 55 *U Chi LR* 73; J Hill 'Public Beginnings and Private Ends—Should Corporate Law Privilege the Interests of Shareholders?' (1998) 9 *AJCL* 21.

E Merrick Dodd Jr championed a view that the management of large companies bore a duty (after ensuring no more than a 'fair' rate of return to stockholders) to ensure that the corporation operated 'in the public interest', 'as a great and good citizen should'.[156] This attracted a trenchantly critical response from one of the earliest law and economics scholars, Adolf Berle, who held fast to the doctrine that the directors were accountable only to shareholders.[157]

Berle's view affirmed an earlier finding of the Michigan Supreme Court in *Dodge v Ford Motor Co*[158] in 1919. In that case, Henry Ford's managerial decision to provide higher wages and better working conditions for the automotive workers in his factories was successfully challenged by shareholders demanding a higher level of dividends—ironically these shareholders were the Dodge brothers who were planning to set up a rival automobile manufacturing plant. Much the same attitude prevailed on the other side of the Atlantic. In the notorious case of *Parke v Daily News Ltd*,[159] an English court found in favour of a minority shareholder who argued that the company's directors were in breach of directors' duties to the company when they caused the company to pay retrenchment benefits to long-serving employees. The company had no strictly enforceable legal obligation to make those payments, so the decision of the directors was treated as an impermissible exercise of directors' powers.

Support for a wider stakeholder approach to corporate governance has grown in recent times in response to a number of high profile corporate scandals, which have unveiled a serious fallacy in the traditional model. The fallacy is that shareholders are always the real risk takers, and that outsiders' contractual claims must be satisfied before the entrepreneurial risk takers may claim their profits. In too many cases, practice has shown that corporate insiders have quarantined or syphoned off the wealth of the enterprise for themselves, leaving outside creditors—including workers—seriously out of pocket. This can happen because of the doctrine of separate legal personality for corporations, and the law's treatment of corporate groups.[160]

Separate legal personality of corporations

It is trite law that a corporation is a separate legal person from the shareholders who created it. As the *Salomon Case*[161] so poignantly illustrated, shareholders are able to contract with their creation, and can secure their own investment in the company by clothing themselves as secured creditors. Many business operators take advantage of this doctrine to set up companies with very little capital—the classic 'two dollar company'—and contribute working capital by way of secured loans. The owners of the shares in such companies have little at stake in the enterprise. If the capital is provided by way of loans, and these are secured by charges over company assets then these

---

156 EM Dodd Jr 'For Whom Are Corporate Managers Trustees?' (1932) 45 *Harv LR* 1154.
157 See AA Berle Jr 'For Whom Corporate Managers Are Trustees: A Note' (1932) 45 *Harv LR* 1365.
158 170 NW 668 (Mich 1919).
159 [1962] Ch 927.
160 See generally JH Farrer 'Legal Issues Involving Corporate Groups' (1998) 16 *C & S LJ* 184.
161 *Salomon v A Salomon and Co Ltd* [1897] AC 22.

charges rank ahead of unsecured creditors in an insolvency. To the extent that they are fixed charges, they rank ahead of priority creditors under s 556 of the *Corporations Act 2001* (Cth). Employees entitled to monetary payments for outstanding amounts say in relation to wages, holiday pay, long service leave or redundancy payments are priority creditors. Who are the real risk takers in such an enterprise? This very common method of corporate financing ensures that shareholders enjoy all the benefits of limited liability, without any need to take any serious entrepreneurial risk. The risk of insolvency is most likely to be borne by the real outsiders—trade creditors who have provided goods and services on credit and have not been able to take security, and workers who have agreed to take some of their remuneration for work in the form of deferred benefits, such as leave entitlements and redundancy benefits.

Corporate groups

The scope for strategic structuring of corporate finance to minimise risk to the owners is multiplied by the use of corporate groups. Australian corporate law treats each subsidiary and related entity in a corporate group as a separate legal person.[162] Each entity is responsible for its own obligations. Creditors (including employees) of one entity cannot launch a claim against another member of the corporate group unless they can prove one of the extremely rare exceptions to the doctrine of separate legal personality, so as to persuade a court to lift the corporate veil.[163] This is so, even where one corporation is a wholly owned subsidiary of another, and shares the same directors.

Controllers of corporate groups can take advantage of this doctrine to quarantine valuable assets in one subsidiary of a group, while ensuring that all of the risky aspects of the business are run through another subsidiary. The action of the James Hardie corporate group in seeking to make provision through only one (underfunded) part of the corporate group for its former workers suffering from asbestos-related diseases caused by their employment is one example of this. Only after a Royal Commission handed down its findings resulting in extensive negative publicity were negotiations conducted with the Australian Council of Trade Unions (ACTU) and a move made by the Hardie group to make more adequate provision for its liabilities to the former employees.[164] The 1998 Waterfront dispute is another example where a corporate restructure was designed to quarantine the assets of the group from obligations to employees.

The waterfront dispute

Prior to September 1997, National Stevedores Holdings Pty Ltd (itself a subsidiary of a listed public company called Lang Corporation Ltd) was parent company to a group of separate subsidiary companies operating in a number of Australian ports. Each of these local subsidiaries owned its own business assets, entered into contracts directly with

---

162 *Walker v Wimborne* (1976) 137 CLR 1, 6–7; *Industrial Equity Ltd v Blackburn* (1977) 137 CLR 567; *Pioneer Concrete Services Ltd v Yelnah* (1986) 5 NSWLR 254.

163 See Farrer, above n 160. See also *Re Willow Fashions (Australia) Pty Ltd (In Liq); Leveque v Downey as Liquidator of Willow Fashions (Australia) Pty Ltd (In Liq)* (unreported, Supreme Court of Victoria, Hayne J, 27 April 1995).

164 See *Report of the Special Commission of Inquiry into the Medical Research and Compensation Foundation* (2004).

shipping companies, and employed its own staff. On 17 September 1997 the group was restructured so that one subsidiary company, Patrick Stevedores Operations (No 2) Pty Ltd, bought and subsequently owned all the valuable fixed assets from these subsidiaries. The purchase moneys were used by the subsidiaries to buy back their own shares from other group companies and to repay debts, so that shareholder funds in these employer companies were substantially reduced.

A second company, Patrick Stevedores Operations Pty Ltd, became the parent of each of the several employer companies, and it entered into non-exclusive Labour Supply Agreements (LSAs) with each of the employer companies, whereby it purchased labour to fulfil its obligations under contracts with outside exporting and importing firms. These LSAs contained a clause, allowing Patrick Stevedores Operations Pty Ltd to terminate the agreements without notice if there was any interruption to the supply of labour due to industrial action. The inevitable industrial action occurred when the Maritime Union of Australia learned that Patrick's was planning to enter into a LSA with a new stevedoring firm, set up by the National Farmers Federation and staffed by non-union labour trained especially for that purpose in Dubai. The strike triggered the termination clause, the employer companies lost their contracts with their parent and consequently had no work and very few assets to pay wages. The controllers, anxious to avoid insolvent trading liability, then put the employer companies into voluntary administration. It was the administrators who took steps to dismiss all the workers.

This transparent scheme to emasculate a strong trade union and restaff the waterfront with non-union labour was eventually thwarted by a successful application for an injunction based on an allegation that the various participants in the scheme had conspired to breach the then recently enacted freedom of association provisions in Pt XA of the *Workplace Relations Act* 1996 (Cth).[165] Ultimately the matter was settled out of court. The risks of litigation proved too costly and unpredictable to both sides. Nevertheless, it is clear that, without the freedom of association rights in the *Workplace Relations* legislation, the scheme may well have succeeded. Yet as David Noakes concluded in an early study of the waterfront dispute, it appeared that the Patrick's group of companies and its directors did not infringe any sections of the *Corporations Law*,[166] although arguably the provisions introduced in Pt 5.8A of the *Corporations Law* in July 2000, which prohibit directors from entering into uncommercial transactions for the purpose of avoiding obligations to employees, might catch some aspects of the Patrick's restructure if it happened now.[167]

Tensions between corporate and labour law

The waterfront dispute provided a shocking lesson for ordinary Australian workers. It demonstrated that the managers of large corporations could legally pursue such

---

165 *Patrick Stevedores Operations No 2 Pty Ltd v MUA* (1998) 195 CLR 1. See further Chapter 10.
166 D Noakes 'Dogs on the Wharves: Corporate Groups and the Waterfront Dispute' (1999) 11 *AJCL* 27, 62. Note: the Corporations Law became the *Corporations Act* in July 2001.
167 See D Noakes 'Corporate Groups and the Duties of Directors: Protecting the Employee of the Insolvent Employer?' (2001) 29 *ABLR* 124.

tactics in fulfilling their primary obligation to maximise profits and protect the capital of corporate shareholders. This kind of corporate group structure, quarantining assets for shareholders in one company separate from the company employing workers, has become a common strategy. It does not, however, always succeed in avoiding obligations to a workforce. In some circumstances, protective industrial laws create obstacles.

The waterfront dispute was by no means the first act of corporate manipulation designed to privilege investors' interests over those of workers. One of the earliest challenges to the *Commonwealth Conciliation and Arbitration Act 1904* (Cth) was brought by an employer company that sought to use the principle of the separate legal personality of the corporation to avoid an obligation to pay award wages to staff. The transmission of business provision in the Act provided that a person taking over a business as a transmittee, assignee or successor would be bound by any award binding the transmitter.[168] In *George Hudson Ltd v Australian Timber Workers' Union*,[169] the employer wished to avoid being bound by the terms of a consent award made with employees. The employer attempted to do this by winding up the company and transferring the business assets, including contracts with staff, to a new company set up for the purpose of taking over the business. This strategy is sometimes referred to as the 'phoenix phenomenon', after the mythical bird that resurrects itself from the ashes of its own funeral pyre. When employees argued that the new employer was a successor to the business according to the terms of the legislative provisions, and was therefore bound to honour the agreement as to wages and conditions, the employer unsuccessfully challenged the constitutional validity of the legislation, claiming that the federal Parliament had no power to override the common law doctrine of privity of contract.

Similar restructuring strategies are still being used. In some cases these are equally unsuccessful precisely because the law's recognition of separate legal personality in the corporation foils the strategy from the outset. *McCluskey v Karagiozis* dealt with a claim from employees of an insolvent company in a corporate group, where the employees, without their knowledge or consent, had been transferred to an undercapitalised subsidiary.[170] In all probability, the purpose of the transfer was to enable the group to 'downsize' and dismiss staff without diminishing shareholder funds by paying out redundancy payments to employees. The scheme failed, because Merkel J found that the transfer of employment contracts had not been effective. Workers are not chattels, to be shifted from one corporation to another without their knowledge or consent. They are contracting parties, whose consent is vital to the creation of a new contract or variation of an old one. In transferring the employees to the subsidiary company their contracts of employment with the original employing corporation had been brought to an end, with no work to do they were made redundant. Justice Merkel held that the former employer, which was a company within the group and did retain assets, remained liable for redundancy entitlements.

---

168 See now *Workplace Relations Act*, Pt 11.
169 (1923) 32 CLR 413.
170 See (2002) 120 IR 147.

This result offers little comfort, however, to workers in company groups that have already been set up to quarantine assets from liabilities to workers, before the engagement of the workers. In those cases, the combined effect of the doctrine of separate legal personality of corporations within a group, and the law's insistence that directors owe fiduciary duties only to the capital investors in the firm, usually leaves workers vulnerable.

While it is possible for the law to protect workers from exploitation through corporate restructuring—for example by express legislative provision,[171] or adoption of the doctrine of joint employment,[172] and unfair contracts provisions offer yet another avenue of protection[173]—this merely exemplifies the ongoing tensions between corporate law and labour law in the new economy.

Rethinking the subject of law in the global era

The legal construction of the corporation and the doctrine of contract have together given the modern firm what Hugh Collins describes as:

> a considerable freedom in law and practice to determine the limits of their boundaries. A firm can decide to produce commodities or services within its own organisation or make contracts outside the firm with independent legal entities for the same work to be performed. Furthermore a firm can operate through numerous corporate entities, corresponding perhaps to different aspects of production, establishing a group of companies managing an economically integrated enterprise.[174]

This has had, and continues to have, profound implications for the structuring of work and the construction of the worker in the global era. As we have seen, the modern corporate business entity has engaged in a number of strategies to operate successfully in the new economy. Employment has changed so that many of the risks and costs of doing business that were once borne by the employing entity now fall on employees or other workers. Furthermore, although the corporation is conceptualised in law as a single entity, a legal person, the reality is that very often its power is not concentrated in one entity but diffused through an interrelated web of companies and networks that can make it very difficult to know where to ascribe legal responsibility for those who are working for it and, therefore, easier for the corporation to evade its responsibilities.

In the process employment has become more precarious. Writing more than a decade ago Breen Creighton, Bill Ford and Richard Mitchell observed:

> The contract of employment is primarily a legal construct, but it is a construct which performs exceedingly significant social, political, and economic functions. It has always been a rather unwieldy tool which bore the conceptual scars of its somewhat confused

---

171 *Workplace Relations Act*, Pt 11.

172 See *Morgan v Kittoschide Nominees Pty Ltd*, above n 97; and *Matthews v Cool or Cosy Pty Ltd; Ceil Comfort Home Insulation Pty Ltd*, above n 99.

173 See *Arrogante & Ors v AOS Group Australia Pty Ltd (in liq)* [2003] NSWIRComm 283, a case brought under *Industrial Relations Act 1996* (NSW) s 106. Note this legislation is now inapplicable to employees of constitutional corporations following the *Work Choices Act*: see *Workplace Relations Act*, s 16(1)(a) and (d).

174 H Collins 'Ascription of Legal Responsibility to Groups in Complex Patterns of Economic Integration' (1990) 53 *Mod L R* 731, 736.

origins. Nevertheless it did, after a fashion, serve its purpose in the context of emergent industrial capitalism. There must, however, be room for serious doubt as to its capacity effectively to discharge its legal, let alone its broader economic and social functions in the circumstances of the later years of the twentieth century.[175]

There words seem even more apposite now we are in the twenty-first century. At the same time, more and more workers are assuming the guise of business. Labour law has sometimes tried to assimilate into its fold some contractors on the basis that the reality is that they are more 'dependent' upon than 'independent' of the business entities for whom they perform work. But this strategy still avoids grappling with the more fundamental problems arising from neo-liberal assumptions about equality of bargaining power in the contractual relations that structure the market and hence fails to address some of the more difficult questions about the nature of power and issues of redistribution in relation to work.

The challenge of new forms of precarious work to law is not simply that courts or tribunals cannot respond appropriately to them. That is true in some instances, but generally courts and tribunals are quite adept at seeing the reality of work relations. But the conceptualisation of work relations as a free contract facilitates exploitation by the more powerful party in work arrangements. For every case that comes before a court or tribunal there are many more that do not. Many workers do not have the power to question the consequences of their 'agreement' to be an independent contractor and are thus left to flounder in the marketplace. Further, courts and tribunals are increasingly prevented from responding to the reality of work relations by the policy behind many statutory laws that encourages the worker to be an independent market operator and insists that corporate actors are dealt with in the commercial arena. The increasing number of people working through a corporate entity prove particularly problematic.[176]

In these circumstances is there a need for a new law of work, one that defines its subject differently? As has been noted at the beginning of this chapter, the binary divide between independent contractors and employees and the dominance of the contract of employment in labour law are in historical terms relatively recent phenomena. While problems of classification are not new, there is a new urgency to these issues: the new forms of work arrangements and the tendency to commercialise work relations are challenging labour law's protective purposes as never before. The disappearance of the traditional subject of labour law threatens labour law itself. As a report prepared for the European Commission commented:

> One of the historic functions of labour law has been to ensure social cohesion. It will only be able to continue to fulfil that function if it is able to accommodate new developments in the way that work is organized in contemporary society and does not revert to covering just the situations it was originally intended to address, which are becoming less typical.[177]

---

175 WB Creighton, WJ Ford and RJ Mitchell *Labour Law Text and Materials* (1993), 31.
176 *Wesoky v Village Cinemas International Pty Ltd* [2001] FCA 32. Cf *Hartnett v Aardvark Security Services Pty Ltd* (1998) 85 IR 315. See also *Eurobodella Shire Council v Dufty* [2004] NSWCA 450. The *Workplace Relations Act 1996* (Cth), except Pts 10 (awards) and 16 (freedom of association), is applicable only to independent contractors who are natural persons: s 4(2).
177 Supiot, above n 49.

Several different strategies have been adopted to respond to this challenge, and they need not be viewed as mutually exclusive, for change and development in law often come through contest and contradiction.

Contesting the boundary between 'employees' and 'independent contractors'

One response to the challenges posed by work arrangements in the global era is to make definitional adjustments legislatively to deal with the problem of 'disguised' employees, those who are really dependent (not independent) contractors. Here the utility and validity of the dichotomy between the two classifications is accepted, but the aim is to make it work effectively. Sometimes all workers in an industry, whether 'contractors' or 'employees', are simply treated the same.[178] In other instances the legislative definition of 'employee' is extended beyond its common law meaning deeming certain workers, like lorry drivers or cleaners or those working through a labour-hire firm, to be employees.[179]

One of the problems with any legislative provision is that in practice it can be fairly inflexible, either because of political obstacles or delay in busy legislative agendas. A more responsive mechanism may be to confer on a designated person or tribunal the power to declare a particular class of workers to be employees (even when they would not be employees at common law).[180] Under the *Industrial Relations Act 1999* (Qld), the Full Bench of the Industrial Relations Commission can exercise such a power on the application of a trade union or its peak body or the Minister. In exercising its discretion a number of factors are identified as potentially relevant considerations:

(a) the relative bargaining power of persons; or
(b) the economic dependency of the class of persons on the contract; or
(c) the particular circumstances and the needs of low paid employees; or
(d) whether the contract is designed to, or does, avoid the provisions of an industrial instrument; or
(e) the particular circumstances and the needs of employees including women, persons from non-English speaking background, young persons, and outworkers; or
(f) the consequence of not making an order for the class of persons.[181]

Such provisions seek to protect vulnerable workers, but again do not challenge the underlying conception of work relations as contractual and the distinction between employees and independent contractors. Furthermore because such procedures have proved largely ineffectual: the remedy is a piecemeal one, depending on others' awareness of the workers' plight and a willingness act on their behalf.[182]

---

178 Eg *Workplace Relations Amendment (Improved Protection for Victorian Workers) Act 2003* (Cth).
179 Eg *Industrial Relations Act 1996* (NSW), Sch 1, Pt 1; *Industrial Relations Act 1999* (Qld), ss 5–6; and *Industrial Relations Act 1979* (WA), s 7.
180 Eg *Industrial Relations Act 1999* (Qld), s 275.
181 *Industrial Relations Act 1999* (Qld), s 275(3). Since the implementation of the *Work Choices* changes on 27 March 2006 this legislation cannot apply to employees under the federal system. See also *Independent Contractors Bill 2006* (Cth).
182 The provision was little used even before 27 March 2006: but see *Transport Workers' Union of Australia, Union of Employees (Queensland Branch) v Australian Document Exchange Pty Ltd* [2001] 1 Qd R 659 (re couriers); and *ALHMWU v Bark Australia* [2001] QIRC 22 (28 February 2001) (re security guards).

The difficulties with the above approaches have led others to propose a presumptive approach: the worker is presumed to be an employee unless it is proved otherwise. Andrew Stewart has argued this is a more effective solution.[183] Stewart also envisages an accompanying legislative declaration that the existence of some factors (such as the power to delegate work to another; the provision of an asset by the worker; or that the labour is used to achieve a result) do not necessarily indicate a contract for services. But that is already implicit in the multiple indicia test. Although placing the burden of proof on the stronger, more powerful party is an advance, it is doubtful that it would make a lot of difference because in practice there is still plenty of scope for bluff and the presumption only has 'real bite' once a matter gets to court.

A desire to foster competitiveness in the market and a belief in freedom of choice resists any of the above moves and tends to insist on the maintenance of the common law approach to determining the boundary between 'employees' and 'independent contractors'. Here if the problem of 'dependent' contractors is acknowledged at all it is only to admit sometimes the need for a minor modification (such as one derived from the taxation system, concerning a requirement to meet the 'results test' or not earn more than 80 per cent income from one source) to be used in conjunction with the common law approach.[184] But even this does not always address the real problem, which is not simply the fact that someone works predominantly for one entity.

The diversity of workers in the global era

An alternative response is to acknowledge that the dichotomy oversimplifies work arrangements, and therefore abandon efforts to classify workers as either employees or independent contractors and instead name the diversity of workers.

In *Hollis v Vabu Pty Limited* McHugh J agreed with the majority judges that the bicycle courier was not an independent contractor, but he thought it inappropriate and inaccurate to describe him as an employee. Justice McHugh reasoned that the new relations of work should not be forced into a dichotomy that was 'based on medieval concepts of servitude'. Instead he preferred to develop the concept of vicarious liability for the changing social conditions by speaking of the courier as the 'agent' of Vabu.[185] And because the courier worked for the economic benefit of Vabu, was described in the contractual documents as the 'representative' of Vabu, and did not contract directly with the public, McHugh J decided that Vabu was liable for his negligence.

The law does in fact acknowledge a variety of work relations. The idea that the worker is an agent of the business entity for whom they work has been recognised before. A worker selling insurance on a commission basis is an example.[186] The law also understands that for the most part those who work in partnerships, those who

---

183 Stewart, above n 24, 270ff.

184 See Australian Parliament, above n 72, Recommendations 2 and 3, and *Income Tax Assessment Act 1997* (Cth), ss 87–15, 87–18, 87–20, 87–25 and 87–30.

185 (2001) 207 CLR 21, 50. Cf *Sweeney v Boylan Nominees Pty Ltd* [2006] HCA 19.

186 See *Australian Mutual Provident Society Ltd v Chaplin* (1978) 18 ALR 385; and *Colonial Mutual Life Assurance Society Ltd v Producers and Citizens Cooperative Assurance Company of Australia Ltd* (1931) 46 CLR 41, 48–9.

drive taxicabs, those who are volunteers or doing work experience, those who are office holders such as members of the armed forces, and members of the clergy, are neither independent contractors or employees.[187] Increasingly there is a wider understanding that many arenas of activity—for instance, those involving sports players, sex workers, prisoners, or children—do constitute labour markets and are therefore very much the province of the law of work.[188] Most of these workers do not fit the traditional industrial paradigm of the employee working at the premises of the employer, for a weekly payment, and some do not have a contractual wages/work bargain. However, as the decision of the High Court in *Ermogenous v Greek Orthodox Community of SA Inc*[189] shows, it is also wrong to presume that there is no contractual or employer–employee relationship. In that case, and contrary to some other cases involving members of the clergy, there was an intention to form contractual relations and Archbishop Ermogenous, the High Court held, did have a contract of employment and was an employee of the incorporated association for which he worked.

Perhaps the more significant issue then is that many statutes ignore the diversity of workers and in the main are concerned with workers as employees or independent contractors. However, policy and law are finding it necessary more and more to respond to the changing nature of work and the diversity of work arrangements. For instance, many services in the marketplace and the community are in effect provided entirely through or subsidised by 'free labour'. Those who provide 'Meals on Wheels', or give of their time to assist children's learning in the classroom, or act as lifesavers, fire fighters or guides at major sporting events, are all familiar examples. The increased use of volunteers has witnessed recent policy and legislative attention to protecting their ordinary paid employment if they are absent on volunteer work,[190] protecting volunteers at work against discrimination and other safety hazards,[191] and insulating volunteers against liability for harm caused by them when at work.[192]

Furthermore the different policy purposes of statutes already means that different classes of workers are specified as protected by different legislative instruments. Occupational health and safety, for instance, is an area where the protection of the law is not restricted to those with a contract of service. The focus of legislation in this area is on the exposure to risks that threaten or jeopardise the health and safety of

---

187 On partnerships see *Brace v Calder* [1985] 2QB 252; *Cam & Sons Pty Ltd v Sargent* (1940) 14 ALJ 162; and *Clarke v Evans* (1989) 32 AILR para 352; on taxi drivers as a bailees of goods see *Jordan v Aerial Taxi Cabs Corp* (2001) 115 FCR 21; on trial work see *Dietrich v Dare* (1980) 30 ALR 407; on members of the armed forces see *Coutts v The Commonwealth* (1985) 157 CLR 911; and on clergy see *Davies v Presbyterian Church of Wales* [1986] 1 WLR 323. With office holders it is usually necessary to refer to the particular statute establishing the office—see M Pittard and R Naughton *Australian Labour Law Cases and Materials* 4th edn, (2003), 69.

188 See the special issue *AJLL* vol 16 no 3, 2003. See also Arup et al (eds), above n 131.

189 (2002) 209 CLR 95.

190 Eg *Workplace Relations Amendment (Protection for Emergency Management Volunteers) Act 2003* (Cth).

191 Eg *Equal Opportunity Act 1984* (SA), s5; *Workplace Injury Management and Workers Compensation Act 1998* (NSW) Sch 1 cls 13 and 16; *Workers Compensation and Rehabilitation Act 2003* (Qld), Div 3 Subdiv 1–2 ss 12–21; *Workers Rehabilitation and Compensation Act 1986* (SA) s 103A; and *Occupational Health Safety and Welfare Act* (SA) s 4(3); *Workers Compensation Act 1951* (ACT), ss 17A–19; and *Work Health Act 1986* (NT), s 3. See also J Murray 'The Legal Regulation of Volunteers' in Arup et al (eds), above n 131.

192 See eg *Commonwealth Volunteers Protection Act 2003* (Cth); *Civil Liability Act 2002* (NSW); *Civil Liability Act 2003* (Qld); *Volunteer Protection Act 2001* (SA); and *Volunteer (Protection from Liability) Act 2002* (WA).

all in the workplace. Although there are still some deficiencies in providing adequate and appropriate coverage to the new forms of work that are flourishing in the new economy,[193] the evidence here is clear that the law has always known about and provided for a much wider range of workers than those who fall within the categories of independent contractor and employee. Discrimination legislation too has always protected a broad range of workers—not only those who are employees, but also contract workers and those in partnerships, and the legislation makes clear its applicability to many of those in newer forms of work such as part-time and temporary employment, and to employment in the public sector.[194] The accepted reason for this is that law protecting human rights is by its nature relevant to *all* workers.

Thus it is evident that the distinction between workers who have contracts *of* service and those who have contracts *for* services has already been abandoned as the touchstone of rights and duties in many statutes regulating work. These statutes often do name and define the workers to whom they apply without reference to those concepts. The question is whether this is the best or indeed the only way forward.[195] While there is no difficulty per se in recognising the diversity of work relations and resisting the pressure to classify workers into two main types, to list every particular type of worker may lead to greater regulatory complexity. For the most part the legislatures in the past have used, and still frequently do use, the concept of employee (sometimes modified) as a 'gateway' category to signify a worker who has access to statutory protections. This gives the law a certain simplicity and coherence. Perhaps what is needed is simply a new conception of the worker as the subject of the law of work.

The worker—a new subject for the law of work?

Law's difficulties in identifying its subject do not arise simply from the existence of a dichotomy between employees and independent contractors but also from the concept of contract underpinning them both. Because of this as soon as law defines its subject, there is always a risk that parties will create work arrangements that fall outside its scope. With contract as the foundation of labour law it is difficult to overcome this problem, for contract necessarily focuses on the agreement of the parties, it implies that the parties' 'choice' is of prime importance. From this it follows that any statutory regulation is portrayed as an interference with or a restriction on their choice and, by extension, contract therefore tends to legitimate any steps that parties might take to avoid (but not evade) that interference. This produces a tension at the heart of the law of work. There are other reasons for calling in to question the use of contract as the conceptual foundation to define the subject of the law of work. The reality is that there is often a power imbalance between parties in a work relation, and yet contract treats the parties as equals, often disguising the real nature of the relation by conceptualising them as two persons, when in most instances one of those legal persons takes a corporate form and

---

193 See Johnstone, above n 125.
194 See *Sex Discrimination Act 1984* (Cth) s 4; *Racial Discrimination Act 1975* (Cth), s 3(1); *Disability Discrimination Act 1992* (Cth) s 4; and *Age Discrimination Act 2004* (Cth) s 5.
195 See the argument in Brooks, above n 29.

is much more powerful than the other. Furthermore many work arrangements can no longer be configured in the form of a bilateral contractual arrangement without losing a sense of the complex realities involved. The contractualisation of work relations has also introduced a hierarchy into law's understanding of work—some (contractual) work relations are more important than other (non-contractual) work relations, which means that for the most part law has ignored the social and economic value of everything from volunteer work in the community to reproductive labour in the home.

Therefore a different and perhaps better strategy is for the law to use the status of the worker as its touchstone and to focus its concern on all who participate in the community through doing work, whether it is paid or unpaid work in the public arena or within familial and friendship relations. Abandoning the existing distinction between employees and independent contractors and all other more specific descriptions, and adopting the more neutral comprehensive label of 'worker' to signify those who are entitled to law's protection has a number of advantages.[196] It would necessarily focus attention specifically on the purpose for asking a question about the worker in law: for example, whether minimum standards ought to apply to a worker, whether the worker or another is responsible for the harm caused by the worker's negligence, or whether the worker is protected from discrimination. The spotlight would be on attaching certain rights and responsibilities to the citizen worker.[197] Most importantly such an approach would provide a new direction in the regulation of work because a move away from contract would remove the regulatory problems that derive from the inevitable power imbalances in work relations and the capacity to contract out of legal protections.

There is no constitutional or legal reason why the 'worker' should not be the touchstone of legislative entitlements in Australia. The dealings of corporations with all manner of workers could be regulated under the corporations power. Many ILO conventions, which can support legislation under the external affairs power, confer benefits on a wider range of workers than is encompassed by the common law concept of 'employee'.[198] The conciliation and arbitration power is not constitutionally restricted to dealing only with disputes between employers and employees.[199] The simplicity of this approach may be appealing for a number of reasons, not least that it would help to make more transparent the connections between all areas of the law that impact upon work. However, difficulties would remain. As a guide to citizens in their work relations, for instance, the use of a generic descriptor such as 'worker' is likely to be of little more assistance than the familiar term 'employee'.

There are two other issues regarding the subject of the law of work that deserve mention here.

---

196 See eg *Employment Rights Act 1996* (UK), s 230(3) definition of 'worker' and see also ss 43K and 230–33; and *National Minimum Wage Act 1998* (UK), s 34–5 (but note exclusions under regulation of young persons, apprentices, trainees on short term trial, and work in family members residing in the same home). See G Davidov 'Who is a Worker?' (2005) 34 *ILJ* 57.

197 See K Ewing *Working Life: A New Perspective on Labour Law* (1996), 46.

198 Eg *Termination of Employment Convention 1982 (ILO No 158)*, Art 2(1): 'This Convention applies to all branches of economic activity and to all employed persons.' See also *Konrad v Victorian Police* (1999) 165 ALR 23.

199 See eg *R v Coldham; Ex parte Fitzsimmons* (1976) 137 CLR 153.

Dependence and precariousness

Many who criticise the current legal distinction between independent contractors and employees do not so much question the utility of the dichotomy itself, but the method of determining the line that separates independent contractors and employees. As risk-taking entrepreneurs, independent contractors are accepted as being different from employees for the purposes of law.[200] The problem is seen as one of sham arrangements, with some dependent employees wrongly categorised as independent contractors. However, in the global era this is too simplistic a view of risk and work. It is obvious that many 'employees', such as casuals, do carry considerable risks and costs of business operations in the marketplace. Furthermore corporate law often works to protect business from risks and costs in the marketplace.

The intended beneficiary of labour law in the industrial era was the employee, identified primarily through this worker's subordination to a powerful, controlling employer. Later more emphasis was placed on the employee's dependence on a (single) employer or the employee's assumed incorporation within the employer's organisation. This employee contrasted with the independent contractor who was assumed to rove freely about the marketplace making agreements to work with a wide range of businesses. In some recent attempts to deal with the problem of the 'dependent' contractor, these understandings are still influential.

Thus one approach to distinguishing so-called 'dependent' from independent contractors is to identify those who perform a certain per centage of work for a single entity. This is the approach favoured in some taxation legislation.[201] It ensures that workers are not treated differently from employees, simply because they have invested in expensive assets that they use when working, if they really work most (up to 80 per cent) of the time for a single business.

One of the drawbacks of this approach, however, is that it assimilates the new worker to the old conception of an employee, one who works mainly for one employer. Perhaps independent contractors who are in business on their own account may not be expected to work all or even most of the time for a single entity, so this distinction may be sensible for the purposes of the collection of revenue through taxation. But in the global era it is no longer true that employees work for a single business entity—there are many casual and part-time employees who have to hold down several jobs with different employers in order to make a living. Working for a number of different entities is therefore not necessarily a characteristic that distinguishes independent contractors from employees. Indeed many so-called independent contractors who contract with a wide range of businesses in the marketplace share many of the concerns of their counterpart casual employees—that is, their work is low paid and they have no security of income or work. Many never earn enough to take up the taxation advantages that are in theory available to all independent operators. The so-called freedom that attends their work is experienced only as precariousness.

---

200 See eg Stewart, above n 24, 261–4.
201 See *A New Business Tax System (Alienation of Personal Services Income) Act 2000* (Cth).

The old labour law, especially the Australian version as traditionally practised in the conciliation and arbitration system, incorporated a redistributive goal. One of the biggest challenges in identifying the worker who is the subject of the law of work in the global era is for law to find a way to pursue those redistributive goals as more and more workers operate in the marketplace but often without enough work or enough decent-paying work. The tendency in this respect is for the line between welfare law and labour law to become blurred as the old division between those 'in work' and those 'out of work' breaks down.

Working inside/outside the market

With the industrial revolution came a division of home and marketplace into two discrete spheres of activity. Reproductive labour, the labour that produces and supports workers in the marketplace and ensures the ongoing maintenance of the community, was 'naturalised' as women's work and the male breadwinner was freed to devote himself wholly to his work in the marketplace. The law governing work played a major role in constructing work and its subjects in accord with this paradigm. The transition from the industrial era to the global era has witnessed a further transformation in the relation between work in the marketplace and work in the home and again law has played (and is still playing) a major role in facilitating this. The law has assisted in creating a new role for women, as part-time workers in the marketplace,[202] and consequently altering the traditional 'breadwinner with dependent spouse and children' model of the family. Yet work in the home remains primarily women's work, despite an increased outsourcing of many of its tasks to the marketplace and despite the encouragement to men to take a greater role in domestic work. However the worker in the private sphere of the home remains an absent subject in the law of work.

Why is this so? And is it necessarily so? A conventional answer has been that it can be presumed that in the domestic sphere there is no intention to create legal relations—but such presumptions do not necessarily accord with reality.[203] Traditionally too, no value is attributed to those work arrangements that are not within the market. But there are various ways of viewing reproductive labour as productive and with a value.[204] Indeed many areas of the law, such as family law, tort and social security law, often have to attribute value to women's work in the home.[205] Perhaps an emphasis on status (worker) rather than contract (employee) would open the possibility of a more inclusive approach to the subject of the law of work, and act as another reminder that the law of work in the global era is necessarily broader than the labour law of the industrial era.

---

202 See Owens, above n 147, on the creation of women's work as part-time work. See also above n 9.

203 Cf *Ermogenous v Greek Orthodox Community of SA Inc* (2002) 209 CLR 95.

204 See M Waring *Counting for Nothing: What Men Value and What Women Are Worth* (1988). See also PF Apps 'Tax Reform, Ideology and Gender' (1999) 21 *Syd LR* 437; and PF Apps and R Rees 'Labour Supply, Household Production and Intra-family Welfare Distribution' (1996) 60 *J Pub Ec* 199.

205 See Graycar and Morgan, above n 8.

part **2**

Contract and Cooperation

Work Relations and the Limits of Contract

5

Private regulation

'Self-regulation' is the mantra of the era of globalisation. Globalisation privileges contracting over traditional forms of public regulation because private regulation is seen to best serve the rising individualism of the global marketplace. Under private contract law, individuals define and regulate their own relationships. In theory at least, contract is inherently flexible. Nevertheless, parties to work contracts negotiate their terms in the shadow of the customs and practices of their working environments, and in the knowledge that should their bargains dissolve into dispute, courts will determine rights and obligations according to a body of common law and equitable principles. This chapter critiques contract law as a model for regulating work relationships. The following Chapter 6 describes and explains the legal principles that define the rights and obligations of parties to work contracts.

This chapter will first examine liberal or 'classical' contract theory,[1] to demonstrate its considerable limitations in regulating long-term work relationships. Classical contract law's standard assumption that autonomous parties freely negotiate to arrive at mutually beneficial bargains disguises the inequality inherent in many work relationships, especially in the relationship that the common law describes as 'employment'. A further assumption—that sufficiently certain contract terms are fixed upon initial agreement—also obscures the reality of many working relationships. Real working relationships—especially those that are classified by the common law as employment relationships—are better described in terms of relational contract theory.[2] Relational contracts 'outline a long-term relation with indeterminate obligations in order to permit flexibility and cooperation'[3] and so require considerable modification of orthodox

---

1   The concept of 'classical contract law' is described by Patrick Atiyah as the general principles of modern contract law developed and elaborated by English courts in the eighteenth and nineteenth centuries: see PS Atiyah *An Introduction to the Law of Contract* 5th edn (1995), 7.
2   See I McNeil 'Contracts: Adjustment of Long-term Economic Relations under Classical, Neoclassical and Relational Contract Law' (1978) *NWULR* 340; CJ Goetz and RE Scott 'Principles of Relational Contracts' (1981) 67 *Va L Rev* 1089; and D Campbell and D Harris 'Flexibility in Long-term Contractual Relationships: The Role of Co-operation' (1993) 10 *JLS* 166.
3   H Collins *Regulating Contracts* (1999), 18.

principles of classical contract law. In particular, relational contract theory explains the emergence of a concept of good faith in the performance of contracts.

Relational contract theory also provides more scope than classical contract doctrine for accommodating contemporary commitments to finding an acceptable 'work/life' or 'work/family' balance for working citizens. Of course, contemporary contract law is also influenced by equitable doctrines, such as the prohibition on unconscionable dealing, and most significantly by statutory interventions, in the form of trade practices and unfair contracts review legislation. This chapter will therefore also outline those influences on so-called 'self-regulation' of working relationships.

Finally, the shortcomings of contract law as a model for expressing collective bargaining will be examined. This has become a particularly important question following the 2005 *Work Choices* changes,[4] which have limited the allowable content of statutory collective bargains, and so prompted trade unions to reconsider options for entering into common law contracts on behalf of an entire workforce.

The emergence of the employment contract

The concept of a contract—a freely entered bargain of negotiated terms and conditions—has dominated legal thinking about the nature of the relationship between workers and those who engage them to work for most of the past century. It was not always so. In fact, the concept of 'employment' as a particular species of contract is a relatively recent phenomenon, born out of the 'Fordist' model of productive enterprise.[5] This model of production—involving the engagement of permanent fulltime workers who provided services on an exclusive basis—is largely responsible for the dominance of employment as the preferred method of engaging labour in industrial economies throughout most of the twentieth century.[6] The transformation that is occurring in the twenty-first century, with the vertical disintegration[7] of Fordist enterprises and the emergence of contracting with many so-called independent 'small business' or 'entrepreneurial' workers, represents a return to earlier forms of engagement. Alain Supiot has reported that '[s]elf-employment prevailed at the turn of the nineteenth century when most workers were farmers (or farm labourers), tradesmen, craftspeople or freelance professionals'.[8]

In those earlier times, mercantile laws and practices together with a body of various statutes, provided the legal framework governing the engagement of labour and the rights and obligations of workers. Public regulation has long been of central importance in the regulation of work relationships, and not always in the interests of worker protection.

---

4   See the *Workplace Relations Amendment (Work Choices) Act 2005*, discussed in some detail in Chapter 3.
5   For a description of 'Fordism' see K van Wezel Stone 'The New Psychological Contract: Implications of the Changing Workplace for Labor and Employment Law' (2001) 48 *UCLA LR* 519, 529–39.
6   For a detailed analysis of the evolution of the modern employment contract see A Merritt 'The Historical Role of Law in the Regulation of Employment—Abstentionist or Interventionist' (1982) 1 *AJLS* 56. See also S Deakin 'The Many Futures of the Employment Contract' in J Conaghan, M Fischl and K Klare (eds) *Labour Law in an Era of Globalization: Transformative Practices and Possibilities* (2002), 193; and J Howe and R Mitchell 'The Evolution of the Contract of Employment in Australia: A Discussion' (1999) 12 *AJLL* 113.
7   H Collins 'Independent Contractors and the Challenge of Vertical Disintegration to Employment Protection Laws' (1990) 10 *OJLS* 35.
8   A Supiot *Beyond Employment:Changes in Work and the Future of Labour Law in Europe* (2001).

The earliest *Statutes of Labourers* of 1349 and 1350, for example, fixed the price of labour and imposed criminal sanctions on workers who abandoned their masters, as a response to severe labour shortages after the decimation of the Black Death.[9] Later, nineteenth-century factories and shops legislation governed the terms and conditions of work and the rights and responsibilities of workers. With the rise of liberalism, private law and particularly contract law began to offer an alternative approach to thinking about the relationship between workers and those who engage them.

Master and servant law

The modern employment contract melds liberal contract theory's conception of a law of obligations created by consensual bargains, with older vestiges of the status-based relationship of master and servant.

Blackstone's Commentaries on the Laws of England[10] included the law dealing with relationships between those who engaged workers in permanent service as part of the law 'Of the Rights of Persons', along with the law concerning relationships between husbands and wives, and parents and children.[11] The master of those times was comparable to the *pater familias*—the father whom the common law allowed to discipline his family. Likewise, the master was permitted to beat his apprentice, 'so it be done with moderation'.[12]

Domestic servants of this time enjoyed some limited advantages from this paternalistic conception of the relationship. Menial servants (that is, those who lived *intra moenia*, that is, as part of the family) were hired from year to year, and the master was obliged to maintain them 'throughout all the revolutions of the seasons, as well when there is work to be done as when there is not'.[13] A mere lack of work to be done did not justify summary dismissal. A master who wanted to be rid of such a servant, even at the end of the year of engagement, was obliged to provide at least three months' notice (a generous period even by present day standards). This was certainly a personal relationship—but it bore none of the characteristics of the freely entered bargain between autonomous parties assumed by liberal contract theory.

Of course, not all workers of that time were domestic servants. Much of the working population was engaged in agricultural labour. These workers enjoyed no security of employment and very limited liberty to choose their employment. While the *Statute of Labourers* was in force, agricultural workers could be compelled to work for prescribed wages and could be punished for deserting a master. Although legal writings about these times may have described these work relationships as contracts, they described a very different species of obligation from the liberal conception of contract as a voluntarily assumed bargain between equals.

---

9   See J Macken et al *Law of Employment;* 5th edn (2002), 3 and R Johnstone and R Mitchell 'Regulating Work' in C Parker et al (eds) *Regulating Law* (2004).

10 See W Morrison (ed) *Blackstone's Commentaries on the Laws of England,* 1765–69, in four volumes (2001).

11 Ibid, Book I, 'Chapter the Fourteenth, Of Master and Servant'. For a critical discussion of Blackstone's classification, and Sir Otto Kahn-Freund's criticism of it, see JW Cairns, 'Blackstone, Kahn-Freund and the Contract of Employment' (1989) 105 *LQR* 300.

12 Morrison, above n 1, 329.

13 Ibid, 327.

A focus on status was understandable in a society still influenced by its feudal origins, and where most work involved agricultural labour or domestic service. For most rural or domestic servants, there was no separation between home and work. Life was work and little else. Industrialisation and urbanisation, however, introduced new types of work, and for many, radically different patterns of life and work. The relationships between masters and workers changed, and so, gradually, did the legal conception of that relationship. The rise of liberalism was particularly influential in reconceptualising the relationship between the master (generally the owner of capital) and the worker, who provided labour. The notion of contract became central to the conception of a whole range of social relationships (even the relationship between citizen and State). Nevertheless, in those relationships we would now call 'employment relationships', or 'contracts *of* service', the vestiges of the status-based relationship have been slow to dissolve.

As Chapter 6 will demonstrate, the incidents of the status-based 'master/servant' relationship had a significant influence on the development of modern employment contract law. The master's prerogative to command is evidenced in the persistence of 'control' as a principal indicia distinguishing an employment relationship from an independent contract. The servant's obligations to obey and to provide loyal and faithful service are evident in the persistence of implied duties of obedience, fidelity and good faith in the employment contract.

Classical contract law theory

As Patrick Atiyah has explained, the general principles of classical contract law were largely formulated by the English courts in the eighteenth and nineteenth centuries.[14] These principles—of offer, acceptance, consideration—implicitly assumed that parties entering into contracts were autonomous actors who had freely negotiated the terms and conditions of their bargains. This notion of 'freedom of contract' justified legal enforcement of those bargains. In a liberal democracy, there was no injustice (in theory at least) in holding parties to the terms of their own voluntarily assumed bargains.

Many of the doctrines of classical contract law are underpinned by the notion of freedom of contract. Principles of construction of contracts assume that the contract contains only those terms that the parties themselves have agreed to assume. So contract law privileges the express terms of a deal (most easily recognised in written form, but express terms can also be oral), and allows the implication of unexpressed terms on the basis that the implied term reflects what the parties themselves would have agreed if they had addressed their minds to the issue. Hugh Collins has opined that implied terms really 'betray judicial perceptions of what obligations should be undertaken by the parties',[15] nevertheless, judicial rationalisations of implied terms frequently hark back to the parties' own choice. This justification applies also to terms implied by custom and usage. A term is implied by custom on the basis that a certain practice is so notorious that all participants in the industry are taken to assume that the practice

---

14 See Atiyah, above n 1, 7.
15 H Collins *Employment Law* (2003), 34.

will also govern their own relationship, unless they expressly provide otherwise. Even terms implied by law (because they are necessary to a particular category or class of contracts) can be expressly excluded by the consent of the parties.[16]

The principles of interpretation also depend upon the assumption that the parties themselves have agreed and defined their own terms. A court testing the meaning of a contract term will ask: what would an 'intelligent bystander' who has witnessed the parties' words and behaviour reasonably infer that the parties themselves intended?[17]

The basis for assessing damages for breach of contract is also rationalised on the assumption that the parties themselves have consented to bear the obligations that the court is now required to enforce. Whereas damages in tort are assessed so as to compensate people for the wrong done to them—to put them back in the position they would have been in, but for the commission of the tort—damages in contract are assessed on the basis that a party is entitled to fulfilment of expectations. One must have what one has bargained for. One must be put in the position that one would be in, if the contract had been properly performed. The common law would not, however, demand actual performance of the promised obligation. The liberal conception of contract as an exchange of economic benefits resisted the development of remedies of specific performance of contractual promises. Courts exercising common law jurisdiction preferred to ascribe some monetary value to the proper performance of the contract and pay that amount in damages. A plaintiff who wanted to enforce actual performance of an obligation under a contract needed the assistance of the equitable jurisdiction. A court of equity could order specific performance where monetary damages were deemed not to be an adequate remedy, and where other discretionary factors (such as interference with the rights of innocent third parties) did not militate against such an order.

The quantification of damages in contract is also influenced by the assumption that contract is about the parties' own voluntarily assumed bargain. Parties who breach a contract will be required to pay for any loss on the principles enunciated in *Hadley v Baxendale*,[18] that is, losses arising 'naturally … according to the usual course of things', or that 'may reasonably be supposed to have been in the contemplation of both parties at the time they made the contract'.[19] The second limb of this rule confirms a principle that contracting parties should only be liable to bear risks that they can reasonably be held to have agreed to bear. Freely given consent is the foundation of orthodox contract law theory.

Freedom of contract

The concept of freedom of contract may have been appropriate at the time of its development to describe the kinds of mercantile transactions of most interest to the common lawyers of the day. A sale of goods for example, required a convenient legal

---

16 An exception are those terms implied by mandatory statutory provisions, for example, the *Trade Practices Act 1974* (Cth), s 74.

17 See *Oscar Chess Ltd v Williams* [1957] 1 WLR 370, 375.

18 (1854) 9 Ex 341; 156 ER 145.

19 (1854) 9 Ex 341, 354; 156 ER 145, 151.

tool for allocating the commercial risks that might arise on a failure of one or other party to perform. The parties themselves could reasonably be assumed to be most knowledgeable about matters such as the quality of the goods, the market price, and a manageable delivery schedule. The inevitable commercial risks arising from such things as market price fluctuations, or delivery delays, could be managed between the parties by this tool allocating responsibility for a variety of anticipated potential outcomes. These bargains could quite reasonably be assumed to be mutually beneficial. Otherwise, the parties would never have agreed to enter into the deal in the first place. The contract law theory supporting this kind of entrepreneurial behaviour understandably valued freedom of contract and certainty.

Unfortunately, not all relationships to which the contract model has subsequently been applied bear the same essential features as these entrepreneurial mercantile transactions. Since the nineteenth century, classical contract law theory has been strained by application to many more complex human interactions. When applied to the typical employment relationship, it can be attacked on various grounds. Indeed, Otto Kahn-Freund has described the contract of employment as a 'figment of the legal mind'.[20]

Employed workers rarely enjoy genuine 'freedom of contract'. Workers generally depend on their jobs for an income, so they have no choice to refuse work entirely. The range of work options available is often limited—more so for those without special skills. Even where alternatives are available, individual workers often enjoy limited opportunities to negotiate terms and conditions with an employer.[21] And even contracts that have been freely and fairly negotiated at the outset may become increasingly unfair following changes of circumstances over the course of a long relationship.

The employment contract, or 'contract of service'

At this point, it is useful to distinguish between the concept of the employment contract, as a 'contract of service', and other contracts 'for services' whereby work is performed. Chapter 4 explained the ways in which this distinction between employment and other 'independent' work contracts can be manipulated. In many instances, notably when highly dependent contractors are engaged exclusively by one enterprise, it has proved to be an unjustly artificial distinction. The distinction has, however, persisted, and it is particularly important in a consideration of the extent to which liberalism's 'freedom of contract' is at all meaningful in the context of relationships through which work is performed. This is because the common law implies a number of terms into employment contracts that are not necessarily present in independent contracts 'for services'.

The concept of 'freedom of contract' in employment relationships can be criticised on several grounds. The employment relationship by definition involves inequality of power. Control, which is one of the factors distinguishing the employee from the non-employee, for example, focuses on the subordination of the worker to the employer's power to command. This inequality often affects the employee's freedom to negotiate

---

20 See O Kahn-Freund *Labour and the Law* 2nd edn (1983), 1–17.
21 A discussion of collective bargaining is reserved for Chapter 11.

terms at the outset of the engagement, and her freedom to resist variations to terms along the way. Furthermore, the terms implied by law into the employment contract (such as the duty to obey) tend to favour the interests of the employer.

Few employees enjoy any real opportunity to negotiate even the explicit terms of their employment contracts—such as remuneration rates, and hours of work. Typically, prospective employees are presented with a 'take it or leave it' offer. Many employment contracts are contracts of adhesion, similar to the standard form contracts that consumers enter into when purchasing insurance or other services. There is no scope at all for negotiation. Sometimes, these non-negotiable terms and conditions of employment are not even disclosed at the time the initial offer of employment is made and accepted. It is common for a written employment contract to be provided to the employee on the day of, or even *after* commencement of duties. Even these documents will not always spell out all of the essential terms of the employment contract. Often matters that become important in a subsequent dispute will not have been determined, nor possibly even contemplated by either party at the time of engagement, and yet they become terms of the contract by implication.

This often happens because of the open-textured nature of many written employment contracts. Employers often deliberately express the terms and conditions of employment in ways that preserve their discretion to apply conditions flexibly, depending on the needs of the business. This is particularly so in the case of the engagement of skilled people, who are employed to achieve results, rather than serve out time. For example, it is not uncommon to find clauses like this in the employment contracts of graduate solicitors and accountants:

> In the light of the professional nature of the firm's business and the need to meet the needs and requirements of clients, as a member of the professional staff, it is expected that you will work such hours as are reasonably necessary to carry out your duties to the satisfaction of the firm, without further remuneration.

This clause fixes the remuneration payable to the employee, but leaves the number of hours to be worked each week to the vagaries of client demand. Typically, 'duties' will not be expressly defined. The employer enjoys the prerogative to allocate duties and responsibilities, and may indeed expect the professional worker to take the initiative of generating productive work for herself. The only apparent control on the number of hours such a professional must work (beyond the limit of twenty-four hours a day set by the laws of nature) is that the employer may demand work only if it is 'reasonably' necessary to satisfy the firm's objective of meeting clients' needs. What is 'reasonable' will depend on such matters as past practices, industry custom, and the business context of the working relationship—all generally matters within the control of the employer. No wonder then, that a culture of working oppressively long hours has developed in many professional spheres, especially in the legal profession, where clients' demands are notoriously complex and urgent.

This illustration demonstrates the nature of 'managerial prerogative'. In contract law terms, it represents the employer's unilateral entitlement to determine important terms of the contract. Managerial prerogative also often extends to other important conditions of employment such as where the work is to be performed, what technology is to be used and how the work is to be organised. The employer's unilateral entitlement to determine the scope of duties is inconsistent with classical contract law's assumption that a contract constitutes freely accepted obligations of a certain nature.

Certainty and fluidity in employment relationships

This raises a second aspect of classical contract law theory that is compromised in the typical employment contract. Classical contract law requires that the terms of the bargain are sufficiently certain, so that a court required to enforce the bargain can be sure it is giving effect to the parties' own agreement. An insufficiently certain bargain will generally be unenforceable, or 'void for uncertainty'. Continuing with the illustration above, it would be exceptional in the extreme for a commercial contract for the provision of legal or accounting services to leave it to the discretion of the recipient of the services to decide how much work was to be done for the agreed payment. This is not unusual in employment contracts, because employment contracts are not like ordinary commercial contracts for services. Whereas the commercial contract involving the retainer of a professional to perform a specific service can be a discrete transaction for performance of a particular task, the employment contract usually describes a continuing relationship, the parameters of which cannot always be contained in preconceived terms. The typical employer of skilled staff expects those staff not only to perform specified duties, but often to exercise their own talents and judgment in devising and executing productive activities to profit the employer's business. This employer will expect such workers to anticipate and develop new business opportunities, and to adjust and adapt to new business environments.

The typical skilled or professional employee will gladly cooperate in these expectations because she also expects to benefit from the continuation of a productive employment relationship. She expects not merely weekly wages, but the benefits promised by a secure income—for example, access to finance to acquire housing and other assets. Long-term engagement undertaking a flexible range of duties allows the employer to acquire valuable skills, experience and professional contacts. This in turn leads to promotion in the employee's career, personal satisfaction and increased social status. The promise of these intangibles—which are often more important to prospective employees than initial pay rates and conditions of work—may explain why people seeking employment are often willing to accept 'take-it-or-leave-it' offers without negotiation, and without insisting on the detailed documentation of terms and conditions of work.

Even where terms and conditions are documented at the outset of an employment relationship, courts will be ready to find that those terms have evolved with the needs of the enterprise. In classical contract law terms, courts will readily accept that by continuing to come to work and perform duties, an employee whose terms and conditions of work have been changed by the unilateral decision of the employer has accepted a variation of the contract, and can no longer complain about the employer's breach of the original terms. For example, in *Quickenden v O'Connor*,[22] an academic who wanted to protest the introduction of new performance review procedures by his employing institution, argued that he ought not to be bound to observe these new procedures that purported to rob him of his contractual right to tenure. The procedures were being implemented as the consequence of a new collectively negotiated enterprise agreement between the university and its academic staff. Dr Quickenden was not himself a member of the union that negotiated the agreement, and claimed therefore to have given no consent to this variation of his original employment contract. The Full Court of the Federal Court rejected Dr Quickenden's argument, on the basis that the 'terms of the contract of employment were *ambulatory* in a number of important respects'[23] (emphasis added) because his original acceptance of an appointment as a lecturer contemplated that conditions of employment would change periodically to accommodate requirements set by new University Senate resolutions, and changes to industrial awards and industrial agreements, regardless of Dr Quickenden's consent. His contract could be, and frequently *was* changed unilaterally as the collective needs of the institution required. (His contract of employment was treated as one variable contract, not as a series of terminations and novations each time his terms of engagement were varied.)

As harsh as this may seem to Dr Quickenden in these particular circumstances, it is in fact a convenient result. Otherwise every institutional decision that varied the precise terms and conditions of employment would cause the termination of employment contracts, and very inconvenient results may follow. For the sake of the argument here, this case shows that employment contracts are not like ordinary commercial contracts. They are not defeated by a lack of certainty. They can be varied without the explicit consent of one party, without necessarily causing the contract to be terminated. In many ways they are more like another relationship uncomfortably included as a species of contract—marriage.

Autonomy and subordination

The above discussion of the employer's capacity to unilaterally vary the terms of an employment contract without necessarily bringing it to an end demonstrate another feature of the typical employment relationship that is at odds with classical contract law theory. It is a rare thing indeed for the employee to wield the same power to vary employment conditions. It is the employer who, by virtue of managerial prerogative, controls the parameters of the relationship. The employee is subordinate to that prerogative. This stands squarely in the face of classical contract law's assumption that parties to freely negotiated contracts enjoy equal legal status, and have acted autonomously in binding themselves to the bargain. If autonomy is a cornerstone of the common law's justification for the enforcement of contracts, then it is missing in

---

22 (2001) 109 FCR 243.
23 Ibid, 265.

many employment relationships. A number of aspects of employment contract law illustrate the employee's subordinate status. The work/wages bargain, for instance, assumes that unless there is an express term to the contrary, the obligation to pay wages is dependent upon the prior performance of work. It is by no means the norm in all commercial contracts that service must precede payment. Insurance premiums, for example, are paid in advance. Theatre tickets are paid for before the performance. Landlords rarely allow for rent to be paid in arrears. Why should the default position in employment assume that service must precede payment? The law and economics scholars, applying game theory, refer to the problem of the 'first mover'.[24] The contract party who is first to perform contractual obligations, must take the risk of the other's default. The first mover is in the weaker position. Should the other default, the first mover will have the problem of seeking redress in the courts. In employment law, the work/wages bargain presumes (in the absence of express agreement or some industrial instrument that provides an alternative method) that this risk is borne by the employee.[25]

The employee's subordinate status is also apparent in an important term implied by law into the employment contract: the duty to obey lawful and reasonable orders. (The extent of this duty is discussed in Chapter 6.) In this aspect, the legal regulation of employment relationships bears greater resemblance to the status-based conception of earlier centuries. As Lord Wedderburn (quoting Sir Otto Kahn-Freund) has written:

> Here then is an ancient tension in the system. For the common law assumes it is dealing with a contract made between equals, but in reality, save in exceptional circumstances, the individual worker brings no equality of bargaining power to the labour market and to this transaction central to his life whereby the employer buys his labour power. This *individual* relationship, in its inception, 'is an act of submission, in its operation it is a condition of subordination, however much the submission and the subordination may be concealed by that indispensable figment of the legal mind known as the contract of employment'.[26]

Relational contracts

The above discussion sought to explain the ways in which the principles of classical contract law developed in the eighteenth and nineteenth centuries to regulate mercantile trading ventures bear little relevance to the typical employment relationship, with its inherent imbalance in bargaining power, its fluid obligations and its indefinite duration. Employment—and also many other long-term relationships for the provision of work—are better described as 'relational' contracts.

Contracts that lack certainty in favour of a mutually convenient fluidity have long been recognised by law and economics scholars as 'relational' contracts.[27] Parties to relational contracts depend upon a mutual commitment to cooperation, in lieu of

---

24 M Trebilcock *The Limits of the Freedom of Contract* (1993), 16.
25 See *Automatic Fire Sprinklers v Watson* (1946) 72 CLR 435, 465.
26 *The Worker and the Law* 3rd edn (1986), 5.
27 See above n 2.

reliance on terms strictly defined at the commencement of their relationship, principally because the nature of their relationships does not permit the easy anticipation of all potential risks. Parties to relational contracts 'are aiming at utility-maximisation indirectly through long-term cooperative behaviour manifested in trust and not in reliance on obligations, specified in advance'.[28] The need for cooperation in these kinds of relationships—long-term joint venture projects, franchises, etc—explains the development in contemporary commercial contract law of obligations of good faith in the performance of contractual obligations.[29] The typical employment relationship reflects this same long term 'relational' nature: expectations of cooperation and flexibility underpin deliberately open-textured obligations.

The studies undertaken by the law and economics scholars tend to focus on large risk-taking enterprises, dealing on equal footing, seeking to maximise mutual welfare. In these deals between giants, the flexibility and cooperation flow both ways. Rarely is that the case in employment relationships. The prerogative to insist on flexibility and cooperation, and the scope to exercise discretionary powers, usually resides only with the employer. Some employees whose skills are in demand, or who enjoy the support of the industrial muscle of a union or employee association, may be able in practice to demand some flexibility. Their legal entitlement to flexibility—outside of limited statutory protections of a right against discrimination on the grounds of disability or family responsibilities—will seldom extend beyond a contractual right to resign on giving a stipulated period of notice. Likewise, under the classic formulation of the employee's duty of fidelity to the employer, it is the employee who owes a duty of cooperation in the employer's business aspirations. Whether the employer is obliged to cooperate in the fulfilment of the employee's expectations from the relationship remains contested ground (as we shall see in Chapter 6).

If courts could be persuaded to apply relational contract theory in an even-handed manner to employment relationships, there may indeed be more scope for finding that employers bear an obligation to deal flexibly with reasonable requests for variations in working time and conditions to accommodate employees' need to balance work with family commitments. At present, employers will owe *contractual* duties to consider and cooperate with employees' reasonable requests to work from home or to vary working hours only if they have given express commitments to consider those requests. (See Chapter 6.)

Modern contract law

Some of the rigidity of classical contract law theory has not survived translation into the twenty-first century. So many modifications must be acknowledged that one might genuinely ask whether contract is indeed dead,[30] despite the dogged loyalty of common law courts to its terminology, if not its true precepts.

---

28 Campbell and Harris, above n 2, 167. See also Collins, above n 3, 18.
29 See generally E Peden *Good Faith in the Performance of Contracts* (2003).
30 See G Gilmore *The Death of Contract* edited by RKL Collins (1995).

Modifications to classic contract law have come through three principal avenues. One is development of common law doctrines themselves, one has been the development of equitable doctrine, which has long played a role in mollifying the rigours of the common law. The other has been through statute, enacted out of parliamentary impatience with the slowness of common law development.

Common law development of 'good faith'

Even in general commercial contract law, where the players are large well-advised parties, Australian law has been willing to acknowledge an emerging duty of 'good faith' in the performance of contracts.[31] Generally, this duty has been called in aid to prevent one party from relying on strict technical contractual rights in a way that unfairly disadvantages the other party. For example, in an appropriate case, a right to terminate a contract for breach will be constrained by a requirement that the right be exercised in good faith, and not capriciously or opportunistically.

The precise scope of good faith obligations continues to be a matter of debate. John Carter and Elisabeth Peden argue that good faith is a tool of construction, inherent in the very essence of contract law as the enforcement of mutually beneficial, consensual private bargains.[32] Contracts are to be construed as if each party intended to allow the other the benefit of the contract.[33] Others have treated good faith as a term that may be implied into a contract, either as a matter of fact if the particular contract required it, or as a matter of law.[34] And there are sceptics who criticise the development of good faith as unfounded in principle,[35] and unnecessary in the light of the availability of equitable remedies in appropriate cases.[36] The greatest scepticism is reserved for assertions that a good faith obligation imposes a requirement of reasonable and not merely honest behaviour by contracting parties. That this debate exists at all is evidence of a softening of the rigidities of classical contract law in the light of contemporary expectations of a certain standard of ethical business practice. Good faith obligations are a legal support for expectations that parties will not abuse contract law by relying on technicalities to harm those with whom they have contracted.

In the employment context, the development of good faith obligations has been paralleled by the emergence of a duty of 'mutual trust and confidence', reciprocated by employer and employee.[37]

---

31 See *Renard Constructions (ME) Pty Ltd v Minister for Public Works* (1992) 26 NSWLR 234, judgment of Priestley J; *Hughes Aircraft Systems International v Air Services Australia* (1997) 146 ALR 1, per Finn J; *Alcatel Australia Ltd v Scarcella* (1998) 44 NSWLR 349; *Burger King Corp v Hungry Jack's Pty Ltd* [2001] NSWCA 187. For a general reference, see Peden above n 29.

32 J Carter and E Peden 'Good Faith in Australian Contract Law' (2003) 19 JCL 1.

33 *Butt v McDonald* (1896) 7 QLJ 68, 70–1.

34 See the cases cited above, n 31.

35 See T Carlin 'The Rise (and Fall?) of Implied Duties of Good Faith in Contractual Performance in Australia' (2002) 25 *UNSWLJ* 99.

36 See IB Stewart 'Good Faith in Contractual Performance and Negotiation' (1998) 72 *ALJ* 370; see also *Service Station Association Ltd v Berg Bennett & Associates* (1993) 45 FCR 84, 96–7 (Gummow J).

37 See Chapter 6.

Equitable intervention

For centuries, courts of equity (originating in the English Court of Chancery) have exercised a discretion to interfere in the strict application of common law rules when common law rights were being asserted against good conscience. Equity's jurisdiction is often explained in terms of the Aristotelian notion that justice cannot be served in every case by the application of a rigid set of rules.

> The Cause why there is a chancery is, for that Mens Actions are so divers and infinite, That it is impossible to make any general law which may aptly meet with every particular Act and not fail in some circumstances.[38]

Equity's principal intervention in contract law has been as a defence for a claim for specific performance or damages for breach. A party claiming the benefit of a contract may be defeated if the other party is able to establish equitable grounds for denying the remedy. Equity achieves this result by asserting that the contract should be vitiated or rescinded, for want of a sound basis. Those grounds may include that the contract was induced by misrepresentation, or by duress or undue influence. In normal circumstances, the relationship of employer and employee would not give rise to any presumption of undue influence, however it would be open to the parties to a particularly oppressive relationship to prove that relationship on the facts, and argue a case of undue influence on the principles espoused in *Johnson v Buttress*.[39] Since the High Court of Australia's decision in *Commercial Bank of Australia Ltd v Amadio*,[40] a further ground for claiming an equitable right to rescission is that the party seeking to enforce the contract has taken unconscionable advantage of a recognised special weakness in the other party. Inequality of bargaining power alone is insufficient to ground a 'special disadvantage'. It would be necessary for an employee to demonstrate some other recognisable constitutional weakness, such as illiteracy, or disability.[41]

Perhaps because of Australia's tradition of industrial awards and dispute resolution by arbitral tribunals, the equitable jurisdiction has developed very little jurisprudence in the field of employment law. Principally, equity has come to the aid of the employer, seeking to enforce the fiduciary aspects of an employee's duties: in claims for breach of confidence,[42] or for accounts of profit or constructive trust over the proceeds of new businesses set up in rivalry with the employer.[43] This reflects the privileged proprietary nature of the law's perception of the employer's interest in the relationship. Equity is very much the handmaiden of property law, and is often called in aid to preserve vested property interests. The employee's interest in the relationship, however, has always been considered to involve no more than a personal right. Equity's persistent

---

38 Lord Ellesmere LC *Earl of Oxford's Case in Chancery* (1615) Mich 13 Jac 1, 21 ER 485.
39 (1936) 56 CLR 113.
40 (1983) 151 CLR 447.
41 See the catalogue of recognised weaknesses in *Blomley v Ryan* (1956) 99 CLR 362, 405 and 415.
42 *Robb v Green* (1895) 2 QB 315.
43 Eg *Green & Clara Pty Ltd v Bestobell Industries* [1982] WAR 1; *Warman International Ltd v Dwyer* (1995) 182 CLR 544.

refusal to order specific performance of contracts for personal services except in the rarest of circumstances means there has been little scope for equitable protection of the employee's interest. The rationale for equity's treatment of the relationship as a personal and never proprietary one accords with the common law's abhorrence of slavery. The worker is never a commodity to be bought and sold. Humans are legal subjects, not objects. However, in the employment context the principle can be blamed for the common law's reluctance to reinstate dismissed workers.[44]

Given the developments in equitable jurisprudence since the 1980s[45] to protect other vulnerable parties to unequal bargains, there is no reason in principle that equity's intervention in contractual relationships to alleviate unconscionable conduct should not also run to protecting employees from exploitation at the hands of employers.[46] Examples of the kinds of situations that may give rise to arguments that an employee should be permitted to escape an unconscionable bargain include agreements to surrender more generous pay and conditions under a collective agreement by signing an Australian Workplace Agreement,[47] and agreements to sign deeds of release, relinquishing rights to make further claims against an employer in exchange for some modest severance benefit.

In practice, however, equitable jurisdiction is exercised only by the most expensive of private law courts. The cases upon which the doctrine of unconscionable dealing have been developed involved considerable sums of money or valuable real estate. It is rare for an employment case to have sufficient at stake to warrant the expense of argument before a Supreme Court exercising equitable jurisdiction. Also, equity's remedies have generally been of limited use to employees. Equity will rescind, but only rarely rewrite,[48] an unconscionable contract, so it will assist an employee only to walk away from a job, not to get fairer treatment. It is possible that a right to rescind for unconscionable dealing will be worth pursuing as a response to an employer's attempt to enforce a restrictive covenant preventing the employee from going to work in a rival enterprise post-employment.[49] On the whole, however, the opportunities for the development of a body of case law on equitable doctrines in employment appear limited, while the ordinary courts remain such forbidding forums for workers.

A role for estoppel?

Since the High Court of Australia's decision in *Waltons Stores (Interstate) v Maher*,[50] Australian law has recognised that the doctrine of promissory estoppel may be used—as a 'sword'—to bring a claim to remedy the harm caused by an unreliable

---

44 See discussion of reinstatement and job security in Chapters 6 and 9.

45 See for instance the high-water mark set by the majority of the High Court of Australia in *Bridgewater v Leahy* (1998) 194 CLR 457.

46 See J Riley *Employee Protection at Common Law* (2005), Ch 5.

47 See Chapter 11.

48 See, however, modern money lending cases, where equity has sometimes rewritten loan contracts to lower usurious interest rates, eg, *Asia Pacific International Pty Ltd v Dalrymple* [2000] 2 Qd R 229.

49 See Chapter 6.

50 (1988) 164 CLR 387.

promise, even where the promise did not meet the requirements for enforceability as a contract. This doctrine would appear on its face to be very useful in the sphere of work relation-ships—although at the time of writing, this potential had not been realised in case law.[51] Many workplace disputes arise because of a mismatch between the terms of that extensive written document presented as a take-it-or-leave it proposition to the worker at the outset (or even after the commencement) of the relationship, and the more informal commitments given as the relationship progresses. Promises of bonuses for performance, or of participation in share option schemes, for instance, may be thwarted by the employer's sudden reliance on a contractual right to terminate on short notice, after the worker has performed to the standard warranting the reward, but before the date for payment of the reward has arrived. The doctrine of promissory estoppel would allow a worker who has detrimentally relied on the promise of the performance-based reward to seek a remedy in equity—for fulfilment of the expectation created by the promise, or at least for reversal of any detriment caused by reliance on the promise.[52]

Few plaintiffs have ever raised such arguments, and on occasions when they have, they have often been defeated by the rejoinder that an employee who simply continues to perform the duties described in the written contract has suffered no detriment from her reliance on the unfulfilled representation.[53] This, with respect, must be wrong. The worker who continues to exhaust herself on the promise of particular rewards has suffered a detriment, in being cheated of the opportunity to decide to do otherwise. Domestic housekeepers who have remained in service on the promise of inheriting money have been able to rely on estoppel to enforce the promise.[54] Other kinds of workers who remained loyal to an employer on the strength of representations that they will enjoy certain rewards deserve similar protection. Development of the doctrine of estoppel in this field may provide a useful antidote to classical contract law's tendency to privilege the terms of written documents even where those documents have not been negotiated, and are barely consulted during the currency of the working relationship.

Statutory intervention

Very early in the history of the development of employment or labour law, statutes were enacted to regulate the raw exercise of power by masters over servants. Today there are still many statutes that regulate particular aspects of the employment relationship, and that provide benefits that the parties themselves cannot escape by private bargain. Examples are state legislation providing for occupational health and

---

51 For a more thorough discussion of the potential use of estoppel in workplace relationships, see Riley, above n 46, Ch 4.

52 There are conflicting opinions on the appropriate remedy for promissory estoppel. See M Spence *Protecting Reliance* (1999); and A Robertson 'Satisfying the Minimum Equity: Equitable Estoppel Remedies after *Verwayen*' (1996) 20 *MULR* 85. This debate is discussed in Riley, above n 46, 107–9.

53 See eg *Bredel v Moore Business Systems Ltd* [2003] NSWCA 117.

54 See *Greasley v Cooke* [1980] 3 All ER 710.

safety standards and workers' compensation arrangements. Industrial statutes also legislate for some minimum standards, and provide procedures for the making of industrial instruments that create enforceable rights.[55]

Contract remains the bedrock beneath these sedimentary layers of regulation. Statutory provisions and industrial instruments are binding upon the parties, but where those provisions and instruments are silent as to a particular matter, a court will fall back upon principles of contract law to determine the issue. Nevertheless, even general commercial contract law has come under challenge from policy makers who have recognised its potential for unjust solutions in cases of unequal bargaining power.

Here we turn our attention to two areas of statutory development. First we examine the *Trade Practices Act 1974* (Cth) and its potential relevance in the field of work contracts. Then we consider statutory unfair contracts review provisions in industrial statutes. The most developed jurisprudence of unfair contracts review of work contracts has emerged from the exercise of the NSW Industrial Relations Commission's jurisdiction under s 106 of the *Industrial Relations Act 1996* (NSW).

Trade practices law

Australian contract law has undergone cataclysmic change since the introduction of the *Trade Practices Act 1974* (Cth). Progressive additions to this statute have extended the obligations on contracting parties to observe certain standards of fair dealing. The *Trade Practices Act* deals not only with competition policy (concerned with supporting an efficient and competitive marketplace in Australia), but also with the protection of certain vulnerable groups, notably consumers (see generally Pt V) and to a lesser extent small businesses.[56] There are cogent arguments for the extension of trade practices protections to employees and other workers.

Behind the post-1996 'Workplace Relations' agenda is an assertion that the employment relationship is *just another commercial exchange* that needs no special regulation. Already, many Australian employees are not covered by industrial instruments, nor unfair dismissal laws, so for them private contract law is already the principal source of legal rights in their employment relationships. If the current trends of individualisation and union exclusion identified by Stephen Deery and Richard Mitchell[57] continue, the future shape of employment regulation in Australia will conform even more closely to ordinary commercial contract law.

The *Trade Practices* legislation has revolutionised ordinary commercial contract law in Australia in a number of ways. We shall focus on those provisions that impose standards of fair dealing in commercial transactions between corporations and individuals. In appropriate cases, those standards of fair dealing can be enforced, despite the wording of any written contract between the parties. Enforcement in the employment context faces a

---

55 Chapters 7 to 9 consider these protections.

56 See Pt IVA ss 51AB and 51AC.

57 See S Deery, and R Mitchell 'The Emergence of Individualisation and Union Exclusion as an Employment Relations Strategy' in S Deery and R Mitchell (eds) *Employment Relations: Individualisation and Union Exclusion, An International Study* (1999).

number of obstacles, although as the cases of *O'Neill v Medical Benefits Fund of Australia*,[58] *Walker v Salomon Smith Barney Securities*[59] and *Magro v Freemantle Football Club Limited*[60] demonstrate, these obstacles are not insuperable. It is useful to outline the provisions on which such a claim will depend. The liability provisions in the Act include:

- s 52, the general prohibition on engaging in 'conduct that is misleading or deceptive or likely to mislead or deceive';
- s 51A, which reverses the onus of proving that a statement as to a future matter was made on reasonable grounds;
- s 51AA, which prohibits 'conduct that is unconscionable within the meaning of the unwritten law, from time to time, of the States and Territories';
- s 51AC, which makes more detailed provisions prohibiting unconscionable conduct in the provision of goods and services involving small businesses (this provision does *not* apply to employment contracts, and is subject to a $3 million limit);
- s 53B, which prohibits misleading conduct in relation to job offers to new recruits.

The remedial provisions comprise:

- s 82, which provides for payment of damages; and
- s 87, which empowers the court to grant a wide range of 'other orders'. It is these 'other orders' that offer the potential for the most useful remedies.

The 'trade and commerce' requirement

Before a successful claim can be brought under ss 52, 51AA or 51AC of the *Trade Practices Act*, it is necessary to show that the conduct complained of was 'in trade or commerce'. This requirement proved an obstacle to an employee in *Concrete Constructions (NSW) Pty Ltd v Nelson*,[61] who complained that the employer (through its vicarious liability for the conduct of a fellow employee) had caused him injury by giving a dangerously false assurance that a grate over an air conditioning shaft was safe. It was not. The claim under the *Trade Practices Act* was unsuccessful because the court held that this communication was internal to the organisation, and so was not made in trade or commerce. The facts of *Concrete Constructions* have been easy to distinguish from cases concerning the negotiation of terms and conditions of employment contracts. A number of decisions of the Federal Court and Supreme Courts such as *Barto v GPR Management Services Pty Ltd*,[62] *Patrick v Steel Mains Pty Ltd*,[63] and *Stoelwinder v Southern Health Care Network*[64] have held that contract negotiations with staff are part of the trading activities of corporations. Some judges have expressed doubt on this point, usually based on Brennan J's observation in *Concrete Constructions* that relief for misleading and deceptive conduct under s 52 must be limited to those claims made in

---

58 (2002) 122 FCR 455.
59 (2003) 140 IR 433.
60 (2005) 142 IR 445.
61 (1990) 169 CLR 594.
62 (1991) 105 ALR 339.
63 (1987) 77 ALR 133.
64 (2000) 177 ALR 501.

the 'capacity as a consumer'.[65] The number of cases that have now allowed claims for breach of s 52 in the course of contract negotiations suggest that Wilcox J's decision in *Barto* is to be preferred.[66]

Grounds for a trade practices claim

Employees who have been ineligible to complain of unfair dismissal under industrial statutes have argued a breach of s 52 of the *Trade Practices Act* when seeking some remedy arising from the termination of an employment contract. The advantages of bringing a s 52 claim in tandem with a contract claim include access to the Federal Court system, and a wider range of remedies under the *Trade Practices Act*. These cases often arise because the employee's expectation of long-term employment has been disappointed by an abrupt dismissal. These claims generally assert that the employer gave oral assurances of long-term engagement, despite the express terms of a written contract allowing termination upon a reasonably short period of notice. The employee's contract law claim is often doomed to failure because the express contractual provision will favour the employer's assertion that there was no binding contract for long-term job security. According to classical contract law principles, written contractual terms are a strong indication that any contradictory verbal assurance is not a binding term of the contract.[67] That does not, however, mean that the verbal assurances carry no legal consequences. At common law they may constitute a misrepresentation that vitiates the contract. Rescission of the contract, however, will be of little value to the employee who is aggrieved by loss of employment. Under the *Trade Practices Act*, those words of assurance may constitute misleading and deceptive conduct, in breach of s 52, and give rise to a claim for damages under s 82, or an injunction or other order under s 87. If the representation was made in recruitment, the employee may also raise s 53B, which explicitly prohibits misleading conduct concerning the 'availability, nature, terms or conditions of, or any other matter' relating to offers of employment.

One of the first obstacles that the employee must overcome is proving that the representation was in fact misleading and deceptive at the time it was made. Sometimes a genuinely intended commitment will be defeated by subsequent circumstances, beyond the reasonable control of the person making the promise. If this is the case, the employee will need to plead s 51A of the Act, which deals with statements concerning future intentions. This section places the onus on the employer to prove that there were reasonable grounds for making the statement of future intentions at the time it was made.

In some cases, a court will be prepared to find that there has indeed been a breach of contract, and will not need to find any remedy for breach of the statute, because expectation damages under contract will adequately and appropriately compensate the

---

65 (1990) 169 CLR 594, 605. See eg *Hearn v O'Rourke* [2002] FCA 1179. Kiefel J relied on similar findings in *Martin v Tasmania Development and Resources* (1999) 163 ALR 79, 97–8, and *Mulcahy v Hydro-Electric Commission* (1998) 85 FCR 170.

66 The NSW Court of Appeal has accepted the validity of a s 52 claim in relation to the terms and conditions of employment in *Saad v TWT Ltd* [1998] NSWSC 282 although it was ultimately decided that the representation was not misleading and deceptive. The Full Court of the Federal Court in *O'Neill v Medical Benefits Fund of Australia* (2002) 122 FCR 455 heard and upheld a claim for breach of s 52 concerning representations made in recruiting an executive.

67 See eg *Gates v City Mutual Life Assurance Society Ltd* (1986) 160 CLR 1, 5–6.

employee.[68] In some cases, the representation will be held to be a contract term, but not a misleading or deceptive representation. For example, in *Saad v TWT Limited*,[69] *Sheldrick v WT Partnership (Aust) Pty Ltd*[70] and *Windross v Transact Communications Pty Ltd*,[71] the respective plaintiffs were able to claim damages for breach of contract, but were not able to prove breach of s 52, because it was held that the representations in each case were made on reasonable grounds at the time they were made.

No requirement of intentional deception

A false representation will be misleading and deceptive even if the person making the statement was unaware of its falsity. 'A corporation may breach s 52 despite the fact that a representation has been made honestly, innocently and without any intention to actively mislead or deceive.'[72] But where the statement concerned some future matter, then liability for a misprediction will depend on whether the person making the representation had reasonable grounds for making the prediction at the time it was made. Section 51A places the onus of proving reasonable grounds for belief on the person making the representation.

Proof of damages

One of the difficulties in using the *Trade Practices Act* in the employment context is the question of damages. Damages under s 82 of the *Trade Practices Act* are assessed on a tort-like basis, that is, the victim of the misleading or deceptive conduct is entitled to be restored to the position he or she would have been in, were it not for the misleading and deceptive conduct. *O'Neill v Medical Benefits Fund of Australia Ltd*[73] provides a convenient example of this principle. Mr O'Neill was an executive employed in a secure position with a large financial institution when he was recruited to what he was assured was a secure long-term position by a recruitment consultant acting for MBF. Despite the assurances that the new job would be long term, Mr O'Neill was made redundant soon after taking up the post. The court held that the representations made to him were made carelessly, without taking any reasonable steps to check their accuracy, and so, with the help of s 51A, Mr O'Neill was able to establish his case for breach of s 52 of the Act. A difficulty arose in assessing damages. If his claim had been successful in contract, he would have been entitled to have expectations assessed, based on the probability that he would have kept the job for the promised long term. The kind of calculation made in cases such as *Gregory v Philip Morris Ltd*[74] and *Bostik (Australia) Pty Ltd v Gorgevski (No 1)*[75] would have been appropriate. In those cases, the employer was obliged to pay

---

68 Eg *Saad v TWT Ltd* [1998] NSWSC 282, *Robert Michael Richman v Pacific Waste Management Pty Ltd* No G378 of 1992 FED No 895.
69 *Saad v TWT Ltd* [1998] NSWSC 282.
70 (1998) 89 IR 206.
71 [2002] FMCA 145 (20 August 2002).
72 See R Steinwall *Annotated Trade Practices Act 1974* (2004), 240 and the body of case law cited in para 71,945.165.
73 (2002) 122 FCR 455.
74 (1988) 80 ALR 455, 482–4.
75 (1992) 36 FCR 20, 32–3.

damages representing the length of time the employee may have been expected to keep the job until he could be dismissed on reasonable grounds. In Mr Gorgevski's case, that was held to be a number of years, until his retirement.

However, rather than pay him an appropriate severance payment on this basis, Mr O'Neill and his counsel were sent away to construct a claim based on what he would have been able to earn had he not been tempted away from his former employer in the first place. In *Magro v Freemantle Football Club Limited*, a football coach who claimed he had been misled into believing he had a secure three-year contract at $100 000 a year, had damages assessed at more than $500 000 under s 82 of the *Trade Practices Act* when it was held that this representation was misleading. It seems an odd result that the damages awarded under s 82 should be higher than any amount the employee would have earned had the contract run its course for the claimed fixed term. Nevertheless, it is a result that arises from the proposition that *Trade Practices* damages must be assessed according to the opportunities that the coach gave up in his former Victorian football club when he relied on the misleading representations.

Section 51AA and other orders under s 87

Since 1993, the *Trade Practices Act* has included further provisions outlawing 'unconscionable' conduct in business dealings between corporations and small businesses. Pt IVA of the Act incorporates s 51AA, which stipulates that corporations must not 'engage in conduct which is unconscionable within the meaning of the unwritten law, from time to time, of the States and Territories'. This provision enables statutory enforcement of contemporary doctrines of equity, with the considerable benefit that the competition watchdog, the ACCC, has standing to bring proceedings to enforce these standards, and the more flexible remedies available under the Act (including orders for variation of contracts under s 87) are made available to litigants. The meaning of the provision has been discussed by the Full Court of the Federal Court in *Australian Competition and Consumer Commission v Samton Holdings Pty Ltd*[76] (a case concerning a dealing over the assignment of a commercial lease):

> Ultimately the language of s 51AA requires identification of conduct able to be characterized as unconscionable in a sense known to the unwritten law. In the context of that law as it presently stands, unconscionable conduct is that which supports the grant of relief on the principles set out in specific equitable doctrines.[77]

In *Samton* the court identified five categories of such relief, including equity's willingness to set aside transactions involving some special disadvantage on one part (typified by the cases of *Commercial Bank of Australia Ltd v Amadio*,[78] *Louth v Diprose*[79]

---

76 (2002) 117 FCR 301. The High Court of Australia has considered the meaning of s 51AA more recently in *Berbatis Holdings Pty Ltd v ACCC* (2003) 214 CLR 51; however, the court restricted its consideration to application of the doctrine of unconscionable dealing in *Commercial Bank of Australia Ltd v Amadio* (1983) 151 CLR 447, and did not consider whether s 51AA also imported a broader range of equitable principles into the *Trade Practices Act* protections.

77 Ibid, 318–19.

78 (1983) 151 CLR 447.

79 (1992) 175 CLR 621.

and *Bridgewater v Leahy*[80]), or some lack of comprehension on one side (as in *Garcia v National Australia Bank Ltd*[81]). The High Court in *ACCC v Berbatis Holdings Pty Ltd*[82] decided that this particular doctrine of unconscionable dealing was captured by s 51AA. The court in *Berbatis* did not go on to consider any of the other categories identified in *Samton*, but neither did it rule out the prospect that those other categories may provide the basis for an argument under s 51AA in the appropriate case.[83]

The third of the five categories outlined in *Samton* is equitable or promissory estoppel. This principle, described briefly above, holds that equity will prevent a party from exercising a legal right in a way that involves unconscionable departure from a representation relied upon by another to his or her detriment. This is precisely the situation that employees such as Mr O'Neill and Mr Magro faced: they relied on representations, seriously made to them, but the employer subsequently chose to ignore the representations and assert a contradictory legal right to terminate a contract of employment on short notice.

The Court in *Samton* cites two estoppel cases in support of the proposition that the doctrine of estoppel is contemplated by s 51AA: *Waltons Stores (Interstate) Ltd v Maher*,[84] and *Commonwealth v Verwayen*.[85] There is a more recent authority on estoppel—*Giumelli v Giumelli*.[86] The significant difference between *Waltons*, *Verwayen* and *Giumelli* lies in the High Court's statements as to the appropriate remedy for estoppel. In *Waltons* a majority held that the appropriate remedy for equitable estoppel was reversal of the detriment suffered by the person relying on the representation. This was the remedy afforded to Mr O'Neill for breach of s 52. *Verwayen* was not so clear on appropriate relief, there being no clear majority on the law. *Giumelli*, on the other hand, held that the plaintiff succeeding in estoppel had a prima facie entitlement to fulfilment of the expectation raised by the representation. This entitlement should only be cut down if there were some reason in equity—such as the intervention of third party rights—which made such a remedy inappropriate. Such a remedy, in a case like Mr Magro's, would have allowed the employer club to simply pay out the remainder of the three-year fixed term contract, which formed the essence of the representation.

The *Samton* judgment leaves open the prospect that employees who would have a case in estoppel could argue a breach of s 51AA and so access statutory remedies. Other kinds of cases, besides those—like *O'Neill* and *Magro*—involving promises of secure employment, may include those where employers have reneged on their representations about performance-based remuneration schemes.

For example, *Canizales v Microsoft Corporation & Ors*[87] (decided under the s 106 of the *Industrial Relations Act 1996* (NSW) jurisdiction to vary unfair work contracts)

---

80 (1998) 194 CLR 457.
81 (1988) 194 CLR 395.
82 (2003) 214 CLR 51.
83 Ibid, 74, 84 and 109
84 (1998) 164 CLR 387.
85 (1990) 170 CLR 394.
86 (1999) 196 CLR 101.
87 (2000) 99 IR 426.

might just as easily have been argued on this basis under s 51AA of the *Trade Practices Act*. Mr Canizales took a position that came with a number of valuable share options that could not be exercised until a certain date. On the strength of firm promises that his employment was secure at least until the options vested, Mr Canizales committed himself to a large debt. The employer resiled from its representation by terminating his employment in a way that was deliberately calculated to deny him the opportunity to exercise his options, shortly before they vested. A court granting him the prima facie right to the benefit of the representation would have granted precisely the same remedy that the NSW Industrial Relations Commission granted under s 106 of *the Industrial Relations Act 1996*—damages calculated to put him in the same position that he would have been in, had he been given reasonable notice, so that his contract of employment would have survived long enough to fulfil the expectation created by the representation.

The appropriate remedial provision to be argued on behalf of an employee in a case like this is s 87, rather than the more limited s 82 damages. Justice Kirby, in dissent in *Marks v GIO Australia Ltd*,[88] opined that s 87 gave the court a broad discretion to make orders that would do justice in the case: 'The *Trade Practices Act* should be construed to achieve its remedial purposes.'[89] In that case (concerning misleading information about loan agreements) Kirby J held that the defendant ought to be made to perform its promise, and that such an order was a permissible exercise of the court's discretion under s 87.

On its face, s 87 promises a broad range of remedies, to enable the court to tailor relief to do justice in the individual case, including variation of contracts.

Further small business protections

Since 1998, the *Trade Practices Act* has included some additional provisions dealing with unconscionable conduct. These provisions were inserted into the *Trade Practices Act* following the Reid Committee Report, *Finding a Balance Towards Fair Trading in Australia*.[90] This report had concluded that, despite the availability of statutory remedies for breach of ss 52 and 51AA, continuing unfair business practices in Australia had left a legacy of stress, marriage breakdown, poor health and even suicide among many small-business owning citizens.[91] The Reid Committee recommended the insertion of s 51AC, which applies to small-business suppliers, and spells out a range of matters by which a court may assess whether a commercial transaction is unconscionable. In addition to the usual concerns with undue influence and inadequate explanation and comprehension of contract terms, s 51AC includes matters related to the relative bargaining strengths of the parties, and even matters concerned with the objective fairness of the transaction according to market standards. For example, s 51AC(4)(f) requires a court to take account of 'the extent to which

88 (1998) 196 CLR 494, 547.
89 Ibid.
90 Report by the House of Representatives Standing Committee on Industry, Science and Technology, May 1997.
91 See *Explanatory Memorandum* to the *Trade Practices Amendment (Fair Trading) Bill 1997*, 2.

the acquirer's conduct towards the small business supplier was consistent with the acquirer's conduct in similar transactions between the acquirer and other like small business suppliers'.

Section 51AC is not available for use by employees—but it is an avenue for redress by the growing armies who have been outsourced to the status of independent contractors.

Conclusions

It is conceded that employee advocates have much work to do to harness the protections of the *Trade Practices Act* in the interests of unfairly treated employees. There are obstacles, and the cases that offer a path forward are presently rare stepping stones. In theory, however, there are sound arguments for extending trade practices protection to this class of commercial dealings—especially if the future of employment regulation in Australia does indeed leave employees to their remedies in commercial contract law. All working citizens ought to be afforded equal treatment before the law with other individuals who enter into bargains with corporations.

Unfair contracts review

Parliaments in many jurisdictions have long recognised the weaknesses of classical contract law to do justice in certain types of dealings between unequally matched contracting parties. Transactions between monopolistic suppliers and consumers, and between financial institutions and small borrowers, have typically been targeted by legislation allowing the review of contracts on the basis of unfairness.[92] These kinds of statutes typically address the remedial shortcomings of the equitable jurisdiction, which generally affords nothing more than rescission of contracts. Rescission is a useless remedy for many of the weaker parties to these kinds of deals. Borrowers under usurious loan contracts still need the money, but they need it on more reasonable interest rate and repayment terms.

The same principles are suitable to work contracts. Workers in sweatshops still need jobs, but on decent wages and conditions. In recognition of this, some parliaments in Australia have enacted provisions for statutory review of unfair work contracts. There are federal provisions for independent contracts in the *Workplace Relations Act 1996* (Cth),[93] and two state jurisdictions, New South Wales and Queensland, have enacted unfair contracts provisions in industrial statutes.[94] These state provisions will have limited operation following the *Work Choices* amendments, which paralysed much state industrial law, including unfair contracts review for all employees of constitutional corporations, even under the *Contracts Review Act 1980* (NSW).

---

92 See for example the *Unfair Contract Terms Act 1977* (UK); *EC Directive on Unfair Contract Terms in Consumer Contracts* 93/13, OJL 95/29, 5 April 1993; *Moneylenders Act 1927* (UK); *Moneylenders Act 1941* (NSW); *Credit Act 1984* (NSW); and *Contracts Review Act 1980* (NSW).

93 *Workplace Relations Act 1996* (Cth), ss 832–4. The *Independent Contractors Bill 2006* (Cth) proposed to repeal these provisions, but re-enact them in special legislation.

94 See the *Industrial Relations Act 1999* (Qld), s 276; the *Industrial Relations Act 1996* (NSW), ss 105–109A.

Nevertheless, it is worth mentioning the NSW provisions because, in half a century of operation, they have produced an extensive jurisprudence on fair dealing at the workplace. That jurisprudence may aid in some measure in interpreting the provisions that remain in federal legislation. Those federal provisions did not attract a great deal of litigation while the state regimes were available to litigants. Now that the state tribunals are closed to many unfair contracts claims, it is possible that independent contractor litigants will consider approaching the Federal Court for a remedy under federal legislation.

Section 106 empowers the NSW Industrial Relations Commission to review any unfair contract or arrangement 'whereby a person performs work in any industry'. The Commission is able to exercise similar powers to those exercised by the Federal Court under s 87 of the *Trade Practices Act* if there has been a breach of those provisions (such as ss 52, 51AA and 51AC) imposing standards of fair dealing in commercial transactions. In its present form, s 106 empowers the Commission (in court session) to declare contracts void or to vary them. This jurisdiction is confined to contracts (or collateral arrangements[95]) 'whereby a person performs work in any industry', which are found to be 'unfair'. 'Unfair' is defined in s 105, in the following terms:

> unfair contract means a contract:
> (a) that is unfair, harsh or unconscionable, or
> (b) that is against the public interest, or
> (c) that provides a total remuneration that is less than a person performing the work would receive as an employee performing the work, or
> (d) that is designed to, or does, avoid the provisions of an industrial instrument.

The federal provisions, which apply only to 'contracts for services', that is independent contracts, also allow for review of contracts that are unfair or harsh, or provide less remuneration than the worker would earn if an employee. The provision allowing review on the basis that the contract is contrary to the public interest was omitted when supervision of unfair contracts review provisions was removed from the Australian Industrial Relations Commission and given to a court. Excision of the public interest consideration was necessary to ensure that the nature of the jurisdiction was not administrative or legislative in character because Federal courts are constitutionally limited to exercising judicial power.[96]

Under the NSW legislation, the Commission may examine the contract at the time it was made, or at any time subsequently, to find that it has become unfair in its terms or in the manner in which the parties have conducted themselves. (The federal provisions allow review of the contract or arrangement as it was made.) The remedial responses available to the NSW Commission include complete rescission (avoidance), variation of the terms of the contract (from its inception or from a later stage), and payment of compensation.

---

95 Section 105.
96 See *Finch v Herald and Weekly Times Ltd* (1996) 65 IR 239.

Origins

Section 106 was enacted with the *Industrial Relations Act* in 1996, but it has its antecedent in s 88F of the *Industrial Arbitration Act 1940* (NSW), enacted in 1959. In early cases testing the scope of the jurisdiction, it was argued that the rationale for s 88F was to defeat the stratagems of employers who sought to avoid their obligations under industrial awards. At a time when most industries were covered by industrial awards fixing wages and conditions for employees, the temptation to save money or enjoy more flexible conditions by engaging workers on independent contracts was no doubt as strong as it clearly is today. Section 88F provided some protection for workers from such schemes. However, as early case law demonstrated, the section was not simply an antidote to the schemes of those allergic to paying award wages. The statute was drafted broadly, and has been interpreted expansively by the courts.[97] In particular, the Commission's discretion could be exercised if the contract or arrangement was found to be 'unfair',[98] or 'harsh or unconscionable'.[99] Award avoidance was only one of the specific instances of unfairness enumerated in paras (d) and (e).

In an early decision on the scope of s 88F, Sheldon J described it as a 'radical law', which 'plays havoc with the classic principles relating to contracts'.[100] Since then, the NSW Commission has developed a vibrant jurisprudence in unfair contracts review, which encompasses employment disputes, independent contracts, franchise agreements, partnership disputes and even cases involving the termination of multimillion dollar commercial distributorships.[101] Many of the employee cases involved executives, who are, after all, the people most likely to enjoy sufficient financial resources to seek legal assistance. A number of multimillion dollar claims[102] prompted the NSW Parliament to amend the statute in 2002 to impose an income threshold of $200 000 for employees and people in partnerships seeking to use the jurisdiction.[103]

An earlier amendment also prohibited use of the provisions by employees if the substance of the complaint was the fact of termination, and not some unfairness in the contract itself. This was to ensure that high-income earners could not subvert the income threshold imposed by the unfair dismissal provisions in Pt 6 of the *Industrial Relations Act 1996* (NSW). Nevertheless the amending provision has been interpreted narrowly so that terminated employees were still able (at least until the enactment of *Work Choices*) to complain of the unfairness of their terms of severance, albeit not about the unfairness of the fact of termination itself.[104]

---

97 See *Stevenson v Barham* (1977) 136 CLR 190, 192.

98 Section 88F(1)(a).

99 Section 88F(2)(b).

100 *Davies v General Transport Development Pty Ltd* [1967] AR (NSW) 371, 373.

101 See *Gough and Gilmour Holdings Pty Ltd v Caterpillar of Australia Ltd* (No 15) [2003] NSWIRComm 173. During 2004, a number of decisions of the NSW Court of Appeal cast doubt on the validity of some of the Industrial Relations Commission's so-called 'commercial case' decisions. We discuss this debate below.

102 *Westfield Holdings Ltd v Adams* (2001) 114 IR 241.

103 See s 108A, introduced by Act No 32 of 2002, effective from 24 June 2002.

104 See s 109A and *Beahan v Bush Boake Allen Aust Ltd* (1999) 93 IR 1.

A jurisprudence of 'fairness'

The NSW unfair contracts review jurisdiction has attracted critics, particularly from the school of legal thought committed to the protection of commercial interests from any uncertainty that arises when judges are afforded 'at large' discretions to disturb contractual commitments. As this chapter has suggested, there are persuasive arguments for questioning the privilege that conventional legal thinking affords to written contracts for the provision of work. The written contract does not always reflect the mutual understandings between the parties. Hugh Collins,[105] writing about relational contract theory generally, describes three 'rationalities' forming the normative framework of a typical business relationship. These are the business relation itself (being the contextual reality of the interdependent relationship of the parties), the business deal, and the contract that documents the deal. In reality, the first two are more important to the parties during their relationship than the third. And yet when common law courts are called upon to resolve disputes, it is the documentation that takes precedence.

If contract law is genuinely concerned with giving effect to the mutual expectations of the parties, there can be no objection to permitting a dispute resolution tribunal to investigate the business deal and the business relationship, and not merely the documentation to determine what terms reasonable parties to such a relationship would have adopted. This is what the NSW Industrial Relations Commission in Court Session does in reviewing contracts and arrangements for fairness. The presiding judge examines the conduct of the parties against benchmarks of what reasonable parties in the same circumstances have done. The Court will ask, for example, what oral representations the employer made to the worker. How were other workers treated in similar circumstances? What industry standards and practices prevail? In *Westfield Holdings Ltd v Adams*,[106] the judge took note of the fact that the Board of the employer company decided to change the rules of the share option scheme to allow pro rata entitlement in a case of redundancy, after they had terminated Mr Adams without affording such a benefit. The benchmark in this case was what other directors of the company decided would be fair should they themselves suffer the same treatment as the unfortunate Mr Adams.

It is true that unfair contracts review is an essentially fact-based jurisdiction. Cases turn on their own facts. The jurisdiction is frequently described as one of morals and not of law.[107] The judge must exercise 'a value judgment reflecting contemporary community values derived from the commonsense approach characteristic of the ordinary, reasonable, hypothetical "standard" member of the community'.[108] But this does not mean that the Commission has exercised its jurisdiction capriciously. An examination of the case law demonstrates the development of recognisable principles, frequently informed by equitable principles, and concepts of procedural fairness.[109]

---

105 Above n 3, 173.
106 (2001) 114 IR 241.
107 *A & M Thompson Pty Ltd v Total Australia Ltd* [1980] 2 NSWLR 1, 14.
108 *King v Cake It Away Pty Ltd* (2005) ATPR 42-059, [84].
109 For a detailed analysis of the jurisdiction up until the end of 2003, see J Phillips and M Tooma *The Law of Unfair Contracts in NSW: An Examination of S 106 of the Industrial Relations Act 1996 (NSW)* (2004).

The boundaries of the jurisdiction

The application of s 106 to cases involving dealings other than employment and labour supply contracts has generated something of a 'turf war' between the NSW Supreme Court and the NSW Industrial Relations Commission. In *Mitchforce v Industrial Relations Commission*,[110] a majority of the NSW Court of Appeal criticised the Commission's expansive view of its jurisdiction, on the basis that the legislature must have intended that the jurisdiction apply only to traditional industrial problems, and not to every commercial contract where one party or other would do some work as a result of the dealing. *Mitchforce* involved a hotel lease, the terms of which had become intolerably onerous for the lessees, who found themselves working for virtually nothing to build up goodwill in a business that they would be required to hand back to the hotel owner. The majority took a somewhat blinkered view of the circumstances, influenced by the law's habit of categorising relationships into rigid taxonomies. This dealing was of the genus *property transaction*, species *lease*. Hence, the majority held that it could not fall within the jurisdiction of a tribunal charged with reviewing contracts and arrangements for the performance of work. Handley JA's dissenting opinion took a broader view based on the economic reality of the arrangement (and arguably more consistent with the High Court of Australia authority in *Stevenson v Barham*[111]), and held that while on its face the contract began as a lease of business premises, the operation of the rent review terms of the contract caused the arrangement to become so onerous that the lessees were working only for the benefit of the hotel owners. The lessees had been 'reduced to the role of managers because the landlord was taking all the profits of the business and leaving them with a loss'.[112]

In many respects the arrangement in *Mitchforce*, while on its face a conventional property lease, typifies the creative structuring of work relationships in the new economy. Those who own capital assets seek to shift as much of the business risk from exploiting those assets onto those who do the work to harvest profit from the assets—but while still reserving an entitlement to skim dividends on a profit-related basis. Turnover-based rents of premises and equipment, royalties for exploitation of patents, designs, trade marks and business systems—these are methods by which capital owners exploit labour. The economic reality is that these kinds of relationships are arrangements under which work is performed, and they are just as susceptible to exploitation as employment and dependent contractor relationships.

Alternatives to contract

The statutory measures described above constitute a modification of the rigidity of classical contract law in the interests of greater equity in business relationships. Essentially, these measures continue to operate within the private contract law model, but allow a

---

110 (2003) 57 NSWLR 212. See also *Solution 6 Holdings Ltd & Ors v Industrial Relations Commission of NSW and Ors* (2004) 60 NSWLR 558.
111 (1977) 136 CLR 190.
112 (2003) 57 NSWLR 212, 250.

judicial discretion to modify or refuse to enforce contract terms. If, as we have argued, classical contract theory is inept in describing the reality of employment relationships, and is therefore inappropriate as an exclusive regulatory tool in this field, what other legal models might be employed in its place? Here we acknowledge other legal models that have conventionally been applied in contexts where work is performed and we consider the potential for creative extension of those models to solve contemporary problems in the regulation of work relationships.

Administrative law

Private contract law is not the only model for regulating relationships. Public law, for example, has developed an alternative model to deal with relationships in which one person (generally the state or its instrumentalities) exercises power over others who are dependent upon and subject to the exercise of that power. Public or administrative law insists that the exercise of such power be for proper purposes (not arbitrary) and rational, and that the governed are entitled to fair procedures, including a right to be heard, and rights to be given reasons. A public law model is intuitively appealing when we contemplate employment by large corporations or public bodies. These bodies wield considerable power and influence. They have the capacity for great influence over the lives and well-being of citizens, and they enjoy certain benefits and privileges in the community, by virtue of the political influence they are able to assert, as productive engines in the national economy.[113] To some extent the unfair dismissal protection regimes enacted federally and by the states reflect an administrative law approach to dealing with the potential problem of abuse of power by such employers. Unfair dismissal protections examine not only whether a dismissal was justified on the basis of contract terms, but whether it was procedurally fair in terms of whether there were consultations, warnings, and opportunities to respond.[114] Concepts of procedural fairness have certainly been adopted in the context of public sector employment. In *Jarratt v Commissioner of Police for New South Wales*[115] the High Court of Australia held that a senior public servant appointed 'at pleasure' and who could be dismissed 'at any time', must still be afforded procedural fairness ahead of any decision to summarily dismiss.

Fiduciary law

Akin in many ways to administrative law, but a creature of the law of private obligations, is the legal model of the fiduciary obligation. This model also concerns the control of the exercise of power.

A fiduciary obligation is notoriously difficult to define. At its heart it is an obligation created when one person (the fiduciary) voluntarily assumes a responsibility to act in the best interests of another person (the beneficiary), who is vulnerable to harm if the fiduciary fails in that responsibility.[116] The paradigm of the fiduciary is the

---

113 See H Collins 'Market Power, Bureaucratic Power and the Contract of Employment' (1986) 15 *ILJ* 1.
114 See Chapter 9 for a discussion of statutory unfair dismissal protection.
115 (2005) 79 ALJR 1581. See also *Ridge v Baldwin* [1964] AC 40, 66.
116 *Hospital Products Ltd v United States Surgical Corporation* (1984) 156 CLR 41, 96–7.

trustee—a person who holds and controls property for the benefit of others. Traditionally employees are a class of fiduciary. The employer, who must trust the employee to carry out duties for the benefit of the employer, is the beneficiary in this relationship. To find that a fiduciary relationship exists is not the end of the matter. The scope of the duties involved, and the extent to which fiduciaries must sacrifice their own interests to those of the beneficiary, depend on the nature of the particular relationship and the extent of the commitment given.[117]

Fiduciary law arose out of the Court of Chancery, so fiduciary obligations are equitable in nature and give rise to equitable remedies, such as injunctions, accounts of profit, and where property is involved, declarations of constructive trust. In the employment context, fiduciary duties have traditionally been applied to find that the employee owes a duty to protect the property and interests of the employer, and may not act in a way that places self-interest above the employer's business interests. The duty of good faith and fidelity in the employment relationship (described in Chapter 6) reflects this obligation. The obligation goes further. In *Victoria University of Technology v Wilson & Ors*,[118] the Victorian Supreme Court found that the fiduciary obligation of a senior employee extended beyond any contractual obligation, so that the employee's interest in a patentable invention created outside of the scope of the employment contract nevertheless belonged to the employer in equity. The imposition of fiduciary duties on the employee reflects the status-based origins of much employment law, which assumes the servant's obligation of loyalty to the master. But what of the new era of contract and cooperation between equal bargaining parties? Can fiduciary law be developed to assist in the regulation of a more equal relationship between workers and employers?

Fiduciary obligations can be owed reciprocally. Partners to a partnership, for example, owe mutual fiduciary duties, also described as duties of 'utmost good faith'. Given that partnership law derives from relationships in which people pool resources and talents to 'carry on a business in common for profit', it is natural that this model should be examined for its potential in the context of a wider range of relationships in which work is performed, especially as we begin to recognise the symbiotic nature of this kind of human exchange.

In the employment context this development has found expression in the development of the concept of a duty of 'mutual trust and confidence' in the employment relationship.[119]

'Property rights' in work

In 'The New Property', Charles Reich coined the concept of a 'property right' in one's job.[120] Other scholars have taken up this idea in analyses of appropriate forms of

---

117 See P Finn 'The Fiduciary Principle' in TG Youdan (ed) *Equity Fiduciaries and Trusts* (1989), 1.
118 (2004) 60 IPR 392.
119 See Chapter 6.
120 (1964) 73 *Yale LJ* 733.

protection for employee rights.[121] On a traditional doctrinal analysis, it cannot be said that a person may have 'property' in a job. At law a property right is one that can be asserted against the whole world, and is able to be transferred (by trade, gift or succession) to others. A job is not such a thing. In the twenty-first century one cannot, for instance, sell one's job or pass it by will to an heir. One cannot take action against a successor to a job, for misappropriating the job. Nevertheless, on a political level, one can understand this assertion of 'property' as a claim to the status and remedies afforded to property rights in our legal system.

Our legal system privileges property rights as inviolable, higher-order entitlements, so the claim that one 'owns' a job, or has tenure over it, is an assertion of an entitlement to enjoy that kind of sacrosanct privilege. In our system, property rights support certain equitable remedies: orders for specific performance, and injunctions, which have traditionally been denied to employees because their legal rights are limited by the fact that their rights derive not from property but from a contract for personal services. So a claim that a job is property and should be protected as property is a claim for the improved protection of entitlements to work, which this range of remedies may offer. A rational response to this claim will identify and specify what type of protection the law should provide to those who hold jobs, and it may be that the kinds of procedural rights and substantive remedies developed in the context of property law should be appropriated to the law of work. One may, for example, identify a range of procedures that must be followed before a job can be taken away, to adequately recognise a person's entitlement to keep a job in the absence of sound reasons that it should be taken away, and these procedures may be borrowed and adapted from the law dealing with leases and licenses to use real and intangible property. Similarly one may seek to improve the remedies for job loss to better approximate remedies that have developed in the context of property law (eg, injunctions and orders for specific performance).

'Human capital'

An emerging literature on the role of workers in enterprise is adopting the concept, of 'human capital'.[122] In recent times, the connection between labour and property expounded by Locke,[123] has developed into a notion that the productive capacity, knowledge and skills of people are assets that may be exploited in business enterprises. An emerging body of law and economics scholarship analyses the contribution of workers in firms in terms of this concept of human capital.[124]

---

121 See eg 'Towards a Property Right in Employment' (1973) 22 *Buffalo LR* 1081; WB Gould IV 'The Idea of the Job as Property in Contemporary America: The Legal and Collective Bargaining Framework' [1986] *BYU Educ & LJ* 886; and MA Glendon *The New Family and the New Property* (1981) 91–5, 151–76, 192–205.

122 See eg K van Wezel Stone 'Knowledge at Work: Disputes over the Ownership of Human Capital in the Changing Workplace' (2002) 34 *Conn L R* 721; C Fisk 'Reflections on the New Psychological Contract and the Ownership of Human Capital' (2002) 34 *Conn L R* 765.

123 See Chapter 1.

124 See eg MM Blair and LA Stout 'A Team Production Theory of Corporate Law' (1999) 85 *Va L R* 247; MM Blair 'Firm-specific Human Capital and Theories of the Firm' in MM Blair and MJ Roe (eds) *Employees & Corporate Governance* (1999); and M O'Connor 'The Human Capital Era: Reconceptualising Corporate Law to Facilitate Labor–Management Cooperation' (1993) 78 *Corn LR* 899.

Our legal system has rapidly developed over the past few decades to create ways for enterprises to capture the produce of work in proprietary form. Examples include the enactment of copyright laws to protect computer programs (once unprotectable because they were conceived of as pure algorithms). A computer program is now a 'literary work' under the *Copyright Act 1968* (Cth). Innovation patents can be granted to trap the value of small innovations, not sufficiently inventive to warrant standard patent protection, but sufficiently commercially valuable to warrant protection. The knowledge economy has sought and obtained legal recognition of the value of its produce. Who should 'own' that new property? All this produce comes from the creativity, skill and effort of labour. And yet traditional employment law presumes that the employer owns it. Katherine Stone argues persuasively that the 'new psychological contract', whereby workers trade their labour not for job security but for career employability, must be accompanied by legal developments recognising the worker's entitlement to ownership rights in their own intellectual capital.[125]

Contract law and collective bargains

One of the most obvious weaknesses of common law contract as a suitable model for regulating the employment relationship in large enterprises is its inherently individualistic focus. The doctrine of privity of contract, which holds that only the parties to a contract will be bound by its obligations or entitled to its benefits, obstructs the use of contract law to enforce collective bargains. Collectively made enterprise bargains are certainly enforceable, but only if they comply with the requirements of statutes. The common law of contract confronts serious difficulties in dealing with a bargain between an employer and a union representing a fluctuating pool of employees. The problems are created by the doctrine of privity, which holds that contracts are enforceable only by the parties who made them, and the common law's insistence that consideration must pass from the person claiming the benefit of the contract. These requirements are notoriously difficult to satisfy in the case of a collective agreement negotiated by a union. *Ryan v Textile Clothing & Footwear Union Australia*[126] provides an illuminating example of these limits of contract law in enforcing collective agreements.

Ryan concerned a redundancy agreement made between a carpet manufacturing firm and the union representing its employees. The agreement, which provided for a level of redundancy benefits in excess of the prevailing industrial award, had never been registered under Victorian or federal industrial legislation.[127] The company had habitually honoured the unregistered agreement, but when receivers and managers were appointed to steer the ailing company through financial difficulties, the receivers sought court directions as to their legal liability to honour those agreements. They

---

125 See above n 5, 576–97. See also J Riley 'Who Owns Human Capital? A Critical Appraisal of Legal Techniques for Capturing the Value of Work' (2005) 18 *AJLL* 1.

126 [1996] 2 VR 235.

127 The agreement, made in 1991, might have been registered under the *Industrial Relations Act 1979* (Vic), which was in force until its repeal with effect from 1 March 1993.

paid out award entitlements to dismissed employees, but they sought directions about the alleged entitlements under the unregistered enterprise agreement. (The receivers wanted to shield themselves from the risk of personal liability to other creditors of the company if they were found to have paid out amounts in excess of the employees' strict legal entitlements.)

The Full Court of the Federal Court held that the unregistered agreement was not legally binding. As it was unregistered, it had no validity under statute. And it did not meet the threshold requirements for enforcement as a common law contract. First, to satisfy the doctrine of privity it was necessary to identify the parties to the agreement. Only contracting parties could enforce the contract. Union officers had signed the agreement, and the union argued that they did so as agents for all employees. The Court could not accept that the union had been authorised to act as agent for each employee purportedly covered by the agreement: some employees were not employed at the time the agreement was made, some were not members of the union, some who were members had not attended the meeting where the vote was taken to enter the agreement, and some who attended the meeting had either abstained or voted against it. The Court held that it was impossible to infer that all of those classes of employees had engaged the union as a bargaining agent. According to the privity doctrine, only those employees who consented to be parties to the agreement (directly or through the union as agent) could be bound by the agreement. And yet the document was drafted in very general terms and purported to apply to all employees.

The doctrine of consideration provided a further obstacle. English (and Australian) contract law adheres to a requirement that to be legally enforceable a contract must be supported by consideration. There must be some exchange of value to support the status of the agreement as a bargain. In *Ryan*, the union argued that its promise of industrial peace was consideration for the promise of redundancy payments to each employee. The Court held, however, that the union's promise could not bind those employees who had not appointed the union as bargaining agent. Those employees, therefore, had not given consideration for the employer's promise. Without consideration, those employees could not be parties to the contract.

The union tried another tack. It argued that the union itself (not the employees) was the party to the contract. The Court held, however, that the union had not provided consideration for the employer's promises. It was the employees who would be doing the work and undertaking the burdens of the contract. The documentation of the agreement made no reference to any promise made by the union that would have provided the consideration needed to support the agreement's enforceability as a common law contract. This particular obstacle might have been overcome had the union entered into the contract by executing a deed. A deed, properly executed and witnessed, precludes the need at common law for consideration. Nevertheless, a deed alone will not resolve the privity problems identified above.

In the result, the receivers were relieved of any liability to continue to honour the unregistered agreement. Had the agreement been registered, it would have been enforceable under statute, but it had no force as a common law contract because it did not conform to contract law rules. In this, we see that our legal system treats different legal subjects unequally. Employees who collectively provide labour to an enterprise have limited means of collective action. Investors who provide capital, however, are assisted by the legal fiction of the separate legal identity of companies. By virtue of its incorporation, there was never any issue in *Ryan* as to whether the company could be a party to an agreement. The separate legal personality conferred on a company upon incorporation enables a multiplicity of investors to act collectively. Decisions of the company board will bind present and future shareholders, those who attended the meetings and those who didn't, those who voted in favour and those who didn't.

The interests of capital have long enjoyed the benefit of this legal fiction that a corporation is a separate legal personality. By this means, capital is able to contract collectively with labour—but labour is atomised into individuals and cannot enjoy the strength of numbers. For many years the common law discriminated against the interests of labour by holding that labourers who joined forces to negotiate even with corporate employers were committing the tort of conspiracy. These weaknesses have since been overcome by statutes, which first conferred immunity from suit on collective industrial action in the United Kingdom, and have subsequently institutionalised forms of collective bargaining. A collective bargain will, however, have force according to the statute under which it is made. It ought not to be relied on as conferring any rights in common contract law. Bargaining under statute is considered in Chapter 11.

The federal *Workplace Relations Act* deliberately restricts the matters that can be included in an enforceable collective workplace agreement. Certain matters that unions have been accustomed to including in enterprise bargains have become 'prohibited content' since the enactment of the *Workplace Relations Amendment (Work Choices) Act 2005*.[128] Unions seeking to circumvent the restrictions of the legislation have investigated the scope for making what they call 'common law agreements by deed', to encompass the matters prohibited in statutory agreements. As a general strategy, the common law agreement has been endorsed in dicta in a number of judicial decisions. In *Electrolux Home Products Pty Ltd v Australian Workers Union*,[129] both McHugh J and Gummow J commented that matters that could not be included in a certified agreement because they did not pertain to the employment relationship could nevertheless be included in an ordinary common law contract.[130] In *Construction, Forestry, Mining and Energy Union v Australian Industrial Relations Commission (The Private Arbitration Case)*,[131] the High Court explained that a collective agreement that exceeded what was allowable under statute could nevertheless be enforceable under the common law: 'the underlying agreement remains and the validity of that agreement depends on the general law, not the legislative provisions'. The important qualification here is that the agreement must be enforceable as a contract under the general law. All of the problems identified in the *Ryan Case* need to be addressed.

---

128 See *Workplace Relations Regulations 2006* (Cth), rr 8.5–8.7, discussed in Chapter 11.
129 (2004) 221 CLR 309.
130 Ibid 355–56, and 368.
131 (2001) 203 CLR 645.

Arguably, the most significant obstacle—ensuring that the terms of the agreement would bind the employer in respect of new employees not engaged at the time the agreement was made—might be resolved by using that most inventive creation of equity—the discretionary trust. While a union may not enter an agreement as an agent for employees who do not exist at the time of the agreement, there is in principle no objection to a union entering into an agreement as a trustee for a class of beneficiaries, defined to include future employees. So long as the requirements of a valid trust are created, the union should be able to enforce the agreement as a trustee on behalf of any of its beneficiaries, and any of the employee beneficiaries should be able to enforce due administration of the trust. A trust can be created over any property, and contractual rights are a form of property. 'It is well established that a contracting party may be a trustee for a third party of that chose in action which is constituted by the benefit of a contract.'[132] Beneficiaries do not have to exist at the time the trust is created, so long as the trust instrument describes with sufficient certainty the class of persons to be benefited, and so long as the trust does not offend the rule against perpetuities. Generally, a clause that causes the trust to cease operation at a definable point in time, no more distant than eighty years, will avoid any risk of perpetuities problems.

Trusts—particularly those used to manage complex multiparty commercial transactions—are sophisticated legal instruments, developed in the commercial world to resolve practical problems created by the highly individualistic doctrines of contract law. Despite neo-liberal rhetoric of individual freedom, human beings will always seek to act collectively. The rise of the corporation is testimony to the effectiveness of cooperative collective enterprise. Just as effective corporate regulation in the interest of the collective benefit of investors has required extensive public regulation through statute, so effective regulation of labour markets in the interests of those who work together requires public regulation supporting forms of collective action. Contract law alone is inadequate to regulate large scale cooperative activity. This issue is revisited in Chapter 11, on enterprise bargaining.

132 JW Carter and D Harland *Contract Law in Australia* 3rd edn (1996), 327.

Rights and Responsibilities under Contract

Introduction

Despite the theoretical criticisms that can be raised against the persistence of contract law reasoning in the workplace context, contract has emerged as the dominant legal model for defining and determining the legal relationship between individual parties to a work relationship. The new orthodoxy of deregulation—the 'widespread displacement of collectively based regulatory strategies in favour of individual mechanisms of worker and employer redress'[1]—has elected contract law as the form of legal regulation most suitable to achievement of its aims of 'flexibility and efficiency'.[2]

In this chapter we analyse the application of the contract model to those work relationships that fall under the rubric of an employment contract. The contract of employment is a particular species of contract encumbered with many legal incidents that do not apply in the usual course to an ordinary commercial contract. (Some of the features of commercial contract law that have developed in the context of non-employment work relationships have been raised in Chapters 4 and 5.)

Even where workers do continue to enjoy the benefits of industrial instruments fixing certain terms and conditions of employment, important obligations will still be regulated by the underlying contract of employment. As we have seen in the jurisprudence emerging from the Federal Court of Australia, orthodox principles of contract law have often been applied strictly in industrial matters—often with results that surprise and confound the industrial players.[3]

In this chapter we examine the principles of construction and interpretation of employment contracts in the light of contemporary workplace practices. Awareness

---

1 J Conaghan 'Labour Law and "New Economy" Discourse' (2003) 16 *AJLL* 9,19.
2 K Klare 'The Horizons of Transformative Labour and Employment Law' in J Conaghan, M Fischl and K Klare (eds) *Labour Law in an Era of Globalization: Transformative Practices and Possibilities* (2002), 3.
3 See eg *Construction Forestry Mining and Energy Union v Amcor Ltd* (2002) 113 IR 112 eg affirmed on appeal in *Amcor Limited v Construction, Forestry, Mining and Energy Union* [2003] FCAFC 57 and reversed on appeal to the High Court of Australia in *Amcor Limited v Construction, Forestry, Mining and Energy Union* (2005) 214 ALR 56. See also *Ramsay Butchering Services Pty Ltd v Blackadder* (2003) 127 FCR 381, also reversed by the High Court of Australia in *Blackadder v Ramsey Butchering Services Pty Ltd* (2005) 221 CLR 539.

of potential liability under statutory unfair dismissal schemes has given rise to a new army of human resources managers and consultants, and to the promulgation of detailed policies and procedures manuals, which have contributed to greater complexity in the interpretation of contractual rights and obligations. On the other hand, many of the most important (and contested) obligations owed by employees and employers remain unwritten, as terms implied by law because of the essential character of the employment relationship.

Consequences of breach

Identifying and interpreting the terms of the employment contract is an essential legal task in any process of dispute resolution, especially when a relationship has broken down. The employer's entitlement to dismiss without incurring costs depends on identifying a sufficiently serious breach of a term of the contract warranting summary dismissal. Likewise, an employee's entitlement to abandon an intolerable working relationship while still claiming entitlement to severance benefits depends on being able to lay the blame for the destruction of the relationship at the employer's feet. In contractual terms, the employee must be able to demonstrate 'constructive dismissal'—that the employer's conduct has signalled a repudiation of the employment contract—which the innocent employee has elected to accept by termination. Contractual analysis continues to form the basis of judicial analysis of the parties' respective entitlements on termination, so it is essential to construe and interpret the contract.

A breach of contract that is not so serious as to allow the innocent party to treat the breach as a repudiation of the contract warranting termination will—in theory at least—give rise to a right to damages, but not a right to terminate. In practice, it is unusual for either employees or employers to claim damages for breach of contract while their relationship remains on foot.

Damages

Whether or not the innocent party is entitled or elects to terminate the contract, breach of contract will give rise to a right to claim damages. Damages in contract law are based on expectation. On the principle that there is no injustice in requiring a person to honour a promise, freely made and for which the person received consideration, contract law requires the party in breach to compensate the other for the loss of the bargain. The innocent party is to be put in the position that party would have been in, had the contract been properly performed.

This is distinguished from compensation in tort. Tort law imposes obligations, not because people have individually and consciously accepted those obligations, but because the community demands certain standards of conduct and care. One person in the community may not burden a neighbour with the cost of intentionally or negligently caused harm. So the appropriate remedy in tort is damages calculated to put the victims in the position they would have been in, had the wrong not been committed.

Because contract law allows damages based on fulfilment of the promises, and not merely on the basis of rectifying harm, construing the contract to establish its terms and interpreting the proper meaning of those terms is an important legal task.

Construction and interpretation of employment contracts

Construction

Contract law, premised as it is on the notion that parties have consented to be bound to their mutual benefit, depends on the assumption that the contract means what the parties themselves intend it to mean. This is tested objectively. What would the reasonably intelligent bystander, hearing all that the parties have said in negotiations, reading all that they have committed to writing, and observing all their conduct, believe to be the terms of their deal?[4]

It is a general principle of contract law that the parties intend to perform their bargain.[5] So contracts will be construed in such a way that each party is taken to agree to do all that they must do to enable the other party to have the benefit of the contract.[6] These principles of construction are often cited in support of the proposition that contract is, in essence, a relationship requiring 'good faith'.[7]

Employment contracts are not among the class of contracts that require writing for enforcement. Simple employment contracts may be constituted by nothing more than the acceptance of a verbal offer of pay in exchange for work. In such an arrangement, it is not unusual for the parties to have given very little express attention to the parameters of their relationship. And yet all contracts of service (employment contracts) are presumed to include many obligations, particularly on behalf of the worker.

Terms are implied into employment contracts by the same legal means as any other type of contract.[8] Terms can be implied in fact, when the particular deal needs such a term to give it 'business efficacy'.[9] Terms can be implied in law, when the contract is of a class or type of contract that the law presumes to include certain responsibilities or obligations.[10] And terms can be implied by custom, if a particular trade or industry always expects those obligations or conditions to be part of their arrangements.[11] Terms will only be implied, however, after construing the express terms of the contract—and these may be oral or in writing.

Express terms

Employment contracts are frequently expressed in very loose terms. Not every aspect of the bargain is written down, nor is every written term included in the same document.

---

4 *Oscar Chess Ltd v Williams* [1957] 1 WLR 370.
5 *Mackay v Dick* (1881) 6 App Cas 251.
6 *Butt v McDonald* (1896) 7 QLJ 68, 70–1.
7 See E Peden 'Incorporating Terms of Good Faith in Contract Law in Australia' (2001) 23 *Syd LR* 222.
8 *Byrne v Australian Airlines* (1995) 185 CLR 410.
9 See *Codelfa Construction Pty Ltd v State Rail Authority of NSW* (1982) 149 CLR 337, 345–6.
10 *Castlemaine Toohey's v Carlton and United Breweries Ltd* (1987) 10 NSWLR 468.
11 *Con-Stan Industries of Australia Pty Ltd v Norwich Winterthur (Australia) Ltd* (1986) 160 CLR 226, 237–8.

Sometimes the employer has several policy documents, perhaps available on an intranet computer database. Often an employee receives nothing more than a letter of appointment itemising very basic matters, such as salary, minimum hours of attendance at the workplace, and notice requirements for termination.

Nevertheless, as with all common law contracts, oral terms can also form part of a contract. Statements made at the time an employee agrees to enter into an employment relationship about important aspects of the work and remuneration can certainly become express, if unwritten, terms of the employment contract, and may subsequently ground a claim for damages in contract by the employee if the employer fails to honour those promises.[12]

Whether an oral statement forms part of the contract of employment or is merely a representation will be determined by applying the general principles of contract law, laid down in such cases as *Oscar Chess Ltd v Williams*[13] and *JJ Savage & Sons Pty Ltd v Blakney*.[14] The essential question is: what, on an objective view, did the parties intend? Was the statement a serious assurance, guarantee or promise that was offered and accepted as part of the deal? Representations of important matters—such as potential earning capacity—made close to the acceptance of the job offer are likely to be treated as terms of the contract and give rise to expectation-based damages.

Representations

A mere representation will not form part of the contract and so will not give rise to a right to expectation-based damages. Nevertheless, a misrepresentation that has induced entry into the contract may give a person a right to rescind the contract. This equitable remedy of rescission recognises that a contract is baseless where there is no real consent. Parties who have been misled or deceived about the bargain cannot be held to have truly consented to participate in it. In the employment context, however, rescission is a somewhat pyrrhic remedy. Occasionally, an employee may wish to walk away from a contract, and may, for instance, wish to avoid the consequences of having signed away certain liberties, for instance, the freedom to compete with the employer.[15] Generally, however, employees will seek compensation for their disappointed expectations in not actually enjoying the benefits they were led to assume would flow from the employment relationship.

Unfortunately, if the source of the disappointment is a mere representation and not a term of the contract, there will be no entitlement to expectation-based damages, but there may be an entitlement to reliance-based damages. Traditionally, the ability to claim any compensation for misrepresentations has arisen in tort—either through the tort of deceit,[16] which depends on proof of fraudulent misrepresentation, or more recently, in negligence, which requires proof that a duty of care has been breached by

---

12 *Saad v TWT Ltd* [1998] NSWSC 282.
13 [1957] 1 WLR 370.
14 (1970) 119 CLR 435.
15 A discussion on restrictive covenants in employment contracts follows at pp 242ff.
16 *Derry v Peek* (1889) 14 App Cas 337.

the giving of negligent advice.[17] In Australia, tortious claims for negligent misstatement have been largely overtaken by statutory developments. Section 52 of the *Trade Practices Act 1974* (Cth)[18] is commonly argued in any case where a person claims to have been misled or deceived by misrepresentations.

Damages for misrepresentations

Breach of the statutory duty not to mislead or deceive still bears the important hallmark of tort claims—compensation is assessed on the basis of reliance. A court will ask what the claimant suffered from relying on the misleading statement.[19] There is no entitlement to be treated as if the representation were in fact true—only to be put back in the position one would have been if the false statement had never been made at all.

In the case of *O'Neill v Medical Benefits Fund of Australia*,[20] for example, an employee who was coaxed into leaving secure employment to join MBF, on a carelessly made promise that the job was a long-term one, was able to claim compensation when this assurance was proved to be misleading and deceptive. The compensation was to be assessed according to the benefits that Mr O'Neill had lost by not continuing in his former secure employment. He was not treated as if he had a contractual entitlement to a long-term job with MBF.

Incorporation of terms from other documents

Terms can be incorporated into a contract by reference. For instance, a letter of appointment may refer to the terms of an award or some collective agreement, or to some policy document, in a way that implies that the parties agree to be contractually bound by the terms of those instruments. It is no obstacle to incorporation of such an instrument that the instrument itself is susceptible to change over time. Parties are taken to have agreed to be bound by the terms of the instrument as it stands from time to time.[21]

Policy manuals

A statement in a letter of appointment asserting that an employee agrees to be bound by the employer's policies and procedures manual will incorporate those policies and procedures into the employment contract, to the extent that the matters contained in the manual create obligations of a promissory nature for the employer or employee. If, in turn, the policies and procedures manual incorporates some other

---

17 *Hedley Byrne & Co Ltd v Heller & Partners Ltd* [1964] AC 465.

18 The *Trade Practices Act 1974* (Cth) applies only to corporations, due to constitutional limitations; however, state Fair Trading Statutes mirror the federal provisions: see *Fair Trading Act 1987* (NSW), s 42; *Fair Trading Act 1999* (Vic), s 9; *Fair Trading Act 1989* (Qld), s 38; *Fair Trading Act 1987* (SA), s 56; *Fair Trading Act 1987* (WA), s 10.

19 For criticism of the tendency to follow tort principles in trade practices claims, see the judgment of Kirby J in *Marks v GIO Australia Holdings Ltd* (1998) 196 CLR 494, 547.

20 (2002) 122 FCR 455.

21 See *Quickenden v O'Connor* (2001) 109 FCR 243 where it was held that the terms of an academic's contract of employment were 'ambulatory' due to the incorporation of the terms of successive enterprise bargains.

document (for example, the terms of a collective agreement) then obligations in that further document may also be incorporated into the employee's contract of employment.[22]

It is important that the particular terms of the policy document are matters that can have contractual effect: they must be matters that are appropriate to an agreement between individual parties. For example, a statement in a policy manual to the effect that the employer adopts and encourages environmentally friendly work practices would not ground a claim in contract by an employee aggrieved to find that the employer failed to recycle paper. Where, however, the policies relate to matters directly affecting the bargain between the parties—including the performance of work, the basis for determining remuneration, procedures for performance review, termination and redundancy—they will create contractual obligations for both the employee and the employer. An employer will not succeed in arguing that a policy manual was binding on the employee alone.[23]

Policy manuals can have a further important influence on the interpretation of contracts, even where it is held that they do not constitute terms of the contract themselves. In *Thomson v Orica Australia Pty Ltd*[24] a policy manual that promised family friendly work practices was used to give substance to the employer's obligation to maintain trust and confidence in the employment relationship. When, by failing to allow Ms Thomson to return to her former position after maternity leave, the employer did not honour the commitment promulgated in its own policy documents, Allsop J held that Orica had breached its obligation to maintain trust and confidence in the relationship.

Accumulated sources—oral, written and by conduct

In an appropriate case, a number of verbal assurances, documents, and consistent practices may be accumulated to find the express terms of an employment contract. For example, *In the Matter of ACN 050 541 047 Ltd*[25] involved employees of the Australian Quality Council Ltd, which administered the Australian Business Excellence Awards before it failed. The letters of engagement for staff had not referred to any redundancy benefits; however, the company had consistently operated a policy of paying three weeks' pay for each year of service whenever employees were made redundant. This practice was demonstrated by a number of written documents, including minutes of Board meetings, a paper written by managers to inform the Board of policies, and letters written to former employees who had been made redundant and had been paid according to the policy. Austin J accepted that together, all of these documents and practices constituted the express terms of the employment contracts, and ordered that the liquidator was contractually obliged to pay the redundancy benefits to the employees, so that these payments took priority according to s 556(1)(h) of the *Corporations Act 2001* (Cth) (which affords a certain priority to employee entitlements in the event of a corporate employer's insolvency).

---

22 *McCormick v Riverwood International (Australia) Pty Ltd* (1999) 167 ALR 689.
23 Ibid. See also *Nikolich v Goldman Sachs JB Were Services Pty Ltd* [2006] FCA 784.
24 (2002) 116 IR 186.
25 [2002] NSWSC 586 (3 July 2002).

Somewhat surprisingly, the explicit terms of an industrial award will not form part of the employment contract unless the parties have expressly incorporated the award into the contract. This follows from the High Court of Australia's decision in *Byrne v Australian Airlines (Byrne)*[26] that terms of an industrial award will not be implied, as a matter of fact, law or custom, into a contract of employment. As we shall see in the discussion of *Byrne* below, an industrial award was formerly often the product of compulsory arbitration, and as such it is not a creature of the mutual consent of the parties. Its legal effect depends upon the statute giving it force, and not upon the general principles of law applying to freely accepted bargains.

Terms implied in fact

Where the express terms of an employment contract (be they oral, written or deducible from conduct) are silent as to some matter that must necessarily form part of the agreement between the parties, a court will imply a term into the contract *in fact*, to fill the gap. Generally, courts refer to the principles in *BP Refinery (Westernport) Pty Ltd v Shire of Hastings (BP Refinery)*[27] when determining whether a term may be implied in fact into a contract that has been committed to writing. The five principles from *BP Refinery* are that the term to be implied must:

1   be reasonable and equitable;
2   be necessary to give business efficacy to the contract;
3   be so obvious that it 'goes without saying';
4   be capable of clear expression; and
5   not contradict any express terms of the contract.

In more informal contracts, these elements will not necessarily be applied rigidly.[28] Following the High Court of Australia's decision in *Byrne*, terms will be implied as a matter of fact into employment contracts only where the term is necessary to make sense of the bargain between the employer and employee.

Byrne concerned a claim by a group of dismissed employees that a 'termination change and redundancy' clause in the industrial award governing their employment was necessarily an implied term of their employment contracts. The employees claimed that the employer had breached this term by summarily dismissing them without following the warning procedures dictated by the award. Further, they claimed this breach of the award gave rise to a right to damages in contract. The argument had been used successfully in *Gregory v Phillip Morris Ltd*,[29] where breach of a similar award clause resulted in an award of contract-based damages to a dismissed employee. In *Bostik (Australia) Pty Ltd v Gorgevski (No 1)*[30] a long-serving employee dismissed for smoking on the job contrary to the employer's safety policy was awarded contract-based damages

26 (1995) 185 CLR 410.
27 (1977) 180 CLR 266, 282–3.
28 JW Carter and DJ Harland *Contract Law in Australia* 3rd edn (1996), 205–206.
29 (1988) 88 ALR 455.
30 (1992) 36 FCR 20.

amounting to several years' salary, on the basis that the award clause effectively gave him a contractual right to employment until retirement age, unless he was dismissed fairly for cause.

In *Byrne*, the High Court held that an award clause was not necessarily implied in fact into the employment contract. To be implied in fact, it is necessary to demonstrate that the clause is necessary to give business efficacy to the contract, and that the proposed clause would necessarily have been accepted by the parties to the contract, as soon as they discovered the need to address the matter at issue. In other words, without the clause, the contract must be unworkable. In the case of an award, the High Court held that there was patently no need to incorporate award terms as contractual obligations, because of the different juridical status of awards.

The High Court held that a federal award had effect according to the provisions of the statute, regardless of the agreement of the parties. Awards were often imposed by Industrial Relations Commissions to settle industrial disputes by arbitration. They did not represent agreement between the parties. They were often imposed as a matter of compulsory compromise, and not always as a matter of willing consent. Hence, they have effect only as dictated by the statute, and not as if they were willingly assumed obligations. Breach of an award attracts the sanctions provided by the statute but does not attract any liability to pay expectation-based damages under the common law of contract. The exception to this will be where an employer has explicitly agreed that the terms of an award form part of the employment contract.

Does this mean that workers whose wages are determined by awards have no contractual right to receive the wages? Early authority establishes that an entitlement to wages arising under an award creates a statutory debt, which can be pursued in the ordinary courts.[31]

Byrne left open the question of whether the terms of a collectively bargained agreement would necessarily be implied in fact into the employment contracts of employees bound by the agreement. Since collective industrial agreements depend on the consent of the employer and either a union or a valid majority of the employees who will be bound, the arguments in *Byrne* have less force. Nevertheless there are other obstacles to the enforcement, as common law contracts, of any form of collective agreement.[32]

Terms implied by law

A term is implied in fact when a particular obligation is necessary to give 'efficacy' to the particular employment contract. The courts justify implication in fact on the basis that the parties to the particular employment contract must necessarily have agreed to the term, if they had addressed their minds to it. Terms are implied by *law* because of the status of the contract as an employment contract. Unless the parties have expressly excluded such terms, these terms are taken to be part of every contract

---

31 *Mallinson v The Scottish Australian Investment Co Ltd* (1920) 28 CLR 66; *Amalgamated Collieries of WA Ltd v True* (1938) 59 CLR 417. See now *Workplace Relations Act 1996* (Cth), s 720.
32 See Chapter 5.

of employment, simply because it is an employment contract. Whether a term is implied in fact or in law is important in determining who bears the onus of proving its existence. A term is implied in law, absent any express exclusion of the term, so it is the party seeking to exclude it that bears the onus of proof.[33]

The terms implied by law into every contract of employment illustrate the persistence of the vestiges of the old master and servant law in the modern contract of employment. Foremost of these implied terms is the employee's duty to obey all lawful and reasonable commands of the employer. This duty is the flip side of the employer's prerogative to command or 'control'. It is one of the features of the employment relationship, which distinguishes this relationship from so-called 'independent' contracts for the provision of services.

The employee's duty of 'good faith and fidelity' or loyalty likewise reflects the subservience inherent in the employment relationship. The employment relationship is one of the classic fiduciary relationships: the traditional duty is a one-sided obligation, owed by the employee to the employer. When students of law first encounter the notion that fiduciary duties protect the 'vulnerable' from the abuse of a power by a trusted person[34] they are apt to mistake the duty in the employment relationship as one owed by the powerful master to the vulnerable servant. It is, however, the master whom the law perceives as vulnerable in this relationship. The employer is vulnerable to the risk that the employee may exploit for her or his own gain the resources provided by the employer—and these resources include business opportunities, contacts, and intellectual property created by the employee during the course of the employment. Fiduciary law traditionally protects employers' interests in preserving and enhancing their capital by exploiting the talents of their workforces. The trade-off (though one not supported at all by any adequate legal sanction) was an expectation that the employer would offer secure employment and engage the employee for a whole working life. In the following discussion, we ask whether the precepts of traditional fiduciary law are still justified in the 'new economy' where employers offer very little job security. Employees with no tenure in their jobs need tenure over the knowledge, skills and contacts they acquire through their work, if they are to survive in a highly mobile workforce.[35]

The employee's duties

The duty to obey

The implied term that the employee owes a duty to obey all lawful and reasonable orders gives the employer considerable scope to manage the workplace. It even permits the employer to unilaterally vary conditions of employment, so long as the employment contract retains its essential character despite the variation.

---

33 *Castlemaine Tooheys v Carlton and United Breweries Ltd* (1987) 10 NSWLR 468.
34 *Hospital Products Ltd v United States Surgical Corporation* (1984) 156 CLR 41, 96–7.
35 See K van Wezel Stone 'The New Psychological Contract: Implications of the Changing Workplace for Labor and Employment Law' (2001) 48 *UCLA LR* 519, 576–97. See also J Riley 'Who Owns Human Capital? A Critical Appraisal of Legal Techniques for Capturing the Value of Work' (2005) 18 *AJLL* 1.

So for example, where the contract itself does not specify particular hours of work, an employer can change hours of work to suit business needs, and an employee will be obliged to comply with the changed hours, so long as the demands are not unreasonable.[36] What is reasonable is determined in the context of the employment relationship itself.

The leading case of *Adami v Maison de Luxe (Adami)*[37] involved a manager of a dancehall who also maintained a remunerative part-time interest as an on-course bookmaker. When the dance hall operator decided to open for Saturday matinee sessions, Adami was unable to attend without giving up his bookmaking. He decided to solve his dilemma by delegating the dancehall work and the employer responded by summarily dismissing him. Adami sued for payment for a reasonable notice period, but failed to persuade the court that the employer's change of operating hours constituted a breach of the employment contract. The employer had exercised its prerogative to command and was entitled to obedience.

The findings in *Adami's case* seem particularly harsh in contemporary times, especially now that employment contract documents—and also industrial instruments such as awards and collective agreements—often spell out duties and hours of work. Where express provisions limit working hours or confine duties to a 'job description', the express provisions will confine the duty to obey. No wonder then that trade unions in earlier years sought to restrict the duty to obey extensive directions by negotiating elaborate awards detailing expected work practices. These kinds of provisions have now been excised from industrial awards.[38]

Professional workers are particularly susceptible to orders to work longer hours and take on additional duties, because of the expectation that the employment contract of a professional—such as a teacher, a doctor, an accountant, a lawyer—is not a 'time service' contract.[39]

Arguably, the employer's own duty to take reasonable care not to expose employees to unnecessary risk of injury or harm should provide an important constraint on the capacity for employers to abuse their prerogative to command. In *Johnstone v Bloomsbury Health Authority*[40] it was held (by a majority of the English Court of Appeal) that this duty of care constrained a hospital employer of a resident doctor from imposing dangerously long hours, even where a literal construction of his contract of engagement permitted back-to-back working shifts. In *Patrick Stevedores (No 1) Pty Ltd v Vaughan*,[41] the New South Wales Court of Appeal unanimously held that the employer's duty to take reasonable care not to expose the employee to unnecessary risk of harm was a necessary corollary of the prerogative to control so many aspects of the employee's working life. Unfortunately, the High Court of Australia has clouded this proposition

---

36 For a discussion of statutory protection of working hours see Chapter 7.
37 (1924) 35 CLR 143.
38 See Chapter 7.
39 *Sim v Rotherham Metropolitan Borough Council* [1987] Ch 216; and *Independent Education Union of Australia v Canonical Administrators* (1998) 157 ALR 531.
40 [1991] 2 WLR 1362.
41 [2002] NSWCA 275.

in *Koehler v Cerebos (Australia) Ltd*,[42] where a woman's claim to damages for a stress-related illness induced by overwork was dismissed on the basis that her contract of employment allowed the employer to require performance of the duties alleged to have induced the illness.

Relationship with industrial and human resources instruments

The extensive scope afforded to the employer's prerogative to command in old case law perhaps explains the impetus for unions to pursue the detailed work classifications and work practices typified by old awards in traditional industries. Express obligations cut down implied terms. Although the terms in an award would—following *Byrne*—have no force as contractual terms in themselves, they prevent the implication into the contract of any obligation contrary to the award. Removing these constraints on the employers' managerial prerogative has been an explicit motive in the award simplification program, promoted by the contemporary 'workplace relations' and 'work choices' agendas.

The introduction of 'Termination Change and Redundancy' (TCR) award terms in the 1980s, and the contemporary statutory provisions mandating that large employers[43] engage fair procedures in disciplining employees, has prompted widespread use—particularly in large organisations with unionised workforces—of policies and procedures manuals. Employers frequently use policy manuals to make explicit the standards of conduct they require at the workplace, and so avoid any allegation that disciplinary procedures have been arbitrary or without adequate warning.

For example, policies governing the use of employer-provided computer facilities and resources have become standard. Accessing 'unauthorised' (notoriously pornographic) Internet sites is frequently prohibited by employer-promulgated policies on Internet and email use. Employees who breach such a policy have breached their duty to obey. If the breach is sufficiently serious, it will give the employer an entitlement to summarily dismiss the employee. In *Kenny v Epic Energy*[44] the AIRC emphasised that the justification for summary dismissal was not the moral quality of the conduct itself—the Commission explicitly disclaimed any entitlement to arbitrate on moral standards—but the employer's prerogative to determine appropriate and permissible uses of its own property, and require obedience. Note that under statutory schemes, summary dismissal for breach of a policy may still be deemed to be unfair if the breach did not constitute a serious repudiation of the contract,[45] and if termination is a disproportionate disciplinary response.[46]

---

42 (2005) 222 CLR 44.

43 Since 27 March 2006, only employers of more than 100 employees have been susceptible to unfair dismissal legislation: see *Workplace Relations Act 1996* (Cth), s 643(10).

44 AIRC, Print S0947, 15 November 1999.

45 See *Pastrycooks Employees Biscuit Makers Employees and Flour and Sugar Goods Workers Union (NSW) v Gartrell* (1990) 35 IR 70.

46 See eg *National Wide News Pty Ltd* AIRC, C2003/1202, 27 August 2003—concerning the reinstatement of workers who knowingly breached a no-alcohol policy.

Orders must be 'lawful and reasonable'

Even in the absence of express contractual limitations, the duty to obey is not completely at large. It is a duty to obey 'lawful and reasonable' orders. This limitation keeps an important boundary between workers' working lives and their rights to a private life, a boundary that is too often placed under stress by the pressures of the 'new economy' demands for greater flexibility and commitment.[47]

'Lawful'

An employee will never be obliged to obey an order that is contrary to other legal obligations, because of the general principle that courts will not enforce agreements to break the law. So an employee will not be in breach of the duty to obey if he or she refuses to assist the employer in a breach of the general law or any statutory obligation. For example, an employee ordered to breach provisions of the corporations legislation by preparing false company reports, or to breach the *Trade Practices Act* by preparing misleading product advertisements, would not be in breach of their contract of employment by failing to comply.

There is a second meaning in the term 'lawful'. The employer is entitled only to command obedience over matters in which the employer has a legitimate interest. The employer's interest is created by the contract, so the parameters of the contract determine what orders are lawful. In this sense, the meaning of 'lawful' overlaps with that of 'reasonable'.

'Reasonable'

A 'reasonable' order is one that falls within the scope of the particular employment contract. The employer may not command an employee in matters of the employee's private life. The duty to obey extends only to matters pertaining to the employment relationship itself.

As an extreme example, an employer is not entitled to send an employee to their death—unless facing death is part of the duties stipulated by the employment contract. In *Ottoman Bank v Chakarian*,[48] the House of Lords decided that a bank teller could not be forced to accept a transfer to a branch in a country in which his life was in peril, at least, not until a change of political administration made the position tolerably safe.[49] As Greg McCarry[50] has explained, the basis of the decision is not that an employer cannot send an employee into personal danger—soldiers and lion tamers are bound to face danger as a matter of course—but that the employer is entitled to command the employee only within the parameters of the employment contract. To be a lawful and reasonable command, the command must fall within the proper scope of the contract. A command that falls outside of the scope of the contract is unreasonable and therefore unlawful.

---

47 See generally R McCallum *Employer Controls over Private Life* (2000).
48 [1930] AC 277.
49 But see *Bouzarou v Ottoman Bank* [1930] AC 271, where the House of Lords held that an employee refusing a transfer into Turkey was lawfully dismissed because the transfer did not subject him to immediately threatened danger or disease.
50 G McCarry, 'The Employee's Duty to Obey Unreasonable Orders' (1984) 58 *ALJ* 327.

The question of what matters fall reasonably within the parameters of the employment contract has produced some contentious litigation. In the *Tramways* case,[51] the High Court of Australia held that an employee must obey all lawful commands, not all commands. One may wear, worship or believe whatever one chooses, in matters not affecting work.

In more recent times, these sentiments have been tested in cases concerning the freedoms of employees to wear what they like to work. Mr Hart wanted to wear a caftan to work as a telecommunications officer.[52] In *Australian Telecommunications Commission v Hart (Hart)*, a majority of the Federal Court held that he was bound to comply with the employer's requirement that he wear more conventional clothing because his position involved dealing with the public and the employer had an entitlement to control its public image. Now that shopfronts for many banks, insurance and telecommunications services are being closed in favour of call centres, it is arguable that these faceless workers should be entitled to dress in any manner that they please, with the possible proviso that they must not cause offence and distraction to fellow workers.[53] A contemporary example is that of a casino worker who ignored the employer's 'grooming policy' by insisting on wearing a tongue stud.[54] The worker claimed that the stud was an invisible, private adornment. However, the AIRC accepted that the policy banning body piercing was reasonable, on the basis that the employer maintained a 'five star image' for the establishment, and also because the worker's capacity for clear speech was impeded by the tongue adornment.

Conduct outside working hours

From *Hart* we discern that the duty to obey extends to any aspect of the employee's conduct that is properly the subject of the employer's control because it affects the performance of work at the workplace. Questions persistently arise over the extent to which the employer may colonise aspects of the employee's persona and private life. Dilemmas arise for workers who spend so much time at work that work becomes their only social life, and their only opportunity to meet companions and potential sexual partners. Questions arise as to the extent to which an employer can insist that workers do not form romantic attachments with co-workers.

If an employee's conduct has a detrimental effect on the conduct of work at the workplace, then the employer is entitled to issue commands in respect of that conduct. So in *McManus v Scott*,[55] the employer was held to be entitled to dismiss an employee for failing to obey an instruction to stop telephoning another worker outside working hours. The male worker's telephone calls amounted to harassment of his female colleague. His

---

51 *Australian Tramways Employees' Association v Brisbane Tramways Co Ltd (Tramways)* (1912) 6 CAR 35.
52 *Australian Telecommunications Commission v Hart (Hart)* (1982) 43 ALR 165.
53 *Boychuk v HJ Symons Holdings Ltd* [1977] IRLR 396.
54 *Fairburn v Star City Pty Ltd* AIRC, PR931032, 6 May 2003.
55 (1996) 140 ALR 625.

conduct had caused her distress, and was the subject of gossip in the workplace. The disruption to workplace harmony was held to be a sufficient ground for the employer to dismiss the male worker.

On the other hand, in *Appellant v Respondent*[56] a male employee who was dismissed for what amounted to seduction of a female co-worker was held to have been unfairly dismissed, because the conduct complained of occurred away from the workplace (albeit during a 'lay-over' between flights), and was no business of the employer.

Submission to testing

The personal autonomy of the employee is also challenged when the employer insists on performing medical or psychological testing on current employees. Where the tests are demanded out of a reasonable concern to protect the employer's business interests, the employee is bound to obey. So in *Anderson v Sullivan*,[57] police officers were obliged to submit to drug tests, because of the employer's interest in ensuring that it presented a credible public image by demonstrating the integrity of its officers. On the other hand, in *Bliss v South East Thames Regional Health Authority*,[58] a demand that a surgeon submit to a psychological examination because he had behaved angrily in disputes with a rival doctor was held to be unreasonable and calculated to destroy the mutual trust and confidence in the employment relationship. Dr Bliss was entitled to treat himself as constructively dismissed and to claim damages for wrongful dismissal by the Health Authority.

Relationship of the duty to obey with the employer's duty of care

The employee's subjection to the employer's control also has important repercussions for the employer's common law duty of care to the employee. It has been consistently held that the employer's prerogative to command brings with it a duty of care to avoid exposing employees to unnecessary risk of harm.[59] This extends not only to physical but also to psychological health.[60]

Johnstone v Bloomsbury Health Authority (*Johnstone*)[61] held that the employer's prerogative to command obedience even in the case of express provisions in the contract is subject to the important limitation that the demands made must not cause harm to the health and welfare of the employee. On the other hand, in *Koehler v Cerebos (Australia) Limited*[62] (a decision that did not refer to *Johnstone*), the High Court of Australia held that an employer bore no duty of care to an employee for

---

56 (1999) 89 IR 407.

57 (1997) 78 FCR 380.

58 [1987] ICR 700.

59 *Crimmins v Stevedoring Industry Finance Committee* (1999) 200 CLR 1, 98; *Schellenberg v Tunnel Holdings Pty Ltd* (2000) 200 CLR 121, 159–160; *State of New South Wales v Seedsman* (2000) 217 ALR 583, 611; *White v Chief Constable of South Yorkshire Police* [1999] 2 AC 455.

60 *Mt Isa Mines Ltd v Pusey* (1970) 125 CLR 383; *Patricks Stevedores (No 1) Pty Ltd v Vaughan* [2002] NSWCA 275.

61 [1991] 2 WLR 1362.

62 (2005); 222 CLR 44; 139 IR 309. See also D Rolph 'No Worries? Employers' Duty of Care for Negligently Inflicted Stress' (2005) 18 *AJLL* 344.

any harm caused by the employer's insistence that the employee perform the work stipulated when the contract was made. The joint judgment of McHugh, Gummow, Hayne and Heydon JJ did, however, leave room for the proposition that an employer's prerogative to exercise powers to command the performance of new duties may be constrained by a duty to consider the employee's welfare.[63] With respect, this view of the employment contract as one in which 'the obligations of the parties are fixed at the time of the contract unless and until they are varied'[64] bears little regard to the reality of employment relationships.[65]

Managing workplace change

The duty to obey reasonable orders has important implications for the management of changes in work practices, particularly when those changes are dictated by technological innovation. The obligation to obey means that an employer can introduce new technology into the workplace, and employees will be required to adapt to its use. So long as the work to be accomplished is sufficiently similar, the contract will not be breached by a requirement to use a new form of technology to achieve the tasks. However, the employer may be required to allow time for adjustment and training.[66] Radical workplace change brought about by the advent of computer technology, and the massive redundancies accompanying technological change in many 'old economy' industries, was the catalyst for the industrial battles that eventually secured the inclusion of TCR clauses in industrial awards. These clauses sought to win rights to consultation and participation in the decision-making surrounding the adjustments to new technology. Award simplification following the introduction of the *Workplace Relations and Other Legislation Amendment Act 1996* (and more recently the *Workplace Relations Amendment (Work Choices) Act 2005*) has excised consultative rights from federal industrial awards, restoring control and management of technological change to the prerogative of management.[67] The Minister has also exercised extensive powers to declare certain matters to be 'prohibited content',[68] to prohibit consultation rights from collective workplace agreements bargains.[69]

The duty of good faith and fidelity

A further aspect of the employment relationship that reflects the former master/servant relationship is the employee's duty to render loyal and faithful service to the employer. This duty is both contractual and equitable. Breach therefore gives rise to a right to terminate the contract and claim damages, and also to a right to equitable remedies,

---

63 (2005) 214 ALR 355, para 37.
64 *Koehler v Cerebos Pty Ltd* (2005) 222 CLR 44, 57.
65 See Chapter 5.
66 See *Creswell v Inland Board of Revenue* [1984] 2 All ER 713, concerning the introduction of computers for tax assessors.
67 See *Workplace Relations Act 1996* (Cth), former s 89A(2) and *the Award Simplification Decision* (1997) 75 IR 272; and current ss 513 and 515.
68 See *Workplace Relations Regulations 2006* (Cth), r 8.5.
69 See Chapter 11.

including injunctions and an account of profits should the employee derive any benefit from breach. Employees who have succeeded in setting up rival businesses in breach of their duties of loyalty have also, in appropriate cases, been held liable as constructive trustees.[70]

In these days where some workers will juggle multiple part-time jobs in an effort to accumulate a sufficient income to manage a decent life, the duty of fidelity creates particular tensions. And in these times of high job mobility and low job security, the extent to which the duty is imposed on employees post-employment, in ways that purport to restrict their ability to take skills, know-how and personal contacts with them into a new job, creates important policy ramifications. If the justification for the new flexibility agenda is efficiency, then surely any restraint on free competition is unacceptable.

The duty during the employment relationship

While the employment relationship subsists, the duty of loyalty means that an employee may not make any secret or unauthorised profit from the employment,[71] and may not compete with the employer, or do anything that would harm the employer's business interests. This does not mean that the employee has no liberty to pursue other business interests outside of work time. The case of *Blyth Chemicals v Bushnell*[72] demonstrates that so long as the outside interest does not compete with the employer, nor hinder the employer's full enjoyment of the energies of the employee in fulfilling the obligations under the contract, there will be no breach of the duty.

A somewhat controversial case is *Hivac Ltd v Park Royal Scientific Instruments Ltd,*[73] in which technically skilled workers were restrained from working for a rival enterprise outside hours, on the basis that their 'moonlighting' allowed a competitive business access to the unique skills necessary to succeed in this industry. The decision must be questionable in the light of contemporary concerns with free competition and abuse of market power.

Post-employment

Problems generally arise when an employee leaves, and seeks to take experience, know-how and client contacts into another business enterprise, either in the service of another employer or to set up business on his or her own account. Disputes arise if the former employer seeks to restrain that activity. The extent to which that is possible depends largely on the terms of the contract itself, the application of the common law doctrine against illegal restraints of trade, and finally on the equitable jurisdiction's reluctance to grant injunctions enforcing covenants in personal service contracts.

---

70 *Green & Clara Pty Ltd v Bestobell Industries* [1982] WAR 1.
71 See *EFG Australia Ltd v Kennedy* [1999] NSWSC 922; *Concut Pty Ltd v Worrell* (2000) 75 AJLR 312.
72 (1933) 49 CLR 61.
73 [1946] ICR 634.

When there is no express contract term prohibiting competition

An employer has no inherent right to prevent a former employee from leaving and going to a competitor. So long as the employee gives the notice required under the contract (or 'reasonable notice' where none is stipulated) leaving to take one's skills elsewhere is not a breach of contract. If an employee leaves without giving the appropriate notice, an employer may seek an injunction preventing the employee from working elsewhere during the notice period, but only if the employer can demonstrate that damages would be an inadequate remedy for breach, and that enforcing the covenant would not have the effect of forcing a person to work for the employer or starve.[74]

Without an effective post-employment restraint covenant, all the employer can protect is its own property rights. An employee can be restrained from exploiting the employer's intellectual property rights, trade secrets, and truly confidential information. The employee can also be prevented from usurping a maturing business opportunity. But the employer cannot prevent an employee from taking away skills developed on the job, general know-how and knowledge, nor the benefit of business associations and contacts developed during the employment. To protect those things, the employer must rely on an express covenant, which goes no further than is reasonable to protect the legitimate interests of the employer.

Intellectual property rights

The common law presumes that in the absence of agreement otherwise, an employer owns any valuable property created by employees in the course of their employment. Section s 35(6) of the *Copyright Act 1968* (Cth) reflects this assumption.[75]

This raises a question about what constitutes creation 'in the course of employment'. Generally, intellectual property (including patentable inventions, designs, works of copyright, and trade marks) will belong to the employer if they are created on the employer's premises, using the employer's resources and equipment, and in working time. What of the new economy employees who do a lot of work at home, are required to provide many of their own tools of trade, and are remunerated for results, not time service? If the property was created as a consequence of performing the work contracted for, it will belong to the employer, even where the property had its genesis in work or creations already owned by the employee prior to taking up the employment.[76]

In *Spencer Industries Pty Ltd v Collins*,[77] a sales manager for a small company selling tyre retreading equipment came up with a new invention for removing old tread from tyres more effectively. He worked on his designs in his spare time, and the employer discouraged him from spending work time or energy on his ideas. He tried to interest his employer in joint exploitation of the invention, and was willing to negotiate an

---

74 Such injunctions are classified as 'garden leave', which is considered at p 265.

75 Section 35(4) makes special provision for journalists to maintain copyright in their work for the purposes of compiling books, but for other purposes the publisher employer owns copyright.

76 See *Redrock Holdings Pty Ltd & Hotline Communications Ltd v Hinkley* (2001) 50 IPR 565.

77 (2003) 58 IPR 425.

improvement in job security in exchange for assigning his rights in the invention to his employer. At first the employer was uninterested in the invention, but later tried to insist that the employee assign his rights as inventor without any consideration. The employee left the enterprise for other employment, and the employer brought a claim of entitlement to the patent in the invention. Branson J held that the invention was not made in the course of Mr Collins' duties as a sales manager, and was therefore his own property. Arguments that he came up with the ideas through his contact with the company's clients and that he owed a duty to pursue the best interests of the company in selling its wares failed to impress the judge. The decision is refreshingly modern, in that it focused not on any assumptions of servitude, but on the terms of the contract between the employer and employee. The employee had not been paid to invent. When he attempted to negotiate for some consideration for the additional inventive work, the employer refused his offer. So no new contract was formed.

Ownership of intellectual property rights is an increasingly important issue. Intellectual property rights are made to mimic real and tangible property rights. Ownership affords a right to exclude others' use and to commandeer all the fruits of exploitation. So an employer who is able to prove ownership of an employee's inventions and creations can obtain an injunction preventing the employee from using the work for her own benefit, or for the benefit of other employers, and can obtain an account of any profits the employee earns by exploiting the work. It is no surprise that intellectual property clauses, purporting to claim extensive rights over the creations of employees, are common in written employment contracts in new economy industries. Intellectual property rights are a highly artificial legal technique for capturing human capital by commodifying creativity. An employer is able to distill the knowledge, ideas and skills of their workforces into products with a shelf life of twenty, fifty or seventy years, depending on the particular protective regime applying to the form of property.

Confidential information

An employer has a right to preserve its intellectual property (including copyright, registered designs, patents and trade marks), its trade secrets, and any truly confidential information related to the business. The employee's duty to respect those rights will run beyond the term of the employment, even where there is no post-employment contractual constraint. This is because the duty arises in equity, not necessarily out of the employment contract. Equity protects the personal obligation to keep confidences.

At times, confidential information is described in terms of property, possibly because the equitable remedies appropriate to protecting the personal obligation to keep confidences are the same as equitable remedies granted for a breach of trust—a court will order an account of profits, equitable compensation, and injunctions to restrain breach of confidence.

But strictly speaking, confidential information is not property under Australian law. This point has been made clear by the High Court of Australia in *Breen v Williams*.[78]

---

78 (1996) 186 CLR 71.

Chief Justice Brennan cited with approval the statement of Lord Upjohn from *Phipps v Boardman*.[79]

> In general, information is not property at all. It is normally open to all who have eyes to read and ears to hear. The true test is to determine in what circumstances the information has been acquired. If it has been acquired in such circumstances that it would be a breach of confidence to disclose it to another then courts of equity will restrain the recipient from communicating it to another. In such cases such confidential information is often and for many years has been described as the property of the donor, the books of authority are full of such references; knowledge of secret processes, 'know-how,' confidential information as to the prospects of a company or of someone's intention or the expected results of some horse race based on stable or other confidential information. But in the end the real truth is that it is not property in any normal sense but equity will restrain its transmission to another if in breach of some confidential relationship.[80]

This principle recognises a general liberty to exploit publicly available information. Information, per se, is not capable of protection as private property under Australian law. Certainly, copyright law can protect the *expression* of ideas and information, but not the ideas or information itself. Copyright is infringed by copying a document, not by reading, digesting and exploiting the information contained within that original expression of ideas. Equity will protect confidential information, but only by imposing a personal obligation on the receiver of the secret not to divulge what they are conscience-bound to protect from disclosure.

This means that an employee can be restrained from using information that is truly confidential, but not information that is publicly available, or that has become part of the employee's own stock of knowledge.[81] Kirby P in *Wright v Gasweld Pty Ltd*[82] set out a list of factors for identifying truly confidential information, including the following:

- How much skill and effort was expended to acquire the information? A lot of skill and effort suggests confidentiality.
- Has the employer jealously guarded the information? If not, it is unlikely to be confidential.
- Did the employer communicate the confidential nature of the information to the employee? The obligation depends on a personal obligation to keep a secret, so it is important that the employee is made aware of that obligation.
- Is there an industry practice in keeping this kind of information confidential?
- Has access to the information been restricted only to senior staff? Wide dissemination suggests lack of any intention to keep information confidential.

---

79 (1967) 2 AC 46, 127–8.

80 (1996) 186 CLR 80. See also *Moorgate Tobacco Co Ltd v Philip Morris Ltd (No 2)* (1984) 156 CLR 414, 438.

81 See *Ormonoid Roofing v Bitumenoids Ltd* (1931) 31 SR (NSW) 347, and more recently, *Triangle Corp Pty Ltd v Carsnew* (1994) AIPC 91–099. Restraining the employee's use of trade secrets and confidential information that cannot be separated from the employee's own know-how and experience may be achieved (subject to the restraint of trade doctrine) by express covenant—or so it has been held, in *Printers and Finishers Ltd v Holloway and Ors* [1964] 3 All ER 731, 736. See *Commercial Plastics v Vincent* [1964] 3 WLR 820, where a contractual restraint was held to be unenforceable because it was unreasonably wide in scope.

82 (1991) 39 IR 256, 271.

Customer lists

An employee who takes away a physical list of customers will breach the duty of confidence.[83] If the list is so elaborate that the employee needs to copy a document or electronic file to obtain and take the information, then it meets the first of the criteria concerning 'skill and effort'. Further, it is likely that an employee who has possession of a list of clients took it while still employed. The obligation of fidelity during the employment relationship—which runs until the termination of the contract upon expiry of the notice period—will protect even non-confidential information. While the contract is on foot, the employee's obligation not to compete for business extends to a prohibition on preparing to compete by copying client lists.[84]

An employer who discovers that such a list has been taken can obtain an injunction ordering return or destruction of the list itself, and an injunction restraining use of the list. The employee is free, however, to use unaided memory and later research to recreate customer lists.[85] If the employee has not taken lists, but simply remembered information, the employee cannot be restrained without an express covenant.[86] An express covenant cannot be in illegal restraint of trade, or it will be unenforceable.

An employer whose customer lists have been taken in breach of a duty of confidence may also claim an account of profits from the former employee, on the basis that the breach of confidence has enabled the employee to gain an advantage that no ordinary competitor, unaided by the special information, would have been able to enjoy.

In *Halliday & Nicholas v Corsiatto*,[87] for example, a former employee of an insurance broking firm downloaded lists of clients a week before leaving his employment to become a sub-broker for a rival firm. The purpose of doing this was to enable him to write immediately to that list of clients as soon as he changed employment, and to secure renewals of insurances on behalf of those clients. The NSW Court of Appeal was prepared to award the former employer an account of profits on the business for a period of twelve months, to reflect the 'head start' or 'springboard' that Mr Corsiatto had secured by using the information.[88]

No perpetual injunction could be granted because the employer did not 'own' the customers. Those customers were free to give their business to whomever they chose. The employee's breach was not to 'steal the customers', but to make an improper use of confidential information that he obtained as a result of his employment, to enable him to compete with the employer more effectively than any stranger to the business would have been able.

It is important that this be remembered. Some of the case law dealing with these kinds of problems adopts the language of property law when referring to client

---

83 See *Robb v Green* [1895] 2 QB 315.
84 Ibid.
85 *Faccenda Chicken Ltd v Fowler* [1987] Ch 117.
86 Ibid. See also *Australian Billboard Connections v Jansen* [2001] VSC 471.
87 [2001] NSWCA 188.
88 See *Wright v Gasweld* (1991) 39 IR 256, 275.

relationships. For example, in *Adler Mallach Holdings Pty Limited v Robertson*,[89] Master McLaughlin referred to a person 'filching' customers.[90] A case decided by the Hong Kong High Court, *Fortune Realty Co Ltd v Chan Hiu Yeung Dick*,[91] described as 'vital assets' of a business such things as 'information relating to the identities of customers' and 'personal contacts between agents and the customers'. More subtly, in *Coordinated Industries Pty Ltd v Elliott*,[92] Hodgson CJ in Equity described the chance of obtaining a contract as an *asset* belonging to an employer who was tendering for that contract.

It is of some concern that use of property terminology begins to blur the precise legal relationships involved in these matters. Describing the customer, and customer relationships, as being 'owned' by the employer risks prejudging the employee's conduct as wrongful when the employee goes on to do business with those customers. The customers are autonomous actors who are entitled to give their business to whomever they please. The employer does enjoy some legal rights to restrict an employee's future engagement with customers, but those rights are limited, and they are based on personal obligations, not on property rights.

It is also interesting to note that in *Halliday & Nicholas v Corsiatto* the Court of Appeal also awarded Mr Corsiatto an allowance for his time, trouble and expertise in securing the renewal business, so that the former employer would not be unjustly enriched by receiving the profits on the business without paying the expenses of his salary.[93] This is an entirely orthodox approach to determining remedies for breach of fiduciary duty.[94]

The maturing business opportunity

Employees cannot tender for business in competition with the employer while still employed, nor can they tender against their former employer after leaving if they are exploiting knowledge of confidential information, such as tender price and conditions, which would not be known in the market.[95] Employees may not usurp a maturing business opportunity by taking over a project commenced while working for the former employer.[96] This doctrine, as expressed in *Coordinated Industries Pty Ltd v Elliott*,[97] is fairly limited. In *Coordinated Industries*, an order was made against a former employee who resigned and after doing so diverted a current project to himself. The court found that the employee had already earned salary from doing the preparatory work on this project, and was now double-dipping, by taking the project off into his own business and earning the ultimate profit on the deal. The court held that it

---

89 [2002] NSWSC 1176, [42].

90 This case concerned a non-compete clause in a sale of business, not a post-employment matter; nevertheless, the cases are comparable because they concern an examination of the nature of the business owner's interest in client relationships.

91 [2001] HKCFI 506.

92 (1998) 43 NSWLR 282, 288.

93 See [2001] NSWCA 188, [30].

94 *Boardman v Phipps* [1967] 2 AC 46. See also *Warman International v Dwyer* (1995) 182 CLR 544.

95 See *Green & Clara Pty Ltd v Bestobell Industries* [1982] WAR 1; *Warman International v Dwyer* (1995) 182 CLR 544.

96 See *Victoria University of Technology v Wilson* (2004) 60 IPR 392.

97 (1998) 43 NSWLR 238.

was improper for him to keep the entire profit from a matter that the employer had already paid him wages to progress. It would appear then that the only cases that should be able to successfully rely on this doctrine are those in which the employee has taken over an existing project upon or after leaving. Repeat business—new projects from old clients—does not fall within this doctrine, as is demonstrated in *Weldon & Co v Harbinson* (*Weldon*).[98]

Weldon involved an employed accountant who, after being trained and working as an integral part of a small practice with a 'father-figure' mentor, decided to set up business on her own in competition with her former employer. Mr Weldon was naturally aggrieved when Ms Harbinson left her employment shortly after being paid a generous performance bonus, and after completing an expensive training conference for which he had paid. Despite Mr Weldon's allegations, there was no evidence in the case that Ms Harbinson had copied any files, or gone about deliberately memorising client information.[99] As soon as she left, she set about compiling her own contact lists, relying on her memory and various publicly available indexes. Bryson J held that she was entitled to do so.

Likewise, the employer complained that in the last two weeks of her employment, while she was working out notice, she told some of her clients that she had resigned and would shortly be setting up her own practice.[100] She did not solicit business at this time and certainly took no instructions from these clients until after she had left. Bryson J held that this conduct was not a breach of her fiduciary duty to the employer. Relying on *Canadian Aero Service Ltd v O'Malley & Anor*[101] and *Coordinated Industries Pty Ltd v Elliott*,[102] the employer attempted to argue that this conduct constituted misappropriation of maturing business opportunities. His argument was that the clients were regular customers who had tax return work done each year, so by letting them know that she would soon be in business on her own she was taking business opportunities that 'belonged' to him.

Bryson J drew a distinction between soliciting clients for repeat business, where the earlier commission has been completed and new work is being contemplated, 'and, on the other hand, interrupting a partly completed or maturing business opportunity by leaving employment and then approaching the customer with the object of taking the job over'.[103]

In the result, Ms Harbinson largely won the case. Bryson J ordered that she pay $500 in respect of some fees she charged two personal clients while still employed. She had, like many professionals, done a small amount of 'family and friends' work in her spare time, usually for no payment at all, but on two occasions she had accepted small payments and had not accounted for them to her employer. Apart from that,

---

98 [2000] NSWSC 272 (7 April 2000).

99 He had, nevertheless, been able to secure an Anton Pillar order in interlocutory proceedings.

100 See also *NP Generations trading as LJ Hooker v Feneley*, (2000) 50 IPR 63, in which it was held that merely contacting former clients to inform them of one's termination was not a breach of the duty of fidelity, even if it resulted in clients deciding to cease giving business to the employer.

101 (1973) 40 DLR (3d) 371, 381–2.

102 (1998) 43 NSWLR 282, 287.

103 *Weldon & Co Services v Harbinson* [2000] NSWSC 389, [78].

none of the orders requested by the plaintiff were made. In a later hearing, Bryson J awarded costs against the plaintiff, in a strongly worded judgment criticising his 'abuse of process'.[104]

Express restraints

Commercially valuable but not strictly confidential information about the employer's business methods, marketing strategies etc, can be protected by an express covenant preventing the employee who now has that information from competing with the employer.[105] Any such covenant must go no further than is reasonable to protect the legitimate interests of the former employer, or it risks being unenforceable as an illegal restraint of trade.

The word 'legitimate' is important. The rights of the employer arise from two legitimate interests:

- the right to protect truly confidential information; and
- the right to protect the special 'customer connections'[106] that the employee has developed in the course of employment with the employer.

Confidential information is dealt with above. Unless information is confidential in the sense described in *Wright v Gasweld*, it cannot support an enforceable restraint. If the information is publicly available, it does not have the required quality of confidence.[107] So information that could easily be constructed from memory and publicly available sources cannot support a restraint.

Customer relationships

Often an employer wishes to protect its established relationships with customers—the 'customer connection'. This is that intangible cement that keeps a customer coming back to a familiar service provider, because of the relationships between the customer and people in the business. When employees leave the business there is a risk that the customers will follow, because the customer identifies the good service with the employee, and not with the business.

To identify the legitimate interest that the employer seeks to protect, we need to step back from any assumption that the employer 'owns the customer', and analyse precisely what it is that is being protected. While employed, the employee developed relationships with customers, and those relationships depended for their success on a number of factors. These include not only the employee's own personable nature, but also the employee's skill and effort (for which the employer remunerated the employee), and the opportunity created by the employer, including all the resources provided by the employer to ensure the success of the relationship. The employer has an interest in preventing the employee from exploiting any particularly close relationship with the customer that has arisen out of that combination of things. The employer has funded the development of that relationship, so the employer has an interest in restraining the employee from taking away the benefit of the relationship.

---

104 Ibid.
105 See *Littlewoods Organisations Ltd v Harris* [1977] 1 WLR 1472, 1479.
106 This term is used in JD Heydon *The Restraint of Trade Doctrine* 2nd edn (1999), 91 ff.
107 *Maggbury Pty Ltd v Hafele Australia Pty Ltd* (2001) 210 CLR 181.

It is the relationship that the employee has with *particular* clients that is protected, not the relationship between the business and *all* of its clients. An employee can only be restrained from exploiting the particular loyalty of the customer to that employee. An employee cannot be restrained from rendering services to any of the former employer's customers—only those with whom a special relationship was developed. Even so, the restraint will only run for so long as is reasonable to protect the former employer's legitimate interest. Generally that interest will allow an injunction against soliciting those clients for a short time—three months was deemed reasonable in *Hitech Contracting Ltd v Lynn*[108]—to give the former employer some time to reassure the customers that another person in the business will be able to adequately fill the shoes of the departing employee. In *Barrett v Ecco Personnel Pty Ltd*,[109] the NSW Court of Appeal upheld a restraint of four months, and allowed a broad interpretation of the notion of 'soliciting' to include accepting an invitation to tender, initiated by the former client.

Restrictive covenants

Relationships with co-workers: 'no poaching' clauses

It has become common, particularly in industries where people work in teams, for employers to seek to restrain employees from inviting co-workers to join them in a new venture. Typically, the employment contract will contain an undertaking that the employee will not 'poach' the employer's other employees by inducing them to leave employment. Here again, practice has begun to adopt property terminology to justify employers' claims to a kind of 'ownership' of their staff. This kind of clause should be entirely unenforceable. Employers do not own staff. The relationship between employer and employee creates personal obligations only, and each employee is entitled to terminate that relationship according to the terms of the contract. So long as the recruiter does not commit the tort of interfering in another's contracts by inducing the employee to breach the terms of the contract[110] (for example, by leaving without giving notice), the recruiter has committed no legal wrong by offering the employee alternative employment. Simply persuading a person to exercise a right to terminate an employment contract with notice does not constitute commission of the tort of interference in another's contractual relationships.

An employer has no legitimate interest to protect in restraining the liberty of movement of employees. They are free to change jobs, even if the change involves them leaving to set up in business with former colleagues. So a restraint that purports to prevent former colleagues from recruiting each other does not protect a legitimate

---

108 2001 NSW LEXIS 1739; BC200108978, 1 May 2001.

109 [1998] NSWSC 545.

110 See eg *Sanders v Snell* (1998) 196 CLR 329 in which the High Court of Australia held that inducing an employer to dismiss without notice (by paying in lieu) constituted the tort of inducing a breach of contract.

interest of the employer and will be an illegal restraint of trade. This was the finding in *Kores Manufacturing Co Ltd v Kolok Manufacturing Co Ltd*[111] in 1958 and this was the view consistently held until at least 1988.[112] In more recent years, however, there has been a disturbing erosion of principle in a number of English cases, where judges have been willing to allow an employer the benefit of clauses purporting to claim an interest in preventing former staff members from recruiting team members.

In *Office Angels Ltd v Rainer-Thomas* (*Office Angels*),[113] a covenant preventing a person from recruiting temp agency staff was upheld. The court in *Hanover Insurance v Shapiro*[114] refused to follow *Office Angels*, on the basis that 'an employer does not have any sort of proprietary interest in a stable team of staff entitling the employer to impose restrictions on the solicitation of staff'. However, in *Dawnay Day & Co Ltd v De Braconier D'Alphen* (*Dawnay*),[115] the English Court of Appeal upheld a restraint preventing investment bond brokers from offering employment to the teams with whom they had worked, on the basis that this industry depended on the operation of experienced and established teams or 'desks' and there was a culture of 'following the leader' in such teams. This case may be explained as an extension of the customer connection cases: the special loyalty built up between team leader and team members was analogous to the special connection with clients. The court was careful to assert that the 'no recruiting' clause would not extend to an absolute prohibition on hiring former colleagues. It may prevent a person from soliciting former colleagues deliberately, but would not prevent the engagement of colleagues who applied for work on their own initiative.

In *TSC Europe (UK) Ltd v Massey* (*TSC*),[116] which conceded that an employer had a legitimate interest in maintaining a stable, trained workforce, the court limited the effectiveness of such clauses to senior or 'key' personnel. These English cases must be questionable. Other recent English authority maintains the faith on the general principle that the employer must have a legitimate interest to protect before a restraint can be enforced. For example, in *FSS Travel & Leisure Systems Ltd v Johnson*,[117] Woolf MR and Millett LJ agreed with Mummery LJ that a highly trained computer programmer could not be restrained from going to a competitor, because the employer could not identify any specific trade secret that they were seeking to protect. They were held not to be entitled to control the 'exercise, after the termination of the employment relationship, of the skill, experience, know-how and general knowledge inevitably gained' by the employee during employment. It is difficult to reconcile this decision with those of arguably less impressive benches in *Office Angels*, *Dawney* and *TSC* that an employer can limit the employment opportunities of remaining staff by upholding no-recruiting restraints given by their colleagues.

---

111 [1958] 2 All ER 65.
112 See P Sales 'Covenants Restricting Recruitment of Employees and the Doctrine of the Restraint of Trade' (1988) 104 *LQR* 600.
113 [1991] IRLR 214.
114 [1994] IRLR 82.
115 [1997] EWCA Civ 1753 (22 May 1997).
116 [1999] IRLR 22.
117 [1997] EWCA Civ 2759 (19 November 1997).

General 'non-compete' clauses

Many employers seek to extract from their employees a commitment not to work for any competitor for a period after the termination of employment. To the extent that these clauses seek to protect a legitimate interest of the employer in stemming the leakage of confidential information or trade secrets from their businesses, they may be enforceable. In *Littlewoods Organisation Ltd v Harris*,[118] Denning LJ allowed that such a clause would be a convenient and acceptable means of protecting such information, when it would be difficult to devise a more specific injunction precluding the use of the confidential information. However, these kinds of restraints must still be able to be justified on the basis that the employer is seeking to protect a legitimate interest—such as confidential information or particular customer connections—and they will still be subject to the restraint of trade doctrine.[119]

The restraint of trade doctrine

Any express covenant must be justifiable in the light of the common law doctrine against restraints of trade, and other equitable constraints on restrictive covenants.[120] The common law doctrine making any restraint of free trade prima facie illegal and unenforceable is an ancient one,[121] based on the notion that people should be able to pursue their own livelihood without restraint, because there is a public interest in free trade and a productive community. These days, we would describe this as the public interest in competition, and of course in Australia we have enshrined such principles in Pt IV of the *Trade Practices Act 1974* (Cth).

The High Court of Australia considered the doctrine against restraint of trade in the context of a dispute over an unpatented design. *Maggbury Pty Ltd v Hafele Australia Pty Ltd (Maggbury)*[122] was not an employment case, but it is relevant to employment cases in a number of respects.

First, the majority decision in *Maggbury* affirmed that the doctrine applies to freely bargained commercial agreements. The argument that an employee agreed to the restraint with open eyes should not be enough to justify enforcing a covenant that would otherwise be an illegal restraint of trade. This warns us that the decisions that have considered restraints from the point of view of equality of bargaining power should be read carefully, lest they be misinterpreted. These cases include *Curro v Beyond Productions Pty Ltd*,[123] in which a restraint that prevented a television presenter from going to a rival television station during the currency of her contract was upheld. The High Court took time to examine the quality of Ms Curro's consent to the restraint,

---

118 [1977] 1 All ER 1472, 1479.

119 See eg *Woolworths Ltd v Olson* (2004) 184 FLR 121, where a six-month non-compete period was upheld to protect strategic commercial information.

120 Particularly, the requirement that these promises must not be extracted by duress, undue influence or unconscionable dealing.

121 For a discussion of its pedigree in Anglo American law, see HM Blake 'Employee Agreements Not to Compete' (1960) 73 *Harv LR* 625.

122 (2001) 210 CLR 181.

123 (1993) 30 NSWLR 337.

and found that she had the benefit of legal advice before signing, she had an attractive alternative offer of employment at the time she signed, and she had not objected to the restraints at the time or sought to have them altered. All these matters go to show that Ms Curro could not establish an *alternative* basis for setting the restraint aside—on the basis of unconscionable dealing. The restraint also had to be tested for reasonableness in the light of the restraint doctrine.

Secondly, *Maggbury* confirms that information that is publicly available and lacks the required quality of confidence cannot be the subject of a valid restraint. Information is free. Any attempt by contract to restrict another's liberty to use freely available information is an illegal restraint, because it offends the common law's interest in free competition. So any post-employment restraint that requires an employee to agree not to contact customers of the employer after leaving cannot be upheld simply on the basis that the customers' names and contact details are confidential. All these things can be found out easily, especially in these days of electronic database and Web searching. Such a restraint will only withstand challenge to the extent that it protects the 'customer connection', described above. That warrants only a very limited time period, sufficient only to allow the former employer time to re-establish a new connection with the customer.

Effective restraints

Not all restraints are illegal. A restraint that goes no further than what is reasonable to protect the legitimate interest of the person taking the benefit of the covenant is acceptable.[124] In the case of employment contracts, post-employment restraint clauses have been upheld.[125] It is the employer who bears the onus of showing that the restraint goes no further than is reasonably necessary to protect the interests of the employer. What is reasonable requires consideration of the purpose of the restraint, and its scope, in time, place and extent of activities.

As to time and place, it is not unusual for employers to use 'cascading provisions', and to draft the restraint in terms that allow severance of any unenforceable elements. In New South Wales, the *Restraint of Trade Act 1976* (NSW), which allows a court to read down a restraint, has encouraged the use of 'blue pencil' or 'cascading clauses', to attempt to save clauses should they be challenged. Such clauses can run a risk of being void for uncertainty, if the various choices contemplate too many permutations to provide a comprehensible restraint.[126]

'In terrorem' effect

Employers who jealously guard their competitive advantages may well seek to prevent employees from taking off with customers by requiring onerous and extensive covenants in employment contracts that would, under challenge, prove to be in illegal restraint of trade. Even a clause that is strictly speaking unenforceable may have the practical effect of intimidating an employee who is not aware of the law. And even a clause that

---

124 See *Lindner v Murdock's Garage* (1950) 83 CLR 628; *Adamson v NSW Rugby League Ltd* (1991) 31 FCR 242.

125 See eg *Hitech Contracting Ltd v Lynn*, above n 94.

126 See eg *Austra Tanks Pty Ltd v Running* [1982] 2 NSWLR 840; *Lloyd's Ships Holdings Pty Ltd v Davros Pty Ltd* (1987) 17 FCR 505.

would not withstand challenge on a full hearing of a claim may support an interlocutory injunction, restricting the employee's freedom for a sufficiently long period to satisfy the employer in the not-so-short time that will elapse before full hearing. An interlocutory injunction need only demonstrate that there is a serious question to be tried, and that the balance of convenience favours the grant of the injunction. And many interlocutory injunctions ultimately decide matters, because the plaintiff with the benefit of an injunction, even for a short time, has little incentive to pursue the matter to hearing.

By including such clauses in contracts, and asserting a willingness to use their economic resources to pursue matters through the courts, employers are abusing their bargaining power, in a way that must be questionable in the contemporary labour market climate.[127]

Our contemporary culture of career and job change means that people expect to move around more than they did in the past. Employers' demands for 'flexibility' have been a major driver in this cultural change. In a climate where employer loyalty to employees is low, redundancies and retrenchments are common, and job security is fragile, rational employees need to keep an eye to their prospects of future employment, and cannot afford to feel the same loyalty to the employer as their grandparents may have done in times of more stable employment. The employer may in fact actively encourage employees to become 'independent contractors', usually to enable the employer to avoid liability for various statutory obligations associated with engaging labour as employees.[128] In such a climate, a 'fair go all round'[129] dictates that the law should be careful to strike an appropriate balance between the interests of employers in preserving the value of their businesses, and the interests of employees in freely pursuing their careers. Katherine Van Wezel Stone argues that this balance does in fact reflect the mutual expectations of the new psychological contract between employer and employees, in a market where job security has been replaced by promises of continued employability as the core commitment of employers in exchange for the reciprocal commitment of workers.[130] Judicial interpretation of contractual commitments needs to recognise these underlying reciprocal commitments.

Effect of the employer's breach of contract on post-employment restraints

Sometimes employees leave their employment for a competitor because of the conduct of the employer. For instance, an employer may terminate the contract directly, or may be responsible for the employee's decision to leave by breaching its duty not to destroy 'mutual trust and confidence' in the relationship.[131] An old line of English

---

127 See Stone, above n 35.

128 Typical reasons for 'contracting out' are to avoid payroll tax, to shift the risks of insurance onto the employee, and often to avoid liability under unfair dismissal laws. See for example *Riste Damevski v Endoxos Pty Ltd* AIRC, PR917597, 9 May 2002; AIRC, PR922380, 13 September 2002, overturned in *Damevski v Giudice* (2003) 202 ALR 494.

129 This expression familiar to industrial lawyers comes from Sheldon J *In Re Loty and Holloway v Australian Workers' Union* [1971] AR (NSW) 95.

130 See Stone, above n 35, 597.

131 This duty is now established in English employment law: see *Bliss v SE Thames Regional Health Authority* [1987] ICR 700; *Malik v Bank of Credit and Commerce International* [1997] 3 WLR 95.

cases[132] suggests that if a contract is breached by the employer by wrongful dismissal of the employee, then the employee is no longer bound by any restrictive covenants in the employment contract restraining post employment competition.

Rock Refrigeration Ltd v Jones[133] is not, however, an entirely secure foundation for this proposition. Only one of the three judges hearing the matter—Morritt LJ—upheld the proposition in *General Billposting* that 'if the contract is terminated because the employer's repudiation has been accepted by the employee then the covenant will no longer bind the employee'.[134] Phillips LJ expressly disagreed with this principle, citing House of Lords authority in *Heyman v Darwins Ltd*[135] for the view that a restraint was a secondary obligation, which the parties intended should operate after termination of the contract, even by breach. Phillips LJ also opined that such a revision would not necessarily be unfair to employees, particularly in the light of contemporary availability of remedies for unfair dismissal (this was an English decision).[136] The remaining judge, Simon Brown LJ, did not decide this particular issue.

If *Rock Refrigeration* has indeed cast doubt on the *General Billposting* principle, then repudiation of the contract by the employer may not discharge the employee's obligations to respect the restraint. Nevertheless, a court called upon to specifically enforce a restraint in such circumstances may hold that the employer's breach of contract is grounds for refusing an order. Such an order is an equitable injunction, and equity's remedies depend upon the claimant being able to show 'clean hands'.

Unfair contracts review

Another potential source of challenge to post-employment restraints is review by a court exercising unfair contracts review powers under a statute. For example, prior to the federal *Work Choices* legislation, employees in New South Wales were able to seek unfair contracts review under s 106 of the *Industrial Relations Act 1996* (NSW).[137] A number of cases challenging restrictive covenants have been heard in this jurisdiction,[138] and it has been held that an employer seeking to enforce a restraint in circumstances where the employer had breached the contract had acted unfairly.[139]

The employee's duty of disclosure

The extent to which the employee's duty of loyalty extends to a duty to report on themselves and others has been subject to some debate. The orthodox view—supported by the somewhat problematic case of *Bell v Lever Brothers*

---

132 Beginning with *General Billposting Co v Atkinson* [1909] AC 118 and culminating in *Rock Refrigeration v Jones* [1997] 1 All ER 1. *General Billposting* has been followed in Australia in *Kaufman v McGillicuddy* (1914) 19 CLR 1.

133 [1997] 1 All ER 1.

134 Ibid, 12.

135 [1942] AC 356.

136 [1997] 1 All ER 1, 20.

137 There are also unfair contracts provisions in federal legislation, which might be used to challenge an unfair restraint in a contract between an employer and an independent contractor.

138 See *Becker v Harry M Miller Attractions Pty Ltd (No 2)* [1972] AR (NSW) 298; *Lumby v Yorkshire-General Life Assurance Co Ltd* [1978] 1 NSWLR 626; *Morgan v Coulson* [1981] 2 NSWLR 801; and *Haddad v S & T Income Tax Aid Specialists Pty Ltd* [1985] 13 IR 16.

139 See *Haddad v S & T Income Tax Aid Specialists Pty Ltd* [1985] 13 IR 16.

(*Bell*)[140]—is that employees have no contractual obligation to disclose their own wrong doing. Failure to disclose one's own misdemeanour will therefore not be a breach of the employment contract. *Bell* concerned a company that paid compensation under an agreement for early termination of the contracts of two executive employees and later discovered that those employees had committed a fraud on the employer company. The employer sought restitution of the compensation payments on the basis of an entitlement to rescind an agreement based on a mistake. The House of Lords held by majority that there was no basis for restitution, because the employees had no duty to disclose their wrongdoing in the course of negotiating the settlement of their claims for termination payments.

This case was raised before the High Court of Australia in *Concut Pty Ltd v Worrell*,[141] which also concerned an executive employee who had breached his fiduciary duty to the company by misappropriating company property. The employee had been employed for a time during which the breach of duty occurred, but it was not discovered until after his engagement had been converted to a short-term contract. The employer terminated the contract, and the employee claimed an entitlement to be paid out for the term of the fixed term contract. He argued, on the basis of *Bell*, that he had no obligation to disclose his earlier wrongdoing when negotiating the new fixed term contract, so failure to disclose could not constitute breach of the contract. He succeeded before the Queensland Court of Appeal, but failed before the High Court, who distinguished *Bell* as a restitution case and held that the employer was not obliged to make a payment of damages to a person who had breached his implied duty of fidelity during the course of the employment relationship.

In any case, there has been some erosion of the broader principle ascribed to *Bell* (ie, the principle that an employee owes no duty to disclose wrongdoing), in cases where an employee has a duty to supervise others. In *Sybron Corp v Rochem*[142] it was held that a senior staff member with supervisory responsibilities did owe a duty to disclose the wrongdoing of others in the firm, even where that disclosure would incriminate himself. Nevertheless, a failure to 'dob in' others will not necessarily constitute a sufficiently serious breach of the employment contract to warrant summary dismissal, especially in the eyes an industrial tribunal exercising a discretion to determine whether a dismissal was harsh, unjust or unreasonable under a statutory regime.[143]

Whistleblowing as an exception

Employees who 'dob' on their employers, however, will be found to be in breach of their duty of fidelity unless they can appeal to a higher public or civic duty[144] or an entitlement or right under legislation.[145]

---

140 [1932] AC 161.
141 (2000) 75 AJLR 312.
142 [1984] 1 Ch 112.
143 See *Wormald Australia Pty Ltd v Harward* (1992) 42 IR 166, 172.
144 *Initial Services Ltd v Putterill* [1967] 3 All ER 145; *Lion Laboratories Ltd v Evans* [1984] 2 All ER 417.
145 See for instance the *Whistleblowers Protection Act 1993* (SA).

Warranty of skill

It is also an implied term of the contract of employment that the employee has the skill to perform the work competently, so under general law an employee may be dismissed summarily for negligent or incompetent work. As with any other implied term, this warranty may be negated by express terms. Employees who disclaim a particular skill or level of experience when applying for a job, and who are taken on regardless on the basis that they will learn on the job, cannot be summarily dismissed for want of skill.[146] They will be entitled to a proper period of notice.

The duty of care

Employees likewise owe a duty of care to their employer in the performance of their work. The extent to which an employer can claim damages from the employee or an indemnity for claims made against the employer is limited by statute.[147]

The duty of care extends to a duty to cooperate in the provision of a safe workplace. (Statutory occupational health and safety regimes also impose obligations of this nature on employees.) Fulfilment of this duty of care has been held to be an 'inherent requirement of the job' for the purposes of defences to discrimination laws. In *X v Commonwealth*,[148] (a case concerning whether the dismissal of a defence forces employee with human immunodeficiency virus [HIV] was unlawful discrimination), McHugh J asserted:

> [C]arrying out the employment without endangering the safety of other employees is an inherent requirement of any employment. It is not merely 'so obvious that it goes without saying'—which is one of the tests for implying a term in a contract to give effect to the supposed intention of the parties. The term is one which, subject to agreement to the contrary, the law implies in every contract of employment. It is but a particular application of the implied warranty that the employee is able to and will exercise reasonable care and skill in carrying out his or her duties.

Where an employee's negligent performance of work under the employment contract causes harm to a third party, the employer will be vicariously liable for that harm. (Except where the employee is granted some statutory immunity,[149] the employee may still be sued by a tort victim, and an employer who has been required to pay for an employee's tort may seek an indemnity from the employee. The *Insurance Contracts Act 1984* (Cth) limits the rights of an employer's insurer to seek indemnity from employees.) In this area, as in the area of employers' duties of care to the employee, the private law of contract and tort has long been supplemented, and at times overridden, by a range of statutory schemes better suited to accommodating the public interest in managing the risks and costs of work-related harms.[150]

---

146 *PIEUA v Jackson & O'Sullivan Pty Ltd* (1957) 1 FLR 175.

147 See eg the *Employees Liability Act 1991* (NSW).

148 (1999) 200 CLR 177, 188.

149 See *Employees Liability Act 1991* (NSW); *Civil Liability Act 1936* (SA); *Civil Liability Act 2002* (WA); *Civil Liability Act 2002* (Tas); and *Civil Liability Act 2003* (Qld).

150 Eg extensive State occupational health and safety statutes regulate duties and liabilities of workplace participants, and workers' compensation schemes deal with compensation and rehabilitation of sick and injured workers.

The employer's duties

Employer's duties

Perhaps because the terms implied by law into the employment contract are largely the fiduciary incidents of the relationship arising from the servant's duty to serve the master, traditional employment contract law implies considerably fewer burdens on the employer in the relationship. Even the duty to pay wages is conditional on the employee's substantial performance of the work (see below). The circumstances in which the employer is obliged to provide work have also been limited. The employer clearly owes the employee a duty of care under the contract of employment and also in tort, and usually under some statute imposing obligations for occupational health and safety.[151]

Perhaps under the influence of statutory developments—especially in protection from unfair dismissal—and perhaps from the emergence in commercial law generally of 'good faith' obligations even in arm's length business dealings, employment contract law has begun to elaborate more reciprocal obligations in the employment relationship. Under English law, and now also under Australian law, the employer has become subject to an emergent duty of 'mutual trust and confidence', although the capacity for this duty to sound in any remedy of its own remains in issue. In Australia, this development is at the most embryonic of stages.[152]

The work/wages bargain

In the absence of any provisions in an industrial instrument or any express contractual term as to the timing of payment, the employer's obligation to pay wages is dependent upon the employee first performing the work. Even where the employee's failure to perform is due to a lock-out by the employer, the employee can claim no wages (though there will be some entitlement to damages for breach of contract, and such damages are likely to be calculated by reference to the amount of wages lost, less any opportunity the employee has had to mitigate that loss).

The principal authority for this proposition is the somewhat peculiar case of *Automatic Fire Sprinklers v Watson*.[153] The case involved the dismissal, contrary to war-time employment regulations, of a man working in an essential industry. Mr Watson asserted an entitlement to be paid indefinitely, despite being given no work, because his dismissal was impermissible under the regulations. In fact, Mr Watson won his case on a construction of the particular regulations; however, the broader principle upheld by the court was that wages follow work, and without the performance of work there is no entitlement to wages, regardless of the reason for non-performance.

---

151 See *Occupational Health and Safety Act 2000* (NSW); *Occupational Health and Safety Act 1985* (Vic); *Occupational Health and Safety Act 1984* (WA); *Occupational Health and Safety Act 1989* (ACT); *Occupational Health, Safety and Welfare Act 1986* (SA); *Workplace Health and Safety Act 1995* (Qld).

152 See A Brooks 'The Good and Considerate Employer: Developments in the Implied Duty of Mutual Trust and Confidence' (2001) 20 *U Tas L Rev* 29; J Riley 'Mutual Trust and Good Faith: Can Private Contract Law Guarantee Fair Dealing in the Workplace?' (2003) 16 *AJLL* 28.

153 (1946) 72 CLR 435.

Despite *Automatic Firesprinkler's* peculiar facts, the case has been persistently cited as authority for this proposition, often prior to the court finding some particular exception to the 'rule' in the case before it. Often, the contemporary circumstances that call the principle into question involve limited industrial action or work bans. Where employees engage in a 'go slow' or 'work to rule' or some other form of limited disobedience, an issue may arise as to whether the employer is obliged to pay the workers. If the employer accepts partial performance of work, the employer must pay for the work and has no common law entitlement to make deductions in respect of underperformance.[154] The employer's acceptance may be deduced from conduct.[155] To avoid payment for underperformance, the employer must issue clear instructions as to the work to be done, and warn employees that performance of other work will not be accepted nor paid for. So long as the employer is consistent, and no senior staff members undermine the instructions by issuing other orders or demonstrating by their conduct that they do not mean to act on the edict of the employer, then the workers can be denied payment.[156]

Case law on this issue has been inconsistent, betraying some judicial reluctance to deny wages to workers who have substantially performed their contracts by attending and providing services that have been accepted by the employer. The English House of Lords considered this problem in *Miles v Wakefield MDC*,[157] a case about a marriage celebrant who refused to perform civil ceremonies on a Saturday. Lords Brightman and Templeman opined that the problem of determining whether the employee should be entitled to payment for the services actually rendered (albeit not the complete range of duties stipulated by his employer) could be resolved by allowing the employee to make a claim based on *quantum meruit*—payment for services rendered and accepted, outside of a contract. The matter has been resolved in Australia by statutory provisions of the *Workplace Relations Act 1996* (Cth), which prohibit payment for periods of industrial action.[158]

The duty to provide work

Traditionally, only employees who are paid on a commission basis,[159] or who work in occupations where publicity is an important aspect of reward, have been able to claim an entitlement to be provided with work. Actors,[160] entertainers, writers, cartoonists, and—in an extension of the cases about entertainers—musical directors,[161] have been held to be entitled to be given the opportunity to perform. In recent years courts have

---

154 *ABEU v National Australia Bank Ltd* (1989) 31 IR 436; *United Firefighters Union of Australia v Metropolitan Fire Brigades Board* (1998) 86 IR 340.
155 *ABEU v National Australia Bank Ltd* (1989) 31 IR 436.
156 *Spotless Catering Services Ltd v Federated Liquor and Allied Industries Employees Union NSW Branch* (1988) IR 255.
157 [1987] 2 WLR 795.
158 Section 507. See Chapter 12.
159 *Devonald v Rosser* [1906] 2 KB 728.
160 *Herbert Clayton v Oliver* [1930] AC 209.
161 *White v Australian and New Zealand Theatres* (1943) 67 CLR 266.

shown a willingness to extend these categories in the case of highly skilled professionals, especially those engaged under contracts for specific projects.[162] In the case of ordinary workers, where the employer pays the stipulated remuneration but fails to provide work, it has generally been held that the employer has not breached the employment contract.[163] The employee's only protection is to offer the required notice for termination and resign the position.

In a world where the development of experience to ensure employability in other enterprises is one of the principal benefits of a job,[164] the reluctance of the law to imply a duty to provide work is problematic and requires review. In *Blackadder v Ramsey Butchering Services Pty Ltd*[165] Callinan and Heydon JJ opined that 'in modern times, a desire for what has been called "job satisfaction", and a need for employees of various kinds, to keep and to be seen to have kept their hands in by actual work have a role to play in determining whether work in fact should be provided'.[166]

Failure to fulfil an implied promise to provide opportunities for skill development should constitute a breach of the employer's obligations, especially where the employer has reserved an entitlement to avoid competition from former employees by the use of restrictive covenants or 'garden leave' provisions. 'Garden leave' describes a situation—common in highly competitive industries where a departing employee may take valuable information or contacts to a rival—where the employer agrees to pay out a long period of notice, without requiring work for that period, on the condition that the employee must not work for anyone else during the notice period. ('Garden leave' can also describe a period of suspension on similar terms.) Problems arise when a departing employee would rather forego the payment and take an often much more remunerative job with a rival. A court may then be asked to consider the former employer's application for an injunction, restraining the departing employee.

Duty to act reasonably?

When the United Kingdom first introduced statutory protection for employees from arbitrary dismissal, a debate arose as to whether an employer owed a duty to 'act reasonably' towards employees. Employers seeking to avoid liability to pay statutory compensation to dismissed employees developed a strategy: rather than fire staff they would use various techniques to goad the employee into resignation. The notion of constructive dismissal, now encapsulated in s 95(1)(c) of the *Employment Rights Act 1996* (UK), was interpreted to include a resignation by the employee after a breach by the employer of its duties under the employment contract. Where the employer's breach was serious enough to constitute a repudiation of the employment contract, the employee was held to be justified in accepting that repudiation and

---

162 See *William Hill Organisation Ltd v Tucker* [1999] ICR 291; *Wesoky v Village Cinemas International Pty Ltd* [2001] FCA 32 (21 February 2001).

163 *Turner v Sawdon* [1907] 2 KB 563; *Mann v ACT Health Commission* (1981) 54 FLR 23.

164 See Stone, above n 35.

165 (2005) 221 CLR 539, 566–67.

166 See J Riley 'Pensioning off Lord Asquith's Cook' (2005) 18 *AJLL* 177.

treating the employment contract as at an end. Because the termination was held to be due to the fault of the employer, this constituted termination by the employer for the purposes of a claim for wrongful dismissal, and gave rise to a claim under the statute.

Circumstances that have been held to constitute a constructive dismissal include:

- unilateral changes to elements of remuneration;[167]
- unilateral demotion;[168]
- harassment, and unjustified criticism,[169] including harassment by work colleagues, in which case an employer may become responsible if the employer fails to intervene in such behaviour;[170]
- institution of precipitate and insensitive inquiries into allegations of misconduct;[171]
- insisting that the employee undergo intrusive medical and psychological examinations,[172] although this will depend on whether the employer has a legitimate business interest in requiring such tests to be taken.[173]

Whether the employer owed employees a duty to 'act reasonably' arose in the context of developing this concept of a constructive dismissal. The English courts were initially most reluctant to concede that employers owed such a duty,[174] no doubt because applying a test of 'reasonableness' to employer conduct would involve courts in assessing business judgments. The reluctance to describe the employer's duty as a positive duty to 'act reasonably' persists in judicial and scholarly discussion of the question; nevertheless it is clear that employers now owe a negative duty, *not* to act in an unreasonable and intolerable manner towards an employee. Also described as a duty to be 'good and considerate',[175] this obligation is now most often expressed as a duty not to act in a way calculated to destroy the relationship of mutual trust and confidence, and is rapidly developing—at least in the United Kingdom—into a duty to deal fairly.[176]

It should be noted that the concept of a 'constructive dismissal'—a repudiation of the employment contract by the employer, which the employee is entitled to accept by termination—appears to be a different concept than that of 'forced' resignation now enshrined in the *Workplace Relations Act* unfair dismissal provisions.[177] The statutory

---

167 *Woods v WM Car Service (Peterborough) Ltd* [1981] ICR 666.
168 *Russian v Woolworths (SA) Pty Ltd* (1995) 64 IR 169.
169 *Lewis v Motorworld Garages Ltd* [1986] ICR 157.
170 See *JV Strong & Co Ltd v Hamill*, EAT/1179/99, 1 December 2000.
171 *Russian v Woolworths (SA) Pty Ltd* (1995) 64 IR 169.
172 *Bliss v South East Thames Regional Health Authority* [1987] ICR 700.
173 *Anderson v Sullivan* (1997) 78 FCR 380.
174 See eg *Western Excavating (ECC) Ltd v Sharp* [1978] ICR 221. See also the discussion in M Freedland *The Personal Employment Contract* (2003), 154–70.
175 *Woods v WM Car Service (Peterborough) Ltd* [1981] ICR 666.
176 See *Johnson v Unisys Ltd* [2003] 1 AC 518. See also D Brodie 'The Heart of the Matter: Mutual Trust and Confidence' (1996) 25 *ILJ* 121; 'Beyond Exchange: the New Contract of Employment' (1998) 27 *ILJ* 79; 'A Fair Deal at Work' (1999) 19 *OJLS* 83.
177 *Workplace Relations Act 1996* (Cth), s 642(4).

provisions imply a requirement that the employee had no choice but resign, whereas the contractual concept allows that the employee may make an election to accept repudiation.

Emergent duty of mutual trust and confidence

The English House of Lords decision in *Malik and Mahmud v Bank of Credit and Commerce International SA (in liq)* (*Malik*),[178] is consistently cited as authority for the existence of a duty of 'mutual trust and confidence' in employment relationships. In *Malik* the House of Lords endorsed the development of a duty articulated in earlier decisions, such as *Courtaulds Northern Textiles v Andrew*,[179] *Woods v WM Car Services (Peterborough) Ltd*,[180] and *Bliss v South East Thames Regional Health Authority* (*Bliss*) [1987] ICR 700.[181] In these earlier cases the duty supported the wronged employees' entitlement to treat their contracts of employment as having been repudiated by the employer and to seek statutory remedies for unfair termination of their contracts—or, in the case of *Bliss*, a common law remedy. *Malik* was important because it represented acceptance by the House of Lords that, in an appropriate case, an employee might also obtain an award of damages for the breach of the duty itself, apart from any remedy arising out of the termination.

Malik was a test case, argued on the basis of assumed facts—ultimately the plaintiffs in the litigation were unable to prove those facts and therefore obtained no compensation for breach of the mutual trust and confidence duty. It was indeed an unusual case, not the least because of the matters that were claimed to constitute the employer's breach of the duty. The employer was a bank that failed under the weight of corruption. The plaintiffs were middle managers of the bank who had been paid out their termination benefits when they lost their jobs through the collapse of the bank, but who were unable to find any alternative employment—allegedly because of the stigma attached to them as a result of their association with the notorious practices of the bank. Counsel for the managers framed the suit as a claim for damages for the bank's breach of mutual trust and confidence in running a corrupt business and so damaging the employees' opportunities to obtain future employment. They argued that this breach gave rise to a claim for loss, which was distinct from any claim related to the termination of the contract itself, or to any claim in tort for defamation for damage to reputation. The House of Lords held that as a matter of law,[182] an employee who could establish a pecuniary loss related to a breach of the duty of mutual trust and confidence could bring an action for such damage, so long as this loss was distinct from any loss suffered as a consequence of termination itself. This proposition has subsequently been confirmed in *Eastwood v Magnox Electric plc; McCabe v Cornwall County Council*.[183]

---

178 [1997] 3 WLR 95.
179 [1979] IRLR 84.
180 [1982] ICR 693.
181 [1985] IRLR 308.
182 When the case came to trial on the facts, the plaintiffs were unable to establish their loss or any entitlement to damages: see *Husain & Anor v BCCI* [2002] 3 All ER 750.
183 [2005] 1 AC 503.

Australian case law has generally accepted *Malik* as authority for the existence of 'an implied term to the effect that the employer would not, without reasonable and proper cause, conduct itself in a manner likely to destroy or seriously damage the relationship of confidence and trust between employer and employee'.[184] Australian academic and professional commentary has documented extensively the acceptance of this new formula in Australian jurisprudence.[185] Questions, however, remain. What is the content of this duty? When is it breached? And most importantly, does it support an independent claim to damages for breach, or does it merely identify an opportunity for an employee to claim compensation for constructive dismissal?

Content of the duty

The mutual trust and confidence obligation should not be misconstrued as a new fiduciary duty owed by the employer to the employee. The mutual or reciprocated duty that the parties share is a duty to the relationship itself, and it is best described in the negative: it is a duty not to abuse or destroy the relationship of trust. If the duty has a fiduciary nature, it lies in the fact that the duty requires that parties perform their obligations and exercise their contractual entitlements for proper purposes—those contemplated by the parties at the outset of their relationship. The mutual trust and confidence obligation has also been described as a principle of construction of employment contracts.[186] This means that all obligations in the employment contract are to be construed on the basis that parties are committed to perform the contract in good faith, and to exercise powers for the purposes that those powers were conferred when the employment relationship was formed. For instance, the employer's prerogative to issue orders should be exercised only for the purpose of pursuing legitimate business interests, and should not be exercised capriciously, to harm or humiliate the employee.

In the field of general commercial contract law, scholars and jurists have debated the existence of a general duty to perform contracts in good faith. While there is general acceptance that such a duty exists, different opinions exist as to the scope and content of such a duty, and in particular, whether such a duty obliges contracting parties to exercise contractual rights 'reasonably', or merely honestly.[187] Those who contest the implication

---

184 *Sea Acres Rainforest Centre Pty Ltd v State of New South Wales* (2001) 109 IR 56, 66. See also *Gambotto v John Fairfax Publications Pty Ltd* (2001) 104 IR 303, 309–11; *Hollingsworth v Commissioner of Police* (1999) 88 IR 282, 318; *Aldersea v Public Transport Corporation* [2001] 3 VR 499, 511–12 *Jager v Australian National Hotels Ltd* (1998) 7 Tas R 437; *Thomson v Broadley & Ors* [2002] QSC 255 (20 June 2002); *Linkstaff International Pty Ltd v Roberts* (1996) 67 IR 381. See also *Irving v Kleinman* [2005] NSWCA 116, [27] where the court refused to strike out a claim based on this duty. The High Court of Australia alluded to the duty in *Koehler v Cerebos* (2005) 222 CLR 44, 55.

185 See A Brooks 'The Good and Considerate Employer: Developments in the Implied Duty of Mutual Trust and Confidence' (2001) 20 *U Tas LRev* 29; J Riley 'Mutual Trust and Good Faith: Can Private Contract Law Guarantee Fair Dealing in the Workplace?' (2003) 16 *AJLL* 28; K Godfrey 'Contracts of Employment: Renaissance of the Implied Term of Trust and Confidence' (2003) 77 *ALJ* 764.

186 See J Riley, *Employee Protection at Common Law* (2005), 76.

187 See eg J Carter and E Peden 'Good Faith in Australian Contract Law' (2003) 19 *JCL* 1; E Peden 'Incorporating Terms of Good Faith in Australian Contract Law' (2001) 23 *Syd LR* 222; T Carlin 'The Rise (and Fall?) of Implied Duties of Good Faith in Contractual Performance in Australia' (2002) 25 *UNSWLJ* 99. For a thorough analysis of good faith in general contract law see E Peden *Good Faith in the Performance of Contracts* (2003). For a study of good faith and fidelity in the employment context, see R McCallum and A Stewart 'The Duty of Loyalty: Employee Loyalty in Australia' (1999) 20 *Comp Lab L & Pol'y J* 155.

that good faith performance requires reasonable behaviour generally express concern that reasonableness is too subjective a concept. However, if 'reasonable' has the same meaning in this context as in the context of the duty to obey lawful and reasonable orders, then an obligation to act in good faith and hence reasonably means no more than exercising rights according to the spirit of the contract itself. Using a contractual right for some extraneous purpose, outside the purposes for which that right was granted, is necessarily *un*reasonable.

Administrative law principles—and in particular, the principle of *Wednesbury* unreasonableness[188]—provide a useful analogy. Those who wield administrative power must exercise discretions for purposes for which the powers were conferred, and not capriciously or irrationally. Administrative law controls abuses of public power—or power conferred by or on behalf of the state. Fiduciary law controls the potential abuse of power in private relationships. Mutual trust and confidence is a comparable tool, for controlling the potential abuse of the power inherent in the typical employment relationship.

'Fair dealing'

Once the English courts were prepared to engage with the terminology of 'reasonable' conduct, it was a short step to articulation of a duty on the employer to deal fairly with employees.[189] In Lord Steyn's dissenting opinion in *Johnson v Unisys Ltd*,[190] he stated that the obligation of mutual trust and confidence could be described as an obligation of 'good faith', or of 'fair dealing'.[191] The notion of 'fair dealing' implies more than merely a prohibition on destroying trust. It suggests a positive duty to deal even-handedly with employees. In some English cases, it has in fact been construed in a way that allowed an employee to claim an entitlement to a new contractual right. For example in *BG plc v O'Brien*,[192] the UK Employment Appeals Tribunal upheld a claim by an employee to receive the benefit of a redundancy package that was never part of his original employment contract.

Mr O'Brien was one of many British Gas (BG) employees made redundant at the same time, but he alone was refused an entitlement to participate in an enhanced redundancy package devised while BG was attempting to retain and motivate staff while winding down its operations. The Employment Appeal Tribunal held that BG's failure to offer Mr O'Brien the same contractual terms as his co-workers was a breach of its implied duty of trust and confidence and in particular its duty to treat employees in a fair and even-handed manner.

On appeal, BG complained that the Tribunal had engaged the implied term of trust and confidence improperly, to force the employer to offer an employee a new contractual right, whereas the implied term could do no more than prohibit the

---

188 From the case of *Associated Provincial Picture Houses v Wednesbury Corporation* [1948] 1 KB 223.
189 See generally Brodie, above n 176.
190 [2003] 1 AC 518.
191 Ibid, 536.
192 [2001] IRLR 496.

employer from 'acting capriciously or negatively so as to destroy or seriously damage' a subsisting relationship. This appeal failed. The Appeal Tribunal said:

> It seems to us that to offer a particular benefit to the entirety of a class of employees bar one is capable of being an act calculated to seriously damage or destroy the trust and confidence between the employer and the employee. If for example, seven out of eight senior employees were awarded a substantial bonus and the eighth was awarded nothing, then he might justifiably think that he was being sent a message—at the least, expressing that the employer had no continuing confidence in him. Where such an act is done without the reasonable and proper cause to which the authorities refer, it is plainly an act that no reasonable employer could take. It would be a breach of what Lord Steyn [in *Johnson v Unisys Ltd*[193]] would call the employer's obligation of fair dealing.[194]

BG took the matter further to the Court of Appeal in *Transco plc (formerly BG plc) v O'Brien*,[195] but failed to have the decision overturned.

Similar reasoning has been applied in disputes about employers' exercise of broad discretions to grant bonuses and pay increases. In *Clark v Nomura International plc*,[196] for example, an equities trader whose base pay was supplemented by substantial performance-based bonuses was awarded damages for the loss of a bonus payment when he was dismissed without cause nine months into a financial year. The English High Court awarded Mr Clark damages of 1.35 million pounds sterling, based on its estimation of the bonus he would have received if the employer had exercised its discretion under the bonus scheme in a rational manner.

These cases demonstrate that—according to English law at least—the employer's duty of 'fair dealing' constrains the exercise of any power or discretion reserved to the employer under the contract.[197] In examining the exercise of such a discretion, the court asks a question similar to that in the administrative law case of *Associated Provincial Picture Houses v Wednesbury Corporation*,[198] concerning review of decisions on the ground of irrationality: was the employer's decision such that 'no reasonable employer would have exercised his discretion in that way'.[199] Other public law concepts, such as natural justice, or procedural fairness, also arise in these cases.[200] These public law concepts are appropriate in the employment context, especially in the case of large corporate employers who exercise considerable influence over the welfare of their workers. Increasingly, our rights at work are being recognised as part of our rights as citizens.[201] It is appropriate that

---

193 Above n 190.
194 [2001] IRLR 496, 500.
195 [2002] IRLR 444.
196 [2000] IRLR 766.
197 See also *Clark v BET plc* [1997] IRLR 348; *Horkulak v Cantor Fitzgerald International* [2003] IRLR 756, [86]; *Cantor Fitzgerald International v Horkulak* [2005] ICR 402, 419–20.
198 [1948] 1 KB 223.
199 [2001] IRLR 766, 774.
200 See eg *TSB Bank v Harris* [2000] IRLR 157.
201 See generally RC McCallum 'Collective Labour Law, Citizenship and the Future' (1998) 22 *MULR* 42; 'Crafting a New Collective Labour Law for Australia' (1997) 39 *JIR* 405.

the exercise of bureaucratic power at the workplace should be subject to similar controls on arbitrary and opportunistic abuse as are applied to ensure rational decision-making by public authorities.

Consequences of breach

While breach of the obligation of mutual trust and confidence supports a finding of constructive dismissal, giving rise to remedies for termination, no Australian case law has yet allowed damages for breach of the obligation per se. Some cases have attempted to use the *Malik* decision to found a claim to damages for stress-related illness, consequent upon dismissal. The obstacle such cases face is the much earlier authority of *Addis v Gramaphone Co Ltd*,[202] which decided that injured feelings alone will not sound in damages for wrongful termination of an employment contract.[203] English cases have allowed such claims, so long as the claimant can establish illness and not merely hurt and distress. The English case law is problematic, as a comparison of *Gogay v Hertfordshire County Council (Gogay)*[204] with *Johnson v Unisys Ltd (Johnson)*[205] demonstrates. In *Gogay*, a social worker who was suspended from her employment pending investigations of a sexual abuse allegation was able to claim damages for a psychiatric illness induced by the precipitate and insensitive manner of the employer's investigation of what proved to be an entirely spurious allegation. This callous investigation was held to constitute a breach of the implied obligation of mutual trust and confidence, which caused compensable psychiatric damage.

In *Johnson*, however, a man who suffered the similar psychiatric harm as a result of an unfairly managed dismissal was not able to recover damages, on the basis that the illness arose out of a dismissal, and dismissal remedies were limited by a statutory scheme. Lord Hoffman held that there was no longer any scope for the implication at common law of a term that the 'power of dismissal will be exercised fairly and in good faith',[206] because Parliament had already covered the field of regulating remedies for termination of employment. The difficulty of this decision when compared with *Gogay* has not escaped the House of Lords' notice. Nevertheless it has been confirmed in *Eastwood v Magnox Electric plc; McCabe v Cornwall County Council (Eastwood & Magnox)*[207] that a plaintiff who can isolate damage suffered independently of any damage consequent upon dismissal will be entitled to claim damages for breach of mutual trust. Those whose misery originates in the circumstances of dismissal will not be so entitled. Oddly, an employer seeking to avoid any risk of a damages claim for psychiatric harm might be encouraged to dismiss an employee precipitately, rather than subject the employee to the long and lingering torture of disciplinary proceedings.

---

202 [1909] AC 488.
203 The result in *Addis* has been subject to a great deal of judicial and scholarly comment and disagreement as to its true effect. See the discussion in Lord Steyn's judgment in *Malik* ([1997] 3 WLR 113), and also the discussion in Brooks above n 185, 57–62.
204 [2000] IRLR 703.
205 [2003] 1 AC 518.
206 Ibid, 541.
207 [2004] 3 All ER 991.

So far, courts in Australia appear to have followed the majority in *Johnson*, as far as awards of damages for psychiatric harm following upon termination have been concerned. In *Aldersea & Ors v Public Transport Corporation*,[208] and in *State of New South Wales v Paige*,[209] Lord Hoffman's refusal to extend the common law into a field already covered by a statutory scheme was followed, on the basis that the claims in these cases also involved claims for psychiatric harm following termination.[210]

Following *Eastwood & Magnox*, it is clear that *Johnson* still leaves room for damages claims where the employee's loss has been caused by some breach of the duty of mutual trust and confidence arising independently of the fact or method of dismissal. English courts have allowed employees to recover losses caused by an employer giving an unfair reference,[211] and by an employer's failure to provide crucial information about access to rights under a pension fund.[212] Under Australian law, there are nevertheless cogent reasons for distinguishing *Johnson*, even where the claim concerns harm consequent upon termination of employment.

The unfair dismissal provisions in Australian legislation do not expressly or even impliedly constrain the jurisdiction of the common law courts in determining contract disputes. They provide an alternative dispute resolution forum and an opportunity to obtain a remedy that the common law has always been loathe to give: reinstatement of an employment relationship. (Compensation is allowed only where reinstatement is deemed inappropriate or inadequate on its own to remedy the unfairness.)

Only low to middle income employees of large enterprises are able to access the jurisdiction. Hence these provisions have a different juridical nature to common law rights and remedies for termination of a contract. The High Court of Australia in *Byrne v Australian Airlines Ltd (Byrne)*[213] held that an obligation created by statute will not necessarily have any impact on a private contract.[214] If a statutory obligation does not create a contractual right, then neither will it destroy one, unless the statutory provision is unambiguous in its intention to do so. It would be surprising if a statutory regime, instituted to provide an accessible jurisdiction for small employment claims based on a socially constructed right to maintain one's job in the absence of serious and genuine reasons for termination, should be construed as intending to curtail the jurisdiction of the ordinary courts to hear contract claims.

---

208 (2001) 3 VR 499.

209 (2002) 60 NSWLR 371.

210 Statutory unfair dismissal cases heard under the provisions in the former federal legislation, the *Industrial Relations Act 1988*, were able to award damages for the hurt feelings. See *Burazin v Blacktown City Guardian Pty Ltd* (1996) 142 ALR 144. Also, an employee who suffers psychiatric harm or whose pre-existing psychiatric condition is exacerbated by treatment at the hands of an employer will have a potential action in tort for breach of the duty to take reasonable care not to expose the employee to health and safety risks: see *Police Service of New South Wales v Batton* (2000) 98 IR 154.

211 See *TSB Bank plc v Harris* [2000] IRLR 157. See also *Spring v Guardian Assurance plc* [1994] IRLR 460, which found that the employer's duty was based in tort.

212 See *Scally v Southern Health and Social Services Board* [1992] 1 AC 294.

213 (1995) 185 CLR 410.

214 See the discussion of *Byrne* above.

Mutual trust and work/life balance commitments?

In any case, the usefulness of the mutual trust and confidence obligation in demonstrating a constructive dismissal ought not to be underestimated. Some employees who have the benefit of generous notice provisions and termination benefits may find that arguing the employer's breach of this obligation will open the door to some remedy for a forced resignation. The 'work/life balance' cases provide illustrations. In *Thomson v Orica Australia Pty Ltd*[215] for example, a high ranking sales woman who returned to work after maternity leave to a much less important position in the company was able to demonstrate that this demotion in status (but not income) was a breach of the obligation of mutual trust and confidence. The demotion also constituted a breach of the *Sex Discrimination Act 1984* (Cth),[216] and that breach gave Ms Thomson an entitlement to a statutory remedy. Ms Thomson's statutory rights were also set out in a human resources policy manual issued by the employer. Allsop J held that this policy gave Ms Thomson an expectation that she would be treated in a particular way on return to work from maternity leave. When Orica disappointed that expectation (by rude treatment as well as refusal to return her to her original job) Ms Thomson quite reasonably lost trust in the employer, and was held to be entitled to treat herself as constructively dismissed. She was then able to bring a claim for damages in contract, in addition to the *Sex Discrimination Act* claim.

This case opens the door to claims for breach of contract, based on the employer's refusal to abide by its own policies, even where those policies have not been incorporated into the contract of employment. A similar argument succeeded before a Federal Magistrate in *Dare v Hurley*[217] where an employer was held to have breached the employment contract by failing to follow the procedures for dismissal set out in its own policy and procedures manual. Where a policy manual gives an employee an expectation of certain treatment, an employer who reneges on the policy—whatever its terms—may be held to have breached its duty not to destroy mutual trust and confidence, and may trigger whatever remedies the employee has on termination. Those policies may include such things as policies allowing flexible working hours to accommodate family responsibilities.[218]

Duty of care

Employers owe a common law duty to take reasonable care to avoid exposing employees to unnecessary risks of injury. This duty is of a tortious nature, but it derives from the contractual relationship between employer and employee. In *Patrick Stevedores (No 1) Pty Ltd v Vaughan*[219] the NSW Court of Appeal held that the duty 'arises from the degree of control that the employer exercises over the lives of the employees'.[220]

---

215 (2002) 116 IR 186.
216 See Chapter 8.
217 [2005] FMCA 844.
218 See J Riley 'Contracting for Work/Family Balance' in J Murray (ed) *Work, Family and the Law* (2005), 182.
219 [2002] NSWCA 275.
220 Ibid, [16].

The duty is not absolute. It will be interpreted in the light of the obligations under the contract. Liability to compensate for any harm will depend on whether the risk that the employee was subjected to was necessary to perform the ordinary course of work.[221] Occupational health and safety statutes also impose statutory duties on employers and others in control of workplaces. This is discussed in Chapter 7.

Patrick Stevedores (No 1) Pty Ltd v Vaughan was a legacy of the notorious waterfront dispute of 1998. Mr Vaughan, a faithful employee with almost thirty years' experience on the waterfront, had been a member of the Maritime Union of Australia and its predecessor since 1970. He was promoted in 1993 to the management staff of the company, so when the waterfront dispute broke out, he found himself uncomfortably on the employer's side of the battle lines. The company insisted on bussing him in to work through abusive and violent picket lines, and on one occasion, failed to provide him with any escort. The stress of this period caused him serious psychological harm, for which he sought compensation from the company. The Court of Appeal rejected the employer's argument that its commercial interest in attempting to break the union monopoly of labour on the waterfront justified placing Mr Vaughan and other managers at risk of abuse and distress. These were not ordinary incidents of work on the waterfront, so the risks were not necessary for the performance of the contracted duties.

The employer's duty of care cannot necessarily be cut down by express terms in the contract. In *Johnstone v Bloomsbury Health Authority*[222] a majority of the English Court of Appeal held that the express terms of a resident doctor's contract of engagement, which—literally interpreted—entitled the hospital to roster him on for extraordinarily long shifts, must be read down in the light of an overarching duty to take reasonable care not to subject the employee to unnecessary risk of harm. On the other hand, the High Court of Australia has held that an employer's duty of care to an employee who suffered a stress-related psychiatric illness as a result of overwork could not recover damages in tort or contract for that injury, because she had expressly agreed in her contract of employment to undertake the work alleged to have caused the injury. The majority decision held that the employer's duty of care to the employee could not be considered 'without taking account of the obligations that the parties owe one another under the contract of employment'.[223]

Of course, even where a contract permits dangerous work, an employer may be in breach of statutory duties under occupational health and safety legislation by requiring the performance of that work. In the important area of work safety, Parliaments have long recognised that private regulation by contract is inadequate to protect the worker's and the community's interest in ensuring a reasonable degree of safety in the workplace. Except in the more esoteric field of psychological and psychiatric harm, contract law has all but vacated the field to statutory schemes for regulating safe work practices and compensating victims.

---

221 See *Koehler v Cerebos Pty Ltd* (2005) 222 CLR 44.
222 [1992] 2 All ER 293.
223 *Koehler v Cerebos (Australia) Ltd* (2005) 222 CLR 44, 53–54. See D Rolph 'No Worries? Employers' Duty of Care for Negligently Inflicted Stress' (2005) 18 *AJLL* 344.

Termination of employment contracts

Under the common law of contract—unaided by industrial awards or statutory protections against unfair dismissal—a contract of employment can be terminated according to its own terms, however harsh they might be, or summarily for a sufficiently serious breach. Termination according to the terms of the contract generally involves the party wishing to terminate giving a stipulated period of notice. In the absence of some express notice period, or any stipulation that the contract is for a fixed term,[224] a contract of employment can be terminated on 'reasonable notice' (see below). The common law is loathe to assume that an employment contract is of perpetual duration. There are no 'jobs for life'.[225]

By the same token, Australian law has not adopted the conception of employment 'at will' prevalent in most states of the USA. Employment at will—where either party can walk away from the relationship at any time, for any reason, with no fear of legal sanction—is arguably not a contractual relationship at all. Contract implies the existence of legally enforceable obligations, breach of which gives rise to a legal remedy.[226]

The evolution of industrial and legislative protections against 'unlawful' and 'unfair' dismissal are dealt with in Chapters 8 and 9. Here we examine the development of purely contractual rights and remedies. From the workers' point of view, orthodox principles of contract law have provided very weak protections for the worker's interest in job security. The most hotly contested disputes concern the employer's right to summarily terminate—without paying any severance entitlements—on the basis of a sufficiently serious breach of contract by the employee; the implied requirement that in all other cases the employer must provide 'reasonable notice' of termination; and the limited remedies available to a party when a contract has been terminated wrongfully.

It is useful to commence with the remedies available on termination, because this demonstrates precisely what is at stake when determining whether the contract has been justifiably or wrongfully terminated, and reveals some of the perceived weaknesses in regulation of the employment relationship by purely private contractual means.

Remedies for wrongful termination

Wrongful dismissal—that is, dismissal without notice when notice is required—does not entitle an employee to reinstatement. The common law judges have almost invariably turned their faces against ordering specific performance of contracts of employment, because of the common law's extreme reluctance to yoke together unwilling partners to a contract for the performance of personal services. There are rare exceptions to this.

---

224 See eg *Reynolds v Southcorp Wines Pty Ltd* (2002) 122 FCR 301.

225 See *Haley v Public Transport Corporation of Victoria* (1998) 119 IR 242.

226 Courts in several US states have accepted that, in appropriate cases, employment can be terminated only for 'just cause', and have granted remedies for breach of contract. See M Lillard 'Fifty Jurisdictions in Search of a Standard: The Covenant of Good Faith and Fair Dealing in the Employment Context' (1992) 57 *Mo L Rev* 1233; S Schwab 'Life-cycle Justice: Accommodating Just Cause and Employment at Will' (1993) 92 *Mich L R* 8; and M Kittner and T Kohler 'Conditioning Expectations: The Protection of the Employment Bond in German and American Law' (2000) 21 *Comp Lab L & Pol'y J* 263.

Where a wrongfully dismissed employee has been denied some significant benefit—such as accrual of a pension benefit—a court may be persuaded to order that the employment contract be continued for a sufficient time to allow the accrual of the benefit,[227] or the determination of some other important entitlement.[228] But such an order will generally not involve any requirement that the work under the contract actually continue to be performed.

In a time when the master–servant relationship involved face-to-face relationships, the common law's refusal to order specific performance may well have been wise, but it is questionable whether a refusal based only on the rationale that parties ought not to be yoked together in an antagonistic relationship is warranted where the employer is a faceless corporation, and the employee could be reinstated to any number of workstations in a large organisation. Statutory schemes, no doubt recognising that modern industrial reality has superseded feudal sensibilities, allow for reinstatement. Nevertheless, the statistics showing that reinstatement is ordered much less frequently than compensation suggest that the industrial commissioners continue to be influenced by the common law's reluctance to force the continuation of failed relationships.[229]

This means that as far as an employee victim of wrongful dismissal is concerned, the only realistically available remedy is damages. Essentially, compensation for wrongful termination is limited to payment of lost remuneration for an appropriate period of notice. This can raise difficulties for employees who are paid on the basis of performance rather than time service. Even where performance-based bonuses are expressed as being at the discretion of the employer, an employee's entitlement to damages for a period of notice can include an amount representing the loss of opportunity or chance to earn performance bonuses. Just because a bonus or performance-related benefit was not a dead certainty does not mean that a court cannot make an assessment of the likelihood of its being earned and give credit for it.[230] 'Mere difficulty in estimating damages does not relieve a court from the responsibility of estimating them as best it can.'[231]

Distress and humiliation

The calculation of damages is constrained by the fact that the employment relationship is conceived of in terms of contract—an economic exchange. In Australia, there is no scope under the general law for payment of damages in respect of disappointment

---

227 Eg *Hill v Parsons* [1972] Ch 305; *Irani v Southhampton and South West Hampshire Health Authority* [1985] ICR 590.

228 Eg employment status for the purpose of an entitlement to join a union: *Turner v Australian Coal & Shale Employees Federation* (1984) 55 ALR 635.

229 The AIRC's Annual Report for 2003–04 showed that of 7044 unfair dismissal claims in all the years since 1996, only 225 resulted in arbitrated reinstatement orders.

230 See *Chaplin v Hicks* [1911] 2 KB 786 and *Howe v Teefy* (1927) 27 SR (NSW) 301 as authority for assessing the loss of a chance in contract damages. See also *Sellars v Adelaide Petroleum NL and Poseidon Ltd* (1994) 179 CLR 332 where the High Court of Australia allowed a claim for a loss of an opportunity or chance of a commercial benefit in a claim for compensation under the *Trade Practices Act 1974* (Cth) for misleading and deceptive conduct. A court will assess the probability of the hypothetical chance or opportunity, and adjust damages to reflect that probability: see *Malec v J C Hutton Pty Ltd* (1990) 169 CLR 638.

231 *Commonwealth of Australia v Amann Aviation Pty Ltd* (1992) 174 CLR 64.

or distress at the loss of the job.[232] The conventional wisdom that an employment contract is an economic exchange, so only the measurable economic consequences of breach should be compensated, has resisted change.[233] Even outrageously humiliating conduct will not sound in damages under common law, because of the common law's refusal to bridge the gap between tort and contract law in the matter of exemplary and aggravated damages. Whereas a flagrant breach of a tortious duty can give rise to exemplary or punitive damages, there is no scope in contract law to punish. A single judge in the NSW Supreme Court, hearing a case of flagrant breach of fiduciary duty by some employees, awarded punitive damages, but this was quickly reversed as heresy in an extensive judgment of Heydon JA (now on the High Court of Australia).[234]

Prior to *Work Choices* this was an area in which some statutory remedies for unfair dismissal have demonstrated a more compassionate response, by recognising the tort-like harm that can be inflicted on a person who is sacked unceremoniously. Tribunals exercising a broad discretion to compensate in lieu of reinstatement for unfair or unlawful dismissal have been willing to award some compensation for shock and humiliation. The dismissed employee in *Burazin v Blacktown City Guardian Pty Ltd*[235] decided under an earlier iteration of the federal statute, was afforded some compensation in respect of a humiliating dismissal; however, the current federal statute has expressly resiled from this position.[236] The AIRC no longer has any authority to award statutory compensation in respect of the manner of a dismissal.

Likewise there is no entitlement to damages for one's inability to find further work as a consequence of a wrongful dismissal. Under the common law, employers do not owe any duty to maintain the employability of the employee. In *Malik*, the House of Lords was careful to distinguish a right to claim damages for an impaired reputation due to the employer's conduct of a corrupt business, and any claimed right to damages for a reputation impaired only by the fact of dismissal. A claim based on an allegation that the employer has, by a flagrantly wrongful dismissal, signalled an imputation that the employee deserved dismissal due to incompetence or misdemeanour, would need to establish a claim in the tort of defamation.

Termination in breach of notice requirements by the employee

Given the usual balance of power in the market for labour there is a temptation to always assume that the law's unwillingness to order specific performance of employment

---

232 Case law persistently cites *Addis v Gramaphone Co Ltd* [1909] AC 488. The principle in *Addis* has been subjected to a considerable amount of judicial and scholarly comment and disagreement as to its try effect. See the discussion in Lord Steyn's judgment in *Malik* [1997] 3 WLR 113, and also the discussion in A Brooks 'The Good and Considerate Employer: Developments in the Implied Duty of Mutual Trust and Confidence ' (2001) 20 *U Tas L Rev* 29, 57–62. In New Zealand, however, *Addis* has been abandoned: see *Stuart v Armourgard Security* [1996] 1 NZLR 484, where an award of damages was made for distress caused by the manner of dismissal. Cf *Nikolich v Goldman Sachs JB Were Services Pty Ltd* [2006] FCA 784.

233 See *Aldersea v Public Transport Corporation* (2001) 183 ALR 545, *Reynolds v Southcorp Wines Pty Ltd* (2002) 122 FCR 301.

234 See *Digital Pulse Pty Ltd v Harris* (2002) 166 FLR 421, overturned in *Harris v Digital Pulse Pty Ltd* (2003) 56 NSWLR 298.

235 (1996) 142 ALR 144. See also *Emerson v Housing Industry Association* (1999) 46 AILR 4-080.

236 See s 654(9).

contracts works to the disadvantage of employees. Employees whose skills are in high demand, and who can find alternative and more highly remunerative work, often seek to take advantage of the law's preference to settle the score between parties by damages by leaving early and failing to serve out the notice period. Employers can—and do—deal with this risk by including in their contracts not only long notice periods (sometimes called 'garden leave' clauses), but also negative covenants restraining the employee from working for a rival enterprise. Where such covenants do not breach the doctrine against illegal restraints of trade, they have been upheld, on the basis that damages provide an inadequate remedy.[237] Even where their legality is dubious, the *in terrorem* effect of a restrictive covenant and a legal threat to enforce it can be very effective against a departing employee.

The extent to which a 'garden leave' clause can be enforced depends on the employer demonstrating that some loss or damage will be caused by the employee leaving early, and payment of damages will not adequately compensate for that loss. In theory an employer can also seek an award of damages against an employee for leaving without giving adequate notice. Damages would be the cost of replacing the employee with a person of equivalent skill, and any additional remuneration that would need to be paid to attract that person, above the amount that the departing employee would have been paid for the period of notice.[238] The cost of hiring staff from a temporary agency for the period of notice provides a convenient measure.

Summary dismissal

Any conduct that constitutes a significant breach of any of the express or implied terms of the contract will warrant summary dismissal under the common law. So disobedience to a lawful and reasonable order of the employer, or breach of the duty of loyalty or of care, will justify dismissal. The cases discussed above in the context of determining the parameters of these obligations provide examples.

The general principle is that the conduct of the employee must demonstrate that the employee is not willing to be bound by the terms of the contract. A minor breach—for instance, refusal to work back late one night for personal reasons—will not necessarily warrant summary dismissal. An employer who purports to dismiss summarily for a minor breach faces the prospect of a successful claim for damages from the employee—but damages will generally involve nothing more than payment for the stipulated, or 'reasonable' period of notice required by the contract.

Constructive dismissal

The introduction of statutory schemes allowing rights to reinstatement, and to more generous compensation for substantively or procedurally unfair dismissals, has given rise to the notion of a 'constructive' dismissal—a dismissal determined to be at the instance

---

237 See *Evening Standard Ltd v Henderson* [1987] ICR 588, 594; *Curro v Beyond Productions Pty Ltd* (1993) 30 NSWLR 337. But see *Network Ten v Fulwood* (1995) 62 IR 43 where the employer's delay in seeking the injunction justified refusal of the application.

238 See *Zuellig v Pulver* [2000] NSWSC 7, [31].

of the employer, even though in fact the employee resigned or appeared to abandon her or his employment. The concept has been important in ensuring that employers are not able to subvert the statutory protections from unfair or unlawful dismissal, which apply to terminations at the initiative of the employer.[239] An employer who goads an employee into resigning can nevertheless be held to have taken the initiative to dismiss, if the employer's conduct amounts to a repudiation of the employment contract. So, a significant demotion imposed without consultation or notice, a withdrawal of important benefits, carping or unwarranted criticism, have all justified a finding that an employee who apparently resigned was—in law—wrongfully dismissed and therefore entitled to damages or statutory compensation.

Termination on reasonable notice

Where a contract stipulates a notice period, the express terms of the contract prevail. If the contract is for a fixed term, and no provision has been made for early termination on notice, then the employee will be entitled to be paid out till the end of the fixed term (subject to any obligation to mitigate losses).[240] Where the contract is for an indefinite duration and no period of notice is stipulated (either in writing or by oral agreement), a notice period may be implied by industry custom, or by law as a 'reasonable' period.

What is reasonable will depend on many factors, including the length of service, the nature of the work, the seniority of the position, qualifications and skills required, age, salary level, prospects of finding new employment, any sacrifices the employee made to take and keep the position, and the effect of termination on accrued entitlements. A judge will weigh the various factors and come up with a figure, rarely more than two years, and frequently less than one year. For example, in *Haley v Public Transport Corporation of Victoria*,[241] the eighteen years' service and specialised skills of an employee were weighed against his relative youth and employability to come up with a period of six months. In *Jager v Australian National Hotels*,[242] a casino manager with very long service in a monopolistic industry was awarded a notice period of two years (although this was overturned on appeal because of the discovery of a statutory rule providing only one month's notice).[243] The system lacks science, but has proven sufficiently predictable for law firms to maintain 'reasonable notice tables', which ascribe points to candidates depending on the various factors, and then tally up the points to find a score with a corresponding notice range. This then forms the basis of settlement negotiations.

An express notice period will not always be applied, where there has been a substantial change in the employment relationship since the time of the initial contract stipulating the notice period. In *Quinn v Jack Chia (Aust) Ltd*,[244] an

---

239 See the discussion above of the development of the employer's obligation of mutual trust and confidence.
240 See for example *Reynolds v Southcorp Wines Pty Ltd* (2002) 122 FCR 301.
241 (1998) 119 IR 242.
242 (1998) 7 Tas R 437.
243 *Australian National Hotels Pty Ltd v Jager* (2000) 9 Tas R 153. Leave to appeal to the High Court from this decision was refused: see *Jager v Australian National Hotels Pty Ltd* H3/2000 (5 April 2001).
244 [1992] 1 VR 567.

employee whose seniority and responsibilities increased over time was held to be working under a new oral contract that superseded the original written contract and its stipulation of one month's notice. The court held that one year was a reasonable notice period under this new contract, taking into account the range of factors including the employer's request that Mr Quinn give up other private business interests to commit more to the job.

An assumption is buried in the reasonable notice calculus: that people who are older, more highly skilled, more highly paid, and in more responsible senior positions, either deserve or need a longer period of notice to adjust to termination of their employment. Conversely, lowly paid process workers are fungible. They can be replaced easily, and equivalent work is plentiful. At a time of massive shifts in technology that has seen the sun set on many of the traditional industries employing armies of workers, these assumptions are questionable.[245] If a notice period is a deferred benefit, rewarding contribution to the enterprise, it seems to be double-dipping that employees on the highest salaries also get more weeks or months compensation. Why is the wage differential not enough? Likewise, if the notice period functions to tide the worker over for a period of unemployment, intuitively one would expect the more lowly paid employees to have greater financial need, since their ability to set aside reserves of savings is commensurately weaker. And yet their lower rate of pay will be compounded by the shorter period of pay. Compulsory minimum notice periods under s 661 of the *Workplace Relations Act 1996* (Cth) are calibrated only to length of service, with an additional accommodation of a further week's notice for people over forty-five years old (so long as they have served at least two years).

Pay in lieu of notice

It is also a breach of the employment contract for an employer to purport to pay out a period of notice and refuse to allow the employee to work out the notice period, unless the contract or some relevant award or industrial instrument allows for pay in lieu of notice.[246] For many employees, pay in lieu is an attractive option, unlikely to prompt complaint, but for others, the opportunity to remain in work while seeking a new position is important for self-esteem and employability. The date upon which the employment contract ends may also be extremely important to the employee. Where notice is given, the contract ends at the end of the notice period. When an employee accepts payment in lieu of notice, the contract terminates on the giving of notice, unless the parties agree to some other official termination date.[247] The date of termination may make an important difference to the accrual of certain benefits—such as long service leave, pension or superannuation entitlements, or vesting rights for share options that have formed part of the remuneration package.

---

245 See G England 'Determining Reasonable Notice of Termination at Common Law: The Implications of *Cronk v Canadian General Insurance Co*' (1996) 4 *Can Lab & Emp Law J* 115.

246 See *Sanders v Snell* (1998) 196 CLR 329.

247 Ibid. See also *Delaney v Staples* [1992] 2 WLR 451.

Frustration of employment contracts

The doctrine of frustration provides that a contract may come to an end, with no fault ascribed to any party, if some circumstance independent of the parties' own conduct has intervened to make performance of the contract a thing entirely different from what the parties themselves contemplated. The absence of fault means that neither party will be responsible to pay damages to the other in respect of the breach. The issue sometimes arises in the employment context when an employee is unable to attend for work due to serious illness[248] or incarceration,[249] and the employer wants to treat the employment relationship as at an end, without affording the employee any notice or other severance benefits.

In such circumstances, an employer may seek to establish that the contract of employment has been frustrated. Serious illness is the more common reason for arguments that a contract has been frustrated to arise. The issue to be decided is 'was the employee's incapacity, looked at before the purported dismissal, of such a nature, or did it appear likely to continue for such a period, that further performance would either be impossible or would be a thing radically different from that undertaken by him and accepted by the employer under the terms of the employment?'.[250] Given the widespread use of sick leave provisions, which demonstrates that the parties have indeed contemplated and made decisions about how to handle sickness, it is unlikely that a court would find that illness—even of a serious nature—has frustrated a contract for continuing service, although it may become an important legal issue in a fixed term contract.

Termination upon a sale of business

Contracts of employment are 'personal' and non-assignable. This means that an employer who sells a business as a going concern to a new owner has effectively terminated the employment contracts of all staff. Those who take up their positions with the new owner will necessarily be entering into new contracts of employment, albeit that their terms and conditions may continue, and they may (as a consequence of an agreement between the vendor and purchaser of the business) carry over accruals of entitlements to such things as long service leave. Employers cannot, as a matter of law, 'sell' the workers with the business. Employees must be informed of the change of ownership of the business, and must consent to establishment of the new employment contract.[251] An employer who sells a business or part of a business and so creates a situation in which the employee can be given no work of the kind the employee was engaged to perform has effectively terminated the employment contract, even—ironically—if the employer continues to pay the employee. The payment will generally be characterised not as wages, but as a settlement of damages for wrongful dismissal.[252]

---

248 Eg *Notcutt v Universal Equipment* [1986] 1 WLR 641; *Finch v Sayers* [1976] 2 NSWLR 540.
249 Eg, *F C Shepherd v Jerrom* [1986] 3 WLR 801.
250 *Finch v Sayers* [1976] 2 NSWLR 540, 557.
251 See *Nokes v Doncaster Amalgamated Collieries* [1940] AC 1014; *McCluskey v Karagiozis* (2002) 120 IR 147.
252 See *Collier v Sunday Referee Publishing Co Ltd* [1940] 2 KB 647. Other legal rights and remedies on transmission of business are discussed in Chapter 9.

Equitable intervention in employment contract law

Grounds for rescission

An employment contract, like any other contract can be vitiated for any of the reasons that a court exercising equitable jurisdiction will allow as an excuse to avoid contractual obligations. The vitiating factors—misrepresentation, mistake, duress, undue influence, unconscionable dealing—challenge the quality of the underlying consent to the relation-ship. Since contract is based on voluntarily assumed obligations, a matter undermining true consent to the bargain or its essential terms will provide an escape hatch.

The considerable weakness, from an employee's point of view, in relying on equity to do justice in cases of misrepresentation, duress, etc, is that the remedy offered is merely rescission. The contract is undone, and the parties go their separate ways. Take for example a contract formed after the employer has misrepresented some important matter, for example, the level of salary, or entitlements to some valuable benefit. An employee discovering this can treat the contract as at an end: a court will refuse any attempt by the employer to enforce the contract, because it will be held to be void from the beginning. There will not, however, be any entitlement to damages based on disappointed expectations created by the misrepresentation. Any right to compensation at all will depend on proof that the misrepresentation breached a tortious duty of care, or amounted to misleading and deceptive conduct for the purposes of s 52 of the *Trade Practices Act 1974* (Cth) or one of its state *Fair Trading* equivalents. And any right to compensation in tort or under statute will be limited to undoing the harm of reliance on the misrepresentation. Employees will need to demonstrate what position they would have been in, but for the misleading representation.[253] Unless they have given up some very valuable benefit to join the firm, it will be difficult to demonstrate any significant loss.[254]

A far better result will usually flow if they are able to demonstrate that the mis-representation was in fact a term of the contract, giving rise to an entitlement to expectation-based damages.[255] So as far as employees are concerned, the benefit of the equitable remedy of rescission is more useful to employees who want to avoid the contract to take up some other opportunity—perhaps an opportunity constrained by a restrictive covenant in the avoided contract. The vitiated contract will have no effect whatsoever, so any contractual undertaking not to compete will be of no effect. Duties of confidence arising in equity, however, will survive regardless of the termination or rescission of a contract.[256]

A further circumstance that may provide a reason for an employee to rely on an equitable right to rescind would be if she had been pressed into agreeing to a variation or a new contract that provided less attractive benefits, or involved a surrender of rights

---

253 O'Neill v MBF (2002) 122 FCR 455.
254 But see *Magro v Fremantle Football Club Ltd* (2005) 142 IR 445.
255 *Saad v TWT Ltd* [1998] NSWSC 282 (29 May 1998).
256 See *Campbell v Frisbee* [2002] EWHC 328 (Ch) [22].

enjoyed under an old one.[257] A body of case law is developing around the signing of Australian Workplace Agreements. These statutory individual bargains, by virtue of their status under a federal enactment, can take away valuable rights under awards, collective agreements, and even state legislation.[258]

Non-employment work contracts

The foregoing discussion has focused on the employment contract as a particular species of contract, involving a range of terms implied by law, ostensibly to give contractual effect to the parties' shared expectations. Many of the implied terms—the duty to obey, the duty of good faith and fidelity—reflect the inherent subservience of employee to employer in the employment relationship.

As Chapter 4 explained, the employment relationship no longer provides the only legal model for work relationships. The rise of the so-called 'independent contractor', and the entrepreneurial, single worker firm, has created an army of workers who fall beyond the reach of traditional employment law. They elude the net of many protective statutory schemes, and they also avoid the implication of these duties akin to those of master and servant. Regulation of these relationships falls to the general commercial law. In practice, those who engage contractors use detailed written contracts that duplicate to a considerable extent many of the obligations implied in employment—notably the obligations to preserve confidential information, to assign intellectual property rights, and to refrain from competition.

Legal status as an independent contractor does not guarantee any truly independent economic status. The underlying economic reality of many relationships between large corporate firms and those whom they engage to perform work demonstrates the same imbalance of bargaining power, the same unilateral imposition of terms and conditions, the same assertion of authority and control and the same potential for abuse and exploitation. In recent decades commercial law has developed tools to protect these small business providers. In Chapter 4[259] we noted the developments in trade practices legislation and Industry Codes of Conduct that have recognised a need for public regulation to contain the potential excesses of a free market. In Chapter 5 we discussed some developments in the common law of contract, including statutory review of unfair or unconscionable contract terms. Cumulatively, these developments are creating a new law of work for post-Fordist business enterprise.

Conclusions

Even for those who are classified as employees, the changing shape of the workplace has created challenges for the persistence of many of the legal incidents of the employment relation. In the case of part-time workers and casual employees, who may need to hold

---

257 For a speculative discussion of the operation of the equitable doctrine of unconscionable dealing in employment contracts see. Riley, above n 186, Ch 5.
258 See Chapter 11.
259 Page 150.

down several jobs to accumulate sufficient income to maintain a family, the boundary between fidelity to one employer and loyalty to another is potentially strained. In a world of short-term contracts, performance-based remuneration, and rapidly changing technology, the mutual expectations of the parties to work contracts do not necessarily reflect the assumptions of the past. Like Captain Cook's slow chronometer in Kenneth Slessor's poem,[260] law tends to have sticky feet as it climbs out of yesterday. But the residue of earlier social conditions and expectations must not be allowed to rob law of its power to find just solutions. If the contract model is valued for its basis in consent, then current expectations of the parties to work relationships must be incorporated into the way the law interprets their implied commitments. In particular, the expectation that workers will acquire valuable skills, experience and contacts that they will be free to exploit in future engagements must not be undermined by a persistent privilege for employers' claims to 'own' those attributes.

---

260 See 'Five Visions of Captain Cook', stanza III, Kenneth Slessor *Selected Poems* (1975).

part **3**

Standards and Rights

Work Standards

Introduction

The concept of 'decent work' has gained increasing purchase around the world due in part to its evocation by the International Labour Organisation (ILO) as the underpinning for its program of economic and social reform in the global era.[1] 'Decent work' is a normative ideal to which all nations are encouraged to aspire. Its attainment requires the adoption of policies and practices that will enable individuals to obtain work that provides an adequate income in conditions where social standards are not compromised and rights are protected. Decent work initiatives traverse areas as diverse as labour and industrial regulation, social security, education and training, taxation, and the regulation of business and the economy, encompassing a consideration of all forms of work in the marketplace and unpaid work. According to the ILO, decent work is work in conditions of freedom, equality and security.

The standards that govern work are all important in giving the concept of 'decent work' more precise content. The word 'standard' has a connotation wider than simply an indication of the terms or conditions that govern work relations. A standard has a normative function: it expresses 'a measure of quantity or quality fixed or approved by some authority'.[2] Thus work standards ultimately represent the basic values of the community in relation to work.

This chapter examines work standards in Australia and focuses primarily upon those operating at the federal level. Attention is devoted first to the regulatory mechanisms establishing these standards. The new *Work Choices* regime and the role of institutions such as the Australian Fair Pay Commission (AFPC), the Award Review Taskforce (ART) and the Australian Industrial Relations Commission (AIRC) are examined against the historical background of award-making and especially the 'test case' process. Secondly, some of the most significant workplace standards in Australia are scrutinised, including the Australian Fair Pay and Conditions Standard (AFPCS). The interdependency of

---

1 International Labour Office, Report of the Director-General *Decent Work* (1999).
2 *R v Galvin; Ex parte Metal Trades' Employers' Association* (1949) 77 CLR 432, 447.

modern workplace standards and the historical, social and economic context in which they are created and in which they operate is emphasised.

Work standards in Australian law have historically been a counterbalance to contract. Common law bargains cannot derogate from them. Some standards now also form part of a safety net of minimum standards and cannot be diminished by statutory bargains. Conventionally standards have secured fairness in work relations. However, the regulatory purposes behind standards are often quite complex and they change over time. The final section of this chapter identifies the way in which regulatory purposes shape the function, form and content of work standards and conceptions of the worker.

Standard setting—the regulatory processes

With the passage of the *Workplace Relations Amendment (Work Choices) Act 2005* (Cth) (*Work Choices Act*), legislation has assumed a dominant role in directly setting workplace standards in Australia. It was not always so. Formerly award standards, produced through a conciliation and arbitration process often conducted as a test case, were much more important. However, the new *Work Choices* system of legislated standards continues to carry traces of the old award standards. Other regulatory mechanisms, such as codes of conduct, may become increasingly important in the future but they are not yet widely used to set basic work standards. However, in some areas they are very important and effective, especially when used in combination with other regulatory mechanisms such as awards, in standard setting. The regulation of outwork in some States provides a good example of this.[3]

Legislating work standards

As a regulatory mechanism for the direct establishment of work standards, legislation has some obvious advantages over the awards made under the old conciliation and arbitration system. For one thing the coverage of legislation is potentially far more comprehensive than awards. If simple and clear, legislative standards have the potential to become better known, and therefore more readily accessible, to a wider variety of workers and businesses than a confusion of multiple and differing standards each of which is only applicable to a very limited range of work relations. Legislation can operate as a simple and uniform 'command and control' mechanism so that those who are subject to it are told in a direct way exactly what to do: as a form of standard setting this can be very effective, especially when backed by strong enforcement mechanisms. However, there is also a down-side to relying upon legislation to establish work standards. Amidst the crowded legislative agenda of modern parliaments, statutes can be somewhat inflexible and therefore less useful tools especially where regular updating

---

3   See eg *Industrial Relations (Ethical Clothing Trades) Act 2001* (NSW) and the mandatory code of practice attached to it, the Ethical Clothing Trades—Extended Responsibility Scheme, which regulates those who fail to sign and comply with the voluntary Homeworkers Code of Practice aimed at ensuring compliance with the relevant industrial award; and *Outworkers (Improved Protection) Act 2003* (Vic). See also C Fenwick 'Protecting Victoria's Vulnerable Workers: New Legislative Developments' (2003) 16 *AJLL* 198.

is necessary to respond to changed conditions. In conjunction with legislative standards it is therefore usually necessary also to have recourse to mechanisms for maintaining the currency of standards. This is often achieved by devolving standard setting powers to an administrative body or by using a regulation-making power to fill out in further detail broader statutory principles.

Commonwealth legislative standards

Australian constitutional arrangements have always been somewhat of an impediment to the enactment of wide and comprehensive work standards in federal legislation. The external affairs power, s 51(xxix) of the *Australian Constitution*, is probably the most appropriate power to support uniform, nationwide workplace standards. It underpins the equality standards contained in the various Commonwealth discrimination statutes.[4] The external affairs power supports the provisions in the *Workplace Relations Act* establishing rights for employees to unpaid maternity, adoption and paternity leave,[5] and prohibiting termination of employment on certain identified grounds.[6] However, since 1996, the corporations power has also been used to support a number of legislative provisions setting work standards, including the rights of individual employees in cases of unfair, harsh or unjust terminations of employment.[7] With the introduction of the *Work Choices* legislation there is now even greater reliance on the corporations power. For instance, the corporations power underpins the Australian Fair Pay and Conditions Standard (AFPCS), which applies to federal employees as defined in s 5 (and Victorian employees according to s 864).[8] The AFPCS is a set of basic work standards governing wages, ordinary hours of work, annual leave, personal/carer's leave and parental leave. At the federal level prior to the introduction of *Work Choices*, work standards on these matters were established primarily by awards.

State legislative standards

In contrast to the Commonwealth Parliament the Australian States have plenary power enabling them to legislate quite comprehensively in relation to workplace standards. The States have standards in their industrial and other laws covering a variety of work-related matters including at least some of those things now dealt with by the AFPCS. All these State legislative standards continue to apply to those who are not employed by constitutional corporations or by other federal employers as defined in s 6. State laws dealing with discrimination in the workplace also continue to regulate a wide range of workers and are not ordinarily inconsistent with the *Workplace Relations Act*: ss 16–17. In addition, State legislation on a wide

---

4 *Racial Discrimination Act 1975* (Cth); *Sex Discrimination Act 1984* (Cth); *Disability Discrimination Act 1992* (Cth); and *Age Discrimination Act 2004* (Cth). See further Chapter 8.

5 See *Workplace Relations Act*, Pt 12 Div 6 and Sch 5 containing the *Workers with Family Responsibilities Convention, 1981 (ILO C 156)*.

6 See *Workplace Relations Act*, Pt 12 Div 4 Subdiv C and Sch 4 containing the *Termination of Employment Convention, 1982 (ILO C 158)*. See Chapters 8–9.

7 *Workplace Relations Act*, Pt 12 Div 4 Subdiv B. See also former s 170CB(1)(c).

8 *Workplace Relations Act*, Pt 7. The AFPCS is discussed in detail below.

range of work-related areas is not excluded by the *Work Choices* amendments: s 16(3). These areas are:

(a) superannuation;
(b) workers' compensation;
(c) occupational health and safety (including the entry of a representative of trade unions to premises for purposes connected with occupational health and safety);
(d) matters relating to outworkers (including entry of a representative of a trade union for purposes connected with outworkers);
(e) child labour;
(f) long service leave;
(g) the observance of a public holiday, except the rate of payment of an employee for the public holiday;
(h) the method of payment of wages or salaries;
(i) the frequency of payment of wages or salaries;
(j) deductions from wages or salaries;
(k) industrial action (within the ordinary meaning of the expression) affecting essential services;
(l) attendance for service on a jury;
(m) regulation of any of the following:
    (i) associations of employees;
    (ii) associations of employers;
    (ii) members of associations of employees or of associations of employers.

Award standards

Historically at both federal and State level it has been industrial awards that have been pre-eminent in the setting of work standards in Australia. Awards contained standards that were in the form of rules establishing future rights and obligations. The work standards set by awards, like those established legislatively, were in effect minimum standards: that is, individuals could always contract above these standards, which expressed the community conception of a fair and reasonable base. In the past the content of awards at both federal and State level was quite wide-ranging covering 'industrial matters' or 'matters pertaining to the relationship between employers and employees'.[9] Even when these 'matters' were given more specific legislative definition, the detail was illustrative rather than exhaustive. Judicial interpretation established the meaning of these expressions, but from a policy and regulatory perspective awards were otherwise generally unrestricted in subject matter. Awards thus once set the terms and conditions of work on a wide range of topics and they provided a comprehensive level of protection.

    With the increasing emphasis on enterprise bargaining in the 1990s, awards changed to provide only what is usually described as a 'safety net' of minimum conditions.

---

9 See Chapter 3, pp 86ff.

In addition between 1996 and 2005 federal awards were restricted to dealing with twenty allowable matters.[10] Although there was some early indication that some States would also restrict the range of matters State awards could govern, this was short-lived and State awards have continued to deal with all industrial matters. However, in the range of matters that can be regulated by awards there is now a significant difference between the federal and State arenas.

The content of federal awards after *Work Choices*

After the *Work Choices* amendments federal awards continue to provide 'minimum safety net entitlements': s 510(a). However, the content of federal awards is now much more restricted than it was previously. The 'allowable matters' with which they can deal are listed in s 513(1) as follows:

(a) ordinary time hours of work and the time within which they are performed; rest breaks, notice periods and variations to working hours;

(b) incentive-based payments and bonuses;

(c) annual leave loadings;

(d) ceremonial leave;

(e) leave for the purpose of seeking other employment after the giving of a notice of termination by an employer to an employee;

(f) observance of days declared by or under a law of a State or a Territory to be observed generally within that State or Territory, or a region of that State or Territory, as public holidays by employees who work in that State, Territory or region, and entitlements of employees to payment in respect of those days;

(g) days to be substituted for, or a procedure for substituting, days referred to in paragraph (f);

(h) monetary allowances for:
  (i) expenses incurred in the course of employment; or
  (ii) responsibilities or skills that are not taken into account in rates of pay for employees; or
  (iii) disabilities associated with the performance of particular tasks or work in particular conditions or locations;

(i) loadings for working overtime or shift work;

(j) penalty rates;

(k) redundancy pay, within the meaning of subs (4);

(l) stand-down provisions;

(m) dispute settling procedures, but only as provided by s 514;

(n) type of employment, such as fulltime employment, casual employment, regular part-time employment and shift work;

(o) conditions for outworkers, but only to the extent necessary to ensure that their overall conditions of employment are fair and reasonable in comparison with the conditions of employment specified in a relevant award or awards for employees who perform the same kind of work at an employer's business or commercial premises.

---

10 *Workplace Relations Act*, former s 89A(2).

Some of these matters are expressed more narrowly than they were previously. 'Cultural leave' has been transformed into the more limited concept of 'ceremonial leave'; the definition of public holidays is more restricted than before; award dispute settling provisions are restricted to the statutorily established model (see also s 514); only certain monetary allowances are now permitted; and redundancy pay provisions cannot apply to those in workplaces with fewer than fifteen employees with the legislation stipulating the time at which and manner in which this calculation is to be made: s 513(4)–(5).

A number of other types of clauses may also be incorporated in federal awards. These include facilitative provisions allowing agreement regarding the way in which award clauses are to be implemented.[11] However, facilitative clauses can no longer require that such agreements be subject to majority approval but must allow individual employees to agree with their employer: s 521. Awards may also contain incidental and machinery provisions: s 522; a model antidiscrimination clause: s 523; and terms about the appointment of a board of reference: s 524.

Since 1996 there have been some explicit restrictions on the content of awards and these have been extended by *Work Choices*. One group of non-allowable matters concerns content relating to 'non-standard' work, especially things that might impose restrictions on the organisational and numerical flexibility of the enterprise: s 515(1)(b)–(h). It has never been possible to restrict the engagement of certain types of workers (such as independent contractors or labour-hire workers) in awards,[12] but now clauses that seek to govern the terms of their appointment and conditions of work are also prohibited (except in an award binding the labour-hire firm in respect of its own workers).[13] Likewise clauses that provide for casuals to convert to ongoing employment are not allowable. As was the case previously it is not possible to restrict the number or proportions of certain types of employment, or the maximum or minimum hours of part-time workers. The other prohibited content is aimed primarily at taking away any institutional support that awards might offer to trade unions and their members: ss 515(a), (i) and (l) and 517–18.[14] From 27 March 2006 award terms about matters that are not allowable award matters ceased to have effect: s 525.

Preserved award terms

After *Work Choices* wages and classifications, which are now included in the Australian Pay and Classification Scales (APCSs), as well as those matters covered by the AFPCS (with the exception of ordinary time matters) are no longer included in the list of allowable award matters. However, awards may still include 'preserved award terms': ss 520 and 527–33. 'Preserved award terms' include entitlements to annual leave, personal/carer's leave, and parental leave, which are all now also dealt with in the AFPCS, as well as to long service leave, notice of termination, jury service, and superannuation (but the

---

11 See below, p 340 on facilitative clauses.
12 *R v Commonwealth Industrial Court Judges; Ex parte Cocks* (1968) 121 CLR 313.
13 Cf *R v Moore; Ex parte Federated Miscellaneous Workers Union of Australia* (1978) 140 CLR 470.
14 See Chapter 10.

latter only until 30 June 2008) that were in an award prior to the introduction of *Work Choices*. In relation to AFPCS matters these 'preserved award terms' can continue to have effect where they are 'more generous' for the individual employee than the AFPCS (and thus the AFPCS does not apply to these employees): ss 529–30 and r 10.3. As a consequence of this there was a rush to 'update' award standards between the passage of the *Work Choices Act* on 14 December 2005 and the coming into operation of its main provisions on 27 March 2006. Employers are only bound in relation to those preserved terms of an award that were binding on them immediately prior to 27 March 2006: s 533. There is a power to exclude by regulation certain matters from the 'preserved award terms' either generally or for certain classes of employees: s 527(8)–(9). This has been done for special maternity leave (SML), provisions relating to transfer to a safe job during pregnancy, compassionate leave, and unpaid carer's leave: r 10.2. Thus in relation to those specific matters, employees are restricted to the AFPCS and cannot access superior award terms.

Standard-setting and State awards

The process for setting standards through awards in the State industrial conciliation and arbitration systems is broadly similar to that which has operated in the federal arena in the past. State industrial commissions are often required, for instance, to take account of the public interest and consider the wider economic impacts of their decision.[15] In the past there has been in practice a loose integration of standards at federal and State level. There was usually a 'flow on' from federal award test case standards, especially wage decisions, to the state jurisdictions, bar contraindications arising from particular state factors and interests or persuasive objections from represented parties, after an appropriate hearing had been convened.[16] However, it should not be thought that this flow on was in any sense automatic, for it was not. Nor should it be thought that in the formation of work standards the influence was all in one direction, from federal to State level. Sometimes reform in relation to a particular work standard was first accomplished in a State jurisdiction before it was accepted at national level. For example, in the mid-1990s the scope of the concept of 'family' to be used for personal leave purposes was controversial, with parties holding differing views especially in relation to families centred upon non-heterosexual relations and the wider kinship groups. Eventually the definition of 'family' adopted by the NSW Industrial Commission influenced that adopted by the AIRC in the *Personal/Carer's Leave Test Case*.[17]

---

15 Eg *Industrial Relations Act 1996* (NSW), s 146(2) provides:
   The Commission must take into account the public interest in the exercise of its functions and, for that
   purpose, must have regard to:
   (a) the objects of this Act, and
   (b) the state of the economy of New South Wales and the likely effect of its decisions on that economy.
16 See, eg, the *Industrial Relations Act 1996* (NSW), ss 48 and 50–2; *Fair Work Act 1994* (SA), s 100; and
   Industrial Relations Act 1979 (WA), s 51.
17 See *State Family Leave Case* (NSW) (1995) 59 IR 1 and *Personal/Carer's Leave Test Case—Stage 2—November
   1995* (1995) 62 IR 48.

Despite the loose harmonisation of federal and State standards in the past there has not been a uniform set of award standards governing work in Australia. The plethora of different standards increasingly became the subject of policy debate. However, the fact that different standards operated in different jurisdictions and in different awards also had transformative potential, opening a space for political action either to forge or resist new standards. Once a particular standard was established at either federal or State level (whether by award or legislatively) the fact that there were some workers and businesses in close geographic proximity who were subject to different 'standards' created pressure for further change. The contest as to which standard should prevail invariably raised arguments not only about the function of standards but also the desirability of conformity to a national norm versus particular State or regional considerations.

After *Work Choices* State awards can continue to bind non-federal employers and employees. However, those employers and employees who were previously covered by State awards but who became covered by the federal *Workplace Relations Act* after 27 March 2006 are no longer covered by awards but by 'notional agreements preserving state awards' (NAPSAs), which may contain 'preserved notional terms' that perform the same function as preserved award terms.[18]

Awards and the role of the AIRC under Work Choices

The peculiar authority of awards, and especially of test case standards, under the old conciliation and arbitration system was very largely explained by the procedures adopted by the AIRC and its predecessors.[19]

Since the introduction of the *Work Choices* amendments federal awards are still intended to provide 'minimum safety net entitlements': s 510(a). The AIRC also continues to have responsibility for awards under the *Workplace Relations Act*, although its powers are now supported by the corporations power rather than the conciliation and arbitration power. In carrying out its responsibilities in relation to awards the AIRC is enjoined by the Act to have regard to 'the desirability of high levels of employment, low inflation and the creation of jobs and high levels of employment'; the decisions of the AFPC and the need for consistency with them; and the importance of awards providing 'minimum safety net entitlements' that are not a disincentive to bargaining: s 511. However, awards have a far less significant place in the new regulatory regime than was the case prior to *Work Choices*.

The general powers of the AIRC in relation to awards are now far more restricted. The main regulatory tasks for the AIRC in relation to safety net standards involve rationalising and simplifying awards: Pt 10, Div 4. The AIRC can no longer make new awards, except as part of the award rationalisation process: s 539. In its function of maintaining awards as an effective safety net of entitlements the AIRC is restricted to varying awards only when it is 'essential' to do so: s 553. Awards are not to include

18 See *Workplace Relations Act*, Sch 8, Pt 3 esp cl 45. See also Chapter 3, pp 126ff.
19 See Chapter 3.

any matters of 'detail or process' that are 'more appropriately dealt with by agreement at the workplace or enterprise level', must not inhibit productivity and efficiency, and cannot have any terms that hinder or restrict productivity 'having regard to fairness to employees': s 568.

Otherwise the AIRC's power to vary awards is restricted to the rationalisation and simplification processes; to removing ambiguities, discriminatory provisions under the process initiated under s 46PW of the *Human Rights and Equal Opportunity Commission Act 1986* (Cth), or provisions contrary to freedom of association under the legislation; and to binding additional persons or organisations: ss 552, 554, 557–63 and 812. Finally, the AIRC's power to revoke awards is also limited to the rationalisation and simplification process, and to where awards are obsolete or no longer capable of operating: ss 555–6. After the processes of rationalisation and simplification awards are thus to be maintained, but everything in the legislative scheme indicates that they are now far less important than legislative standards and workplace agreements and there is little prospect for their development in something akin to the 'dynamic' regulatory system of the past.[20]

Award rationalisation under *Work Choices*[21]

The *Work Choices Act* provides that existing federal awards are to be rationalised and simplified.[22] At the end of 2005 there were still about 2250 federal awards. Rationalisation of awards refers to a process whereby the number of awards will be drastically reduced. The rationalisation of awards is a significant part of the strategy to produce a national system of workplace regulation, and State-based differences are to be eliminated through it: s 535. The actual task of award rationalisation will be undertaken by a Full Bench of the AIRC: s 536. Any awards made in the award rationalisation process must conform to the general provisions of the Act governing award content: see Pt 10, Div 2. Rationalised awards must also specify the employees and employers who are to be bound by them, and they may (but need not) also bind specified organisations. However, the coverage of a rationalised award is dictated by the terms of the award rationalisation request made by the Minister to the AIRC (see below).

Because of the Government's promise that under the *Work Choices* amendments employees would not be worse off than they were previously, preserved award terms cannot be rationalised. The AIRC is under a duty when it reduces a rationalised award to writing to include, and identify as such, any preserved term(s) and also to identify the employers and employees who are bound by the preserved term(s): ss 550 and 567. A rationalised award, therefore, may include a number of different preserved terms on identical matters, each applicable to certain identified employers and employees.

While the AIRC has responsibility for implementing the rationalisation of awards under the *Work Choices* regime, the parameters within which it performs this task are

---

20 J Murray 'The AIRC's Test Case on Work and Family Provisions: The End of Dynamic Regulatory Change at the Federal Level?' (2005) 18 *AJLL* 325.

21 *Workplace Relations Act*, Pt 10, Div 4 ss 534–46.

22 Under the *Work Choices* regime State awards are not subject to this process. Rather they have become NAPSAs: see Chapter 3.

controlled by Ministerial direction, which in turn is influenced by the recommendations of the Award Review Taskforce (ART).

The role of the Minister in award rationalisation

The award rationalisation process is initiated by a request from the Minister and the AIRC is required to undertake the task in accordance with that request: s 534(2)–(6). The request must specify the award rationalisation process and the time frame within which it is to be conducted, although the legislation imposes an outer limit of three years. A rationalisation request must also specify the principles that are to be applied in the process. The Act itself indicates an award rationalisation request may include such matters as the specific awards that are to be rationalised, their coverage, and the matters that may and may not be included in the rationalised awards, although the principles contained in the Minister's request need not be limited to these things. The Minister also has the power to vary or revoke an award rationalisation request. The Government thus has significant control over the award rationalisation process, including the power to intervene in it: s 538.

The Award Review Taskforce

Prior to the commencement of the *Work Choices* amendments the Government established an Award Review Taskforce (ART) to report on and advise it in relation to the federal award rationalisation process and the rationalisation of wage and classi-fication structures. In relation to award rationalisation the ART was specifically asked to recommend to the Minister an approach for rationalising awards on an industry sector basis; whether to permit general coverage of employers and employees according to industry sector based awards; and to consider the issue of award-free employees who are covered by the new federal regime but who do not have workplace agreements. It was also to consider a wide range of related issues including the amalgamation of awards, and the issue of inclusion of 'preserved award entitlements'. The ART issued two discussion papers in December 2005, prior to making its recommendations to the Minister as to the strategy for proceeding at the end of April 2006.[23] Early indications were that an industry approach would be favoured using the Australia and New Zealand Standard Industry Classification (ANZSIC), which has a taxonomy of seventeen divisions, and providing coverage on the basis of common rule.

Award simplification under *Work Choices*[24]

Under the *Work Choices* amendments awards are also to be simplified by the AIRC so that they comply with the new requirements regarding content: s 547. In order to do this, the AIRC will review every award and either vary it so that it complies

---

23 Award Review Taskforce Discussion Paper 'Award Rationalisation' (December 2005); and Award Review Taskforce Discussion Paper 'Rationalisation of Award and Classification Structures' (December 2005), available at <www.awardreviewtaskforce.gov.au>.
24 *Workplace Relations Act*, Pt 10 Div 4 ss 547–51.

with the Act or revoke it if it is obsolete and no longer able to operate. The exact timing and procedure of this review process will be specified by regulation: s 547(3). General principles are to be set down by a Full Bench of the AIRC for the review and simplification process: s 548.

The award review and simplification processes undertaken previously under the former legislation give an indication as to what is involved.

Review of awards, 1993

In 1993 the package of reforms introduced by the *Industrial Relations Reform Act 1993* (Cth) instituted a regular triennial review of awards. The purposes of this s 150A review included overcoming any deficiencies in awards providing 'secure, relevant and consistent wages and conditions of employment'; eliminating discriminatory provisions; and simplifying awards by removing obsolete provisions and ensuring that they were expressed in plain English, so that their overall structure facilitated understanding and they did not contain excessive prescription of detail.[25] The 1993 award review process occurred in the context of moving towards greater regulation through enterprise-based agreements and having awards as only a 'safety net of minimum wages and conditions of employment underpinning direct bargaining'.[26] It was clear that the constitution of the 'safety net' was vitally important to the most vulnerable of workers, because from the early 1990s evidence began to emerge that certain groups of workers, such as women, were losing out through the move to enterprise bargaining. However, it was also apparent that the s 150A review process would not remedy the structural discrimination issues that were evident in a system split between an award safety net and a bargaining stream.[27]

Award simplification, 1996

The transitional arrangements put in place in 1996 required the content of existing awards to be reduced to twenty allowable matters.[28] The subsequent award simplification process was lengthy and required a major allocation of resources by the AIRC. In the *Award Simplification Decision* the Commission indicated how it would go about this process. It gave a meaning to the various listed allowable matters 'consistent with the use of the concepts in industrial relations practice ... [an] ordinary meaning not generous or restrictive' and noted that there was no mutual exclusivity between them.[29] The *Award Simplification Decision* also provided examples of clauses to be removed from awards. Although awards could include things 'incidental' to the allowable matters, the Commission made it clear that this did not expand the list of allowable matters and was not analogous to the implication of contractual terms. Rather it ruled that the statute

---

25 *Industrial Relations Act 1998* (Cth), s 150A.

26 See *Industrial Relations Act 1988* (Cth), s 88A(b) inserted by *Industrial Relations Reform Act 1993* (Cth).

27 T MacDermott 'The Changing Role of the Safety Net: The Australian Industrial Relations Commission's s 150A Review' in P Ronfeldt and R McCallum (eds) *Enterprise Bargaining, Trade Unions and the Law* (1995).

28 See *Workplace Relations and Other Legislation Amendment Act 1996* (Cth), Item 49(7)–(8) governing the interim period and Item 51(6)–(7) for the period thereafter.

29 The *Award Simplification Decision* (1997) 75 IR 272, 276–8.

enabled the Commission to include provisions 'necessary for the effective operation of the award', and required each such provision to be incidental to a particular allowable matter and not merely incidental in some general fashion.[30] The AIRC also ruled that the provision for the inclusion of other 'exceptional matters' in awards was also quite limited.[31]

Constitutional validity of the 1996 award simplification process

The 1996 reforms provided an interim period of eighteen months for parties themselves to apply to the Commission to vary their award in accordance with the new legislation. Where this was not done by mid-1998, the Act itself provided that to the extent that an award provided for matters beyond those allowed in the legislation it 'ceases to have effect' and the Commission was required thereafter to vary the award to ensure its compliance with the statute.

In *Re Pacific Coal Pty Ltd; Ex parte Construction, Forestry, Mining, and Energy Union (Award Simplification Case)*[32] the constitutionality of the 1996 award simplification provisions was challenged by the CFMEU, which wished to preserve a number of award clauses including those giving preference to unionists in the engagement of labour, union right of entry to workplaces, and the 'last on first off' principle in relation to redundancies. The High Court by a narrow majority upheld the validity of the legislation, ruling that under s 51(xxxv) of the *Australian Constitution* the Parliament had the power to enact laws that mandated the effective removal of certain clauses from existing awards. Chief Justice Gleeson focused on the fact that awards are given legal effect by the statute and just as the effect of an award could be extended, so too it could also be restricted.[33] The reasoning in the joint judgment of Gummow and Hayne JJ, with which Callinan J agreed, went further, holding that the terms of an award and its statutory effect were not to be equated. Thus removing the effect of the award under the statute did not alter the award itself, which remained available for other purposes: for instance, it could be given effect at common law if its terms were incorporated into the contract of an employee. According to these judges, just as Parliament can legislate with respect to conciliation and arbitration it may also legislate with respect to the outcome of those processes, provided that the award maintained a connection with the industrial dispute that it settled or prevented.[34] By contrast the dissenting judges (Gaudron, McHugh and Kirby JJ) held that the resultant partial effect of awards after simplification was problematic given that awards were the product of conciliation and arbitration to settle an industrial dispute.[35] Howevejr, the reasoning of the dissentients in the *Award Simplification Case* is perhaps even less persuasive now, given that after *Work Choices* the new simplified awards are

---

30 Ibid, 277–8.
31 *Workplace Relations Act*, former ss 89A(6)–(7), 107 and 120A. See *Safety Net Review—Wages April 1997* (1997) 71 IR 1, 76 (Principle 3.3).
32 (2000) 203 CLR 346.
33 Ibid, 357–9. See also *George Hudson Ltd v Australian Timber Workers Union* (1923) 32 CLR 413.
34 Ibid, 417.
35 Ibid, 395–8, 372 and 442–3.

supported under the corporations and other powers rather than the conciliation and arbitration power.

Under the *Work Choices* amendments, the combined tasks of award simplification and rationalisation in effect involve the construction by the AIRC of sets of rules outlining work standards and these are embodied in documents called awards. These awards are not legislative instruments and are not in themselves legally binding. Rather the document that is an award binds any federal employers, federal employees, and organisations registered under the Act whom it is expressed to bind simply by legislative fiat: s 543. This is no different a legal process to the way in which awards were previously made to be legally enforceable.[36] However, there is now a different constitutional underpinning to the relevant (that is s 543) statutory provision, which means that awards no longer have the same *collective* dimension but rather they set in place *individual* rights.

Pay and classification scales and the role of the AFPC

Terms relating to wages, classification structures, casual loadings and piece rates have been removed from awards since the commencement of the *Work Choices* amendments. The AIRC no longer has any jurisdiction over wage setting. Instead it is the Australian Fair Pay Commission (AFPC) that has the power to conduct wage reviews and to set wages at the national level: s 22. The AFPC can adjust the Federal Minimum Wage (FMW) initially set at \$12.75 by the *Work Choices Act*; determine and adjust special FMWs that can apply to employees who are either juniors, or have a disability or are on traineeships; determine and adjust rates of pay under the Australian Pay and Classification Scales (APCSs); and adjust the default casual loading initially set at 20 per cent by the *Work Choices Act*.

Rationalisation of award wage and classification structures

APCSs may be new or may be derived from wage and classification provisions in federal and State awards (or other pre–*Work Choices* wage setting instruments). At the time of the introduction of the *Work Choices* amendments most awards incorporated a classification structure with a number of different levels. Most awards had around ten and sometimes fewer levels, but some had more. In the *Metal Industries Award*, for instance, there were fourteen classifications with minimum pay rates ranging from \$484.40 to \$1031.10 per week. Thus altogether there were thousands of classifications each setting a minimum pay level for various groups of workers.

The process for rationalising and producing a simpler set of APCSs is to be guided by the ART's recommendations as to how the award classification structures can be simplified, overlap can be reduced, federal and State classifications and wages can be aligned or amalgamated, and equal pay for work of equal value can be achieved. Following upon the ART's first report, the strategy for wage and classification rationalisation was

---

36 See *Workplace Relations Act*, former s 149(1).

determined by the Government, and the ART worked on the draft rationalisation of wages and classifications, which it provided to the AFPC midway through 2006.

The role of the AFPC in wage setting

In exercising its powers regarding wages the AFPC must operate within the parameters set down by the legislation: s 23. The overall objective it must pursue is the promotion of the economic well-being of the Australian people, and in so doing the legislation stipulates that the AFPC is to have regard to the following factors:

(a) the capacity for the unemployed and low paid to obtain and remain in employment;
(b) employment and competitiveness across the economy;
(c) providing a safety net to the low paid;
(d) providing minimum wages for junior employees, employees to whom training arrangements apply and employees with disabilities that ensures those employees are competitive in the labour market.

What is striking about this when compared with the statutory obligations imposed previously on the AIRC in overseeing the safety net of minimum wages is that there is no reference to any need to carry out this task by attending to what might be considered a 'fair' or 'reasonable' wage in the 'context of living standards generally prevailing in the Australian community'.[37] 'Fairness' and 'reasonableness' attend to the importance of social equality and redistributive aims in wage setting. Evaluating wages in a context is critical to ensuring that they enable workers to live with decency. The statutory constraints on the discretion of the AFPC more clearly direct it to contemplating the effect of wage levels on keeping others out of employment.

Next in importance to the above broad parameters, the AFPC is required to have regard to any recommendations of the ART, which are particularly important in relation to the APCSs: s 177. The AFPC must also operate having regard to broadly stated equality principles: s 222. Specifically it must 'apply the principle that men and women should receive equal remuneration for work of equal value', and have regard to 'the need to provide pro-rata disability pay methods for employees with disabilities': s 222(a) and (b). The AFPC is also to take account of the principles in the various Commonwealth discrimination statutes, and the *Workers with Family Responsibilities Convention, 1981 (ILO C 156)*: s 222(c) and (d). The duty of the AFPC is to ensure that its decisions do not contain provisions that discriminate for a broad range of reasons including 'race, colour, sex, sexual preference, age, physical or mental disability, marital status, family responsibilities, pregnancy religion, political opinion, national extraction or social origin': s 222(e). These duties now imposed on the AFPC regarding discrimination are generally the same as those that formerly applied to the AIRC. In the past these did little to advance pay equity claims.[38] This may well be the case in the future too, especially as the AFPC's

---

37 Cf *Workplace Relations Act*, former ss 88A and 88B, esp 88B(2)(a).
38 See below pp 299ff.

duties to consider discrimination principles are expressed as not limiting the general wage setting parameters or its consideration of ART recommendations.

Apart from the above strictures the only other constraints on the AFPC imposed by the legislation is that in exercising its wage setting powers it must ensure that the wages of employees do not fall below the rate to which they were entitled immediately prior to the commencement of the *Work Choices* changes: see for example ss 187, 196 and 214.

In exercising its functions the AFPC can inform itself in whatever way it sees fit, including by commissioning research, consulting with others or monitoring or evaluating its wage decisions: s 24. Some of these powers may enable the AFPC to overcome some of the deficiencies of the previous system. For instance, in *Safety Net Wage Reviews* the AIRC had commented on the need for reliable data on matters such as the needs of the low paid but found that none was forthcoming from the parties.[39] The AFPC is also able to determine the timing and frequency of wage reviews, the scope of any particular wage review, and the manner in which they are to be conducted: s 24. When making decisions in relation to wages the Act requires that the AFPC express its decision in monetary amounts per hour, but this can include a way of calculating a monetary amount per hour for a special FMW or a percentage number for the casual loading. The AFPC is required to present its decisions in writing with reasons, and they must be decisions of the AFPC (and not in the form of majority and dissenting opinions): s 24(4). The date at which its decisions come into effect are a matter for the AFPC: s 24(1)(d). The AFPC also has the power to determine its own procedures: s 27.

In many senses then the AFPC is much more completely in control of the wage setting process than was the AIRC, which was constrained by the conciliation and arbitration power and invariably therefore largely responsive to the submissions of the parties who initiated proceedings and who appeared before it on wage matters. It can also be noted that the AFPC does not have the quite the same level of independence from government as did the AIRC. All the issues over which the AFPC has direct control noted in the above paragraph are also subject to regulation: ss 24(3) and 27(2). The tenure of the AFPC is also more limited than that of the AIRC, with the Chair appointed for no more than five years and other Commissioners for four years: ss 29(2) and 38(2). This can lead, at the very least, to perceptions that the pressures on its independence may at time be more acute and more acutely felt than if there had been a longer tenure (such as appointment till sixty-five years of age as is enjoyed by the AIRC: s 71).

The AFPC has been loosely modelled on the Low Pay Commission (LPC) set up under the *National Minimum Wage Act 1998* (UK), although the LPC makes recommendations direct to government whereas under the *Workplace Relations Act* post–*Work Choices* the power over wage setting is devolved to the AFPC. One of the impacts of the national minimum wage legislation in the United Kingdom has been for allowances and other payments to be abolished or rolled into the basic rate, effectively decreasing rates of pay.[40] This may occur under *Work Choices* too, because the payment

---

39 *Safety Net Review—Wages 2005* AIRC, PR002005 7, June 2005.
40 See *Laird v AK Stoddart Ltd* [2001] IRLR 591; and *Aviation & Airport Services Ltd v Bellfield* [2001] UKEAT 194.

of some monetary allowances and incentive-based payments remain regulated by awards and thus may be bargained away. In the United Kingdom some employers have also restructured their workforce to avoid the minimum wage requirements.[41] There is also no reason why this cannot happen in Australia because the provision for safety net wages under the *Workplace Relations Act* applies only to federal employees but not to independent contractors. Some of the other difficulties that have arisen in the United Kingdom relate to issues of coverage, the calculation of working time especially where work differs from the norm, such as for those who are 'on call', or who are allowed to sleep on shift (for example, workers providing a 24-hour care service).[42] Finally, in the United Kingdom it has been noted that critical to the enforcement of minimum wage standards are workers' knowledge of their rights and access to appropriate, informed advice and assistance. It has also been shown that for especially vulnerable workers having to go first through a grievance procedure before getting a determination from an independent tribunal has proved problematic.[43]

Australian work standards—wages

Work standards reveal much about our understanding of decent work or, to paraphrase the words of Justice Higgins in the *Harvester Case*, of fair and reasonable conditions for human beings living in a civilised community.[44] This chapter pays particular attention to the Australian standards covering wages, working time, annual leave and sick leave, the intersection of work and family and care, and superannuation, as these are among those most critical to the attainment of decent work and therefore a decent life in a civilised community.

Wages

At the centre of social and also legal understandings of work relations is the wages–work bargain.[45] The pay received by a worker is of profound importance. Low wages detract from the dignity of the worker in an obvious economic sense because they preclude or limit access to a decent life. Because workers are so intimately connected to their work, unfair wages signify not simply that the work has little worth but that socially the worker is not valuable, not considered a human being.

Prior to the *Work Choices* changes there has never been a minimum wage set by legislation in Australia. However, since the early years of federation and up to 2005 the AIRC and its predecessors set the wages of workers covered by awards. This 'wage fixing' process became 'centralised' through 'national wage cases', and after the introduction of bargaining in the 1990s the AIRC continued to play a role in determining the award

---

41 *Smith v Hewitson* [2001] UKEAT 489; *Allonby v Accrington & Rosendale College* [2004] IRLR 224.

42 *British Nursing Association v Inland Revenue* [2003] ICR 19 (CA); *Wright v Scott Bridge Construction Ltd* [2003] IRLR (Court of Sessions); and *Walton v Independent Living Organisation* [2002] ICR 688 (CA).

43 B Simpson 'The National Minimum Wage Five Years On: Reflections on Some General Issues' (2004) 33 *ILJ* 22.

44 *Ex parte HV McKay* (*Harvester Case*) (1907) 2 CAR 1.

45 See *Automatic Fire Sprinklers Pty Ltd v Watson* (1946) 72 CLR 435, 465.

wage standards through the annual *Safety Net Reviews*. These wage decisions usually 'flowed on' to State awards. In addition, some State commissions have a power to rule more broadly on wages: the Queensland Industrial Relations Commission, for instance, has the power to set minimum wages for *all* workers through 'general rulings'.[46]

From the basic wage to national wage cases

The history of wage setting standards for award workers in Australia reveals the complex intersection of social and economic factors that influenced the decision-making of the conciliation and arbitration tribunals. Recurrent issues included: the needs of workers; the capacity of business to pay; the impact of wages at both the macroeconomic and microeconomic level including the intersection between the nature of the economy, prosperity and productivity; and the relationship between levels of employment and wages. At various times they each received a differing emphasis.[47]

The first significant wage decision handed down by the Court of Conciliation and Arbitration was determined not under the *Commonwealth Conciliation and Arbitration Act 1904* (Cth) but under the *Excise Tariff Act 1906* (Cth). In the *Harvester Case* Justice Higgins ruled that 'fair and reasonable' wages were to be judged on a needs basis: 'the normal needs of the average employee, regarded as a human being living in a civilized community'.[48] It was a standard intended to ensure 'frugal comfort' for workers and their families. In making his determination Justice Higgins took into account evidence of the household expenditure of the average worker, who was assumed to be a family 'breadwinner', a married man with a wife and three children. To the basic or living wage Justice Higgins added another component for skill or other exceptional qualifications.

The principle in the *Harvester Case* was soon after incorporated into award wage determinations under the *Conciliation and Arbitration Act 1904* (Cth). Thereafter the basic wage was increased from time to time to take account of increases in the cost of living.[49] With the advent of the Great Depression there was a change in emphasis, with greater account taken of the capacity of the employer to pay.[50] Indeed, while the early system of fixing the basic wage was focused primarily on the needs of the worker, as the century progressed greater emphasis was placed on how those needs were to be judged within the broader national economic context. After World War II, redistributive arguments held sway, with prosperity justifying higher rewards to labour. But by the early 1950s regular quarterly cost-of-living adjustments were abandoned,[51] and other macroeconomic issues, especially the impact of wages on inflation and unemployment levels, became predominant.

---

46 *Industrial Relations Act 1999* (Qld), ss 8A and 287.
47 See K Hancock and S Richardson 'Economics and Social Effects' in J Isaac and S Macintye (eds) *The New Province of Law and Order* (2004).
48 *Harvester Case* (1907) 2 CAR 1.
49 See eg *Federated Gas Employees' Industrial Union v Metropolitan Gas Co* (1913) 27 CLR 72.
50 See *Basic Wage and Wage Reduction Inquiry No 1* (1931) 30 CAR 2; *Application for Cancellation—Emergency Reduction of Award Rates* (1932) 31 CAR 305; *Application (No 2) for Cancellation—Emergency Reduction of Award Rates* (1933) 32 CAR 90; and *Basic Wage Inquiry 1934* (1934) 33 CAR 144.
51 *Basic Wage and Standard Hours Inquiry 1952–3* (1953) 77 CAR 477.

The early concept of a basic wage plus margins for skills prevailed until the late 1960s when it was overtaken by the concept of the total wage.[52] From the mid-1970s with rising inflation the 'national wage cases' became a regular review of wages based on indexation to take account of changes in the 'cost of living' with additional increases only being awarded according to formal principles fixed by the Commission.[53] After a period of recession in the early 1980s a 'Prices and Incomes Accord' between the ACTU and the federal Labor Government became a dominant feature of submissions to the Commission in the national wage cases. The Accord ensured that the concept of the 'social wage' remained at the forefront of national wage determination while accepting that unrestrained increases would result in unacceptable levels of unemployment.

The move to enterprise bargaining

From the mid-1980s the national wage cases became the vehicle for driving processes for business to pursue greater productivity through workplaces efficiencies with wage increases increasingly contingent upon industrial reform.[54] A two-tiered wage system was adopted, with adjustments in the lower or first tier at a uniform and flat rate but those in the second tier made dependent upon award restructuring, productivity and efficiency gains. These developments effectively marked the commencement of the decentralisation of wage setting processes in Australia. In 1991 the Commission, referring to its duty to decide matters according to 'equity, good conscience and their substantial merits' and to hear argument from all relevant parties, refused to accede to the submission of the Accord partners for a system of enterprise bargaining but granted a small wage increase to be awarded on a case by case basis as efficiency gains at workplaces were demonstrated. The Commission commented on the radical nature of any move to enterprise bargaining, noting that enterprise bargaining challenged the principle that had been part of the Australian wage fixing system since its inception: that is, 'that the benefits of increased productivity should be distributed on a national, rather than an industry or an enterprise, basis'.[55] Wage increases through enterprise bargaining, it observed, ought be something different to the traditional system of over-award payments, which reflected market not efficiency or productivity considerations. Enterprise bargaining, it observed, would require a new management and workplace culture. A short time later the Commission allowed enterprise agreements to be attached as schedules to awards where there was compliance with the 'structural efficiency principle' it had earlier set down.[56]

---

52 *Basic Wage, Margins and Total Wage Case 1966* (1966) 115 CAR 93; and *National Wage Case 1967* (1967) 118 CAR 655.

53 *National Wage Case 30 April 1975* (1975) 167 CAR 18.

54 See *National Wage Case June 1986* (1986) 14 IR 187; *National Wage Case December 1986* (1986) 15 IR 395; *National Wage Case March 1987* (1987) 17 IR 65; *National Wage Case December 1987* (1987) 20 IR 371; *National Wage Case February 1988* (1988) 22 IR 451; *National Wage Case August 1988* (1988) 25 IR 170; *National Wage Case February 1989 Review* (1989) 27 IR 196; *National Wage Case August 1989* (1989) 30 IR 81.

55 See *National Wage Case April 1991* (1991) 36 IR 120, 158.

56 *National Wage Case October 1991* (1991) 39 IR 127.

Wages under the *Safety Net Reviews*

With the *Industrial Relations Reform Act 1993* (Cth) the industrial regulatory system became formally bifurcated: an award safety net underpinning agreements. In the *Review of Wage Fixing Principles—August 1994* the Commission dealt with the role of arbitration, structural efficiency, enterprise awards, enterprise flexibility provisions, paid rates awards, work value and first awards under the new system.[57] After 1996 with awards restricted to minimum rates, the AIRC set out the principles to deal with the conversion of paid rates awards to minimum rates awards.[58] After that time there were regular *Safety Net Reviews* to adjust award rates of pay and allowances for those who did not get an increase in pay through enterprise bargaining.[59] According to official figures, about one-fifth of those employed in the Australian workforce depended upon the award safety net for wage increases, although this is likely to be an underestimate.[60]

In the *Safety Net Reviews* the AIRC addressed a range of difficult questions concerning the setting of wage standards. In 1997 it established a two-tier system with a flat rate increase of $10 per week for the lowest paid award workers. This decision sought to respond to the problem of the widening gap between workers dependent on the award safety net and those who could achieve wage increases through enterprise bargaining. The majority of the Full Bench of the Commission considered itself constrained to this modest increase because the needs of the low paid were not its only consideration and high levels of unemployment weighed against any greater increase.[61]

Flat rate increases had the inevitable effect of compressing wage relativities in awards, which the AIRC considered to be ultimately unfair to higher-paid employees. Since the earliest years of the conciliation and arbitration system wage relativities had been part of the structure of the labour market, with levels of remuneration supposed to reflect the differing skills of employees, their responsibilities and conditions of work.[62] Therefore in 2001, in the context of a strong and expanding economy, the Commission provided greater increases for those at middle and upper levels in an attempt to reinstate relativities lost in previous years.[63] In 2003 a two-tiered approach was once again adopted, with potential inflationary impacts on the economy put forward as supporting a higher rise to the lowest paid. In this '*Living Wage Case*' much of the argument revolved around the issue of whether the industrial arena was the best place to care for the interests of the low paid or whether this was better done through a tax transfer system. The AIRC ruled it inappropriate to impose wage restraints on the lowest paid workers and burden them with carrying the risks of

---

57 *Review of Wage Fixing Principles August 1994* (1994) 55 IR 144.

58 See *Workplace Relations Act*, former s 89A(3); and *Paid Rates Review* (1998) 123 IR 240.

59 See *Safety Net Review—Wages—April 1997* (1997) 71 IR 1; *Safety Net Review—Wages—April 1998* (1998) 79 IR 37; *Safety Net Review—Wages—April 1999* (1999) 87 IR 190; *Safety Net Review—Wages—May 2000* (2000) 95 IR 64; *Safety Net Review—Wages—2001* (2001) 104 IR 314; *Safety Net Review—Wages—May 2002* (2002) 112 IR 411; *Safety Net Review—Wages—2003* (2003) 121 IR 367; and *Safety Net Review—Wages—2004* (2004) 129 IR 389.

60 ABS, *Year Book 2002: Labour—How Pay Is Set*, Cat no 1301.0, 2002. See C Fenwick 'How Low Can You Go? Minimum Working Conditions Under Australia's New Labour Laws' (2006) 16 *ELRR* 85.

61 *Safety Net Review—Wages—April 1997* (1997) 71 IR 1.

62 The metals industry long set the standard here—see Hancock and Richardson, above n 47, 182–4.

63 *Safety Net Review—Wages—2001* (2001) 104 IR 314.

economic uncertainty. However, it also commented that safety net increases were an 'imperfect and partial mechanism for addressing the needs of the low paid'.[64]

By 2004 there was a positive economic outlook, and all award rates were raised by $19 per week. The Commission was not convinced that this would have a negative impact on employment levels or the take-up of bargaining. Not all employees are capable of bargaining, it pointed out, emphasising once again its statutory duty to maintain 'a safety net of fair minimum wages' for *all* employees.[65] In its final *Safety Net Review Decision*[66] in 2005 the AIRC increased award wage rates by $17 per week thereby lifting the federal minimum award weekly wage to $484.40 per week. It emphasised that low wages had not kept pace with average weekly earnings, that there was a growing wages gap, and unemployment was at record low levels. It did, however, again point to a lack of research evidence on the needs of the low paid and the fact that not all low-paid workers live in low-income households.

In setting wage standards the statutory parameters guiding the decision-maker are clearly of prime importance. Prior to *Work Choices* there was pressure for the AIRC to establish a single minimum wage and require any increases above it to be achieved through enterprise bargaining. In 1994 the Commission rejected submissions to this effect as inconsistent with the purposes of the legislation, which at that time made explicit reference to ensuring 'stable and appropriate relativities based on skill, responsibility and the conditions under which work is performed, and on the need for skill-based career paths'.[67] In its last *Safety Net Review Decision* in 2005[68] the AIRC stressed it was under a statutory duty to consider three categories of factors:

(a) the need to provide fair minimum standards for employees in the context of living standards generally prevailing in the Australian community;
(b) economic factors, including levels of productivity and inflation, and the desirability of attaining a high level of employment; and
(c) when adjusting the safety net, the needs of the low paid.[69]

It was also under a duty to have regard to the need for alteration of wage relativities between awards to be based on skill, responsibility and the conditions under which the work was performed; the special needs of juniors; those in training arrangements; and those with disabilities, as well as a need to adhere to principles of equality and to prevent and eliminate discrimination, and to encourage bargaining.[70]

The function of safety net wages

From the 1990s there was increasing pressure to change the wage fixing system from those who believed that the market should be the primary regulatory site for wages and

64 *Safety Net Review—Wages—2003* (2003) 121 IR 367, [226].
65 *Safety Net Review—Wages May 2004* (2004) 129 IR 389.
66 *Safety Net Review—Wages June 2005* AIRC, PR002005, 7 June 2005.
67 *Safety Net Adjustment and Review—September 1994* (1991) 56 IR 114. See *Industrial Relations Act 1988* (Cth), s 88A(d) as inserted by *Industrial Relations Reform Act 1993* (Cth).
68 *Safety Net Review—Wages June 2005* AIRC, PR002005, 7 June 2005.
69 *Workplace Relations Act*, former s 88B(2)(a)–(c).
70 *Workplace Relations Act*, former ss 88A and 88B(3).

that a tax transfer system or social security payments were better vehicles than safety net adjustments to respond to the needs of the low paid.[71] Lower wages, it was said, would enable business to employ more people. Although the AIRC adopted an *Economic Incapacity Principle* allowing employer parties to an award to make an application to reduce, postpone or phase in the application of an award pay increase at an enterprise on the ground of very serious or extreme economic adversity,[72] the pressure for change continued.

The function of the safety net wage was thus keenly contested. Some argued that there was no evidence that flat rate increases improved the plight of the low paid and that the more urgent need was to ensure that award rates kept pace with community standards, especially because enterprise bargaining brought increasing wage disparities in Australia.[73] It was widely acknowledged that the problems of low-paid workers were not easy to resolve. Some economists pointed out that workers getting the minimum wage represented a broad cross-section of employees, and not all lived in low-income households, and thus increasing the minimum wage might not be the best-targeted way to improve the distribution of *household* income.[74] But the individual rather than the household had for many years been the focus of the industrial system, and in a bifurcated labour market low-paid workers are increasingly dependent upon either others (often family or household members) or welfare payments. Low-paid workers are also often financially penalised for moving into paid work because they lose social security benefits and thus are effectively 'taxed' at a very high rate, which in turn means that even when minimum wages are increased the increase in real income for them is usually much smaller. Influential economists continued to point to the need for better understanding of the relation between labour, tax and welfare law to address the intractable and 'deep seated structural problem of low rates of labour utilisation and high rates of welfare take-up'.[75] *Work Choices* represented a policy decision by the Government on these issues.

The AFPCS standard on wages[76]

Basic pay rates

The AFPCS guarantees a basic rate of pay for federal employees that depends upon whether they are covered by an APCS or not, whether they are paid by the hour or by the task, or whether they otherwise come within a special category: s 182. Thus

---

71 Eg 'ACCI Wants Single Minimum Wage', *Australian Financial Review*, 6–7 February 1999; the submissions of the Howard Government in the *Safety Net Review—Wages—May 2002* (2002) 112 IR 411; and 'Wage Case Will Soon Be a Blast from the Past', Editorial, *The Australian*, 10 November 2004.

72 See *Safety Net Review—Wages—1999* (1999) 87 IR 190, and *Safety Net Review—Wages—2003* (2003) 121 IR 367.

73 D Peetz 'The Safety Net, Bargaining and the Role of the Australian Industrial Relations Commission' (1998) 40 *JIR* 532.

74 S Richardson 'Who Gets the Minimum Wage?' (1998) 40 *JIR* 554; and S Richardson and A Harding 'Poor Workers? The Link between Low Wages, Low Family Income and the Tax and Transfer Systems' in S Richardson (ed) *Reshaping the Labour Market: Regulation, Efficiency and Equality in Australia* (1999).

75 B Gregory 'Where to Now? Welfare and Labour Market Regulation in Australia' in (2004) 30 *ABL* 33. See also B Gregory, E Klug and YM Martin 'Labour Market De-regulation, Relative Wages and the Social Security System' in S Richardson (ed) *Reshaping the Labour Market: Regulation, Efficiency and Equality in Australia* (1999).

76 *Workplace Relations Act*, Pt 7 Div 2 ss 176–222.

employees will fall in one of four categories. First, those employees covered by an APCS are to receive at least the 'guaranteed basic periodic rate of pay' for each of their 'guaranteed hours' (pro-rated for part hours) of work. Secondly, employees who are 'APCS piece rate employees' must be paid at least the APCS specified piece rate for their work. Thirdly, where employees are not covered by an APCS then the FMW will apply to them. Fourthly, junior employees, employees with a disability, or employees to whom training arrangements apply, must be paid a rate equal at least to any special FMW applicable to them.

'Guaranteed hours' are the number of hours a person is contracted to work, excluding any time absent either on authorised leave (whether paid or unpaid, but not public holidays or time off for authorised training) or on industrial action for which the employer is precluded from paying wages under s 507, and including any additional or overtime hours worked: s 183. The statutory default is 38 hours where there are none specified in the contract of employment. Thus the AFPCS only guarantees an employee pay at the basic rate (APCS or FMW) for *all* hours worked, including (reasonable) overtime hours or hours worked on public holidays.

The AFPCS also guarantees that casual employees who have a basic periodic rate of pay under an APCS are to be paid the casual loading under that instrument where it provides for such loading (even if this is lower than the default rate set by the statute). For all other casual employees, that is, those where the AFPC does not specify a casual loading and those covered by a workplace agreement or the FMW, the statute sets a default minimum casual loading of 20 per cent: ss 181–2 and 185–6. This default rate may be altered subsequently by the AFPC, but there will always be only one default loading rate: ss 186–8. Thus it can be seen that after the *Work Choices* changes it is lawful for an enterprise agreement to undermine an APCS casual loading rate that is higher than the default rate but such agreement cannot go below the default rate. For this reason many casuals may end up worse off financially than they were before the introduction of the *Work Choices* reforms. However, where an APCS casual employee has been party to a workplace agreement that is then terminated by one of the parties under s 399(1) that employee becomes entitled to the higher of the APCS or the default casual rate.

Guarantee against the reduction of wages under Work Choices

The AFPCS guarantees to federal employees that their rates of pay cannot fall below the minimum that would have applied to them immediately after the *Work Choices* changes had they then been in their 'current circumstances of employment'. This guarantee works by restraining the AFPC in the exercise of its powers, to adjust the FMW or a preserved APCS, or to determine or adjust a new APCS, or to revoke a preserved or new APCS. In each case the AFPC must ensure that the proposed new rate of pay or the 'resulting guaranteed basic periodic rate' is not lower than the 'commencement guaranteed basic periodic rate' that operated immediately after 27 March 2006. For APCS piece rate employees, this comparative exercise is calculated by considering what would be the wages earned by an 'employee of average capacity', a concept the content of which will surely be contested. In undertaking the comparative exercise for this assessment account must also be taken of any other exercise of power by the AFPC: ss 190–2. There is also a guarantee that when the AFPC adjusts or makes an APCS that is to apply to an employee previously covered by the FMW or a special FMW then the new APCS rate is not lower than the previous relevant FMW rate. This guarantee does not apply to a basic periodic rate included in a preserved APCS (that is, the rate before 27 March 2006) but only when that rate is varied or a new APCS is established. The guarantee also does not apply to a special FMW unless it is expressed to be applicable to the particular APCS, a class of APCSs, or all APCSs: s 193.

It is obvious that the worth of any guarantee against a reduction of wages in the future can only be evaluated in the longer term and will involve a consideration at that time of the real worth of the employee's wage. It will also undoubtedly involve an assessment of other matters such as inflation and social expectations about what is a decent or living wage. It can be noted that the guarantee in *Work Choices* to those who are dependent on minimum wages is simply that the rate of pay will not get worse. There is no guarantee that it will improve. For those many employees who do not have bargaining power to improve their pay *Work Choices* offers no promise that any of the assumed increased wealth in the new economy will be shared.

Frequency of pay

If an APCS makes provision for the frequency with which wages must be paid to an employee then an employer is required to continue to abide by that under the *Work Choices* regime. Where there are no such provisions in the APCS, or an employee is not covered by an APCS, then the employer is required to comply with any frequency provisions in a workplace agreement (if one exists) or a contract of employment. If neither of those instruments makes any such provision then the statutory default period is payment by the fortnight: s 189.

The Federal Minimum Wage (FMW)[77]

The *Work Choices Act* established a standard FMW that is applicable to federal employees, except those who have an APCS pay rate, are APCS piece rates employees, or juniors, employees with a disability or to whom a training arrangement applies. In respect of the latter three groups of employees, the AFPC has power to establish a special FMW but in so doing must make it clear by express statement whether the special FMW is to be a minimum standard for some or all APCSs and for which ones: ss 194–9. There might for instance be a special FMW setting a single junior rate of pay or a scale of rates according to age for all juniors, or for juniors in some industries. The FMW must always be expressed as a monetary amount per hour, although a special FMW may be expressed in terms of a method for calculating that monetary amount, for example as a percentage of another monetary amount. The standard FMW set down by the *Work Choices Act* in 2006 is $12.75 per hour, although this may be altered by the AFPC: s 195. Special FMWs may also be subsequently adjusted by the AFPC: s 200.

---

77 *Workplace Relations Act*, Pt 7 Div 2 Subdiv G, ss 194–200.

Australian Pay and Classification Scales (APCSs) [78]

An APCS is defined in the Act as 'a set of provisions relating to pay and loadings for particular employees': s 201. There are two types of APCS: preserved APCSs, which are derived from wage instruments (such as awards) that operated just prior to the *Work Choices* changes, and new APCSs, which the AFPC may determine under s 214. All APCSs continue to have effect until adjusted or revoked by the AFPC: ss 215–16.

The content of an APCS is outlined under the statute: s 202. An APCS must contain basic periodic rates of pay and/or basic periodic piece rates, where relevant the provisions describing the classifications for which there are different rates of pay, and provisions detailing who is covered by the APCS. APCSs must also contain similar information in relation to casual loadings, as well as any provisions regarding the frequency of payment to casuals. In APCSs wages must be expressed either as a 'basic periodic rate' (that is, a monetary amount per hour), or a monetary amount for piece work, while casual loadings are expressed as a percentage of a basic periodic rate of pay. APCSs, however, cannot contain any provisions establishing automatic adjustments of pay rates and the legislation also limits any provisions that would allow any one other than the AFPC to determine who is covered by an APCS or to adjust rates of pay under an APCS.

The content of a preserved APCS is derived from an award or other instrument that set one or more basic rates of pay or piece rates payable to employees prior to the commencement of the *Work Choices* amendments: s 208. As well as pay rates, the preserved APCS will also include a description of the classifications that are linked to rates of pay, casual loading provisions, provisions regarding pay rates for training, frequency of payment provisions and coverage provisions that were included in the pre–*Work Choices* instrument: see also ss 179–81 and 208. Where such provisions are not expressed in conformity with the requirements of the legislation they will be notionally adjusted to do so. Thus, for example, a weekly or fortnightly pay rate will be translated into an hourly rate.

Any preserved APCSs derived from awards that were adjusted in accordance with the AIRC's *Safety Net Review Case 2004* or that only came into existence after that decision are to be adjusted by the AFPC as part of the first exercise of its wage setting so that they are (if they are not so already) consistent with the AIRC's *Safety Net Review Case 2005*: s 218. For the purpose of the guarantee against reduction in pay this adjusted rate operates as the base rate. There are special provisions relating to the APCSs covering employees with a disability and those to whom training provisions apply: ss 220–1. Whether an employee is covered by an APCS will depend on the coverage provisions it contains, although these cannot be determined by reference to State or Territory boundaries: ss 204 and 206. The guarantee against reductions in pay will dictate that the relevant highest rate will become the basis of any new uniform rate. The *Work Choices Act* operates to guarantee APCS employees (except APCS piece rates employees) that, after the first wage setting adjustment by the AFPC, they will be paid at least either the

---

78 *Workplace Relations Act*, Pt 7 Div 2 Subdiv H–L, ss 201–21.

FMW rate or a special FMW if it is expressed to be a minimum standard for the APCS relevant to a particular employee: ss 182(1), 198 and 207.

Given the broad parameters that govern the exercise of the AFPC's wage setting powers it has been speculated that future increases in pay rates will be fewer than under the old system overseen by the AIRC. There has also been much speculation that there will be pressure on the AFPC to focus only on increases to the FMW rather than the APCS, which will have the effect over time of flattening the wage structure in the safety net. Indeed eventually, it is thought, there may in effect be only a single FMW and a special FMW with all other wages to be set through bargaining. Certainly the Chair of the AFPC has early been reported as indicating that a cut in real wages is a possible outcome. Areas for research that he identified in the first months of the AFPC's operation were the sensitivity of employers and employees to movements in the minimum wage; the sensitivity of higher wage brackets to movements in the minimum wage; and the interaction between the minimum wage and tax and social security systems.[79]

Pay equity

Although the conciliation and arbitration system embraced an aspiration for wage fairness and justice in Australia, its realisation proved more elusive. Sometimes this was a direct expression of legislative policy: junior and trainee rates of pay, for instance, were protected from attack under discrimination principles.[80] However, for the most part the problem of achieving pay equity has been more a practical matter as the absorption of dominant ideologies produced a system that has perpetuated stereotypical views of work value.

Pay equity for Indigenous workers

The struggle for pay equity and wage justice for Indigenous workers is far from over.[81] The original exclusion of Indigenous workers from awards may have been precipitated, or aided, by confusion regarding the legal reach of the federal industrial system: that is, whether the work of Indigenous Australians was the exclusive domain of the States and Territories whose legislation and ordinances did regulate their employment in some detail from an early date.[82] Thus Aboriginal workers were excluded from pastoral awards until the mid-1960s when it was finally accepted that there should be equal pay for Aboriginal stock workers.[83] For many years Indigenous women and girls were employed predominantly as domestic servants in white households, but this work was always excluded from the purview of the conciliation and arbitration system at federal level.[84]

---

79 M Skulley 'Low-paid May Get Less, Says Fair Pay Chief' *Australian Financial Review*, 17 February 2006, 3.

80 *Workplace Relations Act 1996* (Cth), former s 88B(4)–(5) .

81 See G Whitehouse 'Justice and Equity: Women and Indigenous Workers' in Isaac and Macintyre (eds), above n 47.

82 'The aboriginal race' was excluded from the grant of legislative power to the Commonwealth Parliament under s 51(xxvi), *Australian Constitution* of the until changed by referendum in 1967.

83 *Re Cattle Station Industry (Northern Territory) Award* (1996) 113 CAR 651; and *Pastoral Industry Award* (1967) 121 CAR 454, 457–8.

84 The definition of 'industry' in s 4 of the *Conciliation and Arbitration Act 1904* (Cth), excluded 'persons engaged in domestic service'.

The realisation of wage justice continued long after to lag behind the formal recognition of pay equity for Indigenous workers, especially under the impact of some State laws.[85] In many instances Aboriginal and Torres Strait Islanders are still paid and employed in quite a different ways to most other workers: for example, through Community Development Employment Projects (CDEP), which are more akin to a form of social security payment to the community in which the worker lives, rather than a direct payment to the individual workers. The median income of Indigenous Australians is only a little more than half that of non-Indigenous Australians, and Aboriginal and Torres Strait Islander peoples are much more likely to be unemployed. In 2001 the unemployment rate among Indigenous peoples was 20 per cent compared with a little under 7 per cent for the white population.[86]

Pay equity for women

The fight for wage justice for women workers under the conciliation and arbitration system was a lengthy one.[87] In the *Harvester Case* Higgins J (in)famously assumed the worker to be a male breadwinner.[88] The wage principle developed in that decision was later applied differently to women, because they were assumed not to have obligations to maintain a family. The minimum wage, Higgins J said subsequently, could not be based on the 'very exceptional circumstances' where this was otherwise. Women were thus paid less than men, except in those industries where they competed in the labour market with men: then they received the same wage so that they would not be employed in preference to men.[89] The minimum wage for women was first established at around 54 per cent of the male wage, and was based on the costs necessary for a woman to support herself alone.[90]

Thus from the outset Australian wage standards were gendered, with the Conciliation and Arbitration Court refusing to come to the aid of the 'gentle invaders' who trespassed into territory not rightfully theirs. Equal pay where granted was not in recognition of the equality of workers but a stratagem to protect men's jobs. The effect of these early wage principles was to embed gender segregation deeply in the Australian labour market. The history of wage regulation in Australia also shows that when change did come about it was often only in the wake of other social and economic developments, including changes in community attitudes. Laura Bennett has shown that early wage decisions of the Conciliation and Arbitration Court largely reflected existing arrangements. Indeed

---

85 See eg *Bligh v The State of Queensland* [1997] AILR 39. See also S Mudaliar 'Stolen Wages and Fiduciary Duties' [2003] AILR 33.

86 ABS, *Australian Social Trends 2004: Work—Aboriginal and Torres Strait Islander Peoples in the Labour Force* (2004); and *Australian Social Trends 2004: Economic Resources—Incomes of Aboriginal and Torres Strait Islander Australians* (2004).

87 See L Bennett 'Legal Intervention and the Female Workforce: The Australian Conciliation and Arbitration Court 1907–1921' (1984) 12 *Int J Sociol L* 23; R Hunter 'Women Workers and Federal Industrial Law: From Harvester to Comparable Worth' (1988) 1 *AJLL* 147; E Ryan and A Conlan *Gentle Invaders: Australian Women at Work 1788–1974* (1989).

88 (1907) 2 CAR 1.

89 *Rural Workers' Union and United Labourers' Union v Mildura Branch of Australian Dried Fruits Association* (*Fruit Pickers Case*) (1912) 6 CAR 61.

90 *Federated Clothing Trades v Archer* (1919) 13 CAR 647.

throughout the twentieth century the conciliation and arbitration system was more a follower than a leader in the pursuit of wage equality.[91]

Moving away from the principles for wage setting established in the early years was always going to be difficult when the primary basis for the allocation of reward for work was the needs of a worker assumed to be solely responsible for the support of a family. Changes came with the onset of World War II when women were needed to undertake 'men's work'. A Women's Employment Board, with power to override ordinary industrial regulation, was established by the *Women's Employment Act 1942* (Cth) to set wages for women who were working in occupations previously the preserve of men. The Board applied principles that focused more on efficiency, productivity and the value of the work to the employer, although this was initially strongly resisted by employers who challenged the validity of the legislation.[92] The regulation of women's employment in this period was an important step in the gradual move to pay equity for women.

After the war, international developments including the adoption of the *Equal Remuneration Convention, 1951 (ILO C 100)* further highlighted the issue of pay equity for women. The *Conciliation and Arbitration Act* was amended in the postwar era to make it clear that equal pay for the same work or work of equal value to the employer was an industrial matter and to allow for the establishment of a uniform basic wage for women. The Act empowered the Court of Conciliation and Arbitration to determine a basic wage for adult females that was 'just and reasonable' without looking at the industry in which it was performed and directed it to apply the same principles in fixing wages for men and women.[93] In the *Basic Wage Case 1949–50* the female wage had been lifted to 75 per cent male minimum wage.[94] However, the legislation only covered women who were doing the same or similar work to that done by men or work of equivalent value, and thus did nothing to overcome the more profound problems caused by gender segregation of the Australian labour market. In the *Standard Hours and Basic Wage Inquiry 1952–1953*,[95] the Court of Conciliation and Arbitration announced a shift from the emphasis on needs to setting wages at the highest the community could bear.

Equal pay cases

The concept of a family wage continued albeit weakened for the next decade and a half, but during that time there was mounting pressure for equal pay as women's labour force participation increased and as a result of the adoption of legislative initiatives for equal pay in some of the States. In New South Wales legislation required awards to be varied to give women 75 per cent of the male wage plus an appropriate margin for skill

---

91 Bennett, above n 87; and Hunter, above n 87.
92 *Victorian Chamber of Manufactures v The Commonwealth* (1943) 67 CLR 347; *R v Commonwealth Court of Conciliation and Arbitration; Ex parte Victoria* (1944) 68 CLR 485; *Australian Woollen Mills Ltd v The Commonwealth* (1944) 69 CLR 476; and *Australian Textiles Pty Ltd v The Commonwealth* (1945) 71 CLR 161.
93 *Commonwealth Conciliation and Arbitration Act (No 2) 1949* (Cth).
94 (1950) 68 CAR 698.
95 (1953) 77 CAR 477, 495–6.

to implement a policy of equal pay for men and women's work of equal value. Under the legislation women's wages were to rise to 100 per cent by 1963.[96] In 1969 the federal Commission finally accepted that the shift from the basic or minimum wage to a total wage also enabled the adoption of the principle of equal pay for equal work.[97] However, while the decision made an impact in some areas, notably teaching and the public sector, where men and women were doing the same work under an award, it proved impotent in other areas of 'women's work'.

In the early 1970s there followed two more important decisions impacting on pay rates for women. In the 1972 *National Wage and Equal Pay Cases* the Commission went further than its 1969 decision and recognised 'equal pay for work of equal value', although the minimum wage was still not extended to women.[98] However, pressure for this continued following developments in some of the States.[99] In 1974 the *National Wage Case* established the same minimum wage for men and women to be phased in over three years. In so doing the Commission stated that it did not vary wages according to whether workers were single or married, or according to the diversity of their family types. Declaring itself to be 'an industrial arbitration tribunal, not a social welfare agency', the Commission said that care for family needs was a task for government and that it would disregard the family component in fixing the minimum wage. Finally it had turned away from the approach established by the *Harvester Decision*.[100] Its decision also paved the way for the Commonwealth Government to ratify the *Equal Remuneration Convention* in 1974.

Comparable worth

The 'equal pay cases' of the late 1960s and early 1970s had considerable impact, providing clear evidence that the form of wage regulation rather than, say, women's decisions not to invest in their human capital is of prime significance in determining the relative equality in pay between men and women.[101] However, pay equity for women still remained elusive, with the gender segregation of the Australian labour market particularly problematic. In the 1980s there were further attempts to tackle the problem through determinations of work value, a matter that had been raised in an earlier NSW decision.[102]

However, in 1986 the federal Commission refused to embrace the concept of 'comparable worth' because it would involve comparisons of work across different occupations and performed under different awards, which was contrary to the way the system had operated historically.[103] The Commission also saw 'comparable worth'

96 *Industrial Arbitration (Female Rates) Amendment Act 1958* (NSW).
97 *Australasian Meat Industry Employees Union v Meat & Allied Trades Federation of Australia (Equal Pay Case)* (1969) 127 CAR 1142, 1145–6.
98 (1972) 147 CAR 172.
99 See eg *In re State Equal Pay Case* [1973] AR (NSW) 425.
100 *National Wage Case 1974* (1974) 157 CAR 293, 299.
101 B Gregory 'Labour Market Institutions and the Gender Pay Ratio' (1999) 32 *Aust Ec Rev* 273.
102 See *In re State Equal Pay Case* [1973] AR (NSW) 425.
103 *Private Hospitals and Doctors' Nurses (ACT) Award 1972 (Comparable Worth Decision)*(1986) 13 IR 108 and 18 IR 455.

as potentially leading to greater diversification of existing award classifications, just at a time when there were moves to make the centralised system simpler. Women did much to place themselves on the award restructuring agenda at the end of the 1980s, but simultaneously they had to point out that for them the issues were often diametrically opposed to those envisaged by the Commission: what women needed was an increase rather than a reduction in classifications, or a guarantee that there were real career paths and opportunities for training for them.[104] However, award restructuring in the late 1980s never included a general review of entitlements, nor were the transformations effected through the structural efficiency principle appropriated to advance the claims of women to pay equity. In sum the changes made to the structure of regulation through the conciliation and arbitration system in the last two decades of the twentieth century delivered few real benefits to the majority of women.[105] Indeed the move to enterprise bargaining made things worse: wage differentials became greater with enterprise bargaining, impacting most on lower-paid workers, a group in which women are overrepresented.[106]

Work value

After the 'wilderness' years following the failure of the comparable worth case a more significant challenge to the gendered assessment of work value came about through a State initiative.[107] In 1998 following recommendations by a 'Pay Equity Taskforce' and amendments to the *Industrial Relations Act 1996* (NSW), a 'Pay Equity Inquiry' headed by Glynn J of the NSW Industrial Relations Commission was established with the aim of ensuring equal remuneration to men and women doing equal work. The resultant *Pay Equity Report* examined the undervaluation of women's work using particular occupational types to reveal systemic issues of work value.[108] It showed that the traditional factors used to evaluate work, such as qualifications, training, attributes, responsibility, physical conditions, work quality, flexibility of skills, skills, knowledge, supervision, place and importance to the operation overall,[109] have been applied in a way that is deeply gendered.

In evaluating the findings of the 1998 *Pay Equity Report*, Rosemary Hunter has pointed out that it is difficult to identify any clear rule regarding the reasons for the undervaluation of women's work. However, some indicative factors include: female-dominated industry and work; a new industry or occupation, a service industry or

---

104 RJ Owens 'Women, "Atypical" Work Relationships and the Law' (1993) 19 *MULR* 399.

105 See B Pocock 'Women's Work and Wages' in A Edwards and S Magarey (eds) *Women in a Restructuring Australia: Work and Welfare* (1995).

106 *National Wage Case April 1991* (1991) 36 IR 120; and *Review of Wage Fixing Principles—August 1994* (1994) 55 IR 144. See also G Whitehouse and B Frino 'Women, Wages and Industrial Agreements' in (2003) 6 *Aust J Lab Ec* 579; and see A McColgan *Just Wages For Women* (1997) for a comparative assessment of the impact on women of various wage determination structures.

107 See R Hunter *The Beauty Therapist, the Mechanic, the Geophysicist and the Librarian: Addressing the Undervaluation of Women's Work* (2002), 12.

108 *Pay Equity Report*: Reference by the Minister for Industrial Relations pursuant to s 146(1)(d) of the *Industrial Relations Act 1996*, vols 1–3, 14 December 1998. Available at <www.workandfamily.nsw.gov.au/payequity/report/default.html>.

109 *The Vehicle Industry Award 1952* [1968] 124 CAR 295. See also Hunter, above n 87, 152–3.

home-based work; a history of consent awards or agreements with no work value exercise by a tribunal; inadequate application of previous pay principles; a weak union or few union members; small workplaces; high casualisation; lack of recognition of qualifications; and lack of access to training or career path.[110] All factors are not, of course, always present. Librarians, for instance, were generally employed by public authorities and were highly unionised. In some instances special factors were involved, such as the impact of the removal of tariff barriers that increased the transfer of work from factory to home for clothing and textile workers. The *Pay Equity Report* showed that the undervaluation of women's work needed to be assessed on a case-by-case basis and was time-consuming.

Following the *Pay Equity Report* a new 'Equal Remuneration and Other Conditions Principle' was inserted into the wage fixing principles in New South Wales by the Full Bench of the NSW Industrial Relations Commission, whereby if work could be shown to be undervalued then an appropriate adjustment could be made.[111] A claim was then instituted on behalf of librarians for pay justice, and a pay rise averaging 16 per cent was granted recognising that historically there had been an undervaluation of their skills and responsibilities on a gender basis with them being paid much less than other public sector groups with similar characteristics.[112] The case drew upon the *Pay Equity Report's* general findings and its case study of librarians and geologists. Intervening in the case were the national Pay Equity Coalition, Women's Electoral Lobby, and Business and Women's Association of Australia.

The impacts of the *Pay Equity Report* and the *NSW Librarians Case* were far-reaching. Pay equity initiatives were instituted in Victoria and Western Australia,[113] and trade unions began to prepare cases in industries where women predominated and their work had been historically undervalued. Wage justice for childcare workers was one of the first areas targeted and significant decisions increasing their pay were handed down. However, only in New South Wales was the decision specifically grounded on the pay equity principle.[114]

Pay equity after Work Choices

The *Work Choices* changes make it clear that after 27 March 2006 the *Workplace Relations Act* overrides any State or Territory law 'providing for a court or tribunal constituted by a law of the State or Territory to make an order in relation to equal

---

110 Hunter, above n 107.

111 *Re Equal Remuneration Principle* (2000) 97 IR 177; and *State Wage Case 2001* (2001) 104 IR 438.

112 *Re Crown Librarians, Library Officers and Archivists Award Proceedings—Application under the Equal Remuneration Principle* (2002) 111 IR 48.

113 T Todd and J Eveline *Report on the Review of the Gender Pay Gap in Western Australia*, November 2004, available at <www.docep.wa.gov.au>; and *Report of the Victorian Pay Equity Working Party to the Minister for Industrial Relations, Advancing Pay Equity—Their Future Depends on It*, February 2005, available at <www. irv.vic.gov.au>.

114 *Re Miscellaneous Workers Kindergartens and Child Care Centres (State) Award* (2006)150 IR 290, and *Statement by the Full Bench* (2006)150 IR 284. See also *Child Care Industry (Australian Capital Territory) Award 1998 and Children's Services (Victoria) Award 1988 Case*, AIRC, PR954938, 13 January 2005, PR957259, 10 April 2005, PR957914, 10 May 2005, PR959281 and PR959278, 24 June 2005; and *Child Care (SA) Award Work Value Case* [2005] SAIRComm 49 (30 December 2005).

remuneration for equal work of equal value': s 16(1)(c). The legislative provisions endorsing principles of equal pay in a number of jurisdictions are thus inoperative in relation to employees covered by the federal Act.[115]

Following the coming into effect of the *Work Choices* changes, provisions that were first introduced into the Act in 1993 have been retained but in amended form.[116] These provisions were to facilitate the bringing of claims before the AIRC for equal remuneration for work of equal value by either employees, trade unions or the Sex Discrimination Commissioner.[117] They were intended to implement various international conventions, including the *Equal Remuneration Convention 1951 (ILO C 100)*, the United Nations' *Convention on the Elimination of All Forms of Discrimination against Women*, and the *Discrimination (Employment and Occupation) Convention, 1958 (ILO C 111)*, as well as the ILO's *Equal Remuneration Recommendation, 1951 (ILO R 90)* and *Discrimination Employment and Occupation Recommendation, 1958 (ILO R 111)*. However, they were little used, and the AIRC resisted setting down principles under them. In the few cases that were brought intractable problems, including the need to find relevant male comparators, rendered these provisions of little practical value.[118] In short the 1993 reforms proved over the next twelve years to be 'notoriously unsuccessful in achieving their objective'.[119]

The jurisdiction of the AIRC to deal with equal remuneration for work of equal value now sits rather uncomfortably in the new regulatory system because it is the AFPC that otherwise has responsibility for wage determination and wage setting. However, the jurisdiction of the AIRC is very much a residual one. It can only deal with applications where there is no other 'adequate alternate remedy' for an applicant. The AIRC is constrained so that its jurisdiction under this part of the Act does not conflict with the jurisdiction of the AFPC. Thus the AIRC must have regard to decisions of the AFPC, and it cannot deal with any application that would have the effect of setting aside the decisions of the AFPC, for example those determining basic period rates of pay, basic piece rates or the casual loading. It is difficult to predict whether this jurisdiction will prove more useful now that it is virtually the only way to conduct an equal pay hearing.

Under the *Workplace Relations Act* the AFPC is required to apply the principle that men and women should receive equal remuneration for work of equal value: s 222. However, as has been seen earlier it is really recognition of work value that is most significant to achieving pay equity. Despite some of the successes in various pay cases just prior to 2006, genuine pay equity remains an issue not least because women earn significantly less than men, are overrepresented in part-time work, and are less likely than men to have their wages and conditions determined by some form of statutory-supported bargaining mechanism. Indeed prior to 2006 women disproportionately had

---

115 Eg *Industrial Relations Act 1999* (Qld) Ch 2 Pt 5; *Industrial Relations Act 1996* (NSW), s 23; and *Fair Work Act 1994* (SA) s 69(2).

116 *Workplace Relations Act*, Pt 12 Div 3 ss 620–34.

117 *Industrial Relations Reform Act 1993* (Cth), Pt VIA Div 2, ss 170BA–BI.

118 See *AMWU v HPM Industries Pty Ltd* (1998) 94 IR 129. Note also *Automotive, Food, Metals, Engineering, Printing and Kindred Industries and Gunn and Taylor (Aust) Pty Ltd*, AIRC, PR918573, 4 June 2002.

119 Commissioner D Whelan *The Gender Pay Gap: Assessing Possible Futures in the Post-Inquiries Age* (2005).

their wages determined solely by award.[120] As a result of this the outcomes of the award rationalisation process and the APCS are particularly important for women because any removal of skill-based classification structures may make it much harder for women to get above the minimum pay. Any limiting of low-paid workers' access to pay increases has a significant impact on women: as researchers have noted '[l]ow waged workers are principally married people working fulltime and they are principally women'.[121] Eliminating the undervaluation of women's work has the potential to go some way to closing the pay gap between men and women by encouraging a breakdown in the gendered segregation of the labour force. Indeed re-examining the worth of that which is considered 'women's work' in the paid labour market may even lead to changes in the way unpaid or reproductive work is viewed.

Working Time

The evolution of the working-time standard

Time is central to understandings of work and its place in human lives.[122] In Australia, the length of the paid working day became an industrial and political issue as far back as the nineteenth century. In the mid-1850s a number of Australian trade unions were victorious in their struggle for recognition of 'the eight-hour day' and from the mid-1870s colonial parliaments debated the matter after a political push was made to recognise that standard in legislation.[123]

In the early years of the federal conciliation and arbitration system the Australian working-time standard was assumed to be a 48-hour week, 8¾ hours per day on weekdays and 4¼ hours on Saturday. Only in exceptional cases, where the occupation involved excessive travel time or was particularly onerous, was there any deviation from that standard.[124] Thereafter ordinary time hours steadily diminished over the course of the last century. In the *Timber Workers Case (1920)* the maximum ordinary time at work for timber workers was reduced from 48 to 44 hours (eight hours on Monday to Friday and four hours on Saturday),[125] the Conciliation and Arbitration Court ruling that fairness demanded that increased productivity gains achieved through new technology should also result in a reduction of working time. While emphasising that it was not lowering hours simply so that more people would be employed, the Court conceded that lower hours should not be denied simply on the basis that employers might be compelled to employ more people. Observing that some countries already had

---

120 ABS, *Year Book Australia—Labour: Earnings and Benefits*, Cat no 1301.0, 2004, shows that women earned 84 per cent of male average weekly fulltime earnings, but only 65 per cent when part-time work was taken into account. Awards set the earnings of 26.1 per cent of women as opposed to 15.1 per cent of men.

121 Richardson, above n 74, 577.

122 J Conaghan 'Time To Dream? Flexibility, Families and the Regulation of Working Time' in J Fudge and R Owens (eds) Precarious *Work, Women and the New Economy: The Challenge to Legal Norms* (2006).

123 See M Quinlan 'Pre-arbitral Labour Legislation in Australia and Its Implication for the Introduction of Compulsory Arbitration' in S Macintyre and R Mitchell (eds) *Foundations of Arbitration: The Origins and Effects of State Compulsory Arbitration 1890–1914* (1989), 43.

124 *Australian Postal Electricians' Union v Postmaster General and Public Service Commissioner* (1913) 7 CAR 5; and *Australian Builders' Labourers' Federation v Archer* (1913) 7 CAR 210, 228–31.

125 *Australian Timber Workers Union v John Sharp & Sons Ltd* (1920) 14 CAR 811.

a 44-hour standard, the Court concluded that reducing the hours standard by arbitration would avoid the strikes that had occurred elsewhere. Although shortly afterwards the 48-hour standard was reimposed,[126] following amendments that confined jurisdiction over standard working hours to the Full Court, the move to the lower standard was already being adopted at State level in legislation applying to all workers.[127] Some years later the Court accepted that the standard work hours should also be reduced to 44 per week, again allaying concerns about the detrimental economic effects of the decision by pointing to experience elsewhere, especially in the USA.[128]

After World War II ordinary working time was further reduced in federal awards to 40 hours.[129] The Court dismissed employer fears over falls in productivity, expressing confidence that the effects of new technologies would more than compensate. In the postwar context, the decision reflected a view that the benefits of prosperity should flow to workers. At the same time an award clause was added, providing that employees may be required to work reasonable overtime with penalty rates of pay intended to act as a disincentive to excessive hours.

The 40-hour standard along with provision for reasonable overtime remained the norm in most federal awards until the 1980s when there was a further push to reduce ordinary working time to 38 hours.[130] At this time flexible working time arrangements were also introduced in some industries: for instance, a 19-day four-week cycle, where the resultant benefits were identified as the extension of trading hours and increased employment of part-time workers.[131] However, in the *National Wage Case* of 1983 the Commission refused to approve a general reduction in ordinary hours below 38 because of the prevailing difficult economic climate, but allowed unopposed claims where it was satisfied that increased costs were offset by changed work practices.[132] The link between economic considerations, especially productivity, and hours continued to be a focus of the Commission's major wage test case hearings throughout the 1980s and 1990s but no change was made to the working-time standard.[133]

Working-time flexibility

By the beginning of the twenty-first century most awards specified the ordinary hours of working time to be paid at ordinary rates of pay, and also provided that employers could require employees to work reasonable overtime remunerated at penalty rates. However, while awards once always specified exactly when, during the day and the week, ordinary hours (including meal and rest breaks) were to be worked, the modern tendency was to

---

126 *Standard Hours Case* (1921) 15 CAR 1044; and *Australian Timber Workers Union v John Sharp & Sons Ltd* (1922) 16 CAR 649.

127 See eg *Forty-four Hours Week Act 1925* (NSW).

128 *Amalgamated Engineering Union v J Alderdice & Company Pty Ltd and Others (Forty-four Hours Case)* (1927) 24 CAR 755.

129 *Standard Hours Inquiry 1947* (1947) 59 CAR 581.

130 *Re Metal Industries Award 1971* (1981) 1 IR 169.

131 *Australian Bank Employees Union v State Bank (SA)* (1983) 4 IR 132.

132 *National Wage Case—September 1983* (1983) 4 IR 429.

133 See *Inquiry into Wage Fixing Principles April 1981* (1981) 254 CAR 341; *National Wage Case July 1981* (1981) 260 CAR 4; *National Wage Case August 1988* (1988) 25 IR 170; *National Wage Case October 1991* (1991) 39 IR 127.

provide for working-time flexibility. Facilitative clauses allowed ordinary working hours to be arranged by agreement. Such agreements could cover the averaging of hours over a work cycle; the arrangement of ordinary hours in excess of or less than eight per day; the substitution and accumulation of rostered days off; the starting and finishing times of work; and flexibility in taking rostered days off, or time off in lieu of hours worked and its making up. Under this style of award regulation, the so-called standard working day or week in which all workers work at the same time began to disappear in many industries and workplaces.

The boundaries placed around working time in State jurisdictions also became less rigid. New South Wales' legislation stipulated that an employee's ordinary working hours under State awards must not exceed 40 hours either per week or when averaged over a 12-week period or over a period not exceeding 52 weeks for seasonal work.[134] Queensland also provided a broad and fairly flexible definition of ordinary hours of work for periods over a day and a week, the level of overtime penalty payment, and rest pauses for workers not covered by an industrial instrument, such as an award or agreement.[135]

The long-hours problem

Working time is a most significant issue in Australia, which is one of the few OECD countries where the recent trend has been to an increase rather than a decrease in working hours, with around one-fifth of Australia's workforce working more than 50 hours per week.[136] The long-hours problem has come about through an increasing amount of 'overtime' worked. Many workers—especially managers, professionals, and administrators—are often not compensated for these increased work hours. As a consequence, many workers report that long working hours make it very difficult for them to achieve an acceptable work/life balance.[137] The importance of work/life balance was recognised in the early working hours cases, but there it was assumed that time not spent at work could be devoted to leisure because the worker had a spouse who worked in the home.[138] Now with many women also engaged in paid work, work/family/life balance is made even more problematic by the long-hours problem. The other side to this is the short-hours problem of many workers who are underemployed, working fewer hours than they want. Between the long-hours and the short-hours problems, the standard '38 hours' work' week began to disappear.

---

134 *Industrial Relations Act 1991* (NSW), s 22.

135 *Industrial Relations Act 1999* (Qld), ss 9–9A.

136 ABS, *Year Book Australia—Labour: Usual Hours*, Cat no 1301.0, 2004; and JC Messenger (ed) *Working Time and Workers' Preferences in Industrialised Countries: Finding the Balance* (2004).

137 B Pocock et al, *Fifty Families: What Unreasonable Hours Are Doing to Australians, Their Families and Their Communities* (2001).

138 *Australian Timber Workers Union v John Sharp & Sons Ltd* (1920) 14 CAR 811, 847; *Amalgamated Engineering Union v J Alderdice & Company Pty Ltd* (1927) 24 CAR 755, 763; and *Standard Hours Inquiry* (1947) 59 CAR 581. See also A Chapman 'Work/Family, Australian Labour Law and the Normative Worker' in J Conaghan and K Rittich (eds) *Labour Law, Work and Family: Critical and Comparative Perspectives* (2005).

In the *Working Hours Test Case 2002*[139] the AIRC accepted evidence of changes in working time and the generally deleterious consequences of long working hours. The AIRC also noted the wider negative impacts of long hours, such as increased public health costs and the lower productivity levels of those who are overworked. Therefore the Commission inserted a new clause into awards giving workers 'a right to refuse to work unreasonable overtime'. Determination of the reasonableness of overtime was held to require consideration of factors important to both employers and employees, including: the number of hours the employee had worked; occupational health and safety considerations; the employee's personal circumstances and especially family responsibilities; the needs of the workplace; the notice period given; and any other relevant issues. The new clause was available to be included only in those awards with specified hours of ordinary time and provision for payment of overtime. The right to refuse unreasonable overtime was arguably already implicit in existing award provisions and, as the Commission recognised, the new clause scarcely represented any radical change.[140] However, its explicit statement was seen as providing a 'firmer basis' for workers to resist requests for excessive overtime and enabling the long-hours problem to be dealt with up front.[141] The new clause also gave paid breaks to those who had worked extreme hours: identified as 60 hours per week or 26 days over a 4-week period; 54 hours per week or 51 days over an 8-week period; or 48 hours per week or 74 days over a 12-week period.

In the *Working Hours Test Case 2002* the AIRC was not asked to, nor did it, impose any limit on the maximum number of hours that could be worked. However, it rejected the ACTU's submission to incorporate a test of reasonableness into the definition of working hours, because it considered that would undermine the concept of 'ordinary hours' incorporated in most awards and thereby diminish the advantages of certainty and predictability such provisions had for workers and employers.[142] Nor did the *Working Hours Test Case* 2002 deal with the problem of unpaid overtime.

The AFPCS on maximum ordinary hours of work[143]

The *Work Choices Act* introduced for the first time a federal legislative standard on the maximum ordinary hours of work. It applies to all federal employees. Under that standard now incorporated in the *Workplace Relations Act* an employee cannot be required, or indeed requested, to work more than 38 hours per week plus reasonable additional hours: s 226(1). However, it is permissible for an employer and employee to agree in writing to average these hours (including the hours for periods of authorised leave) over a period of up to 12 months: s 226(1)(9)(ii). This agreement may be contained in a workplace agreement or award binding the employer and employee, or they may agree by some other means such as in the contract of employment: s 225.

---

139 (2002) 114 IR 390.
140 See also *Metal Trades Employers Association v Boilermakers Society of Australia* (1963) 4 FLR 333, 334.
141 *Working Hours Test Case 2002*, above n 139, 465.
142 Ibid, 455–6.
143 *Workplace Relations Act*, Pt 7 Div 3 ss 223–6.

What is most striking about the AFPCS working-time standard is the length of the averaging period. The potential to annualise working hours intensifies both the advantages and disadvantages of this form of flexibility. Averaging working hours is advantageous to business because it allows better matching of work schedules to market demands and thereby can reduce labour costs. The payment of penalty rates may be eliminated if periods of 'overtime' are counterbalanced by periods of 'undertime'.

From the employees' perspective there can also be advantages in this form of working-time flexibility. Some employees relish an opportunity to intensify periods at work and hence also for non-work activities, especially if the new hours suit their needs to balance work and family. But in practice averaging does not always work in that way. More often it means that workers have to be available for work at times that suit the needs of the business, and usually over a much great spread of hours with less predictability and for no extra return. Under the AFPCS there are no imposed limits on the number of hours that could be worked in a day, or over a week or a month etc. In addition, the penalty rates premia for working unsocial, as well as long, hours is at best reduced and often disappears altogether with averaging. Thus many employees lose the 'overtime' payments they have relied upon in the past to supplement their income. With averaging the prospect of working 'overtime' only ever emerges towards the latter part of an averaging period, because with averaging one of the goals of employers is to eliminate 'overtime'. Depending on the method of payment of wages, the averaging of working time may also mean that even those workers who do not work 'overtime' may be subject to fluctuations in weekly income having a significant impact on their capacity to pay for housing, food or essential services. Under the AFPCS working-time standard it is possible, at least in theory, for a 'fulltime' employee not to work at all (and perhaps not get paid) for six months and then to work 72 hours per week for the next six months (and get paid a double amount for the period). Even a much less extreme example can impact significantly on workers. In addition, the AFPCS on annual leave and personal leave provides that the accrual rate for those entitlements is based on the nominal hours worked not the hours actually worked after averaging so there can be a mismatch that effectively results in some loss of entitlements.

The potential to control any negative effects from the averaging of hours under the AFPCS rests entirely on the parameters governing the averaging of ordinary time working hours and related matters (payment period, notice of actual hours to be worked etc) contained in the written agreement between an employer and employee. The agreement is absolutely critical to the degree of protection the AFPCS working-time standard affords to the employee (and of course the degree of flexibility it offers to business). Where an employee is agreeing on an individual basis with their employer—perhaps through an Australian Workplace Agreement (AWA) or an ordinary common law agreement—they may be quite vulnerable and experience an overwhelming pressure to 'agree' with any terms their employer presents. Certainly this can be the case where the agreement is incorporated in the offer of employment, and there is no real 'agreement' at all in an employer greenfields agreement.

Where agreement is in a collectively negotiated workplace agreement or an award, there may be stronger protections for employees. The averaging of ordinary time hours can still be incorporated in awards because 'ordinary time hours of work and the times within which they are performed, rest breaks, notice periods and variations to working hours' remains an allowable matter, with the usual exclusion of AFPCS matters from awards not extending to working time: ss 513(1)(a) and 516(2). Some awards will already contain averaging arrangements for ordinary working time. However, where awards provide for averaging agreements under a facilitative provision, this necessarily now refers to an agreement with an individual worker because the *Work Choices* amendments prohibit any proviso of majority agreement: s 521. Even collective workplace agreements may not offer long-term protection to employees because if such an agreement is later terminated the award terms on ordinary hours will lapse because they are not protected terms and thereafter, absent another workplace agreement, the AFPCS will be the only applicable standard for the employee: s 399.

Under the AFPCS ordinary working time standard, an employee may also be requested and required to work 'reasonable additional hours': s 226(1)(b). Such an obligation has long been recognised both at common law as part of an employee's duty of cooperation with their employer and in awards and agreements. Prior to the *Work Choices* amendments, the longstanding practice in Australia under awards and later agreements was for hourly paid employees to be paid penalty rates for any 'overtime' work. However, there is no statement in the AFPCS standard about the rate of pay applicable to the 'additional' hours, and because the standard addresses 'maximum *ordinary* hours of work', absent provisions to the contrary in workplace agreements or awards it is will be open for payment to be made at the ordinary rate.

The reasonableness of any request or requirement to work additional hours is determined under the AFPCS standard by reference to all relevant circumstances: s 226(4). These include, but are not limited to, a list of factors that the statute itemises: the risks to the employee's health and safety; the employee's personal and family circumstances, the operational requirements of the business; the period of notice given by the employer; the notice of refusal by the employee; whether work is on a public holiday; and the hours worked by the employee over the previous four weeks. These are similar to the factors identified by the AIRC in the *Working Hours Test Case 2002* but whereas there they measured the reasonableness of a refusal to work overtime, under the AFPCS the test of reasonableness is attached to the employer's request and requirement.

Finally, the very concept of 'reasonable *additional* hours' is one that is rendered almost meaningless when ordinary hours of work are not fixed in some way. When hours are averaged the idea that time is *additional* to ordinary time only makes sense at the end of the averaging period. There is no test of *reasonableness* to constrain the agreement between the employer and the employee about the period of, and terms governing, the averaging hours under the standard. Reasonableness only becomes an issue *after* the averaged hours have all been worked. The employer who is quite sophisticated in planning working hours to meet the demands of the market may be less likely in any event to require employees to work additional time.

From the above it can be seen that the implementation of the AFPCS working-time standard may mean that one dimension of the long-hours problem, so acute in recent years, may diminish if not disappear altogether. However, the long-hours problem was never simply one about the total number of hours worked. As the AIRC recognised in the *Working Hours Test Case 2002*, the relationship between long working hours and family life is complex and not always negative because the opportunity to work longer hours often means more pay and thus reduces economic stress on families.[144] If workers cannot manage to live decently on the rate of pay for so-called 'ordinary' hours there is always pressure to work more even for 'ordinary' rates of pay. The pressure to work long hours may continue to be exacerbated by the focus on productivity and efficiency in the new economy even despite a widespread adoption of averaging. The long-hours problem is also about unsocial work hours and the impact of working time on family and community life. A flexible, averaged hours standard such as that established by the AFPCS destabilises the old working-time norms, breaks down the distinction between 'fulltime' and 'part-time' work, undermines the notion of a 'normal' working day or week, and in the process changes a wide range of norms underpinning family and community life.

Annual leave

Paid annual leave is one of the most fundamental modern standards attaching to work. Originally annual leave was given only to some workers as a reward for good service, but over time annual leave standards came to recognise that all workers need regular breaks from the workplace to relax and refresh because they are human persons not machines. The entitlement to annual leave ensured that the break away from the workplace did not jeopardise the security of the worker's attachment to the labour market. Most importantly the annual leave break developed as a period of paid leave. Because for most people work is their means to economic survival an entitlement only for unpaid leave would have rendered it an illusory benefit. So basic is the entitlement to annual leave that it has been established in State legislation[145] as well as in awards and workplace agreements. Now there is also an AFPCS annual leave entitlement.

The evolution of the annual leave standard

The widespread enjoyment of paid annual leave is relatively recent. Only in the 1930s and 1940s did workers become entitled to one or two weeks of paid leave. This was further extended in the early 1960s to three weeks, and only in the 1970s did the

---

144 *Working Hours Test Case 2002*, above n139, 437.

145 See *Annual Holidays Act 1944* (NSW); *Industrial Relations Act 1999* (Qld), Ch 2 Pt 1 Div 3; *Fair Work Act 1994* (SA), s 71 and Sch 4; *Industrial Relations Act 1984* (Tas), s 61F(2)(a); *Workplace Relations Act 1996* (Cth), former s 500, Sch 1A, cl (1)(a)—formerly applicable in Victoria; and *Minimum Conditions of Employment Act 1993* (WA), ss 8 and 23–6.

period of four weeks become more widely adopted.[146] Under award provisions workers could usually elect when they would take their annual leave provided that agreement was reached with their employer, although in some industries annual holidays for all employees were scheduled at times to suit the needs of industry. From the 1970s awards also often included an 'annual leave loading' payment, usually of 17.5 per cent, an entitlement originally gained in recognition of the fact that many workers regularly worked overtime and would be economically disadvantaged if their pay reverted to the ordinary rate during their annual leave period.[147] In many instances an entitlement to annual leave only became available after one full year of service was completed, but thereafter usually accrued in proportion to the time worked. The entitlement to annual leave was always cumulative. Casuals were not entitled to paid annual leave.

The initial rationale for annual leave suggested that the opportunities it afforded for refreshment were likely to be maximised when the worker had the chance to take a sustained break from the workplace. Thus initially the leave accrued and was usually taken, as its name implied, once a year. However, in more recent times other pressures began to force a change in the way annual leave was utilised: business wanted more flexibility, and job insecurity meant workers were often reluctant to absent themselves from work on annual leave. In addition, taking annual leave in one or even two large periods did not always accommodate the reality of workers' lives where many were trying to manage the ongoing demands of work and family. In 1994, the *Family Leave Test Case* provided that five days of annual leave could be taken in single days for the purpose of facilitating a balance between work and family.[148] In the *Working Hours Test Case 2002* an application by the Australian Chamber of Commerce and Industry (ACCI) to allow all annual leave to be taken in single days was not granted by the AIRC, which ruled that no evidence had been provided that the system was not working well.[149] Nonetheless, many workplace agreements began to incorporate these more flexible arrangements for leave taking. This trend is picked up in the AFPCS on annual leave.

The AFPCS on annual leave[150]

The provisions of the *Workplace Relations Act* setting out the AFPCS on annual leave provide that all federal employees, except casuals, accrue annual leave for every four weeks of completed service with an employer that is equivalent to 1/13 of the hours worked during that period: s 232(2). Regular shift workers, that is, employees working in a business where shifts are rostered over 24 hours and seven days per week and who regularly work those shifts including on Sundays and public holidays, accrue an extra 1/52 of the hours worked over a year: ss 228 and 232(3). Thus the AFPCS is

---

146 See eg *Annual Holidays Act 1944* (NSW); and *Printing Trades Case* (1936) 36 CAR 738; *Judgment re Annual Leave* (1945) 55 CAR 595; *Annual Leave Case* (1963) 103 CAR 637; and *Annual Leave Cases 1971* (1972) 144 CAR 528.

147 *Annual Holidays Loading Case* (1974) 16 AILR 160.

148 *Family Leave Test Case November 1994* (1994) 57 IR 121.

149 *Working Hours Test Case 2002*, above n 139.

150 *Workplace Relations Act*, Pt 7 Div 4 ss 227–38.

equivalent to four weeks' annual leave per year for those working 38 hours per week, plus an extra week for regular shift workers. Annual leave is calculated by reference to the 'nominal hours worked': see s 229. These are the number of hours of work per week specified in the employee's contract (which may in practice be averaged), but does not include any periods of leave not counting for service (such as parental leave) or time taken on industrial action (see s 507). If the number of hours worked by a fulltime worker are nowhere specified the default number set by the legislation is 38 hours. All annual leave accrues on a pro-rata basis: s 234. Thus, if an employee is a 'part-time worker' for part of a month and a 'fulltime worker' for the other part, leave is calculated accordingly, or if an employee works as a regular shift worker for only part of the year then additional leave is apportioned on that basis. Importantly annual leave does not break the continuity of and counts towards an employee's service, except as prescribed by regulation: s 238.

Under the AFPCS annual leave accrues and must be credited to an employee on a monthly basis, while the additional allowance for regular shift work accrues and is credited on a yearly basis: s 234. An employee is entitled to take any credited leave provided their employer authorises its taking at that time: s 236. In authorising leave an employer is entitled to take account of the operational requirements of the business and the notice given by an employee, but they must not unreasonably refuse (or revoke) annual leave. In some industries there is an annual shut-down, and an employer can require employees to take any accrued annual leave during that period. However, there is otherwise under the AFPCS no minimum or maximum amount of annual leave that is to be taken. Employees may apply to take annual leave for as little as an hour, a few hours, a day, or indeed any amount of time up to the entire amount they have accrued. Thus the AFPCS allows much greater flexibility in taking annual leave than has been possible previously under many awards (or State legislation). While the increased flexibility may have some other immediate benefits to employers and to employees, such arrangements may also mean that in effect some workers give up their only sustained break from the workplace in order to accommodate other pressures in their life, such as balancing work and family.

There is no provision for an 'annual leave loading' under the AFPCS; however, it remains an allowable award matter and is also a 'protected award matter'. Under the AFPCS the employee is required to be paid at least the 'basic periodic rate of pay' that the employee is earning at the time of taking annual leave: s 235. Annual leave is cumulative: an employee who does not take annual leave does not lose it: s 234(4). Thus any annual leave that has not been taken when a worker leaves employment must be paid out. In times of workplace insecurity workers often feel under pressure not to take their annual leave although the consequences of this can be harmful to their health and wellbeing. Because employers carry forward a liability for untaken annual leave they also have an economic incentive for getting their workers to take their annual leave. Under the AFPCS an employer may direct an employee to take annual leave, but only if at the time of the direction the employee has been credited with more than two years' worth of annual leave and the employer may only direct the employee to take a maximum of one-quarter of that leave: s 236(6). For some employers accustomed to ensuring that employees take all their leave on an annual basis these provisions impose a new (and arguably unwanted) constraint.

The most controversial aspect of the AFPCS is that it allows employees to 'cash out' or forgo some of their entitlement to annual leave to a maximum of 1/26 of the hours worked per year (equivalent to two weeks' annual leave): s 233. This entitlement arises only when: the relevant workplace agreement specifically provides for it; the employee elects in writing to cash out an amount of their annual leave; the workplace agreement entitles the employee to be paid in lieu for the foregone leave at least at their basic periodic rate of pay; and the employer authorises the foregone leave. Where an employee has elected to forego some of their annual leave the AFPCS requires the employee to be paid for it 'within a reasonable period': s 233(4).

The capacity to cash out annual leave has the potential to weaken the traditional annual leave standard. The legislation tries to avert fears about this by ensuring that the cashing out of leave is at the employee's written election and by prohibiting the employer from requiring or exerting 'undue influence or undue pressure' on an employee to do so: s 233(3). Nonetheless, in the practical working out of relations these protections are not particularly strong, and in any event it is difficult for an individual to enforce such protections. Where the culture of a workplace is established as one where leave is regularly cashed out by employees it is even more difficult for an employee to resist. Of course, if a workplace agreement does not permit the practice of cashing out annual leave it can not occur. But it is difficult to oppose the inclusion of such a facility in a workplace agreement if one side in the bargaining is pressing for it, because of itself such a facility does not mandate the cashing out of annual leave. With some types of workplace agreement—especially AWAs or employer greenfields agreements—an employee would usually have little choice about agreeing to such a provision. Pressure to cash out annual leave does not necessarily come only from employers. Employees may also see this as an opportunity to generate additional income: in this way employees get to supplement their own low or inadequate pay rate, although they will find themselves in a catch-22 situation if they are wanting more income so they can finance a holiday.

In summary, under the AFPCS there is a further move towards flexibility in taking annual leave, a trend already established prior to the enactment of the *Work Choices* legislation. The capacity to cash out some annual leave was a feature of some workplace agreements prior to 2006 because of the way the old no-disadvantage test operated. The AFPCS has placed a partial brake on this trend by only permitting the cashing out of two weeks' annual leave per year. But it means that in reality the minimum standard for actual leave from the workplace is only equivalent to two weeks per year. This also overstates the position because casuals, to whom the AFPCS on annual leave does not apply, have notionally already cashed out their entitlement altogether. The standard on annual leave is thus one that may be derogated from either fully or partially. This provides little real protection to employees and undermines further the original rationale for a regular break from work. Work relations, even for employees covered by the AFPCS, are thus a little closer to being a mere commercial exchange.

Personal leave

Personal leave encompasses a range of different types of leave that in the past have been known variously as sick leave, bereavement leave and family or carer's leave. In most instances State statutes provided for some, if not all, of these forms of leave,[151] although for the most part awards (and then workplace agreements) were the main source of such entitlements in the past.

The evolution of personal leave
Sick leave

Originally paid sick leave, unlike paid annual leave, was granted to employees without any reference to the quality of the service they rendered to their employer. While workers' compensation and rehabilitation covers (in most cases) illness or injury caused by work, paid sick leave recognises that illness and injury are misfortunes that can befall a worker anywhere and the burden of it should not necessarily jeopardise the security of the worker's income or attachment to the labour market.[152] The entitlement to paid sick leave has been considered so fundamental that generally it has been (and still is) provided for in State legislation,[153] as well as in awards and agreements.

Traditionally the compendium of rights encompassed by 'sick leave' allowed a period of paid leave per annum (generally equivalent to about eight to 10 days) in case of illness or injury for fulltime workers, although the entitlement was often smaller in the first year of employment. In general, sick leave accumulated from year to year. However, given the purpose of sick leave workers were not rewarded for not using it and they were thus not usually entitled to be paid for unused sick leave when they left employment. The conditions on which sick leave could be accessed varied, but generally where absence from the workplace was greater than one day the employer could require a medical certificate to be provided. The entitlement to sick leave was included in most awards at both federal and State levels, and often in workplace agreements.

From sick leave to family leave

With changing demographics, the diversity of family types and the increased participation of women in the labour market, balancing work, family and care obligations in a way that did not jeopardise employment security became an increasingly important issue from the early 1980s. An early practical solution to some of the problems workers with care responsibilities experienced was to use their own entitlements to sick leave to mask their absence from work when caring for others. In the 1990s several test cases saw federal awards recognise and legalise this practice.

---

151 See *Industrial Relations Act 1996* (NSW), s 26; *Industrial Relations Act 1999* (Qld), Ch 2 Pt 2 Divs 1–4; *Fair Work Act 1994* (SA), ss 70–2 and Schs 3–5; *Industrial Relations Act 1984* (Tas), s 61F(2)(b); *Workplace Relations Act*, former s 500 and Sch 1A applying in Victoria; and *Minimum Conditions of Employment Act 1993* (WA), ss 19–22 and 27–8.

152 See *Australasian Meat Industry Employees Union v Metropolitan Export Abattoirs Board* (1944) 53 CAR 19, 21.

153 See above n 151.

After Australia ratified the *Workers with Family Responsibilities Convention, 1981* (*ILO C 156*) in 1990, legislation was enacted to require the AIRC to set up an inquiry into this issue unless an application for a test case on the matter was made before March 1994.[154] A family leave test case was then initiated by the ACTU. The Commission decided to deal with the issues it raised through a package of measures developed in two stages. The underlying approach to the whole question was to increase flexibility for workers primarily through the aggregation and extension of existing leave provisions. In Stage 1, the *Family Leave Test Case—November 1994*, provision was made to allow employees to access up to five days per year of their own sick leave entitlement when they needed to absent themselves from work in order to care of family members.[155] This largely formalised in law the existing practice of many workers.

Personal/carer's leave

A number of matters were left to be determined the following year.[156] In the *Personal/Carer's Leave Test Case* the Commission decided to aggregate a worker's current year entitlements to sick leave and bereavement leave thereby allowing them to access more of their paid leave entitlements for the purposes of providing care. Carer's leave could be taken in periods of less than a single day but was subject to a five-day cap. The entitlements to sick leave and bereavement leave were capped at the existing award rate, in part to address employer concerns with cost. Accumulated sick leave could be accessed for illness, carer's leave (subject to the five-day cap), or bereavement leave (subject to the relevant cap), while any untaken leave accumulated in the ordinary way as sick leave. Although the AIRC conceded that special problems not adequately covered by existing arrangements could arise, it decided not to provide a general entitlement to unpaid leave where, for instance, care was required for someone with chronic illness. However, it did not rule out dealing with this issue in the future.

In both the *Family Leave Test Case* and the *Personal/Carer's Leave Test Case* much attention was devoted to the definition of family responsibilities. Submissions variously urged coverage of responsibilities within traditional heterosexual couple families, same-sex couple families, families as more broadly understood among Indigenous peoples, and any affective relations. Undoubtedly influenced by the intervening *Family Leave Test Case* in New South Wales,[157] the AIRC ruled that the standard should be non-discriminatory and extend to same-sex relations but it framed the clause in terms of care for 'members of a worker's household' in order to protect workers' privacy.

The award standard established was thus not as comprehensive as ideally it might have been. The question of broader kinship relations was left to be determined on a case-by-case basis. The family focus was also quite limited especially as demographic changes—including the ageing population, smaller family size, and increased mobility and hence the geographic dispersion of families—all indicated that a standard that

---

154 *Industrial Relations Reform Act 1993* (Cth), s 170KAA.
155 (1994) 57 IR 121.
156 *Personal/Carer's Leave Test Case—Stage 2—November 1995* (1995) 62 IR 48.
157 *Family Leave Test Case (NSW)* (1995) 59 IR 1.

enabled workers to respond to the care needs of *any* person dependent upon them may well be needed. Friends and neighbours are often as likely as family to be responsible for caring for another.

Flexible family-friendly standards

The amalgamation under the one banner of 'personal leave' of what were previously considered to be different types of leave is one of the most interesting aspects of these test cases of the 1990s. In the *Family Leave Test Case* and the *Personal/Carer's Leave Test Case*, the AIRC also introduced 'facilitative provisions' to provide greater flexibility in the way in which employees could arrange their hours of work or take annual leave or unpaid leave.[158] Previously few awards contained specific family leave clauses, annual leave usually had to be taken in one or two periods, and sick leave was restricted to personal illness. There was little scope to use these various entitlements lawfully for care work. The new provisions allowed: up to a week of annual leave to be taken in single days; time off in lieu of overtime or the working of make-up time at the ordinary rate of pay; and a facilitative clause provided employers and employees could agree to take 'rostered days off' at any time, and in part day amounts, or perhaps bank them to be drawn down later. It was also made clear that employers could agree that employees may take additional unpaid leave to care for a family member who was ill, but the AIRC did not provide any general entitlement to unpaid leave.

The facilitative provisions reflected both the AIRC's acceptance of arguments regarding the problems for workers experiencing work and family conflict and its apprehension about the cost and financial implications of resolving that conflict. The problem of making the system respond to the great variety of individual circumstances was also dealt with by incorporating some internal flexibilities within award clauses. For example, while generally only one employee in any family or household unit would need to take personal/carer's leave it was admitted that on some occasions it might be necessary to allow two employees in a family to take leave together—thus the clause was prefaced by the words 'in normal circumstances' and it was left to the individual employer and employee to determine together what those might be.

In the *Personal/Carer's Leave Test Case* the Commission also adopted 'a positive but cautious' approach to facilitative provisions for part-time work. The caution arose out of a concern that unfairness not creep in and also because of the historic nature of these changes. In the 1990 *Parental Leave Test Case* the Commission had allowed for part-time work for up to two years following the birth or adoption of a child where the employer agreed to this. However many awards still had no general provision for part-time work. The *Personal/Carer's Leave Test Case* provided for the introduction of part-time provisions and pro-rata entitlements into awards through facilitative clauses. Generally these facilitative clauses with respect to part-time work required a majority vote regarding the determination of core working hours for all employees, the ratio of fulltime to part-time workers, and the processes for monitoring part-time work. Within this framework, hours of work and conversion from fulltime to part-time work

---

158 On facilitative provisions, see below p 340.

could then be agreed between individual employer and employee. Part-time work was thus endorsed as a mechanism to enable workers to balance family and work responsibilities.

Two years later the 1996 legislative reforms sought to eliminate restrictions on, and encourage the provision of, part-time work in federal awards.[159] The test case provisions on part-time work were seen in this context as restrictive and were removed in the award simplification process. In this process there were some other minor modifications to the test case clauses: bereavement leave was extended to cover the death of a member of the employee's household, to make uniform the eligibility criteria for all aspects of personal leave; and to enhance further the flexibility of all these entitlements, they were expressed in hours rather than days and made available to be taken in periods of less than a day.[160]

Family Provisions Test Case

The standards established in the test cases in the early 1990s remained in place for almost a decade with only minimal revision and were in most instances replicated at State level.[161] However, difficulties in accommodating work, family and care responsibilities continued to place a great strain on workers. Thus in 2003 a *Family Provisions Test Case*, focusing primarily on parental care responsibilities for children, was initiated. In early 2004 following conciliation, agreement was reached to reorganise personal leave provisions in awards. Sick leave and carer's leave were to become known respectively as 'personal leave for personal injury and illness' and 'personal leave to care for an immediate family or household member'. It was agreed that personal leave could be used even more flexibly, allowing employees to access up to 10 days paid leave per year to attend to care responsibilities. The prospect of additional accrued leave being used for care purposes was seen as a matter for agreement between employers and employees. It was agreed that workers could request unpaid 'emergency leave' where their personal paid leave entitlement was exhausted. Again the period of time was to be a matter of agreement between employers and employees but two days per occasion was a default minimum to be included in awards. Bereavement leave was once again made a separate entitlement for which workers could make application when it was needed. Importantly the conciliated agreement in the *Family Provisions Test Case* also provided that personal leave was to be extended to casuals in the sense that they became 'entitled to not be available to work, or to leave work' for care purposes although they were not paid for this period. The period to which this was to apply was also a matter for agreement between the employer and employee but a default of two days was established.

Claims seeking to protect the longer-term security of workers' connection to the labour market by providing more opportunities to work flexibly were settled by

---

159 *Workplace Relations Act*, former ss 89A(4)–(5) and 143(1C)(b).

160 *Award Simplification Decision* (1997) 75 IR 272, and *Supplementary Award Simplification Decision* AIRC, Print Q5596, 15 September 1998.

161 See eg *State Family Leave Test Case (New South Wales)* (1995) 59 IR 1; and *Re Application for Adoption of Provisions for Family Leave (South Australia)* (1995) 62 IR 403. Some States provided for family and carer's leave by legislation: eg *Industrial Relations Act 1999* (Qld), s 39.

arbitration in the *Family Provisions Test Case*. Some of these claims sought new 'rights' to family-friendly flexible mechanisms so that there would be less scope for their refusal through an exercise of managerial prerogative. They included a right to work part-time up until a child reaches school age, and to request a variation in the hours or place of work that could not be refused unreasonably. Where the request could not be accommodated, a duty was sought to be imposed on employers to investigate reasonable alternatives that could only be refused on the grounds of necessity. There was also a claim to allow employees to 'buy' further leave and to provide for the averaging of wages over a period of time as requested by the employee. In effect such measures, if approved by the AIRC, would have given employees greater rights to utilise workplace flexibility to suit their needs. The claims aimed to set in place standards that would enable workers to make transitions between periods of absence from paid employment, part-time work and fulltime work so that they could manage changes in family and care demands over the life course and at the same time maintain a secure connection to the labour market. The claims reflected developments in other industrialised countries.[162]

The arbitrated decision on these claims in the *Family Provisions Test Case* was handed down in August 2005, just prior to the introduction of the *Work Choices* amendments. As well as new 'right to request' provisions relating to parental leave,[163] parents were also granted 'a right to request' to return to work on a part-time basis so that they could also care for pre-school age children.[164] Under the standard established by the test case the employer must consider a request for part-time work from an eligible employee and can only refuse 'on reasonable grounds related to the effect on the workplace or the employer's business', including 'costs, lack of adequate replacement staff, loss of efficiency and the impact on customer service'.[165] The final orders of the AIRC required an employee wishing to return to work on a part-time basis after parental leave to provide seven weeks' written notice to the employer and required the employer to respond in writing to the request. Because the *Family Provisions Test Case* was handed down very shortly before the enactment of the *Work Choices* legislation, there was frantic activity at both Commonwealth and State level to ensure that these standards were included in awards to become 'preserved conditions' of employment after the legislation came into effect in 27 March 2006.[166]

The AFPCS on personal leave[167]

The AFPCS on personal leave incorporates guarantees relating to paid personal/carer's leave, to unpaid carer's leave, and to paid compassionate leave, and largely replicates the main aspects of this leave as it had developed in test cases. However, it does not

---

162 See esp *Employment Rights Act 1996* (UK); and H Collins 'The Right to Flexibility' in Conaghan and Rittich (eds), above n 138. See also Murray, above n 20, 328–32.

163 See below, p 325.

164 *Parental Leave Test Case* (2005) 143 IR 245; and second week of November final orders. This case is usually referred to as the *Family Provisions Test Case*.

165 Ibid, 333.

166 See also *Family Provisions Case 2005* (2005) 152 IR 364; and 152 IR 367; and *Work and Family Test Case* [2006] SAIRComm 7.

167 *Workplace Relations Act*, Pt 7 Div 5 ss 239–61.

provide the arbitrated right to request flexibility or any of the extended leave options determined in the *Family Provisions Test Case 2005*. Where personal leave is paid it is available to all federal employees except casuals, but eligible casuals are entitled to unpaid personal leave: s 239. Personal leave, whether paid or unpaid, does not break the continuity of the employee's service: ss 260(1) and 261(1). However, while paid leave counts towards service, unpaid leave does not unless so specified in the contract of service or under a law or instrument in force under a law of the Commonwealth or a State or Territory, or as prescribed by regulation: ss 260(2) and 261(2).

Personal/carer's leave includes paid sick leave, available in case of personal illness or injury of the employee, and paid and unpaid carer's leave, which can be used to attend to either a member of the employee's immediate family or household who is ill or injured or in relation to whom an unexpected emergency has arisen: s 244. For paid personal/carer's leave the AFPCS guarantees that at the end of every four weeks' service the employee will have accrued (and be credited with) an entitlement equivalent to 1/26 of the nominal hours worked: s 246. For a 'fulltime' employee this means that over a year there is an entitlement to 10 days paid personal/carer's leave. When employees take paid personal/carer's leave the employer must pay them the amount they 'would reasonably have expected to be paid' had they worked in the period: s 247.

Paid personal/carer's leave is cumulative: s 246(5). While there are no limits imposed in relation to carrying forward such leave for use as paid sick leave, the *Workplace Relations Act* imposes a significant limitation on the use of this leave for care purposes: s 249. In any one year the maximum amount of paid carer's leave is restricted to 1/26 of the nominal hours worked by the employee. Thus fulltime employees can access a maximum of 10 days paid leave for the purpose of caring for or supporting others in their immediate household or responding to emergencies in relation to them.

The AFPCS also guarantees that an employee may take unpaid carer's leave for care purposes for members of the employee's immediate family or household. However, employees are only entitled to such leave where they have exhausted all their paid personal carer's leave or any other 'authorised leave of the same type': s 252. The entitlement to unpaid care leave is restricted to two days per occasion of illness, injury or emergency, and it may be taken in an unbroken period or in separate periods to which the employee and employer agree, either in a workplace agreement or otherwise: s 250. These provisions, both in relation to payment and time restrictions, reveal the still uneasy nature of regulation at the work/family/care interface.

The entitlement to all personal/carer's leave is dependent upon compliance with the notice and document requirements of the legislation: ss 245(1)–(2), 250(2) and 253–6. The statute sets out in some detail the nature of the notice and the period ('as soon as reasonably practicable') within which it is to be provided to the employer: ss 253 and 255; and the form and content of the documentary evidence if the employer requires it: ss 254 and 256.

The legislation excuses employees where compliance with the notice and document provisions is beyond their control: ss 253(4), 254(5), 255(4) and 256(6). However, employees need to exercise great care in relation to these matters for if the employee takes this leave but then fails to comply with the notice and documentation requirements the AFPCS declares that the employee is taken not to have been entitled to the leave: ss 245(2) and 250(3). There are a number of consequences that can flow from this, including that the employee's continuity of service will have been broken by the absence from work, which can affect other entitlements.[168]

Finally, the AFPCS also provides a guarantee of two days' paid compassionate leave to spend time with a person who is a member of the employee's immediate family or household who has a personal illness that poses a 'serious threat to his or her life': s 257(1)(a). The employee is entitled to start such leave at any time while the illness or injury persists. There is also an entitlement for two days' paid compassionate leave after the death of someone in the employee's immediate family or household: s 257(1)(b). Paid compassionate leave is also dependent upon providing any evidence the employer reasonably requires: s 257(3).

While the AFPCS on personal/carer's leave incorporates for the most part the standards established in this area by award test cases over the previous decade and a half before the *Work Choices Act*, there remain significant deficiencies. The periods of leave provided are quite short and can thus only accommodate minor or short-term illness or injury or similarly minor demands for care. In the case of sickness, a worker who has worked for the same employer for a long period and accumulated unused sick leave over the period may be in a better position to cushion some of the serious impacts of not being able to attend work because of illness or injury. Even so, workers with care responsibilities are likely to have cannibalised their own sick leave by taking carer's leave during the period. In this sense the standard still reflects the law's assumption that the normative worker is 'unencumbered',[169] and also privileges those fitting the pattern of the standard worker of the industrial era. In addition, because the AFPCS on personal leave does not incorporate anything like the *Family Provisions Test Case* standards regarding a right to request greater flexibility, it does nothing to assist in a more meaningful way the maintenance of a secure hold on labour market participation over the longer life course.

Parental leave

From the 1970s the increased participation of women in the labour market focused attention on the need to ensure that employment security was not jeopardised when a new child was born or adopted into a worker's family. While there are now legislative provisions both at federal and State level enabling employees to take parental (maternity, paternity and adoption) leave,[170] award provisions established over the last three decades in a series of test cases have been at the forefront of standard setting in this area.

---

168 Cf *Taylor v Walter Fashion Pty Ltd* (1987) 54 SAIR 239.
169 See A Chapman 'Work/Family, Australian Labour Law, and the Normative Worker' in Conaghan and Rittich (eds), above n 138. See also S Berns *Women Going Backwards: Law and Change in a Family Unfriendly Society* (2002).
170 See eg *Industrial Relations Act 1996* (NSW), Ch 2 Pt 2; *Industrial Relations Act 1999* (Qld), Ch 2 Pt 2 Div 1; *Fair Work Act 1994* (SA), s 72 and Sch 5; *Industrial Relations Act 1984* (Tas), s 61F(2)(c); and *Minimum Conditions of Employment Act 1993* (WA), Pt 4 Div 6.

The evolution of parental leave
Maternity leave

Prior to the 1980s pregnancy and childbirth forced most women to leave their paid work. Only a few awards provided maternity leave for women.[171] Usually awards did not prohibit the termination of employment because of pregnancy, although if the woman resumed employment within a specified time after the birth her continuity of employment was not interrupted and there was no loss of entitlement to other benefits. State legislation was usually limited to proscribing employment for a short period after birth.[172] However, by the early 1970s there had been some developments extending protection to women in the public sector.[173]

Against this background the ACTU initiated a *Maternity Leave Test Case*, and in 1979 the Commission granted 12 months unpaid maternity leave as a test case standard for women working in the private sector.[174] This provided security of employment for eligible pregnant women workers, by prohibiting dismissal on the basis of pregnancy and childbirth and entitling them to return to their former position or, where it no longer existed, to a position as near as possible to it. The leave was unpaid although a woman could use her annual leave and long service leave during the maternity leave period provided she was not absent from the workplace for more than 52 weeks. The new standard incorporated two six-week periods of compulsory leave—one before and one after the birth—to allow the mother to recuperate and because medical evidence before the Commission indicated there was a possibility of impaired work performance during this period.

The *Maternity Leave Test Case* also established the procedures required for notifying the employer of the expected birth, the intention to take maternity leave, and its expected duration. Women were entitled to alter their intended period of leave once only, provided their employer agreed. The decision also gave the employer the right, upon the provision of 14 days notice in writing, to require the leave to commence at a certain date prior to the birth in order, to allow certainty in arranging for replacement staff. Other clauses governed the cancellation of maternity leave and the substitution of a period of special unpaid leave or sick leave where a pregnancy terminated without a live birth.

The ACTU also claimed a pregnant woman's right to transfer to a safe job. However, reluctant to interfere with management's prerogative to organise the workplace even where existing practices risked being discriminatory, the Commission was not willing to recognise this as a 'right' that a woman could assert and have enforced. It considered such a 'right' was not practicable from an industrial point of view, and instead simply reposed a discretion in the employer to facilitate a move to safe employment where a medial practitioner certified it necessary.

---

171 Eg *Bank Official's (Federal) (1963) Award* (1969) 128 CAR 215.
172 See eg *Factories, Shops and Industries Act 1962* (NSW), s 50.
173 See eg *Maternity Leave (Australian Government Employees) Act 1973* (Cth).
174 *Re Electrical Trades Union of Australia—Application to Vary Metal Industry Award 1971 re Maternity Leave (Maternity Leave Test Case)* (1979) 218 CAR 120.

In 1979 the justification for 12 months maternity leave was expressed primarily in terms of the special, biological needs of women workers and as allowing the mother adequate time to determine whether she wished to return to the workforce. Maternity leave gave women improved employment security and encouraged their career aspirations, and business also benefited through the retention of their skills.

Adoption leave

A short time later in the *Adoption Leave Test Case* the same entitlements were extended to women who adopted a child under five years of age who has not previously lived continuously with her. The Commission commented that the reasons for maintaining job security and ensuring continued participation in the paid workforce were as applicable to adopting as to natural mothers: adoption leave and maternity leave were 'indistinguishable parts of the same concept'.[175]

Parental leave

The recognition of the social importance of care for all children new to a family paved the way for the recognition of parenting responsibilities. In 1990 a test case standard for parental leave in federal private sector awards was established.[176] It provided a period of 'short' paternity leave: one week to enable men to support their spouse and take care of the family at the time of the birth, or three weeks at the time of adoption as many adoptive parents needed to travel overseas to take custody of the child. In addition, a longer period of 51 (or 49) weeks leave was made available for men who wished to become the primary carer of their new child. This paternity leave carried the same job protection as was afforded to women who took maternity leave. Parental leave thus provided a package for working parents: the period of 'short' leave was designed to be taken concurrently and recognised the different roles that parents play at the time of the birth or adoption, and the remaining period of 'long' leave could be split between them.

The *Award Simplification Decision* produced some minor modifications to the clauses developed in the previous test cases: the requirement to take six weeks' leave prior to the birth of the child was deleted as potentially discriminatory and expressed in facilitative terms, allowing leave to commence anytime within six weeks prior to the birth and permitting the employer to require a doctor's certificate of fitness for ordinary duties, and likewise if the mother elected to return to work earlier than six weeks after the birth.[177]

Parental Leave (Casuals) Test Case

Up until 2001 parental leave had not been able to be accessed by casual employees. Increasingly it was recognised that many so-called 'long-term casuals' were in reality

---

175 *Adoption Leave Case, Retail etc Shop Employees ACT Award 1983 (Adoption Leave Test Case)* (1985) 298 CAR 321, 327.

176 *Parental Leave Test Case* (1990) 36 IR 1.

177 See *Award Simplification Decision* (1997) 75 IR 272, and *Supplementary Award Simplification Decision* Print Q5596, 15 September 1998.

little different from others with 'ongoing' employment.[178] In light of this it was difficult to see why they should also not have similar workplace entitlements. The argument that the casual loading compensated for the lack of rights did not stand up to scrutiny because the loading had never been adjusted to take adequate account of many of these entitlements. Therefore in 2001 the ACTU made an application to extend parental leave to long-term casuals.[179] The application had the support of all the major employer groups (although not the Federal Government), reflecting wide social acknowledgement of the problem of the 'long-term casual' and the fact that the new entitlement would impose no additional costs on business.

The test case set a standard granting access to unpaid parental leave including a right of return to employment to 'eligible casuals' who had been employed on a regular and systematic basis for a period of 12 months, and who had an expectation of ongoing employment. The AIRC made it clear later that this meant there was no automatic flow on of the test case standard to all casuals and all awards.[180] The standard or a similar standard was soon adopted in a number of State awards, and sometimes incorporated into State legislation.[181] Access to parental leave was important in other ways for these casuals, as it is for other employees, for it could also improve their prospect for accessing other workplace rights: for instance, if leave is taken for parental leave purposes the casual's 'continuity' of employment, often a prerequisite for benefits such as long service leave, is not broken.[182]

Family Provisions Test Case 2005

The above standards remained unchanged until the *Family Provisions Test Case 2005*. The claims in this case also sought to extend the period of both short and long parental leaves. In its arbitrated decision the AIRC granted employees a right to request an extension of their existing entitlements to give them up to 24 months 'long' parental leave and eight weeks of simultaneous 'short' leave for both parents immediately after the birth of a child. Parents were required to place their request for an extension of long parental leave four weeks before the date of their intended return to work. The employer had a duty to consider such request but could refuse it on business grounds.[183] In addition, there was agreement in the earlier conciliation phase of this test case that employers had a duty to take 'reasonable steps' to inform workers who were on parental leave of any significant changes at the workplace that would impact on the position

---

178 R Owens 'The "Long Term or Permanent Casual"—Oxymoron or "a Well Enough Understood Australianism" in the Law' (2001) 27 *ABL* 118.

179 *Re Vehicle Industry—Repairs, Services and Retail—Award 1983 (Parental Leave (Casuals) Test Case)* (2001) 107 IR 71.

180 *Automative, Food, Metals, Engineering, Printing and Kindred Industries Union re Graphic Arts—General—Award 2000*, AIRC, PR928884, 19 March 2003.

181 See eg *Parental Leave (Casuals) Test Case* (2002) 110 IR 487; and *Industrial Relations Act 1999* (Qld), ss 15A and 16; and *Industrial Relations Act 1996* (NSW), ss 53 and 57 (the 24-month qualifying period was reduced to 12 months by amendment in 2001).

182 Cf *Taylor v Walter Fashion Pty Ltd* (1987) 54 SAIR 239. On long service leave see *Long Service Leave Act 1976* (ACT); *Long Service Leave Act 1955* (NSW); *Long Service Leave Act 1981* (NT); *Long Service Leave Act 1999* (Qld); *Long Service Leave Act 1987* (SA); *Long Service Leave Act 1976* (Tas); *Long Service Leave Act 1992* (Vic); *Long Service Leave Act 1958* (WA) and *Long Service Leave Order Act 1977* (WA).

183 *Family Provisions Test Case*, above n 164, 333.

to which they would return at the end of parental leave.[184] This aspect of the test case acknowledged that employees on parental leave have a vital interest in their job and that an important aspect of parental leave was assisting workers to maintain their labour force attachment.

The AFPCS on parental leave[185]

The AFPCS on parental leave retreats from the *Family Provisions Test Case 2005* standard and incorporates only provisions broadly similar to those established in the earlier test cases. The AFPCS on parental leave is detailed in 54 sections of the legislation. It divides parental leave conventionally into maternity leave, paternity leave, and adoption leave. The AFPCS applies to all federal employees including 'eligible casual employees', defined as a casual who has been engaged on a 'regular and systematic basis' for a period of at least 12 months, which may be made up of two periods provided the gap between them was not greater than three months, and who but for the expected birth or placement of a child would have a 'reasonable expectation of continuing engagement by the employer on a regular and systematic basis': s 264.[186] Employees are only eligible for parental leave if they have been employed for a continuous period of 12 months with the employer prior to the anticipated date of birth or adoption, or are eligible casual employees: ss 264(2)(b), 282(2)(b) and 300(2)(b). All parental leave provided for under the AFPCS is unpaid. While parental leave also does not break an employee's continuity of service, nor does it count for service, unless that is provided for as a term or condition of the employee's contract, or by law or instrument in force under a law of the Commonwealth, a State or Territory, or as prescribed by regulation: s 316.

The AFPCS on maternity leave

Under the AFPCS there are two different types of maternity leave: special maternity leave (SML) and ordinary maternity leave (OML). Special maternity leave may be taken by a woman who has a pregnancy related illness or whose pregnancy ends within 28 weeks of the expected date of birth otherwise than by the birth of a live child: s 265(1)(a). Ordinary maternity leave is a 'single, unbroken' period of leave taken in relation to the birth or expected birth of a child by the employee: s 265(1)(b).

The maximum period of all maternity leave is 52 weeks: s 266(3). Any period of SML is restricted to the time stated in the medical certificate accompanying the application: s 267. However, other authorised leave (for example, annual leave or long service leave) may be taken in conjunction with maternity leave. Indeed, because maternity leave under the AFPCS is unpaid it is often financially necessary for a woman to take other paid leave (eg annual leave or long service leave) if she is entitled to do so. Although there is some ambiguity in the wording of the *Workplace Relations Act*—in that arguably her authorised leave may not be taken 'because of' the pregnancy, birth etc but simply because she is entitled to it: s 266(1)—the AFPCS allows only a maximum

---

184 Ibid, 353.
185 *Workplace Relations Act*, Pt 7 Div 6 ss 262–316.
186 See also *Workplace Relations Act*, s 638(4).

of 52 weeks away from the workplace: s 266. That is, the standard operates to prevent her taking a longer period of leave from work by the addition of other different types of leave to maternity leave. In addition, her leave is further reduced by any leave (paternity or authorised) her spouse takes during the 52-week period: s 266(3)(b). Thus if some leave, say 'short' parental or annual leave, is taken simultaneously by the mother and her spouse, the period of absence from the workplace may be shorter than 52 weeks.

A pregnant woman still has no right to transfer to a safe job. During her pregnancy if the woman's doctor thinks it inadvisable for her to continue in her present position then if the employer considers it 'reasonably practicable' she can be transferred to a safe job with no other change in her terms and conditions of employment, or if not she may take leave during which she is entitled to the amount of pay she would reasonably have expected during the period: s 268.

Ordinary maternity leave may commence at any time after six weeks before the anticipated birth: s 272. If a woman wishes to continue working during the six weeks prior to birth the employer is permitted to request her to provide medical certification that she is medically fit to do so, and if it is not provided within seven days of this request she may be required by her employer to start OML: s 274. Where the pregnancy ends otherwise than by the birth of a living child a woman must take SML, unless she has already commenced OML. If a child dies after birth the woman's entitlement to OML is not affected, although her employer may cancel the OML provided four weeks' notice of the date of cancellation is given and provided this date is at least six weeks after the date of birth: s 276. If while on OML a woman stops being the primary carer of her child for a 'substantial period' and having regard to that and other relevant circumstances it is reasonable to expect she will not resume this role 'within a reasonable period', the employer may cancel her OML with four weeks' notice: s 277. Ordinary maternity leave may be extended, once by written notice provided to the employer at least 14 days prior to the end of the period of OML, and further extended by agreement between the employer and employee: s 278.

At the end of maternity-related leave a woman has a right to return to her former position, or a new position to which she either was promoted or voluntarily transferred, or to her former fulltime position if she transferred to part-time work during her pregnancy: s 280. However, if she is on OML this entitlement is dependent upon her providing her employer with a further written notice (that is, in addition to the notice implicit in her OML application) to her employer four weeks before the day of her proposed return to work: s 280(1). Where her former position no longer exists, and she is 'qualified and able to work' in another position, then she is entitled to return to work in that position, or if there are two or more such positions the one that is 'nearest in status and remuneration' to her former position: s 280(3)–(5).

The entitlement to both SML and OML depends on the employee fulfilling the documentation requirements set out in the legislation: ss 269–71. To be entitled to SML a woman must make a written application to her employer stating the first and last days of the leave, accompanied by a medical certificate confirming her pregnancy, the expected date of birth and a statement that in the opinion of the medical practitioner she is or will be unfit to work because of a 'pregnancy-related illness' for the stated period: s 269. Where her child did not survive the birth, the medical certificate must supply additional relevant information and the woman must also provide a statutory declaration that she will not engage in conduct inconsistent with her contract of employment during her leave: s 269(3).

To be entitled to OML the employee must provide her employer with a medical certificate stating that she is pregnant and the expected date of the birth at least 10 weeks prior to that expected date: s 270. Then at least four weeks before the woman wishes to take OML she must make a written application requesting OML, stating the first and last days of the period of leave, accompanied by a statutory declaration stating the first and last days of any other authorised leave she intends to take, the similar dates for any paternity or authorised leave her spouse will take, that she intends to be the primary carer of the child when on maternity leave, and that she will not engage in any behaviour incompatible with her contract of employment: s 271.

Thus the *Workplace Relations Act* specifies in some considerable detail notification and documentation requirements that, if not satisfied, can mean that the entitlement to SML or OML is not triggered. The legislation excuses failure to comply with these provisions if the reasons for it are due to 'circumstances beyond her control', and allows documents to be submitted outside the specified times but 'as soon as reasonably practicable' when the non-compliance arises from unforeseen events, such as a premature birth or other compelling reasons: ss 269(4)–(5), 270(4)–(6) and 271(3)–(4) and (6). Nonetheless, just as with personal/carer's leave it is vitally important for employees to comply with the notification and documentation provisions, because failure to do so means there is no entitlement to the leave. If in those circumstances 'leave' is actually taken this can have serious consequences for the employees: if nothing else it means that their continuity of employment will be broken, which may affect their access to other workplace entitlements, or at worst it may provide an excuse for an employer to dismiss.[187] The intersection of the law relating to termination of employment, and to discrimination, as well as understandings of the status of the contract of employment, have shown in the United Kingdom that these detailed statutory notification and documentation requirements can present a minefield for women (and men too in relation to paternity and adoption leave) and have the real potential to render their employment quite precarious if there is a failure of compliance and yet the leave has been taken.[188]

While the AFPCS does not expressly incorporate the *Family Provisions Test Case 2005* provisions into the employer's duty to communicate about significant work changes with the employee on parental leave, it is clear that the legislation assumes that the contract of employment continues during a period of maternity leave. Hence the woman employee is required to state in her application for maternity leave that she will not act in a way that is inconsistent with her contract of employment

---

187 However, termination on discriminatory grounds is unlawful. See Chapter 8.
188 See C Kilpatrick 'Gender and the Legal Regulation of Employment Breaks' in Fudge and Owens (eds), above n 122.

when on leave: ss 269(3)(b)(ii) and 271(5)(d), and equally it envisages that she may terminate her employment while on maternity leave but only by giving whatever notice she is required by law: s 279. It thus stands to reason that the employment contract remains on foot and therefore employers must not act in a way that is contrary to their contractual relation: the duty of mutual trust and confidence, for instance, would require communication with the employee on OML of any relevant changes or developments in the workplace that she should know about.[189]

AFPCS on Paternity leave

The AFPCS provides for the spouses of women who are pregnant and give birth two types of paternity leave, short paternity leave (SPL) and long paternity leave (LPL): s 282(1). Short paternity leave is a period of 'single, unbroken' leave that lasts for only one week and must be commenced in the week following the birth of a child: s 283. It may be taken concurrently with a period of maternity leave: s 284. Long paternity leave is a period of 'single, unbroken leave' that must be taken within 52 weeks of the birth of a child. The definition of 'spouse' includes both present and former spouses, whether in a married or de facto relation. However, it is also restricted to those in heterosexual relationships, because a de facto spouse is defined as 'a person of the opposite sex to the employee who lives with the employee as the employee's husband or wife on a genuine domestic basis although not legally married to the employee': s 263. The legislation thus did not grasp the opportunity to challenge the traditional constitution of the family and make the protections as inclusive as possible.[190]

The AFPCS provisions relating to paternity leave replicate in a general way (but obviously only if relevant for a male spouse) the AFPCS provisions governing maternity leave. Paternity leave is circumscribed in identical ways: it is limited to 52 weeks in total (including other related authorised leave) from which is deducted any periods when the spouse has taken leave: s 283. If the pregnancy of the employee's spouse ends in other than the birth of a living child then the employee is no longer entitled to LPL, but the entitlement to SPL already commenced is not affected: s 291. Where a child dies after birth no entitlement to paternity leave arises after this, but if the employee had commenced LPL then this can continue unless the employee is given notice to return to work: s 292. The provisions governing the end of paternity leave if the employee ceases to be the primary carer of the child, variation of LPL, termination of employment during paternity leave, and return to work after paternity leave are all parallel to those relating to maternity leave: ss 293–6. Virtually the same requirements are also imposed in relation to application, notification and documentation: ss 286–8.

AFPCS on adoption leave

The AFPCS provides for pre-adoption leave (PAL), short adoption leave (SAL) of three weeks, and long adoption leave (LAL): ss 299–300. Employees are entitled to this leave in relation to the adoption of an 'eligible child', who is under five years at the time of

---

189 Ibid, and also B Smith and J Riley 'Family-friendly Work Practices and the Law' (2004) 26 *Syd LR* 396.
190 See A Chapman 'Challenging the Constitution of the (White and Straight) Family in Work and Family Scholarship' in J Murray (ed) *Work, Family and the Law* (2005).

placement and has not lived continuously with the adoptive parent(s) for more than six months at that time, and who is not a child or stepchild of the employee or the employee's spouse: s 298.

There is provision under the statute for a two-day period of PAL in order to attend interviews or examinations to obtain approval for the adoption, although an employer may direct this time to be taken as authorised leave: s 299. On most other matters where relevant the provisions for adoption leave replicate those for both maternity and paternity leave. Thus, for example, SAL may be taken concurrently, but the maximum period of LAL is 52 weeks from which must be deducted other periods of authorised leave. Notification of the proposed adoption must be provided to the employer as soon as the employee receives a placement approval notice, but otherwise generally the documentation and notification provisions also parallel those of maternity and paternity leave: ss 304–7.

Minimum entitlement of all employees to parental leave

Under changes introduced by the *Industrial Relations Reform Act 1993* (Cth) all employees (except casual and seasonal employees) were granted parental leave rights.[191] This legislation was supported by the external affairs power and sought to give effect to the *Workers with Family Responsibilities Convention, 1981 (ILO C 156) and Recommendation, 1981 (ILO R 165)*. These provisions were repealed by the *Work Choices Act*, but it simultaneously re-enacted an identical object provision to maintain the connection to the external affairs power and applied the AFPCS parental leave standard to any other employee who is not a 'subsection [sic] 5(1) employee' providing only that if a casual the employee must come within the definition of 'eligible casual': ss 688–91.

Paid parental leave?

It is notable that the AFPCS standard on parental leave is for unpaid leave, although in the past a few awards have included an entitlement to paid leave.[192] Likewise the entitlement to paid personal/carer's leave is strictly limited to 10 non-cumulative days per year, which if used cannibalise a worker's sick leave entitlement. These standards reflect the long-held assumption in the Australian regulatory system that the costs of reproductive work are an 'externality' to the market. Thus, it is workers, and overwhelmingly female workers, who bear its costs. Where part-time work or options for 'purchased leave' are presented as the solution to work and family conflict they too involve giving up pay (and work in the marketplace). In Australia the conflict between work and family is thus generally dealt with (but never really resolved) by a (usually female) worker absenting herself from the labour market. Therefore law must assume that someone, or the state, financially supports this worker.[193]

---

191 *Industrial Relations Reform Act 1993* (Cth), Pt VIA Div 5, and Schs 13–14.
192 M Baird 'Parental Leave in Australia: The Role of the Industrial Relations System' in Murray (ed), above n 190.
193 RJ Owens 'Taking Leave: Work and Family in Australian Law and Policy' in Conaghan and Rittich (eds), above n 138; and R Owens 'Reproducing Law's Worker: Regulatory Tensions in the Pursuit of "Population, Participation, and Productivity"' in Arup et al (eds) *Labour Law and Labour Market Regulation* (2006).

In relation to maternity leave, the AFPCS does not meet the internationally recognised standard of 14 weeks' paid leave.[194] Paid maternity leave is critical to the recognition of women's equality and especially their right to participate in paid employment. (This is consistent with acknowledging that paid parental leave, or even better paid leave for any worker who is a primary carer to a young child, would encourage even greater equality.) The intense debate that has taken place in recent years in Australia over paid maternity leave has been conducted outside the labour law system under the auspices of the Sex Discrimination Commissioner as part of the Human Rights and Equal Opportunity Commission (HREOC). HREOC's reports anticipated overwhelming resistance if the costs of maternity leave were transferred to employers in the marketplace.[195] HREOC's proposal, for a scheme funded by government and providing a payment to women in paid work for 14 weeks capped at a rate equivalent to the minimum wage, was not endorsed by the main political parties. Ultimately government policy settled on a welfare-style flat rate payment ($3000 when introduced in 2004) to be made to *all* women at the time of birth. While the maternity payment recognises the social contribution of women's reproductive work it does not acknowledge any connection between reproductive and productive labour nor does it encourage women's labour market participation. It thus highlights the convergence of the safety net with welfare entitlements and the different policy goals that attach to the law providing for basic standards in paid work and welfare law. Labour law has effectively said in this area welfare is the only safety net and the only alternative option to increasing protection is through workplace bargaining. This issue thus provides an acute point of debate as to the role of minimum standards in the new economy.

Minimum entitlement — meal breaks[196]

The *Work Choices Act* inserted into the *Workplace Relations Act* provisions setting a statutory minimum entitlement to a meal break. The Act prohibits federal employers from requiring an employee to work for longer than five hours without providing them with an unpaid meal break of at least half an hour: s 607. However, if the employee's terms and conditions of work are regulated by an award, a workplace agreement, or an industrial instrument prescribed by regulation, this meal break entitlement is not applicable: s 608 and r 12.1.

Minimum entitlement — public holidays[197]

The *Workplace Relations Act* also contains a standard in relation to public holidays introduced by the *Work Choices Act*. It provides a federal employee with an entitlement to take a day off work on a public holiday: s 612. The public holidays include the

194 See *UN Convention on the Elimination of All Forms of Discrimination against Women*, and *Maternity Protection Convention, 2000* (ILO C 183).

195 See HREOC, *Pregnant and Productive: It's a Right Not a Privilege to Work while Pregnant* (1999); *Valuing Parenthood: Options for Paid Maternity Leave: Interim Paper* (2002); and *A Time to Value: Proposal for a National Paid Maternity Leave Scheme* (2002).

196 *Workplace Relations Act*, Pt 12 Div 1 ss 607–10.

197 *Workplace Relations Act*, Pt 12 Div 2 ss 611–19.

so-called 'iconic' public holidays of New Year's Day, Australia Day, Good Friday, Easter Monday, Anzac Day, Christmas Day and Boxing Day, and other days declared as public holidays in the States or Territories, but not days substituted for those listed above nor union picnic days or other days excluded by regulation: s 611.

However, this entitlement is qualified because an employer may still request an employee to work on a public holiday and the employee is only entitled to refuse if there are reasonable grounds for doing so: ss 612(2)–(3) and 613. Workplace agreements or awards cannot override this right to refuse on reasonable grounds to work on a public holiday: s 612(4). All relevant factors are to be considered in determining the reasonableness of a refusal, including those listed in the legislation such as the nature of the employment, the employee's reasons and family circumstances, whether there is an entitlement to additional remuneration, and the amount of notice provided: s 613.

The legislation prohibits employers from retaliating against an employee because of a reasonable refusal to work on a public holiday: threatening or taking action either to dismiss such employees, or to injure them in their employment, or to alter their position to their prejudice is unlawful: s 615. Court action seeking a civil penalty and/or compensation in relation to such behaviour may be initiated by a workplace inspector, an affected employee, or trade union to which the employee belongs, and while the applicant bears the burden of proving the reasonableness of the refusal to work, it is the defendants who must prove they did not act for the prohibited reason: ss 616 and 617.

Superannuation

Standards governing superannuation play a significant role in ensuring access to a decent standard of living for workers after, and now often towards the end of, their paid working lives. Thus one of the most important basic work standards in Australia today requires employing businesses to make contributions to their employees' superannuation. Superannuation schemes operate through the mechanism of a trust that manages contributed funds so that on retirement or semi-retirement, usually because of age but sometimes as a result of disability, the former worker is entitled to a lump sum or annuity pension. Until the 1980s there was an ad hoc character to the development of superannuation schemes in Australia, after a number of unsuccessful attempts to establish a national scheme funded by compulsory contributions from earnings.[198] From the mid-1980s superannuation became a focus both of industrial relations agenda as well as an important aspect of national policy.

Historically the insertion in awards of clauses relating to employer-contributed pensions had been doubtful.[199] However, in the mid-1980s the High Court ruled that payments by employers on behalf of their employees into existing superannuation trust funds were matters directly pertaining to employment relations and thus could be regulated by awards.[200] A short while later claims requiring employers to use their best endeavours

198 See D Paatsch and G Smith 'The Regulation of Australian Superannuation: An Industrial Relations Perspective' (1992) 5 *CBLJ* 131 and (1993) 6 *CBLJ* 29.
199 *R v Hamilton Knight; Ex parte Commonwealth Steamship Owners' Association* (1952) 86 CLR 283.
200 *Re Manufacturing Grocers Employees Federation of Australia; Ex parte Australian Chamber of Manufacturers* (1986) 160 CLR 341.

to secure a certain form of superannuation trust fund for their employees were also recognised as matters pertaining to the employment relation.[201] Subsequently, however, the High Court also held that a claim by a trade union to stipulate the identity of the superannuation fund to be utilised by non-trade unionists did not qualify as such a 'matter' and therefore could not be incorporated into an award clause.[202] These principles continue to govern the inclusion of superannuation matters in workplace agreements.[203]

With confirmation in the *Manufacturing Grocers' Case* that the Commission had the jurisdiction to deal with superannuation, a claim was fashioned as part of the Accord Mark II for a 3 per cent superannuation payment instead of a wage rise in return for productivity increases in the *National Wage Case* in 1986.[204] The Commission rejected this at first and made any such payments dependent upon agreement between the parties. However, some months later it issued a 'Statement of Principles relating to Superannuation' and in the following year decided that it would arbitrate in relation to superannuation where agreement on the matter was not reached.[205] Thus 3 per cent employer contribution to superannuation was established for most federal award employees as a substitute for salary increases. The rejection of a claim for a further 3 per cent increase in employer contributions to employees' superannuation by the Commission in 1991[206] precipitated wider policy debate and legislative intervention.

Although there was some federal legislation regulating superannuation from the 1980s, important legislative changes were made in 1992 and these are the foundation of the current regime.[207] The *Superannuation Guarantee Charge Act 1992* (Cth) and the *Superannuation Guarantee (Administration) Act 1992* (Cth) establish a system whereby employers are required to contribute to superannuation funds a percentage (which rose from 3 per cent in 1992 to 9 per cent by July 2002) of the 'ordinary time earnings' of their employees. This legislation applies in relation to most employees, although there were some exceptions, for example those earning less than $450 per month, those working fewer than 30 hours per week and those under 18 years of age or over 70 years, and certain non-resident employees. The legislation is supported by the taxation power, s 51(ii) of the *Australian Constitution*, and so employers incur a liability to pay tax if they fail to make superannuation contributions.

Since 1992 there have been further legislative enactments in the area.[208] These provided federal award employees with a choice as to their superannuation funds meaning they can be no longer required to use a particular superannuation fund. Choice

---

201 *Re Amalgamated Metal Workers Union of Australia; Ex parte Shell Co of Australia Ltd* (1992) 174 CLR 345.
202 *Re Finance Sector Union of Australia; Ex parte Financial Clinic (Vic) Pty Ltd* (1993) 178 CLR 352.
203 See further Chapter 11.
204 *National Wage Case June 1986* (1986) 14 IR 187.
205 *National Wage Case March 1987* (1987) 17 IR 65.
206 *National Wage Case April 1991* (1991) 36 IR 120.
207 See *Superannuation Guarantee Act 1992* (Cth); *Superannuation Guarantee (Administration) Act 1992* (Cth), esp ss 15, 19, 20 27(2) and 28; and *Superannuation Guarantee Charge Act 1992* (Cth).
208 See esp *Superannuation (Government Co-contribution for Low Income Earners) Act 2003* (Cth); *Superannuation (Government Co-contribution for Low Income Earners)(Consequential Amendments) Act 2003* (Cth); *Superannuation Legislation Amendment (Choice of Superannuation Funds) Act 2004* (Cth); *Superannuation Budget Measures Act 2004* (Cth); and *Superannuation Legislation Amendment (Abolition of Surcharge) Act 2005* (Cth). For detail of superannuation standards see CCH *Australian Superannuation Law and Practice*, vols 1–2.

of superannuation funds has been promoted as an important aspect of facilitating portability between funds, something that is particularly important where employees are changing jobs frequently or holding several jobs simultaneously, as well as having advantages of eliminating the duplication of administrative fees.

Some aspects of superannuation policy have been quite controversial: for example, an additional surcharge was for a time imposed on high-income earners as an equity measure but it was also criticised as a disincentive for retirement savings. In addition, as a means of encouraging more people to improve their superannuation it has been made financially advantageous to make contributions to a spouse's superannuation, and a small government subsidy is provided for contributions to superannuation by low-income earners. People are also assisted to make contributions to their superannuation fund even when they are not working, and recent changes enable people to access part of their super funds if they reduce their time working (and their income from work) as they move closer to retirement.

Such is the importance of this superannuation regime that up until 2005 the AIRC was required to have regard to it in making *National Wage Case* or *Safety Net Review* decisions.[209] In the *Superannuation Test Case—September 1994* the Commission made clear that its role with respect to superannuation was to ensure that awards were consistent with the requirements of federal legislation.[210] Once federal awards became only a safety net of minimum terms and conditions they tended to provide little in addition to the legislative entitlements. The logic of continuing to include clauses regulating superannuation in awards was therefore challenged, especially as the taxation power enables comprehensive national legislation on the topic.[211]

It was thus not surprising that the *Work Choices Act* introduced changes so that since 27 March 2006 superannuation has no longer been a matter allowed to be included in awards although it can remain a preserved award entitlement until 30 June 2008: s 527(5). From that date superannuation payments are to be calculated on 'ordinary time earnings' as defined in the *Superannuation Guarantee Act*. This may eliminate some of the issues that have arisen previously regarding the intersection of award provisions and the legislation.[212] Superannuation continues to be a matter that may be included in workplace agreements, but from 1 July 2008 the Commonwealth *Superannuation Guarantee* legislation will set the basic standards in this area.

The importance of superannuation also illustrates the changing nature of the intersection between work and welfare. In the industrial era there was an assumption that the state would provide for those who were not in paid work. Certainly the provision of pensions through employer or industry plans was comparatively rare before the middle of the twentieth century. Now, with the ageing of the population, the anticipated future diminution of government revenue from taxation and decline in the capacity to provide publicly funded pensions, occupational superannuation has become

209 *Workplace Relations Act 1996* (Cth), former s 90A introduced in 1992.
210 (1994) 55 IR 447.
211 See the failed *Workplace Relations Amendment (Superannuation) Bill 1997* (Cth).
212 *Australian Communication Exchange Ltd v Deputy Commissioner of Taxation* (2003) 201 ALR 271.

the cornerstone of national retirement policy in Australia. The idea that all individuals make provision through their productive working life for the years of retirement when they are no longer able to work also fits well with and reinforces neo-liberal values of independence and self-sufficiency that are dominant in the new economy.

While superannuation has become an important workplace standard, it is also one that raises important issues of equity. A decent standard of retirement income through superannuation usually depends on the length of time in waged work as well as the level of income. Superannuation also represents foregone income and poorer workers are less able to benefit from this compulsory form of saving. Therese MacDermott has shown that legislative and regulatory structures have not dealt well with the systemic and structural inequality of women in this area.[213] Many historical factors explain why women's superannuation remains considerably lower than that of men: superannuation spread industry by industry from the 1980s but not initially into areas where women's employment predominated; the exemption of superannuation from the *Sex Discrimination Act 1984* (Cth) was not removed until 1994; the classes of exclusion from employer obligation that were originally allowed were more likely to affect lower-paid workers, predominantly women; and because superannuation benefits are tied to paid work, breaks in the continuity of employment, women's overrepresentation in casual and part-time employment, and problems of pay equity all translate into lower superannuation benefits. The present superannuation subsidies available to low-income workers and the provision of spousal contributions is likely to make little real impact on the retirement prosperity of those who have not had a long history of employment at a relatively decent wage, a problem of increasing dimensions with the proliferation of non-standard forms of work.

The role of work standards in the new economy

Work standards and the standard worker

Work standards commonly perform a number of functions in the law of work. Understanding these roles, and the relation, intersection or hierarchy between them, cannot be separated from an examination of the workers who benefit (or are excluded) from work standards. The 'standard' worker is, as Anthony O'Donnell and others have observed, a 'regulatory pivot'.[214] This is law's normative worker, the one with the characteristics that 'fit' the eligibility requirements of law's standards and who therefore enjoys them most completely. There is a reflexiveness between standards and the construction of law's normative worker. Work standards constitute the standard worker as one who needs certain types of paid or unpaid leave, as one who works a certain length of time whether over hours, days, weeks or years. Traditionally this standard worker was a male, working in a secondary industry (such as the metal trades, building and construction and transport) where there was a strong trade union presence.

---

213 T MacDermott 'Linking Gender and Superannuation' (1997) 2 *Int J Discrimination and Law* 271.
214 See A O'Donnell '"Non-Standard" Workers in Australia: Counts and Controversies' (2004) 17 *AJLL* 89, n 2.

But the needs of the workers of the old economy may be quite different from those in the new economy. As the binary divide between 'standard' and 'non-standard' worker breaks down in the new economy there is renewed debate about the place of standards in the law of work. The growth of non-standard work can be seen as a conscious move to avoid work standards, and standards reinforce this by exempting those in non-standard work. Thus awards under *Work Choices* cannot include provisions regulating the conditions of labour-hire workers or independent contractors (which may include dependent contractors): s 515(1)(g)–(h). When fewer and fewer workers are covered by work standards the role of those standards is further questioned.

A statistical picture of workers and work standards reveals that about one-fifth of workers are directly dependent upon awards to set their pay and that this is the case for women more so than it is for men (in 2002, 26 per cent women compared with 15 per cent of men relied on awards to set their pay). Those dependent upon minimum wages are more likely to be low-skilled workers, in positions such as clerical or service work, and there are a higher proportion of them working in the accommodation, café and restaurant industry than in any other industry, but followed closely by the health and community services sector and the retail sector. In recent years the proportion of workers entitled to paid annual leave and paid sick leave has been diminishing: about four-fifths of men now have access to these benefits compared with a little more that two-thirds of women. However, 90 per cent of employees do have superannuation provided by their employer.[215]

In order to know which workers are covered by particular legislative or award standards a careful examination of the relevant instrument is always required. Only the class of workers defined by the relevant statute or award will enjoy the standards it establishes. Many of the standard terms and conditions applicable to public sector workers, for instance, are established in specific legislation.[216] Care is also needed in assessing access to work standards because the same word may be used differently in different legal instruments or even different sections of the same instrument. There can be 'disjunctions between vernacular, contractual and regulatory vocabularies' in describing certain workers—as indeed there is the case of 'casual' workers.[217] Often too a legal instrument will impose additional eligibility criteria, such as a certain length of time in the service of one employer or an expectation of ongoing employment with that employer, limiting further the access to particular work standards.

Generally federal statutory work standards discussed in this chapter are restricted to certain employees. Most awards make provision for three basic types of employment: fulltime, part-time and casual.[218] While the 'fulltime' employee has 'full' enjoyment of the standards in the award, the part-time employee enjoys its benefits on a pro-rata basis according to the proportion of hours worked when compared to those worked by the fulltimer. However, some State awards still restrict not only the minimum but

---

215 The preceding statistics are taken from ABS, *Year Book Australia: Labour—Earnings and Benefits*, 2004. See also above n 60 and n 120.

216 See eg above n 173.

217 See O'Donnell, above n 214, 101.

218 See *Award Simplification Decision* (1997) 75 IR 272.

also the maximum number of hours a part-timer employee can work. The other major classification found in awards is that of a 'casual'. The definition adopted by the federal Commission in the *Award Simplification Decision* was that 'a casual employee is an employee engaged as such'. Finally, awards also often make provision for other classes of workers, such as apprentices and juniors who are often entitled to some modified form of standards.

The protective function of work standards

The debate over work standards cannot be divorced from their purposes. In standard setting there are usually at play a range of regulatory rationales, usually hierarchically organised with some purposes identified as more prominent and important than others. These rationales can be complimentary, but sometimes too they conflict leaving a place in which political contest thrives and transformative possibilities are presented. This is certainly the case in Australia.

One of the most important roles of the law of work is its protective function. In the nineteenth century Australian factory legislation, like its British predecessor, was enacted to protect vulnerable groups of workers. The emergence of work standards represented, among other things, a policy determination by the state to set a baseline for decent work conditions. With the gradual shift to a contractual understanding of work relations, work standards were understood increasingly as a counterbalance to the superior bargaining power of capital: the standards were to protect vulnerable workers but did not prevent more favourable agreed terms and conditions. Work standards in this sense have always constituted minimum standards.

Where the main purpose of work standards is protective then much of the focus of law ought to ensure effective coverage of vulnerable workers. But as we have seen some workers, such as labour-hire workers, may be treated differently. The geographic isolation in which outworkers labour and the complex contractual chains through which their work relations are structured exacerbate their vulnerability and have prompted special legislative provisions to ensure they are recognised as employees,[219] and in some jurisdictions, innovative combinations of statutes, awards and codes of conduct to provide them with a real access to the protection of basic standards.[220]

However, in the new economy there has been a massive growth of certain groups of workers, who are routinely excluded by both statute and awards from basic work standards. Casuals are the most notable of these. The payment of a monetary 'loading', long a feature of casual work under awards, is often said to compensate for their exclusion from basic work standards. The origins of the loading indicate that it was at first a compensatory supplement for casual male workers whose work did not provide a breadwinner's wage. Secondly, it was intended to deter employers who might use casual employment to deny workers their proper entitlements. Only later did its function as compensatory exchange for rights and entitlements forgone come

---

219 See eg *Industrial Relations Act 1999* (Qld), s 5(1)(g), and *Fair Work Act 1994* (SA), s 5.
220 See above n 3.

more to the foreground.[221] The casual loading rarely fulfils any of these functions effectively.[222] Even if casual loadings provided adequate compensation, the 'cashing out' of basic standards that it represents detracts from their function in protecting vulnerable employees: casual loading arrangements are publicly sanctioned private individual bargains to buy out basic standards. The increasing resistance to the growth of casual labour at the expense of decent part-time work is a recognition that workers often agree to work casually because they have no other option.[223]

Of particular concern has been the position of so-called 'long-term casuals' because the reality of their work lives differs little from that of many others with 'ongoing' employment and hence they are now granted some basic rights in the workplace, such as unpaid carer's leave and unpaid parental leave. This is important because access to parental leave may also improve their access to other workplace rights: for instance, if leave is taken for parental leave purposes the casual's 'continuity' of employment, often a prerequisite for benefits such as long service leave, may not be broken.[224]

However, many of the regulatory efforts to extend the protection of work standards to vulnerable workers depend on assimilating them to a model of the standard worker of the old economy. In the federal arena there remain traces of law's old reticence to provide for outworkers because their access to federal award standards is limited to ensuring that 'their overall conditions of employment are fair and reasonable in comparison with the conditions of employment specified in a relevant award or awards for employees who perform the same kind of work at an employer's business or commercial premises': s 513(1)(o).[225] If there is no old economy comparator they get no protection. Dependent contractors are sometimes excluded from employee status except where they perform the vast proportion of their work for a single business. Their regulation also carries traces of the traditional employment relation of the standard old economy worker. It excludes from law's protection dependent contractors whose work arrangements are more closely analogous to those of the casual worker who has a number of precarious jobs. The problem is illustrated particularly well in relation to casuals. Casuals are offered protection where they have been in an employment relation for a long time and when they expect it to continue. Yet short-term casuals who can never find work lasting for more than a few weeks at a time are excluded. The distinction between long-term and short-term casuals is inevitably arbitrary and the drawing of regulatory lines on this basis invites employment practices designed to avoid responsibility for according workers the protection of work standards. Given the availability of intermediary structures, such as labour-hire firms, through which to organise casual work this is easy to achieve.

---

221 See *Re Metal, Engineering and Associated Industries Award 1998—Part I* (2002) 110 IR 247.

222 Ibid. See also B Pocock, J Buchanan, and I Campbell *Securing Quality Employment: Policy Options for Casual and Part-time Workers* (2004), available at <www.chifley.org.au>.

223 Ibid.

224 See above n 182.

225 See also *Workplace Relations Act*, former s 89A(2)(t), and *Conditions of Employment (Allowable Matters)/The Clothing Trades Award 1982* (1999) 45 AILR 4-029.

In the new economy it is essential to disengage protection and the promise of decent work from its dependency on the employment relation of old. If protection continues to be offered to workers who look most like the standard worker in the old economy then the system is likely to become increasingly dysfunctional. Access to work standards needs to be linked more to participation in the labour market than a certain model of relationship that is steadily disappearing. The old focus on the employment relation also individualises vulnerability, discouraging a wider examination of the systemic features of the organisation of work and an understanding of the importance of the dignity of labour and therefore of the worker.

Work standards in the marketplace of the new economy

In the latter decades of the twentieth century law's regulatory purpose has gradually shifted away from an emphasis on the protection of vulnerable workers towards one that seeks to foster work relations that will facilitate the successful participation of business in the new economy. An important aspect of this is a commitment to allow business to organise its own relations with its workforce with as few externally imposed constraints as possible. The role of the state becomes one of merely establishing processes that will facilitate market relations. There is a growing reluctance to pursue protection for workers in the new economy, especially by broadly applicable standards, which are often seen as an unfortunate example of anti-competitive behaviour.[226] A national system with a strong emphasis on, and trust in, the competitive relations of the market may assume that incentives for business to attract workers through the provision of good conditions of work is the optimal way to secure decent work standards.

Eliminating workplace standards?

At one extreme the neo-liberal logic of 'regulating employment for competition' sees no place for minimum standards in the law of work. Hugh Collins, for example, has argued that in the new economy there is little place for minimum standards except to ensure that wages are sufficient to ensure that individuals work in the paid labour market rather than opt out and rely on welfare. According to Collins any conditions must be able to be justified in light of a new regulatory goal: for instance, recognising the equality of workers and treating them fairly must have the effect of engendering high trust relations and ensuring that they will act in ways that enhance the competitiveness of business.[227] Fixed minimum standards are assumed to impede cooperation in the workplace and harm competitiveness and efficiency in the marketplace. Those who adopt this approach are, if not eager to abolish them altogether, keen to minimise work standards as far as possible. The idea is that there can be at most a limited number of minimum standards with all other terms and conditions governing work set through bargaining.

---

226 Cf *Trade Practices Act 1975* (Cth), s 51.
227 See H Collins 'Is There a Third Way in Labour Law?' in J Conaghan, RM Fischl and K Klare (eds) *Labour Law in an Era of Globalization: Transformative Practices and Possibilities* (2002); and H Collins 'Regulating the Employment Relation for Competitiveness' (2001) 30 *ILJ* 17.

Standards—fixed or flexible?

A slightly different approach, which also adopts the goal of regulating for competition, but at the same time acknowledges that workers can be vulnerable and need protection, sets minimum standards in place but considers them alienable and thus able to be bargained away collectively. Collective bargaining at the workplace is treated as the antidote to the vulnerability of the individual. The ability to bargain away standards at a workplace is seen as ensuring the flexibility necessary to stay competitive: the inflexible application of work standards to all workplaces is anathema. Certainly in Australia work standards (with few exceptions) are no longer a fixed or immutable baseline for work relations but can be modified through facilitative clauses or jettisoned through bargaining. In both cases vulnerable individuals can make these bargains. There is no collective protective shield.

Facilitative clauses in awards

In the award simplification process following the 1996 reforms the Commission was required to ensure that awards were made more flexible. Awards were no longer to set down standards in relation to matters more appropriately dealt with at the workplace level, nor to prescribe work practices that would hinder efficiency or productivity, though the latter reform was tempered by a statutory requirement to ensure fairness to the employee. Where appropriate awards were also to contain facilitative provisions.[228] The AIRC has described these as:

> that part of an award clause which enables agreement at enterprise level to determine the manner in which that clause is applied at the enterprise. A facilitative provision normally provides that the standard approach in an award provision may be departed from by agreement between an individual employer and an employee or the majority of employees in the enterprise or part of the enterprise concerned. Where an award clause contains a facilitative provision it establishes both the standard award condition and the framework within which agreement can be reached as to how the particular clause should be applied in practice.[229]

In the *Award Simplification Decision* the Commission spelled out five general principles governing the use of facilitative clauses. These reaffirmed that facilitative provisions were not to be the occasion for avoidance of award obligations, nor to result in unfairness to employees. They provided for agreements, either individual or collective about the way award provisions would operate at the workplace and could be utilised by both employer and employees. While the Commission might apply certain safeguards regarding their use—such as requiring the recording in time and wage books of agreements made under them, the notification to unions and the provision of an opportunity for them to participate in negotiations where it has members in

---

228 See *Workplace Relations Act*, former ss 143(1B) and (1C).
229 *Safety Net Adjustments and Review—September 1994* ((1994) 56 IR 114, 136. For early comments by the Commission on facilitative provisions see *Third Safety Net Adjustment & Section 150A Review—October 1995 Decision* (1995) 61 IR 326, 255–7.

the workplace and other regular monitoring to evaluate the way such agreements are working in practice—these were essentially 'self-executing', enabling parties at the workplace to change the operation of award provisions away from wider public scrutiny. Facilitative provisions were to be used to promote efficiency and to avoid the need for unnecessary detail in awards.[230]

The Commission also reiterated an earlier statement that specified the type of matters that might be the subject of individual negotiation (including variation to working hours and the time of taking annual leave) and matters that must be subject to collective negotiation (such as ordinary hours of work, 12-hour shifts, public holiday shifts, period of annual leave, annual close-down) and matters that might be negotiated either individually or collectively (such as payment of wages, ordinary hours of work for day workers on weekends, variation to spread of hours, methods of arranging ordinary hours).

However, after *Work Choices* facilitative clauses can only provide for individual agreement and not collective agreement: s 521.

The demise of the no-disadvantage test

The interaction of awards and agreements also shows the way in which the significance of awards is diminished under *Work Choices*. The safety net is lowered by the *Work Choices* amendments because the no-disadvantage test has been removed. While the old no disadvantage test was far from ideal it did require *all* award conditions to be factored in as part of the safety net. After *Work Choices* only the AFPCS, the APCS, and, where relevant, 'preserved award conditions', cannot be undermined by agreements. Another set of award terms and conditions, known as 'protected award conditions', is taken to be included in agreements unless expressly excluded: s 354(2). Protected award conditions are therefore not strongly protected at all and can be bargained away. Once an agreement is in place the award as a regulatory instrument has no more relevance for the parties (although parties may incorporate award terms and conditions in agreements, and their agreement will include protected award conditions unless excluded). More significantly if an agreement is terminated the award as a whole does not revive to bind them again, but only protected conditions: s 399. The termination of an agreement, which can be unilateral, has the potential to wipe out forever more a variety of award provisions.

After the introduction of the *Work Choices* amendments the relationship between the safety net and agreement-making is changed. Henceforward all workplace agreements override and displace awards. Awards are no longer relevant where an employer or employee is bound by a workplace agreement. Workplace agreements may call up provisions from an award, but they will have to do so expressly, unless there is a protected award provision, which will automatically be incorporated in an agreement unless expressly excluded: ss 354–5.

---

230 *Award Simplification Decision* (1997) 75 IR 272, 302–4.

The impact on business of the cost of standards

If the purpose of the law of work is to enhance competitiveness the economic impact of work standards on business and its capacity to pay can also become important considerations. Without business thriving, so the argument goes, there will be no jobs at all but when it does thrive there will be every incentive to raise standards. For this reason the market is said to be the best way to set standards.

None of these considerations are entirely new in Australia where the industrial system has always taken account of the impact of standards on business and its capacity to pay for them. The special circumstances of small businesses are also often put forward as a reason to exempt them from complying with the same work standards as those that apply in large enterprises. In the *Maternity Leave Test Case* this plea for exemption was quickly dismissed by the Commission, which ruled that the difficulties of small business were often exaggerated. In the 1990 *Parental Leave Test Case* the Confederation of Australian Industry requested, unsuccessfully, an exemption for all businesses with fewer than 100 employees. Yet the size of the business continues to be presented as a reason to exclude some workers from work standards.[231]

Who pays?

The question of 'who pays?' is a significant one for understanding the future of work standards in the competitive marketplace of the new economy. Where basic conditions of work are conceived as a 'safety net' it becomes difficult to introduce revolutionary changes to redress previous injustices because the logic of the market assumes that 'a level playing field' already exists. It is argued that the 'extra' costs of 'new' standards (for 'extra' protections) need to be defrayed through bargaining. However, as Kerry Rittich has shown, in relation to many issues there is no 'level playing field' for the market already tends to 'externalise' some costs borne by workers and thereby to discount them altogether.[232] This can be seen in the various Commission decisions dealing with work and family or care issues. The application in the 1979 *Maternity Leave Test Case* was resisted by business on the grounds of cost, but it was pointed out that the proposed leave was unpaid and there was to be no accrual of other entitlements during the leave. The direct costs were thus minimised. The indirect costs, such as arising from the provision of replacement workers, and the uncertainty costs, about whether the employee would return to work, were little different from what would have been incurred anyway if the pregnant worker retired. Providing an avenue for a woman to maintain her job after the birth of a child and remain secure in the paid workforce relieved her of some of the costs of extended absence from the paid workforce, including those associated with the problem of re-entry and loss of skills. However, as unpaid leave, the assumption is that the woman is economically dependent and that she has someone (or the state) who will and can support her for the period she is on leave. This assumption applies more

---

231 See further Chapter 9.
232 K Rittich 'Feminization and Contingency: Regulating the Stakes of Work for Women' in Conaghan, Fischl and Klare (eds), above n 227.

generally for all workers who must take unpaid leave to balance work and family and care. Most major institutional players in the system continue to assume that the costs of reproductive work are to be borne by workers outside the marketplace. For this reason the question of paid leave entitlements to accommodate work and family and care has never been seriously considered as part of the industrial agenda. Rather workers are forced to cannibalise their own existing entitlements or their own place in the labour market to attain this accommodation.

A new standard worker?

The market purposes of law assume a new standard worker. In place of the powerless individual whom capital exploits is a vision of a worker who partners business through a relation built on trust. The relation is one of cooperation not conflict. Such workers are investors in their own human capital who revel in the opportunity to control their own work relations through contract. Little surprise then that contract has infiltrated and transformed work standards. Choice has thus become a component of many work standards: workers can choose to average their hours, and to bargain away half of their annual leave. Through agreements, workers can alienate work standards. If it were accepted that the imbalance of power between capital and labour were a problem of the individual worker facing the might of business, then even a system regulating for competition would need to have in place strong procedural guarantees of freedom of association supporting collective action. However, the Australian regulatory system increasingly places emphasis on fostering the 'free choice' of individuals and trusts in their capacity to protect themselves. For such individuals the majority approval of the collective of workers is painted as oppressive as the power of capital. Work standards can therefore be alienated through individual agreement. The once vulnerable figure of the employee worker thus takes on many of the characteristics of the independent contractor, able to assess the risks and rewards that accompany working in the marketplace and make choices about them.

Social citizenship: work standards as a floor of rights

While some workers in the new economy may thrive in this competitive contractual environment, there remain many low-skilled workers who are unlikely to do so. The 'safety net' metaphor describing work standards suggests that most workers enjoy better terms and conditions. However, for at least a quarter of those in the labour market who have no access to statutory-based enterprise bargaining (whether collective or individual), these legislative and award standards represent simultaneously a 'floor' and a 'ceiling'.[233] Yet for all workers, and for society, there are great risks when work standards can be bargained away. Giving up entitlements to annual leave, for instance, erases the recognition that the worker is a human being in need of refreshment and rest to maintain good health and time to live a life in which work can be balanced with

---

233 See J Conaghan 'Feminism and Labour Law: Contesting the Terrain' in A Morris and T O'Donnell (eds) *Feminist Perspectives on Employment Law* (1999).

family, friends and leisure. Even bargaining away accumulated leave is problematic: pressure may be placed on workers to work long hours and job insecurity can make them reluctant to take a holiday break. When the law of work is reduced to a bargain in which money is often the only thing exchanged for the work, there is an increased risk that labour will be viewed as a commodity divorced from the worker who is a human being.

Another important purpose of work standards is to enable the worker to flourish as a human being. When this is so the nature of the contractual relation in which work is performed in the marketplace is less significant than the status of the worker as such. Every worker will be entitled to fair and reasonable pay, and paid holidays, and sick, personal, parental and care leave. Every worker will be entitled to a decent standard of living in retirement. In order to ensure this, entitlements need to be freed of particular relations: portability of entitlements and proportionality of contribution from anyone for whom any work is done are some of the means that could allow this to happen, but there are also other options.

In a very real sense work standards are here understood as a floor of rights to which all are entitled. There is a sense in which this has long been a purpose of the law of work in Australia. Stuart Macintyre has argued that from the start the system of conciliation and arbitration for the prevention and settlement of industrial disputation imbued Australian workers with more a sense of entitlement than a sense of vulnerability in need of protection.[234]

When recognised as rights, work standards cannot be alienated because they become an important part of what it means to be a human being. However, to suggest that work standards can be seen as rights is not to say that they are fixed or immutable in the sense that they can be considered apart from the context—social, economic, cultural, political and legal—in which they operate. While policy choices, goals and directions are most significant in shaping the present national context, the influence of history and wider global arrangements is also influential. There is an important social dimension to understanding the function of work standards in this way. Where workers flourish as human beings social cohesion is fostered. Work standards as public standards build a sense of community. To acknowledge this is to see that the complex relation between what has been traditionally encompassed within the spheres of labour law and welfare law respectively must be clarified. Australia was once described as having a 'wage earner's welfare state'.[235] However by the latter part of the twentieth century the arbitration system and the state formally eschewed any relation between standard setting and welfare.

Will this be a sustainable approach in the new economy? As basic rights work standards can also benefit business. But these instrumental benefits are secondary to the primary function of work standards as a floor of rights. The function of work standards

---

234 See S Macintyre 'Neither Capital nor Labour: The Politics of the Establishment of Arbitration' in MacIntyre and Mitchell (eds), above n 123, 188.

235 FG Castles 'The Wage Earner's Welfare State Revisited: Refurbishing the Established Model of Australian Social Protection' (1994) 29 *Aust J Social Issues* 120.

as a floor of rights ensures the law of work regards the worker 'as a human being living in a civilized community'. Those words used a century ago by Higgins J in the *Harvester Case*[236] can well be the foundation for a new understanding of the place of work standards in the new economy. They are an Australian aphorism for what is entailed in the concept of decent work.

---

236 (1907) 2 CAR 1, 3.

8 Equality and Diversity at Work

Equality at work

In its 1998 *Declaration on Fundamental Principles and Rights at Work* the International Labour Organization (ILO) reaffirmed the significance of equality, naming it as one of the four fundamental principles and rights applicable to work. Equality at work has always been an important value to the ILO. As stated in the *Declaration of Philadelphia* (1944), it is foundational to the work of that organisation. Equality principles have also been incorporated into many of the ILO conventions, with two of the most important being the *Equal Remuneration Convention, 1951 (ILO C 100)* and the *Discrimination (Employment and Occupation) Convention, 1958 (ILO C 111)*.

The recognition in international law of equality as a fundamental principle and right applicable to work is much more broadly based than its incorporation in the *International Labour Code*.[1] The United Nations *Declaration of Human Rights, 1948* professes the right of everyone to equality before the law: Art 7. The breadth of this right to equality before the law is clearly stated in the *International Covenant on Economic, Social and Cultural Rights, 1976 (ICESCR)*, Art 26:

> All persons are equal before the law and are entitled without any discrimination to the equal protection of the law. In this respect the law shall prohibit any discrimination and guarantee to all persons equal and effective protection against discrimination on any ground such as race, colour, sex, language, religion, political or other opinion, national or social origin, property, birth or other status.

There are also various other United Nations conventions proscribing discrimination in relation to specific groups of people. The *International Convention on the Elimination of All Forms of Racial Discrimination, 1965 (ICERD)* prohibits discrimination on the basis of 'race, colour, descent or national or ethnic origin'. The *Convention on the Elimination of All Forms of Discrimination against Women, 1979 (CEDAW)* seeks to protect women against 'any distinction, exclusion, or restriction made on the basis of sex which has the effect of impairing or nullifying the recognition, enjoyment or exercise by women,

---

1   See generally HJ Steiner and P Alston *International Human Rights in Context* (2000).

irrespective of their marital status, on a basis of equality of men and women, of human rights and fundamental freedoms in the political, economic, social, cultural, civil or any other field': Art 1. Each of these instruments goes further to identify work as a particular area in which equality rights are to be enjoyed. In various terms they state the right of all to work freely; to access equal, just and favourable terms and conditions of employment; to be protected against unemployment and provided with social security support; and the right to equal pay for equal work.[2] Of course these are not the only international instruments to identify rights to equality at work, but they are among some of the most important, and Australia is a party to each of them.

Because equality is considered so fundamental, it is protected in the legal systems of most Western industrialised market economies at the constitutional level. However, Australia stands apart as an exception in this. There is no 'bill of rights', nor any express protection of equality, in the *Australian Constitution*. However, there have been various judicial statements recognising the importance in law of respect for rights that are fundamental to the existence of human beings as free individuals in society, including their right to be treated with dignity and equality.[3] And in Justice Murphy's view the law must necessarily respect the worker as a human being: workers could not be treated as the property or the slaves of another.[4] More pertinently, he also hinted that equality might operate as a constraint on legislative power:

> The Constitution makes no discrimination between the sexes. It may be that an implication should be drawn from its terms that parliament's legislative powers do not extend to authorizing arbitrary discrimination between the sexes.[5]

But to date the view that there is an overarching or constitutional implication of equality, which operates either as an individual right or as a limitation on governmental power, has not received majority judicial support in Australia.[6]

In Australia the legal protection of equality is founded upon statute. All legislatures, Commonwealth, State and Territory, have enacted specific legislation prohibiting certain discriminatory behaviour in areas of public life, including at work. At the federal level there is the *Racial Discrimination Act 1975* (Cth), the *Sex Discrimination Act 1984* (Cth), the *Disability Discrimination Act 1992* (Cth), the *Age Discrimination Act 2004* (Cth), and the *Human Rights and Equal Opportunity Commission Act 1986* (Cth).[7]

---

2   See UN *Declaration of Human Rights, 1948*, esp Arts 2, 4, 7, 22 and 23; *ICESCR* [1976] ATS 5, esp Arts 6–7; *ICERD* [1975] ATS 40, esp Arts 1, 2 and 5(e); and *CEDAW* [1983] ATS 9, esp Arts 1 and 11.

3   See eg *Gerhardy v Brown* (1985) 159 CLR 70, 101–2, and 125–6; and *Mabo v The State of Queensland (No 1)* (1988) 166 CLR 186, 229.

4   See *R v Director-General of Social Welfare (Vic); Ex parte Henry* (1975) 133 CLR 269, 288; and *McGraw Hinds (Aust) Pty Ltd v Smith* (1979) 144 CLR 633, 670.

5   *Ansett Transport Industries (Operations) Pty Ltd v Wardley (Wardley)* (1980) 142 CLR 237, 267.

6   See esp *Leeth v The Commonwealth* (1992) 174 CLR 455; and *Kruger v The Commonwealth* (1997) 190 CLR 1.

7   Hereafter the *Racial Discrimination Act*, the *Sex Discrimination Act*, the *Disability Discrimination Act*, the *Age Discrimination Act*, and the *Human Rights and Equal Opportunity Commission Act*. Unless expressly indicated the discussion in this chapter will focus on federal legislation. For a more complete overview of these statutes and their operation see Human Rights and Equal Opportunity Commission (HREOC) *Federal Discrimination Law 2005* (2005). This chapter will mention from time to time State and Territory discrimination law, but readers ought to consult such legislation, which may differ in detail from the federal law in the area.

The recognition of equality as a fundamental human right in international law is particularly significant for Australia because the constitutionality of its discrimination legislation at the federal level depends largely on the external affairs power,[8] although each of the statutes also claims a wider constitutional basis.[9] The *Human Rights and Equal Opportunity Commission Act* establishes the Human Rights and Equal Opportunity Commission (HREOC), which has broad oversight of human rights and related issues. HREOC also exercises powers under the various federal discrimination statutes. State and Territory legislation specifically proscribing discrimination tends to be contained in a single enactment.[10] In the Australian Capital Territory there is now also a *Human Rights Act 2004* (ACT), recognising certain human rights including equality before the law, freedom of association and freedom from forced work,[11] and other jurisdictions such as Victoria have indicated an intention to pursue a similar course. However, to date such legislation has been focused mainly on civil and political rights rather than a broader range of social, economic and cultural rights.

The first half of this chapter examines in broad outline the principles underpinning federal discrimination law and its operation. These principles are for the most part replicated in State and Territory discrimination law. There is no inconsistency between the discrimination laws at the federal and State and Territory level; they operate side by side. This means in effect there are parallel jurisdictions, and where there is an alleged breach of a discrimination law, complainants must select the jurisdiction in which they wish to bring their action. In some cases there are differences, sometimes significant differences, between the federal and State or Territory discrimination laws and so careful attention is required to the wording of the relevant statutes. The *Workplace Relations Amendment (Work Choices) Act 2005* (Cth) (*Work Choices Act*) made it clear that State and Territory discrimination laws continue to operate and are not overridden by the *Workplace Relations Act 1996* (Cth) (*Workplace Relations Act*).[12] Discrimination statutes have been described as general human rights and social legislation, providing the background legal context against which the more specific labour and industrial statutes regulate work.[13] However, the intersection of discrimination law and labour law is more complex than that statement suggests. The second part of the chapter therefore examines their intersection.

The concept of equality

The concept of equality is critical to understanding the possibilities and limitations of the operation of statutory provisions proscribing discrimination at work.

8　See *Koowarta v Bjelke-Petersen* (1982) 153 CLR 168.

9　See *Racial Discrimination Act*, s 5; *Sex Discrimination Act*, 9; *Disability Discrimination Act*, s 12; and *Age Discrimination Act*, s 10.

10　See *Anti-Discrimination Act 1977* (NSW); *Anti-Discrimination Act 1991* (Qld); *Equal Opportunity Act 1984* (SA); *Anti-Discrimination Act 1998* (Tas); *Equal Opportunity Act 1995* (Vic); *Equal Opportunity Act 1984* (WA); *Discrimination Act 1991* (ACT); and *Anti-Discrimination Act 1992* (NT).

11　See ss 8, 15 and 26.

12　*Workplace Relations Act*, s 16(2)(a).

13　*Wardley*, above n 5.

Formal equality

At a very basic level, equality invokes notions of identity or sameness. At its core is a conviction that all individuals are identical in what it is that makes them human beings, and as such they are entitled to equal respect. From this it follows that everyone is to be treated in the same way. The hallmark of discrimination is thus often identified as different treatment, whether that treatment derives from a rule or norm that is framed for some but not others or manifests in a person's behaviour towards some when compared with that person's behaviour towards others. Viewing equality in this way focuses on the discriminatory rule, norm or action and sees it as aberrant. Discrimination looks as if it is an isolated failing of the one who discriminates. This is a 'formal' or 'procedural' idea of equality.

The human being at the centre of this conception of equality is very much the individual person of classical liberal theory, a pre-social being. On reflection, however, there seem obvious problems with such an approach. First, it is clear that there are many differences between people. Some of these differences appear to be natural, and perhaps even immutable: for instance, only women can give birth to a child; race is not something 'chosen', but something that marks a person from birth; and some people are physically (dis)abled in ways that others are not. Other differences, for example that women are (usually) the primary carers of young children, may be seen to be a product of particular social or cultural arrangements. The differences between people are treated as irrelevant by a formal concept of equality. However, seeing the differences that do exist between people can also suggest that treating everyone as if they were identical may not be appropriate: the same treatment may not have identical impacts. Indeed, treating everyone in the same way may disadvantage some and thus have discriminatory effects.

Substantive equality

A more substantive conception of equality, one that attends to the effects and outcomes of the way individuals are treated, seems to require attention to, and indeed respect for, at least some of the differences between people. By also attending to the outcomes produced by, rather than simply the form of, the rules, norms or behaviours themselves, substantive equality is better equipped to deal with indirect forms of discrimination. Formal equality is ill equipped to deal with systemic or structural inequality. In focusing on whether rules, norms or behaviours are treating everyone in an identical manner, formal equality is apt to ignore underlying assumptions and therefore to fail to identify the way in which social structures and actions may actually create inequality. Substantive equality interrogates the assumptions about an already existing 'level playing field' that are often implicit in a formal approach to equality. Substantive equality recognises that if no account is taken of past discrimination, treating everyone the same can further entrench inequality into the future. Substantive equality thus often demands not 'same treatment' but 'different treatment'. One of the key issues in a substantive approach to equality is identifying which differences should be recognised, which are relevant and which are not. When different treatment is referred to as 'special treatment', the idea of equality as being about sameness is portrayed as the norm and different treatment becomes a deviation that faces a justificatory hurdle.

Equality: benchmarks and comparators

In focusing on identity and difference, both formal and substantive conceptions of equality are usually concerned with comparisons. As such, both raise questions about the kind of being who becomes the benchmark individual when determining if discrimination exists. Models of equality often incorporate stereotypes as a normative ideal. The stereotype might be a white, middle-class and heterosexual man, or a woman as a mother and carer, or a person who is rational, free and exists outside of a social context. Equality under the law is then determined according to the attributes and needs of this stereotype, and in the process other human characteristics are rendered invisible. Formal equality especially tends to ignore anything not represented or needed by this ideal person.

Because of problems with the comparator approach, Sandra Fredman has long argued that there is a great advantage in having a more specific approach to the allocation of rights rather than using the model of formal equality that is dominant in much discrimination legislation.[14] As she points out, the comparator approach never works well, especially for things like pregnancy, and in any event it only delivers to the disadvantaged that which the comparator enjoys, which may or may not be appropriate.

However, a substantive conception of equality also often operates from a comparative framework, by setting up a normative benchmark against which differences and disadvantage are defined, either as relevant and to be taken into account or as irrelevant and to be ignored. By responding to differences, substantive equality often further fixes those differences, and so can risk entrenching them.

Equality as a problem of power in relationships

Historically, formal and substantive conceptions of equality have been conceptualised within a neo-liberal theoretical framework that assumes the individual to be a free and autonomous being.[15] Some feminists and political economists have observed that the problem of inequality is not so much one of sameness or difference but one that it is concerned above all else with questions of power and disadvantage. On this view, discrimination and inequality raise questions about relationships of dominance, subordination and exploitation. Thus to understand the equality of workers there may need to be a focus on whether the powerful or dominant position of some (perhaps those with ready access to work and career opportunities because they are 'unencumbered' by family and care responsibilities) depends upon the subordination and consequent exploitation of others (that is, those workers who have such responsibilities).[16] The exploitation identified by Karl Marx as central to class relations in the capitalist economy

---

14 S Fredman 'Pregnancy and Parenthood Reassessed' (1994) 110 *LQR* 106, 117ff; and S Fredman *Women and the Law* (1997), esp Chapter 7.

15 For a critique see M Thornton *The Liberal Promise: Anti-discrimination Legislation in Australia* (1990).

16 See CA MacKinnon *Feminism Unmodified: Discourses on Life and Law* (1987).

illustrates this kind of inequality.[17] Inequality on this view is not so much a problem of individual pathological action but something imbedded in political, social, economic and cultural structures, such as the state or the market.[18]

A postmodern critique

The analysis of equality in terms of power has also had critics, who note in it a tendency to 'essentialise' certain experiences and cast them as normative.[19] Thus understanding inequality as a manifestation of power imbalance in social relations often assumed homogeneity amongst women, or men, or persons of a particular race, class or age. This insight was extended even further by postmodernist theorists who called into question these very categories. They showed that all attributes, even the ones we tend to think of as natural and immutable (such as sex, race and sometimes disabilities), are constructed by law and society.[20] The postmodern sensibility thus tended to focus on diversity and difference not just between different groups or categories of people but within them as well.

Equality as participation and diversity at work in the marketplace

A diversity approach to equality is now becoming dominant in the marketplace of the global era. As applied to work the diversity approach is said to reach beyond the traditional equality approach to envisage a new workplace in which everyone can work, be valued and flourish. Linked to the diversity approach there have been efforts to kindle afresh the traditional liberal ideal of equality and harness it anew to the purposes of the global marketplace. At the core of the neo-liberal conception of equality remains the idea of the dignity of the individual person and this is linked to traditional values of autonomy and freedom. However, this individual is now recognised as someone who inhabits the global marketplace and is not merely a pre-social being. In this neo-liberal version, equality and its concomitant respect for the individual are not simply valuable in themselves, but hold the key to providing the individual with the good life. In this way equality presents a slight variation on the traditional Kantian ideal of the human being as an end-in-self, which imbues much human rights thinking. The rationale or justification for the diversity approach is generally articulated from an economic perspective rather than an individual rights basis. However, it has been noted that non-economic justifications emphasising more traditional neo-liberal values, such as choice, may prove a more enduring theoretical foundation.[21]

In this neo-liberal articulation, equality is seen as central to enabling human flourishing.[22] It assumes that with equal access to basics—such as education, housing and work—human beings can then be left to exercise their capacities for reason and

---

17 See K Marx *Das Kapital* (1867).

18 See eg CA MacKinnon *Toward a Feminist Theory of the State* (1989).

19 See A Harris 'Race and Essentialism in Feminist Legal Theory' (1990) 42 *Stan LR* 581.

20 See M Davies 'Taking the Inside Out: Sex and Gender in the Legal Subject' in N Naffine and RJ Owens (eds) *Sexing the Subject of Law* (1997).

21 L Barmes and S Ashtiany 'The Diversity Approach to Achieving Equality: Potential and Pitfalls' (2003) 32 *ILJ* 274, 284.

22 See eg MC Nussbaum *Sex and Social Justice* (1999).

choice as to the way they live their lives. This concept of equality is thus also an instrumental and 'procedural' one, in the sense that its focus is predominantly on expressing equality as a right of all individuals to claim access to social institutions (including work) through which they can then build for themselves the good life. It is not otherwise concerned with substantive equality or the way goods are distributed. Equality at work is of particular importance as one of the recognised basics because, commensurate with neo-liberal ideals of the independence of the individual and a 'small state', active participation in the marketplace through work is seen as the way to achieve the economic independence so highly valued in the new economy. Because the marketplace is the domain of this neo-liberal individual the attainment of equality of access to work and the benefits of work is the responsibility of all political, social, economic and legal actors and institutions, whether public or private.

This emphasis on the instrumental value of equality is becoming more and more commonplace. Sitting alongside traditional expressions of formal and substantive equality, it is quite explicit in the ILO's *Global Report, Time for Equality at Work*, which states:

> Discrimination limits the freedom of individuals to obtain the type of work to which they aspire. It impairs the opportunities of men and women to develop their potential, skills and talents and to be rewarded according to merit. Discrimination at work produces inequalities in labour market outcomes and places members of certain groups at a disadvantage. [23]

According to the ILO, equality at work secures 'values of human dignity and individual freedom, social justice and social cohesion'.[24] This approach to equality focuses not just on the individuals who may be discriminated against but asserts that 'the benefits of eliminating discrimination transcend the individual and extend more widely to the economy and society'.[25] This view of equality emphasises not so much the comparison of groups of workers, but the identification of some of the strongest barriers that exclude certain groups from the workplace and its benefits and it demonstrates a commitment to ensuring their inclusion. In Britain this has been referred to as the politics of 'the third way'.[26]

In legal terms, this conceptualisation of equality is seen not only as necessitating laws concerned with the proscription and eradication of discriminatory behaviour but also as encouraging laws that mandate positive duties on those with responsibilities at the workplace, such as business, to prevent discrimination and promote equality and thus ensure that all can participate in the world of work.[27] The ILO *Global Report* talks of 'diversity management' where all individual workers can develop their own talents.[28] Equality becomes 'the responsibility of governments, organizations and individuals to generate change by positive action'.[29] This transformation of equality

---

23 ILO *Time for Equality at Work* (2003), 15. See also K Rittich 'Rights, Risk and Reward: Governance Norms in the International Order and the Problem of Precarious Work' in J Fudge and R Owens (eds) *Precarious Work, Women, and the New Economy: The Challenge to Legal Norms* (2006), 46–50.

24 ILO, ibid, ix.

25 Ibid, ix.

26 See H Collins *Employment Law* (2003), Pt II 'Social Inclusion'.

27 ILO, above n 23, xii; S Fredman 'Equality: A New Generation?' (2001) 30 *ILJ* 145; Collins, ibid; and H Collins 'Discrimination, Equality and Social Inclusion' (2003) 66 *Mod LR* 16.

28 ILO, above n 23, 108.

29 B Hepple *Work, Empowerment and Equality* (2000), 8.

from a negative concept focused on the eradication of certain discriminatory rules, norms or behaviours, to equality as a positive duty makes 'affirmative action' or 'positive discrimination' (as it might have been labelled in the past) not just an exception to equal (same) treatment but the central thing. This idea of equality also confronts some of law's most deeply entrenched conceptions of itself as 'neutral', more comfortably concerned with 'duty bearers' as persons or institutions who are at fault of breaching existing rules and norms rather than as the ones who are in the best position to bring about change.[30]

Although the diversity approach to equality promises to respond to the particularity of the individual person and to be more inclusive because it is not focused so much on categories, its proponents also advocate it as an approach that can be adapted in the workplace to take a more systemic approach to the problem of discrimination. This is to be achieved by focusing on the organisational initiation of change entailing a positive duty to accommodate diversity, rather than simply responding to individual complaints.[31] However, the diversity approach is most often described as operating in the context of large organisations with highly-skilled, knowledge workers. One might be more sceptical as to whether this equality approach is attuned to the needs of those in more precarious forms of work.

In response to this, other commentators have argued that this idea of equality, because it seeks to enable 'fair' participation of everyone in the workforce, is (or can also be) results-oriented and incorporates redistributive goals by ensuring fair participation in the benefits of the marketplace. In this sense, equality may involve special measures for certain disadvantaged groups or individuals.[32] In the context of work, it suggests attention to the needs of all: those who are employed and unemployed, those in the formal and informal sectors of the economy, and those in paid and unpaid work.[33] Equality and discrimination law have thus an important role in ensuring 'social inclusion' or, to put it another way, that there are no barriers that exclude individuals from participating in work, as one of the most important social institutions. However, this social inclusion argument is also based upon certain assumptions. For instance, in relation to care responsibilities it replicates the public/private divide and implies that social value pertains only to paid work. It also depends on accepting that there is a straightforward alliance between the eradication of discrimination and the interests of the marketplace, whereas these may not always be synchronised.

Equality and its interpretation in Australian discrimination legislation

What does this mean for the interpretation of discrimination statutes in Australia? As has been pointed out by Mary Gaudron, former Justice of the High Court of Australia,

---

30 S Fredman 'Providing Equality: Substantive Equality and the Positive Duty to Provide' (2005) 21 *SAJHR* 163.
31 Barmes and Ashtiany, above n 21.
32 Hepple, above n 29.
33 International Labour Office *Decent Work* (1999).

Anglo-Australian jurisprudence has little real developed sense of equality, but it is necessary to build one for discrimination legislation to work effectively.[34]

Australian discrimination legislation defaults to a position of formal equality. At both Commonwealth and State levels, the legislation defines direct discrimination in terms of different and less favourable treatment.[35] This means that the differences between people, say in relation to race or sex, are to be treated as irrelevant. In the case of disability discrimination the statutory formulation varies slightly, acknowledging that those with a disability may be different and require some accommodation.[36]

The proscriptions in the statutes against indirect discrimination do provide protection against situations where the same treatment has discriminatory effects.[37] To this extent substantive equality is also a goal of Australian discrimination legislation. The wording of some discrimination statutes also suggests that other readings of equality are possible. The *Racial Discrimination Act*, for instance, proscribes acts involving any racially based 'distinction, exclusion, restriction or preference' when they have the purpose or effect of 'nullifying or impairing the recognition, enjoyment or exercise, on an equal footing, of any human right or fundamental freedom in the political, economic, social, cultural or any other field of public life'.[38] And in the most recent federal discrimination statute, the *Age Discrimination Act*, the objects refer to the contemporary social and demographic context and 'removing barriers to older people participating in society, especially the workforce'.[39] Both these statutes are thus quite explicit in hinting at equality as a mechanism for social inclusion. However, the normative understanding of equality as sameness is asserted in all the discrimination statutes by their description of other differences in treatment as 'exceptions' or 'exemptions',[40] or sometimes 'positive discrimination' or 'special measures'.[41]

There has been long standing resistance by Australian courts to the idea that disability discrimination legislation, for instance, might play some greater transformative role than simply securing equality of treatment. Considering that

---

34 The Hon Justice M Gaudron *In the Eye of the Law: The Jurisprudence of Equality* (1990).

35 See the definition of discrimination in federal statutes: *Human Rights and Equal Opportunity Commission Act*, s 3; *Racial Discrimination Act*, s 9(1); *Sex Discrimination Act*, ss 5, 6 and 7; *Disability Discrimination Act*, s 5(1); and *Age Discrimination Act*, s 14. See also the following State and Territory provisions: *Anti-Discrimination Act 1977* (NSW), ss 7(1), 24(1), 38B, 39, 49B, 49T, 49ZG and 49ZYA; *Anti-Discrimination Act 1991* (Qld), s 10; *Equal Opportunity Act 1984* (SA), ss 29, 51 and 66; *Anti-Discrimination Act 1998* (Tas), s 14(2); *Equal Opportunity Act 1995* (Vic), s 8(1); *Equal Opportunity Act 1984* (WA), ss 8, 9, 10, 36, 53 and 66A; *Discrimination Act 1991* (ACT), s 8; and *Anti-Discrimination Act 1992* (NT), s 20(1)–(2).

36 *Disability Discrimination Act*, s 5(2). See also *Purvis v New South Wales (Purvis)* (2003) 217 CLR 92, 153 and 162.

37 See the following provisions prohibiting indirect discrimination in federal legislation: *Racial Discrimination Act*, s 9(1A); *Disability Discrimination Act*, s 6; *Sex Discrimination Act*, ss 5(2), 6(2) and 7(2); and *Age Discrimination Act*, s 15. See also the following State and Territory provisions: *Anti-Discrimination Act 1977* (NSW), ss 7(1)(c), 24(1)(b), 38B(1)(b)–(c), 39(1)(b), 49B(1)(b), 49T(1)(b), (3), 49ZG(1)(b) and 49ZYA(1)(b); *Anti-Discrimination Act 1991* (Qld), s 11; *Equal Opportunity Act 1984* (SA), ss 29(2), 51 and 66; *Anti-Discrimination Act 1998* (Tas), s 15; *Equal Opportunity Act 1995* (Vic), s 9; *Equal Opportunity Act 1984* (WA), ss 8(2), 9(2), 10(2), 36(2), 53(2) and 66A(3); and *Discrimination Act 1991* (ACT), s 8 .

38 *Racial Discrimination Act*, s 9.

39 *Age Discrimination Act*, s 3(e)(i).

40 See *Racial Discrimination Act*, s 8; *Sex Discrimination Act*, Pt II Div 4; *Disability Discrimination Act*, Pt II Div 5; and *Age Discrimination Act*, Pt IV Div 4.

41 *Racial Discrimination Act*, s 8(1); *Sex Discrimination Act*, s 7D; *Disability Discrimination Act*, s 45; and *Age Discrimination Act*, s 33.

it 'cannot carry a traffic it was not designed to bear', some judges have pointed out that discrimination legislation is not the only mechanism to counter social disadvantage and should not be interpreted as if it were.[42] Thus the suggestion that the legislation might impose 'positive duties' has been eschewed by the courts. This issue was addressed in the recent case of *Purvis v New South Wales*.[43] Noting that a comparative exercise is inherent to determinations of equality, several High Court judges conceded that the purpose of legislation is critical to the exercise.[44] They went on to observe that:

> Different comparisons may have to be drawn according to whether the purpose is limited to ensuring that persons situated similarly are treated alike, or the purpose is wider than that. In particular, if the purpose of legislation is to ensure equality of treatment, the focus of inquiry will differ from the inquiry that must be made if the relevant purposes include ensuring equality in some other sense, for example, economic, social or cultural equality.[45]

And they continued:

> 'Substantive equality' directs attention to equality of outcome or to the reduction or elimination of barriers to participation in certain activities. It begins from the premise that 'in order to treat some persons equally, we must treat them differently'.[46]

However, the judges then concluded that Australian federal disability discrimination legislation had the principal focus of ensuring 'equality of treatment' rather than 'a substantive conception of equality' and did not explicitly oblige positive action to eliminate discrimination.[47]

The human rights focus of the international conventions they implement and their remedial character suggest discrimination statutes should be given a broad and beneficial interpretation, with any exemptions or defences narrowly construed.[48] Because the discrimination statutes implement international conventions they will be interpreted as reflecting the concepts and terms within those instruments. Many of these incorporate a substantive concept of equality.[49] From a constitutional perspective it is necessary to ensure that the legislation does not extend beyond the convention it implements.[50] Otherwise an identity in the meaning of terms in domestic legislation and the international instrument it specifically implements is to be expected, unless the legislation is expressed more narrowly. This is also true in relation to the concept of

---

42 *Waters v Public Transport Corporation* (*Waters*) (1993) 173 CLR 349, 372. See also *State of Victoria v Schou* [2001] 3 VR 655, 658–9.

43 Above n 36. Note that *Purvis* concerned discrimination in relation to education.

44 *Purvis*, above n 36, 154, referring to Collins, above n 27.

45 Ibid.

46 Ibid, 154–5.

47 Ibid.

48 See *IW v City of Perth* (1997) 191 CLR 1, 12 and 57–8; *Waters*, above n 42, 406–7; *Australian Iron & Steel Pty Ltd v Banovic* (*Banovic*) (1989) 168 CLR 165, 196–7; *QANTAS Airways Ltd v Christie* (*Christie*) (1998) 193 CLR 280, 332–3; and *Purvis*, above n 36, 104.

49 See H Charlesworth and S Charlesworth 'The *Sex Discrimination Act* and International Law' (2004) 27 *UNSW LJ* 858.

50 *Victoria v The Commonwealth* (*Industrial Relations Act Case*) (1996) 187 CLR 416, 511–18.

equality: the statute will reflect the concepts embodied in the international instrument.[51] Nonetheless, some judges have also cautioned against 'adopting the necessarily general forms of aspirational, as distinct from normative, statements found in international instruments as an aid to resolving ... particular questions of construction' in relation to discrimination statutes.[52] Indeed, the judicial approach has been one of careful textual analysis of the relevant legislation, productive of a tendency to a legalistic and narrow approach in reading the words of the statute.[53] Beth Gaze has condemned this so-called 'neutrality' of the interpretative method adopted by Australian courts because it treats discrimination legislation as nothing special and ultimately hinders the social change that the legislation is intended to bring about.[54] In the result even the judges have complained that the language of discrimination legislation in Australia is often 'complex and obscure and productive of further disputation'.[55] Little wonder perhaps that in recent times few discrimination cases have been pursued successfully in the High Court,[56] and there continue to be calls for review and reform of the law.[57]

Discrimination legislation at work

Who is the worker covered by discrimination legislation?

Because of its human rights basis, the scope of discrimination legislation in relation to work is usually broader than traditional labour and industrial relations legislation, and its protections extend to a wide range of workers. Discrimination legislation offers protection generally for all employees, including those in precarious forms of employment such as casuals who have often been excluded by traditional labour law. Coverage also usually extends beyond the employment relation narrowly conceived, to include other workers such as independent contractors working under a contract for services, commission agents, those in partnerships, agency workers, those who seek recognition from qualifying bodies, applicants for positions, and those who hold public or statutory office.[58] Volunteers and those working in the marketplace without pay are another group of workers often ignored by traditional labour law but sometimes

---

51 See *Commonwealth of Australia v Human Rights and Equal Opportunity Commission* (2000) 108 FCR 378, 385. See also *Minister for Immigration and Ethnic Affairs v Teoh* (1995) 183 CLR 273, 287; and *Plaintiff S157 v Commonwealth of Australia* (2003) 211 CLR 476, 492.

52 *Purvis*, above n 36, 156.

53 See *IW v City of Perth*, above n 48, 14–15 and 58; and *Purvis*, above n 36, 105 and 125.

54 B Gaze 'Context and Interpretation in Anti-discrimination Law' (2002) 26 *MULR* 325.

55 *IW v City of Perth*, above n 48, 37.

56 See the comments in *State of New South Wales v Amery* (*Amery*) (2006) 151 IR 431, 452.

57 See G Patmore 'The Disability Discrimination Act (Australia): Time for Change' (2003) 24 *Comp Lab L & Pol'y J* 533; Productivity Commission *Review of the Disability Discrimination Act 1992* (2004); and B Gaze 'The Sex Discrimination Act after Twenty Years: Achievements, Disappointments, Disillusionment and Alternatives' (2004) 27 *UNSWLJ* 914.

58 See eg *Racial Discrimination Act*, ss 3 and 15; *Sex Discrimination Act*, ss 4 and 14–20; *Disability Discrimination Act*, ss 4, 15–21; and *Age Discrimination Act*, ss 5, 18–22. See also *Anti-Discrimination Act 1977* (NSW), ss 8–13, 25–30, 38C–J, 40–45, 49D–K, 49V–ZC, 49ZH–ZN and 49ZYB–ZYH; *Anti-Discrimination Act 1991* (Qld), see Schedule Dictionary 'work'; *Equal Opportunity Act 1984* (SA), ss 30–6, 52–8, 67–70, 72–3, 85B–E and 85G–H; *Anti-Discrimination Act 1998* (Tas), ss 3 and 22; *Equal Opportunity Act 1995* (Vic), ss 13–15 and 30–6; *Equal Opportunity Act 1984* (WA), ss 11–17; *Discrimination Act 1991* (ACT), ss 10–17; and *Anti-Discrimination Act 1992* (NT), ss 31–4.

covered by discrimination legislation.[59] The legislation may also cover workers who may be categorised as providing a service, for example by playing sport under the auspices of a voluntary association.[60]

Given the human rights basis of discrimination legislation there is little justification for the exclusion of any workers from its purview. However, one group of workers often excluded from its protection is those who perform domestic labour for another person in that person's home.[61] The preservation of a distinction between work in the public sphere of the marketplace and the private sphere of the home is increasingly inappropriate, especially as more and more domestic labour is 'outsourced' to the market.

And in relation to which aspects of work?

Commonwealth legislation protects against discrimination in relation to a broad range of issues at work, from the offer of work, to all benefits associated with work including promotion, transfer and training, and the termination of the work relationship.[62]

A note of warning has been raised as to the capacity of discrimination law to respond to the needs of the workplace of the new economy given changes in its nature and structure. As noted above, discrimination law does not exclude those, like casuals or fixed-term employees, who can be described as precarious workers. However, in the new economy all work has become more precarious. Long-term employment is less likely to be the norm, so-called flatter management structures are becoming more common, and rather than seeking a lifelong career in one organisation workers often move from organisation to organisation as a means of promotion and career development. In such an environment where it is often more difficult to identify the decision-makers in an organisation, Katherine Stone has questioned the capacity of traditional discrimination law to respond effectively to the needs of the new worker because it was formulated with certain assumptions about the structure of workplaces that for many no longer hold true. She has also shown that it is harder in the diversified workplace to demonstrate disadvantages flowing from difference.[63] In Australia, the individualisation of work relations often makes it more difficult to assess systemic discrimination.[64]

The prohibited grounds

Because there is neither a constitutional guarantee of equality in Australia nor recognition by the common law of discrimination as a wrong, in order to access a legal remedy it is necessary to establish that there has been discrimination in relation to one of the grounds specifically listed in the statutes. Protection is provided against discrimination

---

59 Eg *Equal Opportunity Act 1984* (SA), s 5 'employee' includes an 'unpaid worker'.
60 See eg *Sex Discrimination Act*, ss 3, 7 and 22; and *Gardner v All Australian Netball Association Limited* (2003) 174 FLR 452.
61 See eg *Racial Discrimination Act*, s 15(5); *Sex Discrimination Act*, s 14(3); *Disability Discrimination Act*, s 15(3); and *Age Discrimination Act*, s 18(3).
62 *Racial Discrimination Act*, s 15; *Sex Discrimination Act*, Pt II Div 1; *Disability Discrimination Act*, Pt 2 Div 1; and *Age Discrimination Act*, Pt 4 Div 2.
63 KVW Stone 'The New Face of Employment Discrimination' in Fudge and Owens (eds), above n 23.
64 See below p 400.

where a person is identified by a prohibited ground, or by a characteristic that appertains generally to those who are identified by such a ground, or by a characteristic imputed to persons who are so identified. Thus discrimination arising from stereotyping in relation to the grounds is also prohibited. In some cases protection is also provided under the statutes to those who are associates of persons identified by the particular ground.[65]

At the Commonwealth level the proscribed grounds include race, colour, descent or national or ethnic origin;[66] sex, marital status, pregnancy or potential pregnancy, and family responsibilities;[67] disability;[68] and age.[69] Following from its constitutional foundations in implementing *ICERD*, the various grounds in the federal *Race Discrimination Act* are all treated as explications of the concept of race. 'National origin', therefore, is not equivalent to 'nationality', but refers to characteristics of a person that are determined at the time of birth and include not just the place of birth but also the national origin of their parents.[70]

Sometimes the statute further defines, often in quite extensive detail, the prohibited grounds. For instance, in the *Disability Discrimination Act*, disability is defined quite broadly to encompass:[71]

(a) total or partial loss of the person's bodily or mental functions; or
(b) total or partial loss of a part of the body; or
(c) the presence in the body of organisms causing disease or illness; or
(d) the presence in the body of organisms capable of causing disease or illness; or
(e) the malfunction, malformation or disfigurement of a part of the person's body; or
(f) a disorder or malfunction that results in the person learning differently from a person without the disorder or malfunction; or
(g) a disorder, illness or disease that affects a person's thought processes, perception of reality, emotions or judgment or that results in disturbed behaviour;

and includes a disability that:

(h) presently exists; or
(i) previously existed but no longer exists; or
(j) may exist in the future; or
(k) is imputed to a person.

Because of the potential for overlapping operation of a number of these sub-grounds, there is nothing decisive about the precise grammatical structure used in this definition.[72] In the end judicial interpretation of the relevant ground is determinative.

---

65 See eg *Disability Discrimination Act*, s 36.
66 *Racial Discrimination Act*, s 9(1).
67 *Sex Discrimination Act*, ss 5–7A.
68 *Disability Discrimination Act*, ss 4(1) and 5–9.
69 *Age Discrimination Act*, ss 5–6 and 14–16.
70 See *Macabenta v Minister of State for Immigration and Multicultural Affairs* (1998) 159 ALR 465.
71 *Disability Discrimination Act*, s 4(1).
72 *Purvis*, above n 36, 157.

The *Human Rights and Equal Opportunity Commission Regulations 1989* (Cth) also declare additional grounds of discrimination to be examinable by HREOC in relation to employment and occupation under the *Human Rights and Equal Opportunity Act*. These include 'age; medical record; criminal record; impairment; marital status; mental, intellectual or psychiatric disability; nationality; physical disability; sexual preference; and trade union activity'.[73]

At State and Territory level the various discrimination statutes cover a diverse range of grounds. There is a substantial overlap between them and the grounds proscribed by the various Commonwealth discrimination laws, but in some instances they are framed more broadly than their Commonwealth counterparts. In Victoria, for instance, discrimination is prohibited in relation to the following attributes: 'age; breastfeeding; gender identity; impairment; industrial activity; lawful sexual activity; marital status; parental status or status as a carer; physical features; political belief or activity; pregnancy; race; religious belief or activity; sex; sexual orientation; or personal association (whether as a relative or otherwise) with a person who is identified by reference to any of the above attributes'.[74] In the Northern Territory, a person is prohibited from discriminating against another on the basis of 'race; sex; sexuality; age; marital status; pregnancy; parenthood; breastfeeding; impairment; trade union or employer association activity; religious belief or activity; political opinion, affiliation or activity; irrelevant medical record; irrelevant criminal record; or association with a person who has, or is believed to have, one of these attributes'.[75]

There are differences between the States and Territories in the grounds of discrimination covered by the legislation. For instance, only in Tasmania and the Northern Territory is it expressly made unlawful to discriminate on the basis of irrelevant medical record, while only Victoria proscribes discrimination on the basis of a person's physical features. Some States (all except New South Wales and South Australia) protect against discrimination on the grounds of political belief or activity. Other States (but not New South Wales, South Australia and Western Australia) prohibit discrimination in relation to participation in industrial activity.[76]

There are also differences in the ways that the various legislatures describe some of the prohibited grounds, which can be significant when applied to the facts of a particular case. Thus, while the federal *Sex Discrimination Act* refers to 'family responsibilities', the Victorian Act uses the expression 'parental status or status as a carer'. On the other hand, some of the grounds covered by Commonwealth legislation are not included at all in the legislation of some States. South Australian legislation makes no mention, for instance, of family responsibilities as a prohibited ground of discrimination. The differences between the various discrimination laws serve to emphasise the importance of carefully examining the relevant statutes (Commonwealth and either State or Territory laws).

---

73 Regulation 4, which implements *ILO C 111*. See also *Human Rights and Equal Opportunity Act*, s 3. There is only a limited regime for the resolution of complaints in relation to these grounds: see below p 381
74 *Equal Opportunity Act 1995* (Vic), s 6.
75 *Anti-Discrimination Act 1992* (NT), s 19(1).
76 Sometimes this type of discrimination is proscribed instead by State industrial laws. However, such laws can no longer cover federal employees: see *Workplace Relations Act*, s 16(2).

Changing social, economic and workplace issues constantly raise policy questions about whether there is a need to add a new ground under discrimination legislation. One way to deal with changing circumstances would simply be to proscribe all discrimination on any irrelevant ground. But the usual response is to increase the grounds listed in the legislation. The proliferation of grounds has been a strong feature of discrimination legislation in recent years. Sometimes it is a matter of one jurisdiction catching up with others. Thus in recent years widespread concern over the ageing of the population and the labour market participation of older workers led to increased efforts to counteract negative stereotypes of older workers as 'old economy' workers.[77] In 2004 new federal legislation, the *Age Discrimination Act*, was enacted even though age discrimination was already prohibited in the States and Territories.

The expansion of grounds delineated in statutes is a useful way of drawing attention more precisely to the nature of some discrimination issues. Thus, although the ground of 'sex' may be relied upon by women to combat (indirect) discrimination in relation to family and care work, because in contemporary society it is they who predominantly undertake this work, when protection is expressly provided in the gender-neutral terms of 'family or care responsibilities' men who challenge the gender stereotype that it is women's role to do this work are also provided with protection. When discrimination legislation fails to define with precision a prohibited ground, it can risk entrenching further structural discrimination (for instance, that women primarily shoulder family or care responsibilities).

A complainant may allege that there is a breach of discrimination legislation on more than one of the proscribed grounds. The different grounds in an enactment are treated as separate; but there is no necessary mutual exclusivity between them.[78] This can be quite significant, especially when the extent of legislative protection differs in relation to the different grounds. The *Sex Discrimination Act*, for example, proscribes discrimination on the basis of 'family responsibilities' only where it is direct and results in a dismissal, but both direct and indirect discrimination affecting a wide range of employment issues is prohibited on the ground of 'sex'.[79]

However, this separation between the various proscribed grounds also means that discrimination legislation has little capacity to address their intersection in people's lives. For example, the issues of race and sex, or race and disability, or disability and age may be so deeply entwined as to be inseparable in a particular factual situation, but for the purposes of the legislation they must be separated and, in practice, often

---

77 See eg Equal Opportunity Commissioners of Victoria, South Australia and Western Australia *Age Limits, Report* (2001); and ACTU and BCA *Age Can Work: The Case for Older Australians Staying in the Workforce, Joint Report* (2003).

78 But see *Thomson v Orica Pty Ltd* (*Thomson*) (2002) 116 IR 186, 225–31, which discusses *Human Rights and Equal Opportunity Commission v Mount Isa Mines Ltd* (1993) 46 FCR 301 where Lockhart J suggested if 'pregnancy' is relied on as a ground there can be no additional reliance upon the ground of 'sex'. See also *Gibbs v Australian Wool Corporation* (1990) EOC ¶92–327; *Bear v Norwood Private Nursing Home* (1984) EOC ¶92–019; and *Marshall v Marshall White & Co Pty Ltd* (1990) EOC 92–304.

79 *Sex Discrimination Act*, ss 7A and 14(3A). See also *Song v Ainsworth Game Technology Pty Limited* (*Song*) (2002) EOC 93–194; and *Escobar v Rainbow Printing Pty Ltd (No 2)* (*Escobar*) (2002) 120 IR 84.

one of the grounds must be identified by the complainant as more significant than another. The consequence of this is that the nuances of some discriminatory behaviour remain invisible to the law.[80]

Discrimination—the legislative concept

The scope of protections offered by discrimination legislation is quite broad in the sense that (with the exception of the *Age Discrimination Act*) it encompasses not only discrimination as might be generally understood but also various forms of harassment and vilification.[81] The legislation also imposes penal sanctions, including imprisonment, for victimising those who seek the protection of the legislation.[82]

In relation to most, but not all, proscribed grounds both direct discrimination and indirect discrimination are prohibited. Direct discrimination essentially involves a situation where a person is discriminated against by being treated differently, on the basis of one of the prohibited grounds, from others who are similarly situated. Indirect discrimination arises where a person, because of their membership of a group defined in accordance with one of the proscribed grounds, is unable to comply with a 'neutral' term, requirement or condition that is reasonable and that others who are not in that group are able to comply with, and the person is disadvantaged as a result. In those few instances where the distinction between direct and indirect discrimination is not made expressly in the legislation, it has been interpreted as implied.[83]

Direct and indirect discrimination have been treated for the most part as mutually exclusive concepts, although this does not prevent an applicant from arguing each in the alternative.[84] In addition, it does not mean that a complainant cannot argue that the same set of facts demonstrates that both types of discrimination have occurred, although in relation to different grounds.[85] For instance, it might be argued that there has been direct discrimination on the grounds of pregnancy or family responsibilities, and indirect discrimination on the grounds of sex. Keeping the two concepts quite distinct can be especially difficult with disability discrimination legislation, because the incorporation of 'unjustifiable hardship' in the definition of direct discrimination imports a consideration of the capacity of the alleged discriminator to accommodate the person's disability, which is an issue more often associated with indirect discrimination.[86]

Direct discrimination—the causative element

Direct discrimination involves a causal relation between the discriminatory behaviour and the proscribed ground. A range of different legislative formulations define this

---

80 See *Trindall v NSW Commissioner of Police* [2005] FMCA 2. See also K Laster and P Raman 'Law for One and One for All? An Intersectional Legal Subject' in Naffine and Owens (eds), above n 20.

81 See *Racial Discrimination Act*, Pt IIA; *Sex Discrimination Act*, Pt II Div 3; and *Disability Discrimination Act*, ss 35–6.

82 See *Racial Discrimination Act*, s 27; *Sex Discrimination Act*, s 94; *Disability Discrimination Act*, s 42; and *Age Discrimination Act*, s 51.

83 See *Human Rights and Equal Opportunity Act*; and *Anti-Discrimination Act 1992* (NT).

84 *Banovic*, above n 48, 171 and 184. See also *Waters*, above n 42, 392–3, and 402.

85 See eg *Commonwealth of Australia v Evans* (2004) EOC ¶93–335.

86 See *Purvis*, above n 36, 127.

causative connection: these include, 'is based on' (*Race Discrimination Act*); 'by reason of' (*Sex Discrimination Act*); 'on the ground of' (*Disability Discrimination Act*); 'because of' (*Age Discrimination Act*). These words are not necessarily identical in meaning: 'based on' for instance seems broader than the other expressions.[87]

It is difficult to replace the words of the statute in order to explain the causative component in direct discrimination. The central issue is to identify why persons claiming to be discriminated against were treated as they were. The focus is on the alleged discriminator's reasons for acting.[88] It is not the same as applying a 'but for' test, which focuses on the consequences for the complainant of the discriminatory behaviour, although it has been said that the 'but for' test may be useful when evaluating collective action, such as the decision of a body corporate.[89]

The requirement of a causal connection means that the unlawful consideration was included in the discriminator's reasons or grounds. A focus on the 'reason' for behaviour may be thought to suggest that it is the alleged discriminator's motive that is at issue. However, it is clear that the alleged discriminator's own articulation of the reason(s) for acting is not determinative. The test is not a subjective one and proof of motive or intention is not necessary. The stated reason, even a genuinely assigned reason, may mask the 'true basis' or the 'real reason' for the action and it is this that must be identified. The stated motive might be relevant to this but it is not determinative.[90] Furthermore, requiring proof of intention could compromise the attainment of the objects of the legislation.[91] No doubt because of this, some jurisdictions have expressly stated that motive is not relevant to the enquiry into causation.[92] While motive, purpose, or effect may all bear on the question of causation, the courts have insisted that those concepts cannot be used as substitutes for the statutory expressions such as 'based on', 'by reason of' or 'on the ground of'.[93] The issue of causation is above all a question of fact. However, it is something that is increasingly difficult to prove, because nowadays few express themselves in a way that might leave them open to an allegation of direct discrimination, although it is not unknown.[94]

Most discrimination statutes require only that the prohibited ground be *a* reason for the action. That is, if there are two or more reasons for certain discriminatory behaviour it is enough that the proscribed ground is one of those reasons, even if that was only a minor reason. However, some statutes, like the *Age Discrimination Act*, require that the proscribed ground be 'the dominant reason' or 'a substantial reason' for the behaviour.[95] This introduces quite serious problems of proof, for it is very difficult to determine which among several reasons dominates especially if the alleged perpetrator makes a contrary assertion.

---

87 *Macedonian Teachers Association of Victoria Inc v Human Rights and Equal Opportunity Commission* (1998) 91 FCR 8.
88 See *Purvis*, above n 36, 137–46.
89 See eg *IW v City of Perth*, above n 48, 32 and 47.
90 *Waters*, above n 42, 359–60. See also *Purvis*, above n 36, 102, 142–4 and 163.
91 See *Waters*, above n 42, 359.
92 See eg *Equal Opportunity Act 1995* (Vic), s 10.
93 *Purvis*, above n 36, 142–3 and 163; *HREOC v Mount Isa Mines* (1993) 46 FCR 301, 322, 327 and 307.
94 But see *Thomson*, above n 78.
95 See eg *Age Discrimination Act*, s 16 (a)–(b). See also *Equal Opportunity Act 1984* (SA), s 6(2).

Apart from these matters the issue of causation is still not without difficulty. A causative relation does have to be shown; mere conjecture is not enough. There must be some evidence. The reasons for refusing to allow a full-time worker to move to part-time employment, for instance, might be said to be totally related to concern that customers do not have to deal with different representatives of the business. It cannot simply be assumed that family responsibilities are also a reason for the decision. However, in such instances if the effects are discriminatory then there may well be indirect discrimination.

Direct discrimination—the comparative element

One of the sustained criticisms of discrimination legislation is that it adopts an inadequate concept of equality based on a sameness/difference approach. With direct discrimination a comparator must usually be chosen, for the issue under most statutes is whether the aggrieved person was treated 'less favourably' than another 'who is in circumstances that are the same or not materially different'.[96] In some cases the determination of a direct comparator has been treated as a relatively straightforward matter, with the workplace circumstances providing an example. In *Kelly* the response to the request for leave by the pregnant woman was compared with that to a co-worker who was not pregnant and was granted leave for another purpose.[97]

However, because this comparator exercise requires a notional comparison with someone who is not identified by the prohibited ground, it is quite artificial. In cases involving a woman seeking leave for pregnancy, comparing her to someone else needing leave is never really the point. She needs temporary leave from work because she is pregnant, and she is disadvantaged if she is not granted it. Removing all consideration of the relevant characteristic usually renders the exercise meaningless.[98] Moreover, when there would be an obvious power imbalance between the situation of the complainant and that of the notional comparator the exercise is made even more futile. When a person has a disability, there can be the additional problem of understanding the disability so as to work out which personal characteristics are to be incorporated into the comparison. This difficulty was evident in the case of *Purvis* where the High Court wrestled with the question of whether a person's mental disability could be disconnected from its physical manifestations.[99] As some of the judges conceded: 'to strip out of those circumstances any and every feature which presents difficulty to a disabled person would truly frustrate the purposes of the Act'.[100]

Indirect discrimination

The statutes also prohibit indirect discrimination that results where a term, condition or requirement that is neutral on its face or is applied to everyone, nonetheless it has a discriminatory effect or impact.[101] The concept of indirect discrimination is particularly

---

96 *Sex Discrimination Act*, s 5(1); *Disability Discrimination Act*, s 5(1); and *Age Discrimination Act*, s 14(a).
97 See eg *Kelly v TPG Internet Pty Ltd* (*Kelly*) (2003) 176 FLR 214, 226–27. However, it is more common for this issue to be contested: see *Dare v Hurley* [2005] FMCA 844, [103]–[104].
98 Thornton, above n 15, 79. See also Fredman, above n 14.
99 *Purvis*, above n 36, 100–1, 131–2, 134–5, 160–1 and 175.
100 Ibid, 160.
101 See above n 37.

important for its capacity to attend to the discrimination that has become an ordinary part of, or is embedded in, the very structure of work arrangements. For instance, the 'last on, first off rule', which once applied almost automatically to organise retrenchment processes, was shown in *Banovic* to discriminate against women who were later arrivals in the workplace because of earlier discriminatory practices in recruitment.[102] In contemporary society the problems encountered by workers with family responsibilities are amongst some of the most common reasons for invoking the assistance of legislation against indirect discrimination.[103]

To establish that there has been indirect discrimination contrary to statute it is usually necessary to show that some term, condition or requirement is imposed, with which a substantially greater number of one group of persons can comply than another, which is not reasonable, and with which the complainant cannot comply. Some statutes adopt a more straightforward approach that requires only proof that the requirement has, or is likely to have, a detrimental impact on, or the effect of disadvantaging, the person who belongs to a particular group and that it is not reasonable.[104]

Discriminatory term, requirement or condition

A broad approach has been taken to the issue of what counts as a term, requirement or condition.[105] It can include, but is certainly not restricted to, a term of a work contract. It extends to all matters of managerial policy and practice. It may be explicit or implicit. For instance, in a workplace, the application of 'breadwinner policies', which reward length of service and seniority or favour those who have been mobile and served in a variety of geographic areas, may well discriminate against workers with family responsibilities who are more likely to have had career breaks to care for children or who need to remain in a limited geographic area because of family responsibilities.[106]

While it is usually not considered difficult to identify the requirement at issue, this is not always so. In *Amery*, a case that concerned a claim of indirect discrimination by a group of casual school teachers, the articulation of the relevant requirement was refined during the course of the litigation.[107] The factual background to the case was that the complainants were female teachers who had relinquished their 'permanent' positions in order to care for young families, but when they returned to employment they were unable to agree to a posting anywhere in the State (which was a requirement for a permanent teacher) because of their family circumstances. Thus they could only hold positions as casual teachers for no such requirement was imposed on that group. However, their complaint was that although they

---

102 See *Banovic*, above, n 48.

103 See eg *Song*, above n 79; *Escobar*, above n 79; *Mayer v Australian Nuclear Science and Technology Organisation* (2003) EOC ¶93–285; *Kelly*, above n 97; *Evans*, above n 85. See also B Gaze 'Quality Part-time Work: Can Law Provide a Framework?' (2005) 15 *Lab Ind* 89; and R Owens 'Engendering Flexibility in a World of Precarious Work' in Fudge and Owens (eds), above n 23, 341–6.

104 See *Sex Discrimination Act*, s 5(2); and *Age Discrimination Act*, s 15(1).

105 See *Foreign Affairs and Trade v Styles* (1989) 23 FCR 251, 257; *Banovic*, above n 48, 185; *Waters*, above n 42, 360, 378 and 393; and *Amery*, above n 56, 452.

106 See eg *Kemp v Minister for Education & State School Teachers' Union of WA Inc* (1991) EOC ¶92–340. Cf *Gardiner v Workcover Authority of New South Wales* [2004] NSWADTAP 1. In *Amery*, above n 56, this issue remained part of the subtext only.

107 *Amery* was a case concerning the *Anti-Discrimination Act 1977* (NSW).

might have the same professional experience and do the same work as permanent teachers, as casuals they were paid inferior wages when compared with permanent teachers.

In the course of the litigation the requirement was generally treated as being simply one of holding 'permanent status'. The distinction between permanent and casual staff and their respective attributes was contained in the *Teaching Services Act 1980* (NSW) and their pay scales were set out in industrial instruments. In a highly technical approach, Gummow, Hayne and Crennan JJ, with whom Callinan J agreed, made a nonsense of the complaint, characterising it as a claim that there was a requirement on casual teachers to cease being a casual teacher! These judges pointed out that the statute structured teaching staff into two *separate* categories imposing different requirements on each: there was no such thing as employment as 'a teacher', only employment either as a permanent teacher or as a casual teacher.[108] Looked at in this way the discriminatory structure of the teaching profession, which was behind the differential pay classifications, remained beyond the reach of the discrimination legislation. The teaching statistics told the story of the impact of this structure. Of all male teachers 79 per cent were employed on a permanent basis, but only 59 per cent of female teachers were so employed. Of those who were employed on a casual basis, 83 per cent were female.[109]

By way of contrast, Gleeson CJ (with whom Kirby J agreed on the requirement point) pointed out that the complainants did not attack the division of teaching staff into two separate groups. They sued the Education Department. The relevant requirement must, therefore, be one imposed by it. Gleeson CJ reasoned that the relevant requirement of permanent status was imposed by the Education Department because it adopted the practice of not making over award payments unless there was permanency. This focused on the way the employer incorporated the pre-existing discriminatory structure into its own behaviour.[110]

Amery shows that the way in which the requirement and its context is characterised can be critical to the success or otherwise of a case. This is seen in many cases. For instance, a refusal to allow a parent to work from home to care for an ill child could be described either as 'a demand to attend at the workplace' or as 'an inflexible demand to attend at the workplace' and whichever is adopted can have very different consequences when it comes to assessing whether or not such a requirement is reasonable.[111]

Indirect discrimination—the comparative element

The comparative element in an indirect discrimination case can be particularly difficult to prove. This is especially so if the legislation requires that a substantially higher proportion of one group can comply with the requirement when compared with the disadvantaged group.[112] In some cases, when discrimination on the basis of disability is at issue, it may be obvious that a greater number or proportion of one group when

---

108 *Amery*, above n 56, 451–52, 481.

109 Ibid, 459.

110 Ibid, 438; and see also 462. Cf *Banovic*, above n 48.

111 See *State of Victoria v Schou* [2004] 8 VR 120, and the contrasting approaches of Phillips JA, 132 and Calloway JA, 136.

112 See *Disability Discrimination Act*, s 6.

compared with another can comply with the relevant requirement, but this is not necessarily so. However, in other cases, especially where the matter is particularly contentious a more precise calculation rather than the assertion of general figures on the basis of assumptions is necessary.[113] In practice it is not always easy for individual complainants to acquire the relevant information. For this reason Margaret Thornton has criticised indirect discrimination, pointing out that the legislation often sets up 'herculean obstacles to be overcome by intrepid complainants'.[114]

Even the determination of the composition of the groups that must be compared, especially the base pool, can prove difficult. It may be necessary to look at the way a requirement operates to work out the comparator groups. In some instances the relevant base pool may be all the workers upon whom the relevant requirement is imposed.[115] But the particular circumstances of those in a workplace may skew results. Thus it may be, as a matter of fact, that more males than females may work part-time in a particular workplace (perhaps they are students), and this could impede a woman who is refused part-time work because she has family responsibilities and wishes to argue she has been subjected to indirect discrimination.[116] Therefore in some instances it may be appropriate to examine this question in relation to the wider population beyond the workplace: the basis of comparison may need to be the population at large or all workforce participants rather than just those at the particular workplace. In *Hickie v Hunt and Hunt*, which involved a refusal to allow a senior lawyer to work part-time, it was observed that in society at large women are less able than men to work fulltime.[117] This approach has on some occasions been rejected.[118] However, where the legislation requires that disadvantage be demonstrated, this approach is more appropriate than a more elaborate calculation of group compositions.

As the High Court made clear in *Banovic*, it is particularly important to ensure that the composition of any base group is not itself affected by pre-existing discriminatory patterns for otherwise present discriminatory practices will simply be masked and consequently further entrenched.[119] In that case a question arose as to whether an ostensibly neutral 'last on first off' rule for retrenchments was contrary to the *Anti-Discrimination Act 1977* (NSW). The minority judges, McHugh J with whom Brennan J agreed, decided the case on the basis of comparing the number of men affected by the requirement as a proportion of men working for the company with the number of women affected as a proportion of women also working for the company. However, the majority judges, Deane, Gaudron and Dawson JJ, insisted that the calculation of

---

113 See *Commonwealth Bank of Australia v Human Rights and Equal Opportunity Commission (CBA)*(1997) 80 FCR 78.

114 Thornton, above n 15, 192. See also R Hunter *Indirect Discrimination in the Workplace* (1992).

115 See eg *Finance Sector Union v Commonwealth Bank of Australia* (1997) EOC 92–889; and *CBA*, above n 113.

116 See eg *Kelly*, above n 97.

117 (1998) EOC ¶92–910. A different way of tackling the problem is to argue this is direct discrimination because a need for part-time work is a 'characteristic generally pertaining to' women with young children: see J von Doussa and C Lenehan 'Barbequed or Burned? Flexiblity in Work Arrangements and the *Sex Discrimination Act*' (2004) 27 *UNSWLJ* 892.

118 See eg *Styles*, above n 105.

119 Above n 48.

the proportions able to comply should not be infected by prior discriminatory hiring practices. They determined the base group not simply on the basis of the numbers of men and women employed at the time of retrenchment but by reference to the time of application for a position in the company in order to counter the earlier tardiness of the company in taking women into employment. The determination of the base is a matter of fact and law.[120]

Reasonableness

Even if a term, requirement or condition has discriminatory effects, if it is reasonable, indirect discrimination under the statutes will not be established. Usually discrimination legislation incorporates reasonableness as part of the definition of discrimination, which means that a complainant must prove that the relevant requirement is not reasonable. However, some statutes reverse the onus of proof, effectively making the reasonableness of the requirement a matter to be raised as a defence to a complaint of indirect discrimination.[121]

The test of reasonableness was early described as being:

> less demanding than one of necessity, but more demanding than a test of convenience ... The criterion is an objective one, which requires the court to weigh the nature and extent of the discriminatory effect, on the one hand, against the reasons advanced in favour of the requirement or condition on the other. All the circumstances of the case must be taken into account.[122]

Sometimes legislative schemes list the specific matters that are to be considered as part of the enquiry into the reasonableness of a requirement. Under s 7B of the *Sex Discrimination Act*, for instance, 'the nature and extent of the disadvantage' the requirement imposes, 'the feasibility of overcoming or mitigating the disadvantage', and 'whether the disadvantage is proportionate to the result sought' to be achieved by its imposition, are the issues to be considered in determining whether an otherwise discriminatory requirement is reasonable. These words indicate a slightly different emphasis than when there is a reference to reasonableness *simpliciter* in the legislation.[123]

The judicial articulation of reasonableness contemplates a weighing of all relevant factors, which may cover a wide variety of issues. The economic situation or the commercial imperatives of the respondent, the impact on the efficiency of the business, the needs of the adversely affected claimant(s), the industrial impact on others at the workplace, will all be relevant.[124] Where a worker suffers some detriment from an employer's action, the whole package of treatment not just a single item needs to be taken into consideration.[125] A failure to consider adequately one of the circumstances

---

120 Ibid, 179.

121 See *Sex Discrimination Act*, ss 7B–7C.

122 *Styles*, above n 105, 263, per Bowen CJ and Gummow J interpreting the *Sex Discrimination Act 1984* (Cth), former s 5(2)(b). In some overseas jurisdictions the expression 'justifiable' is used.

123 See Gaze, above n 54, 348–50.

124 See eg *CBA*, above n 113; *Banovic*, above n 48; and *Amery*, above n 56.

125 *CBA*, above n 113. For a critique see S Tarrant 'Reasonableness in the *Sex Discrimination Act*: No Package Deals' (2000) 19 *U Tas LR* 38.

relevant to the reasonableness of a requirement will open a tribunal's decision to review. Ideally then all the factors have to be considered together, and as the criterion is 'objective' all the perspectives have to be considered at once.[126]

Objectivity in the evaluation of whether a requirement is reasonable is controversial. In the balancing process there may legitimately be different assessments of the weight of some factors. For this reason Kirby J has expressed the view that it is more difficult to demonstrate an error of law by a court or tribunal below and therefore an appellate court ought to be reluctant to disturb its findings on the question of reasonableness.[127] However, determinations of reasonableness at the tribunal or lower court level have often been overturned in the appellate process.[128] In *Styles* the department's reasons of 'tidiness of administration' were held at first instance to have been overstated, and though on appeal the Full Court of the Federal Court judges agreed with this, they reversed the decision because not enough weight was given to the assessment of merit as a factor.[129] In *Amery* a majority of judges who addressed the issue held, contrary to the findings of the majority in the tribunals and courts below, that the imposition of the condition that teachers should have permanent status to receive higher pay rates was reasonable.[130]

Of all the recent cases considering the issue of reasonableness, the *Schou* litigation is the most notorious.[131] In the *Schou* litigation the employer's requirement for a female Hansard reporter to work from the office was held by the courts to be reasonable even though this requirement forced her to resign because of her family responsibilities, and it would have been inexpensive to supply her with a modem and allow her to work from home. The Tribunal twice found that the attendance requirement was not reasonable, and that the employer's objections to it regarding the need for face-to-face interactions among staff and problems of security were overstated. Furthermore, an enterprise agreement promising flexibility, fairness and equity in workplace arrangements was in place. But each time when the matter was appealed, the court ruled differently. In the Victorian Supreme Court, Harper J imposed a high hurdle demanding that it be shown that working from home was 'as efficacious' as working from the employer's office. Despite the earlier different decisions by the Tribunal, in the final hearing in the matter the Court of Appeal of the Supreme Court ruled that it was 'plain beyond argument' that 'on any view' the modem proposal was 'less efficacious (on one or more grounds)' than working from the employer's premises.

In many of these cases it seems that the perspective of the employer or business has tended to dominate. In *Amery* for instance there was considerable attention paid to

---

126 *Waters*, above n 42, 378–9, 383 and 395.

127 *Amery*, above n 56, 468.

128 See eg *Commonwealth of Australia v Human Rights and Equal Opportunity Commission* (1995) EOC ¶92–753; *CBA*, above n 113; *State of Victoria v Schou* [2004] 8 VR 120; *Amery*, above n 56, 438–40.

129 *Styles*, above n 105, overturning *Styles v Department of Foreign Affairs and Trade* (1988) 84 ALR 408.

130 *Amery*, above n 56, 480, 481.

131 This case was brought under the *Equal Opportunity Act 1984* (Vic). See *Schou v State of Victoria* (2000) EOC ¶93–000 and ¶93–101; *Schou v State of Victoria* (2002) EOC ¶93–217; *State of Victoria v Schou* [2001] 3 VR 655; and *State of Victoria v Schou* [2004] 8 VR 120. For comment see T MacDermott and R Owens 'Equality and Flexibility for Workers with Family Responsibilities: A Troubled Union?' (2000) 13 *AJLL* 278; KL Adams 'A Step Backwards in Job Protection for Carers' (2002) 15 *AJLL* 93; Gaze, above n 54; and F Knowles 'Misdirection for Indirect Discrimination' (2004) 17 *AJLL* 185.

the value to the employer of the preparedness of permanent employees to be posted anywhere in the State, the managerial difficulties in administering education across a vast area, and the potential disruptive industrial impacts if payments that departed from the minima set out in the industrial instruments were made.[132] But there was little explicit attention paid to the detriment to the teachers of low wages, or to the advantages to the employer of the services of the temporary teachers. Indeed, in cases dealing with discrimination at work the interpretive approach has often revealed a judicial deference to management's prerogative in determining the way the workplace is organised. In *Schou* Harper J was quite explicit about this:

> When considering in any particular case whether the burden has been discharged, courts and tribunals must act with an appropriate degree of diffidence. The expertise of judges and tribunal members does not generally extend to the management of a business enterprise … and just as the courts, in proper recognition of their lack of relevant expertise, will not in general issue to company directors instructions about how they should manage the businesses under their control, so courts and tribunals concerned with equal opportunity legislation should resist the temptation unnecessarily to dictate to persons who manage, and work on, the shop floor. At the same time, anti-discrimination legislation should be liberally construed. Getting the balance right will often be difficult.[133]

When equality is conceptualised as a human right it is difficult to understand that it can be traded off against business imperatives. However, the test of reasonableness is not articulated within a concept of equality; it is not restricted by reference to the scope and purpose of the legislation. The consideration of a wide range of facts effectively means that practices that are indirectly discriminatory can be justified on grounds not available in cases of direct discrimination. Economic and financial considerations, for instance, can outweigh the effects of the discriminatory disadvantage. This is not possible in a case of direct discrimination, where a statutory exemption is the only way of excusing discriminatory behaviour.[134] Yet if each form of discrimination, direct and indirect, is as objectionable and harmful as the other this is illogical and reduces the capacity of the legislation to tackle the problems of structural discrimination with success. In *Waters* the minority judges, Mason CJ and Gaudron J, saw this and considered that the interpretation of reasonableness should be confined. In their view only the exemptions ought take otherwise discriminatory behaviour outside the operation of the legislation. However, the prevailing view has been that of Brennan J who held that the reasonableness requirement strikes a balance between the putative discriminator's 'legal freedom to impose a requirement' and the interests of persons in the protected category.[135]

No doubt the determination of the reasonableness of a requirement is often difficult and there can be different views about it. However, many of the cases do seem to

---

132 *Amery*, above n 56, 439.
133 See *State of Victoria v Schou* [2001] 3 VR 655, 663.
134 Cf R Dubler 'Direct Discrimination and a Defence of Reasonable Justification' (2003) 77 *ALJ* 514, proposing there should also be a defence of reasonable justification to direct discrimination.
135 *Waters*, above n 42, 379.

underestimate the harm of discrimination and overstate the concerns of business. Acknowledgment of the wrong of discrimination and the statutory purpose of eradicating it suggests that even where discriminatory practices are longstanding, the disruptive and perhaps even costly impacts of removing them may need to be accepted.[136] In some cases this has occurred. In *Banovic* there was judicial acknowledgment of the importance of the maintenance of peaceful industrial relations and a stable workforce that was not subject to industrial disruption because well-established patterns of industrial regulation had been disrupted. However, in the result this did not override concern at the discriminatory nature of those traditional norms.

When the perspective of the business is dominant, there is a risk that those complaining about indirectly discriminatory requirements will be treated as if they are asking for the bestowal of 'a favour', or some 'special treatment' or a 'special advantage'.[137] This risk is intensified because of the dominant understanding of equality as sameness, suggesting that the way not to discriminate is to treat all workers the same. Perhaps paradoxically accompanying the assertion that what is being requested is some form of special treatment, there is also often a fear that to grant it will open the floodgates and make the workplace unmanageable: what if all employees want to work from home? or work part-time? or cannot comply with the roster? Thus it has been noted: '[A] reasonable request made by one employee may place quite unreasonable burdens upon an employer when made by a number of employees.'[138] Of course the floodgates argument simply highlights the way in which workplaces are often structured with a set of assumptions that are premised upon a certain type of worker. In recent times these issues have arisen in a number of cases where women with family responsibilities have been seeking part-time work and their employer has been reluctant to provide it. The cases show that there is most chance of successfully establishing indirect discrimination where flexibility is *already* part of the culture of the workplace.[139] Discrimination legislation to date has thus not proved a particularly powerful tool to effect a transformation of the workplace, to eradicate systemic discrimination although the potential for this would be undeniable if the approach of the courts was a little bolder.

Exemptions, exceptions and special measures

Most discrimination legislation in Australia makes provisions for 'exemptions' or 'exceptions'. Exemptions or exceptions may be granted as a result of specific application to the relevant authority, such as HREOC, or may apply generally as provided in the legislation. In relation to work, one of most important exemptions relates to discriminatory acts done under statutory authority, including things done in compliance with industrial instruments.[140] Where there is an exemption then it places the relevant matters outside

---

136 *Amery*, above n 56, 472–3.
137 *State of Victoria v Schou* [2001] 3 VR 655, 658 and 661.
138 Ibid, 665.
139 *Bogle v Metropolitan Health Service Board* (2000) EOC ¶93–069; *Song*, above n 79; *Escobar*, above n 79; *Mayer*, above n 103. Cf *Kelly*, above n 97.
140 See eg *Gibbs v Commonwealth Bank* (1997) EOC ¶92–877. See below pp 386ff

the concern of the statute. An exemption is the starting point for consideration in a discrimination case. If the facts of the case do demonstrate that it falls within an exemption, then there is no point in going further to consider whether nonetheless there was unlawful discrimination. Thus in a case of disability discrimination, even if overcoming the discrimination would not impose an 'unjustifiable hardship' on an employer, this is of no relevance if the employment is, for example, related to combat duties and thus exempted under the legislation.[141]

General exemptions reflect a legislative policy to allow certain groups or types of businesses to be conducted without having to pay regard to equality principles.[142] This reinforces the perception that there are some domains into which it is inappropriate for the law to intrude. Sometimes these exemptions reflect the potential for clash between two different human rights, such as freedom of religion and equality, or historical arrangements such as the separation of church and state. In deference to the tenets of their belief systems and to avoid injuring the religious susceptibilities of members of particular faiths, religious organisations are often exempted from the proscriptions in discrimination legislation, especially those concerning the grounds of sex, marital status, and sexuality.[143] The width of such exceptions is significant and the policy behind them is often questioned not least because religious organisations are often funded by governments to play a significant role in the community and they employ many people. The exceptions relating to religious organisations are usually not restricted just to the appointment, training and education of clergy and members of religious orders and their performance of functions in the practice of their religion.[144] They often also encompass the employment of persons, for instance in schools conducted in accordance with religious tenets or other church businesses, although very often these exemptions are restricted to discriminatory acts done in 'good faith' to avoid injuring the sensibilities of those who practise the religion.

Sometimes exemptions reflect traditional views about certain kinds of work. Combat in the defence force is one such area.[145] The important High Court case of X v The Commonwealth,[146] considered the rights of a soldier who was HIV positive. Ordinarily such a case would have been considered under the exemption regarding combat and combat-related duties, but at the time the case was brought it was not operative because there were no relevant regulations. However, the courts have accepted that exemptions are to be read strictly according to their terms. Thus the exemptions relating to 'combat or combat-related duties' do not mean there is an automatic exemption from discrimination legislation for the defence forces in relation to all its workers.[147]

Some exemptions reflect and reinforce a view of equality as sameness. Such are the exemptions for 'privileges' granted in respect of pregnancy or childbirth, which only

141 *Disability Discrimination Act*, s 53. See *Commonwealth of Australia v Williams* (2002) 125 FCR 229.
142 These policies have been criticised: see Australian Law Reform Commission *Equality Before the Law: Justice for Women, Report No 64, Pt I* (1994).
143 *Sex Discrimination Act*, ss 37–8, *Age Discrimination Act*, s 35.
144 *Sex Discrimination Act*, ss 37–8.
145 *Sex Discrimination Act*, s 43; and *Disability Discrimination Act*, s 53.
146 (1999) 200 CLR 177.
147 *Commonwealth of Australia v Williams*, above n 141, 237–8.

make sense if equality is understood in this way.[148] The idea that equality generally demands the same treatment is also suggested by the provision of exemptions for 'special measures'.[149] The *Racial Discrimination Act 1975*, for instance, makes an exception for 'special measures', which, following *ICERD*, are designed for the 'sole purpose' of overcoming the negative effects of discrimination, and are not intended to bring about the erection of a system of separate rights for different racial groups.[150] By contrast the *Sex Discrimination Act* exempts acts 'for the purpose of achieving substantive equality'.[151] The *Disability Discrimination Act* exempts acts that are 'reasonably intended' to assist people with a disability to meet their 'special' needs in employment.[152]

In each of the statutory definitions of special measures there is some reference to intention or motive. In *Jacomb v The Australian Municipal, Administrative, Clerical and Services Union* trade union rules preserving the same number of elected executive positions for men and women, although this did not reflect the proportions of the membership, were held to be a special measure to ensure equality in the governance of union matters.[153] The test of 'purpose' was held in this case to be in part subjective, making it necessary to look at the way the matter is viewed by those who claim something is a special measure, although ultimately there must also be an objective assessment.[154]

The status of something as a 'special measure' also depends upon the context in which it operates, especially the nature of the disadvantage it seeks to redress. The elimination of a disadvantage would mean that a measure would no longer qualify as 'special' and thus lose its exempt status under the legislation.[155] In relation to disabilities, special measures are those things that afford opportunities to meet the needs of disabled people where these are different from others. The exemption of 'special measures' from discrimination legislation acknowledges the disadvantage that some groups experience and can play an important role in facilitating their participation in public life including at work.

Defences

Inherent requirements

In contrast to an exemption that places behaviour outside discrimination legislation, a defence provides an internal excuse to discrimination.

Discrimination legislation often provides that it is a defence to conduct that might otherwise be labelled discriminatory if the person discriminated against is unable to fulfil the 'inherent requirements' of the work or satisfy a 'genuine occupational qualification'.[156] As always, attention to the particular wording of the relevant statute

---

148 *Sex Discrimination Act*, s 31.
149 *Racial Discriminations Act*, s 8(1); *Sex Discrimination Act*, s 7D; and *Disability Discrimination Act*, s 45(c).
150 *Racial Discrimination Act*, s 8(1).
151 *Sex Discrimination Act*, s 7D;
152 *Disability Discrimination Act*, s 45(c).
153 (2004) 140 FCR 149.
154 Ibid, 161, 165 and 168–9.
155 Ibid, 169. On this concept see also *Gerhardy v Brown* (1985) 159 CLR 70; and *Kartinyeri v The Commonwealth* (1998) 195 CLR 337.
156 See eg *Sex Discrimination Act*, s 30(1); *Disability Discrimination Act*, s 15(4)(a); and *Age Discrimination Act*, s (4). See also *Workplace Relations Act*, s 659(3) discussed below p 482.

is critical. For instance, the 'inherent requirements' are variously described under the statutes as attaching to the 'employment', 'job', or 'position'. Different connotations may sometimes attach to each of these expressions. [157] Reference to a 'job', for instance, may focus attention more closely on the particular tasks to be performed, whereas a 'position' may indicate that the status in a particular work organisation is also an issue, and employment might refer more widely still to the whole work relationship.

Illustrations of things that might constitute an 'inherent requirement' or a 'genuine occupational qualification' are sometimes included in the legislation. The selection of a person of a certain sex to play a dramatic role, or the employment of a person of a particular sex where this is required in order to conform to social expectations regarding decency and privacy, are two examples.[158] In the cases there are numerous other examples. The requirement that a worker be able to tolerate penicillin if working in a chemical factory where there is exposure to it provides another illustration of the concept.[159]

State discrimination legislation usually provides that this type of defence is available in relation to all discriminatory acts,[160] but its availability is more limited at the Commonwealth level. Under the *Sex Discrimination Act* only those acts at the very beginning of the work relationship, the arrangements for determining who should be offered work and the offer of work in employment or as a commission agent, and acts preventing a contract worker from working or continuing to work are susceptible of being excused by a claim in relation to a 'genuine occupational qualification'.[161] Under the *Disability Discrimination Act* the 'inherent requirement' provision only relates to the offer or termination of employment; the engagement or termination of an agent; allowing a contractor to work or continue to work; the invitation to become a partner, determining who can be a partner, and expulsion from a partnership; in admission to professional bodies; or the allocation of work by employment agencies.[162] The limited availability of the 'inherent requirement' defence has been observed as anomalous and requiring correction by the Australian Parliament.[163]

The interpretation of the defence, excusing what would otherwise amount to discriminatory conduct, impacts upon the protective scope of the legislation. The concept of 'inherent requirements' is not free from difficulty, and the High Court has considered the issue on several occasions. In *Christie* a pilot's employment was terminated when he turned sixty years old because the international rules governing aviation in all but three of the countries serviced by QANTAS did not permit pilots to fly beyond that age.[164] Christie's argument effectively asserted that it would be possible to organise his flight schedules so that he could fly only on routes not governed by the

---

157 See *Christie*, above n 48, 304. Cf *Cosma v QANTAS Airways Ltd (Cosma)*(2002) 124 FCR 504, 511–12.

158 See *Sex Discrimination Act*, s 30(2).

159 *Cramer v Smith Kline Beecham* (1997) 73 IR 470.

160 See eg *Anti-Discrimination Act 1977* (NSW), ss 14, 31, 49D–G, 49J–K, 49V–Y, 49ZB–ZC and 49ZYJ; *Anti-Discrimination Act 1991* (Qld), s 25; and *Equal Opportunity Act 1984* (SA), ss 34, 56, 71 and 85F. Cf *Equal Opportunity Act 1995* (Vic), s 17.

161 *Sex Discrimination Act*, s 30(1).

162 See *Disability Discrimination Act*, ss 15(4)(a), 16(3)(a), 17(2)(a), 18(4)(a), 19(2) and 21(2).

163 *Purvis*, above n 36, 124.

164 See *Christie*, above n 48. Note that this case concerned the interpretation of *Industrial Relations Act 1988* (Cth), ss 170DF(1)(f) and (2), the equivalent of *Workplace Relations Act*, s 569(3).

rules, whereas the airline argued that it was an inherent requirement of his position as an international pilot that he was available to fly all routes. Several years later in *X v The Commonwealth* the High Court considered a claim that the dismissal of a soldier who tested positive to HIV in line with Australian Defence Force policy was justified on the basis of the 'inherent requirements' of his position as a soldier.[165] Both cases were remitted back to the relevant tribunals for final determination on the facts.

There was a wide spectrum of views in these cases on the interpretation of the defence. However, there has been a certain reluctance to elaborate broad binding principles in the cases, with the judges confident that from the facts of particular cases a 'firm jurisprudence' will emerge.[166]

At its narrowest, to say that a requirement is 'inherent' suggests something that is unaffected by factors such as the geographic location of the work, or by the particular workplace context. On this view the terms of a contract or managerial interventions at the workplace, such as the setting of rosters, would not be covered by it.[167] If it were otherwise, employers might be able to evade discrimination legislation. Various synonyms, such as 'essential', 'permanent', 'integral' and 'inseparable', have been used to try to express this view.[168] The argument for a narrow interpretation is strong when the effect of the defence is kept in mind. A successful defence excuses otherwise 'discriminatory' conduct and given the purposes of discrimination legislation should be interpreted narrowly.[169]

However, a broader approach has prevailed. While an inability to do the work will generally suffice, it is also clear that the 'inherent' or 'genuine' requirements of a job are not necessarily limited to the physical capacity to do the work. Something more can be required. The capacity to perform the work in a way that ensures that the workplace is safe for all, be they other workers, clients and customers or the public at large, will also be an integral:

> That is because employment is not a mere physical activity in which the employee participates as an automaton. It takes place in a social, legal and economic context. Unstated, but legitimate, employment requirements may stem from this context.[170]

Compliance with other terms implied in a work contract, such as an ability to keep trade secrets, is something else that would usually be seen as an inherent requirement. Some judges have suggested that the capacity to comply with all legal obligations, whether arising from contract, statute or statutory agreements, may form part of the understanding of the inherent requirements of work.[171]

Nonetheless it is equally obvious that the inherent requirements should not be manipulable or able to be contrived by employers or businesses.[172] If the person wanting

---

165 *X v Commonwealth of Australia (X's Case)* (1999) 200 CLR 177.
166 *Christie*, above n 48, 284.
167 Ibid, 335.
168 Ibid, 340.
169 Ibid, 333; and *X's Case*, above n 165, 228. See also T MacDermott 'Age Discrimination and Employment Law: The Sky's the Limit' (1998) 11 *AJLL* 144.
170 See *X's Case*, above n 165, 187–8, and see also 207–8.
171 Ibid, 209. See also *Christie*, above n 48, 307–8, 316 and 318.
172 Ibid, 208.

work done can simply decree, say in a term of a contract, that something is essential, then the protections of the legislation could easily be evaded by a sham requirement. At the same time, this does not necessarily mean that contractual terms are irrelevant. As Gaudron J observed in *Christie*, if a requirement is essential whether its basis is the employment contract or the conditions governing the employment relationship will be irrelevant.[173] The same issues arise in relation to the question as to whether the nature of the business or the way it is organised can constitute inherent requirements. In *Christie* some judges considered that the ability to participate in the roster bidding system was an inherent requirement of the job, although others left the matter open and when the case was returned to the tribunal to try facts it would have been necessary to determine whether compliance with the ordinary flight roster was an inherent requirement.[174] In *Cosma* the Full Court of the Federal Court confirmed a decision at first instance that working on rotation in a gang was an inherent requirement: this was so as a matter of fairness, because some jobs were more difficult than others, and to minimise the risk of injury.[175] Yet such decisions do not sit easily when work relations are increasingly individualised and there are demands to promote diversity.

In this area of the law similar issues to those that are evident in the calculation of whether a requirement is reasonable can be seen to arise. Again sometimes judges have suggested that, in determining whether something is essential in the way a business is run, there must be 'appropriate recognition to the business judgment of the employer in organising its undertaking and in regarding this or that requirement as essential to the particular employment'.[176] Thus once again there is a risk that a judicial deference to managerial prerogative will translate into a tolerance of discriminatory behaviour and conditions in workplaces and lessen the capacity of the legislation to address systemic discrimination and to bring about workplace change.

A duty to accommodate difference and diversity?

It is common for businesses to organise the workplace according to certain rules. A rostering arrangement is one such example. A requirement to work at the place of business of the employer is another. When these rules are applied to everyone in the workplace the sameness of their treatment will often be characterised as 'equitable, efficient and non-discriminatory' with deviation from the organisational rule said to introduce 'inequality of treatment'.[177] As we have seen, those who cannot comply with the rules and want to be exempted from them are often said to be seeking 'special treatment'. However, if the rules, policies or organisational methods in a workplace are discriminatory in their impact and are not reasonable or do not comprise an inherent requirement of the work, then there will be a breach of discrimination legislation. Can we say, then, that there is a duty to accommodate difference at the workplace?

---

173 *Christie*, above n 48, 295.
174 Ibid, 285–6 and 296.
175 *Cosma*, above n 157, 507, citing the court at first instance.
176 *X's Case*, above n 165, 189–90.
177 See *Christie*, above n 48, 285–6. See above p 373.

The question of whether discrimination legislation actually imposes a positive duty upon business and employers to accommodate diversity and difference by taking positive steps to create a work environment that is inclusive of all is raised more directly in relation to discrimination on the ground of disability. This is because the federal legislation provides an alternative to the inherent requirements defence, that in order to carry out those requirements the person requires services or facilities that would impose an 'unjustifiable hardship' on the employer.[178] As defined by the *Disability Discrimination Act* this requires that 'all relevant circumstances of the particular case are to be taken into account', including the nature of the benefit or detriment likely to accrue to the person, the effect of the disability on the person concerned, the financial circumstances and the estimated amount of expenditure required by the person claiming the unjustifiable hardship, and an action plan regarding the provision of services or the making available of facilities.[179]

The courts have been reluctant to restate the words of the statute. The cases provide many examples where change in the workplace has been effectively required: a policy against sitting at the counter has been modified by the provision of a stool for a disabled worker to be seated and the reorganisation of the workspace so that it was not hazardous;[180] the provision of effective technology to assist workers with visual disabilities and dyslexia.[181] In each case the facts will be important. The provision of a ramp to enable a person in a wheelchair to work from a counter may present no significant difficulty for an employing business, but relocating a person from a remote location on a weekly basis to ensure appropriate access to medical treatment may.[182] One of the arguments for taking a narrow view of what can amount to an 'inherent requirement' under the *Disability Discrimination Act* is that there is always the potential for operational issues to be considered under 'unjustifiable hardship'.[183]

Although some earlier cases suggested that the 'unjustifiable hardship' provision imposed a duty of reasonable accommodation, the High Court rejected this in *Purvis*. It held that the failure to make accommodation was not a breach of the legislation.[184] Nonetheless, as the majority judges also pointed out, in many instances a finding of discrimination will not be able to be avoided where some efforts of accommodation have not been made. Thus 'as a practical matter' an employing business may have to take some positive steps to accommodate a disabled person in order to avoid a finding of discrimination.[185]

However, in most discrimination legislation there is no explicit reference to the concept of 'unjustifiable hardship' and the 'duty' to make accommodation that is

---

178 *Disability Discrimination Act*, ss 15(4)(b), 16(4)(b), 17(2)(b) and 18(4)(b). See *X's Case*, above n 165, 190.
179 *Disability Discrimination Act*, s 11.
180 *Daghlian v Australian Postal Corporation* (2003) EOC ¶93–287.
181 *McNeill v Commonwealth of Australia* (1995) EOC ¶92–714, 78 367; and *Randell v Consolidated Bearing Co (SA) Pty Ltd* (2002) EOC ¶93–216.
182 An example provided in *X's Case*, above n 165, 208–9.
183 See *X's Case*, above n 183, 228.
184 See *Purvis*, above n 36, 105–6, 127, 155 and 159.
185 Ibid, 127 and 159–60.

discussed in the disability arena is usually ignored and held to be irrelevant in the other areas.[186] However, it can likewise be seen that where there is indirect discrimination because a term, requirement or condition is unreasonable, an obvious *practical* (if not legal) effect of discrimination legislation is that change will be required. Of course if the relevant test for indirect discrimination were one of necessity, rather than simply that of reasonableness, discrimination legislation would have an even greater impact.

The duty to provide a workplace free from discrimination and harassment

Harassment at work is a form of discrimination.[187] Some discrimination legislation also effectively imposes positive duties to ensure that the workplace is free from discrimination and harassment. It makes the employer or the business entity responsible for the organisation of a workplace vicariously liable for their employees' or agents' acts of discrimination and harassment. Only where it can be demonstrated that 'all reasonable steps' to prevent the prohibited behaviour have been taken can the liability be avoided.[188]

The law on sexual harassment is well developed here and illustrates the impact of the imposition of vicarious liability under discrimination statutes.[189] A range of facts relevant to the case will be considered to determine if 'reasonable steps' have been taken.[190] Matters such as the provision of training to staff, the development and implementation of an equal employment opportunity (EEO) management plan, and the publication of a discrimination policy are some of the more obvious. But it is clear that it is not enough simply to provide one-off training or to have a written policy. Compliance measures must be made effective. For instance, a policy must be clear, be readily available and be communicated to all in the workplace. But more than this it must be brought to the attention of workers, explained and, where appropriate, training provided in relation to it and perhaps on a regular basis. If the policy provides for contact persons in the organisation they must be accessible.[191] The defence of 'reasonable steps' is equally available to large and small enterprises, but more will usually be expected of a larger organisation with more resources.

The standard imposed by the defence is in most instances quite rigorous: there is an expectation that business and employers will have in place systems to ensure

---

186 Ibid, 121.

187 M Thornton 'Sexual Harassment Losing Sight of Sex Discrimination' (2002) 56 *MULR* 422 points out the dangers of losing the connection between the two.

188 See *Racial Discrimination Act*, s 18A; and *Sex Discrimination Act*, s 106. The concept of vicariously liability under discrimination legislation has been held to be wider than in tort: *Trainer v South Pacific Resort Hotels Pty Ltd* (2005) 144 FCR 402.

189 See G Mason and A Chapman 'Defining Sexual Harassment: A History of the Commonwealth Legislation and Its Critiques' (2003) 31 *Fed LR* 195; J Morgan 'Equality, Morality and Manners' in M Thornton *Public and Private: Feminist Legal Debates* (1995); and C Parker 'Public Rights in Private Government: Corporate Compliance with Sexual Harassment Legislation' (1998) 5 *Aust J HR* 159.

190 In some jurisdictions the legislation provides examples of the factors that will be considered: see eg *Anti-Discrimination Act 1992* (NT), s 105(3).

191 See eg *Evans v Lee and the Commonwealth Bank* (1996) EOC ¶92–822; *Shiels v James & Lipman Pty Ltd* [2000] FMCA 2, [65] and [74]; and *Aleksovski v Australia Asia Aerospace Pty Ltd* [2002] FMCA 81; *Johanson v Blackledge Meats* (2001) 163 FLR 58, 81; *Cooke v Plauen Holdings Pty Ltd* [2001] FMCA 91, [37].

that discriminatory behaviour does not occur. It is preventative action that is required. There is usually no requirement that complainants show that the business or employer authorised the proscribed acts. Of course, where there is knowledge and no action is taken liability will follow.[192] But it is not necessary under federal legislation to show that there was knowledge of the particular acts of discrimination on the part of the defendant.[193]

However, in some jurisdictions discrimination legislation only imposes vicarious liability for some acts of discrimination (such as sexual harassment) and only where the employer or principal authorised, instructed or connived at the behaviour.[194] In *Caton v Richmond Club Limited* a broad interpretation was applied so that 'authorise' also encompassed sanctioning or permitting.[195] In this case it was held that the club knew of the inappropriate and unwanted behaviour because several middle managers knew, although there was never a formal complaint. The managers failed to recognise the behaviour as potentially unlawful, to monitor it, and to take appropriate action such as bringing the sexual harassment policy to the attention of the harasser, all of which effectively permitted the harasser to continue. The tribunal concluded: 'inaction … constitutes implicit authorisation'.[196] Thus to avoid liability there is in practice an obligation on business and employers to take 'reasonable steps' to ensure that the culture of workplaces and the behaviour of those in them is in accord with the legislation.

Affirmative action

There is, however, a general reticence in Anglo-Australian jurisprudence to recognise positive duties. One of the few examples of legislation aiming to mobilise positive action against inequality was first introduced in the mid-1980s. The *Affirmative Action (Equal Opportunity for Women) Act 1986* (Cth), as its name indicates, was concerned only with gender equality. It required the introduction of equity policies and programs in large enterprises, where there were more than 100 employees. This early legislation, which was later extended to cover voluntary bodies including community groups and trade unions, mandated the adoption of an employment equity policy, the appointment of Equal Employment Opportunity (EEO) officers, consultation with trade unions and staff, an analysis of the profile of workers, the setting of targets, and the monitoring and evaluation of progress to meet them.

A review of this legislation was conducted in the late 1990s.[197] Although the research indicated that workplaces covered by the legislation had better outcomes for women vis-à-vis men than those not so covered,[198] there were still deficiencies especially at senior levels in organisations. New legislation, the *Equal Opportunity for Women in*

---

192 *Gilroy v Angelov* (2000) 181 ALR 57.

193 See *Boyle v Ishan Ozden* (1986) EOC ¶92–165; *State Electricity Commission of Victoria v Equal Opportunity Board* (1989) EOC ¶92–259; *McAlister v SEQ Aboriginal Corporation v Lamb* [2002] FMCA 109; *Cooke v Plauen Holdings Pty Ltd*, above n 191.

194 See eg *Anti-Discrimination Act 1977* (NSW), s 53; and *Equal Opportunity Act 1984* (SA), s 91(2).

195 [2003] NSWADT 202.

196 Ibid, [141]–[142].

197 See Independent Committee *Unfinished Business: Equity for Women in Australian Workplaces* (1998).

198 M Gardner et al *Workplace Effects of Affirmative Action Legislation* (1999).

the Workplace Act 1999 (Cth), with the stated aim of eliminating discrimination and fostering consultation in the workplace on EEO issues for women was then enacted. The legislation eliminated all notion of positive treatment or affirmative action, and emphasised that the employment of women must be dealt with on the basis of merit. The equal treatment view of equality was thus reasserted, and gendered assumptions implicit in the concept of merit were not explored.

The *Equal Opportunity for Women in the Workplace Act 1999* (Cth) still requires employers in very large enterprises (those with 100 or more employees, and also higher educational institutions) to develop and implement EEO programs both to eliminate discrimination and to ensure the implementation of measures to secure equal opportunity.[199] Most large businesses have developed discrimination and sexual harassment policies for implementation at the workplace. These policy statements disseminate information about the organisation's EEO program and provide the basis for in-house training. In addition, they usually also establish procedures and mechanisms for dealing with any instances of unlawful discriminatory behaviour within the workplace.

The *Equal Opportunity for Women in the Workplace Act 1999* (Cth) did establish a new process for implementation, requiring the employing business to appoint a person with responsibility to consult with employees and to prepare a profile of the workplace. The next step is for the business itself to identify priority issues, draw up a program of action in relation to them, and then evaluate its effectiveness.[200] The focus in the legislation is thus on facilitating greater self-regulation by business. The 'business case' for diversity and flexibility in the workforce is intended to hold sway.[201] The idea is that the process is outcome-oriented and flexible to suit the needs of the particular workplace. The Equal Opportunity for Women in the Workplace Agency (EOWA), which is set up under the legislation and reports to the Minister, can provide assistance to employers in this process.[202] The employing businesses covered by the legislation should report annually to EOWA, but this reporting can be confidential.[203] The sanction is public shaming, or naming by EOWA, although there can also be exclusion from government contracts, but there is otherwise no formal sanction regime. While there has been a tendency to dismiss the impact of the regime established under the legislation as largely ineffectual, it may also be recognised as making some positive contribution to human rights at least in the workplaces of larger organisations.[204]

The regulatory system of discrimination law

The regulatory system

At the federal level the *Human Rights and Equal Opportunity Commission Act* establishes HREOC, which has regulatory oversight of all federal discrimination

---

199 *Equal Opportunity for Women in the Workplace Act 1999* (Cth), s 6.
200 Ibid, s 8.
201 EOWA *Why Equal Opportunity Makes Sense*, available at <www.eowa.gov.au>.
202 *Equal Opportunity for Women in the Workplace Act 1999* (Cth), ss 8A–12.
203 *Equal Opportunity for Women in the Workplace Act 1999* (Cth), ss 13–19.
204 See C Andrades 'Women, Work, and Unfinished Business: The *Equal Opportunity for Women in the Workplace Act 1999* (Cth)' (2000) 13 *AJLL* 171, 182.

law.[205] HREOC comprises a President, currently the Hon John von Doussa, a Human Rights Commissioner, Race Discrimination Commissioner, Aboriginal and Torres Strait Islander Social Justice Commissioner, Sex Discrimination Commissioner, and Disability Discrimination Commissioner.[206] HREOC has multiple regulatory functions conferred upon it by both the *Human Rights and Equal Opportunity Commission Act* and the various federal discrimination Acts. The functions of HREOC in relation to unlawful discrimination are of two main types. It deals with individual complaints of discrimination and other breaches of federal discrimination legislation involving such matters as harassment, vilification, and victimisation.[207] In addition, it has a broad range of functions that include promoting understanding and compliance with discrimination legislation; developing, fostering and conducting research and educational programs to combat discrimination; preparing guidelines and making recommendations to government; acting as advisor to government regarding legislation; and generally promoting understanding, acceptance and public discussion of human rights in Australia.[208]

The regulatory scheme established in relation to discrimination law is thus a multifaceted one. In an important analysis of this scheme as it applies to the *Sex Discrimination Act* Belinda Smith has observed that its purposes are sometimes competing.[209] From a legal perspective past criticism of discrimination legislation has focused particularly on the way in which the system makes provision for individual remedies and is inadequate to confront the deeper and more systemic problems of discrimination.[210] While not denying the continuing and damaging effects of discriminatory acts and hence the validity of these earlier criticisms, Smith points out that such criticisms tend to ignore the informal and soft regulatory mechanisms that are available under discrimination legislation and she argues these are starting to have an observable impact in developing non-discrimination norms in modern workplaces.

The individual complaint process

In Australia where unlawful discrimination occurs contrary to federal legislation, complaints may be made in writing to HREOC for relief. A complaint may be lodged either by the aggrieved person on their own behalf, or also on behalf of others, or by a trade union on behalf of an aggrieved person or persons.[211] In 'representative complaints' consent by the other person or persons is not necessary, and they may not even be identified individually, just as members of a class, but such a person can always

---

205 Under the various discrimination statutes in the Australian States and Territories there are also established Commissions (or, in New South Wales, a Board) with responsibility for the administrative oversight of the respective legislation.

206 *Human Rights and Equal Opportunity Act*, s 8.

207 Ibid, Pt IIB.

208 *Human Rights and Equal Opportunity Act*, s 11; *Racial Discrimination Act*, s 20; *Sex Discrimination Act*, s 48; *Disability Discrimination Act*, s 67; and *Age Discrimination Act*, s 53.

209 B Smith 'A Regulatory Analysis of the *Sex Discrimination Act 1984* (Cth): Can It Effect Equality or Only Redress Harm?' in C Arup et al (eds) *Labour Law and Labour Market Regulation* (2006).

210 See Thornton, above n 15; Hunter, above n 114; and R Hunter 'The Mirage of Justice: Women and the Shrinking State' (2002) 16 *AFLJ* 53.

211 *Human Rights and Equal Opportunity Commission Act*, s 46P.

withdraw from the complaint.[212] In a representative claim it is important to be clear about the behaviour that is the subject of the complaint and that it affected all the members of the class.[213]

Conciliation

The process for dealing with individual complaints of unlawful discrimination is similar in the various jurisdictions. Following the receipt of a complaint, it is investigated, and there is an attempt to conciliate between the parties. At Commonwealth level the *Human Rights and Equal Opportunity Commission Act* allows HREOC's President to investigate and conciliate in all disputes arising from behaviour that impairs equality of opportunity or treatment in employment or occupation under Commonwealth law.[214] Once a complaint has been lodged with HREOC it is possible to get an interim injunction from the court to maintain the situation as it was immediately before the complaint was lodged.[215] This can be particularly important in affecting the outcome of a case. In most cases conciliation proves an effective means for resolving individual discrimination disputes. However, it remains a private process, and because the ultimate settlement is very often subject to a confidentiality agreement it has a limited capacity to play a wider role in the regulatory system.

Beyond conciliation

The vast majority of cases are settled by conciliation. Under state legislation, where the matter is not resolved in this way it may go on to a further hearing by a tribunal to decide the matter. Appeal to the ordinary courts is then only possible on a matter of law. At the federal level the constitutional doctrine of the separation of powers means that a body that is not a court cannot make a binding determination of rights. Following the decision in *Brandy v Human Rights and Equal Opportunity Commission*,[216] the process for dealing with complaints made under federal discrimination law that are not settled by conciliation was restructured with the passage of the *Human Rights Legislation Amendment Act (No 1) 1999* (Cth).

Where a complaint concerns discrimination on one of the grounds outlined in the *Human Rights and Equal Opportunity Regulations*,[217] HREOC has a power to investigate, and may endeavour to settle it through a conciliation process. If no settlement between the parties is reached, HREOC can only provide a report to the Minister. This report may include a recommendation concerning a remedy, including the payment of compensation, but there is no mechanism for enforcing it.[218]

When there is no conciliated settlement of a complaint made under one of the discrimination statutes, the complainant may take the matter to the Federal Magistrates

---

212 Ibid, s 46PB–46PC.
213 *CBA*, above n 113.
214 *Human Rights and Equal Opportunity Commission Act*, s 11(1)(aa). A detailed account of the various steps in the handling of a complaint can be seen at <www.humanrights.gov.au/legal/reports_hreoca.html>.
215 *Human Rights and Equal Opportunity Commission Act*, s 46PP.
216 (1995) 183 CLR 245.
217 See above n 73.
218 *Human Rights and Equal Opportunity Act*, ss 31(b) and 32(1). Reports are available at <www.humanrights.gov.au/legal/reports_hreoca.html>.

Court, from which there is a further appeal to the Federal Court. In such actions each of the Commissioners appointed under the three Commonwealth discrimination Acts can play a role as *amicus curiae*. The jurisprudence of discrimination law that is emerging from the Federal Magistrates Court is proving very important in creating more public awareness of issues of discrimination in the workplace.

Standard of proof

One of the reasons for the establishment of specialist procedures for dealing with individual complainants under discrimination law was to ensure that there was not an overly legalistic approach to problems. The conciliation process does have many of the advantages of informality when compared with the traditional court processes. However, beyond conciliation at the courts (or tribunals in the States), the process is more formal and there can be significant issues for complainants. For instance, the onus of proof generally falls on the complainant and although sometimes courts and tribunals may be prepared to take notice of well-known facts—say, that part-time work is more generally required by those with family responsibilities—evidence will often be required. With problems of deep systemic discrimination, such as racism, this can often be difficult. On more than one occasion the approach of courts and tribunals has been cautious. Indeed it has been held that although inferences may sometimes be drawn from the facts—for example, when there is no one from a non-English speaking background employed—this is not by itself enough and there is a high standard of proof required when there are serious allegations of discrimination.[219] Proof of the elements of indirect discrimination can be particularly difficult for individuals.[220] The onus of proof in relation to defences, exemptions or exceptions lies with the person arguing for it. Thus, for example, where an employer or business is arguing that accommodating a person with a disability would impose an 'unjustifiable hardship' it is necessary for them to prove that this is so.

Costs

One of the issues affecting the access of individuals to remedies for discrimination is the issue of costs. If individuals are deterred from bringing claims because costs may be awarded against them, the purposes of discrimination legislation are likely to be thwarted. Now that in the federal arena discrimination matters may go forward to the Federal Magistrates Court or the Federal Court, costs may be awarded against unsuccessful litigants.[221] Sometimes there may be some considerations that will influence a court to exercise its discretion to reduce the costs to be paid by the unsuccessful party. In *Jacomb v The Australian Municipal, Administrative, Clerical and Services Union* Crennan J suggested that this could occur where a case was akin to a 'test case' and there could be discerned a particular 'public interest' in its resolution.[222]

---

219 *Sharma v Legal Aid (Qld)* (2002) 115 IR 91. See also J Hunyor 'Skin Deep: Proof and Inferences of Racial Discrimination in Employment' (2003) 25 *Syd LR* 535.
220 See above p 366.
221 *Federal Court of Australia Act 1976* (Cth), s 43; and *Federal Magistrates Act 1999* (Cth), s 79.
222 [2004] FCA 1600, [10]. Cf *Sluggett v Human Rights and Equal Opportunity Commission* [2002] FCA 1060.

Remedies

There is a range of remedial orders, listed in s 46PO(4) of the *Human Rights and Equal Opportunity Act*, available from the courts where discrimination contrary to the federal statutes is proved. These include: orders restraining a respondent from further acts of discrimination; requiring a respondent to take specific actions to redress the loss or damage suffered by an applicant; requiring a respondent to employ or re-employ an applicant; requiring the payment of compensatory damages to an applicant; or requiring variation of the termination of a contract to redress loss or damage; and any other appropriate order.

Employment or re-employment orders

An order of employment or re-employment is particularly significant in supporting the labour force participation of a person who has suffered discrimination. Exclusion from access to employment or loss of employment is very often not something that can be adequately compensated for simply by a monetary award.

In *Song v Ainsworth Game Technology Pty Ltd* an employer had insisted that a woman who worked fulltime change to part-time work if she wanted to absent herself for a short period in the mid-afternoon to transfer her child from school to child care.[223] The inflexibility of this approach, coupled with the fact that there was evidence of others being able to take time out from work (to smoke a cigarette) and that the relevant industrial award would have enabled a more flexible arrangement of her work made it clear that she was discriminated against on the basis of family responsibilities. There were no other problems evident in the work relationship, and so orders were made that Ms Song was to be reinstated and her contract varied to allow her a short break to take her child to childcare in the afternoons.

The appropriateness of an order to employ or re-employ may be affected by the amount of time it takes to resolve a case. However, given the importance of the remedy from the point of view of a worker's labour force participation, there is every reason to determine cases as quickly as possible and to ensure that parties do not act in a way that protracts the proceedings unnecessarily. Re-employment orders, along with other orders that require a business or organisation to act in a way that eliminates the discrimination, such as orders to provide part-time work to workers with family responsibilities or to accommodate better such a worker in a roster, are all particularly significant in impacting on the organisational culture of workplaces.

Damages

Damages in this jurisdiction are awarded on the basis of principles analogous to those in tort.[224] In general this means that the position of the applicant as it would have been had there been no discrimination is compared with their position after the discriminatory

---

223 Above n 79.
224 *Hall v A & A Sheiban Pty Ltd* (1989) 20 FCR 217; *Gilroy v Angelov*, above n 192; and *Leslie v Graham* (2002) EOC ¶93–196.

acts, and the award of damages is intended to put the applicant in the place they would have been in, if unlawful acts had not happened.

Damages may fall into several categories.[225] Special damages are available to cover economic loss such as lost wages, lost superannuation or medical expenses. However, an applicant may also be awarded general damages for humiliation, distress, and loss of dignity. There has been criticism in the past concerning the amounts that have been awarded to compensate for hurt feelings. In part this reflects conflicting views on the nature of these damages. In some cases the compensatory aspect of the damages has tended to keep the amount in check.[226] On other occasions the important public policy aspects of eradicating discrimination have been noted as pointing away from minimising non-economic loss.[227] Although amounts between $5000 and $10000 appear to be the most common, awards of damages always depend on the facts and amounts up to $20000 have been awarded.[228] The damages awarded for non-economic loss may be far greater, especially in a case where there is, for instance, medical evidence that the applicant has suffered major depressive illness over a period of several years as a consequence of a discriminatory dismissal,[229] or in cases of harassment where the nature of the discrimination often means there is a greater element of hurt, humiliation or distress.[230]

The recognition of hurt, humiliation and distress and the provision of damages for them in this jurisdiction is likely to become a significant factor when workers who have been dismissed in a discriminatory way are deciding whether to pursue their case in this jurisdiction or under the *Workplace Relations Act*.[231]

There has been some debate as to whether punitive or exemplary damages are available in this jurisdiction because there is only specific mention of compensatory damages in s 49PO(4). Nonetheless the language of the section also suggests that the listed orders are illustrative rather than exhaustive, and thus the courts ought to retain discretion to award punitive damages where it is appropriate to do so.[232] In some cases aggravated and exemplary damages of a punitive nature have been awarded where there has been an element of maliciousness or particular oppressiveness in a respondent's behaviour. Unnecessary delay caused by a respondent in resolving a case,[233] or by the

---

225 There are summary tables of awards of damages in HREOC, above n 7, Ch 7 'Damages and Remedies'. See also C Ronalds and R Pepper *Discrimination Law and Practice* (2004), Ch 14 'Remedies'. In some state discrimination jurisdictions there is a statutory cap on damages: see eg *Anti-Discrimination Act 1977* (NSW), s 133.

226 See eg in *Song*, above n 79, and *Randell v Consolidated Bearing Company (SA) Pty Ltd* [2002] FMCA 44, where $10 000 was awarded for non-economic loss.

227 See *Horne & McIntosh v Press Clough Joint Venture* (1994) EOC ¶92–591, 77,179; *Mayer*, above n 103.

228 See eg *McKenzie v Department of Urban Services and Canberra Hospital* (2001) 163 FLR 133 ($15000 non-economic loss); and *Oberoi v Human Rights and Equal Opportunity Commission* [2001] FMCA 34 ($18500 non-economic loss). See also the comments in *Catholic Education Office v Clarke* (2004) 138 FCR 121, 149–50.

229 See eg *Commonwealth of Australia v Evans*, above n 85, on appeal reduced general damages from $25000 with interest to $12000.

230 See eg *Bishop v Takla* [2004] FMCA 74 ($20000 non-economic loss); *Gilroy v Angelov*, above n 192, ($20000 non-economic loss); *Shiels v James & Lipman Pty Ltd* [2000] FMCA 2, [79] ($13000 non-economic loss).

231 See below pp 405.

232 *Frith v Exchange Hotel* (2005) 191 FLR 18.

233 *Elliott v Nanda and The Commonwealth* (2001) 111 FCR 240.

introduction of irrelevant evidence designed to further harm an applicant, may be an occasion for aggravated damages.[234] The advantage of exemplary and punitive remedies is that the focus shifts from the complainant to the wrong doing of the respondent.

Discrimination law: soft regulation

Criticism of the effectiveness of the individual remedial process under discrimination legislation is long-standing. Those who are subjected to discrimination are often among the most vulnerable and least able to pursue a claim, and the regulatory role of HREOC is quite limited with no power to initiate and pursue problems of systemic discrimination that it identifies.[235] However, discrimination legislation has always been concerned not only with the provision of remedies for individuals who have been wronged but also with bringing about change in the workplace. HREOC (and its counterpart State regulatory institutions) provide a range of other services, from general educative information throughout the community to delivering specific programs to workplaces. Smith has concluded that, although it does not have the traditional 'big stick' enforcement tools, HREOC has effectively utilised education, persuasion and other technical assistance to bolster, translate and leverage the weak formal mechanisms available to it.[236]

Certainly HREOC and its counterparts are a very useful resource to business in assisting its compliance with discrimination legislation.[237] The availability of guidelines and codes of conduct, such as the *Sexual Harassment Code of Practice*, is an illustration of this. While there is no doubt a desire by many businesses to ensure that they do not sully their own reputation in the area of discrimination, the impact of soft regulatory mechanisms remains arguably much stronger with large enterprises than those that are smaller. It is those larger organisations that are more likely to seek acclaim through 'best practice awards'. In so far as the Australian approach is implementing a range of regulatory responses to the problem of discrimination in the workplace it is conforming to a pattern that is discernible elsewhere in the world and in other areas;[238] however, the absence of a back-up 'big stick' remains a notable problem with this regulatory regime.

Intersections between discrimination and labour law

It is evident that discrimination law has some different objectives from those of traditional labour law. Discrimination law is centred on broad concepts of social equality across a range of areas of 'public' life, of which work is one. In the workplace its focus is the rights of the individual, whatever their workforce status. Labour law has been more focused on the relations of capital and labour in employment relations more narrowly understood and therefore traditionally concerned mostly with the workers who are employees. Nonetheless, its range of concerns in the workplace is wide. In the

---

234 *Font v Paspaley Pearls* [2002] FMCA 142.
235 Smith, above n 209.
236 Ibid.
237 See information provided through HREOC's website, <www.hreoc.gov.au>.
238 B Hepple, M Coussey and T Choudhury *Equality: A New Framework. Report of the Independent Review of the Enforcement of UK Anti-discrimination Legislation* (2000). See also Hepple, above n 29.

past these have tended to coalesce around the concept of fairness, whether that be in the protection of vulnerable workers, the operation of workplace norms in awards and agreements, or the resolution of conflict in the workplace. The focus on fairness has also meant that labour law's lens was in the past often trained on workers collectively and on balancing the interests of capital and labour.

Ever since the introduction of discrimination law in the 1970s its intersection with labour law has been an important issue for workplace participants. Because the two areas of law can be seen as having different concerns, there is no necessary or automatic conflict between them. This was the finding of the High Court when it ruled in *Wardley* that although the pilot's employment was terminated in accordance with the relevant industrial instrument it was, nonetheless, unlawful because in breach of discrimination law.[239] The High Court held that in that case there was no inconsistency between the two laws: the specifics of labour law operated against the background of broad social principles contained in discrimination law. The workplace participants therefore had to comply with the requirements both of industrial instruments, such as awards or agreements, and of discrimination legislation. However, this decision does not resolve all questions about the intersection of discrimination law and labour law.

The coexistence of the two regulatory regimes raised deeper questions about their compatibility,[240] and despite *Wardley* there was always the prospect for collision at the institutional level between the two jurisdictions. What if an industrial instrument itself set up a discriminatory rule or authorised discriminatory treatment? Could an industrial instrument, or the decision of an industrial tribunal, be challenged in the discrimination jurisdiction? These questions point to real issues, for it has not been unusual in the past for industrial instruments to contain discriminatory clauses. Prior to the 1990s it was commonplace for award clauses to be directly discriminatory, for example by prohibiting women from doing certain work or from working at certain times or providing different rates of pay according to the age of the worker.

A more complex problem at the intersection of discrimination and labour law arises where industrial rules and norms that are neutral on their face are indirectly discriminatory in their operation. A 'last on, first off rule', for instance, might discriminate against those who were latecomers to the labour market because of pre-existing discriminatory hiring practices.[241] A requirement of geographic mobility to access certain employment benefits might disadvantage workers with family responsibilities who are not free to move workplaces.[242] These neutral rules play an important part in the very structuring of the workplace and can thus be critical in determining the equality of workers and their opportunities for social inclusion.

The policy and legislative response to the problem of discrimination authorised by industrial instruments has generally been to exempt any actions done in compliance with those instruments from discrimination legislation. Such exemptions are a feature

---

239 *Wardley*, above n 5.
240 M Thornton 'Discrimination Law/Industrial Law: Are They Compatible?' (1987) 59 *AQ* 162.
241 See eg *Banovic*, above n 48.
242 See eg *Amery*, above n 56. See earlier *Amery v State of NSW* [2001] NSWADT 37.

of several federal discrimination statutes, although not the *Racial Discrimination Act*.[243] Where there is such an exemption discriminatory acts authorised by awards or workplace agreements cannot be challenged in the discrimination arena.

However, this is not the approach in all jurisdictions. In New South Wales, the *Anti-Discrimination Act 1977* (NSW) contemplates that complaints might be made under it regarding discriminatory awards or agreements because a 1994 amendment, which came into effect from 8 August 1995, specifically removed the exemption that previously existed in the legislation.[244] This explains how the complex *Amery* litigation came to be instigated in the discrimination arena.[245] That case revolved around the classification by the *Teaching Services Act 1980* (NSW) of teachers into 'officers' and 'temporary employees', a classification that was replicated in the different pay structures of the industrial instruments applying to them.

The integration of discrimination principles into labour law

The damaging effect of allowing the exemption of industrial instruments made under the auspices of labour law regimes was first highlighted in relation to the problems women experienced in the labour market. At the federal level the structural barriers to women's equality and participation in paid work were investigated.[246] The policy resolution to the problem was identified as one of integrating discrimination principles and issues into the industrial jurisdiction. At the federal level this occurred progressively from 1992.[247] In the States similar commitments to the integration of discrimination principles into the industrial arena were made and State industrial legislation was also amended accordingly.[248] This policy response maintains the industrial regime as the arena with prime regulatory responsibility for workplace relations, and redefines discrimination issues as industrial issues.

The discrimination objects of the *Workplace Relations Act*

At the federal level, equality objectives were first included in the *Industrial Relations Reform Act 1993* (Cth). The stated aim was broad ranging: to 'prevent and eliminate discrimination on the basis of race, colour, sex, sexual preference, age, physical or mental disability, marital status, family responsibilities, pregnancy, religion, political opinion, national extraction or social origin'.[249] This goal remains part of the *Workplace Relations*

---

243 See eg *Sex Discrimination Act*, s 40(1); *Disability Discrimination Act*, s 47(1); and *Age Discrimination Act*, s 39(1) and (8).

244 *Anti-Discrimination Act 1977* (NSW), s 54(1).

245 *Amery*, above n 56.

246 See House of Representatives Standing Committee on Legal and Constitutional Affairs, Parliament of Australia, *Half Way to Equal* (1992), 243–4; and Australian Law Reform Commission *Equality Before the Law: Justice for Women*, Report No 69, Pts I–II (1994).

247 See *Workplace Relations Act*, former ss 3(i) and (j), 83BB(2), 88B(3)(c)–(d) and (e), 89A(2) (g)–(h), 89A(8), 93, 93A, 111A, 113(2A)–(2C) and (5), 143(1C)(e)–(f), 143(1D), 150A, Pt VIA Div 2 and Div 5 (and Sch 14), 170LT(7), s 170LU(5)–(6) and s 170VG(1) (and *Workplace Relations Regulations*, former Sch 8).

248 See eg *Industrial Relations Act 1996* (NSW), ss 19, and 169; *Industrial Relations Act 1999* (Qld), s 3; and *Fair Work Act 1994* (SA), ss 3(m)–(n), 79(2) and 99(3)(a) .

249 Section 3(g).

Act though its expression has been modified since 1996 by the addition of prefatory words so that the purpose is one of 'respecting and valuing the diversity of the workforce by helping to prevent and eliminate discrimination …': s 3(m). The 1993 reforms also adverted to the importance of attending to the systemic discrimination against workers with family responsibilities,[250] and in 1996 the aim of 'assisting employees to balance their work and family responsibilities effectively through the development of mutually beneficial work practices with employers' was incorporated in the *Workplace Relations Act* and still remains in place: s 3(l).

The implementation of discrimination objectives in the *Workplace Relations Act* has been achieved primarily by providing mechanisms to eradicate existing discrimination through the imposition of obligations on the various regulatory institutions set up under the Act to take account of the principles of the four federal discrimination statutes in carrying out their duties under the legislation. The post–*Work Choices* regime continues this strategy.

Pay equity under the *Workplace Relations Act*[251]

The Australian Fair Pay Commission (AFPC) has become the primary wage setting institution since the *Work Choices* amendments to the *Workplace Relations Act*. In addition to its obligations to abide by its general wage setting parameters and the recommendations of the Award Review Taskforce, the Act enjoins the AFPC to do a number of things in its decision-making to incorporate equality principles: s 222. Specifically the legislation makes explicit the obligations of the AFPC 'to apply' the principle of 'equal remuneration for work of equal value' to men and women workers; to provide pro-rata pay methods to those with disabilities; 'to take account of the principles' in the four federal discrimination statutes and the principles in the *Workers with Family Responsibilities Convention 1981 (ILO C 156)*: s 222(1)(a)–(d). Finally, the AFPC must 'ensure that its decisions do not contain provisions that discriminate' on any of the grounds spelled out in the objects section of the legislation: s 222(1)(e). Yet the *Workplace Relations Act* makes it clear that special rates of pay for young workers, disabled workers or those on traineeships will not to be treated as a contravention of these equality obligations: s 222(2). Thus various forms of discrimination based on disability and age are explicitly tolerated by the system, and usually justified as a workforce participation measure.

The *Amery* litigation indicates that care is needed in wage setting especially where employees are divided into different classifications that in turn become the gateway to access differing pay levels. In *Amery* there was evidence that significantly fewer women were employed in a permanent capacity with access to the higher pay scales, and they made up a significantly greater number of temporary teachers confined to the lower pay scales. A significant factor in the failure of the complainants' case in *Amery* was that the different classifications, permanent 'officers' and 'temporary employees' were established by statute (and therefore unable to be attacked on equality grounds), and the pay scales that related to them had been first developed

---

250 See also Chapters 3 and 7.
251 See also Chapter 7, pp 299ff.

after an assessment of work value (although equality considerations had never been part of that exercise).

However, if the AFPC were itself to establish such a classification system and related differential pay scales the situation would be distinguishable from that in *Amery*. Its decision could be open to review on the grounds of failure to exercise its discretion according to law as required by s 222. However, the obligations and duties of the AFPC arising from matters contained in s 222 are weakened by the opening words of the section, which state that the matters listed therein do not limit the broad wage setting parameters set out in s 176 (and s 23) and its duty to have regard to the Award Review Taskforce under s 177.

After the *Work Choices* changes the Australian Industrial Relations Commission (AIRC) also retains a power to hear applications relating to claims for equal pay for work of equal value: Pt 12, Div 3.[252] However, this is very much a residual jurisdiction. The AIRC's powers in this area may only be exercised where there is no 'adequate alternative remedy' and where there are no other such proceedings current in another jurisdiction: s 621. Because the statutory scheme provides that the AFPC sets minimum wages and in doing so will apply non-discriminatory principles, the AIRC's jurisdiction is constrained so that its decisions cannot undermine those of the AFPC. The AIRC has no jurisdiction to hear equal pay for work of equal value applications that relate to a basic periodic rate of pay, a basic piece rate of pay or a casual loading where either the employees in both the group w;ho would be covered by the AIRC's order and their comparators are entitled to a guaranteed rate of pay under the AFPCS or the employees in the group who would be covered by the order are entitled to a higher rate of pay than the AFPCS and the comparator group is entitled to a rate of pay equal to the AFPCS: s 622(2)–(5). These restrictions apply whether the source of the employee's entitlement to pay is under a contract of employment, APCS, or workplace agreement: s 622(6). Therefore there are likely to be very few occasions where the AIRC's jurisdiction in this area might be activated.

The *Work Choices* amendments represent a missed opportunity to incorporate provisions in the *Workplace Relations Act* that would ensure pay equity in the future. HREOC has flagged a number of these:[253] the AFPC might have incorporated a specialist pay equity unit; and there could have been provision for individual complaints of pay inequity with simplified procedures such as those found in the *Employment Act 2002* (UK); and there could have been better regulatory oversight through pay equity audits across the whole system.

Awards and equality principles

In performing all its functions under the *Workplace Relations Act* the AIRC has a duty to 'take into account' the need to apply principles relating to equal pay for work of equal value and to prevent and eliminate discrimination: s 104. The obligations 'to take account' of the principles in all four federal discrimination statutes and the *Workers with*

252 See Chapter 7, p 305.
253 HREOC *Submission to the Senate Employment, Workplace Relations and Education Legislation Committee, Inquiry into the Workplace Relations Amendment (Work Choices) Bill 2005* (2005), 2–4.

Family Responsibilities Convention 1981 (ILO C 156) bolster this: ss 105–6. However, 'taking account' of equality principles does not entail that in the end these principles must be determinative. Rather it suggests that there must be at least consideration of discrimination issues even if in the end there are other issues that prove to be more important in leading to a particular determination. Nonetheless, the incorporation of these words in the statute imposes a heavy responsibility on the AIRC to ensure such matters are an important part of its decision-making processes.

The AIRC's power to make and vary awards is now quite restricted,[254] but it is required by the *Workplace Relations Act* to ensure that any awards or related orders made by it do not discriminate: s 568(2)(e). However, the Act also makes clear that an award or order will not infringe this prohibition merely because in relation to particular employment it makes a distinction, or 'discriminates', on the basis of 'the inherent requirements of that employment': s 568(3)(a).[255] These words are the same as those used in the *Disability Discrimination Act* and the *Age Discrimination Act*.[256] However, this concept is not found in the *Racial Discrimination Act*. There is a similar concept in the expression 'genuine occupational qualifications' used in the *Sex Discrimination Act* but there it applies only to the ground of 'sex' and not the other grounds covered by the legislation.[257] Likewise, under the *Disability Discrimination Act* the 'inherent requirements of the particular employment' defence only operates in relation to offers of employment and dismissal, while these same words can clearly relate to a wider range of workplace issues through the operation of s 568(3)(a). The disjunction between the two areas of legislation coupled with the exemption under discrimination legislation for acts done in accordance with industrial instruments means that it is possible for some acts to be authorised under industrial instruments when ordinarily they would be proscribed under discrimination legislation.

Under the *Workplace Relations Act* there is also an exemption for awards or related orders applying to staff employed by a religious institution in accordance with the teachings of the faith where the discrimination is on the basis of those teachings and is in good faith: s 568(3)(b). This means, for example, that awards may allow religious schools to refuse to employ, say, someone who is divorced. Although there are some exemptions relating to religious bodies under federal discrimination statutes, again there is a disjunction between the expression and width and those exemptions created by the *Workplace Relations Act* in relation to awards and award-related orders.[258]

Ever since the AIRC was first required by the legislation to take account of discrimination principles, there have been numerous examples of their influence on the AIRC's decisions in varying awards. Not all applications raising discrimination issues have been successful in the past,[259] but there are also many instances where applications

---

254 See Chapter 3 p 117, and Chapter 7 pp 282–83.

255 See above pp 372–75.

256 *Disability Discrimination Act*, s 15(4)(a); and *Age Discrimination Act*, s 18(4). See also *Workplace Relations Act*, s 659(3), which uses the word 'position' rather than 'employment'.

257 *Sex Discrimination Act*, s 30.

258 See above p 371; *Sex Discrimination Act*, s 37; and *Age Discrimination Act*, s 35.

259 See eg *s 113 Application by Master Builders Association of New South Wales to Vary the National Building and Construction Industry Award 2000* AIRC, PR929454, 26 March 2003 refusing an application to include a provision for part-time work in award to facilitate balancing work and family.

have been successful. The provision of an adequate casual loading has been justified as necessary to allow workers time with their families; requirements to monitor the impact of rosters on the ability of workers to balance work and family life have been put in place; and the inclusion of award provisions aimed at preventing and eliminating discrimination on the basis of age in the offering of voluntary separation packages, provide just a few examples.[260]

After the *Work Choices* amendments one of the few circumstances under which the AIRC is permitted to vary an award is where the award has been referred to it under s 46PW of the *Human Rights and Equal Opportunity Commission Act*: ss 552(1)(d) and 554. Section 46PW provides that a written complaint must first be made to HREOC alleging that an act done under an industrial instrument is discriminatory. Section 46PW complaints may be made either by individuals, who are either aggrieved by the action or are members of a class so aggrieved, or by a trade union. If after examining the complaint the President of HREOC considers that there is unlawful discrimination, the complaint is then referred to the AIRC. Importantly the legislation makes it clear that simply because an act is done in compliance with an industrial instrument does not mean that it is reasonable.[261] As an aside here, it can be noted that even though there is a similar provision in the discrimination legislation in New South Wales, in *Amery* the industrial realities were treated as presenting almost overwhelming evidence of the reasonableness of adhering to the pay scales in the industrial instrument.[262]

The possibility for challenging discriminatory industrial instruments through the s 46PW procedure is an important aspect of integrating discrimination principles into awards. First and foremost a successful case will result in an alteration of the discriminatory rule. This is not necessarily an outcome of ordinary dispute resolution processes under the *Workplace Relations Act* (as to which, see below). The s 46PW process in this sense attacks systemic discrimination. Furthermore s 46PW effectively provides individuals with standing to achieve this, something that is ordinarily unavailable in the industrial arena.

However, a significant limitation of the s 46PW procedure is that the only discriminatory acts that can be the subject of complaint under it are those that are unlawful under Pt II of the *Sex Discrimination Act 1984* (Cth). This explains why the *Workplace Relations Act* provides that the Sex Discrimination Commissioner may intervene in the hearing that the AIRC conducts: s 554(3)(b). However, it also means that all the limitations of the *Sex Discrimination Act* are imported into this procedure. For instance, discrimination on the basis of family responsibilities can only be attacked if the discrimination is direct and results in a termination. More importantly the

---

260 See eg *s 113 Application by the Automotive, Food, Metals, Engineering, Printing and Kindred Industries Union to Vary the Country Printing Award 1959 and the Graphic Arts General Award 2000* AIRC, PR913088, 9 January 2002; *s 113 Application by the Australian Workers' Union to Vary the Pastoral Industry Award 1998* AIRC, PR930781, 30 April 2003; *ACT Department of Health and Community Care and Australian Nursing Federation, Health Services Union of Australian* AIRC, Print M9053, 2 February 1996; *s 113 Application by the Health Services Union to Vary Health Services Union of Australia (Victoria Public sector) Interim Award 1993* AIRC, S Print N7261, 13 December 1996.

261 *Human Rights and Equal Opportunity Act*, s 46PW(8).

262 *Amery*, above n 56, 439.

s 46PW procedure is not available to attack other forms of discrimination based on race, disability or age.

Despite its shortcomings the institutional cooperation put in place by the s 46PW complaint procedure is, at least in theory, a constructive approach. It provides individuals and trade unions with an avenue for instigating complaints about discriminatory conduct arising under an industrial instrument that is different from the ordinary conflict resolution processes under the *Workplace Relations Act*. A process that relies solely on individual complaint is less likely to be effective than where there is also institutional involvement, especially because individuals do not usually have the resources to prove indirect discrimination even if they can identify it in the first place.

The s 46PW procedure was first introduced in 1992.[263] While in theory the role assigned to the President of HREOC and the Sex Discrimination Commissioner under these reforms appeared to be important, they have proved less so in practice. The power of the President of HREOC to refer discriminatory awards and agreements to the AIRC for consideration was never once used prior to *Work Choices* and it is doubtful that the pattern will be any different in the future. The reasons for this are, perhaps, that the s 46PW procedure is not well known to those who might access it, or industrial participants are more comfortable using the ordinary conflict resolution procedures under the *Workplace Relations Act*. Certainly that is likely to be the case where a trade union is involved. In any event as long as a written complaint is required to initiate the s 46PW procedure it is likely to remain under-utilised. However, if the President of the Human Rights and Equal Opportunity Commission had direct access to the AIRC there could be a much better integrated regulatory system of audit and protection for workers.

The *Workplace Relations Act* also provides that awards may contain a discrimination clause: s 523. A model discrimination clause was first adopted by the AIRC as part of the triennial review process that was introduced in 1993 to enable the AIRC to continue monitoring discrimination issues in relation to awards.[264] As part of the triennial review process the AIRC pointed to the important role of individuals and parties in raising concerns about discriminatory instruments, and also welcomed the offer of assistance from HREOC 'in formulating guidelines and assisting in any monitoring of review procedures'.[265] The model clause was later varied to reflect the new aim of valuing diversity incorporated in the 1996 amendments.[266]

The model clause commits parties to achieving the discrimination object of the *Workplace Relations Act*, and to using 'every endeavour' to ensure that neither the provisions nor the operation of the industrial instrument are directly or indirectly discriminatory in their effects, unless in a way exempted by legislation. The insertion

---

263 *Industrial Relations Amendment Act 1992* (Cth), ss 111A–113. See *Sex Discrimination and Other Legislation Amendment Act 1992* (Cth).

264 *Industrial Relations Reform Act 1993* (Cth), s 150A; and *Third Safety Net Adjustment and Section 150A Review* (1995) 61 IR 236.

265 See *Review of Wage Fixing Principles, August 1994* (1994) 55 IR 144; and *Safety Net Adjustments and Review, September 1994* (1994) 56 IR 114.

266 *Award Simplification Decision* (1997) 75 IR 272.

of the model clause in industrial instruments has been noted elsewhere as 'largely educative and illustrative'.[267] There is a hortatory element to the model clause and it may be difficult to use it directly as an enforcement 'stick'; nonetheless, it is one aspect of regulatory commitment by the industrial system to eradicating discrimination in awards and as such is important in itself and ought to weigh strongly in any conflict resolution procedure regarding the discriminatory operation or effect of award terms.

It can also be noted that while industrial instruments, awards and workplace agreements, generally prevail over inconsistent State laws, any terms in them concerning EEO matters have effect subject to State EEO laws, except EEO provisions in State industrial laws: s 17(1)–(2) and r 1.6(1)–(2). While EEO is not defined in the legislation, ordinarily this refers to policies providing that people with equal ability to do a job will have an equal opportunity to access it, whether through hiring or promotion.

Finally, when considering whether safety net provisions (whether the AFPCS, APCSs, FMW or awards) are discriminatory it must be remembered that all safety net terms and conditions only set *minimum* standards. There is no legal restraint preventing any employing business from providing better terms and conditions. Thus an argument of discrimination may sometimes be more properly formulated as one where the employing business has refused to provide a higher standard than the set minimum.[268] For the same reason it may also be more difficult to criticise the regulatory institutions set up under the *Workplace Relations Act* to oversee the safety net.

Workplace agreements and equality principles

With the passage of the *Work Choices* amendments, the Office of the Employment Advocate has regulatory oversight of all agreements under the *Workplace Relations Act*. The Employment Advocate is required to have 'particular regard' to assisting workers balance work and family responsibilities, and to the need to prevent and eliminate all discrimination encompassed in the objects of the legislation: s 151(3). However, a feature of the *Work Choices* changes is that the Employment Advocate plays a minimal role in directly overseeing agreement-making under the Act. Rather the position of that Office in the regulatory scheme is to support the devolution of responsibilities to the parties in the workplace. Thus, for example, the Employment Advocate has no direct responsibility for ensuring that employees who might be vulnerable or in a disadvantaged bargaining position, such as women, people from a non-English speaking background, young people, apprentices, trainees or outworkers, are protected. By way of contrast the AIRC formerly was unable to certify agreements unless satisfied that their terms had been appropriately explained to such groups.[269] Rather the regulatory scheme now envisages that the Employment Advocate will encourage parties to attend to the needs of such workers: s 151(2). However, with no further regulatory back up to ensure compliance by the parties, the protection that this offers to those who are vulnerable in workplace bargaining is considerably weakened.

---

267 *Re State Working Hours Case 2003* (2003) 124 IR 253, 271.
268 See *Amery*, above n 56.
269 *Workplace Relations Act*, former s 170LT(7).

Discriminatory terms are prohibited in workplace agreements: s 356 and r 8.6(1). The proscribed discrimination is that on grounds of race, colour, sex, sexual preference, age, physical or mental disability, marital status, family responsibilities, pregnancy, religion, political opinion, national extraction or social origin. Any terms containing prohibited content are void and the Employment Advocate is required to remove them from the agreement: ss 358–64. While terms that are directly discriminatory may be easy to identify, those that are indirectly discriminatory are unlikely to be. For this reason provisions that void discriminatory terms in agreements have made little impact elsewhere.[270] Under the *Workplace Relations Act* there are also sanctions that are applied to those who either seek to include such terms in agreements or make representations recklessly that such a term does not contain prohibited content: ss 357 and 365–6.

Thus the responsibility for ensuring that discriminatory content is not included in a workplace agreement is effectively devolved to the parties. Before *Work Choices*, the regulatory institution (then the AIRC) bore the onus for compliance via an obligation not to certify discriminatory collective agreements.[271] Because *Work Choices* places such a high emphasis on workplace bargaining, and especially on individual bargaining, it stands to reason that unless there is going to be an extensive supervisory bureaucracy, which admittedly would be out of kilter with the neo-liberal spirit infusing contemporary regulatory systems, there must be an increasing emphasis on self-monitoring backed by the enforcement stick of attached penalties. The effectiveness of such a scheme thus ultimately depends on enforcement, which traditionally has been weak. It has not improved under the current regime.[272]

The *Workplace Relations Regulations* stipulate that a provision in an agreement does not discriminate 'merely because' it provides for rates of pay contained in an Australian Pay and Classification Scale (APCS) or the Federal Minimum Wage (FMW); or relates to 'the inherent requirements of particular employment'; or applies to staff employed by a religious institution and discriminates on the basis of the relevant teachings of the faith and in good faith: r 8.6(2)(a)–(c). In relation to the latter two matters, some of the problems of regulatory gap identified above in relation to awards also apply to workplace agreements.

Dispute resolution in the workplace and equality principles

Ensuring the application of discrimination objectives in any dispute resolution processes conducted under the *Workplace Relations Act* is critical to their effective integration into industrial instruments and work relations. If workplace participants governed by the industrial system know that there is no effective backup or enforcement of discrimination principles when relations break down, then there is little regulatory incentive to incorporate those principles into industrial instruments and to abide by them in the first place.

---

270 See eg *Sex Discrimination Act 1986* (UK), s 6; and L Dickens et al, *Tackling Sex Discrimination Through Collective Bargaining* (1988); and L Dickens 'Collective Bargaining and the Promotion of Equality: The Case of the United Kingdom' (1993).

271 *Workplace Relations Act*, former s 170LU(5).

272 See Chapter 3.

For this reason it is important that the AIRC, which plays a major role in dispute resolution under the legislation, is bound to have regard to the equality principles of discrimination legislation and the *Workers with Family Responsibilities Convention, 1981 (ILO C 156)* in undertaking all of its functions under the legislation: ss 104–6 and Pt 13.[273]

Many of the decisions of the Commission settling disputes prior to *Work Choices* reveal how equality principles can impact during conflict resolution. The AIRC has ordered an employer to review its policy against part-time work and allow female employees returning from maternity leave to move to part-time work, because such a policy was unreasonable when other employees were allowed time off for study and casuals were employed in the business, and it has ordered the provision of safe work to a pregnant employee.[274] On another occasion after a consideration of all the evidence including the circumstances of the industry, the AIRC found that despite quite onerous family responsibilities it was not unreasonable to require a worker to work flexible hours including on Saturdays.[275] In most cases the approach of the AIRC has been one very focused on balancing the interests both of workers and employers, and applying understandings of reasonableness within the industrial context. (This is also evident in its jurisdiction over unfair dismissals. For instance, the AIRC's understanding of the industrial issues in one case led it to find that there was no termination 'at the initiative of the employer' because there was more scope for negotiation over rostering to accommodate the childcare needs of a worker whose resignation was thus precipitate.[276])

However, after *Work Choices* the role of the AIRC in dispute resolution is changed somewhat for it no longer has a power to compel outcomes or arbitrate (except in relation to unfair dismissals) even if acting in the capacity of a private dispute resolution provider: s 701(4)–(5).[277] Sara Charlesworth has previously analysed the construction of complaints settled by conciliation in the industrial and discrimination jurisdictions, highlighting the background structural and cultural tensions between these jurisdictions and their differing dominant frameworks of 'fairness' and 'equality'. Charlesworth argues that the regulatory intersection of discrimination law and industrial law provides a space for tackling issues, such as those involving conflict between work and family from several vantage points.[278] Because the AIRC did not maintain extensive files of its conciliation matters, she drew no conclusion about which was the best jurisdiction in which to pursue a matter, saying that would depend in large measure on the experience and knowledge of advisors. However, it must be remembered that in those instances where there is a complaint of discrimination that can be seen to arise from an industrial instrument, it is not always possible to take an action under discrimination legislation.[279]

---

273 See Chapter 12, pp 556ff.
274 *Australian Liquor, Hospitality and Miscellaneous Workers' Union and The Royal Society for the Prevention of Cruelty to Animals Queensland Inc* AIRC, PR912395, 10 December 2001; *AWU-FIME and Nationalpak Australia Ltd* AIRC, S Print M7155, 22 November 1995.
275 *National Union of Workers and Wooldumpers Australia Pty Ltd* AIRC, M Print R6032, 18 June 1999.
276 *CJ Davies v David Jones* AIRC, Print 927538, 10 February 2002. See below pp 401–405.
277 See further Chapter 12, p 557ff.
278 S Charlesworth 'The Overlap of the Federal Sex Discrimination and Industrial Relations Jurisdictions; Intersections and Demarcations in Conciliation' (2003) *Aust J Lab Ec* 559.
279 See above pp 386–87.

Finally, dispute resolution under the *Workplace Relations Act* may be conducted privately, and it is regrettable that the Act does not impose obligations on these private providers similar to those imposed on the AIRC under ss 104–6, although private providers are constrained from dealing with disputes that have been or currently are being dealt with under discrimination legislation: s 716.

Equality and the regulatory structure governing work

Ever since the regulatory scheme governing work relations has been divided into a safety net of minimum conditions over which is erected a superstructure of terms and conditions forged through workplace bargaining, there has been concern that it incorporates systemic discrimination. The evidence that has emerged to date suggests that there are increasing disparities between the terms and conditions of various groups of workers in Australia, and that these disparities are discriminatory in effect. To date, for instance, considerable evidence has been gathered on the discriminatory impact of the regulatory scheme, especially workplace bargaining, on women.[280]

When bargaining began to be formalised in the early 1990s the AIRC was itself concerned about the impact on workers who would be more vulnerable in bargaining:

> We cannot predict the extent of the disadvantage which female workers will experience if the Commission gives its approval to a scheme of enterprise bargaining. We do accept, however, that enterprise bargaining—especially bargaining for over award payments—places at a relative disadvantage those sections of the labour force where women predominate.[281]

In the face of this the AIRC could only rely on the discrimination provisions incorporated in the legislation.[282] International evidence also indicates that decentralised systems result in greater inequalities between male and female earnings.[283]

Prior to the *Work Choices* amendments, the Government was required to provide biennial reports to Parliament on workplace bargaining highlighting its impacts on women, part-time employees, persons from non-English speaking background and young persons.[284] From these reports it is clear that workplace agreements are scarcely proactive in eradicating discrimination. The official reports show that equity provisions are included in fewer than 40 per cent of agreements. The most common provisions are mere statements of adherence to principles of discrimination and equal employment opportunity. There is little in the way of specific commitment to affirmative action,

---

280 See eg S Charlesworth *Stretching Flexibility: Enterprise Bargaining, Women Workers and Changes to Working Hours* (1997); G Whitehouse 'Industrial Agreements and Work/Family Provisions: Trends and Prospects under "Enterprise Bargaining"' (2001) 12 *Lab Ind* 109; M Baird 'Parental Leave in Australia: The Role of the Industrial Relations System' in J Murray (ed) *Work, Family and the Law* (2005).

281 *National Wage Case April 1991* (1991) 36 IR 120, 173.

282 *Review of Wage Fixing Principles August 1994*, above n 265, 32.

283 See B Gregory 'Labour Market Institutions and the Gender Pay Ratio' (1999) 32 *Aust Ec Rev* 273. See also A McColgan *Just Wages for Women* (1997); and A McColgan *Women under the Law the False Promise of Human Rights* (2000).

284 *Workplace Relations Act*, former s 358A. See Department of Employment and Workplace Relations and the Office of the Employment Advocate *Agreement Making in Australia under the Workplace Relations Act 2000 and 2001* (2002)(*DEWR & OEA 2002*); and *Agreement Making in Australia under the Workplace Relations Act: 2002 and 2003* (2004)(*DEWR & OEA 2004*).

pay equity, achieving gender or ethnicity balance in the workplace, and few provisions for access and equity for Aboriginal and Torres Strait Islander people, cultural leave, or training for part-timers or casuals.

Systemic discrimination arising from the work/family interface has been identified as a critical concern in the contemporary law of work. It is an area in which different regulatory objectives of 'population, participation, and productivity' intersect in some-times conflicting ways,[285] prompting major studies both academic and empirical in recent times.[286]

Under the Australian Fair Pay and Conditions Standard (AFPCS) it has already been noted that balancing work and family is achieved primarily through taking very limited paid leave (the equivalent of ten days personal carer's leave a year for fulltime workers) or unpaid leave from the workplace.[287] In truth this is not so much a balancing of work and family conflict, but avoidance of it through absence from work in order to care for family. Agreements to average working hours are also an option in the safety net but, as we shall see below, the evidence is that the benefits of this for balancing work and family are at best ambiguous. Thus in practice under the safety net, work and family conflict is generally resolved on the backs of (usually female) workers. However, there is no legal mechanism to combat any discriminatory effects that might arise from the operation of the legislated standards that comprise the AFPCS.

The other way to balance work and family, actively promoted by the Government, is the adoption of some form of precarious work, usually as a casual or part-time worker.[288] But this also often effectively amounts to an unpaid absence from work, which in turn means a low(er) income and thus tends also to assume that the worker with family responsibilities is also dependent on another (either a person or the state), whereas the normative worker is unencumbered.[289]

In workplace agreements there has been a strong reliance on flexibility provisions, whether in relation to working time or the taking of leave, to deliver a family-friendly workplace.[290] In the official report of workplace agreements presented in 2004, only 44 per cent of certified (that is, collective) agreements had at least one family-friendly measure if flexible working hours provisions were excluded from consideration, whereas when they were included the proportion jumped to 82 per cent.[291] Almost 31 per cent of AWAs had no family-friendly provisions. And while just on 70 per cent of AWAs were reported as having at least one family-friendly provision, those that apply to women were more likely

285 R Owens 'Reproducing Law's Worker: Regulatory Tensions in the Pursuit of "Population, Participation and Productivity" in Arup et al (eds), above n 209.
286 HREOC *Striking the Balance: Women, Men, Work and Family Discussion Paper* (2005); and Standing Committee on Family and Human Services, Parliament of Australia, *Inquiry into Balancing Work and Family* (2005–6); Murray, above n 280; and J Conaghan and K Rittich *Labour Law, Work and Family: Critical and Comparative Perspectives* (2005).
287 See Chapter 7, pp 320ff.
288 Australian Government, Minister K Andrews *Work and Family: The Importance of Workplace Flexibility in Promoting Balance between Work and Family* (2005).
289 S Berns *Women Going Backwards: Law and Change in a Family Unfriendly Society* (2002); and A Chapman, 'Work/Family, Australian Labour Law and the Normative Worker' in Conaghan and Rittich (eds), above n 286.
290 See *DEWR & OEA 2004*, above n 284, 56.
291 Ibid, 59.

to make provision for flexible hours.[292] Overall, women were more likely than men to have in their AWA provisions on family-friendly flexibility (41 per cent women compared with 31 per cent men), span of hours (35 per cent compared with 31 per cent), averaging of working hours (30 per cent compared with 23 per cent), and absorption of 'extra payments' (42 per cent compared with 41 per cent).

When contrasted with a rigid requirement to attend at a workplace for fixed hours on fixed days, it might appear that a more flexible approach to working time would assist workers to accommodate at least some of their family and care responsibilities. Flexibility may allow them, for instance, to leave work to attend either a medical appointment with an aged relative or a school meeting on behalf of their child. Yet any comprehensive assessment of the real advantages offered by the flexible workplace over the last decade is at best a complex if not a fraught exercise.[293] Working-time flexibility also often means long hours, a greater spread of working hours, and long-shift rosters, all of which have the potential to intensify work and family conflict, and the industrial system is not always responsive to these impacts.[294]

The incidence of other family-friendly provisions in federal agreements shows that on the whole there has not been a lot of attention to work/family issues in bargaining.[295] Over the two reporting periods from 2000 to 2003 there were only slight increases in the provision of flexible annual leave (6 per cent to 9 per cent), paid maternity leave (7 per cent to 10 per cent), paid paternity leave (4 per cent to 7 per cent), paid adoption leave (2 per cent to 4 per cent), paid family leave (3 per cent to 4 per cent), child care (1 per cent to 2 per cent), and part-time work (25 per cent to 26 per cent), counterbalanced by slight decreases in the provision of family/carer's leave (from 27 per cent to 25 per cent) and access to single days of annual leave (13 per cent to 11 per cent).[296] Overall family/carer's leave and part-time work were the most commonly cited family-friendly provisions in certified agreements. Amongst AWAs the most common family-friendly provision highlighted in the official reports was bereavement leave (unpaid in 49 per cent of AWAs, and paid in 47 per cent), with family/carer's leave (unpaid in 25 per cent of AWAs, and paid in 24 per cent) the next most common.[297]

Indeed, the evidence shows there has been little innovation in family-friendly terms in agreements.[298] Many of the examples provided in the official reports also indicate that agreement terms often simply replicate safety net terms and conditions.[299] This, coupled with the fact that awards and collective agreements have operated side by side in the past, may also explain why previously many agreements omitted altogether to deal with

292 Ibid, 95, 100–1.

293 See eg Charlesworth, above n 280.

294 See *Kellogg Brown and Root, Bass Strait (ESSO) Onshore/Offshore Facilities Certified Agreement 2000* AIRC, PR951725, 7 September 2004; overturned by *Kellogg Brown and Root Pty Ltd and Ors and Esso Australia Pty Ltd* AIRC, PR955357, 31 January 2005.

295 DEWR & OEA 2004, above n 284, 49 and Table 3C.

296 Ibid, 57.

297 Ibid, 87.

298 R Mitchell et al *Protecting the Worker's Interest in Enterprise Bargaining: The 'No-Disadvantage' Test in the Australian Federal Industrial Jurisdiction: Final Report* (2004), 48.

299 DEWR & OEA 2004, above n 284, 96.

work/family matters: for instance, very few (only 12 per cent) certified agreements were reported as dealing with parental leave.[300]

Most striking is the limited existence of paid parental (either maternity or paternity) leave after nearly a decade of bargaining under the *Workplace Relations Act 1996* (Cth). The official report in 2004 revealed that only 10 per cent of certified agreements and 8 per cent of AWAs provided for paid maternity leave. The corresponding figures for paid paternity leave (7 per cent and 5 per cent) and paid adoption leave (4 per cent and 4 per cent) were lower still.[301] In 2002–3, seven weeks was the average period of paid maternity leave provided for in certified agreements.[302] Research has shown that the duration of paid maternity leave granted through agreements varies widely, with the average of seven weeks reflecting periods ranging from two to twelve weeks, with the most common period of paid maternity leave in federal agreements being two weeks followed by twelve and six weeks.[303] All these fall below the standards set internationally.[304] Furthermore the entitlement to paid parental leave is found in industries where the workers are highly paid professionals rather than those who occupy lower-paid semi-skilled or unskilled jobs. Paid maternity leave is simply not available to those women employed in more vulnerable positions. Not surprisingly the evidence also suggests that where there is trade union supported bargaining there is a stronger chance of attaining better provisions for paid maternity leave.[305]

The considerable variations in the incidence of family-friendly provisions in workplace agreements reflect, and therefore also reinforce, the sex segregation of the labour market.[306] Paid maternity and paid paternity leave provisions are most common in the education (56 per cent and 43 per cent) and finance and insurance (52 per cent and 37 per cent) sectors, and least common in the mining industry (2 per cent). In the construction industry there has been little provision for part-time work (1 per cent of certified agreements), flexible annual leave (6 per cent), paid family leave (1 per cent), unpaid family leave (2 per cent), or paid parental leave (2 per cent). The same pattern of gendered distribution is observable for equity provisions typically including expressions of commitment to discrimination principles, and is also reflective of patterns noticed in previous years.[307]

Not surprisingly then women are more likely than men to have access to family-friendly provisions in agreements, including paid and unpaid family leave and 'flexible' employment arrangements—such as job sharing, home-based work, and part-time work—although it is quite extraordinary to see provisions such as home-based work touted as being family-friendly when agreements generally expressly provide that such work is not an alternative to family/care arrangements.[308]

---

300 Ibid, 49.
301 Ibid, 57 and 96.
302 Ibid, 71.
303 M Baird, D Brennan and L Cutcher 'A Pregnant Pause: Paid Maternity Leave in Australia' (2002) 13 *Lab Ind* 1.
304 See *Maternity Protection Convention 2000* (*ILO C 183*), which does not require a qualifying period and specifies 14 weeks' pay. See also *Convention on the Elimination of All Forms of Discrimination against Women* (*CEDAW*) (Art 11(2)(b)), in relation to which Australia has a reservation.
305 G Whitehouse 'Industrial Agreements and Work/Family Provisions: Trends and Prospects under "Enterprise Bargaining"' (2001) 12 *Lab Ind* 109.
306 *DEWR & OEA 2004*, above n 284, 58–60.
307 Ibid, 58–9 and Table C. See also R Owens 'Taking Leave: Work and Family in Australian Law and Policy' in Conaghan and Rittich (eds), above n 286, 243–4.
308 Ibid, 70–2. See also M Pittard 'The Dispersing and Transformed Workplace: Labour Law and the Effect of Electronic Work' (2003) 16 *AJLL* 69.

Agreements thus seem to engender a certain kind of bargaining and hence a certain kind of participation at work from men (for example, involving for instance long hours)—and this in turn entrenches further law's understanding of the normative productive worker. In familial relations it is not surprising that the constraints on the productive worker impact and determine constraints upon the other reproductive worker—and this is so at every level of a familial relation from economic relations to the sense of identity through work. Thus it is not surprising that men rarely take advantage of the family-friendly provisions to which they are entitled.[309] The regulatory outcomes of agreement-making have ensured a vicious circle.

Agreements have thus reinforced the gender distribution of reproductive and other unpaid work in the private sphere by constructing provisions that mean women must cannibalise their own entitlements or their time in paid work. Agreements demonstrate little prospect for breaking down existing gendered stereotypes of productive and reproductive labour. Agreements, which have the purpose of making industry more competitive in a global world, will always be unlikely to internalise costs of reproductive labour, which to date have been externalised by the market (and shouldered predominantly by women). Under agreements, it seems that workers will by and large continue to be expected to accommodate family and care responsibilities through cannibalising their own benefits or taking unpaid leave to ensure that these costs remain external to market transactions.

The fact that agreements at most barely replicate rather than improve the safety net standards for work and family, and that their incidence reflects the sex segregation of Australian industry indicates a comfort with labour law reinforcing traditional pictures of the (male) worker. It also represents a failure of this regulatory model imbued with purposes of furthering economic goals (encouraging competition in the marketplace) to effect the substantive social change needed both to protect all workers and to encourage their full participation in all work.

Systemic discrimination seems to be an intractable problem. The workplace relations system is established by legislation and without any recognised constitutional right to equality there is little chance outside of the political arena of undermining it on the basis that it is discriminatory. The problems of indirect discrimination remain equally intractable. That safety net terms and conditions or workplace agreements are indirectly discriminatory is exceedingly difficult to prove. And there can be marked differences in perception over whether terms and conditions of work are disadvantageous. In *Zurek v Hospital Corporation Australia Pty Ltd t/a Warringal Private Hospital* a group of casual nurses argued successfully that the award restructuring process, which sought to de-casualise the industry and provide more part-time work, discriminated against them.[310] Rather than seeing a benefit of long-term increased job security, they considered part-time work would be less flexible and result in a lowering of their pay. The dilemma presented to the women indicates the complexity of the intersection of labour and discrimination law.

---

309 See M Bitman et al *Men's Uptake of Family Friendly Employment Provisions* (2004).
310 (1992) EOC ¶92–459 and ¶92–460.

Unlawful (discriminatory) termination of employment

The one area where the *Workplace Relations Act* provides remedies to an individual employee who has been discriminated against is in relation to termination of employment.[311] Its provisions are intended to implement Australia's obligations under several international instruments,[312] and were first introduced in 1993.[313] After the *Work Choices* amendments the proscription against discriminatory or unlawful termination is retained, although there are some important changes to the remedies available for such terminations. Because the *Workplace Relations Act* after *Work Choices* denies many employees access to a statutory remedy if their dismissal is 'harsh, unjust or unreasonable',[314] it is likely that in the future there will be a greater focus on the remedies for unlawful termination of employment than there has been previously. Furthermore, the various categories of employees who are excluded from accessing unfair dismissal provisions under the *Workplace Relations Act* are not excluded from taking an action in relation to an unlawful dismissal: s 643(6)–(7).

The *Workplace Relations Act* declares that it is unlawful to dismiss an employee for any one or more of the reasons listed in s 659(2), or for reasons that include any one or more of those reasons. This list includes temporary absence from work because of either illness or injury or for reasonable 'voluntary emergency management activity', detailed in s 659(2)(a), r 12.8, and s 659(2)(i); and a limited range of matters relating to trade unionism and employee representation, including membership/non-membership of a union, participation in trade union activities 'outside working hours' or within working hours if the employer has consented, seeking office as or acting as a representative of employees, or filing complaints against an employer for an alleged breach of the law, detailed in s 659(2)(b)–(e). Dismissal of an employee for refusal to negotiate, sign, extend, vary or terminate an AWA is also prohibited: s 659(2)(g).

Section 659(2)(f) sets out a range of discriminatory reasons that render a termination unlawful. They are: race, colour, sex, sexual preference, age, physical or mental disability, marital status, family responsibilities, pregnancy, religion, political opinion, national extraction or social origin. Dismissing an employee for being absent from work during maternity or parental leave is also prohibited, and the *Work Choices* amendments make it clear that such absence cannot of itself be used as an excuse to claim that the employee's position no longer exists: s 659(2)(h) and (5).

There are two exceptions to the prohibition on discriminatory terminations. One concerns situations where a person is employed by a religious institution and is dismissed in 'good faith' to avoid injuring 'the religious susceptibilities' of members of the religion: s 659(4). This could mean, for instance, that an employee who is dismissed because of divorce could not complain that the termination on the basis of 'marital status'

---

311 *Workplace Relations Act*, Pt 12 Div 4 esp Subdiv C.
312 *Termination of Employment Convention, 1982 (ILO C 158); Discrimination (Employment and Occupation) Convention, 1958 (ILO C 111); Workers with Family Responsibilities Convention, 1981 (ILO C 156); and Termination of Employment Recommendation, 1982 (ILO R 165).* See *Workplace Relations Act*, ss 635(1)(e) and 659(1).
313 *Industrial Relations Reform Act 1993* (Cth), Pt VIA Div 3, esp s 170DF and Subdiv C.
314 See further Chapter 9.

was contrary to s 659(2)(f). An employee would also be unable successfully to invoke s 659(2)(h) if the employer could establish that the reason for the dismissal was 'based on the inherent requirements of the particular position': s 659(3). The High Court considered the equivalent provision in the former legislation in *Christie*.[315]

An employee who claims there is a breach of s 659(2) must follow the procedure outlined in the *Workplace Relations Act*.[316] This procedure is at the outset virtually identical to that followed in an unfair dismissal case under the legislation. An application must be lodged within twenty-one days of the termination with the AIRC either by the employee or by a trade union that is entitled to represent the employee: s 643(1) and (3). However, the Commission also has some discretion to vary this time upon an application made during the same period, and need not hold a hearing if there is also an allegation of unfair dismissal: ss 643(14) and 647.[317] The AIRC will convene a conciliation conference, and if this is likely to be unsuccessful it must issue a certificate indicating its view of the merits of the matter: s 650(2).

Because a binding and conclusive determination of a complaint that an employee has been unlawfully dismissed involves an exercise of judicial power, where such a matter is not resolved in a conciliation conference its further resolution can only be in a federal court. After the issue of the certificate by the AIRC an employee has twenty-eight days in which to elect whether or not to commence court proceedings, and must notify the Commission in writing of this decision: s 651. A failure to do so within this timeframe means that the matter cannot be continued, although again the Commission has some residual discretion over this: ss 651(7) and (9) and 663(5). The procedures for election can become complicated because an employee's matter may allege the dismissal was also unfair and the election in relation to all of these matters must be clear. Mistakes can be easily made and may deprive the employee of access to the court. In one such case North J commented in relation to the equivalent former provisions of the Act that they were 'encased in a web of complexity which makes it difficult even for an experienced legal practitioner to follow'.[318]

Under the former equivalent provisions of the *Workplace Relations Act* a small number of unlawful termination cases were pursued through to the courts. The outcomes, as might perhaps be expected, were varied. In some the claim was successfully made out. These include instances where a father who was up all night with an ill asthmatic child was dismissed when he rang in to say he was not able to come to work in the morning;[319] where a disabled person was dismissed as soon as his employer was no longer able to exploit him by underpayment of wages;[320] where a single parent was dismissed because he had turned sixty-five years of age, even though he had indicated he wanted and needed to keep working to support his child;[321] where a single parent

---

315 *Christie*, above n 48. See above, pp 373ff.
316 See *Workplace Relations Act*, Pt 12 Div 4, Subdiv B. See also Chapter 9, pp 432ff.
317 See *Brodie-Hanns v MTV Publishing Ltd* (1995) 67 IR 298 discussed in Chapter 9, p 433.
318 *Bahonko v Southern Health Care Network* [1999] FCA 479.
319 *Thompson v Kertan Pty Ltd* (1995) EOC ¶92–738.
320 *Vickery v Assetta* (2004) EOC ¶93–330.
321 *Peacock v Department of Defence* IRCA, 9800242, July 1998.

who worked part-time had been allowed to take agreed periods of leave when her child became terminally ill but was then sacked five days before the child's death because the employer said it needed a fulltime employee;[322] and where women who were taking maternity leave found themselves without a job.[323] Claims of discriminatory dismissal are rigorously tested in the courts. In *Penwill v National Jet Systems Pty Limited*, although Carr J accepted that in suffering headaches the employee had a 'physical or mental disability', he ruled that it was not her lack of punctuality but her failure to ring and notify when she would be late for work that was the reason for her dismissal.[324]

The relationship of the provisions in the *Workplace Relations Act* governing unlawful (discriminatory) termination of employment both to its provisions governing unfair dismissal and to discrimination legislation is complex. Applicants need to take great care when selecting the jurisdiction in which they will make a claim and the grounds on which they will base their claim.[325] The *Workplace Relations Act* prevents an employee from making an application for unlawful (discriminatory) dismissal under s 659(2) if proceedings in relation to the termination have already been commenced elsewhere. Not until such proceedings are discontinued or have failed for want of jurisdiction can the s 659(2) application be lodged. Likewise once s 659(2) proceedings have commenced an applicant is prevented from commencing other proceedings in relation to the termination: s 674. Proceedings that have been initiated prior to termination and relating to other discriminatory issues that may in fact lead to the termination are not apparently caught by this restriction.[326]

The facts relating to a termination of employment may support claims of unfair dismissal and unlawful dismissal and both can be pursued simultaneously under the *Workplace Relations Act*, provided the employee does not fall within one of the categories excluded from access to the unfair dismissal jurisdiction.[327] Where there are claims of unfair and unlawful (discriminatory) termination and conciliation fails the employee may prefer as a next step to allow the AIRC to arbitrate the unfair dismissal claim. This is likely to be the case where the employee is represented by their trade union, especially if there is a perception that the AIRC is more attuned to the 'industrial' aspects of a case, and in any event because it is less expensive than ultimately having to pursue a case through the courts. Cases may well succeed as an unfair dismissal case where they might fail as an unlawful discriminatory dismissal case.[328] Certainly there are many cases where the AIRC has considered issues in unfair dismissal hearings that concern matters that also might comprise a proscribed ground under s 659(2).[329]

---

322 *Wannberg v Alloa Holdings* IRCA, 960346, 31 July 1996, Ritter JR.
323 See eg *Treadwell v Acco Australia Pty Ltd* [1997] 1440 FCA; and *Laz v Downer Group Ltd* (2000) 108 IR 244.
324 [2002] FCA 5, [50].
325 See HREOC 'Pathways to Resolution' (video), available at <www.humanrights.gov.au/pathways_to_resolution>.
326 *Nott v Australia Postal Corporation* AIRC, PR964228, 18 November 2005, concerning *Workplace Relations Act*, former s 170HB.
327 *Workplace Relations Act*, s 638. See Chapter 9, pp 424ff.
328 Cases such as the *Schou* litigation, above n 131, may provide an example.
329 See eg *Scarpa v Elaeno Nominees* AIRC, PR961595, 19 August 2005 (pregnancy); and *Johnston and Kew Aged Care Pty Ltd t/as Parkland Close* AIRC, Dec1476/98 M Print Q9544, 9 December 1998 (family responsibilities).

Although after the introduction of *Work Choices* the AIRC cannot entertain an application on the ground of unfair dismissal where the termination was made 'for genuine operational reasons or reasons that include genuine operational reasons', a claim of unlawful discriminatory termination does not necessarily fail because of this. A number of cases decided under former provisions of the *Workplace Relations Act* show that such terminations are not inconsistent with it also being shown that there has been unlawful discrimination. It is enough in such cases, it will be recalled, to show that the proscribed reason is *one* of the reasons for the termination of employment. In *Sapevski v Katies Fashion (Australia) Pty Ltd (Sapevski)*[330] a group of women successfully established the termination of their employment was discriminatory. All the women who worked as splitters and packers in a warehouse were dismissed when it was shut down, whereas the men who worked as baggers in a different part of the warehouse were not dismissed. The women were from a non-English speaking background and had little understanding of the separation arrangement put to them by the employer but it was brokered by the union and they had thus accepted it. Their selection for redundancy had been purely on the basis that they were splitters and packers, it being assumed contrary to fact that they could not do the heavier work of bagging. The gender segregation of the workplace thus meant their termination was indirectly discriminatory and thus unlawful.

However, where a business has restructured, employees have by no means always been successful in making out a claim that their termination was also discriminatory. Much can depend on the circumstances of the case and the judicial perception of witnesses. In *Robertson v South*, although it appeared from a reading of the facts that the employee was terminated because she had taken several periods of authorised leave (both annual leave and unpaid leave) to care for her terminally ill husband, there was evident considerable judicial sympathy for a 'volatile' and 'hot head' employer who was trying to survive in a small business but little for the 'aggressive' female employee who failed to establish the claim of discriminatory dismissal.[331]

Sapevski is also interesting for its finding that both direct and indirect discrimination are comprehended by a provision such as s 659(2)(f). The reference in the section to 'reasons' for the termination, and the fact that employers can defend themselves by establishing that there was not a discriminatory reason, might suggest that the section is concerned only with 'direct' discrimination. However, because these legislative provisions implement not just the *Termination of Employment Convention, 1982 (ILO C 158)*, but a range of international conventions that incorporate the concept of indirect discrimination, there are strong reasons for thinking that the ruling in *Sapevski* was made on a sound basis.[332]

---

330 IRCA, 970219, 8 July 1997, Patch JR. On the intersection of operational reasons and discrimination issues under the former provisions of the *Workplace Relations Act* see also *Westen v Union des Assurances de Paris* (IRCA, 17 December 1996, Madgwick J); and *Kenefick v Australian Submarine Corporation Pty Ltd (No 2)* (1995) 62 IR 366, 372–3.

331 (2000) 140 IR 169.

332 Reference was made in the case to CEACR *Report III (Part 4B)* to the 83rd session of the International Labour Conference 1996 (1996).

There are a number of reasons, beyond the convenience that exists for some employees of bringing unfair and unlawful dismissal claims together, why a litigant may choose to pursue an action for an unlawful discriminatory dismissal under the *Workplace Relations Act* rather than under discrimination legislation. The grounds available under the *Workplace Relations Act* are in some respects wider than those available in some jurisdictions: for instance, there is no prohibition of discrimination on the ground of religion in South Australia; and only direct (but not indirect) discrimination is available under federal antidiscrimination law for termination on the basis of family responsibilities.

There may also be other practical differences that figure in the applicants' decision-making. Traditionally complaints have been handled more speedily in the industrial arena when compared with discrimination jurisdictions. In addition, in cases where an employee alleges that they have been dismissed for a reason proscribed by s 659(2), the burden of proof is reversed under the *Workplace Relations Act*.[333] It is not necessary for the employee to prove dismissal contrary to the provision, but employers may defend a case successfully by proving they did not terminate the employment for such a reason. It is not enough for an employer simply to deny that the reason or reasons for the termination included one of the proscribed reasons, and the court in these circumstances will look at all the factors. By the same token it is not necessary for the employer to prove why the employee was dismissed.[334]

However, some of the constraints that the *Workplace Relations Act* imposes, for example limiting the meaning of termination, demotion, and the concept of constructive dismissal,[335] mean that in a number of areas it can have a more limited reach than ordinary discrimination legislation. Likewise, there are now significant differences in the remedies accessible through these different jurisdictions. Under the *Workplace Relations Act* a claimant may seek orders from the Court for a penalty of up to $10 000; reinstatement; compensation; and/or any other order the Court thinks necessary to remedy the situation: s 665. After the *Work Choices* changes, orders for compensation are restricted in terms of quantum: s 665(1)–(4). More significantly, an award of compensation for 'shock, distress or humiliation, or other analogous hurt' caused by 'the manner of the terminating the employee's employment' is prohibited: s 665(2).[336] As these are very often integral to the wrong of discrimination this is a major limitation of the jurisdiction.

Equality and discrimination law: In the shadow of labour law?

Discrimination law often operates in the shadow of labour law. This seems particularly odd given its broad human rights focus. The exemption of discriminatory acts done

---

333 *Workplace Relations Act*, s 664.
334 See *Johns v Gunns* (1995) 60 IR 258 and the cases cited therein.
335 *Workplace Relations Act*, s 642. See further Chapter 9, pp 419–20.
336 See Chapter 9, pp 435–36.

under authority of statute or workplace agreements shows that the casting of this shadow is sometimes a matter of legislative policy. However, the shadow of labour law, and more particularly the emphasis on contract that now dominates it, also subtly affects (or perhaps infects) the interpretation of discrimination legislation. It is sometimes possible to discern an implicit hierarchy in the laws regulating work that places equality issues at the bottom. In *Schou* Harper J commented that discrimination legislation:

> necessitates the interpretation of important legislation in a field, that of employment law, already occupied by the law of contract and by industrial awards and agreements.
>
> The *Equal Opportunity Act* has its place in that field; but courts and tribunals should not, in defiance of its proper construction and without regard for other, long established, claimants, arrogate to it territory which the legislature never intended that it should occupy.[337]

Such comments depict discrimination law as an interloper, an illegitimate intruder, into the realm of workplace relations and as taking a secondary place behind other forms of workplace regulation.

Discrimination law also at times ignores the subtle ways in which the contemporary workplace culture fostered by laws that focus on the competitiveness of industry in the new economy may operate in discriminatory ways. For example, in *Evan's Case*, despite the finding that a single parent had been indirectly discriminated against, Branson J's comments seemingly endorsed the aggressive long-hours culture of modern workplaces, which discourages workers from accessing the workplace entitlements they have:

> The certified Agreement simply establishes the entitlement of NCA staff to leave. It does not provide that all staff who take leave within their respective entitlement must be treated equally when the question of contract renewal arises or anything to like effect … it is not illegitimate for an employer, all other things being equal and provided indirect discrimination is avoided, to favour for re-employment an employee who takes limited leave over an employee who regularly takes a lot of leave, albeit that it is leave to which he or she is entitled.[338]

If only certain workers can access their entitlements the resultant culture makes it more difficult for all workers to balance work, family and life.

Even when equality provisions have been incorporated in labour legislation there is sometimes also a tendency to subordinate their function to the more traditional concerns of labour law and contract. In *Christie* McHugh J did accept that an expansive interpretation to the defence of 'the inherent requirement of the position' was inappropriate in interpreting the legislative provisions proscribing unlawful termination of employment on discriminatory grounds.[339] Nonetheless, he also pointed out, that the prohibition against unlawful (discriminatory) termination operates 'in a context of a free enterprise system of industrial relations where employers and employees have considerable scope for defining their contractual rights and duties' and he went on to imply that it was possible to make contractual arrangements for work that avoided the

---

337 See *State of Victoria v Schou* [2001] 3 VR 655, 660.
338 *Evans*, above n 85, [71].
339 *Christie*, above n 48, 307.

operation of the Act in the absence of a particular legislative provision prohibiting this.[340] With respect, such an approach is inappropriate, and further diminishes prospects for tackling discrimination in the workplace of the global era.

However, transformative possibilities always emerge in law. And it is no different in the area of equality and discrimination. The possibilities for using the common law and contract to counter discrimination are becoming more evident and to some attractive. This is evident in cases such as *Thomson, Rispoli* and *Dare v Hurley* where as well as actions for breach of the discrimination statute, the plaintiffs simultaneously pursued their employers for a breach of contract in failing to comply with their own policies.[341] Where modern businesses espouse a commitment to equality and promote their workplace as one that is free from discrimination, the common law may be used, often with more devastating effect in terms of the damages awarded, to hold them to their promise. In this way contract law may provide one avenue for equality and discrimination to emerge from the shadows in the new economy although the common law is not likely to be effective at tackling the more invidious forms of systemic discrimination.

---

340 Ibid, 307–8.

341 *Thomson*, above n 78; *Rispoli v Merck Sharpe & Dohme* (*Rispoli*) [2003] FMCA 160; and *Dare v Hurley* [2005] FMCA 844. This strategy is discussed in B Smith and J Riley 'Family-friendly Work Practices and the Law' (2004) 26 *Syd LR* 395, 418–26.

9

Security at Work

Security at work in the global era

Security at work is one of the most common concerns of workers in the new economy. Job security along with the opportunity to do interesting work are amongst the attributes most often identified as essential to quality work.[1] Other factors commonly seen as influencing the quality of work include the level of remuneration, working time, the prospects for advancement, the status or prestige of the work in the community, the opportunities afforded to workers to exercise independence and develop their skills, and the quality of interpersonal relations at work. But without job security, all these mean little.

The defining feature of much work over the last two to three decades has been its precariousness. The growth in non-standard forms of work arrangements is a major indicator of this precariousness.[2] Although non-standard work in Australia, and elsewhere, has traditionally been, and remains, a gendered phenomenon affecting women in particular, a characteristic of labour markets in the new economy is the spread of these patterns of work among other groups of workers too.[3] However, the concept of precariousness is one that goes further than simply pointing to the fact that many workers are no longer employed under a traditional or standard contract of employment, that is, to work 'fulltime' on an ongoing basis. The idea of precariousness as it applies to work in the new economy encompasses a much broader range of issues. Insecurity can permeate every aspect of a person's work.

---

1 AE Clark *Measures of Job Satisfaction: What Makes a Good Job? Evidence from the OECD Countries*, (*Labour Market and Social Policy—Occasional Papers* No 34, OECD, Paris, 1998). This study relied primarily on data from a 1989 survey of workers in nine OECD countries, but did not include Australia.

2 See J Fudge and R Owens (eds) *Precarious Work, Women, and the New Economy: The Challenge to Legal Norms* (2006), esp Ch 1.

3 See Fudge and Owens, ibid; B Pocock 'All Change, Still Gendered: The Australian Labour Market in the 1990s' (1998) 40 *JIR* 580; I Campbell 'The Spreading Net: Age and Gender in the Process of Casualisation in Australia' (2000) 45 *JAPE* 68; and Productivity Commission *The Role of Non-Traditional Work in the Australian Labour Market* (2006). See further Chapter 4.

In an early analysis of precarious employment in Europe, Gerry Rodgers and Janine Rodgers probed four defining areas of concern about security at work.[4] These were the degree of certainty about continuing employment; the control workers had over their work, including the degree to which they could have a say through employee associations or trade unions over the pace of work, and their pay and conditions; the extent of legal protections applicable to workers; and the financial rewards workers received for their labour and time spent at work. Since then many scholars have elabora-ted even further the importance of security at work, linking it to understandings of the worker as an autonomous human being, recognition of the contribution that is made to the community through productive labour, and the idea of work as a source of human dignity.[5]

Drawing on the work of Guy Standing, the Australian scholars John Burgess and Iain Campbell have charted eight forms of insecurity affecting the lives of workers in the new economy:[6]

- employment insecurity—when workers can be dismissed or laid off or put on shorter time without difficulty;
- functional insecurity—when workers can be shifted at will or where the content of the job can be altered or redefined;
- work insecurity—when the working environment is unregulated, polluted or entails other things making it dangerous to continue;
- income insecurity—when earnings are unstable, contingency-based or not guaranteed or near poverty;
- benefit insecurity—when access to standard benefits is limited or denied;
- working-time insecurity—when hours are irregular and at the discretion of the employer or insufficient to generate adequate income;
- representation insecurity—when the employer can impose change and need not, or may refuse to, negotiate with the workers' representatives; and
- skills reproduction insecurity—when opportunities to gain and retain skills through access to training and education are limited.

This list serves as an important reminder that there are multiple dimensions to security at work.

However, it may not be helpful to try to define in a complete sense the meaning of security at work. In the new economy it is almost always possible to think of new dimensions to the problem of security. A recent examination of the problem of precariousness as it impacts on women workers identifies a number of matters that do not fall neatly into the categories listed above.[7] For instance, if the focus shifts to

---

4   G Rodgers and J Rodgers (eds) *Precarious Jobs in Labour Market Regulation: The Growth of Atypical Employment in Western Europe* (1989).

5   See eg H Collins *Justice in Dismissal: The Law of Termination of Employment* (1992); and the writing of G Standing, esp 'Globalization, Labour Flexibility and Insecurity: The Era of Market Regulation' (1997) 3 *European JIR* 7; *Global Labour Flexibility: Seeking Distributive Justice* (1999); and *Beyond the New Paternalism: Basic Security as Equality* (2000).

6   J Burgess and I Campbell 'The Nature and Dimensions of Precarious Employment in Australia' (1998) 8 *Labour and Industry* 5, 11–16.

7   Fudge and Owens, above n 2.

security of attachment to the labour market over a lifetime, which is arguably often just as important a perspective as security in a particular job, there might be more attention to the way in which the law deals with employment breaks and facilitates transitions between various types of employment according to the different life stages of a worker.[8] Those responsible for the care of a young child, for instance, may need to be able to reduce their hours of work for a period secure in the knowledge that as the child grows older they will be able to resume a greater participation in the labour market. The costs of accommodating the demands of paid work and care work are an important element in the insecurity many workers experience. More attention might also be paid to those workers who are 'self-employed' who are excluded from the superintendence of traditional labour law. Their terms and conditions of work are sometimes worse than those enjoyed by employees but this is treated as part of the risks inherent in 'commercial arrangements' in the marketplace.[9] There are other issues that can arise at work, such as the problems of harassment or bullying, which may sometimes be treated as occupational health and safety issues, but can equally be seen as matters of equality, or of security.[10] An examination of this list of issues makes it obvious that precariousness may also be experienced by those who remain in so-called standard work, as well as those in the newer non-standard forms of work.[11]

The demise of security at work in the global era has come about in large part because security has come to be seen as opposed to the demands of the market for flexibility, whether it be functional flexibility whereby workers are able to adapt their skills to the changing demands of production, or numerical flexibility, which allows for adjustments or changes in the input of labour to respond more quickly to the needs of the market.[12] Regulatory systems have responded to market demands for flexibility by diminishing the protections for, and the costs of, employing more flexible, non-standard labour. When security at work becomes a cost that business is unwilling to bear, the consequence is that for many the quality of work diminishes. Therefore the challenge is to transform flexibility from a 'neo-liberal shibboleth' into a 'progressive rallying cry'.[13] What is needed perhaps is a 'right to flexibility' that serves equally the interests and needs of employees as it does those of employers,[14] although to date there has been a high degree of scepticism that any promise of flexibility with security, or 'flexicurity', can be fulfilled.[15]

---

8 See C Kilpatrick 'Gender and the Legal Protection of Employment Breaks' in Fudge and Owens, above n 2. See also *Family Provisions Test Case* (2005) 143 IR 245 discussed in Chapter 7, pp 319–20.

9 See J Fudge 'Self-employment, Women and Precarious Work: The Scope of Labour Protection' in Fudge and Owens, above n 2. Note also the proposed *Independent Contractors Act 2006* (Cth).

10 See eg T MacDermott 'The Duty to Provide a Harassment-free Work Environment' (1995) 37 *JIR* 495.

11 See P Brosnan and E Underhill, 'Introduction: Precarious Employment' (1998) 8 *Lab Ind* 1.

12 J Atkinson *Flexibility, Uncertainty and Manpower Management* (1984).

13 See K Klare 'The Horizons of Transformative Labour and Employment Law' in J Conaghan, RM Fischl and K Klare (eds) *Labour Law in an Era of Globalization: Transformative Practices and Possibilities* (2002).

14 H Collins 'The Right to Flexibility' in J Conaghan and K Rittich (eds) *Labour Law, Work, and Family: Critical and Comparative Perspectives* (2005); and R Owens 'Engendering Flexibility in a World of Precarious Work' in Fudge and Owens, above n 2.

15 See S Fredman 'Women at Work: The Broken Promise of Flexicurity' (2004) 33 *ILJ* 299; and S Fredman 'Precarious Norms for Precarious Workers' in Fudge and Owens, above n 2.

Changes in emphases in contractual understanding of work relationships have also impacted on security at work. By the later part of the twentieth century the contract of employment still incorporated traces of earlier notions of medieval servitude in its recognition of the employer's prerogative of managerial control over the worker even though it had discarded long ago any of the pre-industrial hallmarks of security in work, such as the presumption of annual hiring. Modern employees thus had little protection against a capricious employer, who could discard them as they would a thing or piece of property. The simultaneous insistence of contract that the worker is an intentional actor, a human being, did not necessarily sit well with this. Statutory protections, recognising the worker as a human being, were thus introduced as a counterweight to the employers' contractual rights.[16] But these provisions were not initially seen as overly offensive to the contractual understanding of work relations. They could be rationalised as a just, albeit imposed, quid pro quo for the employee's open-ended loyalty and submission to the command and interests of the master's enterprise.

However, the dominance of neo-liberal theory in the global era has since pushed contract to its logical extension. Contract's view of workers as autonomous, intentional beings now insists that workers can know and protect their own interests and that the state ought not to interfere in the work relationship. Security is just another element that might be the subject of a private bargain in the workplace.

In this context the need for the protection of workers, including their security at work, has become keenly contested. The contemporary story of security at work is increasingly packaged in rhetoric that portrays workers as market actors, whose own human capital is the best protection against assaults on their attachment to a particular job. For these workers it is labour market attachment, rather than their security in a particular job or position, that is seen as critical. Such rhetoric seeks to reinforce the view that all workers can be independent, self-reliant beings. It does not acknowledge the reality that for many the only available jobs are low-skilled, and there is strong competition and a large pool of other labour always on standby to replace 'difficult' workers.

This chapter examines three aspects of the law dealing with security in the contemporary workplace in Australia. First, it looks at the ways in which the law is eradicating some of the last vestiges of constraints on the forms of employment and the implications of this for workers' experience of precariousness at work. Secondly, the chapter discusses the statutory protection from dismissal, focusing on unfair dismissal, after the changes introduced into the *Workplace Relations Act 1996* (Cth) by the *Workplace Relations Act (Work Choices) Act 2005* (Cth) *(Work Choices)*. Finally, this chapter examines an issue that is of increasing importance to individual workers, that of privacy in the workplace.

Precarious work

To date the growth of non-standard forms of employment has been one of the clearest indicators of the loss of security by many workers. As Anthony O'Donnell has reminded

---

16 See Collins, above n 5.

us, law's standards are a 'regulatory pivot' around which employees are divided according to the protection law provides them. The 'standard' worker is protected by law, while the 'non-standard' worker is not.[17] When work standards exempt, exclude, or enable the removal of, certain groups from their coverage there is an incentive for business enterprises to enter into particular types of work arrangement and not others. Since the *Workplace Relations Act* was first enacted in 1996 it has been impossible to introduce limits, for instance through award clauses, on work arrangements by imposing a constraint on the numbers or proportions of workers in different classifications—fulltime, part-time or casual—or by placing a limit on the maximum hours that part-timers could work. These provisions remain in the Act after *Work Choices*: s 515(1)(c) and (e).

The conversion strategy for casuals

Prior to the *Work Choices* amendments to the *Workplace Relations Act* the strategy of providing casuals with a right to elect to transfer to an ongoing employment classification was adopted as a means of providing these workers with more security, including improving their access to basic work standards. Thus a 'right of conversion' was inserted in a range of awards[18] for casuals who had been employed on a regular and systematic basis over a specified period of time (usually six or 12 months). The conversion mechanism required the employer to advise such casuals that they had a right to elect to convert from casual employment to ongoing employment, and established a formal notification process by which this was to be done. The outcome of the conversion process was by no means automatic. The clauses, though protective, were only facilitative. They provided a right *to elect* to convert to ongoing employment. An employer might reasonably refuse the request, for instance by pointing to business uncertainty or the impact upon the business. When any resulting dispute was not resolved under the award's grievance procedures there was recourse to the industrial tribunal to resolve the dispute.

The rationale behind conversion clauses, as became evident from the *Secure Employment Test Case*,[19] was that non-standard forms of employment such as casual work (including labour-hire and forms of independent contracting) carried a higher incidence of a range of risks to workers. These risks included a greater chance of non-compliance with occupational health and safety standards, poor wages and conditions of work that did not meet basic award standards, and less access to training and skills development and hence to career development. The repercussions of this then spilled over into

---

17 See A O'Donnell '"Non-Standard" Workers in Australia: Counts and Controversies' (2004) 17 *AJLL* 89, 89 fn 2. See Chapter 7. However, this should not be taken as suggesting that there are no differences within those categories on either side of this binary divide.

18 See eg *Re Metal, Engineering and Associated Industries Award 1998—Part I* (2002) 110 IR 247. Conversion clauses were also inserted in State awards: see eg *Secure Employment Test Case* [2006] NSWIRComm 38; *Metal Industry (South Australia) Award* [2001] SAIRComm 71; *Metal Industry (South Australia) Award—Variation Application No 1607/2001* (SAIRComm, 21 December 2001); *Clerks' (South Australia) Award Casual Provisions Appeal Case* (2001) 108 IR 367; *Clerks' (South Australia) Award—Report to the Full Commission* [2002] SAIRComm 23; *Clerks' (South Australia) Award Casual Provisions Appeal Case* [2002] SAIRComm 39; and *Clerks' (South Australia) Award Casual Provisions Appeal Case* [2002] SAIRComm 50.

19 [2006] NSWIRComm 38.

private life: the uncertainties meant, for instance, that non-standard workers had more limited access to finance.

In so far as a conversion clause provided for a transition between different types of employment the strategy it represented was a welcome one. However, this strategy could be criticised because the outcome was not guaranteed. It also made access to protection a matter of 'choice' by a vulnerable worker, but such 'choice' is never very real especially as by initiating the process the worker risks a hostile response from their employer or, even worse, losing their job.[20] Furthermore, because conversion to ongoing employment meant loss of the 'casual loading', it always represented a difficult option for those who struggle on a low wage.[21] However, the strategy was advocated as one that offered the best way of dealing with the problem of providing protection to long-term casuals.[22]

The impact of Work Choices on precarious work

Since the introduction of the *Work Choices* amendments it is no longer possible to include conversion clauses in awards: s 515(1)(b). This is only one of a number of changes that go further than the 1996 legislation in ensuring that the regulatory system imposes no constraints upon the work arrangements business enters into unless they are agreed.[23]

However, it is not easy to discern whether the new *Work Choices* regime will encourage the further growth of non-standard forms of employment. There are a number of indicators that it will, because the new provisions prohibit award clauses that set the terms or conditions of independent contractors or labour hire workers (at least, in respect to the latter group, in so far as such clauses would purport to bind the host employer for whom the labour hire workers perform work): s 515(1)(g)–(h). The same prohibition is extended by regulation to workplace agreements: r 8.5(1)(h)–(i).

Other provisions in the regulatory scheme are more ambiguous in terms of their likely effect on the encouragement of 'non-standard' work arrangements. For instance, because employees cannot access the unfair dismissal protections if their employer has 100 or fewer employees, and since all employees count for these purposes (except short-term casuals), there is an incentive for employers to employ fewer part-time workers or alternatively to outsource work to independent contractors.[24] Of course, the characterisation of contracts for services as 'commercial arrangements' that are excluded from any of the protective provisions of industrial laws such as the *Workplace Relations Act* is another way of encouraging the growth of these arrangements.[25]

---

20 See *Clerks (South Australia) Award* [2004] SAIRComm 4 for an example of successful conversion in face of protest by the employer. See generally M Smith and P Ewer *Choice and Coercion: Women's Experience of Casual Employment* (1999) on the idea that workers 'choose' non-standard work.

21 For a critique of the conversion strategy see R Owens 'Decent Work for the Contingent Workforce in the New Economy' (2002) 15 *AJLL* 209, 223–9; and Owens, above n 14, 346–9.

22 See B Pocock, J Buchanan, and I Campbell *Securing Quality Employment: Policy Options for Casual and Part-time Workers* (2004).

23 Conversion clauses may still be incorporated in workplace agreements, although this is unlikely to occur except perhaps in collective trade union agreements.

24 See below pp 426–27.

25 See the effect of the proposed *Independent Contractors Act 2006* (Cth).

Conversion clauses worked by assimilating the position of the non-standard casual worker to that of the standard worker. As such they accepted the binary division of employees into these two main types of standard and non-standard employees. However, some of the changes introduced by *Work Choices* have so dramatically transformed the meaning of work standards that they will likely tend to obliterate rather than intensify any binary divide between standard and non-standard employees. Most significant here is the fact that work standards have been effectively diminished, or significantly lowered, in the new system.[26] This means there is less incentive for business to seek to avoid their application to employees. Furthermore, what standards remain in the safety net now function in a way that maximises flexibility (by using the 'hour' as the measure of time for calculating most entitlements, and providing for the possibility of averaging working hours over the year). So there may no longer be any need to resort to non-standard work arrangements to achieve flexibility. Indeed, in so far as there is a loading attached to the employment of some non-standard workers, such as casuals, there are additional costs to engaging these workers that can be easily avoided without sacrificing flexibility by employing them in ongoing positions. That is, after *Work Choices* all work is more precarious.[27] The law regulating the dismissal of employees also makes this clear. The key laws protecting job security have long worked to create a particular model of standard employment.[28] But after *Work Choices* there are considerably fewer employees who meet the new standard.

Protection against unfair dismissal

Two features of the common law of employment presented obstacles to the development of adequate security of employment for workers. The first was the assumption that a contract of employment could be terminated with notice for a good reason, a bad reason, or no reason at all. The common law did not require 'just cause' (such as incompetency, misconduct or redundancy) before an employer could legitimately terminate an employment contract. So an important development in the law of work—achieved primarily through statute but with the assistance of considerable industrial muscle—has been the introduction of some protection (albeit limited) against arbitrary dismissal.

The second obstacle was the common law's refusal to order specific performance of a contract for personal services (except in the rarest and most peculiar circumstances). One of the most significant benefits conferred by the statutory protections against unfair dismissal has been the opportunity to request reinstatement.

Both these obstacles stood in the way of effective remedies for workers who were dismissed from their jobs—and so robbed of their livelihoods—for no good reason.

---

26 See C Fenwick 'How Low Can You Go? Minimum Working Conditions under Australia's New Labour Laws' (2006) 16 *ELRR* 85; and R Owens 'Working Precariously: The Safety Net after Work Choices' (2006) 19 *AJLL* 161. See further Chapter 7.

27 See Owens, ibid.

28 See J-C Tham 'Job Security Laws: Constituting "Standard" and "Non-standard" Employment' in C Arup et al (eds) *Labour Law and Labour Market Regulation* (2006). See also the discussion below on 'Exclusions' from unfair dismissal provisions, p 424.

Where the employer is an individual 'master', the common law's refusal to yoke together unwilling partners by ordering reinstatement of a servant may make some sense, but in contemporary times, when the employer is often a large faceless corporation, there must be less concern that reinstatement will exacerbate conflict. A large organisation can find another workstation for the unjustifiably dismissed worker. Unfair dismissal laws arguably promote greater efficiency for large organisations. They provide a check on capricious conduct by supervising employees, and so support the interests of the corporate employer's shareholders and other investors, in ensuring that managers do not abuse their powers to the detriment of the organisation as a whole.

Nevertheless, Australian law was a long time in developing effective reinstatement remedies for unjustifiably dismissed individual employees.[29] Just how effective these remedies are is now a subject of debate, particularly in the light of later political pressure to undermine protections developed throughout the 1980s and 1990s. *Work Choices* effectively abolished unfair dismissal protection for a great many Australian workers, particularly by prohibiting claims against corporate employers with 100 or fewer employees.[30] These amendments were rationalised as a protection for 'small businesses' whose decisions to take on new staff were said (anecdotally) to be hampered by fear of costly recruiting errors.[31] And in any event the federal jurisdiction has always been limited to those workers who are classified as employees, working under contracts of service within the common law definition (although some state jurisdictions had extended the statutory definition of employee to preclude avoidance of this protection).[32] Independent and dependent contractors are excluded from the jurisdiction.[33] Not surprisingly then, the impact of the amendments introduced by *Work Choices* has been described variously as a move that has transformed a 'work standard' into a 'legal privilege', and as being a step 'back to the future'.[34]

Early influences

The State industrial tribunals had long exercised powers to reinstate workers, as part of their general jurisdiction to make orders in settlement of industrial disputes. In fact, it was a case in the NSW industrial jurisdiction, *Re Loty and Holloway v Australian*

---

29 For a perspective on the development of reinstatement rights, see R McCallum 'Collective Labour Law, Citizenship and the Future' (1998) 22 *MULR* 42. For a history of State and federal introduction of unfair dismissal protection see A Stewart 'And (Industrial) Justice for All? Protecting Workers against Unfair Dismissal' (1995) 1 *Flinders Journal of Law Reform* 85.

30 See *Workplace Relations Act*, s 643(10).

31 For a discussion of the small business proposals identifying the lack of empirical evidence justifying them, see R Barrett 'Small Business and Unfair Dismissal' (2003) 45 *JIR* 87. On the regulation of work and small business generally, see K Wheelwright 'Protecting and Promoting Small and Medium Enterprises: A Role for Labour Law in the New Labour Law Era?' in Arup et al, above n 28.

32 See eg *Industrial Relations Act 1996* (NSW), s 5 and Sch 1; and *Industrial Relations Act 1999* (Qld), s 275. These provisions no longer have any effect on federal employers and employees: see *Workplace Relations Act*, ss 5–6 and 16(1).

33 See the discussion in Chapter 4. For an example of the significance of the distinction, and potential for employers to manipulate their exposure to unfair dismissal laws, see *Damevski v Giudice* (2003) 202 ALR 494.

34 A Chapman 'Unfair Dismissal Law and Work Choices: From Safety Net Standard to Legal Privilege' (2006) *ELRR* 237; and M Pittard 'Back to the Future: Unjust Termination of Employment under the Work Choices Legislation' (2006) 19 *AJLL* 225.

Workers' Union,[35] in 1971, which generated the often-cited concept of a 'fair go all round', which underpins the various statutory schemes, and is still cited in a note to the relevant provision in the *Workplace Relations Act*: s 635. The 'fair go all round' implies that decisions made within this jurisdiction involve a balancing of the interests of all parties involved—employers, employees and any others tangled up in the dispute (such as new employees who have taken over the job). However, this jurisdiction provided a remedy only to those workers whose dismissals occurred in the context of some industrial matter, and whose interests were championed by a trade union. Individual employees unrepresented by unions had no access to reinstatement by a tribunal until the enactment of general unfair dismissal statutes.

The South Australian Parliament was the first in Australia to enact a statute granting individual employees access to a reinstatement remedy in 1973.[36] The South Australian legislation followed an International Labour Organization Recommendation, the *Termination of Employment Recommendation 1963 (ILO R 119)*, now surpassed by the *Termination of Employment Convention, 1982 (ILO C 158)*.[37] Now all States (apart from Victoria, which since 1997 has come under the federal jurisdiction following a reference of industrial matters under s 51(xxxvii) of the *Australian Constitution*) have enacted unfair dismissal laws with a reinstatement remedy. However, the operation of those State provisions has been severely curtailed by the *Workplace Relations Act 1996* (Cth) since 27 March 2006: see s 16.[38]

At the federal level, a general statutory right was slow in coming, largely for constitutional reasons. The Australian Industrial Relations Commission (AIRC) was prepared to draw on *ILO C 158* as well as other developments in this area to establish a standard 'termination, change and redundancy' clause for insertion into federal industrial awards in a test case, the *Termination Change and Redundancy Case*.[39] However, for some time the AIRC was held to lack any power to enforce these award clauses by ordering reinstatement and/or compensation. The AIRC's powers to deal with an individual claiming they had been dismissed contrary to an award were considered to be constrained by its jurisdictional underpinning by s 51(xxxv) of the *Australian Constitution*, which meant it was limited to the settlement of *interstate* industrial disputes by *conciliation and arbitration*. Until the decision in *Re Boyne Smelters Ltd; Ex parte Federation of Industrial Manufacturing and Engineering Employees of Australia*,[40] it had been held that reinstatement of a single worker could not be in settlement of an interstate industrial dispute (because

---

35 [1971] AR (NSW) 95.

36 *Industrial Relations Act 1972* (SA), s 15(1)(e), replaced in 1984 with a more extensive protection in s 34: see A Stewart 'The New Unfair Dismissal Jurisdiction in South Australia' (1986) 28 *JIR* 367. On earlier developments in the United Kingdom see Collins, above n 5.

37 This Convention now forms Sch 10 of the *Workplace Relations Act 1996* (Cth).

38 See *Industrial Relations Act 1996* (NSW), Ch 2 Pt 6; *Industrial Relations Act 1999* (Qld), Ch 3; *Fair Work Act 1994* (SA), Ch 3 Pt 6; *Industrial Relations Act 1979* (WA), s 23A; and *Industrial Relations Act 1984* (Tas), s 30.

39 (1984) 8 IR 34; 9 IR 115. See also A Chapman 'The Declining Influence of ILO Standards in Shaping Australian Statutory Provisions on Unfair Dismissal' (2003) 29 *Monash UL Rev* 104, 110–11.

40 (1993) 177 CLR 446.

a worker could only be located in one state or territory), and the exercise of a power to reinstate would be an exercise of judicial power (a power determining rights) not arbitral power.[41] Earlier cases had also held that a reinstatement order did not involve an 'industrial matter', because it concerned the relationship between an employer and a *former employee*, not employers and their current employees.[42] *Boyne Smelters* (which followed a line of High Court decisions establishing the grounds for a reinstatement jurisdiction)[43] held that an appropriately drafted award clause could confer on the federal tribunal a power to order reinstatements of individual workers in settlement of an interstate industrial dispute: the collective of workers with an eye to the wider implications of a dismissal had a vital interest in such an outcome.

At around this time, however, federal legislation had resolved the problem by enacting the first federal version of unfair dismissal laws, in the *Industrial Relations Reform Act 1993* (Cth) relying constitutionally on the external affairs power, s 51(xxix) of the *Australian Constitution*.[44] However, in one of the first of many amendments that departed from the international standard,[45] the legislation was quickly amended under pressure from employer interest groups to introduce a salary cap for eligibility (so that highly paid non-award workers could not use the jurisdiction), and a cap of six months salary on compensation. The legislation was also challenged by some of the States (lead by the conservative Kennett Victorian Government) and was held to be partially invalid in *Victoria v Commonwealth*.[46] To the extent that former s 170DE(2) protected against dismissals that were merely 'harsh, unjust or unreasonable' but not unlawful, it was held by the High Court not to be appropriate and adapted to implementing the obligations under *ILO C 158* upon which the provisions were purportedly based and as is required by any legislation supported by the external affairs power.[47]

The *Workplace Relations and Other Legislation Amendment Act 1996* (Cth) rewrote the provisions (and there have been further amendments since 1997); however, the protection against dismissals that were 'harsh, unjust or unreasonable', and the remedy of reinstatement in appropriate cases, were essentially maintained, at least for the employees of large enterprises.[48] These new provisions relied primarily on the corporations power, s 51(xx) of the *Australian Constitution*.

---

41 See *R v Gough; Ex parte Cairns Meat Export Co Pty Ltd* (1962) 108 CLR 343; and *R v Gough; Ex parte Meat and Allied Trades Federation of Australia* (1969) 122 CLR 237, 241.

42 See eg *R v Portus; Ex parte City of Perth* (1973) 129 CLR 312, 329.

43 See *Slonim v Fellows* (1984) 154 CLR 505, 515; *Re Ranger Uranium Mines Pty Ltd; Ex parte Federated Miscellaneous Workers' Union of Australia* (1987) 163 CLR 656, 661–6; and *Re Federated Storemen and Packers' Union of Australia; Ex parte Wooldumpers (Victoria) Ltd* (1989) 166 CLR 311.

44 *Industrial Relations Reform Act 1993* (Cth), Pt VIA Div 3.

45 See Chapman, above n 39.

46 (1996) 187 CLR 416, 510–21.

47 This aspect of the decision of the High Court has been criticised as not recognising ILO jurisprudence: see B Creighton 'The *Workplace Relations Act* in International Perspective' (1997) 10 *AJLL* 31, 39–40.

48 For a critique of the 1996 revisions see A Chapman 'Termination of Employment under the *Workplace Relations Act 1996* (Cth)' (1997) 10 *AJLL* 89; and T MacDermott 'Industrial Legislation in 1996: The Reform Agenda' (1997) 39 *JIR* 52.

Reliance on this power meant that (with the exception of those employed in the Territories, or by the Commonwealth) an employee had to be employed by a 'constitutional corporation' in order to bring a claim for unfair (as distinct from 'unlawful') dismissal.[49]

The federal regime for protection against dismissal

The *Workplace Relations Act* still makes provision for employees to seek a remedy in the event they are dismissed. To ensure constitutional validity, this protection against dismissal in the federal statute is divided into protection from 'unlawful' dismissal, and protection from 'unfair' dismissal.

The unlawful dismissal provisions (including provisions requiring notice of termination) are underpinned by the external affairs power and are based on the ILO Convention, *Termination of Employment Convention, 1982 (ILO C 158)*, which is included as a Schedule to the legislation: see ss 636–7, and generally Pt 12, Div 4, Subdiv C and Sch 10.[50] Because of the breadth of the external affairs power, the unlawful dismissal provisions apply to all employees, regardless of whether they work under a federal award or agreement, and whether or not they are employed by a constitutional corporation or other federal employer: ss 636 and 637(3). The specific exclusions from unfair dismissal listed in s 638—explained below—do not apply to unlawful dismissal claims.

The unlawful termination provisions protect against dismissal that is contrary to the standards set by the ILO Convention—discrimination, temporary illnesses or absence, freedom of association, and whistle-blowing: see s 659. The list of discriminatory grounds in s 659(2)(f) comprises race, colour, sex, sexual preference, age, physical or mental disability, marital status, family responsibilities, pregnancy, religion, political opinion, national extraction or social origin.

Like unfair dismissal applications, applications to deal with allegedly unlawful dismissals are also made to the AIRC in the first instance, which will attempt to settle the matter by conciliation. However if conciliation fails, the Commission will issue a certificate under s 650 allowing the applicant to commence proceedings in the Federal Court. Applicants alleging unlawful termination enjoy the benefit of a reversed onus of proof: s 664. The employee is not required to prove that the termination was for a reason proscribed by s 659; however, an employer may defend the proceedings successfully by proving that the termination was for a reason or reasons that did not include the discriminatory reason.

In contrast to the provisions governing unlawful dismissal, the federal regime regulating unfair dismissal depends on a range of powers in the *Australian Constitution*, including the corporations power, the Commonwealth public sector employment power, the trade and commerce power, the Territories power and the referral power: the unfair

---

49 See *Workplace Relations Act*, former s 170CB(1). Victorian employers were also covered, following the Victorian government's reference of industrial matters to the Commonwealth in 1997.

50 For a more detailed discussion of unlawful termination, see Chapter 8.

dismissal provisions apply only to federal employees as defined in s 5 of the *Workplace Relations Act* and to Victorian employees, in relation to whom there has been a referral of power: see ss 636–7 and 858 and Pt 21, Div 7.[51]

'Unfair' dismissal

The influence of contract law

Although unfair dismissal laws are usually described as protective pro-employee legislation derived from international law norms, there is also a strong argument that local developments in employment contract law may have precipitated the statutory enactment of defined rights and remedies, especially in the federal arena. After the insertion into many federal awards of *Termination Change and Redundancy* (TCR) clauses giving federal award workers rights against arbitrary dismissal, a number of cases were brought in which employees sought to obtain contract-based remedies for dismissal in breach of the award clause.[52] The argument made on behalf of the employees in these cases was that the award clause was incorporated into the individual employment contract, giving the employee a contractual right to continue in the job until there was some legitimate reason for dismissal. The consequence of a dismissal in breach of the contract was therefore expectation-based damages. How long would the employee have remained employed, if the contract had not been breached? In the case of Mr Gorgevski—a man with a long and impeccable employment record, apart from a bad habit of smoking on the job contrary to shop floor rules—the Federal Court assessed damages as income until retirement age—a sum of $195 000.

The High Court decision in *Byrne v Australian Airlines Ltd*[53] torched the line of authority suggesting that award clauses were automatically contractually binding—but that decision was not handed down until 1995. Legislation providing statutory remedies—capping compensation at six months' salary—was passed in 1994. The legislation certainly created an entitlement for a wide class of employees to pursue remedies for unfair dismissal; however, it also relieved pressure on the business sector by containing the potential financial risk from applications for unfair dismissal from any employee with the benefit of a *TCR* clause in an industrial award or agreement.

Dismissal

The first element that a federal employee must establish in order to bring a claim for relief under the *Workplace Relations Act* in relation to a dismissal that is harsh, unjust or unreasonable (after of course establishing one's status as an employee) is that there was a 'termination of employment at the initiative of the employer': s 642(1).

---

51 Other 'non-federal' employees, for instance those employed by sole traders, partnerships, or corporations that are not 'constitutional corporations', may still be able to seek redress for unfair dismissal under State law: see above n 38.

52 See eg *Gregory v Philip Morris Ltd* (1988) 80 ALR 455; *Wheeler v Philip Morris Ltd* (1989) 97 ALR 282; *Lane v Arrowcrest Group Pty Ltd* (1990) 99 ALR 45; and *Bostik (Australia) Pty Ltd v Gorgevski (No 1)* (1992) 36 FCR 20.

53 (1995) 185 CLR 410.

This does not necessarily exclude situations where an employee has resigned. Prior to the *Work Choices* changes it was accepted that if the employer's action was the 'principal contributing factor' or resulted 'directly or consequentially' in an involuntary resignation then this amounted to a dismissal 'at the initiative of the employer' for the purposes of the legislation.[54] Thus where the resignation results from a 'resign or be sacked' ultimatum, or if the employee resigns or abandons the employment following the employer's clear repudiation of the employment contract, the termination could be found to be at the initiative of the employer. It was never necessary to show that the employer 'directly coerce[d]' the resignation, although the relevant acts of the employer did need to be of 'sufficient seriousness and proximity' to resignation.[55]

The *Work Choices* amendments introduced a new provision specifying when a resignation may amount to a dismissal for the purposes of the statute. The legislation now requires the employee to prove on the balance of probabilities that they 'did not resign voluntarily' but were 'forced to do so because of conduct, or a course of conduct, engaged in by the employer': s 642(4). As formulated this requirement may be open to an interpretation that is narrower than that of earlier case law. In any event, it has not been unknown for an employer to refuse to accept a 'forced resignation' and require the employee to sign a form attesting that they have resigned for 'personal' or other reasons,[56] and in such situations proof of the circumstances of the resignation while not impossible is also not always easy.

A demotion may also constitute a dismissal.[57] However, changes introduced in 2001 restricted the meaning of termination in the *Workplace Relations Act* to only those cases where there is 'a significant reduction' in remuneration or in the duties of the employee: s 642(3). There is scope for argument on the application of these words in any particular case, and not all demotions will fall within the statutory formula. The facts of *Thomson* illustrate this because there it was her *status*, not her remuneration or her duties, that changed.[58] On her return from maternity leave Ms Thomson was moved to a position where she was paid the same as before and she performed the same duties, but her *status* was significantly affected because of the changed client base allocated to her. In her new position she had many lower value clients rather than a select number of high value clients. Ms Thomson would have found it difficult to show that her demotion was a termination within the wording of the statute. In the new economy status can be extremely important to an employee, more important sometimes than the remuneration or duties performed, and while status will ordinarily be linked to duties and remuneration, the facts of *Thomson* show that this is not always so.

---

54 See *Mohazab v Dick Smith Electronics Pty Ltd* (1995) 62 IR 200, 205; and *Rheinberger v Huxley Marketing Pty Ltd* (1996) 67 IR 154, 160. See also *Russian v Woolworths (SA) Pty Ltd* (1995) 64 IR 169.
55 *Italiano v Bethesda Hospital* [1998] 712 FCA (19 June 1998).
56 *Galvin v Renito Pty Ltd* [1999] FCA 1005.
57 *Advertiser Newspapers Pty Ltd v Industrial Relation Commission of South Australia and Grivell* (1999) 90 IR 211. See former s 170CE(1B).
58 *Thomson v Orica Australia Pty Ltd* (*Thomson*) (2002) 116 IR 186, which was not an unfair dismissal case but a claim in common law and under discrimination law. See also Chapter 5, p 260.

Harsh, unjust or unreasonable

This trilogy of terms, 'harsh, unjust or unreasonable', needs to be understood in the context of the object of ensuring a 'fair go all round': s 635(2). The note to s 635 cites the decision of Sheldon J in *In Re Loty and Holloway and the Australian Workers' Union*, who said:

> The objective in these cases is always industrial justice and to this end weight must be given in varying degrees according to the requirements of each case to the importance but not the inviolability of the right of the employer to manage his business, the nature and quality of the work in question, the circumstances surrounding the dismissal and the likely practical outcome if an order of reinstatement is made.[59]

A dismissal may be harsh, unjust, or unreasonable, without being unlawful, or even 'wrongful' as far as the contract of employment is concerned. A helpful exposition of the meaning of the expression can be found in the judgment of McHugh and Gummow JJ in *Byrne v Australian Airlines Ltd*:

> Thus the one termination may be unjust because the employee was not guilty of the misconduct on which the employer acted, may be unreasonable because it was decided upon inferences which could not reasonably have been drawn from the material before the employer, and may be harsh in its consequences for the personal and economic situation of the employee or because it is disproportionate to the gravity of the misconduct in respect of which the employer acted.[60]

Harsh

A dismissal might be harsh because of the effect it has on the employee concerned: it may be a disproportionately severe punishment, given the relative gravity of the misconduct prompting the termination. An example of a harsh dismissal was the sacking of a bakery worker who refused to undertake a last-minute delivery of goods to a customer on his way home at the end of his shift.[61] Strictly speaking, the refusal to obey this order was a breach of the employee's duty of obedience, but in the circumstances, the punishment was too harsh. Likewise, the sacking of workers who went drinking at lunchtime contrary to their employer's well-published policy forbidding drinking during the working day was held to be a 'harsh' dismissal, despite being for a valid reason, based on a reasonable and justifiable policy.[62] The employees were all long-serving staff members, and inconsistent enforcement of the policy had misled them into believing infringement was not a serious matter.

Factors indicating an unfair dismissal

Cases concerning unfair dismissal depend heavily on their own facts. The legislation provides some guidance in s 652(3) as to what kinds of matters the Commission must have regard to in determining by arbitration whether a dismissal was harsh, unjust or unreasonable. This list includes both substantive and procedural matters.

---

59 Above n 35.
60 (1995) 185 CLR 410, 465.
61 *Pastrycooks Employees, Biscuit Makers Employees and Flour and Sugar Goods Workers Union (NSW) v Gartrell* (1990) 35 IR 70.
62 *Agnew v Nationwide News Pty Ltd* AIRC, PR936856, 27 August 2003, refusing leave to appeal.

The Commission must consider whether there was 'a valid reason for the termination related to the employee's capacity or conduct (including its effect on the safety and welfare of other employees)': s 652(3)(a). Prior to *Work Choices* this provision also included a reference to the 'operational requirements of the employer's undertaking',[63] but this has now been superseded by the 'genuine operational reasons' exclusion.[64]

A valid reason is one that is 'sound, defensible or well founded'.[65] The question of whether the employer had a 'valid' reason for dismissal will often involve analysis of the scope of the employee's duties under the employment contract, including the employee's obedience to the employer's policies. The Commission has taken the view that where an employee breaches their implied contractual duty to obey lawful directions, for example by breaching a company policy that is incorporated in the employee's contract, such as would justify dismissal at common law, then there will be a valid (in the sense of 'sound, defensible or well founded') reason for dismissal.[66] While an employer cannot put in place an unreasonable policy, at the same time the Commission does not interfere with the right of management to run its business; a policy is only unreasonable if no reasonable employer could have adopted it.[67] Termination for a reason unrelated to the employee's duties under the employment contract will not be for a valid reason.

Difficult questions arise over the extent to which the employer is entitled to monitor the employee's private affairs.[68] Some dismissals have been found to be unfair when they have been prompted by the employee's after hours conduct. See for example *Rose v Telstra Corporation Ltd*,[69] where it was held that termination of an employee for brawling in a hotel after hours was 'harsh', because the employer had no entitlement to control the employee's out of hours conduct.[70] Sometimes, however, where after hours conduct has an impact on the employer's business (because animosity between workers spills over into work time or affects the productivity of others in the workplace), it will be a matter of legitimate concern to the employer and so provide a valid reason for dismissal.[71] Cases decided under the common law are helpful in identifying the boundary between the employee's personal life and duty to the employer.[72] Persons who hold positions of trust are more susceptible to out-of-hours control. See for example *Henry v Ryan*,[73] which concerned a police officer who loitered about schools in a state of undress in his spare time, and *Orr v University of Tasmania*,[74] which concerned a professor who engaged in a sexual relationship with

---

63 *Workplace Relations Act*, former s 170CG(3)(a).
64 See below p 424.
65 *Selvachandran v Peteron Plastics Pty Ltd* (1995) 62 IR 371, 373.
66 *Woolworths Limited v Brown* AIRC, PR963023, 26 September 2005, following *Atfield v Jupiters Ltd* (2003) 124 IR 217.
67 *Woolworths Limited v Brown*, ibid.
68 See below pp 444–53 for further discussion of privacy issues in employment.
69 AIRC, Print Q9292, 4 December 1998. For authority that even arrest upon a criminal offence does not of itself constitute misconduct warranting dismissal, see *Commissioner for Railways (NSW) v O'Donnell* (1938) 60 CLR 681, 689, 691–2, 698.
70 See also *Appellant v Respondent* (1999) 89 IR 407.
71 See eg *McManus v Scott Charlton* (1996) 140 ALR 625, 636.
72 See *Rose v Telstra Corporation Ltd*, above n 69.
73 [1963] Tas SR 90.
74 (1957) 100 CLR 526.

a student and so called into doubt his ability to deal objectively with assessment of her academic work.

More senior people may also be treated more stringently if they infringe codes of conduct at work. It depends on all of the circumstances of the case. See for example *Kenny v Epic Energy*,[75] where a manager who had a role in creating and enforcing the company's policy about inappropriate use of computer facilities was dismissed for breaching the policy himself by consulting pornographic Internet sites. His dismissal was held not to be harsh, because as a senior person responsible for giving effect to the policy, he ought to have realised the seriousness of his infringement. On the other hand, in *Hale v Australia and New Zealand Banking Group Ltd*,[76] a senior employee was reinstated by the AIRC after his dismissal for infringement of the company's policy on email etiquette.

The question of whether there was a valid reason for dismissal will not be the only determinant of whether a dismissal was unfair. It is but one factor—albeit an important one—which the Commission must take account of in assessing whether the dismissal was harsh, unjust or unreasonable.[77] Even if there is a valid reason for termination, consideration of other mitigating factors, such as those listed in s 652(3)(b)–(g), may nonetheless make the dismissal harsh, unreasonable or unfair.[78] Employees in larger enterprises will, for example, ordinarily be entitled to a fair process.[79] In *Hale*, for example, the company was held to have a valid reason for termination (breach of its email code of conduct). Nevertheless, its failure to warn Hale that it took a serious view of the inappropriate tone of his email correspondence meant that he had not been afforded procedural fairness, so the dismissal was, in the circumstances, 'harsh'.

Matters going to procedural fairness include whether the employee was given notice of the reason for dismissal, and an opportunity to respond where the reason concerned the employee's own conduct or capacity to do the job: s 652(3)(b)–(c). If the reason was related to performance, the Commission must take into account whether the employee was given warnings about any unsatisfactory aspects of their performance: s 652(3)(d). As the *Nationwide News* case[80] illustrated, the warnings have to be seriously made and clearly understood by the employee to effectively protect the employer from a later allegation of unfair treatment. Also, a non-specific 'pull up your socks' exhortation is unlikely to constitute an adequate warning.[81] Warnings need to specify areas of underachievement and provide guidance and a time frame for improvement. These provisions explain in part the development of performance review systems and the blossoming of 'human resources management' divisions in large firms.[82]

---

75 AIRC, Print S0947, 15 November 1999.

76 AIRC, Print S4068, 14 March 2000.

77 See *Windsor Smith v Lui & Ors* [1998] AILR ¶3–858.

78 See also *Woolworths Limited v Brown*, above n 66.

79 At common law this is not the case: See *Intico (Vic) Pty Ltd v Walmsley* [2004] VSCA 90.

80 Above n 62.

81 See eg *Nicholson v Heaven and Earth Galleries* (1994) 126 ALR 233, 243.

82 Note that the *Workplace Relations Regulations 2006* (Cth) specify that the prohibition on the inclusion of terms relating to 'harsh, unfair and unreasonable' termination in workplace agreements do not also preclude terms making provision for 'a process for managing an employee's performance or conduct': r 8.5(6).

The legislation contemplates that not all businesses will be of a size to develop sophisticated performance monitoring programs. The Commission is to take into account the influence of the size of the employer's enterprise on the procedures followed in dismissals, and whether the enterprise did have access to advice and assistance from human resources management specialists: s 652(3)(e)–(f). These provisions have been in the legislation for some time; however, because the *Work Choices* amendments establish a general exclusion for all business employing fewer than 101 employees, they will now have less work to do.

Exclusions

The federal regime creates a number of exclusions, so that only employees who have an expectation of continuing employment are able bring a claim for unfair dismissal.

First, no one may claim until they have completed a 'qualifying period' of service, determined as either six months, less than six months if the parties so agree in writing, or more than six months if the parties agree in writing and the longer term is objectively reasonable in the light of the nature of the position and the circumstances of the employment: s 643(7).[83] Further exclusions are provided for in s 638, and include people on fixed term contracts, people engaged for a specified task; employees on probation; short-term casuals; trainees on approved fixed term traineeships; seasonal workers; and—in the case of employees who are not employed on conditions derived from a federal award, collective agreement or AWA, or APCS—employees who earn more than a threshold set by the *Workplace Relations Regulations*. This threshold was $64 000 a year in 1997, and is indexed each year according to a formula set out in r 12.6. As at 27 March 2006, the threshold was $94 900.

The *Work Choices* amendments introduced two new and very significant exclusions that hinge on the nature of the employing business: that is, where the employee has been dismissed for a reason that includes a 'genuine operational reason', and where the employee worked for an enterprise employing 100 or fewer employees: s 643(8)–(9).

Genuine operational reasons

One of the most important changes introduced by the *Work Choices Act* is the exclusion of applications claiming unfair dismissal where the termination was for 'genuine operational reasons, or for reasons that include genuine operational reasons': s 643(8). This is further defined as referring to situations where the employer's reasons for dismissing an employee include reasons of 'an economic, technological, structural or similar nature relating to the employer's undertaking, establishment, service or business, or to a part of the employer's undertaking, establishment, service or business': s 643(9). In those cases an employee is not entitled to make an unfair dismissal application, and if they do so, the employer may apply to have the application dismissed. The AIRC is required to hold a hearing into whether the reasons for dismissal included operational reasons, before going any further to determine the application: s 649.

83 Prior to *Work Choices* the qualifying period was three months.

This exclusion proved contentious during the debate preceding the enactment of the *Work Choices Act*. The expression 'operational reasons' as defined in the legislation is potentially very broad. 'Operational reasons' of an 'economic' nature, for instance, might cover situations where a restructure is undertaken to enhance profitability and competitiveness and results in a redundancy, but it might also refer to situations that fall considerably short of the traditional test of redundancy. Under the previous version of the legislation one factor to consider in determining if there was a valid reason for the dismissal of an employee was the 'operational requirements' of the business.[84] This was interpreted quite strictly as indicating that the dismissal was a 'necessary' consequence.[85] The expression 'operational reasons' may not impose such a high hurdle because the terms of the legislation indicate that the operational reason need only be one of any number of reasons and not necessarily the most important of those reasons. An early decision of the Commission pointed out, however, that it is not enough to show there were operational reasons for a restructure. The operational reasons must also necessitate the dismissal.[86]

The 'operational reasons' do need to be 'genuine' and, given that their presence precludes employees from making application for statutory relief when their employment security has been taken away, it seems obvious that something more than a subjective assertion by the employer that they honestly held those reasons ought be required. To indicate the need for genuineness seems to accept that in some instances 'operational reasons' may be proffered that are not genuine. Nonetheless even if a higher objective standard is required the Commission may be reluctant to impose its reassessment of management's judgment in such matters.[87] In addition, most employees will not have the 'capabilities or resources' to challenge the employer's claims regarding operational reasons.[88]

Experience has shown that it is not uncommon for employers to invent needs to restructure and reorganise their businesses when it would be convenient to lose a certain number of staff—particularly where those staff have been difficult or uncooperative in some respect. In *Australasian Meat Industry Employees' Union v Belandra Pty Ltd*,[89] for example, it was held that an elaborate restructuring of a meat works business was motivated by the employer's desire to be rid of unions in the workplace. In other cases, unions have alleged (unsuccessfully) that organisational decisions have disguised attacks on unions. In *National Union of Workers v Qenos Pty Ltd*,[90] for example, the employer engaged in a 'spill and fill'[91] exercise to reduce staff numbers soon after the union commenced a period of protected action for an enterprise bargain, and coincidentally managed to shed quite a number of trade union members in the process. In that case,

---

84 *Workplace Relations Act*, former s 170CG(3)(a).
85 *Nettlefold v Kym Smoker Pty Ltd* (1996) 69 IR 370, 373.
86 See *Perry v Savills (Vic) Pty Ltd* AIRC, PR973103, 20 June 2006.
87 Ibid.
88 See *Koya v Port Phillip City Council* AIRC, PR973045, 13 June 2006.
89 (2003) 126 IR 165.
90 (2001) 108 FCR 90.
91 This involves all positions being vacated, and all employees being invited to reapply for available positions.

although Weinberg J found that some of the supervisors of the employer saw the exercise as 'a perfect opportunity to rid the company of a group of employees who had been particularly irksome', there were still genuine reasons to reduce staff numbers and these motivated the shedding of staff.[92]

Employers who seek to use operational reasons to disguise discriminatory dismissals run the serious risk of successful applications on the basis of unlawful dismissal. The 'operational reasons' exclusion—and other exclusions—apply only to applicants for unfair dismissal. If applicants are able to show that the reasons for the decision to terminate included reasons that would contravene the prohibition on unlawful termination of employment under s 659 they will be able to proceed with that application. So for example, a case such as *Sapevski v Katies Fashions (Australia) Pty Ltd* (*Sapevski*), where a restructure had the effect of terminating the employment of only the women on the shop floor, would still be likely to succeed as an unlawful (discriminatory) termination.[93]

The 'small business' exclusion

Since the enactment of the *Work Choices* amendments, the *Workplace Relations Act* provides that any employer with 100 or fewer employees is not susceptible to a claim for unfair dismissal: s 643(10)–(12). The head count for the purposes of the section includes employees, whether they are employed in an ongoing capacity or otherwise, for example on fixed-term contracts, and whether in a 'fulltime' or 'part-time' position: s 636. Included in the 100 is the employee whose employment was terminated; however, casuals are only included in the count if they have been engaged on a regular and systematic basis for at least 12 months: s 643(10). The legislative provisions also stipulate that the time at which this computation is to be made is to be the earlier of either the time of notice or the time of termination: s 643(12). While the exact impact of this small business exclusion (or, perhaps more accurately, this small to medium business exclusion)[94] may not be clear, there is no doubt that a very large majority of employees will be excluded by it.

The *Work Choices* amendments came as a surprise even to employer advocates. All previous attempts at legislating for what the Government has always claimed to be a 'small business' exemption, designed to overcome the alleged disincentive to employment growth in the small business sector created by fear of the costs of unwarranted unfair dismissal claims, had suggested exempting businesses with up to 15 or 20 employees.[95] However, as the Full Court of the Federal Court in *Hamzy v Tricon International Restaurants trading as KFC* found, the Government's argument that this exemption was necessary for job creation has been based on mere assertion, unsupported by any empirical evidence suggesting that small business employers—or

---

92 Above n 90, 120.

93 IRCA, 970219, 8 July 1997. See Chapter 8, p 404.

94 The ABS defines small business as employing fewer than 20 persons, medium business as employing more than 20 but fewer tha n 200, and large business as employing more than 200: see ABS *Small Business in Australia* (Cat no 1321.0, 2002), and *Counts of Businesses* (Cat no 8161.0, 2004). It is thus difficult to calculate exactly how many are employed by businesses with fewer than 101 employees.

95 See above n 31.

indeed employers in any size of business—have made recruitment and expansion decisions based on any anxiety about the impact of unfair dismissal laws.[96]

As it stands, the exclusion means that there are two classes of employee in Australia—those employed by large organisations have some security against capricious and arbitrary dismissal; those employed in small- to medium-sized enterprises have none. It remains to be seen whether the post–*Work Choices* arrangements will encourage employment growth in the small business sector—or whether they will discourage growth of medium-sized enterprises into larger ones, and perhaps encourage a greater outsourcing of work through the use of short-term labour-hire casuals or independent contractors. It also remains to be seen whether smaller enterprises will have more difficulty in recruiting the most skilled staff, because they are unable to offer the same level of employment security as those employees would enjoy as a matter of law if employed with a large enterprise.

Some concession has been made in the legislation to arguments that large employers may seek to avoid unfair dismissal liability by parcelling their staff into a number of smaller corporate entities. This opportunity is closed off at least partially by s 643(11) of the *Workplace Relations Act*, which holds that an enterprise includes any 'related bodies corporate'—that is, a holding company of another company, or a subsidiary of another company, or a subsidiary of a holding company of another body corporate—within the meaning of s 50 of the *Corporations Act 2001* (Cth).[97] However, as Anna Chapman has pointed out the legislation does not cover those situations where employing businesses also connect to 'associated entities', or a 'related entity', or an 'entity controlled by another entity' under the *Corporations Act*, and so does not take a consistently broad approach to accord with commercial realities.[98] Chapman has also noted that the task of determining whether entities are 'related bodies corporate' involves complex questions of law and fact,[99] often relating to corporations that may be registered in different countries or requiring an assessment of whether there are sham arrangements. As a matter of practical reality most employees will be in no position to test the claims of their employer as to the size of the business.

Fixed-term contracts

The exclusion for employees who have been employed under contracts of employment 'for a specified period of time' have (as the notes to s 638 state) been considered in a number of decisions of the Industrial Relations Court of Australia (which presided over these matters until the change of legislation in 1996). In *Cooper v Darwin Rugby League Inc*[100] Northrop J clarified the position of employees who are given a contract of what appears to be a specific duration (say, three years), but whose employment can

---

96 (2001)115 FCR 78, 94. See further Barret, above n 31; and B Freyens and P Oslington 'The Likely Employment Impact of Removing Unfair Dismissal Protection' (2005) 56 *JAPE* 56.
97 See also *Corporations Act 2001* (Cth), ss 9 and 46–9.
98 Chapman, above n 34, 242–4. See also *Corporations Act 2001* (Cth), ss 9, 50AA and 50AAA.
99 Ibid. For an early decision on the new provisions which demonstrates this see *Baldacchino v Triangle Cables (Aust) Pty Ltd* AIRC, PR972581, 24 May 2006.
100 (1994) 57 IR 238.

nevertheless be terminated before expiry of that term at the initiative of the employer, simply with notice. Such a contract is not in truth a contract for a specified time. Its duration is not predictable at the outset of the contract. It does not necessarily conclude by effluxion of time alone. Likewise von Doussa J in *Andersen v Umbakumba Community Council*[101] held that a contract that merely recorded the 'outer limits' of the contract term was not one for a specified time within the meaning of the exclusion. Von Doussa J did suggest, however, that if the provision in the contract allowing early termination applied only where the employee had breached the contract in some way, a different result may pertain.[102]

Neither will an employer be able to bring an employment relationship within this exclusion simply by offering the employee a series of rolling short-term contracts. In *D'Lima v Board of Management Princess Margaret Hospital for Children*[103] a woman who had been employed as a casual cleaner in a hospital for more than 12 months, ostensibly on a series of one-month contracts, was held to be a continuously employed casual employee, able to access the unfair dismissal jurisdiction when her services were terminated without warning. Although the written contracts stated that the employment expired at the end of a month, the prevailing practice at the hospital was for cleaners to continue working beyond the expiry of the term on the piece of paper. On the other hand, an academic engaged on a one-year fixed-term contract who failed to be appointed when her position was advertised as a continuing position at the end of that contract, was unable to bring a claim for unfair dismissal in relation to the permanent position.[104]

QANTAS Airways Ltd v Fetz[105] illustrated the potential for the exclusion of workers on fixed-term contract to operate unfairly, when a Full Bench of the Commission held that the airline was entitled to dismiss a group of apprentices at the end of their apprenticeships without answering any case of unfair dismissal. Although it was customary for apprentices who had successfully completed their training to go on into skilled positions with the airline, QANTAS decided to achieve a reduction in staff as cheaply as possible (without incurring any liability to large redundancy payouts) by failing to engage a whole generation of their apprentices upon completion of their training. The Full Bench overturned a decision of Ross VP, to find that QANTAS was entitled in these circumstances to the benefit of the exclusion of staff on fixed term contracts.

Probationers

Only a person who has completed a qualifying period (which in the absence of any express arrangements between the parties will be six months) may bring a claim for unfair dismissal: s 643(6)–(7). Additionally, the exclusions in s 638 rule out claims from people who are on probation, where the probation period has been determined

---

101 (1994) 126 ALR 121.
102 Ibid, 126.
103 (1995) 64 IR 19.
104 See *Fisher v Edith Cowan University* (unreported, No WI 1061 of 1996, 12 November 1996), confirmed on appeal in *Fisher v Edith Cowan University* (unreported, No WI96/1453, 2 April 1997).
105 (1998) 84 IR 52.

in advance. It is not enough simply for a new employee to be told that they will be on probation: the period of time must be specified.[106] A period of probation is relevant at the start of the employment relationship: it cannot be introduced afterwards by the employer, say in the form of an extension of the period or as a condition of promotion (or at least not so that such a period excludes the employee from access to the unfair dismissal jurisdiction).[107] The outer limit of the probation period must be stated at the outset.[108] However, where there is a new contract of employment that involves different obligations, as sometimes occurs when there is a change of employment status, say from casual to ongoing employment, then a new probationary period can sometimes be effectively imposed on an employee.[109]

A probation period of more than three months must be 'reasonable having regard to the nature and the circumstances of the employment': s 638(1)(c)(ii)(B). The matters taken into account include how long it would reasonably take an employee to be able to demonstrate sufficient competency in the job. The more complex the range of duties, the greater the time arguably needed to assess the competencies of the employee, and thus the longer the justifiable probation period.[110] Logically, this exclusion will only have an impact on employees whose probation periods are longer than the qualifying period of six months.

In situations where there has been a transmission of business, even if the employees are kept on and do the same job for the new employer, there will be a new contract of employment, and employees will be subjected to a new qualifying period, and depending on the terms may be subject to a new probation period as well, even though perhaps they have been doing the job for many years.[111]

Casuals

Casuals are excluded from accessing the unfair dismissal jurisdiction unless they can show that they have been employed by an employer 'on a regular and systematic basis for a sequence of periods of employment during a period of at least 12 months' with a 'reasonable expectation of continuing employment by the employer': s 638(4). The *Workplace Relations Act* also provides that the 12-month period may be satisfied where there are two shorter engagements of casual employment with the same employer that together total that period, provided no more than three months elapses between them: s 638(5).

The rise of casualisation in many industries—especially, for example, in the retail and hospitality sectors—raises questions about the fairness of excluding casuals from unfair dismissal protection. Effectively, the exclusion of casual workers until they have completed at least 12 months' regular and systematic work with the same employer

---

106 *Makatoa v Arrow Pharmaceuticals Ltd* AIRC, PR951760, 8 September 2004.

107 *Arndt v Crown Business Solutions Pty Ltd* AIRC, PR935154, 22 July 2003.

108 *Olle v De Bono World Centre for New Thinking* AIRC, PRP3932, 12 August 1997.

109 *Jewel v Australasian Corrective Management Pty Ltd* AIRC, PR927056, 24 January 2003. Cf *Clark v Red Rag Pty Ltd* (2004) 54 AILR ¶100–45(51).

110 See *Nicholson v Heaven and Earth Galleries,* above n 81.

111 *Lorimer v Bajo Investments Pty Ltd t/as Subway Windsor* AIRC, PR955605, 8 February 2005.

means that casual workers face at least a year-long 'qualifying period', compared with six months for other employees.[112]

The exclusion of 'short-term' casual workers from unfair dismissal protection has created some confusing case law, particularly in the federal jurisdiction, where—until legislative amendments in 2003—the exclusions were created by regulations.[113] Disputes over the operation of the exclusions identified a disjuncture between common industrial practice, and common law definition. It has become common in Australia for awards and agreements to include a casual classification, under which many long-term workers were engaged, meaning usually that they are paid by the hour and accept a loading on their rate of pay in lieu of benefits such as sick and annual leave. They nevertheless had an expectation of continuing engagement, often according to a very predictable roster. Frequently such a 'casual' is required to notify the employer some time in advance of any anticipated absence from work. The common law, on the other hand, was apt to consider a 'casual' employee as one engaged for a single shift, with each new or subsequent shift treated as a discrete hiring on a new contract. Each separate contract terminated by effluxion of time at the conclusion of the work shift.

In *Reed v Blue Line Cruises*,[114] Moore J in the Industrial Relations Court of Australia held that the master of a ferry boat, who was engaged on a systematic basis and was obliged to obtain permission for periods of leave, was not a 'casual' for the purposes of regulations under the earlier *Industrial Relations Act 1988* (Cth). Justice Moore referred to the ILO's *Termination of Employment Convention, 1982 (ILO C 158)*, which underpinned the constitutional validity of the provisions, and held that the Convention determined the interpretation of 'casual' employment. Casual employment, continued Moore J, was 'informal, irregular and uncertain'.[115]

After the revision of the unfair dismissal provisions by the *Workplace Relations and Other Legislation Amendment Act 1996* (Cth), which based the provisions on the corporations power, a Full Bench of the AIRC held that the ILO Convention's meanings were now irrelevant, and ordinary Australian industrial practice should be applied to find that a casual employee was simply one engaged on casual rates of pay.[116] Consequently, a hotel worker who had been engaged on a regular and systematic casual roster was unable to rely on unfair dismissal protection because he had not been working for a period of at least 12 months.

In *Hamzy v Tricon International Restaurants trading as KFC*,[117] the Full Court of the Federal Court held that (the former) rr 30B(1)(d) and 30B(3) were entirely invalid

---

112 The period of exclusions for casuals is shorter in some States: see eg the *Industrial Relations (General) Regulation 2001* (NSW), r 6(1)(d)(ii), which stipulates a period of six months. State legislation, however, applies only to non-federal employees such as employees of partnerships, sole traders or non-constitutional corporations: see *Workplace Relations Act*, ss 5–7 and 16.

113 See *Workplace Relations Act*, former s 170CC and r 30B(1)(d), later amended by the *Workplace Relations Amendment (Fair Termination) Act 2003* (Cth).

114 (1996) 73 IR 420.

115 Ibid, 425–6.

116 *Bluesuits Pty Ltd t/as Toongabbie Hotel v Graham (Bluesuits)* (1999) 101 IR 28.

117 (2001) 115 FCR 78.

because they purported to exclude all casuals (even those with more than 10 years' association with an employer) unless they had worked on a regular and systematic basis, and had a reasonable expectation of continuity. This exceeded the power to make regulations excluding casuals employed for a short period conferred by the principal Act in the former s 170CC as it was then drafted. The Government tabled amended regulations promptly to correct this problem; however, in *Cetin v Ripon Pty Ltd trading as Parkview Hotel*,[118] a Full Bench of the AIRC found the making of new regulations allowed it to escape any obligation to follow the *Bluesuits* case. In *Cetin*, the Full Bench held that a hotel worker who had been engaged for less than eight months to perform regular nightly shifts on a casual wage was not excluded by the regulations. The Commission relied on a finding in *Hamzy* that there was no material difference in meaning between the expressions 'casual employee' and 'employee engaged on a casual basis', so the new r 30B(1)(d) had the same meaning as the words in Art 2(1)(c) of *ILO C 158* reproduced in Sch 10 of the principal Act and Moore J's findings in *Reed v Blue Line Cruises* should again be adopted. In 2003, the principal Act was amended (with the insertion of s 170CBA, now renumbered as s 638) to reinstate the *Bluesuits* approach, so that employees engaged on a casual basis could not make claims for unfair dismissal until they had been engaged for at least 12 months on a regular and systematic basis.[119]

The question of whether a casual's work is 'regular and systematic' or there is a 'reasonable expectation of continuing employment' will no doubt remain problematic and difficult to resolve in many cases, likewise the question of whether the employee is engaged as a casual or otherwise.[120] The requirements of the legislation by no means guarantee that all long-term casuals can access the unfair dismissal jurisdiction. If work is allocated according to a regular roster there is less likely to be a problem in showing it is 'regular and systematic', although identity of working time is not required. However, should a more flexible arrangement of hours be worked, for instance if a casual employee rings in each week to indicate their availability and often works different hours and sometimes not at all, then there is a greater chance that the requisite regularity will not be found.[121]

Seasonal workers

The *Work Choices Act* introduced a new exclusion for seasonal workers: s 638(8)–(10). According to the *Explanatory Memorandum* to the Act, this new exclusion was made necessary by the inconvenient finding in *SPC Ardmona v Esam and Organ*,[122] where the AIRC held that seasonal fruit-pickers had been engaged for an indeterminate period of time (the length of the season not being predictable at its commencement) so had not been engaged on fixed-term contracts, and were therefore not excluded from the unfair

---

118 (2003) 127 IR 205.
119 *Workplace Relations Amendment (Fair Termination) Act 2003* (Cth). See *Nightingale v Little Legends Childcare* (2004) 134 IR 111.
120 See eg *Dakin v HGC Administrative Services* AIRC, PR967417, 11 January 2006.
121 *Boules v Nestle Australia Limited* AIRC, PR965547, 23 November 2005.
122 AIRC, PR957497, 20 April 2005.

dismissal provisions then in place. Nor could it be said that they were employed on contracts for a specified task, for their contracts were terminable on two days' notice.

Now, the provisions of the *Workplace Relations Act* exclude any worker who is engaged for a season, where the end of the season is uncertain at the commencement of the employment, but is related to the nature of the work and can be objectively determined when it happens: s 638(8). The *Explanatory Memorandum* to the amending legislation gave as examples seasonal fruit-pickers, retail workers engaged to handle a Christmas and post-Christmas sales period, and resort workers engaged for a particular holiday season (by the beach or at the snow, for example). The troops of hospitality workers engaged to cope with tourist inflows during significant sporting events would be another example. Given that the legislation exempts an employer for liability for any dismissal for 'operational reasons', it may be that this new seasonal worker exemption will have little work to do. The absence of fruit on the trees, shoppers in the malls, or holiday-makers on the beach would no doubt cause such a drop-off in trade that an employer could justify dismissals as necessitated by 'economic reasons'.

'High' income earners

When an exemption for 'high' income earners was first introduced in 1994 it applied only to those employees whose wages and conditions were not derived from an award and, after 1996, another federal industrial instrument, either a certified agreement or an AWA. After *Work Choices* employees whose wages and conditions are not derived from a federal industrial award or APCS, or collective agreement or AWA, cannot make an application for an unfair dismissal remedy or any remedy for breach of the minimum notice provisions in s 661,[123] if they earn more than the rate stipulated by the *Workplace Relations Regulations*. At 27 March 2006 this amount was set at $94 000 by r 12.3, and it is indexed annually according to a formula fixed by r 12.6.

Procedures

The procedures for applying for review of an allegedly unfair or unlawful dismissal are intended to encourage speedy resolution of problems, preferably by agreement between the parties themselves. So the legislation requires that aggrieved employees make an application to the AIRC on the required forms no later than 21 days from the date of termination, and agree to submit first to an attempt to conciliate the matter. Only after the Commission has certified that the attempt to conciliate failed will the applicant be entitled to pursue the matter to arbitration (in the case of an unfair dismissal allegation) or litigation (in the case of a breach of a provision in Subdiv C). Applicants for unfair dismissal have only seven days following the issuing of the Commission's certificate to take up the opportunity to continue to arbitration of the matter, and are not able to have that time extended: see s 651(6)(b)(ii) and (8). Applicants for unlawful dismissal have 28 days to decide on their course of action. The Commission is empowered to extend this time upon an extension application, if it considers it would be unfair not to

---

123 See below p 436.

do so: see s 651(6)(b)(i) and (9). In order to expedite matters, the Commission is able to deal with a range of issues, such as determining the number of employees working for a business, 'on the papers', having regard to issues such as the cost of attending hearings for employers, and the need for the Commission to avoid technicalities, but act in a way that is fair and practical: see for example ss 648 and 108–10.[124]

Applications out of time

The Commission does have a discretion to grant time extensions of the initial 21-day period, and will do so if serious injustice would follow from a refusal to grant an extension: s 643(15). However, whether the Commission decides or refuses to extend the time for making an application, there is no right of appeal. Applications for extension of time may be determined without a hearing under the process set out in the Act, which requires the Commission to take account of the costs to the employer of attending: s 648.

A note to s 643(15) cites the former Industrial Relations Court of Australia's decision in *Brodie-Hanns v MTV Publishing Ltd*[125] for the principles to be applied in exercising this discretion to grant an extension. They are, first, that the time limit should prima facie be complied with, unless there is an acceptable explanation for the delay in making the application, which would make it 'equitable' to allow the extension. The fact that the applicant has taken other steps to contest the termination will favour the grant of an extension, because these steps affirm that the employee has not accepted the termination. If the respondent would be prejudiced by the grant of an extension (for example, if they have acted to fill the position left vacant by the termination, in a good faith expectation that no application for reinstatement had been made within the time period), this prejudice will weigh against grant of the extension. Nevertheless, the lack of any such prejudice will not of itself warrant the grant of a time extension. The merits of the claim may also be taken into account when deciding whether to extend time.

The factors taken into account are canvassed in *Sapevski*,[126] a case where a considerable extension was granted to a group of migrant women workers who had suffered indirect discrimination on the basis of gender, and had enjoyed no support from their male-dominated union representatives. The particular factors that influenced a decision to extend in this case included their language difficulties, the fact that the very people who ought to have advised and assisted them (the union representatives) had failed to take up their cause, and the fact that they had protested their dismissal in other ways.

Arbitration

The separation of powers imposed on federal legal institutions by the *Australian Constitution* explains the fact that unfair dismissal applications go to arbitration by the AIRC, while unlawful dismissal applications are heard by the Federal Court. An application based solely on the ground that the dismissal was 'harsh, unjust or unreasonable' will go to arbitration before the AIRC if conciliation fails. The Commission,

---

124 See also *Berryman v Residential Truss Systems Pty Ltd* AIRC, PR973025, 8 June 2006.
125 (1995) 67 IR 298.
126 Above n 93.

as an administrative tribunal, is exercising administrative, not judicial power. In making an order for reinstatement, it is creating new rights, not adjudicating existing legal rights.

Remedies

Reinstatement

The primary remedy for unfair dismissal is reinstatement, and only where reinstatement would be warranted but is inappropriate for some reason, should the Commission order payment of compensation in lieu of reinstatement: s 654. Reinstatement would be inappropriate, for instance, if it appears that it would not be possible to re-establish a 'satisfactory working relationship',[127] although as noted earlier large enterprises can often with relative ease provide a way of overcoming difficulties between personnel.

Despite the supposed primacy of reinstatement as a remedy, in the past very few reinstatements have in fact been ordered. According to the AIRC's *Annual Report* to the end of June 2004, there had only been 225 reinstatements under the federal legislation since the commencement of the *Workplace Relations Act* in January 1997. In that entire period, only 1099 applications resulted in payment of any compensation. Of approximately 7000 to 8000 applications per year, above 75 are resolved by conciliation.[128]

The High Court of Australia has confirmed that a statutory reinstatement order does grant the employee the right to return to work. In *Blackadder v Ramsey Butchering Services Pty Ltd*,[129] an abattoir worker who had the benefit of a reinstatement order was held to be entitled to be given actual work. A majority of the Full Court of the Federal Court (in the face of a vigorous dissent by Moore J) had held that an order for reinstatement meant only that the contract of employment was restored, but this conferred no entitlement upon the employee to be given work unless the employment contract was one of those rare types that included a duty on the employer to provide work. That decision imported the general principle of the common law that employment contracts do not imply any duty to provide work.[130] The High Court reversed this finding, on the basis that the statute had intended to provide a reinstatement remedy restoring the employee to the full benefits of the position enjoyed prior to termination, including the opportunity to increase his earnings because he was paid by piece rates and to gain job satisfaction, as well as vindicating his position.

In practice, the great majority of matters are settled by conciliation (so it is difficult to assess the effectiveness of the statutory provisions in restoring people to their jobs—statistics showing the outcomes of conciliations are not readily available).[131] Of those

---

127 *Ettridge v TransAdelaide* (1998) 80 IR 422, 430. See also *Perkins v Grace Worldwide (Australia) Pty Ltd* (1997) 72 IR 186, 191.

128 AIRC *Annual Report of the President of the Australian Industrial Relations Commission* and *Annual Report of the Australian Industrial Registry*, 1 July 2003–30 June 2004 (2004).

129 (2005) 221 CLR 539.

130 See Chapter 6, p 251.

131 AIRC *Annual Report of the President of the Australian Industrial Relations Commission* and *Annual Report of the Australian Industrial Registry*, 1 July 2004–30 June 2005 (2005), Table 7, 15, shows that between 31 December 1996 and 30 June 2005 approximately 20 per cent of termination of employment matters were not settled by conciliation.

applications that do go to arbitration, most are concluded by an award of some amount of compensation. Compensation under the Act is capped at no more than six months' salary in the case of people whose employment wages and/or conditions are 'award-derived' (that is, derived from an APCS, award or workplace agreement: s 642(6)), and half of the income threshold set by regulations for other applicants: see s 654(11)–(12) and rr 12.5–12.6.

Factors affecting remedy

The appropriate remedy in any particular case will always depend on a consideration of all the facts. Over time the Commission has developed principles that can be of some guidance,[132] but these operate within the overall parameters that the legislation sets in place.

Section 654 of the Act provides guidance to the Commission in determining a fair remedy if the termination has indeed been found to be 'harsh, unjust or unreasonable'. This task involves weighing up employer- and employee-sided factors. On the employer's side, the effect of any order (reinstatement or compensation) on the viability of the employer's business must be considered: s 654(2)(a). On the employee's side, length of service, the benefits that the employee has lost through termination, and whether the employee has made efforts to mitigate that loss are to be taken into account. If the employee has mitigated the loss of income by doing other paid work while waiting for the claim to be heard, the Commission must have regard to that fact: s 654(5).

Since the enactment of the *Work Choices* legislation, any misconduct of the employee that contributed to the employer's decision to terminate the employment must also be considered, and the Commission is obliged to discount any compensation to take account of the employee's contribution to their own misery. The concept is akin to the notion of contributory negligence, introduced by statute into the law of tort. Contributory negligence has never been a factor in determining damages for breach of contract (although contract law has recognised a notion of set-off of damages claims where both parties are in breach). It is interesting that the legislature has chosen to incorporate this particular tort-like concept into the unfair dismissal regime, when it has positively rejected another tort concept—the notion of exemplary or aggravated damages.

An important change made by *Work Choices* is that the Commission is now prohibited from making any award in respect of 'shock, distress or humiliation or any analogous hurt' caused by the manner of dismissal: s 654(9). This is justified (in the *Explanatory Memorandum* to the *Work Choices* legislation) as an incorporation of the ordinary common law principle—from *Addis v Gramaphone Co Ltd*[133]—that an employee is unable to claim any damages for hurt or humiliation, even where the manner of dismissal was especially cruel. The *Addis* principle depends upon

---

132 See *Smith and Kimball v Moore Paragon Australia Pty Ltd* AIRC, PR942856, 20 January 2004.

133 [1909] AC 488. Cf In the United Kingdom where the same issue has arisen under the *Employment Rights Act 1996* (UK) it has been treated simply as a matter of statutory construction: see *Dunnachie Kingston-upon-Hull City Council* [2004] UKHL 36.

the notion that contract law is intended to protect voluntary economic bargains, so damages for breach of contract should be limited to the economic costs of the breach, and ought not to sound in any punitive award (such as the exemplary damages available in tort for intentional harm inflicted upon a victim). Scholarly writings have certainly drawn attention to its deficiencies in the modern employment context, especially given developments in contract law in other areas which recognise non-economic loss.[134]

The *Addis* principle had not been adopted by the Commission in hearing unfair dismissal claims until enactment of this provision. In *Burazin v Blacktown City Guardian Pty Ltd*[135] for example, the Commission allowed an award of compensation to take account of the fact that the employee had been marched unceremoniously off the premises in a most humiliating manner. In *Burazin*, the Commission expressed some criticism of the *Addis* principle. It is certainly true that the relationship between employer and employee is much more than an economic exchange. The employer has the capacity to cause tort-like harm if the employer abuses the prerogative of termination of employment to destroy the employee's self-esteem. Indeed, in New Zealand, the *Addis* principle has been abandoned for common law employment contracts.[136] In Australia, even the statutory scheme—ostensibly designed to redress the harshness and inadequacy of common law remedies—has turned against allowing compensation awards to reflect the bad behaviour of employers, despite the new rule that the bad behaviour of employees must be taken into account. There is an element of doctrinal inconsistency in these rules—tort precepts apply to the employer, but the harsher contract principles apply to the employee. The 'fair go all round' post-2005 leans in favour of a more solicitous concern with the employer's interests.

Minimum notice periods

Under the *Workplace Relations Act* termination of employment for employees (except those in one of the excluded categories) without at least a minimum notice period (or pay in lieu of that period) is unlawful: ss 636–8 and 661.

The statutory scale ranges from one week for employees with less than a year's service, to four weeks for those with more than five years' service. Employees aged more than 45 who have more than two years' service with the same employer are entitled to an extra week's notice. A person who is legitimately dismissed for serious misconduct (illuminated in *Workplace Relations Regulations*, r 12.10) is not entitled to the statutory notice period. Serious misconduct under r 12.10 ranges from theft, fraud and assault at one end of the scale, to 'refusing to carry out a lawful and reasonable instruction that is consistent with the employee's contract of employment' at the other. Intoxication is specifically mentioned as a legitimate reason for summary dismissal. The statutory period cannot be derogated from by a contract to the contrary; although where there

---

134 See eg PRA Gray 'Damages for Wrongful Dismissal: Is the Gramophone Record Worn Out?' in
    R McCallum, G McCarry and P Ronfeldt (eds) *Employment Security* (1994). See above, Chapter 6, p 264.
135 (1996) 142 ALR 144.
136 See *Stuart v Armourgard Security* [1996] 1 NZLR 484.

is no notification term included in the contract the 'reasonable' period of notice that is contractually required might be considerably longer than the period set down by the statute, especially for more senior employees.[137]

Redundancy and severance pay

During the 1970s and 1980s, when technological advancement and changes in the global economy began to change the face of Australian industry, and trade unions were still influential in lobbying for the interests of workers affected by these changes, the concept of payment for 'redundancy' developed. A redundancy meant that the job itself was no longer in existence, not simply that the employee had been dismissed from the job.[138] A redundancy may sometimes arise in circumstances where an employer relocates their business or where there is a transmission of business. However, as the High Court noted in the *Amcor Case* redundancy takes its meaning from context, and in the case of a transmission of business where an employee has their employment terminated with the old employer and 'transfers' to the new employer there will be no redundancy.[139]

Trade unions persuaded industrial arbitrators that it was appropriate that industry should pay additional severance amounts to workers laid off as a result of the obsolescence of their skills following the mechanisation of jobs, and other economic upheavals. Typically, severance pay on redundancy would involve payment of a certain number of weeks' pay for a certain number of years' service—so long-serving and older workers (who were assumed to enjoy weaker prospects of new work through retraining) would receive more substantial benefits than younger workers. So in the *Termination Change and Redundancy Case*[140] in 1984, the AIRC awarded the following additional award benefits for employees who lost their jobs because of genuine redundancy:

- 4 weeks' pay for those with 1 to 2 years' service;
- 6 weeks' pay for between 2 and 3 years' service;
- 7 weeks' pay for between 3 and 4 years' service; and
- 8 weeks' pay for more than 4 years' service.

The Commission made it clear in this decision that these amounts were not payable merely to 'tide over' an employee for a period of unemployment. The Full Bench stated: '[w]e prefer the view that payment of severance pay is justifiable as compensation for non-transferable credits and the inconvenience and hardship imposed on employees',[141] those 'non-transferable credits' being the opportunities that long-serving employees had foregone in continuous service with the one employer. In economic terms, severance or redundancy pay recognises and rewards (to a limited extent) the employee's investment of firm-specific capital in an enterprise.

---

137 See eg *Rankin v Marine Power International Pty Ltd* (2001) 107 IR 117. See also Chapter 6, p 266.

138 *R v Industrial Commission of SA; Ex parte AMSCOL* (1977) 16 SASR 6, 8; *Termination Change and Redundancy Case* (1984) 8 IR 34, 55–6; and *Redundancy Test Case* (2004) 129 IR 155.

139 *Amcor Limited v Construction, Forestry, Mining, and Energy Union* (2005) 138 IR 286, 291, 298–9 and 321. See also *Workplace Relations Act*, Pt 11 on transmission of business.

140 (1984) 8 IR 34.

141 Ibid, 73.

In 2004 the Commission heard applications to vary the earlier standard in a new *Redundancy Case*.[142] It determined that the rationale underpinning the earlier test case was not deficient and it reaffirmed the idea that the standard should be limited to the amount that a worker would have earned until retirement but for the redundancy. Nonetheless it ruled that the scale for calculating redundancy payments ought to be extended in order to take account of some of the non-transferable credits that employees lose on redundancy. Under the new scale the severance payment rate was extended as follows:

* 8 weeks' pay for between 4 and 5 years' service;
* 10 weeks' pay for between 5 and 6 years' service;
* 11 weeks' pay for between 6 and 7 years' service;
* 13 weeks' pay for between 7 and 8 years' service;
* 14 weeks' pay for between 8 and 9 years' service;
* 16 weeks' pay for between 9 and 10 years' service; and
* 12 weeks' pay for more than 10 years' service.

The Commission suggested that applications could be made on an award by award basis to vary the final level of payment where appropriate to take into account of long service leave entitlements that might be lost by some award employees. As in the earlier test case, casuals were still excluded from redundancy benefits, the Commission reasoning that the casual loading represented in part a compensation for redundancy pay.[143]

Since 1984 enterprise agreements in some industries with strong unions have provided considerably more generous benefits than the test case standard. However, for many workers severance pay remains something to which they are only entitled by award, and this entitlement is now more precarious than before. This is because the definition of 'redundancy pay' in the list of award allowable matters has been further restricted by amendments introduced by the *Work Choices Act*: see s 513(1)(k) and (4). Now award provision for 'redundancy pay' must relate to a termination of employment that is either for 'operational reasons' or where the employer is insolvent, and any such provision can only apply where the termination of employment is by an employer with 15 or more employees. Under the 1984 *TCR Test Case* small businesses with fewer than 15 employees had been exempted from award standards covering severance pay.[144] However, in the *Redundancy Case* in 2004 the Commission partially removed this exemption, in the sense that it decided that these employers could be liable for severance payments but only to the level applicable in the old standard; that is, up to a maximum of eight weeks' pay for four weeks' service.[145] However, the *Work Choices Act* has now effectively reinstated the 'small business' exemption.[146]

---

142 (2004) 129 IR 155.

143 Ibid, 225–32.

144 See above n 39.

145 *Redundancy Test Case*, above n 138, 201ff.

146 See also *Workplace Relations Amendment (Work Choices) Act 2005* (Cth), Sch 3A, which operated between 14 December 2005 and 27 March 2006.

It can also be noted that after the *Work Choices* amendments the award right to severance pay may be bargained away: it will not be included in an agreement unless it is specifically 'called up' for it is not a 'protected allowable award matter', and as such if an agreement is terminated it will disappear altogether: see ss 354–5 and 399. Furthermore, prior to the *Work Choices* amendments employees who were made redundant could also bring a case arguing that they were also dismissed in a way that was unfair, perhaps on the basis of the way they were selected for redundancy,[147] or because of the inadequacy of the payouts they received. Now the new 'operational reasons' jurisdictional hurdle prevents this. Finally, after the *Work Choices Act* the duties imposed on employers where 15 or more employees (who are not excluded under s 638(1) or (11)) are made redundant are more limited under the *Workplace Relations Act*. There remains a duty to provide to the Commonwealth Employment Service (CES) details of the terminations, including the reasons, the number and classification of employees affected, and its time: s 660. However, the available remedial action is now more limited. The Commission itself has no power to intervene as it once did, and there is no effective requirement to notify and consult with trade unions. It is no offence for an employer to contravene s 660, although an order may be sought from a federal court in relation to a contravention: ss 662–63.

Protecting entitlements

A rising awareness of the vulnerability of employees whose employers become insolvent owing them accrued wages, leave and redundancy entitlements, has generated debate about the most appropriate means of providing financial backing for employees' interests in job security. At the centre of this issue—possibly the most contentious industrial issue at the turn of the new millennium in Australia—is the question of corporate responsibility.

In the late 1990s there were several crises in 'old economy' heavily unionised industries, notably coal mining and meatworks, that left employees out-of-pocket when employer companies collapsed. Calls for government intervention went unanswered. More cases followed, some transparently engineered corporate insolvencies, to enable shareholders and directors to exit an industry salvaging their own stake, but leaving employee entitlements unpaid. When a relatively small textile firm in a depressed rural community[148] collapsed in January 2000, owing its workers wages and severance benefits, the federal government finally initiated a taxpayer-funded support scheme—the Employee Entitlements Support Scheme (EESS)—to meet a partial payment of lost benefits to employees whose employers became insolvent owing employee entitlements. Following the catastrophic collapse of Ansett Airlines in 2001, on the eve of a federal election, this safety net arrangement was replaced by a more generous plan: the General Employee Entitlements and Redundancy Scheme (GEERS).

---

147 *Sapevski*, above n 93, provides an example.
148 See J Riley 'Bargaining for Security: Lessons for Employees from the World of Corporate Finance' (2002) 44 *JIR* 491 for an account of the collapse of National Textiles Ltd.

GEERS pays unpaid wages, annual leave, long service leave, pay in lieu of notice, and redundancy pay of up to a maximum of 16 weeks pay. Initially, redundancy pay entitlements were capped at eight weeks, but this was changed by a government decision on 23 August 2006. The institution of the EESS and GEERS schemes has been criticised from both sides: as an unwarranted expenditure of public funds to subsidise the costs of private enterprise, and as an insufficiently generous and unreliable measure to meet a pressing matter of national welfare.

At the heart of the matter is the question of corporate responsibility—or more appropriately, corporate *irresponsibility*. Leave and severance entitlements negotiated with employees as part of their remuneration package are a cost of production that should properly be borne by the employer enterprise. In a market economy, the efficiency imperative would dictate that these costs should be borne by the enterprise itself. The doctrine of separate legal entity status of corporations—including separate entity status for each corporation within an elaborate group of wholly owned subsidiaries and related parties—together with shareholders' entitlement to limited liability, has meant that some corporations and their controllers have been able to avoid payment of those costs.

The corporate manipulation that gave rise to the notorious 1998 Waterfront dispute provides an illustration.[149] The controllers of the Patrick Stevedores group of companies saw the potential for ridding itself of a unionised workforce by transferring all employees into an undercapitalised subsidiary in the group. It then allowed that subsidiary to become insolvent, and purported to dismiss the workforce on the basis that they were redundant. Meanwhile, a newly formed labour-hire company, which engaged Dubai-trained ex-military, was engaged to provide stevedoring services to the other companies in the group, which held the benefit of contracts to provide stevedoring operations. The strategy came to grief because a well-advised union brought successful proceedings for an interim injunction to stop this strategy, on the basis that the scheme was in breach of the freedom of association provisions in the *Workplace Relations Act 1996* (Cth).[150] Ultimately, the matter was settled between the Maritime Union and the employers out of court. The costs and risks of litigation proved too high for all antagonists. Nevertheless, the case brought to light a developing practice of strategic organisation of corporate enterprise to quarantine exposure to the costs of employment by employing staff through separate subsidiaries—often undercapitalised.[151] Not all schemes have proved successful.[152] Courts have become willing to scrutinise such arrangements carefully, to ensure that employees have given informed consent to such arrangements.

This problem, created to some extent by our legal system's adherence to strict principles of corporate law, has provoked industrial and political responses. Various schemes to ensure that corporate employers—or at least industry generally—bear their own costs of production have been proposed.

---

149 See *Maritime Union of Australia v Patrick Stevedores No 1 Pty Ltd* (1998) 77 FCR 456; *Patrick Stevedores Operations No 2 Pty Ltd v Maritime Union of Australia* (1998) 77 FCR 478; and (1998) 195 CLR 1.

150 See former Pt XA.

151 For a detailed and illuminating account of the dispute see D Noakes 'Dogs on the Wharves: Corporate Groups and the Waterfront Dispute' (1999) *AJCL* 27.

152 See *McClusky v Karagiozis* (2002) 120 IR 147.

Trust-based schemes

The Metal Workers union, anxious to establish an iron-clad guarantee of payment for its members, has promoted employer contributions to a dedicated trust fund (similar to investment-style superannuation funds). The first manifestation of this proposal was the ManuSafe Trust. Subsequently, the ManuSafe trust has been replaced by a similar National Entitlements Security Trust fund (NEST).

A trust fund solution would have the dual benefit that it ensures that each employing enterprise meets the full costs of its own labour force, and it resonates with general public sentiment about how the problem should be solved. Media reports frequently refer to employers betraying the trust of employees by losing the employees' money. Of course, from a legal perspective, employee entitlements are not customarily 'held in trust'. The employees are owed a debt—often a contingent debt. Under the legal system they are characterised as unsecured creditors, and they line up with all other unsecured creditors in any division of the employers assets on insolvency. They take a privileged position in the creditors' queue by virtue of the priorities provisions in s 556 of the *Corporations Act* 2001 (Cth)—after secured creditors and liquidators costs, but before floating charges and trade creditors. To give legal effect to the lay person's expectation that the entitlements should be treated as 'belonging to the employee', so that the employee has a proprietary and not merely a personal claim against the employer, it would be necessary to establish some kind of trust whereby the employer dedicated certain property to be held by trustees for the benefit of any employee with a claim for unpaid entitlements. That property need not be cash, alienated from the employer's business into a separate fund. It could be a security interest (like a mortgage or a charge), over some asset used in the enterprise.

Employers (no doubt supported by the banks and other traditional secured creditors whose interests may be compromised by employee entitlement trusts) have resisted these proposals. So there has been considerable industrial action, particularly in the automotive industry, in support of collective bargaining claims for employers to contribute to trust schemes.

Industrial action taken in support of claims for compulsory contributions to the ManuSafe Trust was held to be unprotected in *Transfield Pty Ltd v AMWU*,[153] on the grounds that the claim did not constitute an 'industrial matter' and so could not legitimately form the basis of a certified agreement under *Workplace Relations Act 1996* (Cth). This decision by Munro J in the Australian Industrial Relations Commission has subsequently been criticised.[154] Arguably, a claim by employees that the employer set aside funds to ensure payment of accruing entitlements is a matter pertaining to the relationship between the employer who owes the benefit and the employees for whom the promised benefit forms a component of their expected remuneration.

Now, whether the inclusion of such a provision in a workplace agreement is possible will depend on two matters: whether it is a matter *directly* pertaining to the relationship between the employer and employee, according to the principles enunciated most

---

153 AIRC, PR908287, 30 August 2001 (see (2002) 51 AILR ¶4–538(43)).
154 *Electrolux Home Products Pty Ltd v AWU* [2001] FCA 1600.

recently in the *Electrolux*[155] decision of the High Court of Australia, and—most importantly—whether the government decides to expressly prohibit such content under extensive powers to table regulations under s 356 of the *Workplace Relations Act* sometime in the future. (No express prohibition was in force at 27 March 2006). The fact that a particular commitment may not be able to be included in a statutory workplace agreement does not necessarily mean that a willing employer could not agree to such terms in an ordinary common law contract with a trade union. The problems of collective common law agreements were discussed in Chapter 5. So long as these problems can be addressed by appropriate drafting, there appears to be no obstacle to employers and unions reaching an agreed solution to this problem.

Insurance-based solutions

The NSW Department of Industrial Relations, and the Australian Labor Party have supported the concept of a compulsory insurance scheme, where employers pay premiums against the risk of insolvency. Like other forms of insurance, such a scheme would pool the risks of insolvency and the costs of paying entitlements to redundant workers across the whole of the industry. Most proposals of this sort have included exemptions from premiums for small business. At the time of writing no such scheme has been instituted, and in the light of the insurance industry crisis in 2001–2002, it seems unlikely in the short term that any underwriters for such a scheme could be found.

Welfare-based solutions

The Employee Entitlements Support Scheme (EESS) introduced in 2000, and its successor, the General Employee Entitlements Redundancy Scheme (GEERS) introduced in 2001, represent a sizable contribution by taxpayers to underwrite the costs of failed industry.[156] GEERS is an administrative scheme that (at the time of writing) was not supported by legislation.

GEERS eases some of the pain suffered by some employees whose employers fail, but it is not a universal scheme. Not every person who loses a job because an employer company fails is entitled to any payment. The GEERS rules, administered at the discretion of the department, pay benefits that are supported by awards, certified agreements or other industrial instruments (such as Australian Workplace Agreements), and written contracts. Many industrially weak, award- and agreement- free workers enjoy no severance benefits. Their entitlements are limited to any unpaid wages and accrued holiday pay, plus payment for a statutory notice period stipulated in s 661 of the *Workplace Relations Act 1996*. If GEERS makes a payment to any employee, GEERS takes the place of that employee in the queue of creditors in the company's liquidation. This right of subrogation to the employees' claims explains the government's interest in a proposal to raise the priority of employees' claims in the ranking of preferential creditors

---

155 *Electrolux Home Products Pty Ltd v Australian Workers Union* (2004) 221 CLR 309.
156 On 23 August 2006, Minister Kevin Andrews announced that the federal government had paid out nearly $700 million under EESS and GEERS since the inception of these schemes: see <http://mediacentre. dewr.gov.au/mediacentre/Minister Andrews/Releases/GEERS.htm>.

in s 556 of the *Corporations Act 2001* (Cth) from a position after secured creditors (for example, banks) to a position ahead of secured creditors. A super-priority would enhance the government's chance of recouping the considerable costs of the scheme.

Criticism of GEERS

One of the main criticisms of the GEERS scheme as a universal welfare measure is that it is by no means universal. It continues to reinforce the privileges of those classes of workers who enjoy redundancy benefits under industrial instruments. As a case involving the collapse of the Australian Quality Council Ltd demonstrated,[157] even employees who enjoy redundancy benefits under a company policy will not necessarily receive any payment from GEERS if the employer fails, because the department has taken a strict view of what constitutes a contractual entitlement to severance or redundancy pay.

In that case, GEERS contested a decision by the liquidators of a company to pay redundancy payments to clerical workers who lost their jobs as a result of the collapse. The company had established a practice of paying redundancy benefits, and although there were no expressly written contracts of employment that explained the policy, there were Board minutes and inter-office memoranda establishing the practice. Justice Austin was prepared to say that the contracts of employment of these workers did include a term—expressed in verbal assurances and supported by these internal records—that redundancy benefits would be paid. This meant that the liquidators were entitled to make these payments to the workers as preferential creditors, and GEERS—which had refused to recognise the entitlement itself—could not claim to rank above those payments. (GEERS had paid the workers in respect of unpaid wages, but not redundancy, and now claimed to be entitled to claim reimbursement of those wages from the liquidator ahead of payments to other creditors, including the workers' redundancy claims.)

This case made it clear that workers without written contracts or industrial award or agreement coverage will not benefit by the scheme. Employees who have no redundancy benefits at all may well be confused by a system that pays taxpayer dollars to more highly paid and industrially strong groups of employees when an employer goes bust. And of course the unemployed who have neither jobs nor income to lose have reason to criticise the dedication of government funds to people who have (in their eyes) been fortunate enough to enjoy the benefits of employment.

Clearly, in the light of these criticisms, calls by the unions for the extension of GEERS to cover all entitlements of workers are politically inept. That would mean that taxes paid by the working poor would need to be earmarked to cover the generous redundancy benefits of, for example, unionised airline pilots.

Changes to corporate laws

Along with the introduction of the EESS in 2000, the federal government enacted a new Part in the insolvency chapter of the *Corporations Act*—Pt 5.8A, 'Employee Entitlements'. This Part includes any 'uncommercial transactions' deliberately entered into by company directors for the purpose of avoiding payment of employee entitlements

---

157 *In the Matter of ACN 050 541 047 Ltd* [2002] NSWSC 586.

as an act warranting directors' personal liability for payment of those entitlements.[158] Such conduct is also a contravention of civil penalty provisions, and attracts potential fines and disqualification orders.[159] The rationale for this amendment was to address a potential moral hazard problem. Directors knowing that their employees could claim against a taxpayer-funded guarantee scheme might be tempted to engineer a corporate insolvency in a way that preserved funds for other purposes, and left employee entitlements to be paid by the government. These punitive provisions seek to outlaw such conduct.

Further changes have been proposed to the priorities scheme, to elevate employee claims ahead of the banks in a winding up. Such a proposal has no doubt been prompted by the heavy demands of the GEERS scheme on public funds. If the government makes a payment to an employee under the GEERS scheme, the government is subrogated to the employee's claim against the liquidator of the company. This means that the government takes the place of the employee in the queue of creditors. A change to the priorities scheme would not only enhance the payment of employees directly by liquidators; it would also raise the government's place in the creditors' queue and improve the recovery rate for the GEERS scheme.

More radical changes to corporate law to allow a court to pierce the corporate veil and make other companies within a corporate group responsible to meet obligations to employees of a failed subsidiary or sibling entity have been proposed, but have failed to attract any serious debate.[160] The shareholder-centred model of corporate enterprise, which privileges the freedom of entrepreneurs to manage risk through full exploitation of limited liability, is far too entrenched in Australian commercial practice.

Privacy at work

Privacy is an aspect of security at work that is somewhat different from the things traditionally considered under that heading, but it is one that has become more topical in recent times. An obvious reason for this is that developments in technologies have made possible greater intrusions (for example, through testing, monitoring and surveillance) into workers' lives than ever before. Law has often lagged behind these developments.

The concept of privacy is one 'plagued by lack of precision', but it is generally taken to be founded in respect for human dignity and the personal autonomy of the individual.[161] Most discussions of a 'right to privacy' emphasise the autonomy of the individual and a person's sovereignty over the self through the associated values of consent and choice. Privacy is thus also often understood as an aspect of human liberty. In this respect it is not surprising that the resurgence in neo-liberal thinking in the global era has prompted an awakening of concerns about the protection of the individual worker's privacy.

---

158 For a detailed analysis of these provisions see D Noakes 'Corporate Groups and the Duties of Directors: Protecting the Employee or the Insolvent Employer?' (2001) 29 *ABLR* 124.

159 See *Corporations Act 2001* (Cth), Pt 9.4B.

160 See eg the failed *Employment Security Bills* introduced by ALP members in both houses of federal Parliament in 1999, following the waterfront dispute.

161 See *Australian Broadcasting Corporation v Lenah Game Meats* (2001) 208 CLR 199, 225–6. See also M Crompton, Federal Privacy Commissioner 'What is Privacy?', Speech to the *Privacy and Computer Security in the Information Age Conference* (2001).

In addition, many aspects of contemporary work, such as the long hours spent by many at work, have also meant that the line between people's work lives and their private lives has often become increasingly blurred, prompting a re-examination of concepts such as privacy. The law has generally accepted that employer controls may extend beyond the workplace, at least in situations where ostensibly 'private' behaviour also impacts on the business of the employer.[162] Likewise the law accepts issues that are often seen as deeply personal or private, such as personal grooming and dress, may be subject to employer direction at the workplace.[163] The law has tended to assume that when people are at work they leave behind their 'private' world, and come under the direction of the employer. Certainly the conventional understanding is that the law does not countenance the use by employees of their employer's property for their own private (non-work) purposes.[164] Thus, for example, there is no automatic legal right to privacy for personal mail delivered to work addresses. Employers are entitled to open and inspect all mail received by employees at work, although without warning the employee in advance this is not likely to engender a relation of trust and confidence. In any event it is good practice for such mail to be opened in the presence of the employee concerned and for there to be a policy in the workplace identifying that this may occur.[165] However, the law has been less quick to deal with questions about what are the limits of employer power in relation to privacy in the workplace.[166]

Concern with privacy and its protection by law is not in itself new. The importance of the protection of a 'right to privacy' is recognised in international law, both in Art 12 of the *Universal Declaration of Human Rights*, as well as Art 17 of the *International Covenant on Civil and Political Rights*. There are also now in place international codes of conduct, such as the ILO's *Code of Practice on the Protection of Workers' Personal Data, 1997*[167] and the OECD *Guidelines on the Protection of Privacy and Transborder Flows of Personal Data*, which indicate international recognition that privacy is a matter of increasing importance.[168] Well before the adoption of these instruments, indeed almost a century ago, Samuel Warren and Louis Brandeis in the USA wrote about the then contemporary threat to the 'right to be left alone', and argued that the common law should extend its protection beyond the physical integrity of persons and their

---

162 R McCallum *Employer Controls Over Private Life* (2000), 37–8. See also Chapter 6, pp 231–32.

163 *Australian Telecommunications Commission v Hart* (1982) 43 ALR 165. See also Chapter 6, p 231.

164 This is so even when the issue may appear to be work-related: see *Australian Municipal, Administrative, Clerical and Services Union v Ansett Australia Ltd* (2000) 175 ALR 173 where an employee who was a trade union official was sacked for using her work email to communicate with other trade union members.

165 NSW Privacy Commissioner/Lawlink NSW Report *Privacy & Private Mail, Email, Lockers, Drawers & Computers At Work*, available at <www.lawlink.nsw.gov.au>.

166 Prior to the enactment of the *Work Choices Act* the managerial prerogative of the employer, which in many cases precipitated actions ostensibly interfering with the privacy of employees, was indirectly kept in check because the majority of employees had access to a legal remedy for unfair dismissal.

167 Adopted by a meeting of Experts of Workers' Privacy, convened in October 1996 following resolution of the Governing Body of the International Labour Organization, November 1995: available at <www. ilo. org>.

168 OECD *Recommendation of the Council Concerning Guidelines Governing the Protection of Privacy and Transborder Flows of Personal Data*, 23 September 1980: available at <www.oecd.org>. These guidelines were developed for the OECD by a group of experts led by Hon Justice MD Kirby, then of the Australian Law Reform Commission.

property to comprehend a wider notion of the right to an inviolate personality of the individual.[169] In other jurisdictions, like the United Kingdom, Canada and New Zealand, the legal protection of a 'right to privacy' has developed considerably since that time.[170] After hints from several High Court Justices there is perhaps reason to think that there may be like developments in the common law in Australia.[171] However, the most that might be said at the moment is that the recognition of a 'right to privacy' at common law is at best inchoate.[172]

In the employment context the doctrine of mutual obligation of trust and confidence in relation to employment contracts can almost certainly be developed to impose restraints on employers, say if they were inappropriately to require an employee to undergo testing or if they were to use covert methods of surveillance at the workplace.[173] Although the common law may need to be relied upon increasingly in the global era, this is not to deny that it also has some deficiencies arising from the incremental nature of case law and the expense of litigation.[174] This is one of the reasons that increasingly there is a turn to statutory and other regulatory mechanisms to deal with issues of privacy, including at work.

Privacy and gathering information in the workplace

Since 2001 the application of the *Privacy Act 1988* (Cth), which is underpinned by the external affairs power in s 51(xxix) of the *Australian Constitution*, has been extended from government departments and agencies to cover private sector organisations, including partnerships, trusts and individuals.[175] However, the *Privacy Act* exempts small business with an annual turnover of $3 million or less, registered political parties, Commonwealth government agencies, and State or Territory authorities or prescribed instrumentalities.

Under the *Privacy Act* private sector employers are bound by the 10 National Privacy Principles (NPPs) established under the Act, unless they elect to be bound by a Privacy Code approved by the regulator, the Federal Privacy Commissioner.[176] The NPPs govern the use of 'personal information', which is defined as 'information or an opinion (including information or an opinion forming part of a database), whether true or not, whether recorded in material form or not, about an individual whose identity is apparent, or can be reasonably ascertained from the information or opinion'.

---

169 S Warren and L Brandeis 'The Right to Privacy' (1890) 4 *Harv LR* 193.

170 See generally JDR Craig *Privacy and Employment Law* (1999).

171 *Australian Broadcasting Corporation v Lenah Game Meats*, above n 161, 248–9. See also G Taylor 'Why is There no Common Law Right to Privacy?' (2000) 26 *Mon U L Rev* 235, and D Butler 'A Tort of Invasion of Privacy in Australia?' (2005) 29 *MULR* 399.

172 A 'right to privacy' might also include a tort of harassment: see eg *Grosse v Purvis* [2003] *Aust Torts Reports* ¶81–706, 64 187, which involved stalking.

173 See Chapter 6, p 232. See also J Riley *Employee Protection at Common Law* (2005), 71.

174 See the discussion by J Sempill 'Under the Lens: Electronic Workplace Surveillance' (2001) 14 *AJLL* 111, 128–33.

175 *Privacy Amendment (Private Sector) Act 2000* (Cth). See also legislation in some of the States covering privacy issues: eg *Privacy and Personal Information Act 1998* (NSW), *Invasion of Privacy Act 1991* (Qld), and *Information Privacy Act 2000* (Vic).

176 *Privacy Act 1988* (Cth), ss 6, 18BB, and Sch 3.

The NPPs require among other things that personal information should generally not be used or disclosed for any purpose (a 'secondary purpose') other than that for which it was collected (the 'primary purpose') without consent; impose obligations on those who collect information to ensure its accuracy and currency; protect the information; and require organisations to be open about the collection of information, and provide individuals with the access to their information.

The *Privacy Act* regulates even more strictly the gathering of 'sensitive information', which includes information about a person's racial or ethnic origin; political opinions; membership of a political association; religious beliefs or attitudes; philosophical beliefs; membership of a professional or trade association; membership of a trade union; sexual preferences or practices; criminal record; or health information. The NPPs preclude the gathering of this information from individuals unless they consent to its collection; the collection is required by law; or the collection is necessary to prevent a serious or imminent threat to the life or health of any individual where the individual is physically or legally incapable of giving consent to the collection or physically unable to give consent.[177]

However, under the *Privacy Act* there is an exemption for 'employee records'. 'Employee records' is broadly defined and covers the engagement, training, disciplining, resignation or termination of employment of an employee; the terms and conditions of employment of an employee; the employee's performance or conduct, hours of employment, salary or wages, personal and emergency contact details; the employee's membership of a professional or trade association or trade union membership; the employee's recreation, long service, sick, maternity, paternity or other leave; and the employee's taxation, banking or superannuation affairs.[178] This means that any information in such records may be passed on to others—for instance a future employer. However, the NPPs do apply to the collection of personal data from prospective employees, because the 'employee record' exemption only applies to personal information relating to a current or former employee. Once a person is hired, information gathered about the employee in the recruiting process is no longer covered by the NPPs; however, if the prospective employee is unsuccessful the information obtained through the recruitment and selection process remains subject to the NPPs.[179]

The exemption of 'employee records' from privacy law has been subjected to much discussion and criticism.[180] The original exclusion of 'employee records' under the *Privacy Act* represented a policy view that privacy issues relating to employees ought to be dealt with under the *Workplace Relations Act*.[181] Issues of privacy at the workplace are clearly matters that may be incorporated in workplace agreements, provided they

---

177 *Privacy Act 1988* (Cth), s 6 and Sch 3 cl 10.

178 *Privacy Act 1988* (Cth), ss 6, 7B(3).

179 See P Armstrong and B Cox 'Privacy, Health Information and Employee Records: Implications of New Commonwealth Privacy Laws' (2001).

180 See eg Attorney-General's Department and Department of Employment and Workplace Relations *Employee Records Privacy: A Discussion Paper on Information Privacy and Employee Records* (2004); and Australian Law Reform Commission (ALRC) *Essentially Yours: The Protection of Human Genetic Information in Australia* (2003) recommending against this exclusion at least in relation to genetic information: see Ch 34 and Recommendation 34.1.

181 See Commonwealth of Australia, *Parliamentary Debates*, House of Representatives, 12 April 2000, 15749 (Hon Daryl Williams, Attorney-General).

are dealt with in a way that enables them to be described as a matter that pertains to the employment relationship.[182] However, there is increasingly a perception that privacy rights are too serious and complex a matter to be left simply to workplace agreements, which are often nothing more than an agreement between the employer and the individual employee, and that privacy rights may be too important to be subject to waiver through workplace agreements.[183] From the employer perspective, there can also be quite legitimate reasons for establishing processes that might be seen as an invasion of privacy outside the workplace, and making these conditional upon the agreements of workers will not always be appropriate.

Despite the exemption of 'employee records' from the *Privacy Act*, those handling information about employees should nonetheless proceed cautiously, as is signalled by notes to the *Workplace Relations Act*.[184] Not all information about employees may fall within the relevant definitions activating the exemption in the *Privacy Act*. In particular, employers ought to be particularly careful about the way they manage and record information about, say, an employee's leave from work for reasons relating to illness or other family circumstances. In addition, although the *Privacy Act* only imposes limited obligations on employing businesses, and only on a limited range of employing business, in relation to employees' personal and sensitive information, the requirements imposed by discrimination statutes will usually constrain employers in relation to 'sensitive information'. Discrimination statutes are also not confined either to those who operate businesses with a turnover of $3 million or less or to actions in relation only to workers who are employees.[185] Certainly the discrimination statutes protect workers, including prospective workers, who may be required to undergo testing (for example, pregnancy, genetic, medical or psychological testing), by constraining the use of information in test results. In effect the discrimination statutes indirectly, and in some instances directly,[186] operate also to preclude such testing unless it can be justified, for example as an occupational health and safety requirement or as relevant to the requirements of the job. However, prospective workers do not always feel empowered to press such arguments and discrimination can also be difficult to prove. Otherwise there is little explicit regulation of employee testing in the workplace and the law provides little guidance on how an employer may legitimately approach such matters. For instance only one Australian State, New South Wales, has specific legislation concerning the use of polygraph testing. The *Lie Detectors Act 1983* (NSW) makes it an offence if a person uses an instrument or apparatus to monitor (among

---

182 *Workplace Relations Regulations*, r 8.7. In *Australian Services Union v Fuji-Xerox Australia* AIRC, PR952518, 15 October 2004, an agreement certified under the *Workplace Relations Act*, former s 170LJ contained provisions regulating privacy issues. See also Sempill, above n 174, 118; and R McCallum and A Stewart 'The Impact of Electronic Technology on Workplace Disputes in Australia' (2002) 24 *Comp LL & Pol'y J* 19, 39–40. The legislation of some States specifically envisages that 'surveillance' in the workplace is such a matter: see eg *Industrial Relations Act 1996* (NSW), s 6; and *Industrial Relations Act 1999* (Qld), Sch 1, cl 24.

183 See esp the considerations noted in Victorian Law Reform Commission (VLRC) *Workplace Privacy: Final Report* (2005); and ALRC, above n 180, Ch 34.

184 See notes accompanying *Workplace Relations Act*, ss 253–7, 269–71, 286–8, 304–7 and 748.

185 See generally Chapter 8. See also M Otlowski 'Employers' Use of Genetic Test Information: Is there a Need for Regulation?' (2002) 15 *AJLL* 1, 9–20.

186 See esp *Equal Opportunity Act 1995* (Vic), ss 100–1; *Anti-Discrimination Act 1991* (ACT), s 23; and *Anti-Discrimination Act 1992* (NT), s 26.

other things) the physiological reactions of a person for any 'prohibited purpose', which covers 'matters relating to employment' including 'an application for or offer of employment'.[187] In the new area of genetic screening there are no specific regulations in Australia that address the situation of employees, although changes in the law in this area have been recommended.[188]

Surveillance at work

The surveillance of workers is at the forefront of concerns regarding privacy in the contemporary workplace. There may be quite legitimate reasons for an employer wanting to establish surveillance at the workplace. These include ensuring the security of the business and the workplace, including by preventing and detecting fraud or other wrongdoing by employees, or monitoring compliance with occupational health and safety regulations or discrimination law.[189] Employers may also wish to use surveillance as a means of monitoring and thereby controlling employee performance at work, especially if the workplace is geographically dispersed. Concerns about unwarranted intrusions into employee privacy through surveillance have become more acute because of the ready and cheap availability, and the sophisticated nature, of modern computer and technological developments in this area. In addition to the more traditional visual or acoustic devices, employers can now also utilise systems of surveillance that include electronic trails to retrace keystrokes made by an employee on a computer keyboard and locational key-cards or global positioning system (GPS) instrumentation to map every movement of a worker whether in the factory, the office or beyond.

In relation to security (direct surveillance) matters, the privacy of all workers is protected to some extent by the ordinary law. Thus an employer must obtain the consent of an employee before searching that employee's person, otherwise this may amount to an assault. Likewise, any unauthorised access to an employee's bag or personal effects, including a locker supplied by the employer, is likely to constitute a trespass to goods. However, in many workplaces the consent and hence legal authority to undertake such searches can easily be incorporated as a condition of work through a clause in the contract of employment or as part of a workplace policy. The reality is that an insistence on consent provides employees with little effective right to prevent invasions of their privacy by the activity of security staff. As noted above, the idea that consent is adequate to deal with matters of privacy at work has been questioned from both employer and employee perspectives.[190]

The regulation of surveillance in the workplace by the state therefore tends to balance the interests of workers in privacy with any legitimate business interests of the

---

187 *Lie Detectors Act 1983* (NSW), ss 4–5.

188 See ALRC, above n 180; and VLRC, above n 183. For a discussion of this issue see also Otlowski, above n 185 and D Keays, 'The Legal Implications of Genetic Testing: Insurance, Employment and Privacy' (1999) 6 *Journal of Law and Medicine* 366.

189 The use of surveillance for such purposes is evident in many cases: see eg *Byrne v Australian Airlines Ltd* (1995) 185 CLR 410; and *Digital Pulse Pty Ltd v Christopher Harris &Ors* [2002] NSWSC 33.

190 See NSW Law Reform Commission, Report 98, *Surveillance: An Interim Report* (2001); and see above n 183.

employer in surveillance. In the recent report into *Workplace Privacy* by the Victorian Law Reform Commission, the concept of proportionality is adopted because it expresses this balancing approach and provides a sound basis for comprehensive regulation of privacy in the workplace.[191] The report works from the premise that employers must not unreasonably breach the privacy of employees. A proportionality test can be used to evaluate the acts and practices of employers and ensure that they were only undertaken for purposes 'directly connected' to the employer's business and in a manner proportionate to those purposes using the least privacy-invasive measure. This means that the greater the intrusion the more safeguards that are needed. The report also suggests that employers should be under an obligation to take reasonable steps to inform and consult with employees and provide adequate safeguards in relation to any acts or practices they adopt that impact on employee privacy.

However, to date the law has not always been developed in the light of overarching principles. For the most part it has been adapted as new issues and problems emerge. There are a number of different statutes that regulate surveillance by listening devices. At the Commonwealth level, s 6(1) of the *Telecommunications (Interception and Access) Act 1979* (Cth) regulates the interception (listening or recording) of a communication that passes over a telecommunications system. However, this legislation exempts any interception of calls made to or from a premises lawfully occupied by the person listening to or recording the call. Employers' monitoring and recording of employees' telephone calls are thus not caught by the terms of the Act.

The States and Territories also have in place legislation regulating the use of listening devices,[192] and these statutes do not contain such exemptions. This legislation (which it is not specific to the use of listening devices by employers) generally prohibits the installation or use of a listening device to overhear, record, monitor or listen to any private conversation without the express or implied consent of the parties to the conversation.[193] Private conversation is generally defined in terms that suggest it is 'carried on in circumstances that may be reasonably taken to indicate that any party to the conversation desires it to be confined to the parties to the conversation'.[194]

The *Surveillance Devices Act 1999* (Vic) and *Surveillance Devices Act 1998* (WA) go somewhat further and impose limitations on the use, again by anyone and not just employers, of listening devices, optical surveillance devices and tracking devices. For example, under the *Surveillance Devices Act 1999* (Vic) a person must not install, use or maintain a video surveillance device to record visually or observe a private activity to which the person is not a party without the express or implied consent of each party to the activity.[195] 'Private activity' is defined as an activity carried on in circumstances

---

191 See above n 183.

192 On one view, the *Telecommunications (Interception) Act 1979* (Cth) 'covers the field' in this area and thereby constitutionally ousts the operation of State laws in this area: see *Edelstein v Internal Committee of NSW* (1986) 7 NSWLR 222, 230; and *Miller v Miller* (1978) 141 CLR 269.

193 See eg *Listening Devices Act 1984* (NSW), s 5(1) and (3); *Listening and Surveillance Devices Act 1972* (SA) s 47(3)(a); *Listening Devices Act 1991* (Tas), s 5(1) and (3); and *Listening Devices Act 1997* (ACT), s 4(1). See also *Invasion of Privacy Act 1991* (Qld), s 43(1)–(2); *Surveillance Devices Act 1999* (Vic), ss 3, 6(1); *Surveillance Devices Act 1998* (WA), s 5(1), 5(3).

194 See eg *Listening Devices Act 1972* (SA), s 3.

195 *Surveillance Devices Act 1999* (Vic), s 7.

that may reasonably be taken to indicate that the parties to it desire it to be observed only by themselves, but does not include (a) an activity carried on outside a building or (b) an activity carried on in any circumstances in which the parties to it ought reasonably to expect that it may be observed by someone else: s 3. Julian Sempill has noted that the *Explanatory Memorandum* to this Act stated that the circumstances in which parties to an activity ought reasonably expect that they may be observed by someone else include 'activities in places accessible to the public and activities in those parts of the workplace accessible to other employees or invitees of the workplace' but not 'activities in those parts of the workplace where the parties to the activity may exclude others from observing the activity, such as an office with covered windows'.[196] Sempill concludes that this means most employees, except those in high-status positions with offices that can be closed off to others, are able to be placed under visual surveillance. The Victorian Act also provides that a person must not install, use or maintain a tracking device to determine the geographical location of a person or object without the express or implied consent of the person or the person controlling the object.[197] The Western Australian Act has very similar provisions. The *Surveillance Devices Act 1999* (Vic) also only offers a limited protection to employees: each of the possible limitations on an employer's use of visual, acoustic or electronic devices can be avoided if the employer obtains the express or implied consent of employees and employees are often not in a position where they feel powerful enough not to agree to an employer's request.

The surveillance of email use by employees provides a good illustration of the complexity and often confusion that can exist in the area of surveillance at the workplace. It is usually assumed that the basic legal position is that because the employer owns the equipment through which emails are sent and received at work, the equipment should be used solely for the business of the employer and therefore it is lawful for the employer to access and read employees' emails.[198] However, some commentators have suggested that the interception of email messages by employers may contravene s 7 of the *Telecommunications (Interception and Access) Act 1979* (Cth), at least if it involves the interception and copying of emails before they reach the employee, although the provision would not extend to monitoring or reading emails once they have been received.[199]

The collection, storage, use and disclosure of emails may also be subject to the federal *Privacy Act* to the extent that the information contained in the emails concerns persons who are not employees and therefore it is information that would not be covered by the 'employment record' exemption. The Federal Privacy Commissioner has released *Guidelines on Workplace Email, Web Browsing and Privacy, 2000*[200] to assist organisations in developing their own internal policies governing the use of emails and the Internet at work. The *Guidelines* emphasise the importance of bringing a policy to the attention

---

196 Sempill, above n 174.

197 *Surveillance Devices Act 1999* (Vic), s 8.

198 J Nolan 'Employee Privacy in the Electronic Workplace Pt 1: Surveillance, Records and Emails' [2000] *PLPR* 51.

199 N Dixon *Employees and the Internet—Issues for the Private and Public Sector Employees Research Brief* (2001).

200 The *Guidelines* are available at <www.privacy.gov.au>.

of employees, of making explicit in it what is and is not permitted in the workplace, of indicating what information may be logged by the employer and who has a right to access the logs to monitor them, and of stressing the security of the Internet at the workplace. Good policies are reviewed on a regular basis and are clearly expressed so that they can be easily understood in the workplace. The *Guidelines* are not legally binding, but they do indicate matters that might be considered by the Privacy Commissioner in any case of a complaint that the *Privacy Act* had been breached. To the extent that employers follow these *Guidelines* in order to avoid having to defend such a claim, it could be said that the *Guidelines* regulate employers' interception and monitoring of emails.

New South Wales is the only jurisdiction to have legislation that expressly addresses the issue of computer surveillance at the workplace.[201] The *Workplace Surveillance Act 2005* (NSW) prohibits surveillance of employees at the workplace by camera, computer or tracking device unless they are given prior written notice of at least fourteen days in advance (unless a more limited time frame is agreed).[202] The notice must detail the nature of the surveillance and its duration. There are additional requirements imposed that vary according to whether camera, computer, or tracking devices are to be employed. Thus any computer surveillance can only be conducted in accord with a policy at the workplace, which has been brought to the attention of employees in advance in such a way that it is reasonable to assume they will comprehend its meaning. Where the computer is provided by the employer, it may also be monitored away from the workplace. Under the NSW legislation employers may block delivery of emails or access to websites only where this is notified as part of a policy, or where it is necessary to comply with other legislation (such as the *SPAM Act 2003* (Cth)) or to secure the integrity of the computer system, or to prevent material that is offensive or may harass others. In relation to camera surveillance the *Workplace Surveillance Act 2005* (NSW) requires the camera to be clearly visible and for signs to be posted in the area where the camera operates.[203] Where a tracking device is fixed to a vehicle, it must also have a clearly visible notice.[204]

Covert surveillance at the workplace is even more tightly restricted by the *Workplace Surveillance Act 2005* (NSW). The seriousness of covert surveillance is underlined by the legislation, which makes it a criminal offence for an employer to embark on such a course of action without first getting approval from a covert surveillance authority (CSA) such as a magistrate.[205] Covert surveillance is in any event only permitted if the employer has a reasonable suspicion that the employees to be monitored have acted unlawfully, and other matters (such as whether the employer has taken other steps to address the issue) will be relevant to the issuing of an approval for covert surveillance. The authority granted by a CSA will be for a limited period, and a report must be made at the end of the period. The Act makes clear that any covert surveillance cannot be used to monitor the performance of an employee.

---

201 *Workplace Surveillance Act 2005* (NSW), ss 12, 17.
202 Ibid, s 10.
203 Ibid, s 11.
204 Ibid, s 13.
205 Ibid, ss 19–22 and see also ss 23–38.

The *Workplace Surveillance Act 2005* (NSW) regulates the surveillance of employees when 'at work', either when they are at the workplace working or when working elsewhere, and it prohibits any surveillance at other times.[206] There are some areas of the workplace, such as bathrooms and changerooms, where surveillance is not allowed at all.[207] The legislation also imposes strict controls on the use or disclosure of any surveillance records gathered, permitting only those things that are for the legitimate purposes of the business, the enforcement of the law, or the prevention of serious injury or damage to persons or property.[208]

The *Workplace Surveillance Act 2005* (NSW) is broadly in conformity with international principles, such as the ILO's *Code of Practice on the Protection of Workers' Personal Data, 1997*, which state that monitoring should always be advised in advance, that covert monitoring should only be conducted in accord with legislation or if there is suspicion of criminal activity or other serious wrongdoing, and that there should only be continuous monitoring of employees if required for ensuring health and safety or the protection of property.[209] However, it can be seen that in Australia there are at present a wide range of different provisions regulating privacy at work. While some jurisdictions have been actively developing the law in this area in recent years, others have done little and in those circumstances employees remain quite vulnerable.

It is also evident that there are widely differing approaches to the choices of regulatory mechanisms. In some instances surveillance, and other intrusions on privacy, are subject only to the consent of the individuals concerned and in other cases there are legislated standards. Much of the legislation applies a very strict regulatory approach, making it a criminal offence to breach privacy standards. Thus the *Workplace Surveillance Act 2005* (NSW) imposes criminal liability on employers that are in breach of any of its provisions, and on any directors or managers who knowingly authorised or permitted the contravention.[210] In this sense it does not discriminate in relation to the seriousness of the activity. By way of contrast the Victorian Law Reform Commission (VLRC) has recommended a 'lighter touch' approach to regulation of privacy at work. This is also the approach that is adopted by the *Privacy Act 1988* (Cth). The VLRC suggests advisory codes of practice for email monitoring and over video surveillance. However, for acts or practices that are a potentially greater threat to privacy, such as genetic testing, drug and alcohol testing or covert surveillance, it proposes mandatory codes of practice. The VLRC has also noted that genetic testing or covert surveillance will rarely be warranted and ought be directly authorised by the regulator.

---

206 Ibid, ss 5, 16.
207 Ibid, s 15.
208 Ibid, ss 18, 36–8.
209 Principle 6.14.
210 *Workplace Surveillance Act 2005* (NSW), s 43.

part **4**

Freedom of
Association

Freedom of Association at Work

Introduction

Although the general principle of freedom of association is one that is well accepted in international law and very often also in national or domestic law, its actual content, scope and nature has been the subject of vigorous debate. Especially contentious has been the question of the relationship between the understanding of freedom of association relevant to other spheres of life—political, cultural, religious—and that applicable to work relations. This debate has been particularly intense in places like Europe, Canada, and the USA, where there is protection of freedom of association at a higher, constitutional level.[1] The debate is one that is also extending to international law, especially because rights at work are presented more frequently now as human rights.[2]

This debate is also occurring in Australia. Here there is no express constitutional guarantee of freedom of association in the *Constitution*, although an inchoate implied constitutional freedom exists in relation to 'political' association.[3] A neat dichotomy between 'political' and 'industrial' or 'work-related' associations is not easily sustainable,[4] but as with other fundamental values, the protection of freedom of association in Australia must be found primarily in the ordinary law, in statute or at common law.

A central issue in much of this debate is whether freedom of association is an individual or a collective right, whether it is a right of individuals merely to join together in association or a right also to act collectively. In the labour arena the view of scholars

---

1 There is a vast literature in this area. See eg Council of Europe *Freedom of Association* (1993), 163–201; J Fudge '"Labour is Not a Commodity": The Supreme Court of Canada and the Freedom of Association' (2004) 67 *Saskatchewan LR* 425; TI Emerson 'Freedom of Association and Freedom of Expression' (1964) 74 *Yale LJ* 1; and RW McGee 'The Right to Not Associate: The Case for an Absolute Freedom of Negative Association' (1992) 23 *UWLA Law Rev* 123.

2 See P Macklem 'The Right to Bargain Collectively in International Law: Workers' Right, Human Right, International Right' in P Alston (ed) *Labour Rights as Human Rights* (2005).

3 See eg *Kruger v Commonwealth* (1997) 190 CLR 1, 91–3, 115–16, 119–20; and *Mulholland v Australian Electoral Commission* (2004) 220 CLR 181, 225–26, 277–78.

4 See eg R Doyle 'The Industrial/Political Dichotomy: The Impact of Freedom of Communication Cases on Industrial Law' (1995) 8 *AJLL* 91.

has traditionally been that freedom of association must be a freedom to act collectively otherwise it would be a meaningless sham.[5] The jurisprudence of the International Labour Organization (ILO) also sees freedom of association as a vehicle to pursue and protect the interests of industrial players by collective action. However, aside from some rare judicial comments to the contrary,[6] the common law has generally been antagonistic to collective action, especially to any form of industrial action, even in support of collective bargaining.[7] In the contemporary law of work in Australia statute law has been developed against this background.

This chapter first looks at the influence of liberal theory on understandings of freedom of association. It then moves on to examine international law in relation to the freedom, in particular the jurisprudence of the ILO both generally and as it has been applied to legal developments in Australia. Under ILO conventions, freedom of association means not only a freedom to join together in association, but also a freedom to bargain collectively and, where necessary, to take industrial action. The protection of freedom of association under the *Workplace Relations Act 1996* (Cth) (*Workplace Relations Act*) as an individual right to associate and to disassociate is examined in this chapter, while bargaining and industrial action are dealt with in more detail in Chapters 11 and 12. This chapter concludes by examining trade union membership in contemporary Australia, and exploring some ideas about the future development of trade unions in the new economy.

Freedom of association—individual or collective right?

The liberal ideal of freedom of association

The principle of freedom of association has a long history in Western liberal thought. At the centre of much philosophical and legal thought about the freedom are assumptions about the nature of the individual. In classical liberal theory the individual is a rational, free and independent being, who exercises a sovereign-like control over every action and engagement in the world. Autonomy is thus the most important characteristic of the individual. In classical liberal theory the individual exists, fully formed so to speak, prior to any social interactions. Already complete in the world of nature, the individual can be easily threatened by others in social relations. Only by exercising free choice and consent to control relations and associations with others does the individual remain a subject. For the bounded autonomous individual of Western liberal thought, association with others always carries the potential for harm as much as for fulfilment.

The primacy of this individual in Western thought has provided the basis for much of contemporary law's understanding of the principle of freedom of association. In classical liberal theory, freedom of association is an important extension of the autonomy of the individual and as such it has two interrelated aspects: a 'positive' freedom to associate,

---

5   See eg Lord Wedderburn 'Freedom of Association or Right to Organise?' (1987) *IRJ* 244, 252.
6   See *Crofter Handwoven Harris Tweed Co v Veitch* [1942] AC 435, 463.
7   See Chapter 12 regarding the common law and industrial action. See also *Colleymore v Attorney-General* [1970] AC 538.

and a 'negative' freedom not to associate. Indeed, in classical liberal theory, freedom not to associate is of far greater importance than freedom to associate, because it is this negative freedom that is necessary to preserve intact the very essence of the person.

This liberal ideal of freedom of association is often elaborated in more general discussions about constitutional or fundamental rights.[8] According to classical liberal theory, life, liberty and property are the only inherent rights of the individual and must remain inviolate. Otherwise the interests of individuals are incommensurable. Therefore, the adherents to liberal theory are sceptical about the common good, and common values of individuals in association. Work rights are not considered fundamental or special and cannot be converted to such through association. Furthermore, in liberal theory the state must respect the rational, free and independent individual. Thus even if the state is not hostile to associations it is likely at most to be 'neutral', neither facilitating nor preventing them. However, in liberal theory the state will always be positively justified in protecting the individual against any semblance of forced association, and so freedom not to associate rather than freedom to associate will if anything be its primary focus.

In the global era the dominance of neo-liberal theory has meant that it has been the classical liberal view of freedom of association that has most frequently been applied directly to work relations by governments keen to adapt to the competitive world of the new economy. Furthermore this very individualised understanding of freedom of association has been seamlessly incorporated into the legal culture because the common law doctrines of contract and property have become the 'natural' law of the marketplace.[9]

Freedom of association—the individual 'in' relations

There have also been many criticisms of the classical liberal and neo-liberal approach to freedom of association. In an extensive study of labour law and freedom of association Sheldon Leader has powerfully put the argument that the nature of a right cannot necessarily be extrapolated from the nature of the bearer of the right.[10] Indeed in Western thought there can also be found acknowledgment of the interdependency of individuals in society. De Tocqueville, for instance, wrote that:

> The most natural privilege of man, next to the right of acting for himself, is that of combining his exertions with those of his fellow creatures and of acting in common with them. The right of association therefore appears ... almost as inalienable in its nature as the right of personal liberty. No legislator can attack it without impairing the foundations of society.[11]

---

8 The liberal ideal of freedom of association is clearly articulated by a number of US scholars: see Emerson, above n 1; McGee, above n 1; and R Raggi 'An Independent Right to Freedom of Association' (1997) 12 *Harv CR-CL LR* 1.

9 See Lord Wedderburn 'Freedom of Association and Philosophies of Labour Law' (1989) 18 *ILJ* 1. Wedderburn discusses the influence on freedom of association of neo-liberal philosophers, such as Friedrich A von Hayek (see *Law, Legislation and Liberty: A New Statement of the Principles of Justice and Political Economy* vol 1 'Rules and Order' (1976). See also the work of other influential liberal philosophers: eg R Nozick *Anarchy, State and Utopia* (1974).

10 S Leader *Freedom of Association: A Study of Labor Law and Political Theory* (1992), esp 33–4.

11 Alexis de Tocqueville *Democracy in America* (1946), vol I Ch XII, 203.

While de Tocqueville viewed freedom of association as a secondary, or derivative, right, the idea that it facilitates social action also opens up other and perhaps more productive ways of thinking about individual human beings 'in' relations.

Canadian jurisprudence shows how such ideas have been developed in modern legal systems. According to the Canadian view an important aspect of freedom of association is that it recognises:

> the profoundly social nature of human endeavour ... As social beings, our freedom to act with others is a primary condition of community life, human progress and civilised society.[12]

This acknowledges that an individual never stands completely alone, absolutely independent of others, but is a social being. However, this sentiment is not simply the idea that any individual achievement is linked to the cooperation and assistance of others, though that is also an important point to be made. Rather the idea can be taken further so that freedom of association becomes in fact a necessary pre-condition for individuals to have a meaningful social existence. In order to attain full potential as a human being, the individual must be able to associate with others: freedom of association can therefore be seen as necessary for '[i]ndividual self actualisation through relations with others'.[13] Understood in this way the individual remains at the centre of the conception of freedom of association but association has become a positive opportunity rather than a negative threat.

Freedom of association as a collective value

A view of freedom of association that suggests a relational understanding of the individual is not all that far removed from some of the traditional explanations by labour lawyers of the freedom as a collective value. Thus some considerable time ago C Wilfred Jenks wrote about freedom of association in the following way:

> In an age of interdependence and large-scale organisation, in which the individual counts for so little unless he acts in co-operation with his fellows, freedom of association has become the cornerstone of civil liberties and social and economic rights alike. It has long been the bulwark of religious freedom and political liberty; it has increasingly become a necessary condition of economic and social freedom for the ordinary citizen.[14]

For Jenks there were two starkly opposed alternatives in work relations—either they were characterised by freedom, importantly through freedom of association, or by conditions of slavery. Jenks was writing specifically about labour law, and he went on to note that freedom of association played a critical role in the industrial era, an era of mass production where the economic concentration of power had rendered individual craftsmen powerless. Jenks thus regarded freedom of association as not simply an individual right but something to be used collectively by labour as a countervailing

---

12 *Reference Re Public Service Employee Relations Act (Alberta)* [1987] 1 SCR 313, 365.
13 *Lavigne v Ontario Public Service Employees Union* [1991] 2 SCR 211, 343.
14 CW Jenks *Human Rights and International Labour Law Standards* (c 1960), 49.

power to the might of capital to secure a redistribution of wealth in a capitalist economy. It is this understanding of freedom of association that became particularly important in international labour law.[15]

Freedom of association and the citizen worker

There is one other important aspect to freedom of association at work, and that is as an expression of the voice of workers and the mechanism through which they participate as subjects in decisions at work. Without coming together in association the worker is unlikely to have a voice in the workplace. Freedom of association thus recognises the citizen worker and at the same time performs a role that is also supportive of the wider democratic society. In a significant way, the vitality of a constitutional democracy depends on the degree to which *all* relationships in the community reflect a commitment to the individual as a subject, as an active participant engaging in a creative way, rather than as an object subordinate to the power of another, in social relations. If, as Carole Pateman argued, the lives of citizens cannot be compartmentalised, participation in the democratic community is learned through practice, a practice that occurs as much in work relationships as in other more strictly political relationships.[16] The separation of 'private' working lives from 'public' community lives, or the division of 'social and economic' lives as separate from 'political' lives, is an impossibility, and freedom of association becomes an important bridge between them.

Freedom of association—individual or collective?

From the foregoing it can be seen that the idea that freedom of association must be conceived of as either a collective or an individual right or value is perhaps over simplistic. There is perhaps no reason why freedom of association cannot be understood as an individual, human right, while at the same time acknowledging that it also has a peculiar collective function in relation to work relations. This is the way that understandings of freedom of association are developing in international labour law.

Freedom of association in international law

Freedom of association is recognised as a fundamental right in many international instruments. A general right to association and a freedom from compulsion to associate is part of international instruments such as the *United Nations Declaration of Human Rights 1948*, the *International Covenant on Civil and Political Rights 1966* (*ICCPR*), and the *International Covenant on Economic, Social and Cultural Rights 1966* (*ICESCR*). Each of these instruments also acknowledges specifically the importance of freedom of association in work relations. Thus the *United Nations Declaration of Human Rights, 1948* refers to the right of workers to join in trade unions for the protection of their interests: Art 20. The right to form and join trade unions is also

---

15 See below pp 462 ff.
16 See eg C Pateman *Participation and Democratic Theory* (1970).

explicitly mentioned in the *ICESCR* (Art 8(1)), along with the right of trade unions to form national and international federations and to function without interference: Arts 8(1)(b)–(c). Significantly the *ICESCR* also makes explicit mention of the 'right to strike', although this is qualified as being a right that must be 'exercised in conformity with the laws of the particular country': Art 8(1)(d). The right to form and join trade unions is also recognised in the *ICCPR* (Art 22(1)), and the *First Optional Protocol* to the *ICCPR* provides that the United Nations' Human Rights Committee can hear complaints from individuals or governments if a signatory state fails to protect the rights enshrined in the convention adequately. The Human Rights Committee has interpreted both the *ICESCR* and the *ICCPR* as also supporting collective bargaining.[17]

However, it is two of the conventions of the International Labour Organization (ILO), the *Freedom of Association and Protection of the Right to Organise Convention, 1948 (ILO C 87)* and the *Right to Organise and Collective Bargaining Convention, 1949 (ILO C 98)*, which are of first importance in protecting freedom of association in work relations in international law. Indeed both the *ICESCR* and the *ICCPR* underline this by stating an intention to support and not derogate from *ILO C 87*.[18]

Some writers have expressed the view that the principle of freedom of association is so fundamental that it should be regarded as a part of international customary law.[19] Whether or not that is so, Australia has ratified, and is therefore bound by, all of the major international conventions regarding freedom of association that have been mentioned here.[20]

Freedom of association and the International Labour Organization

Freedom of association has been one of the core, foundational values of the ILO. Reference to freedom of association is found in the *ILO Constitution*, as it was originally in 1919 and as revised in the early 1940s, and in the *Declaration of Philadelphia*.[21] In 1998 the ILO's *Declaration of Fundamental Principles and Rights at Work* announced to the world that freedom of association is one of the four most important issues in the workplace of the new economy.

The ILO conventions on freedom of association

The *Declaration of Fundamental Principles and Rights at Work* reiterated the major significance of *ILO C 87* and *ILO C 98*, both of which were adopted by the ILO

---

17 See Macklem, above n 2, 72–3.
18 See *ICESCR*, Art 8(3); and *ICCPR*, Art 22(3).
19 G von Potobsky 'Protection of Trade Union Rights: Twenty Years Work by the Committee on Freedom of Association' (1972) 105 *Int Lab Rev* 69, 83.
20 Australia ratified *ILO C 87* and *ILO C 98* in 1973, *ICESCR* in 1975, *ICCPR* in 1980, and the *First Optional Protocol* to the *ICCPR* in 1991. Australia has also endorsed a variety of other international instruments, such as the OECD *Guidelines for Multi-National Enterprises* that also express support for freedom of association: see Chapter 2, p 70.
21 See now *ILO Constitution*, Art 41; and see originally the *Treaty of Versailles*, Art 427. See further Chapter 2.

Conference soon after World War II. The effort to frame general freedom of association conventions under the auspices of the ILO was not without difficulty, notwithstanding the fact that as early as 1921 there was a convention concerning the right to association in the agricultural sector.[22] However, twice after this in 1927 and 1947, the ILO Conference failed to get agreement between the delegates of workers and those of employers and business on a general convention on freedom of association, with the sticking point being the inclusion of terms referring to the 'freedom to join and freedom not to join' in the proposed convention. Apart from *ILO C 87* and *ILO C 98*, the principles of freedom of association are now also enshrined in a range of other ILO conventions, which in some instances supplement *ILO C 87* and *ILO C 98*.[23] But it is *ILO C 87* and *ILO C 98* that are the most important of the ILO conventions on freedom of association.[24]

ILO C 87 focuses especially on the formation and independent governance of organisations of workplace participants. It protects the right of both workers and employers to come together, establish, join and administer organisations without interference: see especially Arts 2–4. These same rights extend to affiliation with other organisations in federations and internationally, and to freedom from external administrative interference or restrictions in any aspect of their governance and conduct: Arts 5–6. An important aspect of *ILO C 87* is Art 10 recognising that the freedom to form and join organisations is one for the purpose of 'furthering and defending the interests' of the members of the association. Thus the freedom of association protected by the convention extends beyond a simple coming together to actually doing things together, in association.

ILO C 98 supplements the provisions of *ILO C 87*. It sets down the rights of workers to adequate protection against anti-union discrimination, in all phases of work relations with special emphasis on protection in relation to selection for, or termination of, employment, as well as guaranteeing that workers are free to engage in union activity, either during working time with the consent of employers or outside the workplace: Art 1. *ILO C 98* further provides that trade unions shall be free from the interference of employers, including through the provision of funding, and that there shall be appropriate regulatory mechanisms to ensure and protect that independence: Arts 2–3. Employer-funded workers' organisations, for instance, are not an expression of the freedom of workers to associate.

The function of freedom of association, as guaranteed in *ILO C 98*, is to enable collective bargaining between employers and employee organisations. Under Art 4

22 *Right of Association (Agriculture) Convention 1921 (ILO C 11)*.

23 See eg *Workers' Representatives Convention, 1971 (ILO C 135); Workers' Representatives Recommendation 1971 (ILO R 143); Rural Workers' Organization Convention, 1975 (ILO C 141); Rural Workers' Organization Recommendation, 1971 (ILO R 143); Collective Bargaining Convention, 1981 (ILO C 154) and Collective Bargaining Recommendation, 1981 (ILO R 163)*.

24 On the ILO and freedom of association see generally B Creighton 'Freedom of Association' in R Blanpain and C Engels (eds) *Comparative Labour Law and Industrial Relations in Industrialized Market Economies* (2001); J-M Servais *International Labour Law* (2005), Pt II Ch 1 'Freedom of Association and Social Dialogue'; and L Swepston 'Human Rights Law and Freedom of Association: Development through ILO Supervision' (1998) 137 *Int Lab Rev* 169.

the duty of signatories to the convention is to put in place measures that 'encourage and promote' collective agreements. That is, there is a duty on states to take positive action in this area and to enable industrial players to have the freedom to select the level of collective bargaining in which they engage. The convention enshrines collective bargaining as the most important mechanism through which workers can protect and advance their economic and social interests.

Although not expressly provided for in *ILO C 87* or *ILO C 98* the jurisprudence of the ILO has interpreted freedom of association and the right to bargain collectively as including a right to take industrial or strike action.[25] This extends to include sympathy and other supportive action and strikes in which workers put forward wider (political) claims.[26] However, *ILO C 87* also requires worker and employer organisations to 'respect the law of the land' provided that it 'shall not be such as to impair, nor shall it be so applied as to impair' freedom of association: Art 8. The ILO has thus accepted that there may be procedural controls in relation to strike action imposed by national law: for example, national law may insist on a period during which parties must attempt to resolve matters by conciliation, or may require strike ballots, provided the limits are reasonable and do not impose substantial restrictions on the right to strike.[27]

The ILO conventions on freedom of association except some categories of workers from their protections, and allow for national regulation in relation to them. Public sector workers engaged in the administration of the state are excluded from *ILO C 98*: Art 6. Members of the armed forces and the police are also to be subject to national law: *ILO C 87*, Art 9(1); and *ILO C 98*, Art 5. ILO jurisprudence also recognises that limits in relation to the right to strike operate in relation to all 'essential services', the interruption of which 'would endanger the life, personal safety or health of the whole or part of the population', provided that safeguards are in place to protect the industrial interests of the relevant workers.[28]

The focus of the ILO conventions on freedom of association as a collective right extends well beyond the understanding of the freedom in many national constitutional and legal systems, which often tend to have a very limited and 'individualised' conception of the freedom.[29] It is noticeable that the ILO conventions have nothing to say about a right to dissociate or not to belong to an association. As was pointed out above, for some years the ILO failed to develop a convention on freedom of association because of debate over this very issue in relation to the wording of a convention. Nevertheless, it has been

---

25 See *ILO C 87*, Arts 3, 8 and 10. See also R Ben-Israel *International Labour Standards: The Case of Freedom to Strike* (1988); J Hodges-Aerberhard and A Odera de Dios 'Principles of the Committee of Freedom of Association concerning Strikes' (1987) 126 *Int Lab Rev* 543; B Creighton 'The ILO and the Protection of Fundamental Human Rights in Australia' (1988) 22 *MULR* 239, 248; and Swepston, above n 24, 182.

26 See ILO, *Freedom of Association and Collective Bargaining: General Survey of the Report on the Freedom of Association and the Right to Organise Convention (no 87) 1948, and the Right to Organise and Collective Bargaining Convention (no 98) 1949* (1994), [168].

27 See ILO *Freedom of Association: Digest of Decisions and Principles of the Freedom of Association Committee of the Governing Body of the ILO*, (1996), [498], [508]–[511]. See also Swepston, above n 24, 182.

28 See the comments in *Complaint against the Government of Australia presented by the International Federation of Airline Pilots Association (IFALPA)*, Report No 277 of the Committee of Freedom of Association *(Case No 1511)* 1991.

29 See above ns 1 and 8.

said that it is not inconsistent with the collective nature of freedom of association to provide legal protection for those who do not wish to join or who wish to resign affiliation from a particular association.[30] Indeed, others have gone further to argue that unless there is a freedom 'not to' as well as a freedom 'to' then it makes little sense to refer to a 'freedom' at all. At the same time the point has been made that seeing the freedom of association in this way is not the same as saying that it is a 'negative freedom'.[31]

Although freedom of association as expressed in ILO conventions and in the jurisprudence explicating them focuses on collective aspects, it also necessarily incorporates a range of protections that must be enjoyed by individuals. For instance other rights, such as those to be free from arbitrary arrest, to enjoy a freedom of expression and freedom of speech and assembly, the right to a fair trial, and protection of trade union property, have all been recognised by the ILO as playing a significant role in the protection of freedom of association.[32]

The *Global Reports* on freedom of association

While the body of ILO jurisprudence that has developed under *ILO C 87* and *ILO C 98* has focused primarily upon encouraging states to ensure the protection of freedom of association under their own domestic law, the rhetoric at the ILO exhorting adherence to the freedom has now shifted somewhat. Labour rights are increasingly being articulated anew as 'human rights' protecting the dignity of workers and needing to be advanced on a global scale. As a result international labour law, it is claimed, is changing to find a 'third way' emphasis on the importance of the freedom as an 'international right'.[33] These developments are driven in large part by the particular nature of the challenges that the ILO sees the global era posing to freedom of association and other fundamental principles and rights at work.

Two of the earliest *Global Reports,* issued by the ILO as part of its follow-up to the *Declaration of Fundamental Principles and Rights at Work 1988,* address the issue of freedom of association.[34] The reports articulate a dual aspect to the rationale underpinning freedom of association. On one level, the *Global Reports* continue to emphasise that the freedom serves the traditional functions of protecting employees in their dealings with employers and ensuring decent wages and conditions at work. Both of the *Global Reports* on freedom of association thus reinforce the importance of closing the 'representational gap' in the modern world of work, collective bargaining, and the right to strike without which collective bargaining 'risks being inconsequential—a dead

---

30 See B Creighton 'The ILO and the Protection of Fundamental Human Rights' (1998) 22 *MULR* 239, 248; and Swepston, above n 24.

31 L Betten *International Labour Law: Selected Issues* (1993), 75–82.

32 See ILO, *Freedom of Association and Collective Bargaining: General Survey of the Report on the Freedom of Association and the Right to Organise Convention (No 87) 1948 and the Right to Organise and Collective Bargaining Convention (No 98) 1949* (1994). See also Swepston, above n 24, 177.

33 See Macklem, above n 2.

34 International Labour Office, *Your Voice at Work* (2000); and International Labour Office, *Organising for Social Justice* (2004). These *Global Reports* now replace the *General Surveys on Freedom of Association,* which had previously been provided to the International Labour Conference in 1956, 1957, 1959, 1973, 1983 and 1994.

letter'.[35] The *Global Reports* make particular mention of the risks—including low wages and conditions, and discrimination and arbitrary treatment—attendant on the increasing individualisation of labour relations and make a claim for the primacy of workers' and employers' self-determination in setting their preferred style of collective bargaining, whether at enterprise or industry levels.

The *Global Reports* also look to bolster support for freedom of association by identifying it as a principle with a special role to play in the new economy, supporting economic, social and political processes.[36] In particular, the ILO seeks to ensure that freedom of association becomes one of the central processes for bringing about a fair sharing of the fruits of the progress promised by the new economy. Unless freedom of association is protected everywhere, so the argument of the *Global Reports* goes, the intensity of competition in the global marketplace will impose an extreme test of survival of the fittest because the absence of the freedom in some jurisdictions will only invite business to threaten to take production away from those jurisdictions where it is protected.

The strategy of the ILO is therefore one of promoting freedom of association as a fundamental principle and right that can serve the purposes of the modern global agenda. Couched in the language of cooperation rather than conflict, freedom of association for labour is said to carry reciprocal benefits for capital. It promises to engender trust and cooperation by securing a voice for workers, and thereby providing a means for the mutual ownership of the problems in the workplace and allowing a more wide-ranging input into the resolution of those problems. It also provides an organised forum for the management of conflict, which is in turn envisaged as lessening industrial disputation. All of this, so it is said, will result in greater predictability of business conditions and also enable workers to better adapt to the demands of flexibility, innovation and productivity in the contemporary workplace.[37] The invitation is to see workers as partners in, and not a hindrance to, global expansion. 'Freedom of association' is portrayed as a natural corollary to 'freedom of enterprise' and marking out a 'high road' to international competitiveness.

The stress in the *Global Reports* is on the importance of social dialogue, including all forms of negotiations, consultations and exchanges of information between governments, workers and employers on social and economic policy. Representation and voice are seen as complements to good governance and corporate social responsibility in the new economy. The idea is that freedom of association will allay fears and insecurity and dispel social unease.

However, the *Global Reports* also remind member states that they continue to play an important role in preserving the freedom, and comment once again that the trend to the individualisation of work relations is a major threat to freedom of association, because it reinforces the inequality of bargaining power between the parties, exposes workers to a greater risk of abuse and threatens decent work standards. The continuing role of governments in promoting collective bargaining is stressed as a particularly

---

35 International Labour Office, *Your Voice at Work*, ibid, 37.

36 See esp International Labour Office, *Organising for Social Justice*, above n 34, 1, 5, 7, 74–77.

37 See esp International Labour Office, *Your Voice at Work*, above n 34, 16–19, 23.

important one, and Australia is singled out for negative comment as a country where the government is content simply to allow parties to 'choose' themselves between collective and individual bargaining.[38] In addition, the severe restrictions on the right to strike in Australia, especially in relation to secondary boycotts and solidarity or sympathy action, have also been specifically averted to by the ILO in the *Global Reports* as inconsistent with freedom of association.[39] The *Global Reports* thus highlight a number of issues about freedom of association in Australia that have been of concern to the ILO for a considerable period through its usual monitoring processes.[40]

Decisions of the Committee on Freedom of Association regarding Australia

The ILO's Committee on Freedom of Association (CFA) is the main supervisory committee charged with dealing with complaints that there has been a breach by member states of their obligations under *ILO C 87* and *ILO C 98*. Since its establishment in 1951, the CFA has dealt with a number of complaints against Australia. Between 1990 and 2005, there were four such cases.[41]

In *Case 1511*, the CFA dealt with complaints lodged by the International Federation of Air Line Pilots Associations relating to the airline pilots' dispute of 1989–90.[42] In that dispute the airline pilots tried to bargain collectively outside the guidelines for wage negotiations set under the conciliation and arbitration system, and in pursuit of their claims they instituted industrial action first by working restricted hours and then by resigning en masse.[43] As a result of their actions the pilots' union was effectively excluded from the conciliation and arbitration system, its existing awards were cancelled, and new awards incorporating many of the elements of the airline contracts that the pilots had been resisting were put in place. The pilots were also sued at common law and ordered by the Victorian Supreme Court to pay $6.48M for the damages caused by their actions.

Case 1511 first dealt with the right to bargain collectively. The jurisprudence of the ILO has not held that the conventions require national law to contain provisions requiring employers to bargain collectively, or recognising an organisation of workers for the purpose of collective bargaining. Rather Art 4 of *ILO C 98* simply requires states to put in place measures that *encourage* and *promote* collective bargaining. There is no duty on member states to enforce collective bargaining by compulsory means.[44] The CFA therefore held that Australia had not breached its obligations in respect of collective bargaining.

Case 1511 also raised the issue of protection of the right to strike in Australia. In relation to some aspects of this issue the pilots were not successful. The CFA ruled

---

38 Ibid, 37.

39 Ibid, 38.

40 On the role of ILO supervisory bodies, see Chapter 2.

41 These cases may be accessed from the ILO website: <www.ilo.org.>. A number of earlier cases concerning Australia are also available on the website, including *Case No 1324*, *Case No 1371*, *Case No 1345* and *Case No 1415*.

42 *Case No 1511*, above n 28. See KP McEvoy and RJ Owens 'On a Wing and a Prayer: the Pilots' Dispute in International Context' (1993) 6 *AJLL* 1.

43 A more detailed account of this dispute is provided in Chapter 12, pp 547–50. See also KP McEvoy and RJ Owens 'The Flight of Icarus: Legal Aspects of the Pilots' Dispute' (1990) 3 *AJLL* 87.

44 See International Labour Office *Freedom of Association: Digest of Decisions and Principles of the Freedom of Association Committee of the Governing Body of the ILO* (1985), [614]–[615].

that the decision of the pilots to work only the hours between 'nine and five' was not in accordance with national law, and specifically the directions and rulings of the AIRC, and so Australia did not breach *ILO C 87*. The CFA acknowledged that the right to strike might be curtailed where the interruption of services would endanger the life, personal safety, or health of the whole or part of the population.[45] However, it also made it clear that there was a proviso to this, requiring protections to be put in place for any workers who could not defend their own interests through industrial action, including strikes.

Case 1511 was the first case in which the CFA examined the operation of the common law in relation to industrial action in Australia. Perhaps this explains why there was some tentativeness by the CFA in criticising the common law, even though the common law when left to operate unconstrained by statute clearly inhibits the power of workers to press their demands effectively through collective bargaining.[46] However, *Case 1511* resiled from condemning in the strongest terms the fact that the operation of Australian common law left no place for any strike action at all because, as the CFA noted, the case as it had evolved was quite different from a normal strike situation. The CFA, however, drew to the attention of the Committee of Experts on the Application of Conventions and Recommendations (CEACR) its concern over this aspect of the case, and called on the Australian government to do all in its power to see that the damages were not collected from the pilots' union.

In the next Australian case, *Case No 1559* initiated by complaint of the Confederation of Australian Industry, the CFA questioned whether a 1991 amendment to s 189 of the *Industrial Relations Act 1988* (Cth), which required trade unions to have 10 000 members in order to register under the legislation and to access the federal conciliation and arbitration system, breached the principles of freedom of association in *ILO C 87* and *ILO C 98*. This requirement had been put in place by the Commonwealth Parliament in furtherance of a policy to encourage a reduction in the number of trade unions in Australia and thereby also reduce the exposure of business to destructive demarcation disputes where trade unions battled among themselves for coverage in a workplace or an industry. The registration of trade unions under the Act had always been precluded if there was already registered a trade union to which members might 'conveniently belong', but this had not prevented demarcation disputes.

The CFA held the membership requirement in the legislation was a breach of the freedom of association principles, and as a result of *Case No 1559* the Australian Parliament amended its legislation in 1993 to make all trade unions with at least 100 members eligible for registration under the Act. Three years later in 1995, an 'observation' of the CEACR noted with satisfaction this and other changes that had

---

45 The powers of the Australian Industrial Relations Commission to suspend and terminate bargaining periods, and thus remove the immunity for industrial action, now go beyond this: see esp *Workplace Relations Act*, s 430(3)(c)(i)–(ii).

46 For further discussion of the operation of the common law in the pilots' dispute see McEvoy and Owens, above n 43. See also Chapter 12, pp 545–50.

been made by Australia to the legislation with the aim of ensuring compliance with the International Labour Code.[47]

In *Case No 1963* there was a complaint by international and Australian trade unions that the handling of the waterfront dispute involving the Patrick group of companies in 1998 constituted a breach of the principles of freedom of association and collective bargaining.[48] The ILO found that there had been anti-union discrimination against the Maritime Union and its members. The CFA held that although the union had a 'monopoly' position on the waterfront this had been achieved through voluntarism. In deciding this case, the CFA recalled the basic principle that voluntary trade unionism should be respected, and it recommended that the Australian government take action to prevent the training and deployment of replacement personnel when workers were legitimately on strike.[49] The facts of the case did not bring this dispute within the exceptions applicable to essential services, as defined by the ILO.[50] The CFA responded to the argument that individual Australian Workplace Agreements were being used in the dispute to undermine collective bargaining, by calling upon the Australian Government to amend the *Workplace Relations Act* to ensure that it enshrined the principles in the *International Labour Code*, especially *ILO C 98*, Art 4. Finally the CFA requested that it be kept informed by the Australian Government of further developments. However, Australia did not change its law in response to the decision in this case.

In *Case No 1963* part of the complaint made was also that the trade unions had been threatened with legal action by the Australian Competition and Consumer Commission (ACCC) for engaging in secondary boycotts contrary to ss 45D, 45DB and 45E of the *Trade Practices Act 1974* (Cth). The CFA reiterated the view of the ILO that a total prohibition on sympathy action could contribute to the abuse of workers and that sympathy strike action was to be permitted under ILO principles, at least where the primary strike it supported was itself lawful. The CFA thus reinforced earlier critical comments made by the ILO concerning the provisions regarding secondary boycotts in Australian legislation,[51] and it also drew this issue to the attention of the CEACR.

---

47 See *Complaint against the Government of Australia Presented by the Confederation of Australian Industry (CAI) and the International Organisation of Employers (IOE)* Report Nos 281 and 284 of the Committee of Freedom of Association (*Case No 1559*) 1992; and CEACR *Individual Observation Concerning Convention No 87 Freedom of Association and protection of the Right to Organise, 1948 Australia*, 1995.

48 *Complaint against the Government of Australia Presented by the International Confederation of Free Trade Unions (ICFTU), the International Transport Workers' Federation (ITF), the Australian Council of Trade Union (ACTU) and the Maritime Union of Australia (MUA)*, Report No 320 of the Committee of Freedom of Association *(Case No 1963)* 2000. See also J Murray 'Australia in the Dock: The ILO's Decision on the Waterfront Dispute' (2000) 13 *AJLL* 167, and G Biffl and J Isaac 'Globalisation and Core Labour Standards: Compliance Problems with ILO Conventions 87 and 98. Comparing Australia and other English Speaking Countries with EU Member States' (2005) 21 *IJ Comp LL & IR* 405, 424. For an account of the dispute itself see G Orr 'Conspiracy on the Waterfront' (1998) 11 *AJLL* 159, and RC McCallum 'A Priority of Rights: Freedom of Association and the Waterfront Dispute' (1998) 24 *ABL* 207. See also Chapter 12, p 552.

49 See *Digest of Decisions and Principles of the Freedom of Association Committee* 4th (revised) edn 1996, [292].

50 See text accompanying n 45 above.

51 *Case No 1963*, above n 48, [234]–[236]. See also *Digest of Decisions and Principles of the Freedom of Association Committee*, 4th (revised) edn 1996, [486]; and Report of the Committee of Experts, Report III, Part 1A, 1999, 206. For a striking example of the use of the *Trade Practices Act* in relation to industrial action and secondary boycotts, see *AMIEU v Mudginberri Station Pty Ltd* (1987) 74 ALR 7; and for comment see M Pittard 'Trade Practices Law and the Mudginberri Dispute' (1988) 1 *AJLL* 23. See further Chapter 12, pp 553ff.

In *Case No 2326* the CFA dealt with a complaint against the Federal Government by the ACTU and the Trade Unions International of Workers of the Building, Wood and Building Materials Industries in relation to the *Building and Construction Industry Improvement Bill 2003 (2003 BCII Bill)*.[52] The complaints argued that the then proposed legislation interfered with the right to strike by requiring secret ballots to initiate industrial action, by setting mandatory cooling-off periods, by prohibiting industrial action once an agreement was in force even if the agreement did not deal with the matter that was the subject of the industrial action,[53] and by introducing severe penalties for all other industrial action. The complaint also argued that the right to collective bargaining was restricted by the provisions of the proposed *2003 BCII Bill*, which prohibited 'pattern bargaining', made 'project agreements' unenforceable, limited agreements to certain matters and prohibited industrial action in relation to other matters, placed procedural hurdles in the way of negotiating and certifying agreements, gave wide supervisory powers to a Building and Construction Commission, and denied government funding to contractors covered by agreements that did not meet the government's code. However, in the course of hearing the matter the *Bill* lapsed and new legislation was enacted omitting a number of matters that had been the subject of the complaint to the CFA and thus it did not go on to consider them.[54]

However, in considering the remaining matters, the CFA referred back to its criticisms of the *Workplace Relations Act* and the *Trade Practices Act* in *Case No 1963* and criticised the apparent broadening of their effects in relation to the building industry.[55] It criticised in particular the extension of rights to a broader range of parties to sue in relation to industrial action, the extension of civil penalties and criminal penalties to all those who 'aided, abetted, counselled or procured the contravention, induced the contravention by threats or promises or otherwise, were directly or indirectly knowingly concerned in or party to the contravention, or conspired with others to effect the contravention' of the legislation.[56]

In the result, the CFA requested the Australian Government to amend its laws and to keep the ILO informed of relevant developments. In particular, the CFA requested that excessive impediments, penalties and sanctions against industrial action be removed; and that parties themselves be able to determine the level of bargaining (for example, whether at a single workplace or with multiple employers). It also requested a review of, and amendment to the relevant code and guidelines, regulating collective bargaining; a guarantee that the Australian Building and Construction Commissioner could not interfere with the organisation of trade unions; the removal of disproportionate penalties; and that the Government continue to consult with both employer and employee organisations on the development of regulation.

---

52 *Complaint against the Government of Australia Presented by the Australian Council of Trade Unions (ACTU) and Supported by the Trade Unions International of Workers of the Building, Wood and Building Materials Industries* Report No 338 of the Committee on Freedom of Association *(Case No 2326)* 2005.

53 Thus overriding the approach in *Australian Industry Group v Automotive, Food, Metals, Engineering, Printing and Kindred Industries Union* (2003) 130 FCR 524.

54 Similar provisions to those complained of in *Case No 2326* have now been incorporated in the *Workplace Relations Act* through the amendments made by the *Work Choices Act*. See Chapters 11 and 12.

55 See *Case No 2326*, above n 52, [445]–[446].

56 Ibid, [444].

In the majority of the above cases the Australian Government failed to respond in a positive way to the CFA, either ignoring the requests from the CFA or defending its own policies, thus again demonstrating that the effectiveness of the supervisory mechanisms of the international legal order are still mediated by responsiveness and action at the national level.[57]

The CEACR's observations on freedom of association in Australia

Since the *Workplace Relations Act* came into force at the beginning of 1997, several areas of concern have been consistently raised in the individual observations of the ILO's Committee of Experts on the Application of Conventions and Recommendations (CEACR) in relation to Australia's compliance with *ILO C 87* and *ILO C 98*.

One of the primary concerns in the reports of the CEACR on Australia between 1999 and 2006 in relation to *ILO C 87* has related to the restrictions and limitations in the *Workplace Relations Act* on the taking of strike action.[58] In addition to noting that all industrial action is severely restricted by the availability of common law actions, the CEACR has been concerned that industrial action has only enjoyed limited protections under the *Workplace Relations Act*, and has been otherwise controlled through the use of injunction, and the imposition of civil liabilities.[59] The CEACR has commented that the effect of the legislation has been to allow industrial action to be taken only in relation to a quite restricted range of matters, that is, those pertaining to the employment relationship.[60] In addition, there has been a prohibition on secondary boycotts and sympathy action, and the restrictions in relation to demarcation disputes and industrial action where it inflicts 'significant damage to the economy' go beyond the exceptions recognised by the ILO as necessary to protect 'essential services'.[61] The CEACR has also commented on the fact that the *Workplace Relations Act* has prohibited not only payment to workers for periods of industrial action but also industrial action to secure any such payment. While this is not strictly inconsistent with the conventions, the CEACR has observed that to preclude payments uniformly in all cases is inappropriate.[62]

The observations of the CEACR have also highlighted the ongoing concern of the ILO with the restrictions imposed on secondary boycotts by the *Trade Practices Act 1974* (Cth), and with several provisions of the *Crimes Act 1914* (Cth), notably s 30J, which

---

57 See Chapter 2.

58 See CEACR *Individual Observation Concerning Convention No 87, Freedom of Association and Protection of the Right to Organise, 1948 Australia* (1999); CEACR *Individual Observation Concerning Convention No 87, Freedom of Association and Protection of the Right to Organise, 1948 Australia* (2001); CEACR *Individual Observation Concerning Convention No 87, Freedom of Association and Protection of the Right to Organise, 1948 Australia* (2003); CEACR *Individual Observation Concerning Convention No 87, Freedom of Association and Protection of the Right to Organise, 1948 Australia* (2004); and CEACR *Individual Observation Concerning Convention No 87, Freedom of Association and Protection of the Right to Organise, 1948 Australia* (2006).

59 See *Workplace Relations Act*, former ss 127, 170ML, 170MT and 170MU discussed in CEACR *Individual Observation Concerning Convention No 87, Freedom of Association and Protection of the Right to Organise, 1948 Australia* (1999).

60 See *Workplace Relations Act*, former s 170LI restricting agreements to 'matters pertaining' to the employment relationship.

61 See *Workplace Relations Act*, former ss 170MM and 170 MW. In relation to the last point the ILO understands essential services to be those whose interruption 'would endanger the life, personal safety or health of the whole or part of the population': see *Case No 1511*, above n 28.

62 See *Workplace Relations Act*, former s 187AA–187AD. See CEACR *Individual Observation Concerning Convention No 98, Right to Organise and Collective Bargaining, 1949 Australia* (1998).

makes it is an offence to be involved with any industrial action where the Governor-General has issued a proclamation that it is 'a serious industrial disturbance prejudicing or threatening trade or commerce with other countries or among the states', and s 30K, under which it is an offence to obstruct or hinder the performance of services by the Australian Government or the transport of goods or persons in international trade.

There are a number of aspects relating to the regulation of agreement making by the *Workplace Relations Act* prior to the *Workplace Relations Amendment (Work Choices) Act 2005* (Cth) *(Work Choices Act)* that have also been criticised by the CEACR.[63] The clear ILO view is that it should be open to the parties themselves to determine the level at which they engage in collective bargaining. Thus a legislative requirement that bargaining be conducted at the single businesses level, making it virtually impossible to have industry-wide or multi-employer agreements, does not accord with ILO jurisprudence.[64] Furthermore, the provisions of the legislation covering collective agreements made directly with employees and greenfields agreements have been criticised because they either excluded the trade union or did not permit the worker to select the trade union with whom the employer reaches the agreement.[65] The limited scope of matters (that is, only those things pertaining to the employment relationship) able to be addressed in bargains made under the *Workplace Relations Act* has continued to draw adverse comments from the CEACR, as has the lack of any requirement to engage in good faith bargaining.[66]

Above all it has been the emphasis on individual bargaining through individual Australian Workplace Agreements (AWAs) as opposed to collective bargaining that has come in for the most consistent criticism by the CEACR. Associated with the structural support for individualised over collective bargaining under the Act, the CEACR has commented particularly on the vulnerability of workers to discrimination on the basis of membership of a trade union because of the operation of AWAs. Although the *Workplace Relations Act* included some provisions protecting workers against discrimination in relation to freedom of association,[67] the CEACR questioned their adequacy generally but especially at the point of hiring.

In 2005 the CEACR placed significant emphasis on the fact that in *Maritime Union of Australia v Burnie Port Corporation Pty Ltd*[68] the Federal Court held that to offer an AWA as a condition of employment did not amount to duress (and hence discrimination on the basis of membership of a trade union) under the *Workplace Relations Act* because there was no pre-existing relationship between employer and employee. Similarly, the CEACR was also of the view that the decision in *Australian Workers' Union v*

---

63 See CEACR *Individual Observation Concerning Convention No 98, Right to Organise and Collective Bargaining, 1949 Australia* (1998); CEACR *Individual Observation Concerning Convention No 98, Right to Organise and Collective Bargaining, 1949 Australia* (2000); CEACR *Individual Observation Concerning Convention No 98, Right to Organise and Collective Bargaining, 1949 Australia* (2005); and CEACR *Individual Observation Concerning Convention No 98, Right to Organise and Collective Bargaining, 1949 Australia* (2006).

64 See *Workplace Relations Act*, former s 170LC(4).

65 See *Workplace Relations Act*, former ss 170LK and 170LL.

66 Good faith bargaining requirements were removed from the legislation in 1996.

67 See the discussion of the *Workplace Relations Act*, former Pt XA, below pp 474ff.

68 (2000) 101 IR 435. See discussion below, p 478.

BHP Iron-Ore Pty Ltd[69] raised concerns in respect to discrimination on the basis of trade union membership. In that case the Federal Court held that there was no such discrimination where a wage increase was made contingent on employees forfeiting a collective agreement and signing an AWA. In coming to its decision the Court had emphasised that the AWAs were offered to *all* employees, but employees who did not sign were able to continue in employment under the collective agreement. Although no dismissals occurred, the CEACR was of the view that this decision indicated that the legislation was inconsistent with Art 1(2)(b) of *ILO C 98*, which protects against 'acts which "otherwise" prejudice a worker by reason of union membership or because of participation in union activities'. The possibility of employers insisting on AWAs and refusing to bargain collectively with employees through their designated trade union has also been taken by the CEACR as a breach of the right to bargain collectively.

The CEACR has also consistently indicated concern about discriminatory termination of employment on the basis of trade union membership because of limitations and restrictions on access to remedies for dismissal under the *Workplace Relations Act*. It has viewed the protections against dismissal as inadequate, especially in relation to a refusal to sign an AWA, because it has always been possible to exclude by regulation specified classes of employees either based on the terms and conditions relating to their termination or where problems are deemed to be incurred because of 'the particular conditions of employment' or 'the size or nature of the undertaking in which they are employed'.[70] The interaction of the relevant provisions of the *Workplace Relations Act* has been judged by the ILO to carry greater risks to trade union members. The ILO has also asked for information to be provided about the break down of trade union membership amongst various types of employment, given the exclusion of persons engaged on fixed term contracts or for a specific project and those earning more than the remuneration threshold, as well as earlier proposals to exclude the employees of small businesses from access to remedies for termination of employment.[71] Finally, the ILO has also been concerned about potential discrimination against trade unionists who seek multi-business agreements.[72]

In a further series of individual observations and direct requests in 2006 the CEACR continued to request the Australian Government to respond to a range of matters that had previously been brought to its attention. It also enquired about some emerging issues. It noted, for instance, that the right to collective bargaining in the higher education sector was threatened because funding incentives were contingent on the offering of AWAs, and it repeated that parties ought themselves be able to determine the content of their agreements, including whether bargaining fees ought be paid by non-trade

---

69 (2000) 106 FCR 482; and see the discussion below, p 480. See also D Noakes and A Cardell-Ree 'Individual Contracts and the Freedom of Association: *Australian Workers' Union v BHP Iron-Ore Pty Ltd* [2001] FCA 3' (2001) 14 *AJLL* 89; and see generally D Quinn 'To Be or Not To Be a Member—Is That the Only Question? Freedom of Association under the *Workplace Relations Act*' (2004) 17 *AJLL* 1.

70 See *Workplace Relations Act*, former ss 170CC and 170CK(2)(g).

71 See CEACR *Individual Observation Concerning Convention No 98, Right to Organise and Collective Bargaining, 1949 Australia* (1998); CEACR *Individual Observation Concerning Convention No 98, Right to Organise and Collective Bargaining, 1949 Australia* (2000) seeking information about the exclusion of employees of small businesses under the then proposed *Workplace Relations Amendment (Unfair Dismissals) Bill*.

72 See *Workplace Relations Act*, former ss 170LC, 170MU, 170ML, 298K, and 298L.

unionists who took the benefit of union negotiated agreements.[73] However, at the time of the preparation of the CEACR's report for 2006 the amendments introduced by the *Workplace Relations Amendment (Work Choices) Act 2005* (Cth) (*Work Choices Act*) were still in the future and had not been notified to the ILO.

Freedom of association in Australia after *Work Choices*

Few of the concerns that have been expressed by the ILO's supervisory committees in the years leading up to 2006 are likely to have been alleviated by the amendments made by the *Work Choices Act* to the *Workplace Relations Act*. Indeed, in almost all respects the concerns of the ILO are likely now to intensify.[74] The wider issues of bargaining and industrial action are examined in Chapters 11 and 12, but first we turn to the provisions dealing specifically with the protection of freedom of association under the *Workplace Relations Act* following the amendments introduced by the *Work Choices Act*.

A brief historical overview

Evaluating Australia's compliance with the principles of freedom of association in ILO conventions has always been a slightly awkward exercise because of the way in which work was traditionally regulated under the conciliation and arbitration system. That system historically adopted a 'collectivist' approach to the regulation of work. Trade unions always played a key role, and registration under the *Commonwealth Conciliation and Arbitration Act 1904* (Cth) and its successors brought to them a range of benefits. However, the system was predicated on the provision of an alternative to the strike as a means of resolving industrial disputation, rather than recognition of the right to strike.[75]

Only with the enactment of the *Industrial Relations Reform Act 1993* (Cth) did Australia really purport to give effect in a more direct way to the principles of freedom of association in *ILO C 87* and *ILO C 98*. Then for the first time in Australia there was some limited protection, during the period of bargaining for an agreement, for the right to strike. Although the legislation did not otherwise remove common law liability for strikes, it made it more difficult in all instances to take action at common law. Instead parties were required first to make application to the Australian Industrial Relations Commission (AIRC) and only when the matter could not be speedily resolved there was a certificate issued that enabled application to the courts.[76]

The changes made to the legislation in 1996, however, weakened Australia's compliance with its international obligations under *ILO C 87* and *ILO C 98*. The enactment of the *Workplace Relations and Other Legislation Amendment Act 1996* (Cth) meant

---

73 See CEACR *Individual Observation Concerning Convention No 98, Right to Organise and Collective Bargaining, 1949 Australia* (2006); CEACR *Individual Observation Concerning Convention No 87, Freedom of Association and Protection of the Right to Organise, 1948 Australia* (2006); CEACR *Individual Direct Request Concerning Convention No 98, Right to Organise and Collective Bargaining, 1949 Australia* (2006); and CEACR *Individual Direct Request Concerning Convention No 98, Right to Organise and Collective Bargaining, 1949 Australia* (2006).

74 See C Fenwick and I Landau 'Work Choices in International Perspective' (2006) 19 *AJLL* 127.

75 See Chapter 3, pp 81ff.

76 On the 1993 changes see G McCarry 'Sanctions and Industrial Action: The Impact of the *Industrial Relations Reform Act* (1994) 7 *AJLL* 198.

that many of the practices that had previously supported trade union security began to be undermined.[77] However, the greatest impact on freedom of association under the 1996 laws came from the redirection of the regulatory system away from collective work relations and towards a greater emphasis on individualism, especially through the introduction of individual AWAs.[78] The *Workplace Relations Amendment (Work Choices) Act 2005* (Cth) has continued down this track.[79] The 1996 legislative changes were also quite explicit in providing protection only for an individualised conception of freedom of association, and the *Work Choices Act* also continues this development.

Now freedom of association as an individual right is expressly protected in the *Workplace Relations Act 1996* (Cth), Pt 16, which contains elaborate provisions making unlawful certain conduct by various labour market participants. This Part was originally introduced into the Act in 1996 as Pt XA, at the same time as amendments outlawing preference clauses and 'closed shop' arrangements (that is, arrangements whereby an employer agreed to employ only union members).[80] Given that Pt XA was introduced among a range of measures designed to reduce the power of trade unions in Australian workplaces, it is fair to say that Pt XA was intended to support a new freedom *not* to associate.

Part XA replaced former ss 334, 335 and 336 of the *Industrial Relations Act 1988* (Cth). These earlier provisions prohibited conduct of employers intending to harm employees and potential recruits because of their involvement with trade unions as members or organisers. Some balance was provided by former s 320, which allowed for, and protected, 'conscientious objection' to trade union membership. On the whole, the form of protection for freedom of association in the 1988 legislation had guarded employees' rights to join together and act collectively. The new Pt XA, however, configured the right as an individual freedom, to join or not to join a union: it provided, as Gray J observed, for a 'counterpart freedom' or one which 'in metaphorical terms ... assumed that freedom to join and freedom not to join are two sides of the one coin'.[81] The objects of Pt XA expressed an intention to protect the freedom of association of employees, employers and independent contractors. Like other aspects of the *Workplace Relations Act*, its validity was anchored to the corporations power in s 51(xx) of the *Australian Constitution*, not to the external affairs power in s 51(xxix). The post-1996, Australian version of freedom of association was not the conception enshrined in ILO instruments.

Part XA became Pt 16 of the *Workplace Relations Act* following the renumbering of the Act by the *Workplace Relations Amendment (Work Choices) Act 2005*. *Work Choices*

---

77 See P Weeks *Trade Union Security Law: A Study of Preference and Compulsory Unionism* (1995) for an examination of the relevant law and practice prior to 1996. See also R Naughton 'Sailing into Unchartered Seas: The Role of Unions under the Workplace Relations Act' (1997) *AJLL* 112.

78 For a discussion of these developments see B Creighton 'The Workplace Relations Act in International Perspective' (1997) 10 *AJLL* 31, 43-49; and A Coulthard 'The De-collectivisation of Australian Industrial Relations: Trade Union Exclusion under the *Workplace Relations Act 1996* (Cth)' in S Deery and R Mitchell (eds) *Employment Relations: Individualisation and Union Exclusion* (1999). See generally, Chapter 3.

79 The impact of the *Work Choices Act* on bargaining and industrial action is discussed in Chapters 11 and 12.

80 The *Workplace Relations and Other Legislation Amendment Act 1996* (Cth) repealed former s 122 allowing for preference clauses in awards, and s 170RA(2) allowing for preference clauses in enterprise agreements, and amended s 94, to prevent the AIRC from including in any award a provision which would infringe Pt XA. For the earlier history, see Weeks, above n 77.

81 *Employment Advocate v Williamson* (2000) 111 FCR 20, 26.

also introduced some subtle but important amendments to the provisions. Part 16 contains almost the only provisions in the Act that are also applicable to independent contractors as well as employees. The current form of the legislation is best understood by first explaining the shape of the original Pt XA provisions, and some of the more significant judicial decisions on those provisions. Many of the *Work Choices* amendments appear to have been made in response to these earlier decisions of which the government disapproved.

The 1996 provisions

The main work of the former Pt XA was done by former ss 298K and 298L. These provisions set out that certain conduct (listed in s 298K) was prohibited if done for a reason that included a prohibited reason (listed in s 298L). Section 298K applied particularly to conduct by employers; however, additional provisions in ss 298N–298S applied to conduct by employees and by industrial associations.

Section 298M prohibited an employer from inducing employees or independent contractors to stop participating in unions. Trade unions attempted to rely on this provision in a number of cases—notably litigation surrounding the restructuring of working arrangements at BHP mines in the Pilbara region.[82] As is explained below, the testing of former s 298M revealed very weak protection for collective union activity under these 1996 freedom of association laws.

A number of other provisions supported the essential framework of prohibitions. One of the most important was former s 298V, which provided for a reversed onus of proof so that the burden would fall on any person defending an allegation of breach of these provisions to prove that they did not engage in prohibited conduct for a prohibited reason. A reversed onus of proof still exists in s 809.

Policing of the new laws was left in the hands of the Employment Advocate. The Federal Court of Australia was given jurisdiction to hear applications concerning breaches of the provisions and was empowered with a range of remedies.

Prohibited conduct by employers

According to former s 298K(1) an employer could not do or threaten to do any of the following in respect of an employee or potential employee:
- dismiss an employee;
- injure an employee in his or her employment;
- alter the position of an employee to the employee's prejudice;
- refuse to employ another person as an employee; or
- discriminate against another person in the terms or conditions on which the employer offers to employ the other person as an employee.

These prohibitions are now contained in s 792(1).

According to former s 298K(2) a person engaging workers under contracts for services (so-called independent contracts) could not do or threaten to do the following, if it was for, or included, a reason prohibited by s 298L:

---

82 See *Australian Workers' Union v BHP Iron Ore Pty Ltd* (2000) 96 IR 422 (interlocutory injunction granted by Gray J); (2000) 102 FCR 97 (appeal to Full Court of the Federal Court); and (2001) 106 FCR 482 (final determination by Kenny J).

- terminate a contract for services that he or she had entered into with an independent contractor;
- injure the independent contractor in relation to the terms and conditions of the contract for services;
- alter the position of the independent contractor to the independent contractor's prejudice;
- refuse to engage another person as an independent contractor; or
- discriminate against another person in the terms or conditions on which the person offers to engage the other person as an independent contractor.

These prohibitions are now contained in s 792(5).

Prohibited reasons

A long list of reasons was prohibited under s 298L. In summary, they included:

- The person was or proposed to become a member or official of an industrial association.
- The person was not or did not propose to become a member or official of an industrial association.
- The person (if an independent contractor) engaged non-union employees, or refused to pay dues to an industrial association.
- The person has refused to join in industrial action.
- The person, if an employee, has refused to consent to or vote in favour of a union collective agreement.
- The person has proposed or participated in a secret ballot about an industrial matter.
- The person is entitled to the benefit of an industrial instrument or order of an industrial body. (This was former s 298L(1)(h).)
- The person made or proposed to make a complaint, take proceedings, or give evidence in proceedings, under an industrial law.
- The person—being a member of an industrial association seeking better industrial conditions—is dissatisfied with his or her conditions.
- The person was absent from work to perform duties as an officer of an industrial association, in circumstances where leave was requested but unreasonably refused.

These prohibited reasons are now reflected in s 793. It was not necessary in relation to either former s 298K(1) or former s 298K(2) to show that a prohibited reason was the sole or even the dominant reason for the prohibited conduct.

Illustrations of breach

Case law preceding the enactment of these provisions gave a wide meaning to the notion of an injury in employment. In *Squires v Flight Stewards Association of Australia*,[83] for example, Ellicott J held that an employee who had been stood down on full pay had been injured in his employment, despite suffering no immediate financial detriment.

---

83 (1982) 2 IR 155.

A number of cases testing s 298K(1)(d)—refusal to employ a person—struggled with the question of whether an employer could defend such an allegation merely by showing that there was no longer any vacancy to be filled.[84] For example, could an employer with two vacancies to fill and a choice of three candidates deliberately avoid choosing one of the candidates because he or she was a union activist? Once the two jobs were filled with the other two candidates, could the employer escape liability by proving the absence of a further vacancy? *Burnie Port Corporation Pty Ltd v Maritime Union of Australia* held not.[85] *Australasian Meat Industry Employees' Union v Belandra Pty Ltd.*[86] confirmed that an employer could not escape liability merely by manipulating a situation where no vacancies for employees existed.

The *Belandra* case provides an illuminating example of the way in which former ss 298K and 298L operated as a control on employers' ability to manipulate their obligations to deal with trade unions and comply with collective workplace agreements. The facts of the case—especially in respect of the corporate structures involved—were complicated. One particular man with long experience in the cattle industry—who called himself Joseph Catalfamo—owned and controlled (either directly or as a de facto director) a number of related companies in the business of slaughtering cattle to supply beef to Coles Supermarkets Australia Pty Ltd. Initially, the various abattoirs in the group employed staff directly according to certified agreements made with trade unions under the former s 170LJ of the *Workplace Relations Act*.

After a fire destroyed one of the abattoirs, staff employed by that company in the group were dismissed, on the basis that there was no work for them. However, they were not paid any severance pay according to the redundancy provisions in their certified agreement, because they were told that there was an intention to set up again and rehire them. This occurred in June 2001. By March 2002, however, Mr Catalfamo had changed his mind, and decided to restructure the businesses in a way that would not involve the direct employment of any staff. The former employees were paid their severance entitlements. Many of them did, however, find that they were offered work doing the same jobs, slaughtering meat in Belandra-owned abattoirs, under the same management as before and for the purpose of supplying the same major buyer. However they were offered these jobs as labour-hire employees, and they were employed on individual AWAs.[87] Their trade union brought an action under former s 298K complaining that they had been dismissed and/or injured in their employment, and they had been refused employment, because they were trade union members and were entitled to the benefit of a particular industrial instrument.

Belandra sought to defend its conduct as a legitimate corporate restructuring. Mr Catalfamo argued that following the big fire his group of related companies faced potential insolvency and needed to be reorganised. He decided to stick with the 'core' business of purchasing cattle and owning abattoirs, and so acquired another abattoirs

---

84 See eg *CFMEU v BHP Steel (AIS)* [2000] FCA 1008, and *Burnie Port Corporation Pty Ltd v Maritime Union of Australia* (2000) 104 FCR 440.

85 Ibid.

86 (2003) 126 IR 165, 185.

87 AWAs and other forms of statutory workplace agreements are explained in Chapter 11.

site. Rather than engage directly in the business of slaughtering beasts itself, however, this cattle- and land-owning company contracted with a management company to operate the abattoirs. A man who had formerly been engaged as the site manager of the burned premises was invited to set up his own company, which would then contract with the land-owning company to slaughter the cattle. This new operations company employed supervisory staff directly, but decided to engage all production staff through a separate labour-hire company. The labour-hire company engaged former Belandra process workers on AWAs.

Belandra tried to avoid liability on the basis that it was not an employer at all any more, that it had no vacancies, and that its reasons for its strategy were business survival. It failed to persuade the Federal Court on any of these arguments. As is explained below, former s 298V provided for a reversed onus of proof. Mr Catalfamo bore the burden of proving that the prohibited reasons were not among the reasons motivating the strategy. The Court relied on the reversed onus of proof, and also on the fact that the legislation required that a prohibited reason need only be one of many reasons, and not the 'sole or dominant reason' for conduct.[88]

The *Belandra* decision also provided a very useful analysis of 'International law and the law of other jurisdictions' in respect of freedom of association in the course of analysing Parliament's intentions as to the appropriate interpretation and application of former ss 298K and 298L.[89] Justice North clearly took the view that international law instruments were a relevant context for understanding the Australian provisions.

Prohibitions for industrial associations

Former s 298P prohibited industrial associations (which can be associations of employees, independent contractors or employers) or their officers or members from taking or threatening to take any industrial action against an employer because the employer was a member or officer of an industrial association. This provision also prohibited any form of coercion to press an employer to join or resign membership of such an organisation. Former s 298Q similarly prohibited industrial associations from coercing employees to join or to participate in trade union activities; former s 298R concerned industrial associations' conduct towards their own members; and former s 298S dealt with industrial associations' conduct in respect of independent contractors. In essence, all of these provisions supported a protection for all workers and those who engaged them from any kind of coercive pressure in relation to their decisions about participation in collective industrial activity.

Protection for trade unions?

Former s 298M provided that 'an employer, or a person who has engaged an independent contractor, must not (whether by threats or promises or otherwise) induce an employee, or the independent contractor … to stop being an officer or member of an industrial association'. This provision has been replaced by s 794, which adds a prohibition on

---

88 (2003) 126 IR 165, 227.
89 Ibid, 208–26.

inducing an employee or independent contractor (by threats, promises or otherwise) to become or remain a member or officer of an industrial association.

The implications of former s 298M were tested in *Australian Workers' Union v BHP Iron Ore Pty Ltd*,[90] a case arising out of BHP's strategy to use individual workplace agreements to manage labour costs in its Western Australian mining operations.

Some time in 1999, BHP began investigating a potential takeover of another mining company, and in the course of its due diligence enquiries discovered that the target company enjoyed lower labour costs, principally because it engaged staff on individual workplace agreements made under the prevailing Western Australian industrial legislation. The takeover never proceeded. However, following these investigations, BHP adopted an industrial strategy whereby it refused to negotiate a new collective enterprise agreement with the trade unions representing the industrial interests of its workforce, and instead offered various incentives to individual employees to sign up to individual workplace agreements. One of the more generous incentives was an opportunity to cash out accrued sick leave entitlements. For a long-serving employee who had enjoyed good health, this represented an offer of several thousands of dollars.

Several trade unions joined together in an application for an injunction to stop BHP from continuing with this strategy, on the basis that BHP's conduct breached both s 298K and s 298M. (There were also other claims, not directly relevant to the freedom of association concerns.)

The s 298K claim was based on the argument that the employees who opted to remain on collective bargains were being discriminated against, because they were not granted the increased pay and incentives. Justice Gray, hearing the initial application for an injunction, held that there was a serious question to be tried on this point;[91] however, his decision on this issue was overturned on appeal to a full bench.[92] The Full Court of the Federal Court determined that there was no breach of s 298K, because all employees were offered the option of the individual agreements.

Justice Gray had also accepted that there was a serious question to be tried that BHP had breached s 298M. By the time of the hearing before Gray J, some 40 per cent of BHP employees had accepted the individual agreement offer and resigned their trade union membership. This provided sufficient evidence (particularly for the purposes of an interim injunction) that BHP had induced those employees to resign their membership of the trade union, not by threats or promises, but 'otherwise'. This aspect of the decision was upheld on appeal to the Full Court of the Federal Court.[93]

In the course of these interlocutory hearings, the Federal Court expressed a view, consistent with an earlier decision in *Davids Distribution Pty Ltd v National Union of Workers*,[94] that the *Workplace Relations Act* (as it stood then, in 2000) continued to maintain a central role for trade union collective bargaining, so the freedom of association

90 (2001) 106 FCR 482.
91 (2000) 96 IR 422.
92 (2000) 102 FCR 97.
93 Ibid, 121.
94 (1999) 91 FCR 463.

provisions should be interpreted in the light of a commitment to maintain the survival of trade unions. Citing some decisions from the USA,[95] and the *Davids Distribution* case,[96] the Full Court of the Federal Court held that what is protected by freedom of association laws is 'the right to participate in protected union activities, including the taking of collective industrial action against an employer to seek to obtain better industrial conditions'.[97] Strategies designed to undermine trade union presence in a workplace so as to defeat collective bargaining were therefore arguably in breach of s 298M.

At the final hearing of these issues, however, Kenny J held that BHP had not breached any of the freedom of association provisions.[98] Justice Kenny held that BHP was motivated by legitimate business concerns and had not undertaken the strategy for the purpose of causing employees to resign their union membership. The employer had an entitlement under the legislation to choose to use individual agreements, and was under no obligation to engage in collective bargaining. Justice Kenny rejected arguments that the refusal to bargain collectively breached s 298M. She held that the role of a trade union at a workplace where the employer exercised its prerogative to refuse to bargain collectively 'may well differ', but the trade union could still maintain a role in other activities, for example, in representing employees in grievances. This decision makes clear that the freedom of association rights in Australian federal law from 1996 to 2005 did not support a *right* to collective bargaining. If anything, the *Work Choices* amendments, which came into effect in March 2006, have cemented this view.

Reversed onus of proof

As the *Belandra* and *BHP* cases—and a number of other interlocutory applications—demonstrated, the reversed onus of proof in these matters can be very influential in determining the outcome of a case. Although the trade unions in the BHP litigation ultimately lost their case, they gained an extra year of time in which to broker an industrial solution to the problem with the employer.

A number of high profile cases alleging breach of the freedom of association provisions have been effectively determined at the interlocutory stage. For example, the waterfront dispute,[99] which concerned allegations that the employer and other parties had conspired to injure the maritime employees in their employment because they were members of the Maritime Union of Australia, was effectively resolved by industrial negotiation following the grant of an injunction largely favouring the union's cause. The legal issues were never ultimately determined in a full trial. The High Court decision that put an end to a string of court skirmishes over this matter concerned the validity of an order for an interim injunction. The most that can be said about this case is that the High Court held that there was a serious question to be tried that the employer parties in this case had conspired to breach former s 298K. Given the reversed onus

95 *American Ship Building Company v National Labor Relations Board* 85 S Ct 955, 965 (1965); and *National Labor Relations Board v Brown* 85 S Ct 980 (1965).
96 (1999) 91 FCR 463, 500.
97 (2001) 102 FCR 97, 118-19.
98 (2001) 106 FCR 482, 543.
99 *Patrick Stevedores Operations No 2 Pty Ltd v Maritime Union of Australia* (1998) 195 CLR 1.

of proof under former s 298V, the case demonstrates no more than that the employer parties were not able to establish that there was *not* a serious question to be tried.

A reversed onus of proof is very valuable to a plaintiff when the matters in question concern matters that are only within the knowledge of the defendant. The defendant's motives and state of mind are naturally such matters, so it makes eminent sense to leave the defendant with the burden of establishing their own motives. A reversed onus of proof applies also in the case of allegations of unlawful dismissal for discriminatory reasons under s 659: see s 664. A consequence of a reversed onus of proof is that a 'tied result' falls to the plaintiff. If the court does not know whom to believe, then the defendant has not met the burden of proof and loses the case.

In the case of interlocutory injunctions the court's task is to determine whether there is a serious question to be tried, and where the balance of convenience lies. This second consideration requires the court to consider the harm that may flow from granting, and also from refusing, the injunction.

The party winning its argument in such a case generally enjoys a tactical advantage in the negotiations that frequently follow applications for interim injunctions. Industrial problems are often too urgent to loiter in court lists. Both sides need to negotiate a solution to keep a business running and workers in gainful employment. If a trade union wins an injunction stopping an employer from continuing on a particular path—as it did in the *BHP Case*—then it may have won a considerable negotiating advantage.

Following the *Work Choices* amendments, the reversed onus of proof in s 809 will not apply in the case of applications for interim injunctions. Arguably a number of interim applications heard under the former rules may have been decided differently without the reversed onus of proof. The practical consequences of such a change may be to tilt the playing field somewhat in the negotiations that inevitably pursue an interim injunction hearing.

Remedies

The Federal Court was empowered under former s 298U to grant a range of remedies for contravention of Pt XA, including pecuniary penalties of up to $10 000 for bodies corporate and $2000 for individuals; orders of reinstatement or re-engagement; compensation orders; injunctions including interim injunctions; and any other order that the court deemed necessary to stop the conduct or remedy its effects.

Section 298X specifically provided that contravention of Pt XA was not an offence, and so attracted no criminal sanctions. From a regulatory point of view, civil penalties are often deemed a more effective means of controlling market behaviour than criminal sanctions. Although criminal penalties appear to be more serious, imposition of a criminal sanction requires proof of an offence 'beyond reasonable doubt' and according to strict rules of evidence. Prior to the 1996 changes, when breaches of freedom of association laws were criminal offences, successful prosecutions were rare. Civil penalties, however, require proof on the lesser civil standard—on the balance of probabilities. Cases are easier to prove and penalties more frequently imposed; hence the sanctions are arguably more effective. Similar regulatory strategies have been adopted in Australian corporations and trade practices regulation, where the prime objective of regulation is inducing compliance with the law.

Freedom of association after Work Choices

The *Work Choices* legislation re-enacted Pt XA as a new Pt 16 in essentially the same form, though with some subtle but important modifications. The inclusion of additional statements in the 'objects' section, indicating that the legislation is intended to provide effective relief when breached and remedies that penalise and deter, signals a further tightening in the laws: see s 778(c)–(d).

The *Work Choices Act* inserted new general provisions in the *Workplace Relations Act* that prohibit 'a person' engaging or threatening to engage in action aimed at coercing the other person or a third person to join or not join an industrial association, or to remain or cease to be in such an organisation: s 789. Making false or misleading statements about another's obligations to be an officer or a member of an industrial association, or their need to disclose their status as such, or their obligations regarding membership or non-membership in order to benefit from an industrial instrument is also prohibited: s 789. Industrial action relating to membership of an organisation is also prohibited: s 791.

Other changes in the legislation include some small but significant changes to the prohibited reasons, no reversed onus of proof for interim injunctions, elaboration of the provisions dealing with industrial associations and their conduct towards other labour market participants, some new prohibitions on false and misleading statements and boycott-like conduct, and changes to the remedies available for employees.

When the prohibited reason involves entitlement to an industrial instrument

The backbone provision setting out prohibited conduct by employers is now s 792, and in substance this generally mirrors former s 298K. Likewise, s 793 containing the prohibited reasons follows the wording of former s 298L. There are a number of relatively small, but not unimportant changes to this pair of provisions. The legislation now makes clear that a prohibited reason covers not only the situation where a person 'proposes to become' a member of an industrial organisation but also where a cessation of membership is planned: s 793(1)(b).[100] The reference to an industrial entitlement is updated to also refer to the Australian Fair Pay and Conditions Standard as well as to other industrial instruments: s 793(1)(i).

Another change to what is now s 792 is that a new subsection now provides that a person does not refuse to engage another if they do not intend to engage someone: see s 792(7). This amendment purports to overcome the interpretation by North J of the former provision in the *Belandra* case, because there the employer did not intend to employ anyone at the time.[101]

---

100 In *Construction, Forestry, Mining and Energy Union v Hamburger* (2003) 127 FCR 309 comments were made regarding the absence of the latter words in the former provisions.

101 See JHC Colvin, G Watson, and N Ogilvie *An Introduction to the Industrial Relations Reforms* (2006), 111, n 13.

Another important change concerns the interaction between ss 792(1), 792(5) and 793(1)(i) (formerly s 298L(1)(h)). According to s 792(4) and 792(8), if the reason for any prohibited conduct is that the employee or independent contractor is entitled to the benefit of a particular industrial instrument then this must be not merely one reason, but the 'sole or dominant' reason for the conduct.[102] This amendment is explained as a legislative response to some case law on the former provisions.

A number of actions brought by employees under the former provisions arose in the context of business restructuring. The *Belandra* case described above was one of them. Where an employer's plans to restructure operations were motivated by reasons that included a desire to save on labour costs by utilising different forms of engagements, or new industrial instruments, it was open to trade unions to argue that the employer had breached the freedom of association provisions by injuring employees in their employment for reasons that included the employees' entitlement to the benefit of certain industrial instruments.

A contentious example of such a case was *Greater Dandenong City Council v Australian Municipal Clerical and Services Union*.[103] The case concerned a local government's decision to outsource its community care services. Its principal reason for deciding to outsource these services to a private provider (rather than continue to engage its own employees to undertake the services) was budgetary pressure. It called for tenders, and a consortium of former employees lodged a tender for the work. The employees' tender, however, was priced on the basis that the employees would continue to enjoy their existing pay and conditions under an industrial instrument. The council selected the least expensive tender offer—from an organisation called Silver Circle, whose lower price was based on lower labour costs. The successful tenderer subsequently offered employment to the former employees.

Madgwick J at first instance[104] held that the council had breached the freedom of association provisions because it had discriminated against the employees on the basis that they were entitled to the benefit of pay and conditions set by a particular industrial instrument. The council appealed Madgwick J's decision to a Full Court of the Federal Court, but the appeal was dismissed in circumstances that demonstrated the significance of two aspects of the former provisions—the requirement that the prohibited reason be only one of a number of reasons motivating conduct, and the reversed onus of proof under s 298V. The Full Court of the Federal Court dismissed the appeal by a two-to-one majority.

The judgment of Merkel J was most illuminating. He held that the council had been motivated by an obligation—brought about by external pressures—to follow a competitive tendering process in making its decision on outsourcing these services. Nevertheless, the council had not met the burden of proving that the employees' entitlement to certain industrial benefits was not among the many reasons motivating

---

102 Although *Workplace Relations Act*, s 792(5) and (8) refers to the protection of independent contractors, such protection is largely irrelevant because they cannot be entitled to the benefit of an industrial instrument or the AFPCS as is relevantly required by s 793(1)(i).

103 (2001) 112 FCR 232.

104 (2000) 101 IR 143.

the council's decision. Arguably, Merkel J may have allowed the appeal (or indeed, Madgwick J may have refused the initial application) if the council only needed to demonstrate that the employees' entitlement to the benefits of an industrial instrument were not the sole or dominant reason for its decision to accept the cheaper tender.

Thus, this small but important amendment by the *Work Choices* legislation will ensure that the freedom of association laws do not present an impediment to business restructuring where the motivation for reorganisation can be described as general economic efficiency. It should be remembered, however, that the requirement under s 792(8) that the prohibited reason be the 'sole or dominant' reason for prohibited conduct applies only to claims based on s 793(1)(i), that the employee had the benefit of an industrial instrument. It does not apply if the complaint concerns an allegation that the reason for harming the employee was the employee's participation in a trade union.

A number of claims have been brought under the freedom of association provisions on this ground.[105] But not all such claims have succeeded. For example, in *National Union of Workers v Qenos Pty Ltd*,[106] a trade union failed to establish that a 'fill and spill' strategy (whereby an employer makes all positions vacant, and requires employees to apply again for their jobs) was not motivated by prohibited reasons, even though the practical effect of this strategy was to terminate the employment of a number of trade union activists.

Reversed onus of proof and interim injunctions

Section 809 provides that where any application is made under s 807 for a breach of Pt 16, and there is an allegation that conduct was carried out for a particular reason or with particular intent, then it is to be presumed that the conduct was carried out for that reason unless the respondent proves otherwise. This provision therefore shifts the onus of proof to the person whose state of mind is under scrutiny. Section 809(1) restates former s 298V; however, s 809(2) provides that the reversed onus of proof does not apply to any application for an interim injunction. Cases such as *Australian Workers' Union v BHP Iron Ore Pty Ltd*,[107] which may have turned on the burden of proof, are therefore likely to be decided differently after *Work Choices*.

The conduct of industrial associations

The prohibitions on activities of industrial associations in former ss 298P–298S are now spelled out more fully in ss 796–802, in ways that capture a wide range of industrial relationships. Some of the elaborations of these provisions made by the *Work Choices* amendments are explained by the findings in earlier cases. For example, in *Australian Building Construction Employees and Builders' Labourers' Federation v Employment Advocate*,[108] the Full Court of the Federal Court unanimously dismissed an appeal by

---

105 See eg *Communications, Electrical, Electronic, Energy, Information, Postal, Plumbing and Allied Services Union of Australia v ACI Operations Pty Ltd* (2005) 147 IR 315.
106 (2001) 108 FCR 90.
107 See above ns 91–92.
108 (2001) 114 FCR 22.

the Employment Advocate[109] against a decision finding that some union officials who tried to persuade some sub-contractors on a building site to join the trade union to avoid trouble had not breached former s 298S.

The problem with this case was that the wording of former s 298S required that the person against whom industrial action was taken or threatened must be an employer. In this case, all of the relationships at the building site were independent contracts. The words of the Court, indicating that Parliament had clearly 'placed limits on the scope of several subsections of the Act', were clearly heeded by the legislative drafters of the *Work Choices* amendments. It would appear that the new s 799(2)(b) would now catch the particular conduct complained of in this case.

New prohibitions on false and misleading statements

A new s 805 makes it unlawful to make false or misleading representations about a person's obligations to pay bargaining fees, or join industrial associations. This provision is likely to be the legacy of *Employment Advocate v Williamson*,[110] a case in which the Employment Advocate failed to secure an order against a union official who wore a hat bearing a sticker with the words 'no ticket—no start' when he was talking to contractors at a building site.[111] The *Explanatory Memorandum* to the *Work Choices Bill* explained the new s 805 in the following terms: 'An example of a false or misleading statement about membership would be a representation that describes a building site as a 'no ticket no start' site or a union site in a way that suggests or implies that a person must be a member of an organisation to enter or work on that site.'[112]

Boycott-like conduct

Section 804, headed 'Discrimination against employer in relation to industrial instruments', was introduced into the legislation by the *Work Choices* amendments. It is drafted in terms of 'first persons' discriminating against 'second persons' on the basis that the second person does or does not engage employees on certain industrial instruments. The language is reminiscent of the secondary boycott provisions in ss 45D and 45E of the *Trade Practices Act 1974* (Cth).

The *Explanatory Memorandum* to the *Work Choices* legislation explained that this section 'would only apply to discrimination on the basis of the particular type of industrial instrument (for instance, that the instrument is an AWA or a collective agreement) or who the agreement is made with, rather than anything contained in the agreement'.[113] Section 804 would catch conduct by a head contractor who refused to engage a subcontractor because the subcontractor's employees were covered, say, by a collective agreement to which an organisation was not a party or by an AWA.

---

109 See *Hamberger v Construction, Forestry, Mining and Energy Union* (2000) 104 IR 45.

110 (2001) 111 FCR 20.

111 In this case a majority of the Full Court of the Federal Court held that some of the evidence was inadmissible, because conversations with the trade union shop steward had been secretly taped without his knowledge, and a confrontation had been contrived in order to incite a response from him.

112 *House of Representatives Workplace Relations Amendment (Work Choices) Bill 2005, Explanatory Memorandum*, 383.

113 Ibid, 388.

On its face, s 804 appears to be wide enough to prohibit any kind of boycott of a particular business on the basis of the boycotter's disapproval of the business' work practices. For example, campaigns by trade unions in some industries to encourage the end users of goods and services to insist that their suppliers meet certain labour standards, would appear to be caught by this prohibition on 'discrimination' against a person on the grounds that they do or do not engage staff on a particular kind of industrial instrument. If, for example, a department store refused to stock clothing unless the supplier could guarantee that all employees engaged in making the clothing were paid according to a particular award or collective agreement, then it would appear that the department store may have infringed s 804. Similarly, a construction company employer who chose to engage its own staff on trade union collective agreements would not be free to select only sub-contractors who also engaged staff on similar union collective agreements.[114] Section 804, on its face, appears to restrict citizen's liberties to choose with whom they will do business, if their choices are influenced by their own ethical standards and values in respect of decent working conditions for others.

Protected industrial action (explained in Chapter 12) is exempted from this prohibition, so a person may discriminate on these grounds if they do so in the context of taking legitimate industrial action during the course of a properly notified bargaining period for a collective workplace agreement.

Objectionable provisions

Sections 810–812 provide that any provision in an industrial instrument, including an award or any kind of workplace agreement, or in any other written or unwritten agreement or arrangement requiring or permitting any infringement of the freedom of association provisions, is void, and therefore unenforceable. The inclusion of 'written or unwritten agreements or arrangements' means that any common law agreements, including those made orally and informally, that would support a 'no ticket no job' policy at a work site would be void. The definition of 'objectionable provisions' has been further elaborated by the *Work Choices* amendments, to make clear that it also comprehends any provisions in industrial instruments or other agreements that, directly or indirectly, require either encouragement or discouragement of, or support for or opposition to, trade union membership, as well as provisions for bargaining services fees and clauses contrary to Pt 16: see s 810 (1)(c)–(d). An agreement that an employer 'first consult' unemployed union members who are suitably qualified when employing labour would, under these new provisions, be likely to be void,[115] as certainly would any agreement that requires an employer to distribute membership forms for a particular trade union to new employees and encourage their membership of a trade union.[116]

---

114 See *Employment Advocate v Barclay Mowlam Construction Limited* (2005) 139 IR 237 involving a breach of *Workplace Relations Act*, former s 298K(2)(d) for refusing to use an independent contractor whose employees were not members of a union and who had AWAs.

115 Cf *Office of the Employment Advocate v Construction, Forestry, Mining and Energy Union* (2003) 126 IR 468, where such a clause was held to be only 'procedural' in character, governing the order in which potential workers were contacted. Such provisions would also now infringe the new prohibitions on preference clauses in workplace agreements.

116 Cf *McDonald's Australia Ltd v Shop Distributive and Allied Employees Association* (2004) 132 IR 165.

The expansion of the 'objectionable provisions' arrangements under this Part of the Act, thus complements the new prohibitions on any clauses in workplace agreements that might provide support for trade union membership.[117]

Remedies

Section 807 provides that the Federal Court or now also the Federal Magistrates Court can make a range of orders in relation to a person who has contravened Pt 16. These include an order to pay a pecuniary penalty, to pay compensation to any person who suffered damage as a result of the contravention, and 'any other order that the court considers appropriate'. The maximum pecuniary penalties are up to 300 penalty units for bodies corporate and 60 penalty units for individuals.

The 'other orders' allowed under s 807(1)(c) include injunctions, and 'any other orders that the court considers necessary to stop the conduct or remedy its effects'. While there is no longer any specific mention of reinstatement or re-engagement of a worker (as was the case under former s 298U), these 'other orders' arguably offer the potential for such an order, if a court were persuaded reinstatement was the most appropriate way to remedy the effects of a dismissal that infringed s 792. Likewise damages could also be ordered to be paid to an injured party.

Whereas under the 1996 provisions the Employment Advocate bore the burden of policing freedom of association contraventions, under the 2006 amendments, the Workplace Inspectorate undertakes this task. Applications alleging breach can be brought by a workplace inspector; any person affected by the contravention; or any person prescribed by the regulations: s 807.[118]

The role of workplace inspectors expanded considerably following the *Work Choices* amendments, just as the role of trade unions in policing workplace laws was constricted, particularly by amendments to the trade unions' former rights of entry to workplaces. Since union rights of entry have historically supported a role for worker collectives in supervising compliance with industrial and occupational health and safety laws, awards and agreements, it is appropriate to recognise (albeit briefly) the role of those rights here.

Union rights of entry

On one view, affording employee representatives a role in inspecting compliance with workplace laws and industrial instruments is the pinnacle of a privatisation of regulation. The direct stakeholders in the system of regulation take a role and bear the expense of policing compliance with standards. Nevertheless, the *Work Choices Act*, consistently with its general preference for reduced trade union involvement at workplaces, has instituted greater reliance on a centralised taxpayer-funded bureaucracy to undertake inspections for compliance. These provisions appear also to be motivated by a desire to overcome the inconvenient and unwanted consequences of a number of earlier decisions in the Federal Court and the Australian Industrial Relations Commission.

---

117 See *Workplace Relations Regulations 2006* (Cth), rr 8.5(1)(a)–(g), (2) and (7). See further Chapter 11.
118 No regulations had been tabled at the time of writing.

Once upon a time, union rights of entry could be included as award provisions, but they are now not allowable award matters and are prohibited matters for any workplace agreement: ss 518 and 356 and r 8.5(1)(g). The *Workplace Relations Act*, Pt 15 codifies all rights of entry under industrial laws, except where those rights are exercised legitimately under State occupational health and safety laws.[119] Part 15, Div 5 nevertheless provides that federal laws prevail over rights of entry under State occupational health and safety laws for 'constitutional corporations' and other employers subject to the federal statute. This overcomes the decision by French J in *BGC Contracting Pty Ltd v Construction, Forestry, Mining and Energy Union*, which recognised that a trade union registered under State law could exercise rights of entry under a State industrial law in relation to employees who were subject to federal AWAs.[120]

On one view, the *Work Choices* amendments that restricted rights of entry were a response to a perceived abuse by militant unions going on 'fishing expeditions' to gain tactical advantages in their negotiations for collective agreements.[121] On another, they represent a further assertion of the view that trade unions are interfering 'third parties' and a denial of their legitimate role as representatives of collective worker interests.

Right of entry permits

Prior to the *Work Choices* amendments, the provisions of the *Workplace Relations Act* gave quite broad powers to trade union officials to enter workplaces and investigate breaches of the Act, including awards and agreements and orders of the AIRC.[122] After the *Work Choices* changes a union seeking to exercise a right of entry under the *Workplace Relations Act* must first obtain a permit under s 740, and this may be issued by the Industrial Registrar subject to conditions. Section 742 sets out mandatory conditions that permit holders must meet to prove that they are 'fit and proper' persons to hold a permit.

Permits can be used to enter premises to investigate breaches of industrial laws or instruments, but only after the owner of the premises is given at least 24 hours (and no more than 14 days) notice of a specified date of entry, and if the notice particularises the suspected breach.

Under the former law there was an issue as to whether particulars were required on entry notices. In *Victorian Association of Forest Industries v Construction, Forestry, Mining and Energy Union*,[123] a Full Bench of the AIRC decided that Parliament had not expressly stipulated this requirement, so it was unnecessary for an entry notice to contain details of the alleged breach. This is clearly another of those decisions that the government considered went the wrong way. Nevertheless, there are at least two good reasons for

---

119 See *Workplace Relations Act*, s 16(1)(e), 1(3)(c). See also *Workplace Relations Regulations*, rr 15.1–15.8.

120 (2004) 140 FCR 53.

121 See eg *Victorian Association of Forest Industries and CFMEU*, AIRC, PR939097, 9 October 2003, and where rights of entry notices were served on sixteen employers in the timber industry during the same week after bargaining periods had been initiated to negotiate new agreements with those employers.

122 See eg *Australian and New Zealand Banking Group v Finance Sector Union*, AIRC, PR951766, 8 September 2004. For an examination of earlier changes in the law regulating the rights of trade unions to enter workplaces see W Ford 'Being There: Changing Union Rights of Entry under Federal Industrial Law' (2000) 13 *AJLL* 1.

123 Above n 121.

the Full Bench's conclusion in this case. Particulars may identify the individual employee complainant, and render that person susceptible to victimisation; and particularisation may give an offending employer an opportunity to hide evidence.[124]

Permits can also be issued and used to enter premises for the purposes of holding discussions with employees, but only with employees who 'wish to participate', and only during the meal breaks in working hours: ss 760–761. The same notice requirements apply: s 763. The constraints in the legislation on the right of trade unions to enter the workplace make general recruiting drives at workplaces more difficult than in the past.

The law and future of trade unions in the new economy

Challenges to trade union membership

All around the world trade union membership has been declining in recent times, resulting in a wide 'representational gap' in the contemporary world of work.[125] Australia presents a very stark example of this wider, general decline. Because of their important place in the conciliation and arbitration system in the industrial era, trade unions once flourished in Australia with membership reaching a peak in the years after World War II when 63 per cent of Australian workers belonged to a trade union.[126] In 1976 just over half of employees in Australia still belonged to a trade union, but thereafter numbers began to drop. Between 1986 and 1996 trade union membership reported by employees declined by one-third.[127] In the decade following from 1995, trade union membership in Australia again fell by one-third, from 33 per cent of the workforce to 22 per cent. As is the case elsewhere, in Australia there are stronger membership rates amongst those who work fulltime (22 per cent) than amongst those who are part-timers (17 per cent), and public sector workers are more highly unionised (47 per cent) than those working in the private sector (17 per cent).[128]

The reasons for the decline in trade union membership are complex. It is commonplace to suggest that trade unions are simply out of place in the new economy: not only do they have no direct interest in work relations, being at most third-party interveners, but also their collectivist tradition marks them as anti-competitive cartels, hostile to the values of the market. Yet trade unions are no more a cartel than the corporation that represents a collection of shareholders. Through the medium of the transnational corporation that latter collective is flourishing in the new economy.

In the face of the dominance of neo-liberal theory trade unions have not been able to adapt easily to the emergence of the global economy. The ILO has noted that freedom of association, and especially collective bargaining, does not seem to be generally feasible on a global scale, except perhaps in a few industries such as the maritime industry.[129]

---

124 See eg *AFMEPKIU & Caltex Australia Ltd* [2002] NSWIRComm 1067.
125 See International Labour Office *Your Voice at Work*, above n 34, 7–23.
126 See D Peetz *Unions in a Contrary World: The Future of the Australian Trade Union Movement* (1998), 26, examining ABS figures for the period 1911–96.
127 ABS *Trade Union Members, Australia, August 1996* Cat no 6325.0, 1997; and ABS *Employee Earnings Benefits, and Trade Union Membership*, Cat no 6310.0, 2001.
128 ABS *Employee Earnings Benefits, and Trade Union Membership* Cat no 6310.0, 2006.
129 See International Labour Office, *Organising for Social Justice*, above n 34, 84–7.

In many instances the international trade union movement has offered support to locally based organisations,[130] but in terms of practical assistance it has played a predominantly coordinating role bringing together locally based organisations. In one such example, the support of local trade unions for maritime workers forced the ship the 'Neptune Jade' to voyage on around the globe in search of a place to off-load its cargo.[131] The possibility of such transnational action always depends to a large extent upon local law, which has generally suppressed industrial action for the purposes of wider solidarity among workers. Certainly that has always been the case in Australia.[132]

From this it can be more easily appreciated that the decline of trade unions does not exist as a phenomenon wrought out of any independently operating socio-economic exigencies of the new economy. It is something that has also been policy driven and for the most part it is regulatory changes that have helped to transform and diminish the role of trade unions.[133] In the new economy the law has recast freedom of association so that it conforms to the logic of the market and even mimics the interests of capital. Disagreement, in the form of collective action, is only permitted in the making of certain bargains closely defined as to subject matter and confined to deals with other individual (albeit often corporate) players. Once the deal is struck it is not just that the bargain binds, but that there is little possibility for the expression of other interests or views. Secondary boycotts and other forms of sympathy strike are resisted because they confront the logic of the market. Laws contrary to secondary boycotts and sympathy strikes destroy alternative relations and alliances, being designed especially to break any sense of solidarity between wider groups of workers. Law's 'neutrality' in the market is in this sense deeply political.

All this is evident in the transformation of Australian labour law from the industrial to the global era.[134] Since the mid-1990s the reform of labour law in Australia has seen the dismantling of the once sanctioned *de jure* and de facto protections for trade union security.[135] Freedom of association has become an individual right, and its prospects for supporting collective action diminished. The regulatory system set in place by the *Workplace Relations Act*, with its emphasis on non-trade union bargaining, the exit of employers from collective bargaining through the emphasis on individual bargaining, and continued restrictions on industrial action, has been designed to bring about the demise of trade unions in Australia. The changes introduced by the *Work Choices Act* are clearly designed to weaken trade unions even more.[136]

---

130 See eg the role of international trade unions in *Case No 1511* and *Case No 2326*: see above pp 467ff.

131 See also J Atleson 'The Voyage of the Neptune Jade: Transnational Labour Solidarity and Obstacles at Domestic Law' in J Conaghan, RM Fischl, and K Klare (eds) *Labour Law in an Era of Globalization: Transformative Practices and Possibilities* (2002).

132 See eg *Caledonian Collieries Ltd v Australasian Coal and Shale Employees Federation (No 1)* (1930) 42 CLR 527.

133 See F Radday 'The Decline of Union Power—Structural Inevitability or Policy Choices?' in Conaghan, Fischl and Klare (eds), above n 131, applying this insight in the wider global context.

134 See Chapter 3.

135 See Weeks, above n 77.

136 See A Forsyth and C Sutherland 'From "Unchartered Seas" to 'Stormy Waters': How Will Trade Unions Fare under the Work Choices Legislation?' (2006) 16 *ELRR* 215; A Forsyth and C Sutherland 'Collective Labour Relations under Siege: The Work Choices Legislation and Collective Bargaining' (2006) 19 *AJLL* 183; S McCrystal 'Smothering the Right to Strike: Work Choices and Industrial Action' (2006) 19 *AJLL* 198; and J Fetter 'Work Choices and Australian Workplace Agreements' (2006) 19 *AJLL* 210.

Other challenges to the organisation of trade unions, and to freedom of association and 'representational security', have come from the segmentation of the workforce into a variety of different labour markets, a process itself encouraged by regulation. The ILO has noted the diversity of issues and concerns in different labour markets.[137] Thus in the public sector, services often continue to be privatised because of on-going budget constraints, and with union membership remaining high in this sector there continues to be a strong potential for confrontation. In the agricultural sector, the problems of remoteness and seasonality of work pose particular issues for the organisation of workers. Migrant labour is often ignored or treated as a threat by other workers in the trade union movement. Labour law's silence on domestic workers leaves a 'twilight zone' in the so-called private and non-market sphere. In addition, organising for the informal economy, and for many of those who are labelled entrepreneurial workers but whose conditions of labour are often little different from those of the traditional employees demands new approaches.

Because of the 'commercialisation' of many work relationships, the recognition by the ILO that freedom of association does not hinge on working under a contract of employment is of particular significance.[138] As noted above, the freedom of association provisions in Pt 16 of the *Workplace Relations Act* are expressed as applicable to independent contractors as well as to employees and employers, thus ostensibly providing protection for *all* workers. However, for these workers the freedom is even more truncated than it is for others, because the *Workplace Relations Act* provides them with no rights to bargain collectively nor to take industrial action. Rather it is the *Trade Practices Act 1974* (Cth), especially Pt IV governing restrictive trade practices, which regulates the making of commercial deals in the marketplace. Under this Act many aspects of freedom of association that are treated as commonplace under labour law regimes, such as collective bargaining over pay and allocation of work and threatened industrial action, have traditionally been unlawful.[139] There have been some exceptions. For instance, it is possible to get an authorisation from the Australian Competition and Consumer Commission providing immunity from the exclusive dealings provisions of the *Trade Practices Act 1974* (Cth) if it can be shown that there is a 'net public benefit' to undertake action that would otherwise be in breach of Pt VII, s 45 of the *Trade Practices Act*.[140] However, the clash of regulatory assumptions that this entails makes it difficult to envisage that a more fully elaborated version of freedom of association could be incorporated as part of the regulation of the market.[141]

---

137 International Labour Office *Your Voice at Work*, above n 34, 13; and International Labour Office, *Organising for Social Justice*, above n 34, 33–47.

138 International Labour Office *Your Voice at Work*, above n 34, 13.

139 See eg *Gallagher v Pioneer Concrete (NSW) Pty Ltd* (1993) 113 ALR 159. See also S McCrystal 'Regulating Collective Bargaining: Employees, Self Employed Persons and Small Business' in C Arup et al (eds) *Labour Law and Labour Market Regulation* (2006).

140 See eg ACCC Determination, *Authorisation granted to Australian Swimmers Association Incorporated, Authorisation No A40106* (2006), permitting collective bargaining with Swimming Australia Ltd.

141 However, reform of the law has been discussed in this area for some time. See Australian Competition and Consumer Commission (ACCC) *Authorising and Notifying Collective Bargaining and Collective Boycott Issues Paper* July (2004); and Commonwealth of Australia *Review of the Competition Provisions of the Trade Practices Act*, prepared by D Dawson, J Segall and C Rendall (2003) available at <http://tpareview.treasury.gov.au/content/report.asp>. See also *Trade Practices Legislation Amendment Bill 2005* (Cth).

Trade unions: new functions and new forms

In the ILO's *Global Reports* there is a keen awareness that the right to freedom of association in the global era is one that is unlikely to be effective if expressed only through a trade union performing traditional functions and organised in traditional ways. Again there is debate about these issues across the globe. Some have argued that the reality is that the traditional representational and regulatory functions of trade unions have diminished, leaving the delivery of services and political representation and a role in public administration (assisting in implementing and delivering government policy) as the main function of trade unions.[142] Others have been more optimistic about trade unions rebuilding their traditional functions in the global era.[143]

The *Global Reports* identify a future need for innovative and productive 'partnerships' between trade unions, employers and community groups.[144] Alain Supiot has also argued that it is necessary for the old 'pyramid structure' of mass unionism to give way to more networked arrangements if trade unions are to respond to 'the expansion and fragmentation of the interests they represent' and to look after the diversity of workers in the new economy.[145] Indeed, there is a growing recognition that if all workers are to be reached, there will be a need for wider, community-based organisation as well as the more traditional shop floor organisations. The focus of many trade unions is thus now on extending their traditional role by building alliances with other groups to get a wider perspective on issues of concern to workers.[146]

The highly effective 'Justice for Janitors' campaign in the USA provides a model for innovative relations between trade unions and other groups, ranging from religious organisations, the police and community groups. In this productive alliance the working conditions of some of the poorest 'unorganisable' workers have been improved.[147] This campaign was mobilised through the Service Employees International Union (SEIU), which recognised that these workers could never attend union meetings because of their other responsibilities, including for their children and families, and so took the campaign to the workers and their community. The 'Justice for Janitors' campaign was not simply about improved wages and working conditions. It was also about human dignity and justice and raised awareness about the multitude of affronts to the immigrant groups to which the janitors belonged.

There have been a number of examples of similar activist coalitions between trade unions and other groups in Australia. The Fairwear campaign, which has addressed the working condition of outworkers in the clothing and textile industry, is one. The 'Clean Start' campaign aimed at improving the working lives of cleaners and security guards is another. It is modelled specifically on the 'Justice for Janitors' campaign. Sponsored by the Liquor, Hospitality and Miscellaneous Workers Union it aims to

---

142 See eg K Ewing 'The Function of Trade Unions' (2005) 34 *ILJ* 1.

143 See eg ACTU *Unions @ Work: The Challenge for Unions in Creating a Just or Fair Society* (1999); and ACTU *Future Strategies: Unions Working for a less Fairer Australia* (2003).

144 See esp International labour Office *Your Voice at Work*, above n 34, 17.

145 A Supiot *Work, Law and Social Linkages* (1999), [25]–[26].

146 See M Crosby *Power at Work: Rebuilding the Australian Union Movement* (2005).

147 See International Labour Office *Organising for Social Justice*, above n 34, 102.

galvanise community groups, migrant groups, poverty action groups and religious groups to raise awareness, including among property owners and managers, by asking them to sign on to ten principles, including a commitment to freedom of association and to fair wages.[148]

The success of these campaigns has also prompted greater awareness of the advantages of developing associations that are focused not only on the person 'at work' and thus defined by a craft, trade or industry, but also on the whole identity of the person, including race, gender, nationality, social class and religious affiliations.[149] Part of the attraction of these 'identity-based' unions for those who advocate them as a response to the challenges of globalisation is an understanding that traditional trade unions have not always been open to the needs of new entrants to labour markets.[150] Understanding the differences in the interests of workers is one way of responding better to their needs, especially if the prevailing powerful group is operating in ways that are exclusionary. Contrary to this, others have argued that such movements carry the seeds of destructive fragmentation of the interests of workers and thus deflect trade unions in their efforts to win true change in the workplace.[151] This critique suggests that 'identity-based' organisations place too strong an emphasis on the characteristics that identify workers prior to their entry to the workplace and can therefore downplay the ways in which identity continues to grow and be changed by participation at work. This critique suggests that it is more important for workers to stress the things they have in common rather than their differences.

Political contest and debate about the nature and role of the trade union movement will play an important role in forging the future of freedom of association in labour law. Because the principle that 'labour is not a commodity' underpins the freedom, the traditional function of organising for collective bargaining will no doubt continue to be a central goal of trade unions in the future. However, the insight that those in work relations invariably associate not just to advance their economic interests 'but to build and enrich their lives and the lives of their families and communities through horizontal networks and organisations that provide social support and cultural expression'[152] suggests that other functions and roles will also continue to develop.

---

148 The website for the Clean Start campaign can be found at <http://lhmu.org.au/lhmu/campaigns/Clean_Start/>. See also the Fairwear campaign website at <www.fairwear.org.au>.

149 See eg ML Ontiveros 'A New Course for Labour Unions: Identity Based Organizing as a Response to Globalization' in Conaghan, Fischl and Klare (eds), above n 131.

150 See eg M Crain 'Images of Power in Labour Law: A Feminist Deconstruction' (1992) 33 *Boston College LR* 481 on traditional trade union views of women's isssues.

151 See M Selmic and MS McUsic 'Difference and Solidarity: Unions in a Post-Modern Age' in Conaghan, Fischl and Klare (eds), above n 131.

152 Fudge, above n 1, 446.

Bargaining

Enterprise bargaining

Enterprise bargaining describes a market-based system for regulating working wages and conditions that leaves determination to the participants working within the business enterprise itself. Those who engage labour (usually managerial or executive staff appointed to act in the best interests of the capital owners of the firm), and those who represent the interests of the labour force to be engaged (usually trade unions or some other form of representative organisation), negotiate wages and conditions of work to apply to certain categories of workers within the enterprise. In Australia, enterprise bargaining provides a mechanism for the determination of wages and conditions above the safety net described in Chapter 7, for those categories of employees who enjoy some market power.

This chapter explains (briefly) the rationale for the introduction of enterprise bargaining in Australia (Chapter 3 provided a fuller discussion of the introduction of enterprise bargaining in the broader historical and political context of Australian labour market regulation), and maps out the principal features of the current federal model. Collective workplace bargaining is considered first, and discussion of a newer development—individual workplace bargaining—follows. Although these individual Australian Workplace Agreements (AWAs) are included in the legislation as a form of workplace bargain, it is questionable whether they bear any of the characteristics of conventional enterprise bargaining. Research to date suggests that most AWAs are not bargained or negotiated at all, but are presented as 'take it or leave it' standard form contracts to individual employees.[1] Certainly, one novel instrument introduced with the *Work Choices* reforms in 2005 bears no resemblance to any kind of bargain: the employer greenfields agreement, by which an employer determines unilaterally what working conditions will be established for a new business enterprise prior to the engagement of any of the workers who will be bound by those conditions: *Workplace Relations Act 1996* (Cth), s 330.

---

1   See eg R Mitchell and J Fetter 'Human Resource Management and Individualisation in Australian Labour Law' (2003) 45 *JIR* 292.

The chapter concludes with an examination of the transmission of business rules, which determine the fate of these workplace bargains when businesses change hands.

Terminology

Enterprise bargaining has operated in a number of jurisdictions in Australia. Often the terms used to describe these kinds of bargains differs. Some jurisdictions talk of 'EBAs' (enterprise bargaining agreements), some (including the *Workplace Relations Act* in force before the introduction of *Work Choices*) used the term 'certified agreement' or 'CA', in recognition of the fact that enterprise agreements required certification before they became enforceable. Similarly, some jurisdictions referred to 'registered agreements'.

Earlier iterations of federal law recognised non-union collective agreements as 'enterprise flexibility agreements', or 'EFAs'. Now, the federal system uses the term 'workplace agreements' to refer to a range of statutory bargains, individual and collective, that can be made under the *Workplace Relations Act 1996* (Cth). This chapter will use the expression 'enterprise bargain' as a generic term to describe bargains that can be made under statutes to regulate working conditions in a business enterprise. When we are referring specifically to the types of enterprise bargains that can now be made under current Australian federal law, we use the terms of the statute, including 'workplace agreement', 'collective workplace agreement' and 'Australian Workplace Agreement' or 'AWA'.

The rationale for enterprise bargaining

Chapter 3 explained the peculiarly Australian system of conciliation and arbitration of industry-wide awards, now in demise following the enactment of the *Workplace Relations Amendment (Work Choices) Act 2005* (Cth). The conciliation and arbitration model dominated the Australian industrial relations landscape from the turn of the twentieth century until the early 1990s. It was subjected to critical review during the 1980s, at both federal and state levels.

At the heart of these investigations was concern that the arbitration system reinforced uncompetitive work practices and disadvantaged Australia as a trading nation in global markets. The award system was criticised for applying the improved wages and conditions won by industrially strong unions across an entire industry sector, without regard to the productive capacity of individual enterprises to pay.[2] Under the award system, a centralised wage-fixing body would determine a fair standard of wages and conditions for classifications of work, after hearing submissions from unions, employer peak bodies, governments and other interested parties (for example, charitable organisations such as the Brotherhood of St Lawrence, and social welfare organisations such as the Australian Council of Social Services). The arbitral tribunal would make a determination taking into account a range of criteria, including workers' needs for a

---

2   See eg Ministerial Discussion Paper *Getting the Outsiders Inside—Towards a Rational Workplace Relations System in Australia* (1999); Department of Employment, Workplace Relations and Small Business *Breaking the Gridlock: Towards a Simpler National Workplace Relations System—Discussion Paper 1, The Case for Change* (2000).

living wage, employers' capacity to pay, and macroeconomic concerns, such as impact on inflation, the trade balance and levels of unemployment. Frequently, the award would reflect a compromise between conflicting demands. Often no party would leave the tribunal contented with the outcome. The tribunals have had to contend with criticisms of bias from both sides of the capital/labour divide.

In looking abroad for alternatives, it is not surprising that Australian policy-makers determined to adopt an enterprise bargaining model, similar to the model used in the USA. Enterprise bargaining, US-style, promised a system that would encourage enterprises to work productively and competitively. Whereas the award system spread wage rises across a whole industry-sector, regardless of the productive capacity of individual enterprises, an enterprise bargaining system claimed to ensure that only those enterprises sufficiently productive to support wage rises would negotiate them.

Such, at least, is the rhetoric. The strength of the traditional conciliation and arbitration system was that it provided some check on abuses arising from the 'usual, but unequal, contest, the "higgling of the market" for labour, with the pressure for bread on one side and the pressure for profits on the other'.[3] Enterprise bargaining institutionalises the higgling of the marketplace as the appropriate mechanism for determining wages and working conditions. Single business enterprise bargaining—such as has now been introduced at the federal level in Australia—limits the opportunities for workers to act effectively to pursue their interests across an industry sector or a broader community. Single business bargaining defines the collective of worker interests according to the parameters of the employer's single business enterprise.

The *Industrial Relations Reform Act 1993* (Cth) (enacted by the Keating Labor Government) introduced two streams of collective enterprise bargaining at the federal level—union bargaining, and a contentious instrument called an 'enterprise flexibility agreement', which could be made by employers directly with their workforces, without union involvement. The *Workplace Relations and Other Legislation Amendment Act 1996* (Cth) (arguably the most significant piece of legislation enacted by the Howard Coalition Government in its first term of office) revised the collective bargaining provisions, left in place two collective streams (union and non-union certified agreements), and introduced the even more contentious Australian Workplace Agreement (AWA), to enable employers to strike individual workplace agreements that (having the force of federal statute) allowed employers to do what common law employment contracts could not achieve. AWAs allowed employers to contract out of the protections of industrial awards and certain state statutory obligations. The 1996 reforms left in place a no-disadvantage test, providing a somewhat questionable protection for workers against the erosion of award conditions.[4] The *Work Choices* reforms in 2005 abolished this no-disadvantage test, and introduced a number of modifications to the processes for making workplace bargains designed to facilitate and encourage employers to use AWAs.[5]

---

3   *Ex parte HV McKay* (*Harvester Case*) (1907) 2 CAR 1, 3.

4   See R Mitchell et al 'What's Going on with the No-Disadvantage Test? An Analysis of Outcomes and Processes under the *Workplace Relations Act 1996* (Cth)' (2005) 47 *JIR* 393.

5   See A Forsyth and C Sutherland 'Collective Labour Relations under Siege: The *Work Choices* Legislation and Collective Bargaining' (2006) 19 *AJLL* 183. These changes have been discussed in Chapter 3.

The adoption of an enterprise-bargaining system does not—as we have seen in Chapter 7—completely dissolve the role of a safety net of minimum wages and mandated working conditions, nor does it preclude reliance on a purely common law contract model for settling terms and conditions of work in any workplace. It is, however, necessary to understand the relationship between enterprise bargaining and the safety net, and to distinguish statutory enterprise bargaining from common law contracting.

Relationship with the safety net

Chapter 7 explained the safety net of minimum wages and working conditions provided by the *Workplace Relations Act 1996* (Cth). The Australian Fair Pay and Conditions Standard (AFPCS)—supplemented in respect of some employees by the remains of the award system—underpins statutory workplace bargaining. A workplace agreement—collective or individual—will have no force to the extent that it undermines the minimum conditions provided by the AFPCS: s 172(2).

Employees who had the benefit of conditions better than the AFPCS may also continue to enjoy those 'protected award conditions' so long as they are not persuaded to bargain them away. Section 354 provides that a range of matters from a prior award will be protected, so long as a workplace agreement does not expressly exclude them: s 354(2)(c). These matters include:

- rest breaks;
- incentive-based payments and bonuses;
- annual leave loadings;
- paid time off for State or regional public holidays;
- monetary allowances for:
- employment-related expenses, skills or responsibilities, or disabilities associated with particular work or working conditions (presumably wet-weather allowances would be included);
- overtime or shift work allowances;
- penalty rates;
- outworker conditions; and
- any other matter stipulated in Regulations.

If an employer wants to dispense with any prior award conditions about these matters, it will be necessary to include express provisions in the workplace agreement overriding those conditions.

This provision for protected award conditions was enacted in an attempt to satisfy the government's commitment (during the marketing campaign supporting the introduction of the *Work Choices* legislation) that no worker would be obliged to be worse off under the proposed regime. Of course, any worker without the market power to resist a reduction in working conditions enjoys no such guarantee. In effect, the guarantee simply ensures that any reductions of conditions must be transparent on the face of any new workplace agreement.

Other important protective standards are also immune from erosion by enterprise bargaining. Notably, State laws on occupational health and safety and workers' compensation are preserved by s 17(2), and State antidiscrimination laws are not overridden by an enterprise bargain, by virtue of s 16(2).[6] A list of 'non-excluded matters' in s 16(3) allows States to continue to regulate some issues relevant to working conditions—notably long service leave—but federal agreements can still be made to override those non-excluded matters if parties elect expressly for this.

Relationship with private contract

A system of enterprise-based bargaining is contractual in form and underlying philosophy. The parties choose their own terms, and are bound to honour their own consensual agreements. Agreements contain dispute resolution clauses—also determined voluntarily—to govern how the parties will resolve issues of interpretation and application, should grievances arise. Why then is there any need for legislation? Why can the common law of contract not provide adequately for the making and enforcement of such bargains? In Chapter 5 we discussed why collective enterprise bargains create problems for contract law, in an examination of *Ryan v Textile Clothing & Footwear Union Australia*.[7]

Essentially, a collective bargain raises problems with privity of contract. A workable collective enterprise bargain needs to be able to bind newcomers to the workplace, and any individual dissentients to its making. Following the *Electrolux* decision,[8] in which the High Court clarified that only a very narrow range of matters could be contained in a statutory workplace agreement, trade unions began investigating the potential to use common law collective agreements to bargain over a wider range of concerns.[9] The efficacy of such agreements remains a matter of debate. Certainly, a statutory regime that provides the means of creating instruments that will bind all workers in an enterprise on a majority-rules basis, and can even be made to bind successors to the business enterprise, overcomes all of the complexities involved in satisfying the general law requirements for making an effective and enforceable multiparty contract.

The obstacles thrown up by general contract law to the making of collective agreements to bind a whole workforce do not, however, explain the need for statutory provisions to support the introduction of *individual* enterprise bargains, such as AWAs. The rationale for AWAs is nevertheless quite simple: ordinary common law contracts are overridden by statute. Awards and collective enterprise agreements certified under statutes have the force of statutory law and therefore override any inconsistent contractual arrangements. Employers can enter common law contracts to provide more generous benefits than an award, workplace agreement or statute allows, but cannot contract out of the minimum obligations determined by awards or collective enterprise bargains.

---

6   See Chapter 9 for an explanation of standards of protection against unlawful discrimination on the grounds of characteristics such as sex, sexual preference, race and disability.

7   [1996] 2 VR 235.

8   *Electrolux Home Products Pty Ltd v Australian Workers Union (Electrolux)* (2004) 221 CLR 309.

9   See Chapter 5 at p 217.

To ensure that corporate employers could make enforceable individual agreements with workers, unhindered by the existence of more generous provisions in any applicable awards, certified collective agreements or even state legislation, it was necessary for the federal government to create a form of individual agreement that would carry the status of federal law. An AWA can undermine an award or collective workplace agreement, even though a common law employment contract cannot. A workplace agreement properly made under a statute will override any common law contract providing for lower standards than the award or certified bargain. An AWA, however, can trump them all—contract, award and collective bargain alike.[10]

This fact was clearly demonstrated in *McLennan v Surveillance Australia Pty Ltd*,[11] where the full Federal Court held that a trainee pilot was not obliged to repay a sum of money under a training bond when she left her employment before working out the period of service stipulated in the bond. Her employment was governed by an AWA, which provided that the employer would provide training, and did not stipulate any conditions upon the provision of training. The bond agreement was a separate contract she was required to sign upon obtaining approval for a special training scheme. It had not been filed with the Employment Advocate as a variation to her existing AWA. The full Federal Court (overturning a decision of a South Australian magistrate upholding the bond as a common law contract) held that the bond agreement did not bind her because it imposed a more onerous condition upon her than she enjoyed under the AWA.

Workplace agreements under the federal Act

This chapter focuses on federal enterprise bargaining and the processes for making and enforcing those bargains. Generally, all Australian States (with the exception of Victoria, which referred industrial matters to the Commonwealth in 1997) have legislated to support collective bargaining.[12] State legislation provides a largely similar framework for collective bargaining as the federal statute, although the role of Industrial Relations Commissions varies considerably in the different systems. Compared with the federal jurisdiction, for example, New South Wales' legislation provides a greater role for the NSW Industrial Relations Commission in monitoring bargaining and in creating its own 'Principles' for collective bargaining.[13] Western Australia and Queensland have also experimented with individual workplace

---

10 See *Workplace Relations Act 2006* (Cth), s 348(2), and see *Workplace Relations Regulations*, r 8.5(8), which prohibits any workplace agreement from containing a clause restricting the ability of the parties to make AWAs.

11 (2005) 142 FCR 105.

12 See *Industrial Relations Act 1996* (NSW), Pt 2 Div 1; *Industrial Relations Act 1999* (Qld), *Industrial Relations Act 1984* (Tas), *Industrial Relations Act 1979* (WA) as amended by the *Labour Relations Reform Act 2002* (WA), and *Fair Work Act 1994* (SA), Pt 1.

13 See *Industrial Relations Act 1996* (NSW), ss 29–47, and *Re Principles for Approval of Enterprise Agreements: Application by Minister for Industrial Relations* (1996) 70 IR 437. For general comment on the NSW system, see S Jamieson 'Enterprise Agreements in NSW: A New Era?' (1992) 5 *AJLL* 84; J Shaw 'A Balanced Industrial Relations Reform Package for New South Wales' (1996) 38 *JIR* 57.

agreements.[14] Until an amendment in 2005 South Australian legislation allowed an enterprise agreement to be made by a single employee, by virtue of a definition of 'group of employees' that included a single employee; however, that provision—s 4(2) of the *Fair Work Act 1994* (SA)—has since been repealed.

By virtue of s 16 of the *Workplace Relations Act 1996* (Cth) the federal provisions now override any State industrial laws providing avenues for workplace bargaining for any employer who falls within the definition of employer in s 6 of the federal Act. This means that the great majority of employer enterprises—all of those that are incorporated—can no longer make binding enterprise agreements under State industrial laws. Given the facility for even very small businesses to incorporate under the *Corporations Act 2001* (Cth)—there is now a need only for one shareholder and a single director for a corporation to be formed[15]—the need for corporate status is no serious hurdle to the promulgation of federal workplace agreements throughout the private sector in Australia. Readers with an interest in the State systems are advised to consult specialist works.[16]

The single business requirement

Federal workplace agreements can only be made by eligible employers for 'single businesses' (s 322), although there is some scope for 'multiple business agreements' if the Employment Advocate is satisfied that it is in the public interest to allow a multiple business agreement (ss 331–2) notwithstanding the pressing objectives of the legislation to discourage bargaining beyond the boundaries of a single enterprise. This discouragement is particularly apparent in the prohibitions on pattern bargaining: ss 431 and 439.

Multiple business agreements have been allowed, for instance, in the case of franchises, where the franchisee employers are, strictly speaking, separate businesses. In *Shop Distributive and Allied Employees Association and McDonald's Restaurants*,[17] for example, the AIRC allowed the certification of a multiple business agreement covering nine McDonalds franchises in the ACT, because the businesses carried on by the franchisees were 'identical in character … operated in an identical manner and … provided identical products which are priced identically'.[18] Because of the overriding interest of franchisor and franchisees in maintaining uniform wages and conditions in these cloned businesses, multiple business agreements were held to be appropriate and not to disturb the overall regulatory agenda.

It appears that business owners who choose to use a group of separate corporate entities to segregate their workforces for all other purposes can still enter into the one multiple business agreement to fix working conditions for staff across the group of companies. For example, in *Dome Coffees Australia—Certified Agreement 2004–2007*,[19]

---

14 See Western Australian Workplace Agreements (WAWAs), and Queensland Workplace Agreements (QWAs).
15 *Corporations Act 2001* (Cth), ss 114 and 201A.
16 See for example the loose-leaf encyclopaedia, *The Australian Labour Law Reporter*, published by CCH. State public sector employment is also a specialist area of concern.
17 AIRC, PR915681, 22 March 2002.
18 Ibid, [4].
19 AIRC, PR945864, 16 April 2004.

three separate companies owned a number of coffee shops operating under the business name of Dome Coffees. Dome Coffees Australia Pty Ltd had a 50 per cent interest in each of the companies, either directly or through another subsidiary, the remaining capital being contributed by investors taking no part in management. The registration of a multiple business agreement was allowed in respect of all thirteen of the Dome Coffee sites, on the basis that the businesses shared operations. They had a single management structure, a commonality of interest, a common mission and vision statement for employees, and a common corporate culture. Customer complaints for all businesses were centrally managed.

Types of agreement

The federal Act provides for several kinds of workplace agreement. Australian Workplace Agreements, or AWAs, are made by employers with individual employees, although as is explained below, this does not necessarily make them idiosyncratic, personally tailored agreements. Standard form AWAs are as common as standard form car insurance contracts. Employees are frequently presented with a complete agreement, and offered no invitation at all to engage in any serious negotiation of terms. Individual employees have a statutory right to engage a bargaining agent to negotiate an AWA for them: s 334.

Employers may also make collective agreements, either directly with employees under s 327, or with a union under s 328, so long as the union has at least one member employed in the enterprise who will be bound by the proposed agreement.

Greenfields agreements

Employers starting up new businesses or projects may also make 'greenfields' agreements, either with a union that represents the industrial interests of the kinds of employees likely to be engaged by the business (under s 329), or—most peculiarly—with them-selves. An employer greenfields agreement made under s 330 of the Act allows an employer to make and lodge an agreement, binding itself in respect of employees whom it has not yet engaged to do any work. The absence of any opposing party at the time that such an agreement is made challenges the notion that it is in fact any kind of agreement or bargain at all. Nevertheless, an employer greenfields agreement will operate in the same way as any other workplace agreement, except that it enjoys a considerably shorter nominal duration. Employer greenfields agreements can be made for only one year, compared with five years for a two-party agreement: s 352(1)(a). This gives the employer a twelve-month 'honeymoon' period, in which it can proceed to operate a business and lock in labour costs and work practices without the fear of disruption from protected industrial action. Part 9 of the Act (described in Chapter 12) allows parties negotiating collective workplace agreements to take industrial action to support their claims, but this entitlement is hemmed around with many restrictions, one of which is a prohibition on taking action during the currency of a workplace agreement: ss 494–5.

What matters can be included in an agreement?

The legislation mandates certain basic content for a valid workplace agreement. It must contain a nominal expiry date, no more than five years after its commencement (s 352); it must contain a dispute settlement procedure, and if it fails to do so, it will be taken to include the model procedures set out in Pt 13 of the Act.[20] If it is intended that the agreement will exclude or vary any 'protected award conditions' (described above, in the discussion of 'relationship with the safety net'), it must expressly deal with those matters. A workplace agreement will be presumed to include any protected award conditions unless those conditions are expressly excluded.

If parties wish to call up terms from previous awards or agreements, they must stipulate expressly the terms to be included. A common practice of incorporating terms of awards and agreements by reference can now only be adopted in respect of an award or agreement that bound the employer immediately before the making of the workplace agreement. State awards and agreements cannot be incorporated by reference: s 355(6)(a). These provisions have the effect of forcing parties to expressly incorporate any terms they wish to continue from any past awards or agreements, other than an immediately preceding federal instrument.

Section 348(1) of the Act provides that only one workplace agreement can have effect in respect of a particular employee at any time. The *Explanatory Memorandum* to the *Workplace Relations Amendment (Work Choices) Bill 2005* explained this provision as an encouragement for parties to use comprehensive agreements.[21] It does mean that in the event that a prevailing AWA is silent as to some important matter, parties will no longer be able to look to an award or collective agreement that would otherwise have covered that employee to fill the gaps.

Prohibited content

Section 356 provides that certain content may be prohibited from inclusion in a workplace agreement by Regulations, and if a matter is prohibited, the Employment Advocate must expunge it from any agreement already lodged. An employer knowingly or recklessly lodging an agreement that contains prohibited content is liable to a civil penalty: s 357.

The *Workplace Relations Regulations* do in fact prescribe a long list of prohibited matters in Regs 8.5 to 8.7.

Matters supporting union influence in the workplace

Regulation 8.5 prohibits a long list of matters, most of which concern provisions that were once common in union collective agreements, to support the functioning of the union at the workplace. These included employer commitments to allow for automatic deduction of union dues from wages, paid leave to attend union training or meetings, and rights for unions to communicate with the workforce. Other matters in the list prohibit clauses—also common in old union-negotiated agreements—restricting the employer's liberty to engage personnel through labour hire or independent contracting.

---

20 See Chapter 12.
21 *Explanatory Memorandum*, 166.

Regulation 8.5(8) also prohibits any restriction on engaging staff on AWAs. The full list of matters in r 8.5(1) is:

(a) deductions from the pay or wages of an employee bound by the agreement of trade union membership subscriptions or dues;

(b) the provision of payroll deduction facilities for the subscriptions or dues referred to in paragraph (a);

(c) employees bound by the agreement receiving leave to attend training (however described) provided by a trade union;

(d) employees bound by the agreement receiving paid leave to attend meetings (however described) conducted by or made up of trade union members;

(e) the renegotiation of a workplace agreement;

(f) the rights of an organisation of employers or employees to participate in, or represent an employer or employee bound by the agreement in, the whole or part of a dispute settling procedure, unless the organisation is the representative of the employer's or employee's choice;

(g) the rights of an official of an organisation of employers or employees to enter the premises of the employer bound by the agreement;

(h) restrictions on the engagement of independent contractors and requirements relating to the conditions of their engagement;

(i) restrictions on the engagement of labour-hire workers, and requirements relating to the conditions of their engagement, imposed on an entity or person for whom the labour-hire worker performs work under a contract with a labour-hire agency;

(j) the forgoing of annual leave credited to an employee bound by the agreement otherwise than in accordance with the Act;

(k) the provision of information about employees bound by the agreement to a trade union, or a member acting in a representative capacity, officer, or employee of a trade union, unless provision of that information is required or authorised by law.

A further list of matters is prohibited in rr 8.5(2) to 8.5(9). These include any terms that discourage or encourage union membership, or would be objectionable under s 810 of the Act, which prohibits any terms in an agreement that would breach freedom of association rights. Likewise, terms that would allow parties to the agreement to take industrial action are prohibited. Industrial action is regulated completely by Pt 9 of the Act.

Matters providing remedies for unfair dismissal

Regulation 8.5(5) prohibits terms providing rights or remedies against unfair dismissal. Unfair dismissal is codified by Pt 12 Div 3 of the Act.[22]

The exclusions provided in the statute cannot be avoided by making a workplace agreement. Nevertheless, it is arguably still possible for an employer to agree to confer rights to procedural fairness on dismissal in a common law employment contract. These rights would operate as contractual terms, and the employee would need to seek a remedy for breach of contract in the ordinary courts. There would be no recourse, as under the Act, to the Australian Industrial Relations Commission. The prohibition on

---

22 See Chapter 9.

such matters in a workplace agreement arguably means no more than that a union cannot organise protected industrial action to support a claim to such provisions in a statutory workplace agreement.

In any event, this prohibition may produce some inconvenient results in practice. Regulation 8.5(6) stipulates that a term is not prohibited under r 8.5(5) 'to the extent that it provides a process for managing an employee's performance or conduct'. This would suggest that a workplace agreement can include performance management procedures, which include policies for reviewing performance, providing warnings of underperformance and opportunities to respond or correct deficiencies prior to any disciplinary action. If such a term were included in an AWA, and it were breached by the employer (for instance, by summary dismissal without first pursuing the stipulated processes), it seems clear that the employee would be entitled to bring proceedings against the employer for breach of the AWA. Under s 721 of the Act, an employee who suffers damage as a result of a breach of an AWA can bring an action to recover any loss suffered in an eligible court.[23] It would appear then, that there is still the prospect for an agreement to contain terms that would ultimately lead to a remedy for unfair dismissal.

Prohibition on discriminatory terms

Regulation 8.6 prohibits any terms in an agreement would be discriminatory; however, it preserves the same kinds of excuses for employers that are permitted under the unlawful dismissal rules in s 659 of the Act (discussed in Chapter 8). The text of r 8.6 is reproduced here:

(1) A term of a workplace agreement is prohibited content to the extent that it discriminates against an employee, who is bound by the agreement, because of, or for reasons including, race, colour, sex, sexual preference, age, physical or mental disability, marital status, family responsibilities, pregnancy, religion, political opinion, national extraction or social origin.

(2) For the purposes of subregulation (1), a provision of an agreement does not discriminate against an employee or class of employees merely because:
    (a) it provides for a rate or rates of pay that comply with a rate or rates of pay that are contained in the Australian Pay and Classification Scale or a special Federal Minimum Wage that would otherwise apply to the employee or class of employees; or
    (b) it discriminates, in respect of particular employment, on the basis of the inherent requirements of that employment; or
    (c) it discriminates, in respect of employment as a member of the staff of an institution that is conducted in accordance with the teachings or beliefs of a particular religion or creed:
        (i) on the basis of those teachings or beliefs; and
        (ii) in good faith.

---

23 See Chapter 12 at pp 558–59.

Matters not pertaining to the employment relationship

Regulation 8.7 prohibits any content dealing with a matter that 'does not pertain to the employment relationship', except to the extent that it is a machinery term, or a matter that is incidental or ancillary to a legitimate matter in the agreement. This provision derives from former law, which provided that enterprise bargains could include any 'matter pertaining' to the employment relationship. It is to be expected that the new Regulation will be interpreted in the light of case law on the old provisions, so an explanation of that body of law is useful here.

The former enterprise bargaining provisions adopted the language of a body of case law concerning what constituted an 'industrial matter' for the purposes of federal legislation dependent upon the conciliation and arbitration power.[24] The words in s 51(xxxv) of the *Constitution* required that federal labour laws should be for the purposes of conciliation and arbitration of interstate industrial disputes, so it was important to establish what constituted an 'industrial' dispute. This body of case law (developed throughout the time when industrial awards could be made about all industrial matters and not just the allowable matters now listed in s 513) established that an industrial matter was a matter that pertained to the relationship between an employer *as employer*, and the employees as employees. In *R v Kelly; Ex parte Victoria*,[25] the High Court of Australia held that a matter was not an industrial matter 'simply because it is a matter with respect to which persons who are employers and employees are disputing'.[26]

Nevertheless, the boundary between matters pertaining to the employment relationship and thus appropriate for inclusion in an industrial instrument, and those that do not concern the employment relationship, has not always been easy to map. For example, *R v Kelly* concerned a dispute over the trading hours of butchers' shops—a matter that the union took some interest in because of the pressure it placed on its members' working hours. The court held that *working* hours were a matter pertaining to the employment relationship, but *trading* hours were a matter of managerial prerogative. It was no matter that the latter created enormous pressure for the extension of the former.

Some of the contentious matters in the past have concerned the automatic de-duction of union fees and contributions to union-controlled superannuation funds. *R v Portus; Ex parte ANZ Banking Group Ltd*,[27] followed by *Re Alcan: Ex parte Federation of Industrial, Manufacturing and Engineering Employees*,[28] decided the automatic deduction claims against the unions. The dispute was characterised as concerning the relationship between the employer and a union who was seeking to force the employer to act as a collecting agency. A claim directed at strengthening the union was not, without more, a matter pertaining to the employment relationship. These decisions have since been reaffirmed by a majority of the High Court in *Electrolux*,[29] discussed below.

---

24 See Chapter 3.
25 (1950) 81 CLR 64.
26 Ibid, 85.
27 (1972) 127 CLR 353.
28 (1994) 181 CLR 96.
29 (2004) 221 CLR 309.

The superannuation cases proved more contentious. In *Manufacturing Grocers' Employees Federation of Australia; Ex parte Australian Chamber of Manufacturers*[30] it was held that the entitlement to participate in a superannuation scheme and the means of funding the scheme were matters pertaining to the employment relationship; however, in *Amalgamated Metal Workers Union of Australia; Ex parte Shell Co of Australia Ltd*,[31] a union's attempt to influence an employer's decision about how to treat surpluses in a defined benefit superannuation fund were unsuccessful to the extent that the claims imposed obligations on the employer not *as employer*, but as the recipient of the property of a trust of which employees were beneficiaries. The only claim that was held to be a matter pertaining to the employment relationship in this case was one that required the employer to 'use its best endeavours' to exercise its influence in the interests of employees.[32]

In *Re Finance Sector Union of Australia; Ex parte Financial Clinic (Vic) Pty Ltd*,[33] a union claim that compulsory superannuation contributions should be made to the union-sponsored industry fund was held, by a four-to-three majority of the High Court, to fail the test. The minority in this case (Brennan CJ, Dawson and McHugh JJ) held that the claim that all contributions should be made to a single industry fund could be characterised as a matter pertaining to the employment relationship because it was a means of avoiding potential discrimination against those employees who belonged to the union.[34] This finding was based on the view that an employer free to choose a fund for non-union members may elect to contribute to a self-managed superannuation fund that invested in the employer's own business, and this would create incentives to employ non-unionists ahead of unionists.

These specific issues have now been resolved in other ways;[35] however, the cases still illuminate how courts will reason to determine what is, and what is not, a matter pertaining to the employment relationship. To the extent that federal *Workplace Relations Regulations* prohibit content that fails that test, this case law remains useful precedent in any consideration of what is an appropriate matter for inclusion in a workplace agreement.

Other disputes have concerned the levying of compulsory bargaining fees on non-union members who would otherwise 'free-ride' on the efforts of unions to bargain for improved wages, and security for employee entitlements. The bargaining fees claim (which had conflicting results in various jurisdictions) was ultimately resolved at the federal level by the legislature passing an Act outlawing any claims for compulsory bargaining fees: see the *Workplace Relations Amendment (Prohibition of Compulsory Union Fees) Act 2003* (Cth).

The dispute resolved in the *Electrolux* case[36] arose before the passing of this amending statute. In *Electrolux*, the High Court held that a claim by a union that employers

---

30 (1986) 160 CLR 341, 356.
31 (1992) 174 CLR 345.
32 See Chapter 7.
33 (1993) 178 CLR 352.
34 Ibid, 364.
35 See Chapter 7.
36 (2004) 221 CLR 309.

agree to ensure that non-union member employees paid a bargaining agents fee to the union in respect of the union's services in negotiating the agreement was not a 'matter pertaining to' the employment relationship, within the terms of former s 170LI of the Act. The claim was characterised by the majority reasons[37] as a claim involving the creation of an agency relationship between the employees and the employer, for the purposes of making payment of an obligation owed by the employees to the union. This agency arrangement was characterised as the provision of a benefit to the union, not a benefit to employees, so fell outside the scope of matters pertaining directly to the employment relationship. The *Electrolux* decision evidences a narrow interpretation of what matters can be included in a collective agreement or AWA. Matters having an 'indirect, consequential and remote effect on that relationship'[38] cannot be included.

Nevertheless, as Kirby J noted in his dissenting opinion in *Electrolux*, whether a matter is within the scope of the employment relationship is something upon which equally well-informed people may disagree.[39] Take, for example, a claim that employers provide some sort of security to guarantee payment of employee entitlements in the event of the employer's insolvency.

In *Transfield Pty Ltd v AMWU* (*Transfield*)[40] Munro J in the Australian Industrial Relations Commission held that a claim that the employer contribute specifically to the ManuSafe trust fund set up and controlled by the union to protect members' severance entitlements in the case of employer insolvency, failed the test. Munro J held that the clause could not be identified as a simple claim that the employer should make provision for the payment of contingent liabilities to employees, because of certain features of the ManuSafe trust vehicle. It provided a broad discretion for the trustees to apply surpluses to a range of objects, and it also provided for portability of entitlements when employees left jobs voluntarily.[41] Since the claim was held not to be a matter pertaining to the employment relationship, it could not be included in a certified agreement under former s 170LI, and any action taken in support of the claim did not enjoy protection under former ss 170ML and 170MT.[42]

The *Transfield* decision does, however, leave open the door for unions that are prepared to rephrase claims as simple demands that employers establish measures to provide adequate protection for entitlements (so long as the Minister does not decide to prohibit such content by making further regulations to that effect). Arguably a claim that an employer provide as part of the package of remuneration an entitlement to beneficial interest in some security over property held by the employer, contingent upon the employer's failure to pay entitlements as and when they fell due, may be characterised as a matter pertaining directly to the relationship between the employer

---

37 The majority was formed by four separate judgments: Gleeson CJ; McHugh J; Gummow, Hayne and Heydon JJ; and Callinan J. Each of these reasons adopted the characterisation of the clause determined by Merkel J at first instance.

38 (2004) 221 CLR 309, 325.

39 Ibid, 377–78.

40 (2002) 51 AILR ¶4.538(43); AIRC, PR908287, 30 August 2001.

41 Merkel J of the Federal Court criticised Munro J's reasoning on this issue in *Electrolux Home Products Pty Ltd v AWU* (2002) 51 AILR 4-534, [2001] FCA 1600.

42 This conclusion has been confirmed in *Electrolux* (2004) 221 CLR 309.

as an employer, and the employee, as a worker with a direct interest in guaranteed remuneration for services.

Of course, if the negotiating parties want to reach agreement about a non-industrial matter, there is nothing to prevent them doing so. In *CFMEU v AIRC*[43] the High Court noted that agreements between employers and employees about matters that are not strictly 'matters pertaining to the employment relationship' can still form the basis of valid commercial contracts enforceable under the general law. They just can't be lodged as workplace agreements under the *Workplace Relations Act* and enjoy the benefit of the various statutory provisions (including the entitlement to take protected action in support of a proposed agreement). The want of consideration, which proved an obstacle to the enforcement of an unregistered certified agreement in *Ryan v Textile Clothing and Footwear Union Australia*,[44] could be overcome by using a deed.[45]

The role of institutions

Office of the Employment Advocate

The enterprise bargaining model is based on contract law principles—parties are bound by their own agreement, and not by an award decision made by an arbitral tribunal. Institutions therefore play a limited role in agreement-making. The Office of the Employment Advocate plays a registry role, in accepting lodgment of agreements, variations of agreements and terminations. The only kind of agreement that the Employment Advocate will vet prior to lodgment is a proposed multiple business agreement, which must be authorised by the Employment Advocate under s 332 to ensure that there are legitimate public interest reasons for allowing the employer to avoid the requirement that agreements must relate to single businesses. The Employment Advocate also plays a policing role in removing prohibited content (described above) from any agreement that has been lodged.

Workplace inspectorate

Generally, policing the observance of workplace agreements is left largely to the parties themselves; however, the workplace inspectors (whose powers are generally dealt with in Pt 6 of the Act) also have standing to initiate proceedings for breach of any of the provisions of Pt 8: see ss 404 and 405. Workplace inspectors also have standing under s 718 to bring actions for civil remedies for breach of any kind of workplace instrument.

Unions' rights to monitor compliance with workplace agreements are controlled by Pt 15 of the Act, which regulates unions' rights of entry into workplaces. Unions will have standing to bring actions for breach of workplace agreements if they are parties to the workplace agreement themselves, or if they are requested to represent an employee aggrieved by a breach of an agreement that binds at least one person who is a union member: s 718.

---

43 (2001) 203 CLR 645.
44 (1996) 2 VR 235.
45 See Chapter 5, p 216.

AIRC

Formerly, the AIRC had a role in collective agreement-making. It was the body certifying agreements and applying the no-disadvantage test. This role ceased with the enactment of the *Work Choices* legislation. Except in the case of pre-reform certified agreements, which continue to operate under the pre-reform Act according to the modifications provided by Sch 7 of the Act, the AIRC has no continuing role in collective agreement-making, variation or termination. Now lodgment of all kinds of agreements, both individual and collective, and all variations and terminations of post-reform agreements, rests with the Employment Advocate.

The AIRC has, however, maintained its role as a referee, 'keeping the field' as parties to collective workplace agreements negotiate their agreements. Parties intending to initiate a bargaining period must notify the AIRC and the other negotiating parties of their intention under s 423, and the AIRC will thereafter play a supervisory role over the bargaining process. Like a sports referee, the AIRC can blow the whistle on certain unacceptable play or even call the game off by exercising a power to suspend or terminate a bargaining period under ss 430–433. If a bargaining period is terminated because it is causing significant threats to safety, welfare or the Australian economy, the AIRC can make a workplace determination under Pt 9 Div 8. However, apart from this power, the AIRC has very limited opportunity to intervene in the results of bargaining. At its heart, bargaining is a self-regulatory model. The parties themselves determine the outcomes, and their relative bargaining strengths will inevitably be reflected in those outcomes. The Commission's role in the management of industrial conflict is considered in Chapter 12.

Collective bargaining

Although collective and individual workplace agreements are now all dealt with by the Employment Advocate, according to a common set of rules for lodgment, variation and termination, there are nevertheless some important conceptual and practical differences between collective and individual agreements. From a practical perspective, collective enterprise bargaining presents a number of challenges that must be addressed in an effective regulatory scheme. These include:

- collective choice mechanisms—how to determine when decisions have been made that will bind each individual in the enterprise, perhaps despite the individual's own apathy or resistance;
- procedures for negotiation of terms—the rules of the negotiating game, which determine how parties bargain, given that not every individual will participate in the bargaining process;
- mechanisms for breaking deadlocks, and imposing some resolution on parties that may be contrary to the first preferences of some or all of the persons who will be bound.

A number of other issues are common to both collective and individual agreement making:

- mechanisms for officially recognising binding agreements;
- mechanisms for varying agreements and recognising the binding effect of variations;
- duration of agreements—how and when they will cease to apply; and
- coverage of agreements especially after some change in the enterprise's structure or ownership.

Coverage of agreements after a transmission of business is explained at the conclusion of this chapter.

Collective choice mechanisms

Any form of collective agreement-making confronts the problem of finding an appropriate collective choice mechanism. When a group of people want to make a bargain, some mechanism must be found to determine when sufficient consensus is reached to settle the terms of that agreement, despite some individuals' dissent. Where the interests of the members of the collective are relatively homogenous, arriving at consensus is easier than when the interests of the group are heterogeneous.[46]

This explains why collective bargaining is more effective in industries where workers have similar work patterns and similar needs and priorities. Unions traditionally were very effective in pressing for the interests of the typical fulltime male breadwinner, whose interests included discouragement of part-time work, penalty rates for overtime and unsociable hours, and progressive pay scales through a highly calibrated series of job skills classifications. The entry of women, part-time workers, people with preferences to work outside the nine-to-five paradigm, and people whose careers are likely to be interrupted with long periods of leave, have challenged the effectiveness of collective bargaining—because the interests to be represented are more diverse. Prospects for finding a core of common interests are weakened. A challenge for the union movement in the twenty-first century is to find ways of accommodating diversity in the workforce.

Unanimous agreement is notoriously difficult to obtain, so collective choice mechanisms generally involve some kind of system for identifying whose choices are to be preferred. Two methods of voting are common: voting to elect a representative decision-maker, and direct voting for the agreement itself. The present federal collective bargaining system favours direct voting. With the exception of the anomalous category of greenfields agreements (where no workers are engaged at the time they are made) all proposed collective workplace agreements, whether made with unions or not, must be put to all current employees who will be bound. A majority of the workforce must approve the agreement—but what kind of a majority? In the federal system, 51 per cent of employees in favour is sufficient to establish an agreement. In fact, if the employer takes a formal vote of employees, it is necessary only that more than 50 per cent of

---

46 See H Hansmann 'Worker Participation in Corporate Governance' (1993) 43 *U Tor LJ* 589.

those employees who cast a valid vote agree—see s 340(2)(b)(i)—so a large number of abstainers can mean that an agreement will come into force with the conscious support of only a minority of the workforce.

One might question whether this level of majority is sufficient to ensure adequate protection of employee interests, particularly in an increasingly diverse workforce. Other choices have been made. In New South Wales, for instance, a collective agreement made directly with employees without union involvement must have the support of 65 per cent of the employees affected before it can be certified.[47]

Procedures for negotiating terms

An employer who wants to make a collective workplace agreement need only 'take reasonable steps' to ensure that all employees have 'ready access to the agreement in writing' and an information statement, for seven days before the agreement is approved: s 337. The information statement must tell the employees when and how their agreement is to be sought, explain that they are entitled to engage a bargaining agent, and contain any other information that the Employment Advocate gazettes as a requirement from time to time. Hence, it is possible that collective workplace agreements can be made on a take it or leave it, non-negotiable basis under the current federal provisions.

Generally, however, collective enterprise bargaining systems typically provide for real negotiation, and to this end recognise the right of parties to flex industrial muscle in the course of bargaining to reach an agreement. Industrial action taken in the context of bargaining to establish an agreement is legitimate in such systems. It should be remembered that industrial action can be taken by both sides. Workers may strike, picket or impose more limited work bans, and employers may lock out workers. Many of the most acrimonious disputes in Australia's industrial history have involved aggressive employer tactics of this kind.

Industrial action taken in the course of negotiating a new agreement constitutes an 'interests' dispute, and is considered to be legitimate in an enterprise bargaining system. Industrial action taken during the currency of an agreement, however, is illegitimate. Any dispute that arises over the terms of an agreement—how it should be interpreted and applied in a particular set of circumstances—is a 'rights' dispute that must be settled according to the terms of the dispute resolution clause in the agreement. The parties may not take industrial action to force a compromise of existing rights.

As is explained in Chapter 12, however, under the common law in Australia most kinds of industrial action constitute legal wrongs. The withdrawal of one person's labour represents a breach of contract justifying termination. The withdrawal of the labour of a whole workforce constitutes a conspiracy to injure the employer in its trade, and interference in contractual relationships. A picket line may constitute the tort of intimidation. The *Workplace Relations Act* provisions recognise that some collective agreements will indeed be negotiated—especially those initiated by unions—and allow

---

47 See *Industrial Relations Act 1996* (NSW), s 36(4).

for negotiating parties to take 'protected industrial action', without taking the legal risks associated with vigorous bargaining tactics. To enjoy this immunity from common law consequences, however, bargaining conduct must conform to a strict set of procedures.[48] Parties who want to shelter under the protected action provisions need to be scrupulous about playing the bargaining game according to the rules set out in Pt 9 of the Act.

Controls on industrial action—both protected and unprotected—are discussed more fully in Chapter 12. This section outlines the procedural requirements for creating and lodging a valid collective workplace agreement.

Initiating a bargaining period

A party wishing to initiate a collective workplace agreement must give the other parties and the Commission at least seven days' notice of this intention, and the notice must particularise the business to be covered, the employees to be bound, the matters to be dealt with, and a proposed nominal expiry date (and any further matters stipulated by Regulations). While a properly notified bargaining period is on foot, the parties may take protected industrial action in support of their claims; however, this right to take action is hemmed around by elaborate restrictive procedures (including the requirement that all employee industrial action must be authorised by a vote taken in a secret ballot).

These secret ballot provisions in Pt 9 Div 4 were finally enacted in the *Work Choices* legislation, after a number of earlier attempts, beginning with the *Workplace Relations (More Jobs Better Pay) Bill 1999*. Earlier proposals were generally resisted on the basis that secret ballots create an expensive administrative burden and have not been proven to make a difference to outcomes in any case. The notion that secret ballots are needed to prevent irrationally militant union organisers from stirring up unnecessary trouble against the inclinations of a more moderate 'silent majority' was tested some time ago in a study by Ron McCallum.[49] This study suggested that, on the contrary, union leadership tended to moderate and control inflamed tempers among the rank and file.

Nevertheless, elaborate secret ballot provisions now preclude any employee organisation from taking industrial action until that organisation has applied to the AIRC for an order authorising the taking of a secret ballot, created a roll of voters, and complied with all of the legislative provisions, and any regulations or orders of the Commission in taking the poll. If any industrial action is planned, a further notice of the intention to take industrial action must be served on the other parties at least three days in advance: s 441(3). Without these notices, any industrial action will not be protected: s 441(1).

Section 494 stipulates that no industrial action can be taken during the term of a current collective workplace agreement or workplace determination. All workplace agreements must stipulate a nominal expiry period no more than five years from commencement: s 352. The parties may not take any industrial action during a current agreement, even if the industrial action pursues a claim over a matter not dealt with in the current workplace agreement or determination: see s 494(1).

---

48 See ss 447 and 448 discussed in Chapter 12.
49 See R McCallum 'The Mystique of Secret Ballots: Labour Relations Progress v Industrial Anarchy' (1975–76) 2 *Mon LR* 166.

This provision reverses the court's finding in the *Emwest* case.[50] In that case, an enterprise agreement had been made between the employer and the union in 2000; however, the parties expressly agreed to defer any negotiation of redundancy provisions until 2001. When the union attempted to reopen negotiations over redundancy entitlements, and initiated a bargaining period in support of their claims, the employer filed proceedings against the union in the Federal Court, claiming that the union had committed an offence by breaching former s 170MN—the provision prohibiting the taking of any industrial action during the term of a certified agreement. Justice Kenny's decision that this section did not apply to industrial action over matters not contained in the agreement was upheld by a Full Bench. In a particularly robust decision, Marshall J stated that the employer's interpretation of the law in this case would lead to unfairness and inflexibility that may ultimately undermine the collective bargaining regime.[51] Marshall J gave as an example the prospect that employers and employees may wish to settle paid maternity leave claims by collective bargaining. An interpretation that would make parties wait some years until the expiry of a workplace agreement that contained no such provisions would hinder the effective operation of the legislation to resolve issues of current public concern.

Nevertheless, when the *Work Choices* amendments were enacted, they contained the current provision that precludes the taking of any industrial action while an agreement is within its nominal expiry date, even where some hitherto unforeseen matter has arisen for negotiation. Parties are entitled to reach amicable agreements for varying a collective agreement within its nominal expiry date, but they cannot initiate a new bargaining period and take any industrial action in support of claims for new matters. Given that workplace agreements can now have nominal expiry dates five years out from their commencement (the former law provided a three-year maximum term), the prohibition on negotiating new matters presents some concerns for prospects for workplace bargaining to deal with evolving workplace issues, especially as there is no longer any mechanism for such issues to be dealt with as test cases before the AIRC.

'Good faith' bargaining?

After initiating a bargaining period, and before commencing any industrial action, parties must 'genuinely' try to reach an agreement. Failure to do so will run the risk that the Commission will exercise its powers under s 430(2) to suspend or terminate the bargaining period. Industrial action taken without first making a real attempt to negotiate a solution will not be protected action: s 444.

This obligation to 'genuinely try to reach agreement' is as close as the federal legislation comes to an obligation to bargain in good faith. The concept of 'good faith bargaining' is well understood in North America as an important assumption in any enterprise bargaining system. Good faith bargaining is mandated in New Zealand's *Employment Relations Act 2000*,[52] in ss 42B–42D of the Western Australian *Industrial*

---

50 *Australian Industry Group v Automotive, Food, Metals, Engineering, Printing & Kindred Industries Union (Emwest)* (2003) 130 FCR 524.

51 Ibid, 542.

52 See the definition of good faith in s 4, and s 32, which deals with the meaning of good faith specifically in the context of collective bargaining. See also G Anderson 'Transplanting and Growing Good Faith in New Zealand Labour Law' (2006) 19 *AJLL* 1.

Relations Act 1979 (introduced by amendments passed in 2002), and in s 146 of Queensland's *Industrial Relations Act 1999*. Section 76A of the *Fair Work Act 1994* (SA), adopts the terminology of 'best endeavours bargaining'.

The *Industrial Relations Reform Act 1993* (Cth), enacted by the Keating Labor Government, contained a provision—former s 170QK—empowering the AIRC to make orders that parties must bargain 'in good faith'. This section was repealed by the *Workplace Relations and Other Legislation Amendment Act 1996* (Cth). Several decisions of both the AIRC and the Federal Court suggest that an obligation to genuinely try to reach agreement is akin to an obligation to negotiate in good faith.[53]

There is no express provision empowering the AIRC to make orders to force parties to the bargaining table. In *Asahi Diamond Industrial Australia Pty Ltd v AFMEU*,[54] a Full Bench refused an application for an order to force the employer to negotiate with a union, as beyond power. This is a deliberate policy choice by the Federal Government. Attempts by Democrat senators to introduce good faith bargaining provisions into the *Workplace Relations Act* have been firmly rejected by the Government, on the explanation that such an obligation would be vague and may be open to interpretations that would hinder the free exercise of bargaining power by the parties.

Nevertheless, the Commission's role as referee of the bargaining game, able to blow the whistle when parties have failed to 'genuinely try to reach an agreement' in s 430, has allowed it some scope to test bargaining conduct against a good faith standard.[55] What kind of conduct does 'genuine' or 'good faith' bargaining require? In *Joy Manufacturing*, the employer sought an order under former provisions for terminating an existing certified agreement in the public interest. The Commission held that the employer's conduct in breaking off negotiations, refusing to respond to union proposals, switching precipitately to a non-union agreement (made directly with employees by sidestepping the union), and instigating a 'livelihood-destroying level of lockout action' were matters going to a finding of bad faith. The employer was nevertheless able to obtain the order it sought, because it had cured its bad faith conduct by subsequently terminating its bargaining period, removing the lockout, and volunteering to allow the Commission to exercise its powers under former s 111 to make orders resolving the stand-off. (The AIRC's powers to make such orders were removed with the *Work Choices* amendments.)

Section 32 of the New Zealand *Employment Relations Act 2000* is pragmatic in its advice to parties: good faith requires parties to use their best endeavours to agree to an orderly process for bargaining, to meet regularly, to consider and respond to each other's proposals, and to provide information to support their own claims. The Western Australian statute also prescribes practical guidance. 'Bargaining in good faith' under s 42B of the *Industrial Relations Act 1979* (WA) includes communication and explanation of one's position, meeting regularly at reasonable times, face-to-face; disclosing relevant information; acting honestly and openly and not capriciously changing the agenda;

---

53 See *AMIEU v G & K O'Connor* (1999) 97 IR 261.
54 (1995) 59 IR 385.
55 See eg the *National Tertiary Education Industry Union v Australian Higher Education Industrial Association* (2000) 48 AILR 4–309; *Joy Manufacturing Co Pty Ltd* [2000] AILR ¶4–341; and *Community and Public Sector Union v Sensis Pty Ltd* (2003) 53 AILR 100.

recognising bargaining agents; providing reasonable facilities to unions and employee associations to allow them to carry out their functions; and adhering to agreed outcomes and commitments. The Western Australian Commission in Court Session is empowered to make a code of good faith, by s 42C of the Act. Section 42D, however, clarifies that the good faith obligation does not require a party to agree to include any matter in an industrial agreement, nor to agree to enter an agreement at all.

The 'best endeavours bargaining' provisions of s 76A of the *Fair Work Act 1994* (SA) mandate the following bargaining practices:

(a) meeting at reasonable times and places to negotiate;
(b) explaining their positions;
(c) disclosing relevant and necessary information;
(d) acting openly and honestly;
(e) not 'capriciously' adding or excluding issues from the negotiations;
(f) adhering to agreed procedures;
(g) adhering also to agreed outcomes and commitments; and
(h) meeting their own timetables.

Those who support the inclusion of a good faith obligation in the bargaining provisions do so on the basis that such an obligation would support the view that the enterprise bargaining system is intended to support a process of 'real and not illusory negotiation and general agreement'.[56] If bargaining is to be more than merely a process whereby the employer places on the table a 'take it or leave it' offer that the employees must accept without negotiation, some procedures ensuring an orderly and respectful exchange of proposals is warranted. Ironically, the current provisions, enacted by the *Work Choices* amendments, do include some practical indications of the kinds of con-duct that constitute 'genuine' bargaining—but only in respect of pattern bargaining. In determining whether a negotiating party 'is genuinely trying to reach an agreement' for a single business, the following matters pursuant to s 421(4) are relevant:

(a) demonstrating a preparedness to negotiate an agreement that takes into account the individual circumstances of the business or part;
(b) demonstrating a preparedness to negotiate a workplace agreement with a nominal expiry date that takes into account the individual circumstances of the business or part;
(c) negotiating in a manner consistent with wages and conditions of employment being determined as far as possible by agreement between the employer and its employees at the level of the single business or part;
(d) agreeing to meet face-to-face at reasonable times proposed by another negotiating party;
(e) considering and responding to proposals made by another negotiating party within a reasonable time; and
(f) not capriciously adding or withdrawing items for bargaining.

---

56 *Schanka v Employment National (Administration) Pty Ltd* (1999) 166 ALR 663, 695.

One of the many peculiar provisions in the new Act, however, is s 421(6), which provides that this definition of genuine bargaining does not affect the meaning of the same phrase in other sections of the legislation. This suggests that the legislative drafters recognised that these procedures may provide valuable assistance to parties (and the AIRC) seeking guidance as to what kind of behaviour constituted genuine bargaining. They were happy to impose these practical requirements on unions to discourage pattern bargaining, but were afraid of imposing any mandatory procedures for negotiation on employers.

No pattern bargaining

'Pattern bargaining' is the term used to describe union campaigns across an industry or a number of workplaces directed towards securing common or at least comparable wages and working conditions. Pattern bargaining undermines the 'single business' enterprise bargaining agenda. In addition to the specific provisions requiring the AIRC to suspend or terminate a bargaining period where it finds that parties are engaged in pattern bargaining (see s 431), there are provisions restricting the taking of protected action to those parties who are to be bound by the proposed single business agreement. Any industrial action taken in concert with non-parties (including action taken in concert with workers in the same industry, but in different enterprises) loses its status as protected action: s 438.[57]

The prohibition on pattern bargaining applies to all parties negotiating workplace agreements, not just unions. The definition of 'pattern bargaining' does not single out conduct by unions: see s 421. Nevertheless, it is a generally a term confined to the behaviour of industry-wide union activity. Employers who want the convenience of fixing a common set of wages and conditions for a number of separate employing entities can apply for authorisation of a multiple business agreement under s 332.

Processes to ensure fair negotiation

Disclosure

A system based on contract principles—with its assumption that free negotiation of a consensual bargain will produce the most efficient outcome—favours full disclosure as the means of ensuring fairness. Information asymmetry is a cause of market failure, so the solution (according to this theory) is to ensure that parties are fully informed and have adequate time to process information before making a binding decision. Employees are therefore to be given access to the written agreement at least seven days in advance of approval.[58] Section 337 does not specifically require a personal copy to be given to each employee. Employers must 'take reasonable steps to ensure that all eligible employees in relation to the agreement either have or have ready access to the agreement in writing

---

57 For interpretation of action taken 'in concert', see *Australasian Meat Industry Employees Union v Meat & Allied Trades Federation of Australia* (1991) 40 IR 303; *Australasian Meat Industry Employees' Union v Mudginberri Station Pty Ltd* (1985) 9 FCR 425 and *J-Corp Pty Ltd v Australian Builders Labourers Federated Union of Workers (WA Branch) (No 1)* (1992) 44 IR 264, all decided prior to the enactment of the 1996 *Workplace Relations* reforms.

58 Section 337. Former s 170LK(2) required fourteen days.

during the period': s 337(1). Nevertheless, merely reading an agreement aloud and posting a single copy on a notice board was held to be inadequate in *Re Australia Meat Holdings Pty Ltd*,[59] decided under an earlier iteration of this provision. Employees may waive the right to ready access to the agreement under s 338.

Employees must be advised that they are entitled to be represented by a bargaining agent: s 337(4). If any employee takes up this invitation, the bargaining agent must be allowed reasonable time to consult with the employer: s 335(3). Employees are entitled to receive an information statement about the agreement, but this need contain only information about the time and manner in which the employer intends to seek approval for the agreement, notice of their rights to appoint a bargaining agent, and any other information gazetted by the Employment Advocate: s 337(4).[60] The requirement pre–*Work Choices* that employees must receive an explanation of the terms of the proposed agreement, and how it compared with their existing entitlements, has been abandoned.[61] In practice, employers used to disseminate a table comparing the new and old terms; however, this was not necessary where the employees were already aware of their exist-ing rights.[62] Post–*Work Choices*, the onus is on employees to inform themselves of the differences between a proposed agreement and former working conditions. Pre–*Work Choices* provisions requiring that any employees who have special needs for interpretation or explanation (for example, non-English speaking migrant workers, women and young people) must be given appropriate assistance have also disappeared from the legislation.[63]

So long as these very minimal requirements are met, the employees can be asked after seven days to approve the agreement. If a vote is taken, an agreement is approved if a majority of employees casting a valid vote approve it. No vote is necessary under s 340(2)(b). Approval can be given informally by a majority of employees.

Dealing with the risk of coercion and misrepresentation

The legislation also recognises the risk that a consensual process may be corrupted by coercive and deceptive tactics, so includes statutory protections from duress and coercion[64] and false and misleading statements.[65] These are civil remedy provisions, so that any person bound by the agreement or a workplace inspector can bring proceedings for a fine of up to sixty penalty units against a person who has used threats or coercion, or who has deliberately or recklessly misrepresented some matter, in connection with the making of a workplace agreement. An agreement affected by such conduct will nevertheless remain on foot, and binding on the parties, until a court orders that the agreement be declared void or varied under s 409. The sanctions against coercion apply to both sides of the bargaining table: both unions and employers have faced complaints about coercive conduct. Even formalised and notified industrial action taken

---

59 (1995) 62 IR 241, 250.
60 On 11 April 2006, Special Gazette No S 54 was published, containing the required information statements.
61 This requirement was in former s 170LK(7).
62 See *Re Application by Deckway Pty Ltd (t/as Lilianfels Blue Mountains)* [1995] AILR ¶3–067, 1, 280.
63 See former s 170LT(7).
64 Section 400.
65 Section 401.

in the genuine belief that a proposed agreement was certifiable fell foul of the former prohibition on coercion (s 170NC) when it was held that the proposed agreement contained a clause that did not pertain to the employment relationship.[66]

There is an inherent tension in a system that positively encourages industrial conflict and sanctions industrial action, but prohibits any form of coercion. In the *Electrolux* case for example, it was necessary for the matter to be litigated all the way to the High Court before it was clear whether industrial action was protected—and therefore exempt from sanction under former 170NC—or unprotected. Once a majority of the High Court held that the action was unprotected, it was held that the union's action was coercive, even though the employer side had conceded that the union had taken the action in good faith, believing that the claim was genuinely part of a properly notified bargaining period.

Dealing with the risk of discrimination

A collective mechanism that by definition favours majority rule may not only exclude the interests of minorities, but positively disadvantage those minorities at the expense of a majority. For example, hamburger chain Hungry Jack's and a union representing its workers attempted to register a collective workplace agreement that improved remuneration for fulltime career staff at the expense of lower rates of pay at the junior and casual levels.[67] Before *Work Choices*, collective workplace agreements had to be examined by the AIRC prior to certification. In this case the AIRC refused certification because it was not prepared to countenance an agreement that redistributed benefits between different classes of employees. Since the introduction of *Work Choices* there are no longer any legislative provisions requiring any institutional watchdog to vet agreements on the basis of fair dealing or discrimination between different employees; however, discriminatory content is prohibited from agreements by r 8.6, and so may be excised from a workplace agreement, if it comes to the attention of the Employment Advocate. This regulation prohibits any term of an agreement that would discriminate between employees on the grounds of race, colour, sex, sexual preference, age, physical or mental disability, marital status, family responsibilities, pregnancy, religion, political opinion, national extraction or social origin. The regulation excuses discrimination on the basis of the inherent requirements of the job, or to protect religious sensibilities. Discrimination between employees on the grounds of union affiliation is prohibited in the Act itself by s 402.

Protection from disadvantage

A clear regulatory shift is apparent in the *Work Choices* changes—formerly, compliance with certain mandated standards was policed at the point of authorising use of an agreement by the certification process. To some extent this minimised the more serious casualties of an enterprise bargaining system that inherently favours the strong over the weak. Now, there is little official supervision of bargaining and agreement-making, and

---

66 See *Electrolux* (2004) 221 CLR 309.
67 *SDA Hungry Jacks (South Australian and Northern Territory Group) Certified Agreement 2002* AIRC, PR928575, 10 March 2003.

parties must look out for their own interests and initiate their own litigation to address any breaches of standards. This raises particular concerns for the weak and disadvantaged worker in the Australian labour market.

Earlier iterations of the federal enterprise bargaining provisions, and the continuing provisions in many of the States, have dealt with the particular vulnerability of the weakest in the community by applying a no-disadvantage or 'no net detriment' test before allowing any enterprise bargain to be made. This test has been abandoned at federal level, and replaced instead with the legislated minimum conditions of the AFPCS, described in Chapter 7. Although no longer in place at the federal level, some discussion of the operation of a no-disadvantage test is warranted as an illustration of the risks that industrially weak workers do face from a market-based enterprise bargaining system.

The no-disadvantage test

In the federal system before *Work Choices*, a no-disadvantage test mediated the relation between collective and individual statutory bargains and the safety net of awards. The test was introduced in 1992, and it was considered to be particularly important upon the introduction of new 'enterprise flexibility agreements' that, for the first time, recognised statutory collective agreements made between employers and employees without the involvement of unions.[68]

When the Howard Government first tabled the *Workplace Relations and Other Legislation Amendment Bill* it sought to dispense with the no-disadvantage test and substitute it with a set of statutory minimum entitlements that would have applied universally to all employees. This strategy—ultimately effected by the *Work Choices* legislation—was designed to take control of the safety net away from the AIRC and beyond the influence of unions. The opposition and minority parties, which controlled the balance of power in the Senate in 1996, refused to endorse this change,[69] so a version of the no-disadvantage test was retained. The new test in former Pt VE (now repealed by *Work Choices*) was subtly but importantly different from the earlier test.

Under the new test, the AIRC was required to examine a proposed agreement against an award, or against an award 'designated', at the request of either the employer or a union party to an agreement, as an appropriate benchmark where there was no award binding the parties to the agreement.[70] The AIRC was required to apply a global test. Only if 'on balance' approval of the agreement would result in a reduction in the overall terms and conditions of the employment, would the agreement fail the test.[71] This meant that reduction in any specific entitlement would not cause the agreement to fail the first stage of the test. Only if the overall package disadvantaged the employees when compared with the benchmark award was the AIRC required to take the further step of examining those trade-offs against public interest.

---

68 There are similar tests in state legislation: see eg *Industrial Relations Act 1996* (NSW), s 35(1)(b); *Industrial Relations Act 1999* (Qld), s 160; and *Fair Work Act 1994* (SA), s 79(1)(e)(iii).

69 The Senate was persuaded by the Senate Economics Reference Committee's *Report on the Consideration of the Workplace Relations and Other Legislation Amendment Bill 1996*, August 1996 at para [4.176], that the government's preferred strategy would 'almost guarantee a worsening of employment entitlements' for the industrially weak in the community.

70 Former s 170XF.

71 Former s 170XA.

Even if an agreement did fail this global comparison it could nonetheless still be certified or approved if it was not contrary to the 'public interest' to do so.[72] The AIRC undertook this second test of public interest, even for AWAs. Agreements that were made as part of a strategy to deal with a short-term crisis or aid in the revival of a business, for instance, would satisfy this part of the test.[73] The no-disadvantage test thus meant that with limited exceptions (such as antidiscrimination, occupational health and safety, statutory termination provisions) most standards could be negotiated away.

When first introduced in 1992 the no-disadvantage test was stated as intended to protect 'well established and accepted standards which apply across the community, such as maternity leave, standard hours of work, parental leave, minimum rates of pay, termination change and redundancy provisions and superannuation'.[74] While this goal was reiterated in 1993 it was obvious then and even more so in 1996 that standards could be reduced, especially following the amendment requiring that any reduction had to be judged only as 'not contrary to the public interest' rather than in the public interest.[75]

In an important empirical study of the operation of the no-disadvantage test, Richard Mitchell and others have observed that determining 'disadvantage' by means of the global comparative exercise was inherently problematic.[76] The difficulty, if not impossibility, of evaluating the exchange is implicit in some of the comments made by the Commission in its decisions. Some commissioners said that it could not be applied 'purely as a mathematical exercise', and questioned the possibility of erasing basic work standards by reducing them to a monetary value.[77] The Commission rejected agreements that effectively bargained away all conditions for a dollar sum as inconsistent with its statutory duty to maintain a safety net of fair minimum wages *and* conditions.[78] However, there were numerous instances of agreements that cashed out basic entitlements. Although the Commission indicated some unwillingness to allow the complete bargaining away of sick leave and annual leave, many decisions cashed out

---

72 See Chapter 3 at p 90 for a discussion of public interest.

73 Former s170LT(4).

74 See Commonwealth, *Parliamentary Debates*, Senate, 7 May 1992, Minister for Industrial Relations, 2519. See also Commonwealth, *Parliamentary Debates*, House of Representatives, 28 October 1993, Minister for Industrial Relations, 2777. See also *The EFA Test Case*, (1995) 59 IR 430, 456; *The Tweed Valley Processors Enterprise Flexibility Agreement 1995* AIRC, Print M6526, 26 October 1995; *Re Application by Deckway Pty Ltd (t/as Lilianfels Blue Mountains)* AIRC, Print L4744, 16 January 1995; *Arrowcrest Group Pty Ltd re Metal Industry Award 1984* (1994) 36 AILR 402. Other community standards have included the provision of safe transport late at night for juniors: *Re Application by Toys R Us (Australia) Pty Ltd* (1994) AILR 1283; and more recently Whelan C in *Kellogg Brown and Root Pty Ltd; Worley ABB Joint Venture; Corke Instrument Engineering Pty Ltd* PR95172, 7 September 2004, held that it was a community standard to ensure that fathers could participate in family life.

75 See *Workplace Relations Act* 1996 (Cth), former ss 170LT(3) and 170VPG(4). See also J Riley et al *Workplace Relations: A Guide to the 1996 Changes* (1997), 324 and 332–3.

76 See R Mitchell et al *Protecting The Worker's Interest in Enterprise Bargaining: The 'No Disadvantage' Test in the Australian Federal Industrial Jurisdiction, Final Report Prepared for the Workplace Innovation Unit* (2004). Cf *Re MSA Security Officers Certified Agreement 2003* AIRC, PR937654, 15 September 2003.

77 See *Shop Distributive and Allied Employees Association v Bunnings Building Supplies*, AIRC, Print P6024, 21 October 1997.

78 See *Australian Municipal, Administrative, Clerical Services Union re Clerks (Breweries) Consolidated Award, 1985*, AIRC, Print S6443, 26 May 2000.

accumulated leave.[79] Prior to the abolition of the test by *Work Choices*, there was a trend demonstrating a gradual increase in the number of agreements in which the entitlements established in basic standards were 'cashed out'.[80] Thus under the no-disadvantage test the 'safety net' was already shrinking.[81] At least now with the AFPCS fixed in legislation, the benchmark is clear, albeit much lower than before.

Mechanisms for breaking deadlocks

There will be times when parties cannot reach agreement. Given that parties are entitled to take industrial action without fear of any legal sanction during a bargaining period, a 'Mexican stand-off' has the potential to be very damaging. For example, an employer in the meat industry sustained a lockout of employees for as long as eight months in pursuit of a change in working conditions.[82] Where parties have not genuinely tried to negotiate an agreement,[83] where unions have engaged in pattern bargaining,[84] or a demarcation dispute,[85] or where industrial action taken in a bargaining period has caused significant harm to a third party,[86] or generally endangered life, safety, health or welfare, or caused 'significant damage to the Australian economy or an important part of it',[87] the Commission has power to suspend or terminate a bargaining period. If the AIRC terminates a bargaining period under s 430(3) for endangering life, safety, welfare or economic stability, it must first give the negotiating parties between twenty-one and forty-two days to resolve the matters in dispute, and if they do not settle an agreement within that time, a Full Bench of the AIRC must make a workplace determination under Pt 9 Div 8 to resolve the disputed matters. A workplace determination may deal only with the disputed matters, and in making it, the Full Bench must regard the following factors only:

(a) the matters at issue;
(b) the merits of the case;
(c) the interests of the negotiating parties and the public interest;
(d) how productivity might be improved in the business or part of the business concerned;

---

79 Some cases disallowed complete cashing out of sick leave provisions, because of the public importance of allowing sick workers to recuperate: *Automotive, Food, Metals, Engineering, Printing and Kindred Industries Union v Tweed Valley Fruit Processors Pty Ltd* (1995) 61 IR 212, 233; *Re Independent Order of Oddfellows of Victoria Friendly Society* (1996) 65 IR 129; *Re Fabricorp Pty Ltd Enterprise Flexibility Agreement 1995* (1996) 64 IR 370.

80 See for example *Silver Chain Registered Nurses Agreement 1997*, AIRC, Print S1403, 27 May 1997; *Greyhound Pioneer Australia Ltd Certified Agreement*, AIRC, Print P8624, 5 February 1998; *Mountacastle Pty Ltd Enterprise Agreement*, AIRC, Print M2260, 22 December 1998; *Just Cuts (Canberra and Queanbeyan) Agreement 2000–2003*, AIRC, Print P7746, 4 July 2000. Cf *Timevalue Pty Ltd t/a Aussie World and the Ettamogah Pub, re Aussie World Employee's Certified Agreement 2002–2005* AIRC, PR923952, 23 October 2002. See also R Mitchell et al, above n 4, and Mitchell et al, above n 76.

81 See O Merlo 'Flexibility and Stretching Rights: The No Disadvantage Test in Enterprise Bargaining' (2000) 13 *AJLL* 207, 223.

82 See *Australasian Meat Industry Employees Union v GK O'Connor Pty Ltd* AIRC Print S0987, 17 November 1999; upheld by the Full Bench in Print S 2371, 12 January 2000.

83 Section 430(2).

84 Section 431.

85 Section 430(8).

86 Section 433.

87 Section 430G(3).

(e) the extent to which the conduct of the negotiating parties during the
     bargaining period was reasonable;
(f) incentives to encourage parties to pursue negotiated outcomes at a later stage;
(g) the employer's capacity to pay;
(h) decisions of the AFPC;
(i) any other factors specified in the regulations.[88]

A workplace determination operates as a collective workplace agreement, and is generally subject to the provisions of the Act relating to collective agreements, with the exceptions in s 506(2). For example, a workplace determination cannot contain any prohibited content. A workplace determination can have a nominal expiry date of no more than five years from commencement, but it can cease to apply in respect of an employee before the end of its nominal expiry if the employee becomes bound by a new workplace agreement: s 506(4).

The limited scope of workplace determinations means that they represent only the most minimal remnant of the AIRC's former powers of conciliation and arbitration, and are most unlikely to provide any avenue for militant unions to circumvent the *Work Choices* insistence that any wage rises or improvements in conditions above the safety net must be agreed by the employer and cannot be imposed. The provisions that existed before *Work Choices* was introduced allowed the AIRC to break a deadlock by making an award, unlimited by the restrictions on allowable award matters in former s 89A. Nevertheless, on the rare occasions that the Commission made one of these special s 170MX awards, it considered itself bound to make a minimum safety net award only. In the long-running Hunter Valley mining dispute, for instance, the union requested the Commission to terminate a bargaining period and made a s 170MX award, in the hope that the Commission would look favourably on their claims.[89] The award made by the Commission in that case reflected the earlier minimum safety net award with only minor changes.

A party to a workplace agreement is able to unilaterally terminate that agreement after its nominal expiry date, by lodging a declaration to that effect with the Employment Advocate: s 393. This means that once an agreement has run its term, a party seeking a new agreement can give ninety days' notice and then initiate a bargaining period for a new agreement. Failure to reach a bargain may result in one of these minimalist workplace determinations replacing the former agreement. Or it may result in parties returning to the safety net described in Chapter 7.

Recognition of binding agreements by lodgment

Once a collective agreement has been approved by a majority of employees (either by a vote or 'otherwise'), it must be lodged with the Employment Advocate within fourteen days, together with a declaration in the form required by the Employment Advocate and published in the Gazette. The Employment Advocate is expressly

---

88 Section 504(5).
89 *Construction, Forestry, Mining and Energy Union v Coal & Allied Operations Pty Ltd* AIRC, Print R9735, 7 October 1999.

exonerated from any obligation to check the accuracy of the declaration, or to test whether the requirements for approval have in fact been met: s 344(5). It will be up to a person bound by the agreement to bring any irregularities to the attention of a court for remedy. Section 341 prohibiting lodgment of an agreement without obtaining approval is a civil penalty provision, attracting a fine of up to sixty penalty units, and a person bound by the putative agreement has standing to bring an action for variation or avoidance of the agreement under s 409. A note to s 344(2) states that ss 137.1 and 137.2 of the *Criminal Code* create offences for providing false or misleading information or documents. Failure to lodge an agreement, and failure to issue employees with a copy of the Employment Advocate's receipt of lodgment within twenty-one days, are each civil penalty provisions, attracting fines of up to thirty penalty units.

The Employment Advocate issues receipts for lodgment (s 345) and the employer is responsible for notifying employees that the workplace agreement has been lodged: s 346.

Recognition of variations of agreements

The long potential nominal expiry dates for collective workplace agreements (increased from three to five years by the *Work Choices* legislation) may be expected to result in more activity seeking to vary agreements during their currency. The Act provides a mechanism for variation by agreement, and the processes for obtaining agreement to a variation reflect the processes for originating an agreement: see Pt 8 Div 8. Variations must be approved by a majority of employees under s 373, and be lodged with the Employment Advocate under s 375. There are penalties for lodging a variation that has not been duly approved by a majority of employees: s 374. No protected industrial action can be taken during the currency of a workplace agreement. A workplace agreement can also be terminated during its currency with the approval of a majority of employees: s 386. There are no provisions, however, for early variation or termination of agreements without approval.

Duration

Collective workplace agreements must stipulate a nominal expiry date, no more than five years from commencement. An agreement does not automatically cease to apply beyond that date unless the agreement itself contains a sunset clause that deals with termination: s 392. Even where an agreement provides for its own termination, a party to the agreement must give fourteen days' notice to the other parties and then lodge a declaration with the Employment Advocate that the agreement is to be terminated: s 392(4). Collective agreements can be terminated earlier than the nominal expiry date with the approval of the parties: s 381. The procedures required for early termination reflect the procedures for approving and lodging the agreement, and include providing information statements to employees at least seven days beforehand (s 384), obtaining their approval by majority (either by taking a vote or 'otherwise'),[90] and lodging a declaration within fourteen days of approval: s 388. If a vote is taken, a majority of employees casting a valid vote must approve early termination.

Under former provisions, an agreement would remain in force until a replacement agreement was negotiated. If the parties failed to negotiate a replacement agreement after the nominal expiry date, the employer, a union bound by the agreement, or a majority of employees bound was able to apply to the AIRC under former s 170MH to have the agreement terminated. After hearing all parties, the AIRC was required to terminate the agreement if it considered that it would not be contrary to the public interest to terminate it. Since the enactment of *Work Choices*, parties to a collective workplace agreement have been able to unilaterally terminate an expired agreement by lodging a declaration under s 393 with the Employment Advocate. The party seeking termination must take reasonable steps to inform other parties to the agreement of the intention to lodge this declaration at least ninety days before it is intended to lodge. An employer using this procedure may give undertakings about the terms and conditions of employment it will provide following unilateral termination, and the employer will be bound by any such undertakings until a new agreement is approved and lodged.

There is no obligation on employers to seek to negotiate a new collective agreement. Employers may unilaterally terminate an agreement after its nominal expiry date using this ninety-day notice provision, and return to reliance on the AFPCS. Sometimes, an employer will seek to negotiate the introduction of AWAs when a collective agreement has expired. The BHP litigation[91] (discussed in Chapter 10) demonstrates that the employer has no obligation to collectively bargain with employees. The legislation, as currently drafted, allows the employer the choice to opt for individual bargains, or to strike no bargain at all and rely only on the safety net. It is only industrial reality— the strength (or otherwise) of worker collectives, the convenience or otherwise of collective negotiation—which operates to persuade employers to engage in collective bargaining.

Employers are free to negotiate individual Australian Workplace Agreements (AWAs) with employees even while they are bound by a current collective agreement.[92] If an employee agrees to enter into an AWA, the collective agreement will have no effect in respect of that employee's employment. Former provisions that precluded the operation of an AWA until the expiry of an earlier collective agreement (unless the collective agreement expressly allowed for AWAs) were repealed with the *Work Choices* reforms. The *Workplace Relations Regulations* now prohibit the inclusion in a collective agreement of any term that 'directly or indirectly restricts the ability of a person bound by the agreement to offer, negotiate or enter into an AWA'.[93]

---

90 Section 386(2).
91 See *Australian Workers' Union v BHP Iron Ore Pty Ltd* (2000) 106 FCR 482.
92 See s 348(2).
93 Regulation 8.5(8).

Individual enterprise bargaining

Australian Workplace Agreements

One of the most contentious reforms of the *Workplace Relations and Other Legislation Amendment Act 1996* (Cth) was the introduction of a statutory individual bargain, called Australian Workplace Agreements (AWAs). The rationale for the introduction of a statutory individual contract was that it would support complete 'flexibilisation' of working conditions (and of course labour costs) by enabling bargains to be struck with individual workers, but in a way that would escape the weaknesses inherent in relying on ordinary common law contracts to regulate employment conditions. A common law contract cannot avoid award conditions, or override the minimum terms set by an applicable collective agreement. And it can certainly not escape the application of State legislation imposing minimum protective standards. An AWA made under a federal enactment has the status of federal statutory law and so overrides both the common law, and any contradictory State laws. So by adopting an AWA an employer can avoid the application of State laws, and also any awards[94] or collective agreements.[95] From the employee's perspective, this enables—in theory at least—the personal tailoring of working conditions. The only restrictions are those imposed by the AFPCS. As Chapter 7 explained, some of those standards—notably working time, and a proportion of annual leave—can still be bargained away to some extent by making an AWA.

Although described as a form of 'workplace bargain', in practice AWAs tend most often to be made as standard 'take it or leave it' offers. All staff of a particular classification are often given the same AWA—much like a standard insurance contract or other contract of adhesion.

It should be remembered that—for the constitutional reasons explained in Chapter 3—AWAs have only ever been able to be made by 'constitutional corporations', employers in the Territories and Victoria, and the Commonwealth government. (Now all new federal agreements can only be made by employers who meet the definition in s 6 of the *Workplace Relations Act*.) Because they are made with individuals, AWAs bear the well-recognised risks of unequal bargaining. These are addressed in the statute to some extent by provisions requiring disclosure of the terms, time to consider before signing, and protection from duress and coercion. AWAs made with minors (people under eighteen) must be signed by a responsible parent or guardian: s 340(1)(c).

In the early years of AWAs, the take-up rate by private sector employers was relatively low, and this tended to be blamed on the procedural requirements for making and seeking approval of AWAs, and on the requirement that any AWA must pass the no-disadvantage test. For very large workforces, the former requirements for approval were arguably burdensome. Attempts to simplify the processes for making AWAs were presented to Parliament in the form of amending Bills on several occasions between 1999 and 2004, but because these allegedly onerous procedures also formed part of the

---

94 See s 349.
95 See s 348(2).

protection for workers against too easy erosion of award protections and collectively bargained benefits, a fiercely independent Senate had been unwilling to agree to these amendments.

The *Work Choices* amendments in 2005 finally achieved the Government's objective of removing these disincentives for making AWAs. The procedural requirements were simplified considerably by the *Work Choices* reforms, and the no-disadvantage test (described above) has now been abandoned. AWAs are not vetted at all for their substantive content by the Employment Advocate. They must simply be signed and lodged. Nevertheless, an AWA is still subject to the limitation that it cannot undermine the basic safety net of wages and working conditions. To the extent that an AWA provides for lower wages or worse conditions than the AFPCS, the AWA will not be enforceable: s 172(2).

At the time of writing, it was too early to assess whether the take-up of AWAs would increase as a result of these reforms. Certainly, the government has been doing its best to encourage the take up of AWAs, especially in sectors of the labour market where it has particular influence. The contentious Higher Education Workplace Relations Requirements,[96] for example, represent an attempt by the government to lean on universities to make AWAs with their staff, instead of relying on their long-established practice of negotiating union collective agreements.

Where an employer is working in an industrially weak union-free territory, where there are no applicable awards or collective agreements, it remains doubtful whether AWAs offer the employer any advantages. Such employers may prefer to save themselves the trouble of making any agreements at all, by relying solely on the AFPCS.

Content of AWAs

The content rules for AWAs are the same as for collective workplace agreements. They must include a nominal expiry date, allowing a nominal duration of no longer than five years: s 352. They must include dispute resolution procedures (or else they will be assumed to contain the Pt 13 model dispute resolution procedures, explained in Chapter 12): s 353. They must explicitly override any protected award conditions if they intend to do so: s 354. And they must not contain any 'prohibited content', determined by the Government from time to time in regulations: s 356. The same content is prohibited for all workplace agreements, and is explained above.

Processes for making AWAs

Information disclosure

An employer who intends to make an AWA with an employee must provide the employee with 'ready access' to the agreement in writing at least seven days before seeking the employee's approval of the AWA. (Under the former provisions, an AWA could not be signed less than fourteen days after a written copy had been provided to the employee.) The employer must also provide an information statement that

---

96 See the *Higher Education Legislation Amendment (Workplace Relations Requirement) Act 2005* (Cth).

tells the employee when and how the employer proposes to obtain agreement, that the employee may engage a bargaining agent, and any other information required by the Employment Advocate and published in the government Gazette: s 337(4). The employee can, however, waive the entitlement to be given ready access to the agreement for seven days, but this waiver must be in writing and dated: s 338. The employer no longer has any obligation (as under former s 170VPA) to explain the effect of the agreement. Employee signatures must be witnessed, and if the employee is a minor, an 'appropriate person' (such as a parent or guardian, but *not* the employer) must sign for the employee.

Freedom from coercion

Employees are entitled to appoint a bargaining agent, and the employer must not refuse to deal with a properly appointed agent: s 334. Employees asked to sign AWAs enjoy the same protection from coercion and duress (s 400) and false and misleading statements (s 401) as apply for collective workplace agreements. An existing employee is not allowed to be terminated for failing to negotiate an AWA. This would constitute an unlawful dismissal under s 659(2)(g), and a breach of the freedom of association provisions under ss 792 and 793(1)(i), which provide that being 'entitled to the benefit of an industrial instrument' (which includes an award or collective workplace agreement) is a 'prohibited reason' for the purpose of the sanctions against dismissal. There is no longer any provision in the Act for employers to take advantage of the protected action provisions by locking out employees in the course of bargaining to introduce AWAs (see former s 170WB). Under the former provisions, AWA industrial action by employers was not uncommon.[97]

The case law on coercion or duress in relation to the making of AWAs is somewhat unsatisfactory. In *Schanka v Employment National (Administration) Pty Ltd*,[98] Moore J held that a 'sign or else' ultimatum given to employees who were transferring from a government authority to the same jobs with privatised agencies did constitute duress. However, in *Burnie Port Corporation Pty Ltd v Maritime Union of Australia (Burnie Port)*,[99] the Full Court of the Federal Court decided that a threat not to employ new recruits unless they agreed to sign an AWA did not contravene former s 170WG(1). The *Burnie Port* decision has been enshrined in a new provision. Section 400(6) provides that 'to avoid doubt, a person does not apply duress … merely because the person requires another person to make an AWA as a condition of engagement'.

In Bill form, s 104(6) had initially used the word 'employee' instead of 'person', raising the prospect that the legislation intended that existing employees could also be given 'sign or resign' ultimatums. The rectification of this provision prior to enactment, together with the continuation of unlawful dismissal protection under s 659(2)(g) and s 793(1)(i), indicates that a distinction is to be drawn between new and old employees. It is legitimate to make a 'take it or leave it' offer to new employees, but not to existing

---

97 See *AMIEU v Peerless Holdings Pty Ltd* (2000) 48 AILR 4-351(16).
98 (2001) 112 FCR 101.
99 (2000) 101 IR 435.

employees.[100] The distinction is justified on the basis that it is illegitimate to threaten existing employees with the loss of a job, whereas it is entirely legitimate to simply fail to offer a job to a new recruit. With respect, this distinction is not entirely satisfactory. In both cases, opportunities for ongoing employment are equally important to the candidates. Each type of candidate is equally susceptible to making a decision against their interests by necessitous circumstances. In the *Burnie Port* case, the new recruits were seeking work in depressed economic circumstances, where employment prospects were scarce. By agreeing to an AWA they would forfeit an entitlement to an industry-wide award that would otherwise apply. In practical terms, it is difficult to see why the second class of vulnerable workers—those without any job at all—should enjoy less protection, and should be exposed to the prospect of working side by side doing the same work with others who have the benefit of more generous pay and conditions.

Processes for approval

Within fourteen days of signature, the employer must lodge the AWA with the Employment Advocate: s 342(1). It must be accompanied by a declaration in the required form. There is no longer any requirement (as under former provisions) that the employer must provide a statement advising the Employment Advocate whether all comparable employees have been offered the same agreement. Any content in an AWA that is discriminatory will be prohibited content under r 8.6. The Employment Advocate is not required to check for such content prior to issuing a receipt for lodgment. Prohibited content can be removed subsequently. Section 402 prohibits any discrimination on the basis of union membership. The employment relationship will be governed by the AWA from the time of lodgment: s 347(1).

An AWA must include a dispute resolution clause, and if it does not, it will be taken to have included the provisions set out in Pt 13: s 353.

Variation and termination

AWAs may be varied or terminated by agreement, by the same processes involved in the initiation of an AWA. They may also be terminated without agreement, so long as their nominal expiry date has passed, by one of the parties giving the other party ninety days notice of an intention to lodge a declaration with the Employment Advocate that the agreement is to be terminated: s 393. This declaration must be lodged with the Employment Advocate (s 395), who must issue a receipt to the employee: s 396.

Supporting the high trust 'human resources management' model?

Much of the rhetoric surrounding the introduction of AWAs assumed that this instrument, and its capabilities for personal tailoring, would support the provision of flexible working conditions, and promote the objectives of the high trust human resources management

---

100 For cases decided under the former provisions in respect of existing employees, see *Canturi v Sita Coaches Pty Ltd; Napoli v Sita Coaches Pty Ltd* (2002) 116 FCR 276, and *Australian Services Union v Electrix Pty Ltd* (1999) 93 IR 43.

paradigm of contemporary employment. AWAs would be made in a spirit of cooperation and trust, to the mutual benefit of both parties. Early commentary on AWAs was skeptical of these claims.[101] Whether experience has supported these aspirations has been hotly debated.[102] Most of these studies, however, have examined the operation of AWAs made under the old rules that still provided extensive procedural protections and a no-disadvantage test. Time alone will tell how the new rules affect the culture of Australian workplaces.

Transmission of business rules

Coverage after changes in enterprise structure or ownership

Collective workplace agreements (and awards before them) are instruments designed to settle the wages and working conditions for a single business. A business, however, is not a legal person. It is an accumulation of assets (tangible and intangible), owned by a legal person or persons. The employer in an employment relationship is the legal person who owns the business, not the business itself. If an employer sells a business, or loses the entitlement to own and control those assets for some other reason (perhaps insolvency), a question arises as to whether any new owner will be bound by any industrial instruments made between the former owner and the employees of the business.

Industrial legislation has long contained provisions ensuring that the terms of settlement of an industrial dispute continue to bind transmittees, successors and assignees of businesses, at least for a time, subject to some qualifications. The rationale for such provisions was considered in an early High Court of Australia decision determining a challenge to a provision for the transmission of industrial awards in the old *Commonwealth Conciliation and Arbitration Act 1904* (Cth). In *George Hudson Ltd v Australian Timber Workers' Union*,[103] an employer attempted to avoid the consequences of an agreement struck with employees by winding up his company and transferring the business to a newly incorporated entity. In upholding the constitutional validity of the provision defeating this stratagem of award-avoidance, the Court focused on fair treatment of the employees who had relied on the award, and held that there was no injustice in binding successor employers to an award, 'because a successor to a business could not become so without knowing the statutory obligations of his predecessor to his employees'.[104]

Until the introduction of enterprise bargaining, disputes over transmitted awards were relatively rare, because the transmittee or assignee of the business was likely to already be a respondent to the industry-wide award, either directly or through membership of an industry association. If the new employer was not a respondent, it was a simple enough matter for a union to take steps to 'rope in' the new employer to an existing award. So the most significant transmission of business cases for awards

---

101 See R McCallum 'Australian Workplace Agreements: An Analysis' (1997) 10 *AJLL* 50.
102 See R Mitchell and J Fetter 'Human Resources Management and Individualisation in Australian Labour Law' (2003) 45 *JIR* 292.
103 (1923) 32 CLR 413.
104 (1923) 32 CLR 413, 435.

were in essence demarcation disputes.[105] The real issue in those cases was not whether the employer was to be bound by an award, but which award? Which of two unions would have coverage of the new workplace?

Single business enterprise bargaining has created many more opportunities for transmission of business disputes. The widespread adoption of workplace agreements has created many more problems when businesses are sold or restructured. The new owner may already be bound by the terms of some other very different industrial instrument. The very reason for the restructure or sale of the business may be to reorganise work practices, so that an old workplace agreement will not be appropriate to pursue new plans.

Trent Sebbens[106] has suggested that the transmission of business tests developed in the context of transmission of arbitrated awards[107] ought not to be applied to the transmission of single enterprise workplace agreements, because such agreements do not, and never have, played any safety net role. While it may make sense to preserve an arbitrated industry-wide award despite a change in business ownership (especially where the change involved some sham corporate structure designed to avoid the award), it makes less sense to bind the new operator of a restructured enterprise to the terms and conditions of an enterprise-specific bargain made between the operator and workers of an earlier incarnation of that business. On the other hand, the consensual bargains struck between workers and enterprises ought not to be easily discarded by corporate stratagems, designed only to allow one party to the bargain a liberty to avoid its commitments before they expire. As Sebbens notes, there is a balance to be struck between competing interests—on the one side is the workers' interest in stable wages and conditions, and on the other is the business sector's interest in fostering 'economic development through organizational flexibility'.[108] It should be remembered of course that the latter interest also protects the interest of capital owners in improving profits at the expense of working wages and conditions.

Most of the case law on transmission of business provisions concerns former s 149 of the *Workplace Relations Act 1996* (Cth). This provision, together with more recently enacted provisions dealing with collective workplace agreements and AWAs, has now been replaced by a new Pt 10 of the Act. The case law on s 149 continues to be of use, however, in identifying when a business has in fact been transmitted, assigned or transferred to a successor. Not all business ownership restructures will trigger the provisions, as is demonstrated by the decisions of the High Court in *PP Consultants Pty Ltd v Finance Sector Union of Australia* (*PP Consultants*),[109] and *Minister for Employment*

---

105 See eg *Re Australian Industrial Relations Commission; Ex parte Australian Transport Officers Federation* (1990) 171 CLR 216.

106 TD Sebbens, 'Wake, O Wake—Transmission of Business Provisions in Outsourcing and Privatisation' (2003) 16 *AJLL* 133, 146–7.

107 See the 'substantial identity' test for public sector enterprises, articulated in *Re Australian Industrial Relations Commission; Ex parte Australian Transport Officer Federation* (1990) 171 CLR 216, and the 'business characterisation' test from *PP Consultants Pty Ltd v Finance Sector Union of Australia* (2000) 201 CLR 648.

108 Sebbens, above n 106, 170.

109 (2000) 201 CLR 648.

and Workplace Relations v Gribbles Radiology Pty Ltd; Gribbles Radiology Pty Ltd v Health Services Union of Australia (Gribbles Radiology).[110]

In *PP Consultants*, St George Bank decided to close one of its rural branches, and instead appointed the pharmacy next door to act as its agent in offering retail banking services to customers. The pharmacy took over the premises formerly occupied by the bank, and engaged two of the bank's former staff to perform the same essential duties that they had performed for the bank. These employees continued to wear the red livery of the bank. Although the employees continued to do precisely the same work, in the same place, it was held that their industrial award had not transmitted in the course of this rearrangement of banking services. The majority held that a 'substantial identity' test, developed in earlier cases concerning public sector reorganisations and which focused on the nature of the duties performed by the employees, ought not to be applied in the case of a private sector arrangement. In private sector cases, it was necessary to examine the legal character of the business in the hands of its former owner, and compare that with the legal character of the business in the hands of the new owner. Only where those businesses bore the same legal character should it be held that a transmission of business had occurred for the purposes of continuation of a federal industrial award. In this case, it was held that the character of the business transferred had changed. Whereas the bank had operated a full-service banking business, relying on the margins between lending and borrowing for its profits, the pharmacy was operating only as a fee-for-service agent. The pharmacy was not operating a bank. This case offers a clear path forward for private enterprises to avoid existing awards and agreements by outsourcing specific business functions to labour-hire organisations.

In *Gribbles Radiology*, a group of doctors had contracted with a radiology service provider to operate from premises within their medical centre, for the convenience of easy referral of clients. The medical practice owned the equipment and held a head lease on the premises. When the medical practice re-tendered for the business, Gribbles won the contract, and took over the operation of the radiology practice, employing the same radiologists who had worked there under previous management. When Gribbles withdrew from the business and dismissed the employees, the employees claimed an entitlement to be paid out severance pay according to the terms of their award. Gribbles refused. The full Federal Court found, in favour of the employees, that Gribbles had succeeded to the radiology business, even though it had not had any dealings directly with the original business operators. This decision was subsequently overturned by the High Court. The High Court agreed with the Federal Court that 'succession' to a business (unlike 'transmission' or 'assignment') did not require any direct dealing between the old and new proprietors. However, a majority of the High Court held that a succession of a business necessarily involved the new operator acquiring some tangible or intangible assets formerly owned by the former operator.

The majority proposed a two-step test. The first step involves identifying what the business or part of a business is in the particular context, and the second involves

---

110 (2005) 214 ALR 24.

identifying what assets of that business are now enjoyed by the putative successor. In this case, the employees failed at the second step. Although the same assets were being used to operate the business (the premises, the equipment), these were all in the ownership of others (the medical practice). There was no assignment of any lease over premises or equipment. Nevertheless, Gribbles now enjoyed the same contractual rights as the former operator had enjoyed, albeit under a newly drawn contract, and not by way of assignment. Gribbles enjoyed the right to use the premises and equipment owned and controlled by the medical practice, and the right to receive referrals from the practice. Like *PP Consultants*, this decision demonstrates that the protection for employees' working conditions provided by transmission of awards and agreements is of limited benefit in the new world of business networks. Where workers are engaged not by monolithic enterprises, but by an interlocking network of discrete entities who provide services under contract to each other, there is much greater scope for restructuring to defeat any transmission of working entitlements.

Transmission rules

In a case where there has in fact been a transmission of business according to the tests described above, the provisions in Pt 10 of the Act will apply. Part 10 was enacted with the *Work Choices* reforms, and it covers all kinds of instruments—awards, AWAs, and collective agreements. The same essential rules have been made for all of them. Transitional provisions in Schs 6 and 9 of the Act make essentially the same rules for all other statutory instruments—transitional federal awards,[111] pre-reform certified agreements and AWAs,[112] preserved State agreements, and 'notional agreements preserving State awards' or 'NAPSAs'.[113]

These rules maintain some protection for employees following a sale or restructure of the business they work in, but with significant limitations, compared with the former law. First, only 'transferring employees' will have the benefit of any industrial instrument that transmits with a business to a new employer. Under the former rules, an instrument would bind the new employer in respect of any employees engaged in the acquired business. The new rules provide that the instrument will apply only to those employees who were engaged by the former business owners. (This rule potentially provides an incentive for a new business owner to decide not to engage the employees of the old employer.)

Transferring employees will only be covered by the transmitted instrument for so long as they do work of the same nature as the work they did for the old employer. If the nature of their employment changes, they will not continue under the old instrument.

Most importantly, the new owner will be bound by the transmitted instrument for a maximum period of only twelve months—not indefinitely (until variation by agreement or Commission order) as under the former provisions. The only instruments that do not

---

111 See Sch 6, cl 72G(4).
112 See Sch 9, cl 14.
113 See Sch 9, cl 23. These instruments are explained in Chapter 3.

have this twelve-month shelf life are transmitted Australian Pay Classification Scales. They already state the minimum entitlement for employees engaged in a particular classification of work.

A new employer can shorten the twelve-month period by seeking the transferring employees' agreement to a termination, under the provisions for early termination in Pt 8 of the Act. They may also negotiate new AWAs[114] or collective agreements with transferring employees;[115] however, the employees cannot be forced to accept new agreements during the twelve-month transmission period. Even if a transmitted collective agreement or AWA is past its own nominal expiry date, it cannot be terminated unilaterally by the incoming employer during the twelve-month period: see s 588(2) for collective agreements and s 584(1) for AWAs.

The same rules apply for pre-reform instruments. Parties can agree to terminate pre-reform certified agreements, AWAs or preserved State instruments, but they cannot make a unilateral application to have the instrument terminated earlier than the twelve-month transmission period according to the termination provisions in former s 170VM(3) or (6) for AWAs or former ss 170MH and 170MHA for certified agreements, even if the transmitted agreement is past its own nominal expiry date.

A transmitted agreement will have no effect once there are no longer any transferring employees engaged by the new employer. A new employer who decides to engage the old employer's employees will not, however, be able to dismiss those workers for the 'sole or dominant reason' that they have the benefit of the transmitted instrument. That would be in breach of the freedom of association protections in ss 792 and 793 of the Act (explained in Chapter 10). The new employer will, however, be able to dismiss those employees for 'operational reasons' under s 643(8), if such reasons genuinely exist.[116]

Any party bound by a transmitted award or collective workplace agreement can apply to the AIRC for an order that the award or agreement should not bind the incoming employer at all, or should bind for a period shorter than twelve months.[117] The legislation is silent as to the matters that the AIRC must take into account in making such an order.

Anti-avoidance provisions

An employer who does not wish to be bound by an instrument binding the vendor of the business can avoid it by not engaging any of the vendor's employees. However, vendors cannot circumvent the protection for transferring employees by making employees redundant shortly before transmission if the purchaser intends to hire those employees. If the employees are dismissed within a month of the transmission, and are engaged by the new employer within two months of the transmission, the employees will be transferring employees, entitled to the benefit of the provisions: s 581(2).

114 See s 585(3).
115 See s 587(3). See Sch 9, cl 12(2) for pre-reform agreements.
116 See Chapter 9 at pp 424ff.
117 See s 590 for collective workplace agreements, and s 595(5) for awards. The AIRC has no power to make orders in respect of transmitted AWAs.

The transmission rules will not apply to a transmission that occurs only because an old employer who is not a constitutional corporation decides to incorporate the business and transfer employees to the new corporate entity. Schedule 9, cl 10(5) provides that a transmitted pre-reform certified agreement made by an unincorporated employer with a union to resolve an industrial dispute will not cease to operate after twelve months if the only reason for the transmission was that the employer adopted the corporate form to opt into the new workplace relations system. There appear to be no similar provisions for transitional awards. Presumably, then, if an employer bound by a transitional award decided to incorporate to opt into the new system, the new corporation would be bound by the transitional award for no longer than the twelve-month transmission period.

Notification and lodgment requirements

New employers are required to notify transferring employees of their entitlements under a transmitted instrument within twenty-eight days of employing the employee (s 602) and lodge those notices with the Employment Advocate within fourteen days of the transmission date: s 603.

Priorities

Only one workplace agreement can govern the employment of any given employee at any particular time: s 348(1). But which one? The proliferation of forms of industrial instruments has created some complexity. The priority rules—which exhibit a policy preference for localised, enterprise-based bargaining, preferably between employers and their individual employees—may be stated thus:

- An AWA operates to the exclusion of any award or collective agreement that would otherwise apply to that employee's employment: 353(2). Since collective agreements cannot preclude the making of AWAs by individual employees, this means that where a collective agreement applies generally at a workplace, it will nevertheless not bind the employer in respect of any employee who has signed an AWA.
- In the absence of any AWA, a collective agreement operates to the exclusion of any award, or any State law, outside the specific exclusions in s 16 of laws relating to occupational health and safety, workers' compensation, apprenticeship, and any other matter stipulated by the *Workplace Relations Regulations*: s 349.
- If a new collective agreement is made while an earlier one is in operation (that is, the old agreement has not been terminated by agreement, and is still within its nominal expiry date), then the new agreement will not take effect until the nominal expiry date of the old agreement: s 348(3).
- In the case of a transmission of business where the employer acquiring the business is already bound by an existing workplace agreement, the employer will be bound only by the transmitted workplace agreement in respect of the transferring employee. The transferring employee's employment will not be governed by the

new employer's existing workplace agreement, until the transmitted agreement is terminated by agreement, or else expires after the twelve-month transmission period: s 586.

Dispute resolution

Once an agreement is made it is binding for its stipulated term or until it is terminated early by agreement. It is an important object of the enterprise bargaining system that once lodged, bargains should underwrite a period of industrial stability for enterprises by mandating an interregnum of up to five years between each period of renegotiation. During the agreement, however, issues frequently arise concerning interpretation of the agreement, and how it should apply to a particular situation. Workplace agreements must contain dispute resolution mechanisms for dealing with these kinds of issues.[118] Pt 13 of the *Workplace Relations Act* deals with dispute resolution processes, and provides a default model dispute resolution process to be used where agreements have failed to stipulate any processes. This process requires that parties 'genuinely attempt to resolve the dispute at workplace level' before resorting to the assistance of any other processes. Importantly, however, parties do not forfeit any rights they may have to litigate any matter arising under an agreement: s 693. The dispute resolution provisions are discussed in Chapter 12.

---

118 Section 353.

Conflict at Work: Rights and Resolutions

Managing industrial conflict

Even within the new paradigm of cooperative workplace relations, some industrial conflict is inevitable. Cooperation is an ideal that is rarely perfectly achieved. There will always be times when parties cannot agree, when a bargaining deadlock must be broken, when disagreement over the interpretation of an agreement must be resolved. And of course, under the old 'industrial relations' paradigm, the very purpose of law was seen to be the management of an inherent conflict between the interests of capital and labour.[1] A desire to avoid a repeat of the damaging industrial disputes in the shearing and maritime industries in the 1890s was an important motivation for those who framed the federal industrial power in Australia's *Constitution* to provide for conciliation and arbitration of interstate industrial disputes. So although this chapter comes last, it deals with an issue of fundamental importance: law's power to intervene in, and resolve, industrial conflict.

Conflict arises in a number of contexts. On the one hand, there is conflict directed towards winning new rights for oneself, and imposing new responsibilities on others. This kind of conflict is strategic conflict—the flexing of industrial muscle for the purpose of pressing a case for the recognition of certain interests. Typically, these kinds of disputes are termed 'interest' disputes, because they concern the assertion of interests, with the intention of establishing new rights. On the other hand, there are disputes over the interpretation and application of existing industrial instruments in particular situations. These are typically termed 'rights' disputes, because they concern the interpretation and application of existing rights.

This chapter will consider interests disputes first. This involves an examination of the collective bargaining provisions in the *Workplace Relations Act*, and particularly those provisions that allow negotiating parties to take 'protected' industrial action. It also involves an examination of the statutory and common law sanctions against any

---

1 'The purpose of labour law is to regulate, to support and to restrain the power of management and the power of organized Labour': O Kahn-Freund *Labour and the Law* 2nd edn (1977).

industrial action, that does not enjoy the statutory immunities allowed to protected action. Protected action can only be taken during a properly notified bargaining period. Once an agreement is made and lodged, legitimate 'interest' disputation is at an end, until the relevant agreement expires.

While workplace agreements are in force, disputes may arise about the interpretation of those agreements, about their application to particular circumstances, and about alleged breaches. This chapter also considers the legal mechanisms available to parties to resolve these kinds of disputes.

The common law context

Before proceeding to an examination of the current statutory controls on industrial conflict, it is important to acknowledge some historical influences. All industrial action—including strikes, pickets and boycotts—has traditionally been unlawful under the common law. Indeed, even the formation of trade unions was for a long time considered to constitute criminal activity.[2] For workers to agree among themselves to withdraw their labour was certainly a criminal conspiracy.[3] An early conspiracy of this nature was punished by transportation to New South Wales.[4] The British *Combinations Act 1799* made it a criminal offence for workers to make any agreement among themselves to raise wages, reduce hours, limit work, or interfere in any way with the master's business.[5] Under the British *Master and Servants Acts* of 1747, 1765 and 1823, a servant could be imprisoned for up to three months for going on strike or absconding from work. It was not until the *Trade Union Acts* of 1871 and 1876 that trade unions were granted immunity from suit for conspiracy in restraint of trade.[6]

The traditional Australian system of conciliation and arbitration maintained the fundamental principle that a strike intending to cause harm to the employer's business constituted an actionable tort—possibly one or more of a number of 'industrial torts' (described below)[7]—however, common law suit against unions by employers was discouraged by the facility to notify a dispute under the prevailing industrial legislation, and to have the dispute settled, either by conciliation or compulsory arbitration. Except for a brief period from the enactment of former s 334A by the *Industrial Relations Reform Act 1993* (Cth) until its repeal in 1996, there has been no general 'right to strike' in Australia.[8] Strikes were, despite common practice, illegal. It was unusual, however, for employers to take common law action because the industrial machinery offered a more efficient means of resolving disputes and achieving what the employers really wanted—a return to work. Nevertheless, it is important to remember that special

---

2   See PG Gahan 'Dead Letters? An Examination of Union Registrations under Australian Colonial Trade Union Acts 1876–1900' (2000) 13 *AJLL* 50.

3   *Quinn v Leathem* [1901] AC 495.

4   See *R v Loveless* (1834) 174 ER 119.

5   Above n 2, 5

6   For a general study on the development of Australian Trade Union law see JH Portus *The Development of Australian Trade Union Law* (1958).

7   For a detailed explanation of the legal principles of the industrial torts, see AJ Stewart 'Civil Liability for Industrial Action: Updating the Economic Torts' (1984) 9 *Adel L R* 358.

8   K Ewing 'The Right to Strike in Australia' (1989) 2 *AJLL* 18.

industrial laws and procedures have always operated within the shadow of the common law's intolerance for any kind of industrial action.

Industrial action under the *Workplace Relations Act*

Since 1996 there has been a very limited right to take protected industrial action during a bargaining period for a single business collective workplace agreement, but there has been no right to strike in support of claims to coverage by an industrial award, apart from during the short period of time when former s 334A remained on the statute books. The enterprise bargaining regime (described in Chapter 11) legitimates the use of industrial muscle, but only for so long as it conforms to the strict rules of the game.

What is industrial action?

Industrial action is defined in s 420 of the *Workplace Relations Act* to mean any of the following:

(a) the performance of work by an employee in a manner different from that in which it is customarily performed, or the adoption of a practice in relation to work by an employee, the result of which is a restriction or limitation on, or a delay in, the performance of the work;

(b) a ban, limitation or restriction on the performance of work by an employee or on the acceptance of or offering for work by an employee;

(c) a failure or refusal by employees to attend for work or a failure or refusal to perform any work at all by employees who attend for work;

(d) the lockout of employees from their employment by the employer of the employees.

The definition, although apparently wide enough to contemplate a failure to attend work due to illness, is read in the context of the statutory purpose of defining 'industrial' action, so only action that has the character of industrial disputation is captured.[9]

The statutory definition specifically excludes any action taken by employees that has been authorised or agreed to by the employer. Arguably, a limited work ban such as that imposed by the bank employees in *Australian Bank Employees' Union v National Australia Bank Ltd*[10] might be held to be impliedly authorised by the employer, if managerial staff acquiesced in the performance of a lesser range of duties.

One of the consequences of a finding that action taken by employees is industrial action is a prohibition on payment for at least four hours of time on the day that the action took place: s 507. If the employer has agreed to or acquiesced in the taking of the action (for example, the holding of a stop work meeting, or an alteration of duties that are the subject of a dispute), then the action will not fall within the definition of industrial action and the employer will not be obliged to withhold wages, and may

---

9 *Automotive, Food, Metals, Engineering, Printing and Kindred Industries Union v The Age Company Limited* AIRC, PR946290, 11 May 2004.

10 (1989) 31 IR 436.

thereby avoid escalating an acrimonious dispute. On the other hand, an employer who wants to treat the action as industrial action and withhold wages should take steps to make it clear to employees that any limited work restriction—however minor—is not authorised. See for example the steps taken by the employer in *Spotless Catering Services Pty Ltd v FLAIEU*.[11] Clear instructions given to employees were held to be sufficient to indicate the employer's refusal to acquiesce in a particular work ban (a refusal to serve items of food on a particular new menu), without the necessity for the employer to actually lock employees out.

Industrial action taken out of a reasonable concern about an imminent risk to health or safety is also excluded by the statutory definition; however, if employees wish to take advantage of this carve-out, they bear the onus of establishing that their apprehension of a safety risk was reasonable, and that they complied with all reasonable directions of the employer to do other available work, at the same or another site: s 420(1)(g).

It is important to note that the definition of industrial action also contemplates employer industrial action. The lock-out is a powerful tool in the hands of employers, and has been used effectively to bring about widespread change in the working conditions in some industries in Australia—notably the meat processing industry. See for example the long running dispute dealt with by the Australian Industrial Relations Commission (AIRC) in *Australasian Meat Industry Employees Union v GK O'Connor Pty Ltd*.[12] Section 420(3) defines a lock-out as any occasion on which 'the employer prevents the employees from performing work under their contracts of employment without terminating those contracts'.

Protected industrial action

Any industrial action (as defined in s 420) taken in pursuit of a collective workplace agreement made under Pt 8 of the *Workplace Relations Act* is immune from any common law action (with important exceptions) so long as the parties comply strictly with the bargaining rules stipulated in the legislation.[13] These immunities include protection from dismissal or injury in one's employment: s 448. This means that employees taking protected action cannot be demoted or lose any entitlements; however, they may nevertheless be stood down, and they have no entitlement to remuneration for the period of industrial action: s 448(2).

All parties taking protected industrial action (employers, unions and employees) will be immune from suit for any of the industrial torts (described below); however, this immunity does not extend to immunity from suit for action that has involved 'or is likely to involve' personal injury, wilful or reckless property damage or misappropriation of property, or defamation: s 447.

Protected industrial action will also not be susceptible to statutory sanctions against industrial action. The AIRC may not grant a s 496 stop order (described below) ordering

---

11 (1988) 25 IR 255.

12 AIRC, Print S0987, 17 November 1999.

13 Note that protected action cannot be taken in pursuit of an AWA, which means that employers who lock out employees in a campaign to introduce AWAs in a workplace do not enjoy the immunities of protected action.

the action to cease: s 496(13). Also, the industrial combatants will not be susceptible to any sanction under s 400 (which is an offence provision) for coercive conduct: s 400(2).

Requirements for protection

Since the *Work Choices* amendments taking effect early in 2006, the requirements for securing protection for industrial action have become so onerous that many commentators have predicted that protected industrial action will become rare indeed. The procedures now require that unions intending to flex industrial muscle for the purpose of persuading an employer to agree to a log of claims for a collective agreement, must take a number of steps before stopping work. Pattern bargaining is strictly prohibited, so the first step is to identify the single business or part of a business proposed to be covered by the desired workplace agreement.

The union or employees opening negotiations must give at least seven days' written notice to the employer and to the AIRC that they intend to initiate a bargaining period: ss 423 and 427. This notice must be accompanied by detailed particulars, identifying the types of employees to be covered by the proposed agreement, the matters proposed to be included in the workplace agreement, a nominal expiry date, and any other matter required by regulations: s 426.

Both parties must then 'genuinely try to reach agreement' before taking any industrial action: s 444. Failure to do this renders the whole bargaining process susceptible to an order by the AIRC that the bargaining period be suspended or terminated under s 430. It the AIRC does suspend or terminate a bargaining period, no protected industrial action can be taken.

Before a union can organise any industrial action, it must make an application to the AIRC for permission to hold a secret ballot to obtain the authorisation of employees for the particular action planned: s 445. The secret ballot provisions are extensive: ss 449–93. They are also supported by extensive regulations dictating the processes for administering a ballot: rr 9.4–9.23.

First the AIRC must grant the application, then the ballot must be held, and at least 50 per cent of employees must vote in the ballot. At least 50 per cent of validly cast votes must favour taking the action, before the action will enjoy protection: s 478. There is an exemption from applying for and holding a secret ballot if the union or employees are taking industrial action in response to employer industrial action. So an employer who initiates industrial action by locking out employees will lose the benefit of the brake on employee industrial action provided by these secret ballot provisions.

Once the ballot is taken, the industrial action must also be 'duly authorised' by a committee of management of the union itself: s 446. Once authorised, the union must give the employer at least three days' notice that particular industrial action is to be taken (s 441), and this must occur within thirty days of the secret ballot: s 478(1)(d). During any industrial action, the union must comply with any procedural directions or orders made by the AIRC: s 443. Failure in any of these requirements will cause the industrial action to be unprotected by the immunities in the statute.

Exclusions

Any one of a number of circumstances will rob purported protected action of its protected status.

If the union is engaging in pattern bargaining (meaning that it is attempting to obtain the same agreements across a number of different enterprises), the industrial action will not be protected (s 439) and the AIRC must terminate any bargaining period initiated to support such agreements: s 431. Similarly, if any persons who will not be bound by the single business enterprise agreement once made are participating in the action by 'acting in concert with' negotiating parties, the industrial action will not be protected: s 438. The meaning of acting 'in concert' with others has been judicially considered in connection with the secondary boycott provisions under the *Trade Practices Act 1974* (Cth). (The secondary boycott provisions are outlined below.) In *J-Corp Pty Ltd v Australian Builders Labourers Federated Union of Workers (WA Branch) (No 2)*,[14] French J of the Federal Court held that acting in concert meant more than acting simultaneously. It was necessary that parties be shown to be acting with a community of purpose. Union officials who merely offer advice to parties taking industrial action will not necessarily be acting in concert with the strikers: see *Australasian Meat Industry Employees Union v Meat & Allied Trades Federation of Australia*,[15] and *Australasian Meat Industry Employees' Union v Mudginberri Station Pty Ltd*.[16]

If the proposed collective agreement contains any prohibited content (explained in Chapter 11) any action taken in support of the agreement will not be protected: s 436. This much was decided in the *Electrolux* decision.[17] That decision also demonstrated that taking industrial action in good faith, believing the action to be protected, will nevertheless expose the combatants to penalties for breach of the coercion provisions in s 400 (formerly s 170NC).

Protected action cannot be taken while employment at the workplace is covered by another workplace agreement that is still within its nominal expiry period. This is so, even if the existing agreement does not deal with the matters proposed in the new agreement: ss 440 and 494. Section 440 defeats the finding of the Federal Court in *Australian Industry Group v Automotive, Food, Metals, Engineering, Printing & Kindred Industries Union*,[18] which allowed a union to take protected industrial action in support of a new workplace agreement dealing only with redundancy matters, while an earlier agreement specifically excluding redundancy, was still on foot.

Finally, if any of the procedural requirements explained above are not followed to the letter, the industrial action will be unprotected, exposing participants to the risk of legal sanctions.

---

14 (1992) 46 IR 263.
15 (1991) 40 IR 303.
16 (1985) 9 FCR 425.
17 *Electrolux Home Products Pty Ltd v Australian Workers Union* (2004) 221 CLR 309.
18 (2003) 130 FCR 524.

No work, no pay

Protected action is still industrial action, and will trigger the operation of s 507, which prohibits any payment of wages for periods of industrial action.[19] Strikers—including those who undertake limited work bans—acquire no immunity from loss of wages so long as the employer objects to, and does not acquiesce in their behaviour.[20] Since the enactment of *Work Choices*, the minimum amount of time that a striking employee must be docked is four hours for any day on which industrial action was taken. Given that a thirty-minute stop work meeting will incur the same deduction from wages as one of four hours' duration, it is not surprising that during the first industrial negotiations involving the ferries on Sydney Harbour after the introduction of *Work Choices*, services stopped for four hours. No work, no pay. No pay, no work.

Dealing with deadlocks

If parties negotiating an agreement cannot reach agreement, despite taking industrial action, the AIRC has a power under s 432 to suspend bargaining for a 'cooling off' period on the basis that such an order may assist the parties to resolve issues. Application for a 'cooling off' suspension can be made by a party to the negotiations, and the AIRC must give all parties an opportunity to be heard before making an order. The AIRC also has powers to suspend a bargaining period where protected action is causing significant harm to a third party, for example, the proprietors of other businesses dependent upon supply from the enterprise in conflict: s 433. An application for such an order can be made by the person or organisation affected, or by the Minister.

Where protected action is causing serious harm to the community, the AIRC has a power to suspend or terminate a bargaining period: s 430(3). The AIRC may make such an order on its own initiative, or on application by a negotiating party or the Minister, if it finds that the protected action threatens 'to endanger the life, the personal safety or health, or the welfare, of the population or part of it; or to cause significant damage to the Australian economy or part of it': s 430(3)(c). The AIRC had this power under former s 170MW of the Act. In 2006, *Work Choices* introduced an additional provision enabling the Minister to intervene directly to terminate a bargaining period by making a declaration under s 498. So if the Minister is not satisfied with the AIRC's assessment of the public interest, the Minister can take matters in hand personally. If the Minister chooses to exercise this power, he or she may also forbid the initiation of a new bargaining period to deal with the contentious matters: s 498(6).

If the AIRC or the Minister terminates a bargaining period for reasons of public safety or economic welfare, the matters remaining in dispute may be resolved by a Full Bench of the AIRC making a workplace determination under Pt 9 Div 8. Workplace determinations are more limited than former s 170MX awards, which could be made by the AIRC to resolve an acrimonious dispute, and could include matters other than

---

19 *Independent Education Union of Australia v Canonical Administrators, Barklay Street, Bendigo* (1998) 157 ALR 531.

20 See s 420 definition. See also *ABEU v National Australia Bank Ltd* (1989) 31 IR 436, for an illustration of the way in which an employer may be seen to impliedly authorise industrial action.

allowable award matters. Although a workplace determination is stated to operate as if it were a workplace agreement (s 506), it may only deal with the limited range of matters that were in issue at the time that the bargaining period was terminated. The Full Bench's discretion to make these determinations is constrained by the matters listed in s 504, and they appear to be heavily weighted in favour of finding that the employer enterprise ought not to be burdened with any obligation that it is unwilling to accept. The factors include 'how productivity might be improved in the business', 'the employer's capacity to pay', and 'decisions of the AFPC [Australian Fair Pay Commission]'. The AFPC's brief is to provide the barest of safety nets for employees.

If experience under the former provisions that enabled the AIRC to make a s 170MX award to resolve a dispute following compulsory termination of a bargaining period is any indication of the way the post–*Work Choices* provisions will operate, then it appears that employees are unlikely to secure improvements in working conditions by pressing a dispute to the point of a need to make a workplace determination. The AIRC's determination of a s 170MX award in *Construction Forestry Mining and Energy Union v Coal and Allied Operations Pty Ltd*[21] demonstrated that the AIRC treated itself as bound to make only a minimum safety net award when exercising these powers. It refused to exercise its powers to tip the balance of bargaining power in favour of a union that was losing an industrial battle to improve working conditions.

A recipe for more conflict?

The extensive regulation of the bargaining process has opened up scope for a considerable amount of litigation over whether procedures have in fact been complied with, and whether the AIRC has exercised its own discretions properly in making directions and orders concerning bargaining periods. Arguably, the introduction of protection for certain industrial action, and the detailed provisions marking out protected from unprotected action, have encouraged a new legalism, which has exacerbated rather than ameliorated industrial conflict.

Consider for example the progress of the Hunter Valley coal mining dispute in the late 1990s. The parties—a multinational resources corporation and an established trade union—found themselves before the AIRC or the Federal Court on several occasions in their efforts to resolve this acrimonious dispute.

In November 1997, Boulton J was persuaded to terminate a bargaining period under the powers conferred on the AIRC under former s 170MW—now s 430(3)(c)(ii)—on the basis that the action was destructive of the public interest. The union sought this order so as to invigorate the Commission's powers under former s 170MX to make an award that was not limited by the constraints on allowable award matters in s 89A. (Now the AIRC would be required to make a workplace determination to resolve the limited matters under dispute: see s 503.) The employer successfully appealed Boulton J's decision before a Full Bench in January 1998, but then the union sought judicial review of the Full Bench decision before the Full Court of the Federal Court.

21 AIRC, Print R 9735, 7 October 1999.

In November 1998, the Federal Court held that the Full Bench had committed a jurisdictional error, and remitted the matter to the Full Bench to be reheard. In May 1999, a new Full Bench restored Boulton J's original order. The matter then went to hearing to determine an award, and the Full Bench made the award in October 1999 (nearly two years after the original order). Meanwhile, the employer appealed the Federal Court's decision quashing the original Full Bench decision to the High Court of Australia. The High Court overturned the Full Court of the Federal Court decision, and reinstated the first Full Bench decision. It is difficult to see that this highly juridified process promotes industrial harmony and facilitates efficient dispute resolution. Arguably, the old system, which empowered the AIRC to step in to resolve disputes by conciliation and arbitration, was more effective in reaching timely solutions to industrial conflict than the legal processes revealed by the *Coal and Allied* litigation. The new Ministerial power to terminate bargaining periods by declaration may prompt more cases of judicial review of administrative action.

Unprotected industrial action

By restricting the jurisdiction of the AIRC to intervene between warring parties to an industrial dispute at an early stage in conflict, the new regime has in many respects reinvigorated recourse to common law suits. The threat to bring tort action against a negotiating party has again become a common weapon of industrial warfare. Until the *Work Choices* amendments, former s 166A provided that any person intending to take tort action against another party for damage caused by unprotected industrial action was first obliged to obtain a certificate from the Commission. The Commission had seventy-two hours to resolve the dispute, before the party seeking the certificate was entitled to continue with the filing of a suit against the union in the courts. This requirement gave the AIRC a window of time (albeit a very narrow one) in which to broker a truce. Section 166A did not apply to any action brought in respect of conduct resulting in personal injury or property damage or conversion, nor for any complaint arising out of a demarcation dispute, an unlawful claim for strike pay, or any conduct that was in breach of a direction given by the AIRC or any State industrial authority. Section 166A was repealed by *Work Choices*, so that parties are no longer constrained in their ability to litigate a dispute. Even where parties have committed themselves to resolving disputes by some alternative dispute resolution procedure in an agreement, they may nevertheless take court action to resolve any dispute: s 693.

Persons affected by unprotected industrial action may seek a remedy under tort law, or a statutory injunction under the *Workplace Relations Act* s 496, or—in the case of a secondary boycott—may seek a *Trade Practices Act 1974* (Cth) remedy. Each of these kinds of actions is explained below.

Common law action for industrial torts

On an individual level, a refusal to perform work according to the terms of the engagement is a breach of contract, and if it signals a repudiation of the contract, gives rise to an employer's right to terminate the contract summarily. Collective withdrawal of labour also risks characterisation as an industrial tort. Inducing a person to breach a contractual obligation with a third person constitutes a tort committed against the third person. For instance, in *Sanders v Snell*[22] it was held that the action of a Minister in persuading a public servant to dismiss another without giving the proper notice required by the contract was a tortious act. Under the common law the actions of unions in organising strikes may constitute a number of industrial torts: inducing breach of contract, conspiracy to injure the employer in its trade or business, and possibly intimidation.

During the years of conciliation and arbitration, industrial tort cases were rare. Two notable examples occurred because the unions involved deliberately stepped outside the prevailing rules of the industrial system. In *Dollar Sweets Pty Ltd v Federated Confectioners Association of Australia*,[23] for example, the strikers were seeking shorter hours in breach of an industry-wide consensus that no further claims for shortened hours would be made. The strikers and picketers who were successfully sued for a number of torts (including assault and intimidation because of their threatening behaviour towards people entering the factory) were defying the orders of an industrial tribunal. They deliberately stepped outside the informal protections offered by the former system of conciliation and arbitration, and found themselves subject to the rigors of a common law that is entirely antipathetic to disruptive industrial action.

Likewise the notorious airline pilots' dispute[24] occurred because the pilots' federation objected to the Accord principles imposing wage restraints that had been agreed between the ACTU, the government and the employer peak bodies. The pilots took the view that these restraints were appropriate to nine-to-five workers, but not to highly skilled pilots who worked in stressful jobs entailing exceptional demands. To demonstrate their point, they organised industrial action that involved members working only between the hours of 9 am and 5 pm. This of course meant the cancellation of many flights, especially long haul flights. Because the action was as much a reaction against the prevailing Hawke Labor Government's industrial relations agenda as a strike against employers, the Government intervened in the action by providing the services of the air force to make some flights to help break the strike. The employers terminated the contracts of the pilots, and advertised overseas for pilots. The pilots' union placed their own advertisements in these international magazines, warning overseas pilots not to become 'scabs', because if they did so they would inevitably lose their new Australian jobs when the strike had been resolved and the Australian pilots were restored to their positions.

The employers took action in tort against the pilots' federation and individual officers of the federation, and succeeded. (Next time you catch an international flight with a foreign airline, and hear a familiar Australian accent, remember the striking airline pilots. Many of them were never re-employed in Australia.) The airline pilots' dispute was an incredibly complex one. Many aspects of the dispute are now of limited interest because they concerned an analysis of the now largely defunct arbitral powers of the

---

22 (1998) 196 CLR 329.
23 [1986] VR 383.
24 *Ansett Industries (Operations) Pty Ltd v Australian Federation of Airline Pilots (Pilots' Case)* (1989) 95 ALR 211.

AIRC. However, the case remains significant for its detailed analysis of the elements that will go to prove the commission of one of the industrial torts. For that reason, a study of those aspects of the decision is provided here.[25]

The Pilots' Case

The airline employers first brought actions for damages for breach of contract against individual pilots, but discontinued these proceedings and instead pursued tort actions against the Australian Federation of Airline Pilots (AFAP) and fourteen of its members, including the president, the vice-presidents and the salaried executive director. Five causes of action were argued:

- interference with contractual relations;
- unlawful interference with trade or business;
- conspiracy (constituted by the mass resignations of the pilots);
- action on the case for intentionally inflicting harm (according to the principles in *Beaudesert Shire Council v Smith*[26]); and
- intimidation (by way of the warning notices published in international magazines to deter others from applying for employment with the airlines).

Brooking Justice exhaustively examined the evidence for each of these claims, and found on the facts that the mass resignations did not constitute conspiracy, nor did the advertisements in overseas press constitute intimidation. He did not consider the claim for the 'action on the case'. He did, however, find for the plaintiffs on the claims based on the tort of interference with contractual relations, and the tort of unlawful interference, or intentional infliction of economic loss by unlawful means. He assessed damages at $6.48m, which was a significant sum in 1990, especially when one considers that liability for this sum was to be shared by individual union officials.

Interference with contractual relations

The tort of interference with contractual relations requires a plaintiff to prove that the defendant has induced another to breach a contract. In this case, two kinds of contractual relationship were identified: the employment relationships between the airlines and the pilots, and the contracts of carriage between the airlines and their customers.

The argument concerning the employment contracts was that the AFAP and its officers had induced the rank and file members of the union to take strike action. A finding against the union therefore involved finding that taking strike action was necessarily a breach of the employment contract. This is in fact a contentious point. Lord Denning in *Morgan v Fry*[27] suggested that strike action suspended, but did not necessarily terminate, a contract of employment. In *Hall v GMH Ltd*,[28] Keely J opined

---

25 For a comprehensive analysis of the entire dispute see KP McEvoy and RJ Owens 'The Flight of Icarus: Legal Aspects of the Pilots' Dispute' (1990) 3 *AJLL* 87. See also KP McEvoy and RJ Owens 'On a Wing and Prayer: The Pilots' Dispute in the International Context' (1993) 6 *AJLL* 1.

26 (1966) 120 CLR 120.

27 [1968] 2 QB 710, 728.

28 (1979) 45 FLR 272, 279.

that a strike, although a breach of the employment contract, need not always be a sufficiently serious or fundamental breach to justify termination. In this case, after failing to persuade the court that they enjoyed a general right to strike, the union argued that it was an implied term of the pilots' employment contracts that they should be able to take strike action without rendering themselves liable to dismissal. The union attempted to rely on its own rules and procedures manuals, which the employer had acknowledged in its dealings with union, and which contemplated occasions when industrial action may be taken. Brooking J dismissed this argument and held that the union's action in encouraging members to go out and remain on strike constituted an inducement to breach their contracts.

The essential elements of the tort of interference with contractual relations, set out by Wells J in *Woolley v Dunford*,[29] are:

- there must be knowing and intentional interference without justification;
- there must be proof of interference with a contract not discharged nor finally performed, and binding on a third party;
- the interference may lead to a breach, or may simply hinder performance;
- the interference may be direct or indirect;
- the interference must be unlawful. Where the interference is direct, unlawfulness is found in the persuasion or inducement itself, but where it is indirect there must be some independent unlawfulness in the means of the interference;
- the breach or defective performance need not itself be actionable;
- the defendant must know of the contract, but constructive knowledge is sufficient; and
- the interference must be intentional.

In the pilots' case, the airlines alleged that the AFAP and its officers had directly induced breaches of contract by issuing the directive that the pilots should not attend for work outside the hours of 9 am to 5 pm. The unlawful act was the inducement to breach the employment contract, which required cooperation with the airlines' flight schedules. The AFAP clearly knew that the employment contracts existed, and intended that the contracts should not be perfectly performed. The AFAP argued that it had not induced the striking pilots to go on strike at all. The pilots themselves, as members of the union, had taken the decision themselves and authorised their union to coordinate their action. Although 95 per cent of the pilots present at meetings had voted in favour of resolutions to strike, Brooking J rejected this view of the facts. He relied instead on authority in *South Wales Miners' Federation v Glamorgan Coal Mining Co*[30] for the proposition that a union giving directions for industrial action remains responsible for that action, despite acting on the express authority of its members. Brooking J also rejected the AFAP's argument that the striking pilots had acted willingly. According to Wells J in *Woolley v Dunford* 'it is immaterial that the contract-breaker … yields readily or is even a willing party to the breach'.[31] The implications of this decision for unions

---

29 (1972) 3 SASR 243, 266–8.
30 [1905] AC 239.
31 (1972) 3 SASR 243, 290–1.

in the current environment are clear: unions and union officials will not be able defend themselves from personal liability for the tort of interfering in contractual relationships, on the basis that they are simply carrying out the instructions of their constituencies.

Unlawful interference with trade or business

The essential elements of this tort are the commission of an unlawful act with the intention of and causing damage to the plaintiff. In *Daily Mirror v Gardner*[32] Lord Denning MR held that if one person interferes with the trade of another using unlawful means then that person has committed a tort, even in the absence of conspiracy, intimidation or interference with contractual relations. Authority for the existence of this tort derives principally from English case law.[33]

In this case, Brooking J held that the AFAP had given the nine-to-five directive with the intention of injuring the plaintiff airlines, so as to secure industrial advantages for themselves. The requirement that the union's conduct be unlawful was satisfied by two arguments: that inducing the breaches of employment contracts was unlawful in itself, and that the action also constituted a breach of s 312 of the *Industrial Relations Act 1988* (Cth), which imposed a criminal penalty on officers of associations who encouraged or incited their members to ignore the terms of a binding industrial award. This provision was part of the AIRC's armoury for protecting arbitrated awards from being undermined. Brooking J allowed the alleged breach of s 312 to count as an unlawful act, without there being any actual prosecution of the union for that supposed breach.[34] This demonstrates a peculiar consequence of the availability of this tort action: a statutory offence provision that does not itself exhibit any intention to confer a private right of action on any person affected by the breach may nevertheless found an essential element in a tort claim brought by that person. This appears to contradict authority in *Williams v Hursey*,[35] where Fullager J (with whom Dixon CJ concurred) said: '[I]t does not follow that an action will lie at the suit of an individual … who has suffered loss by the commission of the offence … It is only in a limited class of case that a statutory prohibition accompanied by an express criminal sanction can be held to create a duty enforceable by civil proceedings.'

A defence to the tort: justification

The AFAP attempted to argue that its actions were justified by its legitimate role in furthering the industrial interests of its members. Brooking J rejected this argument. It was an argument suggested, however, by the House of Lords decision in *Lonrho*.[36] *Lonrho* concerned an allegation of conspiracy by unlawful means; however, it may

---

32 [1968] 2 QB 762, 783.

33 See *Ex parte Island Records* [1978] 3 All ER 824; *Lonrho Ltd v Shell Petroleum Co Ltd (Lonrho)* [1981] 2 All ER 456; *Metall und Rohstoff v Donaldson Lufkin & Jenrette Inc* [1989] 3 All ER 14; *Merkur Island Shipping Co v Laughton* [1983] 2 WLR 778; *Hadmor Productions v Hamilton* [1982] 1 All ER 1042. See RJ Mitchell 'Liability in Tort for Causing Economic Loss by the Use of Unlawful Means and its Application to Australian Industrial Disputes' (1976) 5 *Adel LR* 428, 451–3.

34 For an analysis of this aspect of the decision, see McEvoy and Owens, above n 25.

35 (1959) 103 CLR 30, 79.

36 *Lonrho* [1981] 2 All ER 456.

equally apply to an action for causing damage by unlawful means. The House of Lords suggested that the defence of justification may be available even where the means used are independently unlawful.[37] The conclusion in *Lonrho* was that the tort is made out only where the predominant intention of the defendant is to cause harm to the plaintiff. That is, if the defendants' predominant concern was to further its own trade interests and damage to the plaintiff was only secondary, the tort will not be made out. This aspect of the *Lonrho* decision has not, however, been followed uniformly in all subsequent English decisions.[38]

Implications of the *Pilots' Case*

Following the enactment of the *Work Choices* amendments, the *Workplace Relations Act* contains a great many offence and civil penalty provisions aimed at curbing the industrial activities of unions. The airlines case demonstrates that unions—and their individual office bearers—are susceptible not only to statutory fines and injunctions for breach of these provisions, but may also be liable in tort for damages suffered by an employer (or indeed any other person affected) as a result of any action taken that is made unlawful by those myriad provisions. Strikes, boycotts and pickets have always been susceptible to common law action in the past, but the system of conciliation and arbitration set up to regulate industrial disputation meant that such actions were relatively rare. The new regulatory framework imposes none of those disincentives or impediments to litigation.

Statutory injunctions under the *Workplace Relations Act*

Tort action is nevertheless subject to the usual expenses and delays involved in all forms of litigation. Parties affected or threatened by unprotected industrial action may choose the quicker route of seeking and obtaining a stop order under s 496 of the *Workplace Relations Act*. Any unprotected action is susceptible to such an order. (Circumstances that will cause industrial action to lose it protected status are outlined above.)

Section 496 is the successor to former s 127. This new statutory injunction has evolved from an earlier injunctive power conferred on the AIRC to call a halt to destructive industrial action occurring the public sector. In 1996, s 127 was amended to extend the power to the private sector, and to empower the AIRC to issue such orders whenever unprotected industrial action was happening, threatened, impending or probable. After 1996, s 127 did not require that the AIRC determine that the action was causing any particular dangers to personal or public welfare before issuing a stop order. Nevertheless, in its own interpretation of the power, the Commission showed some caution. For instance, in *Coal & Allied Operations Pty Ltd v AFMEPKIU*[39] (another episode

---

37 For a discussion of *Lonrho* and its implications see M Otlowski 'The Demise of Conspiracy by Unlawful Means?' (1989) 2 *AJLL* 107.

38 See eg *Hadmor Productions v Hamilton* [1982] 1 All ER 1042, and *Lonrho plc v Fayed* [1989] 2 All ER 65.

39 (1997) 73 IR 311.

in the long-running Hunter Valley mine dispute), a Full Bench of the Commission held that just because industrial action was not protected by the statutory immunities did not mean that it would necessarily be 'unlawful' action. Factors other than the requirements for protected action status had to be considered, including Australia's obligations under International Labour Organisation (ILO) treaties protecting freedom of association and rights to collective bargaining, which at the time were still preserved in the objects clauses in former s 3 of the *Workplace Relations Act*. In particulars, 3(k)—which has survived the *Work Choices* changes as s 3(n)—describes an object of the Act as 'assisting in giving effect to Australia's international obligations in relation to labour standards'. Hence, the AIRC held that the ILO conventions supporting freedom of association and rights to bargain collectively should be respected, and the AIRC should exercise some restraint in issuing s 127 orders. This interpretation of its own powers was consistent with the permissive wording of former s 127: it stated that the AIRC 'may' issue a stop order, not that it must do so.[40]

The *Work Choices* amendments substantially rewrote these provisions so that the AIRC is now obliged to issue a stop order whenever it 'appears' that unprotected action is happening, is threatened, impending or probable, or is being organised. Section 496 orders can be issued against industrial action being taken in State industrial systems wherever the threatened industrial action is likely to cause substantial loss or damage to a constitutional corporation: s 496(2). Applications for these orders can be brought by any person affected, or likely to be affected, by the industrial action, or by a peak body, and the AIRC can also make an order on its own initiative: s 496(4). The AIRC has only forty-eight hours to determine applications. If it is unable to reach a conclusion within that time, it is obliged to make an interim order that the action cease, unless it would be contrary to the public interest to do so: s 496(5)–(7).

The first case to test s 496 involved an application made against the Transport Workers Union who had organised industrial action during the currency of a preserved collective State agreement with a nominal expiry date of 31 December 2007. Hamberger SDP held that the elements for grounding an order were established: industrial action was happening; it was industrial action taken by employees of a constitutional corporation; and the industrial action was not protected. Hence, the AIRC was bound to make the order. 'There is no need to determine that the industrial action is "illegitimate" as was the case for s 127 applications under the unamended Act.'[41] The TWU had argued that they were not susceptible to the order because they were an organisation registered in New South Wales under the *Industrial Relations Act 1996* (NSW). Hamberger SDP held that a s 496 order can be made against 'any person', and that since person was defined to include an organisation, an organisation registered in New South Wales was also a person susceptible to an order.

---

40 For an analysis of the law applying former s 127, see V di Felice 'Stopping or Preventing Industrial Action in Australia' (2000) 24 *MULR* 310.

41 See *TNT Australia Pty Ltd Riteway Transport Pty Ltd t/as Riteway Express and Transport Workers' Union of Australia* AIRC, PR971471, 10 April 2006. This decision was subsequently appealed to a Full Bench, and the orders were amended: see AIRC, PR973028, 15 June 2006.

Consequences of a stop order

A party who breaches a s 496 order can be taken to the Federal Court, which has power under s 496(10) to issue an injunction. Refusal to obey a Federal Court injunction renders a person liable to proceedings for contempt of court—so ultimately one's liberty is at stake. The path towards imprisonment for industrial action is more tortuous now than it was in the nineteenth century, but the common law's intolerance for strikers has returned to cast a shadow over trade union activity.

Potential to curb political protests?

The potential for such an extensive power to be used to curb political protest is of considerable concern in a community where there has historically been a close association between political and industrial issues. In the 1970s in Sydney, for example, it was the building workers unions (and Jack Mundy in particular) who led protests against the destruction of heritage buildings and imposed 'green bans' in protest against overdevelopment of the urban landscape. The notorious waterfront dispute of 1998,[42] in which many ordinary Australians participated, was as much a general protest against the callous manipulation of corporate structures (with tacit government encouragement) to rob working citizens of rights and entitlements, as it was a contest between a particular organisation and its employees. This concerted attack on the maritime unions by a coalition of political and employer parties was deeply resented by the broader Australian community and they joined in protest on the waterfronts. In more recent times the trade union movement has been involved in general awareness campaigns over safety at work, and unions in the higher education sector have been concerned with the erosion of academic freedom threatened by the so-called Higher Education reforms.

The statutory stop order under s 496 makes it mandatory for the AIRC to order people to cease any industrial action that comes within the broad definition in s 420, that is, where the protest involves disturbing anyone's normal working arrangements. If any withdrawal of labour outside the parameters of 'protected action' for single enterprise bargaining is susceptible to injunction, important political freedoms are at risk. Workers are citizens too. They speak as both workers and as citizens through their participation in the workforce.[43]

This issue was squarely raised in *CEPU v Laing*,[44] a dispute essentially triggered by anti-union industrial relations law changes in Western Australia. Workers in the State's power stations engaged in industrial action as a political protest against the Western Australian government's introduction of industrial legislation allowing individual contracting. The union's argument in that case was that their industrial action was a legitimate exercise of their freedom of political speech. While the *Australian Constitution* does not recognise this as an individual right, it prohibits any exercise of legislative or executive power that unreasonably constrains the

---

42 See *Patricks Stevedores Operations No 2 Pty Ltd v Maritime Union of Australia* (1998) 195 CLR 1.
43 See R McCallum 'Collective Labour Law, Citizenship and the Future' (1998) 22 *MULR* 42.
44 (1998) 159 ALR 73.

freedom.[45] This argument failed to impress the court, and a stop order was granted. Under current legislation, the AIRC has no discretion to refuse an application for an order if it finds that industrial action is happening. There is certainly no discretion to weigh in the balance any civil or political rights of the industrial combatants.

Secondary boycotts

A primary boycott concerns a dispute directly between an employer and the employer's workforce. A secondary boycott occurs when a person who is not a party to a negotiation for an agreement joins in industrial action to bring additional pressure to bear on one side of a dispute between an employer and employees. For example, imagine that oil refinery workers are in dispute with their employer. If the Transport Workers' Union were to persuade its members to refuse to make any deliveries for the oil refineries in order to bring more pressure on the oil refineries to meet the demands of their own workers, then the transport workers would be engaged in a secondary boycott. Since January 1997, a secondary boycott constitutes a breach of the *Trade Practices Act 1974* (Cth) and renders those engaging in the boycott liable to fines, damages and injunctions ordered by the Federal Court under the *Trade Practices Act*. The Australian Competition and Consumer Commission (ACCC) has standing to bring an action against a union engaging in secondary boycott activity, even if the corporation affected by the conduct does not wish to take any action. Fines under the *Trade Practices Act* are substantial—a union may be fined up to $750000 under s 76(1A)(a) for each act in breach of the secondary boycott provisions. Other remedies include injunctions under s 80, damages under s 82 for any person who suffers loss or damages as a consequence of breach of the provisions (and damages can be very substantial), and any 'other orders' under s 87 that the court deems appropriate in the circumstances.

Secondary boycott provisions were first enacted by the Fraser Liberal Government in 1977. The insertion of these provisions into trade practices legislation signalled the Government's view that this type of conduct ought to be regulated alongside other anti-competitive market conduct. On this view, a secondary boycott was an abuse of market power, and ought to be regulated as such. The provisions remained in the *Trade Practices Act 1974* until the Labor Government removed them and enacted different boycott provisions in the *Industrial Relations Act 1988* (Cth). The Labor Government's philosophy was that secondary boycotts formed part of the fabric of industrial disputation and were more properly regulated by the industrial statute, under the supervision of the AIRC. In 1996, the Howard Liberal Government restored the provisions, in an allegedly 'simplified' form (although the 1996 provisions are more detailed and consume many more pages of text) to the *Trade Practices Act*. This restoration is testimony to the Howard Government's commitment to regulating all conduct that affects market competition under the provisions of Pt IV of the *Trade Practices* legislation.

---

45 See eg *Nationwide News Pty Ltd v Wills* (1992) 177 CLR 1; *Australian Capital Television Pty Ltd v Commonwealth* (1992) 177 CLR 106; and *Lange v Australian Broadcasting Corporation* (1997) 189 CLR 520.

A particular advantage of inclusion of the provisions in the *Trade Practices Act*, as far as the Federal Government is concerned, is the ability for the competition watchdog, the ACCC, to police the provisions, regardless of the inclinations of the parties to disputes.[46] Successive Ministers for Employment and Workplace Relations have expressed frustration with the unwillingness of employers to take the full benefit of their legal rights in punishing illegal industrial action. The ACCC provides an alternative plaintiff/prosecutor, who need not be concerned with the practical industrial costs of pursuing action against parties with whom they wish to continue doing business in the future.

Identifying a secondary boycott

The secondary boycott provisions, now in ss 45D–45EA of the *Trade Practices Act 1974* (Cth), prohibit concerted conduct by two persons (the first and second persons) that interferes with the supply of goods or services from a third person to a fourth person (the target), where the purpose of the conduct is to cause substantial loss or damage to either the third or the fourth party, or to cause a substantial lessening of competition in the market. Because the *Trade Practices Act* provisions are underpinned constitutionally by the corporations power in s 51(xx) of the *Constitution*, it is necessary that either the third or the fourth person be a corporation.

For example, in *Wribass Pty Ltd v Swallow*,[47] meat packers at a Tasmanian abattoirs black-banned the supply of meat to a supermarket that proposed to sell meat on a Saturday morning. (The case pre-dated the freeing up of butchers' trading hours.) In this case, the Tasmanian union's branch secretary was held to be the first person, the union was the second person, the wholesaler was the third person, and the supermarket was the fourth person target of the boycott. In *Utah Development Co v Seamen's Union*[48] tug pilots imposed a black ban on ships sailing under flags of convenience. The tug pilot workers and their union were held to be the first and second persons, the tug owners and operators were the third person, and the fourth person target was the ship owner.

Section 45DB prohibits a 'three person' type of boycott: a person must not, in concert with another, engage in conduct that prevents or substantially hinders the third person from engaging in international trade or commerce. This provision depends upon the trade and commerce power in the *Constitution* for its validity.

All of these provisions catch activities by unions, because the union and its members count as multiple separate persons. Just as in the airlines dispute (described above) the union was held to have induced its members to act, even though the union acted on a resolution by its members, so in a secondary boycott action a union will be treated as a separate person from the members authorising its actions.

The legislation is also designed to catch any deals done between workers and their own employers that would have the effect of bringing industrial pressure on a target. For example, in *Leon Laidley Pty Ltd v TWU*,[49] a dispute arose because Leon Laidley

---

46 See for example *ACCC v Automotive, Food, Metals, Engineering, Printing & Kindred Industries Union* [2004] ATPR 42–002.
47 (1979) 38 FLR 92.
48 (1977) 1 ATPR ¶40–049.
49 (1980) 28 ALR 589.

Pty Ltd was using non-union labour to transport its bulk fuel supplies from Amoco (a large oil supplier). The Transport Workers' Union (TWU) boycotted Amoco, to bring pressure on it to stop supplying Leon Laidley. Leon Laidley succeeded in obtaining an injunction under former s 45D against the TWU; however, the TWU subsequently came to an agreement with Amoco to settle the industrial action, and a term of that agreement involved Amoco agreeing not to supply Laidley. Under ss 45E and 45EA, these kinds of deals are now prohibited.

Protest action alone (picketing) is not sufficient to attract the sanctions of the *Trade Practices Act*. In *Gisborne Garden & Building Supplies Pty Ltd v Australian Workers Union*,[50] a protest over dismissals of workers staged at the gates of a garden centre was held not to contravene the Act. The protest did not in fact prevent any supply to the premises, except to the extent that suppliers decided of their own volition not to deal with the business.

Consumer boycotts

At first glance, the secondary boycott provisions would appear to catch consumer and environmental lobby group boycotts.[51] However, consumer and environmental boycotts are specifically excluded from the legislation, so long as the boycotts do not involve taking any industrial action: see s 45DD(3).

Dispute resolution

Orderly dispute resolution

A dispute—even an interests dispute—need not result in industrial action. Although the *Workplace Relations Act* appears to encourage actual industrial action by providing protections, it also encourages parties to use alternative dispute resolution mechanisms of a facilitative nature to resolve their differences without disturbance to work and productivity. Part 13 of the Act, dealing with dispute resolution generally, also provides that the AIRC may be engaged by the parties to resolve an interests dispute, using techniques such as arranging for conferences: s 706(2). The AIRC is expressly forbidden, however, from arbitrating any interests dispute, or making any determination of parties' rights: s 706(4).

The AIRC—and private dispute resolution providers—may also play a role in determining rights disputes, that is, disputes over the interpretation and application of awards, agreements and other industrial instruments.

Disputes over workplace agreements and other industrial instruments

Disputation does not necessarily cease after negotiating parties have reached and lodged workplace agreements. Like all contract documents, workplace agreements are often ambiguous, or fail to anticipate certain eventualities, so disputes arise over

---

50 [1998] FCA 1323.

51 See eg *Australian Wool Innovation Ltd v Newkirk* [2005] ATPR 42–053, which concerned a boycott of Australian wool exporters by a group called the 'People for the Ethical Treatment of Animals'.

the interpretation of rights, and over the application of terms and conditions to certain circumstances. There will also be disputes that arise when one or other party inadvertently, negligently or deliberately breaches an agreement.

Every workplace agreement is required to include a dispute resolution clause. Any agreement lodged without one is deemed to include the model dispute resolution process described in s 694 in Pt 13 of the Act.

Consistently with the Howard Government's push towards the privatisation of industrial disputation, these dispute resolution procedures encourage the settlement of disputes at the workplace level, first by some internal grievance handling procedure, and then by use of alternative dispute resolution machinery. The model process in s 694 sets out the following hierarchy of steps that must be taken should a dispute arise over any instrument containing the model provisions (either expressly or by default):

1   Parties must genuinely try to resolve matters at the workplace level: s 695.
2   If parties are unable to resolve the matter at workplace level, they may agree to seek the assistance of a mutually acceptable alternative dispute resolution service provider: s 696(1) and (2).
3   If parties cannot agree on whom to appoint, either party may notify the Registrar that the parties have not been able to agree on an alternative dispute provider: s 696(3).
4   The Industrial Registrar must provide an information statement prescribed by *Workplace Relations Regulation* 13.1, and must give the parties fourteen days to consider their options.
5   If the parties still cannot agree, a party may apply to the AIRC to have the matter resolved by the AIRC.

If this final step is reached and the AIRC is appointed to resolve the dispute, the AIRC's powers are limited by s 701(4). It does not have power to compel persons to do anything, to make an award to resolve the matter, to make any orders in respect of the matter, or to appoint a board of reference to oversee the matter, even if the parties agree that the AIRC should do such things: see s 701(5). The AIRC can arbitrate the matter or determine the respective rights or obligations of the parties only if the parties have agreed that the AIRC should do so. Hence, the model process set out in the Act does not confer on the AIRC any power to finally settle any matter, unless the parties expressly agree to it.

The model process set out in the legislation is to be used to resolve disputes over the following kinds of matters:

- the terms of a workplace agreement where the agreement contains or is deemed to contain the model process: s 353;
- the application of a workplace determination: s 504;
- the application of an award: s 514;
- entitlements under the Australian Fair Pay and Conditions Standard: s 175; and
- entitlements to meal breaks (s 609), public holidays (s 614), and parental leave (s 691) under Divs 1, 2 and 6 of Pt 12 of the *Workplace Relations Act*.

The model does not necessarily apply to all workplace agreements made under Pt 8 of the Act. Parties to workplace agreements are free to make their own provisions for dispute resolution, and they may include in their agreements a term appointing the AIRC as a private mediator and arbitrator. If they do so, the AIRC will have the power to do whatever the agreement permits, including arbitrate on the dispute; however, it will not have the power to make any binding orders: s 711(2).

The AIRC's private arbitration powers

Some explanation of the history of the AIRC's private arbitration powers is warranted. Under the former provisions (s 170LW), the AIRC had a power to accept the role of private arbitrator when parties made agreements to that effect. Disputes arose over whether the AIRC could exercise the full range of its arbitral powers when fulfilling this private arbitration function, or whether it was constrained by the provisions in former s 89A to arbitrate only over allowable award matters. This difficulty was settled by the High Court of Australia in *Construction, Forestry, Mining and Energy Union v Australian Industrial Relations Commission*.[52] There, the Court held that when exercising powers conferred under a clause in a certified agreement, the Commission derived its arbitral power from the contract between the parties, and was therefore not restricted by the limitations on its award-making powers under former Pt VI of the Act. In particular, it was not limited to resolving matters that fell within the list of what were then twenty allowable award matters in former s 89A.[53]

In the course of the judgment, the High Court noted in an aside that this dispute concerned a single business. A single business could not be involved in an 'industrial dispute', according to the definition that was then included in s 4 of the Act, since that definition necessitated an interstate dimension. None of the provisions in Pt VI of the Act dealing with the Commission's powers to settle industrial disputes would therefore apply to its exercise of powers conferred by s 170LW and a certified agreement to settle single business disputes. This aside left open room for argument in subsequent cases before the AIRC that if the dispute resolution clause was part of an agreement made to resolve an industrial dispute, the necessary interstate dimension would be present, so s 89A would apply in such a case. Duncan SDP accepted this argument, but was overturned by a Full Bench of the Commission in *Finance Sector Union of Australia v GIO Australia Ltd*.[54] The effect of the Full Bench decision was that where parties to an agreement appointed the AIRC to act as a conciliator and arbitrator, the AIRC had the same powers as any other professional mediator and arbitrator would have, if they were appointed to perform a service of dispute resolution by consent of the parties. The powers to be exercised by the AIRC would be governed by the agreement made by the parties themselves. Any matter included in the agreement could therefore be resolved by arbitration, whether it was an allowable award matter or not.

52 (2001) 203 CLR 645.

53 See also *Maritime Union of Australia v Australian Plant Services Pty Ltd* (2001) 50 AILR 4–511; *Appeal by Shop, Distributive and Allied Employees Association re Big W Certified Agreement 2000*, AIRC, PR924554, 12 November 2002; *Finance Sector Union of Australia v GIO Australia Ltd*, AIRC, PR928618, 12 March 2003.

54 AIRC, PR928618, 12 March 2003.

The *Work Choices* provisions continue this logic so long as the parties have expressly provided to confer such powers on the AIRC. They may equally decide to confer these powers on a private dispute resolution provider under s 713. As Carolyn Sutherland has noted, following the introduction of former s 170LW, the AIRC experienced a significant expansion in its workload as a private arbitrator. Sutherland postulated that this was because parties respected the Commission's established expertise in industrial dispute resolution, and often found it more palatable to accept the decision of a mutually respected external expert than to 'lose face' by agreeing to compromise on an issue themselves.[55]

Transitional instruments

The model process will not automatically apply to disputes over rights under transitional awards (that is, those surviving for the benefit of employees of excluded employees for no more than five years after the *Work Choices* commencement on 27 March 2006). Nevertheless, Sch 6, cl 11 of the Act provides that the AIRC must 'encourage' parties to resolve disputes at workplace level before exercising its transitional dispute resolution powers.

Schedule 7 of the Act preserves the pre–*Work Choices* law for any old certified agreements, so they will continue to be governed by the dispute resolution procedures allowed under former s 170LW. So the AIRC will continue to be able to perform a private arbitration function in respect of these pre-reform agreements.

Pre-reform AWAs will continue to operate on the basis that their original dispute resolution clauses are effective. Schedule 7, cl 17(1)(a) preserves the operation of former s 170VG(3), which required all AWAs to contain a dispute resolution clause. Any AWA without such a clause was taken to include the model clause set out in the old *Workplace Relations Regulations*, Sch 9.

Final resort to litigation

Although the Act encourages alternative dispute resolution techniques—conferencing, mediation, assisted negotiation, neutral evaluation, case appraisal and conciliation—to facilitate a consensual resolution of disputes, parties maintain an ultimate right to litigate a dispute: s 693. The Federal Court and Federal Magistrates Court have jurisdiction under ss 847–50 to interpret awards and workplace agreements, and to deal with any dispute arising over provisions of the *Workplace Relations Act*.

The Federal Court has ultimate jurisdiction to interpret workplace agreements under s 849, and may make a range of orders enforcing those rights, including orders for the recovery of underpaid wages under s 720. A party who has suffered loss or damage as a result of a breach of an AWA may seek an award of damages under s 721.

Standing to pursue remedies

The *Workplace Relations Act* provides for a range of remedies for breach of the Act, or any award or agreement made under it. Section 718 provides a table showing who may

---

55 C Sutherland 'By Invitation Only: The Role of the AIRC in Private Arbitration' (2005) 18 *AJLL* 53.

pursue remedies for breach of any provision or instrument. Any party who is bound by an award or agreement can sue for breach. Unions have rights to bring actions, so long as they have at least one member bound by the award or agreement. If the matter concerns an AWA, they may act only on the request of an employee: s 718(5).

Workplace inspectors also have standing to pursue a breach.

Small claims

A person who has a small claim, amounting to no more than $5000, may choose to bring proceedings under the small claims procedures in s 725 of the Act, before a Magistrates Court.

Civil penalties

The *Workplace Relations Act* extensively employs the regulatory technique of imposing civil penalties for breach of provisions. Whereas criminal offences must be proved according to the more difficult criminal standard of proof—beyond reasonable doubt—civil actions need only meet the civil burden of satisfying the court on the balance of probabilities. Standing to bring actions for civil penalties is given to persons affected by a breach of the statute or an instrument made under it, and also to workplace inspectors. The court may order that a civil penalty be paid not only to the Commonwealth, but to a registered organisation or a workplace inspector who has brought the proceedings: s 715.

Bibliography

Adams, K Lee 'A Step Backwards in Job Protection for Carers' (2002) 15 *Australian Journal of Labour Law* 93.

Alben, Elissa 'GATT and the Fair Wage: A Historical Perspective on the Labour-Trade Link' (2001) 101 *Columbia Law Review* 1410.

Alston, Philip (ed) *Labour Rights as Human Rights* (Oxford University Press, Oxford, 2005).

Alston, Philip 'Core Labour Standards' and the Transformation of the International Labour Rights Regime' (2004) 15 *European Journal of International Law* 457.

Alston, Philip 'Facing Up to the Complexities of the ILO's Core Labour Standards Agenda' (2005) 16 *European Journal of International Law* 467.

Anderson, Gordon 'Transplanting and Growing Good Faith in New Zealand Labour Law' (2006) 19 *Australian Journal of Labour Law* 1

Apps, Patricia F 'Tax Reform, Ideology and Gender' (1999) 21 *Sydney Law Review* 437.

Apps, Patricia F and Rees, Ray 'Labour Supply, Household Production and Intra- Family Welfare Distribution' (1996) 60 *Journal of Public Economics* 199.

Arthurs, Harry 'Labour Law Without the State' (1996) 46 *Toronto Law Journal* 1.

Arthurs, Harry 'Reinventing Labour Law for the Global Economy: The Benjamin Aaron Lecture' (2001) 22 *Berkley Comparative Journal of Labor and Employment Law* 271.

Arup, Chris 'Labour Market Regulation as a Focus for a Labour Law Discipline' in Mitchell, Richard (ed) *Redefining Labour Law: New Perspectives on the Future of Teaching and Research* (Centre for Employment and Labour Relations Law, Occasional Monograph Series No 3, Melbourne, 1995).

Arup, Chris, Gahan, Peter, Howe, John, Johnstone, Richard, Mitchell Richard and O'Donnell, Anthony (eds) *Labour Law and Labour Market Regulation: Essays on the Construction, Constitution and Regulation of Labour Markets and Work Relationships* (Federation Press, Sydney, 2006).

Arup, Chris, Howe, John, Mitchell, Richard, O'Donnell, Anthony and Tham, Joo-Cheong 'Employment Protection and Employment Promotion: The Contested Terrain of Australian Labour Law' in Biagi, Marco (ed) *Job Creation and Labour Law: From Protection towards Pro-action*, (Kluwer Law International, The Hague, 2000).

Astor, Hilary and Chinkin, Christine *Dispute Resolution in Australia*, 2nd ed (LexisNexis Butterworths, Australia, 2002).

Atiyah, Patrick S *An Introduction to the Law of Contract*, 5th ed (Clarendon Press, Oxford, 1995).

Atleson, James 'The Voyage of the Neptune Jade: Transnational Labour Solidarity and Obstacles at Domestic Law' in Joanne Conaghan, Richard M Fischl, and Karl Klare (eds) *Labour Law in an Era of Globalization: Transformative Practices and Possibilities* (2002).

Australian Bulletin of Labour Special Issue on Casual Employment, vol 27, (National Institute for Labour Studies, Flinders University, 2000).

Australian Bureau of Statistics *Australia's Most Recent Immigrants*, Cat No 2053.0 (ABS, Canberra, 2004).

Australian Bureau of Statistics *Australian Labour Market Statistics 2004: Feature Article—Changes in Types of Employment* (Cat No 6105.0, Canberra, October 2004).

Australian Bureau of Statistics *Australian Social Trends 2000: Work* (Cat No 4102.0, Canberra, 2000).

Australian Bureau of Statistics *Australian Social Trends 2002: Work—Paid Work: Working from Home* (Cat No 4102.0, Canberra, 2002).

Australian Bureau of Statistics *Australian Social Trends 2004: Economic Resources—Incomes of Aboriginal and Torres Strait Islander Australians* (Cat No 4102.0, Canberra, 2004).

Australian Bureau of Statistics *Australian Social Trends 2004: Work—Community Service Workers* (Cat No 4102.0, Canberra, 2004).

Australian Bureau of Statistics *Characteristics of Small Business Australia* (Cat no 8127.0, Canberra, 2005).

Australian Bureau of Statistics *Earnings and Hours of Employees* (Cat No 6303.0, Canberra, 1996–2004).

Australian Bureau of Statistics *Employee Earnings Benefits, and Trade Union Membership*, (Cat no 6310.0, Canberra, 2001).

Australian Bureau of Statistics *Employee Earnings Benefits, and Trade Union Membership* (Cat no 6310.0, Canberra, 2006).

Australian Bureau of Statistics *Forms of Employment* (Cat no 6359.0, Canberra, 2005).

Australian Bureau of Statistics *Trade Union Members, Australia, August 1996* (Cat no 6325.0, Canberra, 1997).

Australian Bureau of Statistics *Year Book Australia 2002: Labour - How Pay is Set* (Cat No 1301.0, Canberra, 2002).

Australian Bureau of Statistics *Year Book Australia 2004: Feature Article—Usual Hours* (Cat No 1301.0, Canberra, 2004).

Australian Bureau of Statistics *Year Book Australia 2004: Labour—Earnings and Benefits* Cat No 1301.0, Canberra, 2004).

Australian Bureau of Statistics *Year Book Australia 2005: Labour—Employed Persons* (Cat No 1301.0, Canberra, 2005).

Australian Bureau of Statistics *Year Book Australia: Labour 'Feature Article—Changes in Types of Employment'*, *Australian Labour Market Statistics* (Cat no 6105.0, Canberra, October 2004).

Australian Bureau of Statistics, *Australian Social Trends 2004: Work—Aboriginal and Torres Strait Islander Peoples in the Labour Force* (Cat No 4102.0, Canberra, 2004).

Australian Chamber of Commerce and Industry *Modern Workplace: Modern Future—A Blueprint for the Australian Workplace Relations System 2002–2010* (ACCI, Canberra, 2002).

Australian Competition and Consumer Commission (ACCC) *Authorising and Notifying Collective Bargaining and Collective Boycott Issues Paper* (July 2004). Available at <www.accc.gov.au/content/index.phtml/itemId/554792/fromItemId/314462>.

Australian Council of Trade Unions *Future Strategies for the Trade Union Movement* (ACTU, Congress Paper, Melbourne, 1987).

Australian Council of Trade Unions *Future Strategies: Unions Working for a Fairer Australia* (2003). Available at <www.actu.asn.au/public/papers/Organising.html>

Australian Council of Trade Unions *Statement of Accord by the Australian Labor Party and the Australian Council of Trade Unions Regarding Economic Policy* (ACTU, Australia, 1983).

Australian Council of Trade Unions *Submission on Australia's Position for the November 2001 WTO Ministerial Meeting* (ACTU, Australia, July 2001).

Australian Council of Trade Unions *Unions @ Work: The Challenge for Unions in Creating a Just and Fair Society: report of the ACTU Overseas Delegation 1999* (ACTU, Australia, 2002). Available on line at < http://www.actu.asn.au/public/papers/unionswork/>.

Australian Government, Minister K Andrews *Work and Family: The Importance of Workplace Flexibility in Promoting Balance between Work and Family* (Australian Government, Canberra, 2005).

Australian Law Reform Commission *Equality Before the Law: Justice for Women*, Report No 69, Parts I and II (Commonwealth of Australia, Sydney, 1994).

Australian Mines and Metals Association *A Model of Internal Regulation of Workplace Employee Relations: Discussion Paper* (February, 2002).

Australian Mines and Metals Association *Beyond Enterprise Bargaining: The Case for Ongoing Reform of Workplace Relations in Australia* (July, 1999).

Australian Parliament Joint Standing Committee on Treaties *'Who's Afraid of the WTO? Australia and the World Trade Organisation'* (Australian Parliament, Canberra, September 2001).

Australian Parliament, Senate Economics References Committee *Outworkers in the Garment Industry* (Canberra, December 1996). Available at <http://www.aph.gov.au/SEnate/committee/economics_ctte/completed_inquiries/1996-99/outworkers/report/contents.htm>.

Australian Productivity Commission (P Laplagne, M Glover and T Fry) *The Growth of Labour Hire Employment in Australia* (Staff Working Paper, Melbourne, February 2005).

Award Review Taskforce *Discussion Paper 'Award Rationalisation'* (Canberra, December 2005) available at <www.awardreviewtaskforce.gov.au>.

Award Review Taskforce *Discussion Paper 'Rationalisation of Award and Classification Structures'* (Canberra, December 2005) available at <www.awardreviewtaskforce.gov.au>.

Baccaro, Lucio *Civil Society, NGOs and Decent Work Policies: Sorting out the Issues* (International Institute for Labour Studies, Geneva, 2001).

Baird, Marian 'Parental Leave in Australia: The Role of the Industrial Relations System' in Jill Murray (ed) *Work, Family and the Law (Special Issue of Law in Context*, vol 23) (Federation Press, Sydney, 2005).

Baird, Marian, Brennan, Deborah and Cutcher, Leanne 'A Pregnant Pause: Paid Maternity Leave in Australia' (2002) 13 *Journal of Labour and Industry* 1.

Barmes, Lizzie and Ashtiany Sue 'The Diversity Approach to Achieving Equality: Potential and Pitfalls' (2003) 32 *Industrial Law Journal* 274.

Bellace, Janice and Rood, Max G (eds) *Labour Law at the Crossroads: Changing Employment Relationships* (Kluwer Law International, The Hague, 1997).

Ben-David, Dan, Nordstrom, Hakan and Winters, L Alan *Trade, Income Disparity and Poverty* (World Trade Organisation, Special Studies 5, Geneva, 1999).

Ben-Israel, Ruth *International Labour Standards: The Case of Freedom to Strike* (Kluwer, Boston, 1988);

Benjamin, Paul 'Who Needs Labour Law? Defining the Scope of Labour Protection' in Joanne Conaghan, Richard M Fischl and Karl Klare, (eds) *Labour Law in an Era of Globalization: Transformative Practices and Possibilities* (Oxford University Press, Oxford and New York, 2002).

Bennett, Laura 'Legal Intervention and the Female Workforce: The Australian Conciliation and Arbitration Court 1907–1921' (1984) 12 *International Journal of the Sociology of Law* 23.

Bennett, Laura 'Women Exploitation and the Australian Child Care Industry: Breaking the Vicious Circle' (1991) 33 *Journal of Industrial Relations* 20.

Bennett, Laura *Making Labour Law in Australia: Industrial Relations, Politics and Law* (Lawbook Co, Sydney, 1994).

Berle Jr, Adolf A 'For Whom Corporate Managers Are Trustees: A Note' (1932) 45 *Harvard Law Review* 1365.

Berns, Sandra *Women Going Backwards: Law and Change in a Family Unfriendly Society* (Ashgate, Burlington, 2002).

Betten, Lammy *International Labour Law: Selected Issues* (Kluwer, Deventer, The Netherlands, 1993).

Bickerdyke, Ian, Lattimore, Ralph, and Madge, Alan *Business Failure and Change: An Australian Perspective* (Productivity Commission Staff Research Paper, AusInfo, Canberra, 2000).

Biffl, Gudrun and Isaac, Joe 'Globalisation and Core Labour Standards: Compliance Problems with ILO Conventions 87 and 98. Comparing Australia and other English Speaking Countries with EU Member States' (2005) 21 *International Journal of Comparative Labour Law and Industrial Relations* 405.

Bitman, Michael, Hoffman, Sonia and Thompson, Denise *Men's Uptake of Family Friendly Employment Provisions* (Australian Government Department of Family and Community Services Policy Research paper No 22, Canberra, 2004).

Blackett, Adele 'Whither the Social Clause: Human Rights, Trade Theory and Treaty Interpretation' (1999) 31 *Columbia Human Rights Law Review* 1.

Blackshield, Tony and Williams, George *Australian Constitutional Law and Theory: Commentary and Materials*, 3rd ed (Federation Press, Sydney, 2002).

Blair, Margaret M 'Firm-Specific Human Capital and Theories of the Firm' in Blair, Margaret M and Roe, Mark J (eds) *Employees & Corporate Governance* (Brookings Institution Press, Washington DC, 1999).

Blair, Margaret M and Stout, Lynn A 'A Team Production Theory of Corporate Law' (1999) 85 *Virginia Law Review* 247.

Blake, Harlan M 'Employee Agreements Not to Compete' (1960) 73 *Harvard Law Review* 625.

Blanpain, Roger R 'The Kenneth M Piper Lecture: Transnational Regulation of the Labour Relations of Mutinational Enterprises' (1982) 58 *Chicago Kent Law Review* 909.

Bohle, Philip, Quinlan, Michael et al *Managing Occupational Health and Safety: A Multidisciplinary Approach*, 2nd ed (Macmillan Publishers Australia Ltd, South Yarra, 2000).

Braithwaite, John and Drahos, Peter *Global Business Regulation* (Cambridge University Press Cambridge, 2000).

Brett, Bill *International Labour in the 21st Century: The ILO—Monument to the Past or Beacon for the Future* (Epic Books, London, 1994).

Brodie, Douglas 'A Fair Deal at Work' (1999) 19 *Oxford Journal of Legal Studies* 83.

Brodie, Douglas 'Beyond Exchange: the New Contract of Employment' (1998) 27 *Industrial Law Journal* 79.

Brodie, Douglas 'The Heart of the Matter: Mutual Trust and Confidence' (1996) 25 *Industrial Law Journal* 121.

Brooks, Adrian 'Myth and Muddle—An Examination of Contracts for the Performance of Work' (1988) 11 *University of New South Wales Law Journal* 48.

Brooks, Adrian 'The Good and Considerate Employer: Developments in the Implied Duty of Mutual Trust and Confidence' (2001) 20 *University of Tasmania Law Review* 29.

Broomhill, Ray and Sharp, Rhonda 'The Changing Male Breadwinner Model in Australia: A New Gender Order?' (2004) 15 *Labour and Industry* 1.

Brown, Drusilla K *International Trade and Core Labour Standards: A Survey of the Recent Literature* (Labour Market and Social Policy—Occasional Papers No 43, OECD, Paris, 2000).

Business Council of Australia *Enterprise-based Bargaining Units: A Better Way of Working* Report to the Business Council of Australia by the Industrial Relations Study Commission (Business Council of Australia, Melbourne, 1989).

Cairns, John W 'Blackstone, Kahn-Freund and the Contract of Employment' (1989) 105 *Law Quarterly Review* 300.

Callus, Ron, Morehead, Alison, Cully, Mark and Buchanan, John *Industrial Relations at Work: The Australian Workplace Industrial Relations Survey* (AGPS, Canberra, 1991).

Campbell, David and Harris, Donald 'Flexibility in Long Term Contractual Relationships: The Role of Co-operation' (1993) 20 *Journal of Law and Society* 166.

Cappuyns, Elisabeth 'Linking Labour Standards and Trade Sanctions: An Analysis of their Current Relationship' (1998) *Columbia Journal of Transnational Law* 658.

Carlin, Tyrone 'The Rise (and Fall?) of Implied Duties of Good Faith in Contractual Performance in Australia' (2002) 25 *University of New South Wales Law Journal* 99.

Carter, John and Harland, David *Contract Law in Australia*, 3rd ed (Butterworths, Sydney, 1996).

Carter, John and Peden, Elisabeth 'Good Faith in Australian Contract Law' (2003) 19 *Journal of Contract Law* 1.

Cassel, Douglass 'Corporate Initiatives: A Second Human Rights Revolution?' (1996) 19 *Fordham International Law Journal* 1963.

Castel, Robert 'Work and Usefulness to the World' (1996) 135 *International Labour Review* 615.

Castells, Manuel *The Rise of the Network Society* (Blackwells, Cambridge, MA, 1996).

Castles, Frances G 'The Wage Earner's Welfare State Revisited: Refurbishing the Established Model of Australian Social Protection' (1994) 29 *Australian Journal of Social Issues* 120.

Cattui, Maria Livanos *Letters to the Editor*, Fin Times, 24 Mar 1999 cited in Taylor, Alexis M 'The UN and the Global Compact' (2001) 17 *NY Law School Journal of Human Rights* 975.

CCH *Australian Labour Law Reporter*, vols 1–4 (CCH Australia Ltd).

CCH *Australian Superannuation Law and Practice*, vols 1–2, (CCH Australia Ltd).

Champion, Karen Vossler 'Comment, Who Pays for Free Trade? The Dilemma of Free Trade and International Labor Standards' (1996) 22 *North Carolina Journal of International Law and Commercial Regulation* 181.

Chapman, Anna 'Challenging the Constitution of the (White and Straight) Family in Work and Family Scholarship' in Jill Murray (ed) *Work, Family and the Law (Special Issue of Law in Context*, vol 23*)* (Federation Press, Sydney, 2005).

Chapman, Anna 'Work/Family, Australian Labour law and the Normative Worker' in Conaghan, Joanne and Rittich, Kerry (eds) *Labour Law, Work and Family* (Oxford University Press, Oxford and New York, 2005).

Charlesworth, Hilary 'The Australian Reluctance about Rights' (1993) 31 *Osgoode Hall Law Journal* 195.

Charlesworth, Hilary 'Transforming the United Men's Club: Feminist Futures for the United Nations' (1994) 4 *Transnational Law and Contemporary Problems* 421.

Charlesworth, Hilary and Charlesworth Sara 'The *Sex Discrimination Act* and International Law' (2004) 27 *University of New South Wales Law Journal* 858.

Charlesworth, Hilary and Chinkin, Christine *The Boundaries of International Law: A Feminist Analysis* (University Press, Manchester, 2000).

Charlesworth, Hilary, Chiam, Madelaine, Hovell, Devika and Williams, George 'Deep Anxieties: Australia and the International Legal Order' (2003) 25 *Sydney Law Review* 423.

Charlesworth, Sara 'The Overlap of the Federal Sex Discrimination and Industrial Relations Jurisdictions: Intersections and Demarcations in Conciliation' (2003) 6 *Australian Journal of Labour Economics* 559.

Charlesworth, Sara *Stretching Flexibility: Enterprise Bargaining, Women Workers and Changes to Working Hours* (Human Rights and Equal Opportunity Commission, Sydney, 1996).

Charlesworth, Sara *Unrewarded: Women in Community Services. A review of overaward payments in Victorian Local Government* (Human Rights and Equal Opportunity Commission, AGPS, Canberra, 1994).

Charnovitz, Steve 'The Influence of International Labour Standards on the World Trading Regime: A Historical Overview' (1987) 126 *International Labour Review* 565.

Charnovitz, Steve 'Trade Employment and Labour Standards: The OECD Study and Recent Developments in the Trade and Labour Standards Debate' (1997) 11 *Temple International and Comparative Law Journal* 131.

Chin, David 'Servant or Serf? Severance Pay on Transmission of Business and the Right to Choose an Employer (2003) *Australian Journal Of Labour Law* 172.

Chin, David *A Social Clause for Labour's Cause: Global Trade and Labour Standards—A Challenge for the New Millennium* (Institute of Employment Rights, London, 1998).

Collins, Hugh 'Ascription of Legal Responsibility to Groups in Complex Patterns of Economic Integration' (1990) 53 *Modern Law Review* 731.

Collins, Hugh 'Discrimination, Equality and Social Inclusion' (2003) 66 *Modern Law Review* 16.

Collins, Hugh 'Independent Contractors and the Challenge of Vertical Disintegration to Employment Protection Laws' (1990) 10 *Oxford Journal of Legal Studies* 35.

Collins, Hugh 'Is There a Third Way in Labour Law?' in Joanne Conaghan, Richard M Fischl, and Karl Klare (eds) *Labour Law in an Era of Globalization: Transformative Practices and Possibilities* (Oxford University Press, Oxford and New York, 2002).

Collins, Hugh 'Market Power, Bureaucratic Power and the Contract of Employment' (1986) 15 *Industrial Law Journal* 1.

Collins, Hugh 'Regulating the Employment Relation for Competitiveness' (2001) 30 *Industrial Law Journal* 17.

Collins, Hugh *Employment Law* (Oxford University Press, Oxford, 2003).

Collins, Hugh *Regulating Contracts* (Oxford University Press, New York, 1999)

Collins, Hugh, Davies, Paul and Rideout, Roger (eds) *Legal Regulation of the Employment Relation* (Kluwer Law International, London, 2000).

Collins, Hugh, Ewing, Keith and McColgan, Aileen *Labour Law Text and Materials* (Hart Publishing, Oxford, 2001).

Colvin, John HC Watson, Graeme and Ogilvie Nicholas *An Introduction to the Industrial Relations Reforms* (LexisNexis Butterworths, Australia, 2006).

Commonwealth Department of Family and Community Services Consultation Paper 'Building a Simpler System to help Jobless Families and Individuals' (12 December 2002). Available at <www.facs.gov.au/welfare_reform>.

Commonwealth of Australia *Review of the Competition Provisions of the Trade Practices Act*, prepared by The Hon Daryl Dawson, Jillian Segall and Curt Rendall (Canprint Communications Pty Ltd, Canberra, 2003), available at <http://tpareview.treasury.gov.au/content/report.asp>.

Commonwealth *Parliamentary Debates*, House of Representatives, 28 October 1993 Minister for Industrial Relations, 2777

Commonwealth *Parliamentary Debates*, House of Representatives, 28 October 1993, Minister for Industrial Relations, 2777–89.

Commonwealth *Parliamentary Debates*, House of Representatives, 28 October 1993, Minister for Industrial Relations, 2777–89.

Commonwealth *Parliamentary Debates*, Senate, 7 May 1992, Minister for Industrial Relations, 2519

Commonwealth *Parliamentary Debates*, Senate, 7 May 1992, Minister for Industrial Relations, 2519–20.

Commonwealth *Parliamentary Debates*, Senate, 7 May 1992, Minister for Industrial Relations, 2519–20.

Commonwealth, *Parliamentary Debates*, House of Representatives, 30 July 1903.

Conaghan, Joanne 'Feminism and Labour Law: Contesting the Terrain' in Anne Morris and Therese O'Donnell, (eds) *Feminist Perspectives on Employment Law* (Cavendish Publishing Limited, London, 1999).

Conaghan, Joanne 'Labour Law and 'New Economy' Discourse' (2003) 16 *Australian Journal of Labour Law* 9.

Conaghan, Joanne 'The Invisibility of Women in Labour Law: Gender-neutrality in Model Building' (1986) 14 *International Journal of Society and Law* 377.

Conaghan, Joanne 'Time to Dream? Flexibility, Families, and the Regulation of Working Time' in Judy Fudge and Rosemary Owens (eds) *Precarious Work, Women, and the New Economy: The Challenge to Legal Norms* (Hart Publishing, Oxford and Portland Oregon, 2006).

Conaghan, Joanne and Rittich, Kerry (eds) *Labour Law, Work and Family* (Oxford University Press, Oxford and New York, 2005).

Conaghan, Joanne, Fischl, Richard M and Klare, Karl (eds) *Labour Law in an Era of Globalization: Transformative Practices and Possibilities* (Oxford University Press, Oxford and New York, 2002).

Cooney, Sean 'A Broader Role for the Commonwealth in Eradicating Foreign Sweatshops?' (2004) 28 *Melbourne University Law Review* 290.

Cooney, Sean 'Testing Times for the ILO: Institutional Reform for the New Political Economy' (1999) 20 *Comparative Labour Law and Policy Journal* 365.

Cordova, Efren 'Some Reflections on the Overproduction of International Labour Standards' (1993) 14 *Comparative Labor Law Journal* 138.

Cossman, Brenda and Fudge, Judy *Privatization, Law and the Challenge to Feminism* (Toronto University Press, Toronto, 2002).

Coulthard, Amanda 'Non Union Bargaining: Enterprise Flexibility Agreements' (1996) 38 *Journal of Industrial Relations* 339.

Coulthard, Amanda 'The De-collectivisation of Australian Industrial Relations: Trade Union Exclusion under the *Workplace Relations Act 1996* (Cth)' in Stephen Deery and Richard Mitchell (eds) *Employment Relations: Individualisation and Union Exclusion* (Federation Press, Sydney, 1999).

Council of Europe *Freedom of Association* (Kluwer Academic Publishers, Dordrecht and Boston, M Nijhoff , Norwell, MA 1993).

Crain, Marion 'Images of Power in Labour Law: A Feminist Deconstruction' (1992) 33 *Boston College LR* 481.

Creighton Breen 'Freedom of Association' in Roger Blanpain and Christian Engels (eds) *Comparative Labour Law and Industrial Relations in Industrialized Market Economies* (2001).

Creighton Breen 'The ILO and the Protection of Fundamental Human Rights in Australia' (1998) 22 *Melbourne University Law Review* 239.

Creighton, Breen 'Employment Security and 'Atypical' Work in Australia' (1995) 16 *Comparative Labor Law Journal* 285.

Creighton, Breen 'Enforcement in the Federal Industrial Relations System: An Australian Paradox' (1991) 4 *Australian Journal of Labour Law* 197.

Creighton, Breen 'One Hundred Years of the Conciliation and Arbitration Power: A Province Lost?' (2000) 24 *Melbourne University Law Review* 839.

Creighton, Breen 'The Forgotten Workers: Employment Security of Casual Employees and Independent Contractors' in Ron McCallum, Greg McCarry, and Paul Ronfeldt (eds) *Employment Security* (Federation Press, Annandale NSW, 1994).

Creighton, Breen 'The Future of Labour Law: Is there a Role for International Standards?' in Catherine Barnard, Simon Deakin and Gillian S Morris (eds) *The Future of Labour Law: Liber Amicorum Bob Hepple* QC (Oxford ; Portland, Or. : Hart,, 2004).

Creighton, Breen 'The ILO and the Protection of Fundamental Human Rights in Australia' (1998) 22 *Melbourne University Law Review* 239.

Creighton, Breen 'The ILO Convention No 138 and Australian Law and Practice relating to Child Labour' (1996) 2 *Australian Journal of Human Rights* 293.

Creighton, Breen 'The Internationalisation of Labour Law' in Richard Mitchell (ed) *Redefining Labour Law: New Perspectives on the Future of Teaching and Research* (Centre for Employment and Labour Relations Law Occasional Monograph Series No 3, Melbourne, 1995).

Creighton, Breen 'The Workplace Relations Act in International Perspective' (1997) 10 *Australian Journal of Labour Law* 31.

Creighton, Breen 'Transmission of all Parts of a Business: A Neglected Issue in Australian Industrial and Employment Law' (1998) 26 *Australian Business Law Review* 162.

Creighton, Breen and Mitchell, Richard 'The Contract of Employment in Australian Labour Law' in Lammy Betten (ed) *The Employment Contract in Transforming Labour Relations* (Kluwer Law International, The Netherlands, 1995).

Creighton, Breen and Stewart Andrew *Labour Law: An Introduction* (1990).

Creighton, Breen and Stewart, Andrew *Labour Law*, 4th ed (Federation Press, Annandale NSW, 2005).

Creighton, Breen and Stewart, Andrew *Labour Law: An Introduction*, 3rd ed (Federation Press, Sydney, 2000).

Creighton, Breen, Ford, William and Mitchell, Richard *Labour Law Text and Materials*, 2nd ed (The Law Book Company Limited, Sydney, 1993).

Crock, Mary and Lyon, Kerry (eds) *Nation Skilling: Migration, Labour and Law in Australia, Canada, New Zealand and the United States* (Desert Pea Press, Sydney 2002).

Crosby, Michael *Power at Work: Rebuilding the Australian Union Movement* (Federation Press, Sydney, 2005).

D'Antona, Massimo 'Labour Law at the Century's End: An Identity Crisis? in Joanne Conaghan, Richard M Fischl, and Karl Klare (eds) *Labour Law in an Era of Globalization: Transformative Practices & Possibilities* (Oxford University Press, Oxford and New York, 2002)

Davidov, Guy 'Who is a Worker?' (2005) 34 *Industrial Law Journal* 57.

Davies, Margaret 'Taking the inside out: Sex and gender in the legal subject' in Ngaire Naffine, and Rosemary Owens (eds) *Sexing the Subject of Law* (Lawbook Company and Sweet and Maxwell, North Ryde NSW, 1997).

Davies, Margaret and Naffine, Ngaire *Are Persons Property?: Legal Debates about Property and Personality* (Ashgate, Aldershot, England, 2001).

Davies, Paul and Freedland, Mark (eds) *Kahn-Freund's Labour and the Law*, 3rd ed (Stevens, London, 1983).

de Tocqueville, Alexis *Democracy in America* (Vintage Books, Random House, New York, 1945).

de Wet, Erika 'Labour Standards in the Globalized Economy: The Inclusion of a Social Clause in the General Agreement on Tariff and Trade/ World Trade Organisation?' (1995) 17 *Human Rights Quarterly* 443.

Deakin, Simon 'The Evolution of the Contract of Employment 1900–1950' in Whiteside, Noel and Salais, Robert (eds) *Governance, Industry and Labour Markets in Britain and France* (Routledge, London, 1998).

Deakin, Simon 'The Many Futures of the Contract of Employment' in Joanne Conaghan, Richard M Fischl, and Karl Klare (eds) *Labour Law in an Era of Globalization: Transformative Practices and Possibilities* (Oxford University Press, Oxford and New York, 2002).

Deakin, Simon and Wilkinson, Frank 'Rights vs Efficiency? The Economic Case for Transnational Labour Standards' (1994) 23 *Industrial Law Journal* 289.

Deakin, Simon and Wilkinson, Frank *The Law of the Labour Market: Industrialization, Employment and Legal Evolution* (Oxford University Press, Oxford, 2005).

Deery, Stephen and Mitchell, Richard (eds) *Employment Relations: Individualisation and Union Exclusion—An International Study* (Federation Press, Sydney, 1999).

Deery, Stephen and Mitchell, Richard 'The Emergence of Individualisation and Union Exclusion as an Employment Relations Strategy' in Stephen Deery, and Richard Mitchell (eds) *Employment Relations: Individualisation and Union Exclusion—An International Study* (Federation Press, Sydney, 1999).

Deléchat, Corinne, Lunat, M, Richards, A and Torres, Raymond *Trade, Employment and Labour Standards: A Study of Core Worker's Rights and International Trade* (OECD, Paris, 1996).

Department of Employment and Workplace Relations and Department of Family and Community Services *Building a Simpler System to Help Jobless Families and Individuals*, Consultation Paper (Commonwealth of Australia, Canberra, 2002).

Department of Employment and Workplace Relations and the Office of the Employment Advocate *Agreement Making in Australia under the Workplace Relations Act: 2000 and 2001* (Commonwealth of Australia, Canberra, 2002).

Department of Employment and Workplace Relations and the Office of the Employment Advocate *Agreement Making in Australia under the Workplace Relations Act: 2002 and 2003* (Commonwealth of Australia, Canberra, 2004).

Department of Employment, Workplace Relations and Small Business *Breaking the Gridlock: Towards a Simpler National Workplace Relations System—Discussion Paper 1*, The Case for Change, (Commonwealth of Australia, Canberra, 2000).

Di Felice, Victor 'Stopping or Preventing Industrial Action in Australia' (2000) 24 *Melbourne University Law Review* 310.

Dickens, Linda 'Collective Bargaining and the Promotion of Equality: The Case of the United Kingdom' (Interdepartmental Projects and Activities, Working Paper No 12, International Labour Office, Geneva, 1993).

Dickens, Linda, Townley, Barbara and Winchester, David *Tackling Sex Discrimination Through Collective Bargaining: The Impact of Section 6 of the Sex Discrimination Act 1986* (Equal Opportunities Commission, Research Series, HMSO, London, 1988).

Dodd Jr, E Merrick 'For Whom are Corporate Managers Trustees?' (1932) 45 *Harvard Law Review* 1145.

Donaldson, Thomas and Dunfee, Thomas W 'Toward a Unified Conception of Business Ethics: Integrative Social Contract Theory' (1994) 19 *Academy of Management Review* 252.

Doyle, Rachel 'The Industrial/Political Dichotomy: The Impact on the Freedom of Communication Cases on Industrial Law' (1995) 8 *Australian Journal of Labour Law* 91.

Dubler, Robert 'Direct Discrimination and a Defence of Reasonable Justification' (2003) 77 *ALJ* 514.

Encel, Sol *Age Can Work: The Case for Older Australians Staying in the Workforce* (Report to the Australian Council of Trade Unions and Business Council of Australia, Sydney, April 2003).

Encel, Solomon, Australian Council of Trade Unions and Business Council of Australia *Age Can Work: The Case for Older Australians Staying in the Workforce, Joint Report* (Social Policy Research Network, University of New South Wales, Sydney, 2003).

England, Geoffrey 'Determining Reasonable Notice of Termination at Common Law: The Implications of *Cronk v Canadian General Insurance Co*' (1996) 4 *Canadian Labour and Employment Law Journal* 115.

Equal Opportunity Commissions of Victoria, South Australia and Western Australia and the Australian Employers Convention *Age Limits: Age-Related Discrimination in Employment Affecting Workers Over 45* (Australia, March 2001).

Evatt Foundation *Unions 2001: A Blueprint for Trade Union Activism* (Evatt Foundation, Sydney, 1995).

Ewing, Keith 'Australian and British Labour Law: Differences of Form or Substance?' (1998) 11 *Australian Journal of Labour Law* 44.

Ewing, Keith 'Social Rights and Constitutional Law' [1999] *Public Law* 104.

Ewing, Keith 'The Function of Trade Unions' (2005) 34 *Industrial Law Journal* 1.

Ewing, Keith 'The Right to Strike in Australia' (1989) 2 *Australian Journal of Labour Law* 18.

Ewing, Keith *Working Life: A new perspective on Labour Law* (The Institute of Employment Rights, Lawrence & Wishart, London, 1996).

Fairbrother, Peter, Paddon, Michael and Teicher, Julian (eds) *Privatisation, Globalisation and Labour: Studies from Australia* (Federation Press, Sydney, 2002).

Farrer, John H 'Legal Issues Involving Corporate Groups' (1998) 16 *Corporations and Securities Law Journal* 184.

Fenwick, Colin 'How Low Can You Go? Minimum Working Conditions Under Australia's New Labour Laws' (2006) 16 *Economic and Labour Relations Review* 85.

Fenwick, Colin 'Protecting Victoria's Vulnerable Workers: New Legislative Developments' (2003) 16 *Australian Journal of Labour Law* 198.

Fenwick, Colin 'Regulating Prisoner's Labour in Australia: A Preliminary View' (2003) 16 *Australian Journal of Labour Law* 284.

Fenwick, Colin 'Shooting for Trouble? Contract Labour Hire in the Victorian Building Industry' (1992) 5 *Australian Journal of Labour Law* 237.

Fenwick, Colin and Landau, Ingrid 'Work Choices in International Perspective' (2006) 19 *Australian Journal of Labour Law* 127.

Fetter, Joel 'Work Choices and Australian Workplace Agreements' (2006) 19 *Australian Journal of Labour Law* 210.

Fetter, Joel and Mitchell, Richard 'The Legal Complexity of Workplace Regulation and Its Impact upon Functional Flexibility in Australian Workplaces' (2004) 17 *Australian Journal of Labour Law* 276.

Finn, Paul 'The Fiduciary Principle' in Timothy G Youdan (ed) *Equity Fiduciaries and Trusts* (Carswell, Toronto, 1989).

Fisk, Catherine 'Reflections on the New Psychological Contract and the Ownership of Human Capital' (2002) 34 *Connecticut Law Review* 765.

Ford, William 'Being There: Changing Union Rights of Entry under Federal Industrial Law' (2000) 13 *Australian Journal of Labour Law* 1.

Ford, William 'Reconstructing Australian Labour Law: A Constitutional Perspective' (1997) 10 *Australian Journal of Labour Law* 1.

Ford, William 'The Constitution and the Reform of Australian Industrial Relations' (1994) 7 *Australian Journal of Labour Law* 105.

Ford, William J 'Politics, the Constitution and Australian Industrial Relations: Pursuing a Unified National System' (2005) 38 *Australian Economic Review* 211.

Ford, William J *An Independent Review of the Amendments to the Industrial Relations Act 1979 made by the Labour Relations Reform Act 2002* (A Report for the Minister for Consumer and Employment Protection, Perth WA, 2004).

Forsyth, Anthony and Sutherland, Carolyn 'Collective Labour Relations Under Siege: The Work Choices Legislation and Collective Bargaining' (2006) 19 *Australian Journal of Labour Law* 183.

Forsyth, Anthony and Sutherland, Carolyn 'Collective Labour Relations Under Siege: The Work Choices Legislation and Collective Bargaining' (2006) 19 *Australian Journal of Labour Law* 183;

Forsyth, Anthony and Sutherland, Carolyn 'From "Unchartered Seas" to "Stormy Waters": How Will Trade Unions Fare under the Work Choices Legislation?' (2006) 16 *Economic and Labour Relations Review* 215;

Fox, Charlie *Working Australia* (Allen & Unwin, Sydney 1991).

Frazer, Andrew and Nyland, Chris 'In Search of the Middle Way: The ILO and Standard Setting' (1997) 10 *Australian Journal of Labour Law* 280.

Fredman, Sandra 'Equality: A New Generation?' (2001) 30 *Industrial Law Journal* 145.

Fredman, Sandra 'Precarious Norms for Precarious Workers' in Judy Fudge and Rosemary Owens (eds) *Precarious Work, Women and the New Economy: The Challenge to Legal Norms* (Hart Publishing, Oxford and Portland Oregon, 2006).

Fredman, Sandra 'Pregnancy and Parenthood Reassessed' (1994) 110 *Law Quarterly Review* 106.

Fredman, Sandra 'Providing Equality: Substantive Equality and the Positive Duty to Provide' (2005) 21 *South African Journal on Human Rights* 163.

Fredman, Sandra *Women and the Law* (Oxford University Press, Oxford, 1997).

Freedland, Mark *The Personal Employment Contract* (Oxford University Press, Oxford, 2003).

Friedman, Milton 'The Social Responsibility of Business is to Increase Profits' in Hoffman, W Michael and Moore, Jennifer Mills (eds) *Business Ethics: Readings and Cases in Corporate Morality* (McGraw-Hill, New York, 1984).

Friedman, Milton 'The Social Responsibility of Business to Increase Profits' (13 September 1970) *The New York Times Magazine* 32.

Fudge Judy '"Labour is Not a Commodity": The Supreme Court of Canada and the Freedom of Association' (2004) 67 *Saskatchewan Law Review* 425.

Fudge, Judy 'A New Gender Contract? Work/Life Balance and Working Time Flexibility' in Joanne Conaghan and Kerry Rittich (eds) *Labour Law, Work and Family: Critical and Comparative Perspectives* (Oxford University Press, Oxford and New York, 2005).

Fudge, Judy 'Self-Employment, Women, and Precarious Work: The Scope of Labour Protection' in Judy Fudge and Rosemary Owens (eds) *Precarious Work, Women and the New Economy: The Challenge to Legal Norms* (Hart Publishing, Oxford and Portland Oregon, 2006).

Fudge, Judy and Owens, Rosemary 'Precarious Work, Women, and the New Economy: The Challenge to Legal Norms' in Judy Fudge and Rosemary Owens (eds) *Precarious Work, Women, and the New Economy: The Challenge to Legal Norms* (Hart Publishing, Oxford and Portland Oregon, 2006).

Fung, Archon, O'Rourke, Dara and Sabel, Charles 'Realizing Labour Standards: How Transparency, Competition and Sanctions Could Improve Working Conditions Worldwide' (2001) 26 *Boston Review* 1.

Fung, Archon, O'Rourke, Dara and Sabel, Charles *Ratcheting Labour Standards: Regulation for Continuous Improvement in the Global Workplace* (World Bank Group Social Protection Unit Discussion Paper No 0011) (World Bank Group, Washington DC, May 2000).

Gahan, Peter and Mitchell, Richard 'The Limits of Labour Law and the Necessity of Interdisciplinary Analysis' in Richard Mitchell (ed) *Redefining Labour Law: New Perspectives on the Future of Teaching and Research* (Centre for Employment and Labour Relations Law, Occasional Monograph Series No 3, Melbourne, 1995).

Gahan, Peter G 'Dead Letters? An Examination of Union Registrations under Australian Colonial Trade Union Acts 1876–1900' (2000) 13 *Australian Journal of Labour Law* 50.

Gardner, Margaret, Peetz, David, Brown, Kerry and Berns, Sandra 'Workplace Effects of Affirmative Action Legislation' Research commissioned by the Department of Workplace Relations and Small Business on behalf of the independent committee conducting the Regulatory Review of the *Affirmative Action (Equal Opportunity for Women) Act 1986*, a paper presented at the Association of Industrial Relations Academics of Australia and New Zealand Conference, Adelaide, February 1999 (Copy on file with the authors).

Gastells, Manuel *The Rise of the Network Society* (Blackwell Publishers, London, 1996).

Gaudron, The Honourable Justice Mary 'In the Eye of the Law: The Jurisprudence of Equality' (The Mitchell Oration 1990, Adelaide, 24 August 1990).

Gaze, Beth 'Context and Interpretation in Anti-discrimination Law' (2002) 26 *Melbourne University Law Review* 325.

Gaze, Beth "Quality Part-time Work: Can Law Provide a Framework? (2005) 15 *Labour and Industry* 89.

Gilmore, Grant *The Death of Contract*, 2nd ed (with forward by Ronald K L Collins (Ohio State University Press, Columbus, 1995).

Ginters, Peteris 'The Transmission of Business Provisions in the Workplace Relations Act 1996 (Cth): Reaffirming the Primacy of the 'Substantial Identity Test" (1999) 12 *Australian Journal of Labour Law* 211.

Giudice, The Hon Justice Geoffrey, President of the Australian Industrial Relations Commission, an *Address to the Bar Association of Queensland Industrial and Employment Law Conference* (20 April 2001, available at <www.airc.gov.au>).

Giudice, The Hon Justice Geoffrey, President of the Australian Industrial Relations Commission, 'The Industrial relations System in Victoria: A Unitary IR System?' (18 October 2002, available at <www.airc.gov.au>).

Glendon, Mary Ann *The New Family and the New Property* (Butterworths, Toronto, 1981).

Godfrey, Kelly 'Contracts of Employment: Renaissance of the Implied Term of Trust and Confidence' (2003) 77 *Australian Law Journal* 764.

Goetz, Charles J and Scott, Robert E 'Principles of Relational Contracts' (1981) 67 *Virginia Law Review* 1089.

Gould IV, William B 'The Idea of The Job as Property in Contemporary America: The Legal and Collective Bargaining Framework' [1986] *Brigham Young University Law Review* 886.

Graycar, Regina and Morgan, Jenny *The Hidden Gender of Law*, 2nd ed (Federation Press, Sydney, 2002).

Greenfield, Kent 'The Place of Workers in Corporate Law' (1998) 39 *Boston College Law Review* 283.

Gregory, Bob 'Labour Market Institutions and the Gender Pay Ratio' (1999) 32 *The Australian Economic Review* 273.

Gregory, Bob 'Where to Now? Welfare and Labour Market Regulation in Australia' (2004) 30 *Australian Bulletin of Labour* 33.

Gregory, Bob, Klug, Eva and Martin, Yew May 'Labour Market De-regulation, Relative Wages and the Social Security System' in Sue Richardson (ed) *Reshaping the Labour Market: Regulation, Efficiency and Equality in Australia* (Cambridge University Press, Australia, 1999).

Griffin, Gerard, Nyland, Chris and O'Rourke, Anne 'Trade Promotion Authority and Core Labour Standards: Implications for Australia' (2004) 17 *Australian Journal of Labour Law* 35.

Group of 151 Industrial Relations, Labour Market and Legal Academics, Australian Parliament, Submission to the Inquiry into the Workplace Relations Amendment (Work Choices) Bill 2005, Senate Employment, Workplace Relations and Education Legislation Committee, *Research Evidence about the Effects of the 'Work Choices' Bill* (November 2005). Available at <www.aph.gov. au/Senate/committee/eet_ctte/completed_inquiries/index.htm>.

Gryst, Roma *Contracting Out: A case study of how the use of agency workers in the SA Power Industry is reshaping the employment relationship* (ACIRRT Working Paper No 59, University of Sydney, Sydney, 2000).

Gunningham, Neil and Johnstone, Richard *Regulating Workplace Safety: Systems and Sanctions* (Oxford University Press, Oxford, 1999).

Gunningham, Neil *Industrial Law and the Constitution* (Federation Press, Sydney,1988).

Gunter, Hans 'The Tripartite Declaration of Principles concerning Multinational Enterprises and Social Policy' in Roger Blanpain (ed) *International Encyclopedia for Labour Law and Industrial Relations* (Kluwer Academic Publishers, London, 1992).

Hadfield, Gillian 'Problematic Relations: Franchising and the Law of Incomplete Contracts' (1990) 42 *Stanford Law Review* 927.

Hall, Philippa and Fruin, Di 'Gender Aspects of Enterprise Bargaining: the Good, the Bad and the Ugly' in David Morgan (ed) *Dimensions of Enterprise Bargaining and Organisational Relations* (UNSW Studies in Australian Industrial Relations, No 36, Sydney, 1994).

Hall, Richard *Labour Hire in Australia: Motivation, Dynamics and Prospects* (ACIRRT Working Paper, University of Sydney, 2002).

Hancock, Keith 'Work in an Ungolden Age' in Ron Callus, and Russell Lansbury (eds) *Working Futures: The Changing Nature of Work and Employment Relations in Australia* (Federation Press, Sydney, 2002).

Hancock, Keith and Richardson, Sue 'Economics and Social Effects' in Joe Isaac and Stuart Macintyre (eds) *The New Province of Law and Order: 100 Years of Australian Industrial Conciliation and Arbitration* (Cambridge University Press, Australia, 2004).

Hancock, Keith *Report of the Committee of Review on Australian Industrial Relations Law and Systems*, vols 1–3 (Australian Government Printing Service, Canberra, 1985).

Hansmann, H 'Worker Participation in Corporate Governance' (1993) 43 *University of Toronto Law Journal* 589.

Hansmann, Henry 'Worker Participation in Corporate Governance' (1993) 43 *University of Toronto Law Journal* 589

Harris, Angela 'Race and Essentialism in Feminist Legal Theory' (1990) 42 *Stanford Law Review* 581.

Hayek, Friedrich von A *Law, Legislation and Liberty: A New Statement of the Principles of Justice and Political Economy* vol 1 'Rules and Order' (Routledge & Kegan Paul, London, 1976).

Hepple, Bob 'A Race to the Top? International Investment Guidelines and Corporate Codes of Conduct' (1999) 20 *Comparative Labour Law and Policy Journal* 347.

Hepple, Bob 'New Approaches to International Labour Regulation' (1997) 26 *Industrial Law Journal* 353.

Hepple, Bob 'Restructuring Employment Rights (1986) 15 *Industrial Law Journal* 69.

Hepple, Bob 'The Future of Labour Law' (1995) 24 *Industrial Law Journal* 303.

Hepple, Bob Coussey, Mary and Choudhury, Tufyal *Equality: A New Framework. Report of the Independent Review of the Enforcement of UK Anti-discrimination Legislation* (Hart, Oxford, 2000).

Hepple, Bob *Labour Laws and Global Trade* (Hart, Oxford, 2000).

Hepple, Bob *Social and Labour Rights in a Global Context: International and Comparative Perspectives* (Cambridge University Press, Cambridge, 2002).

Hepple, Bob *Work, Empowerment and Equality* (International Institute for Labour Studies, Public Lectures, Geneva, 2000).

Heydon, John D *The Restraint of Trade Doctrine*, 2nd ed (Butterworths, Sydney,1999).

Higgins, Henry Bournes 'A New Province For Law and Order: *Industrial Peace through Minimum Wage and Arbitration*' (1915) 29 *Harvard Law Review* 13.

Hill, Jennifer 'At the Frontiers of Labour Law and Corporate Law: Enterprise Bargaining, Corporations and Employees' (1995) 23 *Federal Law Review* 204.

Hill, Jennifer 'Public Beginnings and Private Ends—Should Corporate Law Privilege the Interests of Shareholders?' (1998) 9 *Australian Journal of Corporate Law* 21.

Hodges-Aerberhard, Jane and Odera de Dios Alberto 'Principles of the Committee of Freedom of Association concerning Strikes' (1987) 126 *International Labour Review* 543.

House of Representatives Standing Committee on Employment, Workplace Relations and Workforce Participation *Making it Work: Inquiry into Independent Contracting and Labour-Hire Arrangements* (Parliament of Australia, Canberra, August 2005).

House of Representatives Standing Committee on Family and Human Services *Inquiry into Balancing Work and Family* (Parliament of Australia, Canberra, 2005).

House of Representatives Standing Committee on Industry, Science and Technology *Finding a Balance—Towards Fair Trading in Australia* (Parliamentary Paper Number 83/97, AGPS, Canberra May 1997).

Howe, John 'The Job Creation Function of the State: A New Subject for Labour Law' (2001) 14 *Australian Journal of Labour Law* 242.

Howe, John and Mitchell, Richard 'The Evolution of the Contract of Employment in Australia: A Discussion' (1999) 12 *Australian Journal of Labour Law* 113.

HR Nicholls Society *Arbitration in Contempt*, the proceedings of the inaugural seminar of the HR Nicholls Society held in Melbourne 28 February-2 March, 1986. (HR Nicholls Society, Melbourne,1986).

HREOC 'Pathways to Resolution' (video), available at <www.humanrights.gov.au/pathways_to _ resolution>.

HREOC *Submission* to the Senate Employment, Workplace Relations and Education Legislation Committee, Inquiry into the *Workplace Relations Amendment (Work Choices) Bill 2005* (2005). Available at < http://www.aph.gov.au/Senate/committee/eet_ctte/completed_inquiries/index.htm>.

Human Rights and Equal Opportunity Commission *A Time to Value: Proposal for a National Paid Maternity Leave Scheme* (HREOC, Sydney, 2002).

Human Rights and Equal Opportunity Commission *Just Rewards* (AGPS, Canberra, 1992).

Human Rights and Equal Opportunity Commission *Pregnant and Productive: It's a right not a privilege to work while pregnant* (HREOC, Sydney, 1999).

Human Rights and Equal Opportunity Commission *Striking the Balance: Women, Men, Work and Family*, Discussion Paper (HREOC, Sydney, 2005).

Human Rights and Equal Opportunity Commission *Valuing Parenthood: Options for Paid Maternity Leave: Interim Paper* (HREOC, Sydney, 2002).

Human Rights Watch *Trading Away Rights: The Unfulfilled Promise of NAFTA's Labour Side Agreement* (April 2001) available at www.hrwatch.org.

Human Rights Watch, *Corporate Social Responsibility: letter to the United Nations* http://www.hrw.org/press/2000/07/hrw-ltr-july.htm.

Hunter, Rosemary 'Representing Gender in Legal Analysis: A Case/Book Study in Labour Law' (1991) 18 *Melbourne University Law Review* 305.

Hunter, Rosemary 'The Mirage of Justice: Women and the Shrinking State' (2002) 16 *Australian Feminist Law Journal* 53.

Hunter, Rosemary 'The Production of Precarious Work' in Judy Fudge and Rosemary Owens (eds) *Precarious Work, Women and the New Economy: The Challenge to Legal Norms* (Hart Publishing, Oxford and Portland Oregon, 2006).

Hunter, Rosemary 'The Regulation of Independent Contractors: A Feminist Perspective' (1992) 5 *Corporate and Business Law Journal* 165.

Hunter, Rosemary 'Women Workers and Federal Industrial Law: From Harvester to Comparable Worth' (1988) 1 *Australian Journal of Labour Law* 147.

Hunter, Rosemary *Indirect Discrimination in the Workplace* (Federation Press, Sydney, 1992).

Hunter, Rosemary *The Beauty Therapist, the Mechanic, the Geoscientist and the Librarian: Addressing the Undervaluation of Women's Work* (ATN WEXDEV, University of Technology, Sydney, 2000).

Hunyor, Jonathan 'Skin Deep: Proof and Inferences of Racial Discrimination in Employment' (2003) 25 *Sydney Law Review* 535.

Hyde, Alan 'A Closer Look at the Emerging Employment Law of Silicon Valley's High Velocity Labour Market' in Joanne Conaghan, Richard M Fischl, and Karl Klare (eds) *Labour Law in an Era of Globalization: Transformative Practices and Possibilities* (Oxford University Press, Oxford, 2002).

Independent Committee *Unfinished Business: Equity for Women in Australian Workplaces*, Regulatory Review of the Affirmative Action (Equal Employment Opportunity for Women) Act 1986 (AGPS, Canberra, June 1998).

International Labour Organization 'Private Initiatives and Labour Standards: A Global Study' (ILO GB 23/WP/SDL/1, Geneva, October 1998). Available at <www.unglobalcompact.org/gc/unweb. nsf/webprintview/ilostudy.htm>.

International Labour Organization *A Future Without Child Labour: Global Report under the follow-up to the ILO Declaration on Fundamental Principles and Rights at Work*, Report of the Director- General, International Labour Conference, 90th session 2002, Report IB (International Labour Office, Geneva, 2002).

International Labour Organization *Decent Work in the Informal Economy* Report VI, International Labour Conference, 90th session, (International Labour Office, Geneva, 2002).

International Labour Organization *Decent Work* Report of the Director-General, International Labour Conference 87th Session, (International Labour Office, Geneva, 1999).

International Labour Organization Director-General's speech 'Decent Work for Women: ILO's Contribution to Women 2000' (follow up after the Fourth World Conference on Women held in Beijing in 1995, Geneva, 24 March 2000).

International Labour Organization *Final Report on the Impact of Globalisation* Working Party on the Social Dimensions of the Liberalization of International Trade, (GB 276/WP/SDL/1, International Labour Office, Geneva, 1999).

International Labour Organization *Freedom of Association and Collective Bargaining: General Survey of the Report on the Freedom of Association and the Right to Organise Convention (no 87) 1948 and the Right to Organise and Collective Bargaining Convention (no 98) 1949* (International Labour Office, Geneva, 1994).

International Labour Organization *Freedom of Association and Collective Bargaining: General Survey of the Report on the Freedom of Association and the Right to Organise Convention (no 87) 1948 and the Right to organise and collective Bargaining Convention (no 98) 1949*, Report III (Part 4B), International Labour Conference, 81st session, 1994, (International Labour Office, Geneva, 1994).

International Labour Organization *Freedom of Association: Digest of Decisions and Principles of the Freedom of Association Committee of the Governing Body of the ILO* (International Labour Office, Geneva, 1996).

International Labour Organization *Freedom of Association: Digest of Decisions and Principles of the Freedom of Association Committee of the Governing Body of the ILO* (International Labour Office, Geneva, 1985).

International Labour Organization *Gender: A Partnership of Equals* (Bureau for Gender Equity, International Labour Office, Geneva, 2000).

International Labour Organization *Global Employment Trends for Women 2004* (International Labour Office, Geneva, 2004).

International Labour Organization *Organizing for Social Justice: Global Report under the Follow-up to the ILO Declaration on Fundamental Principles and Rights at Work*, Report of the Director-General, International Labour Conference, 92nd Session Report I(B) (International Labour Office, Geneva, 2004).

International Labour Organization *Overview of developments in other international organizations and bodies relevant to the work of the Working Party*, Report of the Working Party on the Social Dimensions of Liberalization of International Trade, to the Governing Body of the ILO, 277th Session, March 2000, GB 277/16 GB 277/WP/SDL/2 (International Labour Office, Geneva, March 2000).

International Labour Organization 'Part-time work', *Conditions of Work Digest*, vol 8, no 1, (International Labour Office, Geneva, 1989).

International Labour Organization *Seventh Survey on the effect given to the 1977 Tripartite Declaration* (ILO Governing Body docs GB 280/MNE/1/1 and BG 280/MNE/1/2, 280th session Geneva, March 2001).

International Labour Organization *Stopping Forced Labour: Global Report under the Follow-up to the ILO Declaration on Fundamental Principles and Rights at Work*, Report of the Director-General, International Labour Conference, 89th Session Report I(B) (International Labour Office, Geneva, 2001).

International Labour Organization *The Employment Relationship*, Report V(1), International Labour Conference, 95th Session, 2006 (International Labour Office, Geneva, 2005).

International Labour Organization *The ILO and Standard Setting and Globalisation* Report of the Director General, International Labour Conference 85th Session, (International Labour Office, Geneva, 1997).

International Labour Organization *The ILO Tripartite Declaration of Principles concerning Multi National Enterprises and Social Policy—Ten Years After* (International Labour Office, Geneva, 1988).

International Labour Organization *Time for Equality at Work: Global Report under the Follow-up to the ILO Declaration on Fundamental Principles and Rights at Work*, Report of the Director-General, International Labour Conference, 91st Session Report I(B) (International Labour Office, Geneva, 2003).

International Labour Organization *World Labour Report 1997–98* (International Labour Office, Geneva, 1997).

International Labour Organization *Your Voice at Work: Global Report under the Follow-up to the ILO Declaration on Fundamental Principles and Rights at Work*, Report of the Director-General, International Labour Conference, 88th Session Report I(B) (International Labour Office, Geneva, 2000).

Isaac, Joe and Macintyre, Stuart (eds) *The New Province of Law and Order: 100 Years of Australian Industrial Conciliation and Arbitration* (Cambridge University Press, Australia, 2004).

Jackson, David *Report of the Special Commission of Inquiry into the Medical Research and Compensation Foundation* (NSW Government, Sydney, September 2004).

Jamieson, S 'Enterprise Agreements in NSW: A New Era?' (1992) 5 *Australian Journal of Labour Law* 84.

Jamieson, Suzanne 'Enterprise Agreements in NSW: A New Era?' (1992) 5 *Australian Journal of Labour Law* 84

Jenks, Clarence W *Human Rights and International Labour Law Standards* (London Institute for World Affairs, Stevens, London, c 1960).

Johnson, Lyman 'New Approaches to Corporate Law' (1993) 50 *Washington and Lee Law Journal* 1713.

Johnstone, Richard 'Paradigm Crossed? The Statutory Occupational Health and Safety Obligations of the Business Undertaking' (1999) 12 *Australian Journal of Labour Law* 73.

Johnstone, Richard and Mitchell, Richard 'Regulating Work' in Christine Parker, Colin Scott, Nicola Lacey, and John Braithwaite (eds) *Regulating Law* (Oxford University Press, Oxford, 2004).

Johnstone, Richard and Wilson, Therese 'Take Me to Your Employer: The Organisational Reach of Occupational Health and Safety Regulation' (2006) 19 *Australian Journal of Labour Law* 59.

Johnstone, Richard *Occupational Health and Safety Law and Policy* (LBC Information Services, Pyrmont NSW, 2004).

Kahn-Freund, Otto 'Blackstone's Neglected Child: The Contract of Employment' (1977) 93 *Law Quarterly Review* 508.

Kahn-Freund, Otto 'On Uses and Abuses of Comparative Law' (1974) 37 *Modern Law Review* 1.

Kahn-Freund, Otto 'Servants and Independent Contractors' (1951) 14 *Modern Law Review* 504.

Kahn-Freund, Otto *Labour and the Law* (Stevens, London, 1972).

Kahn-Freund, Otto *Labour and the Law*, 2nd ed (Stevens, London, 1977).

Kent, Ann 'Australia and the International Human Rights Regime' in Cotton, James and Ravenhill, John (eds) *The National Interest in a Global Era: Australia in World Affairs 1996–2000* (Oxford University Press, Melbourne, 2002).

Kilpatrick, Claire 'Gender and the Legal Regulation of Employment Breaks' in Judy Fudge and Rosemary Owens (eds) *Precarious Work, Women, and the New Economy: The Challenge to Legal Norms* (Hart Publishing, Oxford and Portland Oregon, 2006).

Kinley, David 'Human Rights as Legally Binding or Merely Relevant?' in Stephen Bottomley, and David Kinley (eds) *Commercial Law and Human Rights* (Ashgate, Aldershot UK, 2002).

Kirby, The Honourable Justice Michael 'Industrial Conciliation and Arbitration in Australia—a Centenary Reflection' (2004) 17 *Australian Journal of Labour Law* 229.

Kittner, Michael and Kohler, Thomas 'Conditioning Expectations: The Protection of the Employment Bond in German and American Law' (2000) 21 *Comparative Labor Law & Policy Journal* 263.

Klare, Karl 'The Horizons of Transformative Labour and Employment Law' in Joanne Conaghan, Richard M Fischl, and Karl Klare (eds) *Labour Law in an Era of Globalization: Transformative Possibilities and Practices* (Oxford University Press, Oxford and New York, 2002).

Knowles, Fiona 'Misdirection for Indirect Discrimination' (2004) 17 *Australian Journal of Labour Law* 185.

Kollmorgen, Stuart 'Towards a Unitary National System of Industrial relations?' (1997) 10 *Australian Journal of Labour Law* 158.

Kucera, David '*The Effects of Core Worker's Rights on Labour Costs and Foreign Direct Investment: Evaluating the Conventional Wisdom*' (ILO, International Institute for Labour Studies, Decent Work Research Program, DP/130/2001, Geneva, 2001).

Langille, Brian A 'Core Labour Rights—The True Story (Reply to Alston)' (2005) 16 *European Journal of International Law* 409.

Laplagne, Patrick, Glover, M and Fry, Tim *The Growth of Labour Hire Employment in Australia* (Australian Productivity Commission, Melbourne, 2005).

Laster, Kathy and Raman, Padma 'Law For One and One For All? An Intersectional Legal Subject' in Ngaire Naffine and Rosemary J Owens, (eds) *Sexing the Subject of Law* (Lawbook Company and Sweet and Maxwell, North Ryde NSW, 1997).

Lavarch, Michael *Half Way to Equal: Report of the Inquiry into Equal Opportunity and Equal Status for Women in Australia'* (House of Representatives Standing Committee on Legal and Constitutional Affairs, AGPS, Canberra, 1992).

Leader, Sheldon *Freedom of Association: A Study of Labor Law and Political Theory* (Yale University Press, New Haven, 1992).

Leary, Virginia A 'Human Rights at the ILO: Reflections on Making the ILO More User Friendly' in Pedro Nikken and Antonio Cancado-Trinidade (eds) *The Modern World of Human Rights: Essays in Honours of Thomas Buergenthal* (Inter-American Institute of Human Rights, San Jose, Cost Rica, 1996).

Leary, Virginia A 'Workers' Rights and International Trade: The Social Clause' in Jagdish Bagwati and Robert E Hudec (eds) *Fair Trade and Harmonization: Prerequisites for Free Trade* (MIT Press, Cambridge MA, 1996).

Lee, Eddy 'Globalisation and Labour Standards: A Review of the Issues' (1997) 136 *International Labour Review* 173.

Lillard, Monique C 'Fifty Jurisdictions in Search of a Standard: The Covenant of Good Faith and Fair Dealing in the Employment Context' (1992) 57 *Missouri Law Review* 1233.

Lloyd, Vincent and Weissman, Robert 'Against the Workers: How IMF and World Bank Policies undermine Labor Power and Rights' (2001) 22(9) *Multinational Monitor* 7–13.

Locke, John *Two Treatises of Government: a critical edition with an introduction and apparatus criticus by Peter Laslett* (Cambridge University Press, Cambridge, 1960).

Ludeke, The Honourable Justice JT 'What Ever Happened to the Prerogatives of Management?' (1991) 33 *Journal of Industrial Relations* 395.

Ludeke, The Honourable Justice JT 'Whatever Happened to Managerial Prerogative?' (1992) 66 *Australian Law Journal* 11.

MacDermott, Therese 'Age Discrimination and Employment Law: The Sky's the Limit' (1998) 11 *Australian Journal of Labour Law* 144.

MacDermott, Therese 'Labour Law and Human Rights' in David Kinley (ed) *Human Rights in Australian Law* (Federation Press, Leichhardt NSW, 1998).

MacDermott, Therese 'Linking Gender and Superannuation' (1997) 2 *International Journal of Discrimination and Law* 271.

MacDermott, Therese 'The Changing Role of the Safety Net: The Australian Industrial Relations Commission's s150A Review' in Paul Ronfeldt and Ron McCallum (eds) *Enterprise Bargaining, Trade Unions and the Law* (Federation Press, Sydney, 1995).

MacDermott, Therese and Owens, Rosemary 'Equality and Flexibility for Workers with Family Responsibilities: A Troubled Union?' (2000) 13 *Australian Journal of Labour Law* 278.

Macintyre, Stuart 'Neither capital nor labour: the politics of the establishment of arbitration' in Stuart MacIntyre and Richard Mitchell (eds) *Foundations of Arbitration: The Origins and Effects of State Compulsory Arbitration 1890–1914* (Oxford University Press, Melbourne, 1989).

Macken James J, McGarry, Greg, Moloney, Carolyn *The Common Law of Employment* (Lawbook Company, Sydney, 1978).

Macken, James, O'Grady, Paul, Sappideen, Carolyn, and Warburton, Geoff *Law of Employment*, 5th ed (Lawbook Company, Sydney, 2002).

MacKinnon, Catharine *Feminism Unmodified: Discourses on Life and Law* (Harvard University Press, Cambridge MA, 1987).

MacKinnon, Catharine *Toward a Feminist Theory of the State* (Harvard University Press, Cambridge MA, 1989).

Macklem, Patrick 'The Right to Bargain Collectively in International Law: Workers' Right, Human Right, International Right' in Phillip Alston (ed) *Labour Rights as Human Rights* (Oxford University Press, Oxford and New York, 2005).

Marshall, Thomas H *Citizenship and Social Class* (Cambridge University Press, Cambridge, 1950).

Marx, Karl *Das Kapital: Kritik der politischen Oekonomie* (Verlag von Otto Meissner, Hamburg, and LW Schmidt, New York, 1867).

Mason, Gail and Chapman, Anna 'Defining Sexual Harassment: A History of the Commonwealth Legislation and Its Critiques' (2003) 31 *Federal Law Review* 195.

Maupin, Frances 'Revitalization Not Retreat: The Real Potential of the 1998 ILO Declaration for the Universal Protection of Workers' Rights' (2005) 16 *European Journal of International Law* 439.

McCallum, Ron 'Australian Workplace Agreements: An Analysis' (1997) 10 *Australian Journal of Labour Law* 50.

McCallum, Ron 'Collective Labour Law, Citizenship and the Future' (1998) 22 *Melbourne University Law Review* 42.

McCallum, Ron 'Crafting a New Collective Labour Law for Australia' (1997) 39 *Journal of Industrial Relations* 405.

McCallum, Ron 'Industrial Citizenship' (Paper presented at Australian Labour Law Association Second National Conference, University of Sydney, 25 September 2004).

McCallum, Ron 'International Standards in Industrial Relations and their Application in Australia' (1995) 2 *The Judicial Review* 163.

McCallum, Ron 'The Internationalisation of Australian Industrial Law: The *Industrial Relations Reform Act 1993*' (1994) 16 *Sydney Law Review* 122.

McCallum, Ron 'The New Millennium and the Higgins Heritage: Industrial Relations in the 21st Century' (1996) 38 *Journal of Industrial Relations* 294.

McCallum, Ron 'The New Work Choices Laws: Once Again Australia Borrows Foreign Labour Law Concepts' (2006) 19 *Australian Journal of Labour Law* 98.

McCallum, Ron and Stewart, Andrew 'The Duty of Loyalty: Employee Loyalty in Australia' (1999) 20 *Comparative Labor Law and Policy Journal* 155.

McCallum, Ron *Employer Controls over Private Life* (University of New South Wales Press, Sydney, 2000).

McCallum, Ron *Independent Report Prepared for the Victorian Industrial Relations Taskforce* (The State of Victoria, Melbourne, August 2000).

McCallum, Ronald 'Justice at Work: Industrial Citizenship and the Corporatisation of Australian Law', The Kingsley Laffer Memorial Lecture (2005)' (2006) 48 *Journal of Industrial Relations* 131.

McCallum, Ronald C 'A Priority of Rights: Freedom of Association and the Waterfront Dispute' (1998) 24 *Australian Bulletin of Labour* 207.

McCallum, Ronald C 'Australian Workplace Agreements: An Analysis' (1997) 10 *Australian Journal of Labour Law* 50.

McCallum, Ronald C 'Enhancing Federal Enterprise Bargaining: *The Industrial Relations (Legislation Amendment) Act 1992* (Cth) (1993) 6 *Australian Journal of Labour Law* 63.

McCallum, Ronald C 'The Mystique of Secret Ballots: Labour Relations Progress v Industrial Anarchy' (1975–76) 2 *Monash University Law Review* 166.

McCallum, Ronald C, 'The Mystique of Secret Ballots: Labour Relations Progress v Industrial Anarchy' (1975–76) 2 *Monash University Law Review* 166.

McCallum, Ronald C, Pittard Marilyn J, and Smith, Graham F *Australian Labour Law: Cases and Materials* 2nd ed(Butterworths, Sydney, 1990).

McCann, David 'First Head Revisited: A Single Industrial Relations System under the Trade and Commerce Power' (2004) 26 *Sydney Law Review* 75.

McCarry, Greg 'Sanctions and Industrial Action: the Impact of the *Industrial Relations Reform Act* (1994) 7 *Australian Journal of Labour Law* 198.

McCarry, Greg 'The Employee's Duty to Obey Unreasonable Orders' (1984) 58 *Australian Law Journal* 327.

McCarry, Greg *Aspects of Public Sector Employment Law* (Lawbook Company, Sydney, 1988).

McColgan, Aileen *Just Wages For Women* (Clarendon University Press, Oxford, 1997).

McColgan, Aileen *Women Under the Law the False Promise of Human Rights* (Longman, Essex, 2000).

McCrystal, Shae 'Regulating Collective Bargaining: Employees, Self Employed Persons and Small Business' in Chris Arup, Peter Gahan, John Howe, Richard Johnstone, Richard Mitchell and Anthony O'Donnell (eds) *Labour Law and Labour Market Regulation* (Federation Press, Sydney, forthcoming).

McCrystal, Shae 'Smothering the Right to Strike: Work Choices and Industrial Action' (2006) 19 *Australian Journal of Labour Law* 198;

McEvoy, Kathleen P and Owens, Rosemary J 'On a Wing and a Prayer: the Pilot's Dispute in the International Context' (1993) 6 *Australian Journal of Labour Law* 1.

McEvoy, Kathleen P and Owens, Rosemary J 'The Flight of Icarus: Legal Aspects of the Pilots' Dispute' (1990) 3 *Australian Journal of Labour Law* 87.

McGee Robert W 'The Right to Not Associate: The Case for an Absolute Freedom of Negative Association' (1992) 23 *University of West Los Angeles Law Review* 123.

McGinley, Gerald P 'The Status of Treaties in Australian Municipal Law: The Principle in *Walker v Baird*' (1990) 12 *Adelaide Law Review* 367.

McMahon, J F 'The Legislative Techniques of the International Labour Organization' (1965–66) 41 *British Year Book of International Law* 1.

McNeil, Ian 'Contracts: Adjustment of Long-term Economic Relations under Classical, Neoclassical and Relational Contract Law' (1978) 72 *Northwestern University Law Review* 854.

McNeil, Ian 'Values in Contract: Internal and External' (1983) 78 *Northwestern University Law Review* 340.

Méda, Dominique 'New Perspectives on Work as Value' (1996) 135 *International Labour Review* 633.

Merlo, Omar 'Flexibility and Stretching Rights: The No Disadvantage Test in Enterprise Bargaining' (2000) 13 *Australian Journal of Labour Law* 207.

Merrit, Adrian 'Control v Economic Reality: Defining the Contract of Employment' (1982) *Australian Business Law Review* 105.

Merritt, Adrian 'The Historical Role of Law in the Regulation of Employment—Abstentionist or Interventionist' (1982) 1 *Australian Journal of Law & Society* 56.

Messenger, Jon C (ed) *Working Time and Workers' Preferences in Industrialized Countries: Finding the Balance* (International Labour Organization, Routledge, London, 2004).

Mills, C P 'The Contract of Employment: Control is Economic Reality' (1982) 10 *Australian Business Law Review* 270.

Ministerial Discussion Paper *Getting the Outsiders Inside—Towards a Rational Workplace Relations System in Australia* (Australian Government, Canberra, 1999).

Mitchell, Richard (ed) *Redefining Labour Law: New Perspectives on the Future of Teaching and Research* (Centre for Employment and Labour Relations Law, Occasional Monograph Series No 3, Melbourne, 1995).

Mitchell, Richard 'Liability in Tort for Causing Economic Loss by the Use of Unlawful Means and its Application to Australian Industrial Disputes' (1976) 5 *Adelaide Law Review* 428.

Mitchell, Richard 'State systems of conciliation and arbitration: the legal origins of the Australasian model' in Stuart Macintyre and Richard Mitchell (eds) *Foundations of Arbitration: The Origins and Effects of State Compulsory Arbitration 1890–1914* (Oxford University Press, Melbourne, 1989).

Mitchell, Richard and Fetter, Joel 'Human Resource Management and Individualisation in Australian Labour Law' (2003) 45 *Journal of Industrial Relations* 292.

Mitchell, Richard and Fetter, Joel 'Human Resource Management and Individualisation in Australian Labour Law' (2003) 45 *Journal of Industrial Relations* 292

Mitchell, Richard and Naughton, Richard 'Australian Compulsory Arbitration: Will It Survive into the Twenty-First Century?' (1993) 31 *Osgoode Hall Law Journal* 265.

Mitchell, Richard, Campbell, Rebecca, Barnes, Andrew, Bicknell, Emma, Creighton, Kate, Fetter, Joel and Korman, Samantha 'What's Going on with the 'No Disadvantage Test'? An Analysis of Outcomes and Processes Under the Workplace Relations Act 1996 (Cth)' (2005) 47 *Journal of Industrial Relations* 393.

Mitchell, Richard, Campbell, Rebecca, Barnes, Andrew, Bicknell, Emma, Creighton, Kate, Fetter, Joel and Korman, Samantha *Protecting The Worker's Interest in Enterprise Bargaining: The 'No Disadvantage' Test in the Australian Federal Industrial Jurisdiction* (Final Report prepared for the Workplace Innovation Unit, Industrial Relations Victoria, Melbourne, 2004).

Mitchell, Richard, O'Donnell, Anthony and Ramsay, Ian 'Shareholder Value and Employee Interests: Intersections between Corporate Governance, Corporate Law and Labour Law' (Research Report, Centre for Corporate Law and Securities Regulation and Centre for Employment and Labour Relations Law, University of Melbourne, Melbourne, June 2005).

Morgan, Jenny 'Equality, Morality and Manners' in Margaret Thornton (ed) *Public and Private: Feminist Legal Debates* (Oxford University Press, Melbourne, 1995).

Morrison, Wayne (ed) *Blackstone's Commentaries on the Laws of England*, 4 volumes (Cavendish, London, 2001).

Mudaliar, Sanushka 'Stolen Wages and Fiduciary Duties: A Legal Analysis of Government Accountability to Indigenous Workers in Queensland' [2003] *Australian Indigenous Law Reporter* 33, (vol 8, p 1, available at <www.austlii.edu.au/au/journals/AILR/2003/33.html>).

Murray, Jill (ed) *Work, Family and the Law (Special Issue of Law in Context*, vol 23*)* (Federation Press, Sydney, 2005).

Murray, Jill 'A New Phase in the Regulation of Multinational Enterprises: The Role of the OECD' (2001) 30 *Industrial Law Journal* 255.

Murray, Jill 'Australia in the Dock: The ILO's Decision on the Waterfront Dispute' (2000) 13 *Australian Journal of Labour Law* 167.

Murray, Jill 'Social Justice for Women? The ILO's Convention on Part-time Work' (1999) 15 *International Journal of Comparative Labour Law and Industrial Relations* 3.

Murray, Jill 'The AIRC's *Test Case on Work and Family Provisions*: The End of Dynamic Regulatory Change at the Federal Level?' (2005) 18 *Australian Journal of Labour Law* 325.

Murray, Jill 'The International Regulation of Maternity: Still Waiting for the Reconciliation of Work and Family Life' (2001) 17 *International Journal of Comparative Labour Law and Industrial Relations* 25.

Murray, Jill 'The Legal Regulation of Volunteers' in Christopher Arup, Gahan, Peter, Howe, John, Johnstone, Richard, Mitchell Richard and O'Donnell, Anthony (eds), *Labour Law and Labour Market Regulation* (Federation Press, Sydney, forthcoming).

Murray, Jill *International Legal Trends in the Reconciliation of Work and Family Life* (Report prepared for the ACTU's submission in the Family Provisions Test Case 2004, April 2004).

Murray, Jill *Transnational Labour Regulation: The ILO and EC Compared* (Kluwer Law International, The Hague, 2001).

Naughton, Richard 'Natural Justice in the Australian Industrial Relations Commission' (1993) 35 *Journal of Industrial Relations* 3.

Naughton, Richard 'Sailing into Unchartered Seas: The Role of Unions under the Workplace Relations Act' (1997) *Australian Journal of Labour Law* 112.

Naughton, Richard 'Self Regulation of Australian Workplaces' (1999) 12 *Australian Journal of Labour Law* 131.

Naughton, Richard 'The New Bargaining Regime under the *Industrial Relations Reform Act*' (1994) 7 *Australian Journal of Labour Law* 147;

New South Wales Department of Industrial Relations *Behind the Label—The NSW Government Clothing Outwork Strategy—Issues Paper* (Department of Industrial Relations, Sydney, December 1999).

New South Wales Industrial Relations Commission *Pay Equity Inquiry: Reference by the Minister for Industrial Relations pursuant to s146(1)(d) of the Industrial Relations Act 1996*, volumes 1–3 (NSWIRC, Sydney, 1998).

Niland, John and Clarke, Oliver (eds) *Agenda for Change: An International Analysis of Industrial Relations in Transition* (Allen & Unwin, Sydney, 1991).

Niland, John and Clarke, Oliver *Agenda for Change: An International Analysis of Industrial Relations in Transition* (Allen & Unwin, North Sydney, 1991).

Niland, John *Transforming Industrial Relations in New South Wales: A Green Paper* (NSW Government Printing Office, Sydney, 1989).

Noakes, David 'Corporate Groups and the Duties of Directors: Protecting the Employee of the insolvent Employer?' (2001) 29 *Australian Business Law Review* 124.

Noakes, David 'Dogs on the Wharves: Corporate Groups and the Waterfront Dispute' (1999) 11 *Australian Journal of Corporate Law* 27.

Noakes, David and Cardell-Ree, Andrew 'Individual Contracts and the Freedom of Association: *Australian Workers' Union v. BHP Iron-Ore Pty Ltd* [2001] FCA 3' (2001) 14 *Australian Journal of Labour Law* 89.

Nossar, Igor, Johnstone, Richard and Quinlan, Michael 'Regulating Supply Chains to Address Occupational Health and Safety Problems Associated with Precarious Employment: The Case of Home-Based Clothing Workers in Australia' (2004) 17 *Australian Journal of Labour Law* 137.

Note: 'Towards a Property Right in Employment' (1974) 22 *Buffalo Law Review* 1081.

Nozick, Robert *Anarchy, State and Utopia* (Blackwell, Oxford, 1974).

Nussbaum, Martha C *Sex & Social Justice* (Oxford University Press, New York and London, 1999).

Nyland, Chris and Castle, Rob 'The ILO and the Australian Contribution to the International Labour Standards Debate' (1999) 41 *Journal of Industrial Relations* 355.

O'Connor, Marleen 'The Human Capital Era: Reconceptualizing Corporate Law to Facilitate Labor-Management Cooperation' (1993) 78 *Cornell Law Review* 899.

O'Donnell, Anthony ''Non-Standard' Workers in Australia: Counts and Controversies' (2004) 17 *Australian Journal of Labour Law* 89.

O'Donnell, Anthony and Mitchell, Richard 'Immigrant Labour in Australia; The Regulatory Framework' (2001) 14 *Australian Journal of Labour Law* 269.

O'Higgins, Paul ''Labour is Not a Commodity'—an Irish Contribution to International Labour Law' (1997) 26 *Industrial Law Journal* 225.

OECD *Economic Survey of Australia 2004: Policies to Lower Unemployment and Raise Labour Force Participation* (OECD, Paris, 2005).

OECD *Trade, Employment and Labour Standards: A Study of Core Workers' Rights and International Trade* (OECD, Paris, 1996).

Ontiveros, Maria L 'A New Course for Labour Unions: Identity Based Organizing as a Response to Globalization' in Joanne Conaghan, Richard M Fischl and Karl Klare (eds), *Labour Law in an Era of Globalization: Transformative Practices and Possibilities* (Oxford University Press, Oxford and New York, 2002).

Orr, Graeme 'Conspiracy on the Waterfront' (1998) 11 *Australian Journal of Labour Law* 159.

Orr, Graeme 'Unauthorised Workers: Labouring Beneath the Law?' in Chris Arup, Peter Gahan, John Howe, Richard Johnstone, Richard Mitchell and Anthony O'Donnell (eds) *Labour Law and Labour Market Regulation* (Federation Press, Sydney, 2006).

Otlowski, Margaret 'The Demise of Conspiracy by Unlawful Means?' (1989) 2 *Australian Journal of Labour Law* 107.

Owens, Alexandra 'Testing the Ratcheting Labour Standards Proposal: Indonesia and the Shangri-La Workers' (2004) 5 *Melbourne Journal of International Law* 169.

Owens, Rosemary 'Engendering Flexibility in a World of Precarious Work' in Judy Fudge and Rosemary Owens (eds) *Precarious Work, Women and the New Economy: The Challenge to Legal Norms* (Hart Publishing, Oxford and Portland Oregon, 2006).

Owens, Rosemary 'Reproducing Law's Worker: Regulatory Tensions in the Pursuit of "Population, Participation and Productivity"' in Chris Arup, Peter Gahan, John Howe, Richard Johnstone, Richard Mitchell and Anthony O'Donnell (eds) *Labour Law and Labour Market Regulation* (Federation Press, Sydney, 2006).

Owens, Rosemary J 'Commentary: Lionel Murphy and Gender Issues' in Michael Coper and George Williams (eds) *Justice Lionel Murphy: Influential or Merely Prescient?* (Federation Press, Sydney, 1997).

Owens, Rosemary J 'Law and Feminism in the New Industrial Relations' in Ian Hunt and Chris Provis (eds) *The New Industrial Relations In Australia* (Federation Press, Sydney, 1995).

Owens, Rosemary J 'Taking Leave: Work and Family in Australian Law and Policy' in Joanne Conaghan and Kerry Rittich (eds) *Labour Law, Work and Family* (Oxford University Press, Oxford and New York, 2005).

Owens, Rosemary J 'The 'Long Term or Permanent Casual' - Oxymoron or 'a well enough understood Australianism' in the Law' (2001) 27 *Australian Bulletin of Labour* 118.

Owens, Rosemary J 'The Future of the Law of Work' (2002) 23 *Adelaide Law Review* 345.

Owens, Rosemary J 'The Peripheral Worker: Women and the Legal Regulation of Outwork' in Margaret Thornton (ed) *Public and Private: Feminist Legal Debates* (Oxford University Press, Melbourne, 1995).

Owens, Rosemary J 'The Traditional Labour Law Framework: A Critical Evaluation' in Richard Mitchell (ed) *Redefining Labour Law: New Perspectives on Teaching and Research* (Centre for Employment and Labour Relations Law, Occasional Monograph Series, The University of Melbourne, 1995).

Owens, Rosemary J 'Women, 'Atypical' Work Relationships and the Law' (1993) 19 *Melbourne University Law Review* 399.

Owens, Rosemary J 'Working in the Sex Market' in Ngaire Naffine and Rosemary J Owens (eds) *Sexing the Subject of Law* (Sweet and Maxwell, London and LBC Information Services, Sydney, 1997).

Paatsch, Dean and Smith, Graham 'The Regulation of Australian Superannuation: An Industrial Relations Perspective' Part I (1992) 5 *Corporate and Business Law Journal* 131.

Paatsch, Dean and Smith, Graham 'The Regulation of Australian Superannuation: An Industrial Relations Perspective' Part II (1993) 6 *Corporate and Business Law Journal* 29.

Pahuja, Sundhya 'Trading Spaces: Locating Sites for Challenge within International Trade Law' (2000) 14 *Australian Feminist Law Journal* 38.

Parker, Christine 'Public Rights in Private Government: Corporate Compliance with Sexual Harassment Legislation' (1998) 5 *Australian Journal of Human Rights* 159

Parkinson, John E *Corporate Power and Responsibility: Issues in the Theory of Company Law* (Clarendon Press, Oxford and Oxford University Press, New York, 1993).

Parliament of Victoria, Economic Development Committee *Inquiry into Labour Hire Employment in Victoria* (Government Printer for the State of Victoria, Melbourne, June 2005).

Pateman, Carole *Participation and Democratic Theory* (Cambridge University Press, Cambridge, 1970).

Pateman, Carole *The Sexual Contract* (Polity Press, Cambridge, 1988).

Peden, Elisabeth 'Incorporating Terms of Good Faith in Contract Law in Australia' (2001) 23 *Sydney Law Review* 222.

Peden, Elisabeth *Good Faith in the Performance of Contracts* (LexisNexis Butterworths, Sydney, 2003).

Peetz, David 'The Safety Net, Bargaining and the Role of the Australian Industrial Relations Commission' (1998) 40 *Journal of Industrial Relations* 533.

Peetz, David *Unions in a Contrary World: The Future of the Australian Trade Union Movement* (Cambridge University Press, Cambridge, 1998).

Perez-Lopez, Jorge F 'Promoting International Respect for Worker Rights through Business Codes of Conduct' (1993) 17 *Fordham International Law Journal* 1.

Phillips, Jeffrey and Tooma, Micheal *The Law of Unfair Contracts in NSW : An examination of section 106 of the Industrial Relations Act 1996 (NSW)* (Lawbook Co, Pyrmont NSW, 2004).

Picciotto, Sol and Mayne, Ruth (eds) *Regulating International Business: Beyond Liberalisation* (MacMillan Press Ltd in association with Oxfam Houndmills, Baskingstoke, 1999).

Pittard, Marilyn 'Collective Employment Relationships: Reforms to Arbitrated Awards and Certified Agreements' (1997) 10 *Australian Journal of Labour Law* 62.

Pittard, Marilyn 'Rethinking Place of Work: Federal Labour Law Framework for Contemporary Home-based Work and its Prospects in Australia' in Jill Murray (ed) *Work, Family and the Law (Special Issue of Law in Context*, vol 23*)* (Federation Press, Sydney, 2005).

Pittard, Marilyn 'The Dispersing and Transformed Workplace: Labour Law and the Effect of Electronic Work' (2003) 16 *Australian Journal of Labour Law* 69.

Pittard, Marilyn 'Trade Practices Law and the Mudginberri Dispute' (1988) 1 *Australian Journal of Labour Law* 23.

Pittard, Marilyn 'Unfair Dismissal Laws: The Problem of Application to Small Business' (2002) 15 *Australian Journal of Labour Law* 154.

Pittard, Marilyn and Naughton, Richard *Australian Labour Law: Cases and Materials*, 4th ed (LexisNexis Butterworths, Sydney, 2003).

Pocock, Barbara 'Women's Work and Wages' in Anne Edwards and Susan Magarey (eds) *Women in a Restructuring Australia: Work and Welfare* (Allen & Unwin, Sydney, 1995).

Pocock, Barbara *The Work/Life Collision* (Federation Press, Sydney, 2003).

Pocock, Barbara, Buchanan, John and Campbell, Iain *Securing Quality Employment: Policy Options for Casual and Part-time Workers in Australia* (Chifley Research Centre, Canberra, 2004).

Pocock, Barbara, van Wanrooy, Brigid, Strazzari, Stefani and Bridge, Ken *Fifty Families: What unreasonable hours are doing to Australians, their families and their communities* (A report commissioned by the ACTU, Australia, July 2001).

Pocock, Barbara (ed) *Strife: Sex and Politics in Labour Unions* (Allen and Unwin, Sydney, 1997)

Portus, J H *The Development of Australian Trade Union Law* (Melbourne University Press, Carlton Victoria, 1958).

Productivity Commission *Economic Implications of an Ageing Australia*, (Productivity Commission Research Report, Canberra, 2005).

Prugl, Elisabeth 'What is a Worker? Gender, Global Restructuring, and the ILO Convention on Homework' in Mary Meyer and Elisabeth Prugl (eds) *Gender Politics in Global Governance* (Rowman and Littlefield Publishers, Lanham Maryland, 1999).

Quick, John and Garran, Robert Randolph *The Annotated Constitution of the Australian Commonwealth* (Angus & Robertson, Sydney,1901)

Quinlan, Michael "Pre-arbitral' labour legislation in Australia and its implications for the introduction of compulsory arbitration' in Stuart Macintyre and Richard Mitchell (eds) *Foundations of Arbitration: The Origins and Effects of State Compulsory Arbitration 1890–1914* (Oxford University Press, Melbourne, 1989).

Quinn, David 'To Be or Not To Be a Member—Is That the Only Question? Freedom of Association under the *Workplace Relations Act*' (2004) 17 *Australian Journal of Labour Law* 1.

Radday, Frances 'The Decline of Union Power—Structural Inevitability or Policy Choices?' in Joanne Conaghan, Richard M Fischl and Karl Klare (eds) *Labour Law in an Era of Globalization: Transformative Practices and Possibilities* (Oxford University Press, Oxford and New York, 2002).

Raggi, Reena 'An Independent Right to Freedom of Association' (1997) 12 *Harvard Civil Rights-Civil Liberties Law Review* 1.

Raynauld, Andre and Vidal, Jean-Pierre *Labour Standards and International Competitiveness: A Comparative Analysis of Developing and Industrialised Countries* (Edward Elgar Publishers, Northampton Mass, 1998).

Reich, Charles 'The New Property' (1964) 73 *Yale Law Journal* 733.

Reith, The Hon Peter, Ministerial Discussion Paper *Getting the Outsiders Inside—Towards a Rational Workplace Relations System in Australia* (24 March 1999). Available at <www.simplerwrsystem.gov. au/discussion/outsidersinside.htm>.

Report of the Senate Standing Committee on Legal and Constitutional Affairs, *Company Director's Duties* (AGPS, Canberra, November 1989).

Report of the Special Commission of Inquiry into the Medical Research and Compensation Foundation (David F Jackson QC, Special Commissioner, September 2004). Available at <www.cabinet.nsw.gov.au>.

Richardson, Sue 'Who Gets the Minimum Wage? (1998) 40 *Journal of Industrial Relations* 554.

Richardson, Sue and Harding, Ann 'Poor Workers? The Link Between Low Wages, Low Family Income and the Tax and Transfer Systems' in Sue Richardson (ed) *Reshaping the Labour Market: Regulation, Efficiency and Equality in Australia* (Cambridge University Press, Australia, 1999).

Riley, Joellen (with chapters by McCarry, Greg and Smith, Megan) *Workplace Relations: A Guide to the 1996 Changes* (LBC Information Services, Sydney, 1997)

Riley, Joellen 'Contracting for Work/Family Balance' in Jill Murray (ed) *Work, Family and the Law (Special Issue of Law in Context*, vol 23*)* (Federation Press, Sydney, 2005).

Riley, Joellen 'Mutual Trust and Good Faith: Can Private Contract Law Guarantee Fair Dealing in the Workplace?' (2003) 16 *Australian Journal of Labour Law* 28.

Riley, Joellen 'Pensioning off Lord Asquith's Cook' (2005) 18 *Australian Journal of Labour Law* 177.

Riley, Joellen 'Who Owns Human Capital? A Critical Appraisal of Legal Techniques for Capturing the Value of Work' (2005) 18 *Australian Journal of Labour Law* 1.

Riley, Joellen *Employee Protection at Common Law* (Federation Press, Sydney, 2005).

Rittich, Kerry 'Feminization and Contingency: Regulating the Stakes of Work for Women' in Joanne Conaghan, Richard M Fischl, and Karl Klare (eds) *Labour Law in an Era of Globalization: Transformative Practices and Possibilities* (Oxford University Press, Oxford and New York, 2002).

Rittich, Kerry 'Rights, Risk, and Reward: Governance Norms in the International Order and the Problem of Precarious Work' in Judy Fudge and Rosemary Owens (eds) *Precarious Work, Women, and the New Economy: The Challenge to Legal Norms* (Hart Publishing, Oxford and Portland Oregon, 2006).

Rittich, Kerry *Recharacterizing Restructuring: Law, Distribution and Gender in Market Reform* (Kluwer International, The Hague, 2002).

Robertson, Andrew 'Satisfying the Minimum Equity: Equitable Estoppel Remedies after *Verwayen*' (1996) 20 *Melbourne University Law Review* 85.

Robinson, Mary *Business and Human Rights: A Progress Report* (2000) available at <www.unhcr.ch/business.html>.

Rolph, David 'No Worries? Employers' Duty of Care for Negligently Inflicted Stress' (2005) 18 *Australian Journal Labour Law* 344.

Ronalds, Chris and Pepper, Rachel *Discrimination Law and Practice* (Federation Press, Sydney, 2004).

Rothnie, Warwick A 'Restoring the Frontiers of an Unruly Province: Intergovernmental Immunities and Industrial Disputes' (1985) 11 *Monash University Law Review* 120.

Rubin, Paul 'The Theory of the Firm and the Structure of the Franchise Contract' (1978) 21 *Journal of Law and Economics* 223.

Ryan, Edna and Conlan, Anne *Gentle Invaders: Australian Women at Work 1788–1974* (Penguin Books Australia Ltd, Victoria, 1989).

Ryan, Edna *Two Thirds of a Man: Women and Arbitration in New South Wales 1902–08* (Hale and Ironmonger, Sydney, 1984).

Sales, Philip 'Covenants restricting recruitment of employees and the doctrine of the restraint of trade' (1988) 104 *Law Quarterly Review* 600.

Salzman, James 'Labour Rights, Globalisation and Institutions: The Roles and Influence of the Organization for Economic Cooperation and Development' (2000) 21 *Michigan Journal of International Law* 769.

Schwab, Stewart 'Life-cycle Justice: Accommodating Just Cause and Employment at Will' (1993) 92 *Michigan Law Review* 8.

Sebbens, Trent D "Wake, O Wake'—Transmission of Business Provisions in Outsourcing and Privatisation' (2003) *Australian Journal Of Labour Law* 133.

Selmi, Michael and McUsic, Molly S 'Difference and Solidarity: Unions in a Post-Modern Age' in Joanne Conaghan, Richard M Fischl and Karl Klare (eds) *Labour Law in an Era of Globalization: Transformative Practices and Possibilities* (Oxford University Press, Oxford and New York, 2002).

Senate Economic Reference Committee's *Report on the Consideration of the Workplace Relations and Other Legislation Amendment Bill 1996*, August 1996. Available at <www.aph.gov.au/senate/committee/economics_ctte/completed_inquiries/1996-99/workplace/report/index.htm>.

Sennett, Richard *The Corrosion of Character: The Personal Consequences of Work in the New Capitalism* (WW Norton and Company, New York, 1998).

Servais, Jean-Michel *International Labour Law* (Kluwer Law International, The Hague, 2005).

Shaw, Jeff 'A Balanced Industrial Relations Reform Package for New South Wales' (1996) 38 *Journal of Industrial Relations* 57.

Shearing, Clifford 'A Constitutive Conception of Regulation' in Peter Grabosky and John Braithwaite (eds) *Business Regulation and Australia's Future* (Australian Institute of Criminology, Canberra, 1993).

Shklar, Judith *American Citizenship: The Quest for Inclusion* (Harvard University Press, Cambridge MA, 1991).

Short, Mark, Preston, Alison and Peetz, David *The Spread and Impact of Workplace Bargaining: Evidence from the Workplace Bargaining Research Project* (Department of Industrial Relations, AGPS, Canberra, 1993).

Simpson, Brian 'The National Minimum Wage Five Years On: Reflections on Some General Issues' (2004) 33 *Industrial Law Journal* 22.

Skulley M 'Low-paid May Get Less, Says Fair Pay Chief' *Australian Financial Review* 17 February 2006, 3.

Slessor, Kenneth *Selected Poems* (Angus & Robertson, London, 1977).

Smith, Belinda 'A Regulatory Analysis of the *Sex Discrimination Act 1984* (Cth): Can It Effect Equality or only Redress Harm?' in Arup, Chris, Gahan, Peter, Howe, John, Johnstone, Richard, Mitchell Richard and O'Donnell, Anthony (eds) *Labour Law and Labour Market Regulation* (Federation Press, Sydney, 2006).

Smith, Belinda and Riley, Joellen 'Family-friendly Work Practices and The Law' (2004) 26 *Sydney Law Review* 395.

Smith, Meg and Ewer, Peter *Choice and Coercion: Women's Experience of Casual Employment* (Evatt Foundation, University of NSW, 1999).

Spence, Michael *Protecting Reliance* (Hart Publishing, Oxford, 1999).

Spencer, David and Altobelli, Tom *Dispute Resolution in Australia: Cases, Commentary and Materials* (Lawbook Co, Sydney, 2005).

Standing Committee on Family and Human Services, Parliament of Australia, *Inquiry into Balancing Work and Family* (Current Inquiry, 2005–6).

Stanworth, Celia 'Working at Home—A Study of Homeworking and Teleworking' (Institute of Employment Rights, London, 1996).

Starke, JG 'The High Court of Australia and the Rule in *Walker v Baird* [1892] AC 491' (1974) 48 *Australian Law Journal* 368.

Steiner, Henry J and Alston, Philip *International Human Rights in Context*, 2nd ed (Oxford University Press, Oxford and New York, 2000).

Steinfeld, Robert *The Invention of Free Labor: The Employment Relation in English and American Law and Culture* (University of North Carolina Press, Chapel Hill, 1991).

Steinwall, Ray *Annotated Trade Practices Act* 1974 (LexisNexis Butterworths, Chatswood NSW, 2005).

Stevens, Greg *Report of the Review of the South Australian Industrial Relations System* (Workplace Services, Adelaide, November 2002).

Stewart, Andrew '"Atypical" Employment and the Failure of Labour Law' (1992) *Australian Bulletin of Labour* 217.

Stewart, Andrew 'Civil Liability for Industrial Action: Updating the Economic Torts' (1984) 9 *Adelaide Law Review* 359.

Stewart, Andrew 'Federal Jurisdiction over Industrial Management Matters: the Demise of Managerial Prerogative' (1988) 1 *Australian Journal of Labour Law* 70.

Stewart, Andrew 'Federal Labour Laws and New Uses for the Corporations Power' (2001) 14 *Australian Journal of Labour Law* 145.

Stewart, Andrew 'Redefining Employment? Meeting the Challenge of Contract and Agency Labour' in (2002) 15 *Australian Journal of Labour Law* 235.

Stewart, Andrew 'The AIRC's Evolving Role in Policing Bargaining' (2004) 17 *Australian Journal of Labour Law* 245.

Stewart, Andrew 'The Federated Clerks Case: Managerial Prerogative in Retreat?' (1985) 59 *Australian Law Journal* 717.

Stewart, Ian 'Good Faith in Contractual Performance and in Negotiation' (1998) 72 *Australian Law Journal* 370.

Stone, Katherine *From Widgets to Digits, Employment Regulation for the Changing Workplace* (Cambridge University Press, Cambridge, 2004).

Supiot, Alain *Beyond Employment: Changes in Work and the Future of Labour Law in Europe* (Oxford University Press, Oxford, 2001).

Supiot, Alain *Work, Law and Social Linkages* (International Institute for Labour Studies, Geneva, November 1999).

Sutherland, Carolyn 'By Invitation Only: The Role of the AIRC in Private Arbitration' (2005) 18 *Australian Journal of Labour Law* 53.

Sutherland, Carolyn 'Dispute Resolution in the Changing Workplace—A Delegated Responsibility?' (Paper presented at Australian Labour Law Association Second National Conference, University of Sydney, 25 September 2004).

Swepston, Lee 'Human Rights Law and Freedom of Association: Development through ILO Supervision' (1998) 137 *International Labour Review* 169.

Swepston, Lee 'Supervision of ILO Standards' (1997) 13 *International Journal of Comparative Labour Law and Industrial Relations* 327.

Sykes, Edward I and Glasbeek, Harry J *Labour Law in Australia* (Butterworths, Sydney, 1972);

Tarrant, Stella 'Reasonableness in the Sex Discrimination Act: No Package Deals' (2000) 19 *University of Tasmania Law Review* 38.

Taylor, Alexis M 'The UN and the Global Compact' (2001) 17 *New York Law School Journal of Human Rights* 975.

Terry, Andrew 'Business Format Franchising: the Cloning of Australian Business' in Franchisors Association of Australia *Business Format Franchising in Australia* (Legal Books, Sydney, 1991).

Textile Clothing and Footwear Union of Australia *The Hidden Cost of Fashion* (TCFUA, Sydney, 1995).

Thornton, Margaret 'Discrimination Law/Industrial Law: Are They Compatible?' (1987) 59 *Australian Quarterly* 162.

Thornton, Margaret 'Sexual Harassment Losing Sight of Sex Discrimination' (2002) 56 *Melbourne University Law Review* 422.

Thornton, Margaret *The Liberal Promise: Anti-Discrimination Legislation in Australia* (Oxford University Press, Melbourne, 1990).

TI Emerson 'Freedom of Association and Freedom of Expression' (1964) 74 *Yale LJ* 1.

Trebilcock, Michael *The Limits of Freedom of Contract* (Harvard University Press, Cambridge MA, 1993).

Tully, Kate *Women and Enterprise Bargaining: Who Benefits?* (National Women's Consultative Council, AGPS, Canberra December 1992).

Twining, William *Globalisation and Legal Theory* (Butterworths, London, 2000).

United Nations Development Program *Human Development Report 1999* (Oxford University Press, New York, 1999).

Valticos, Nicolas 'International Labour Standards and Human Rights: Approaching the Year 2000' (1998) 137 *International Labour Review* 135.

van Wezel Stone, Katherine 'Knowledge at Work: Disputes over the ownership of Human Capital in the Changing Workplace' (2002) 34 *Connecticut Law Review* 721.

van Wezel Stone, Katherine 'Labour and Corporate Structure: Changing Conceptions and Emerging Possibilities' (1988) 55 *University of Chicago Law Review* 73.

van Wezel Stone, Katherine 'Labour and the Global Economy: Four Approaches to Transnational Labour Regulation' (1995) 16 *Michigan Journal of International Law* 987.

van Wezel Stone, Katherine 'The New Psychological Contract: Implications for the Changing Workplace for Labor and Employment Law' (2001) 48 *UCLA Law Review* 519.

Victorian Industrial Relations Taskforce *Independent Report of the Victorian Industrial Relations Taskforce* (Victorian Industrial Relations Taskforce, Melbourne, 2000).

von Doussa, The Honourable John and Lenehan, Craig 'Barbequed or Burned? Flexibility in Work Arrangements and the Sex Discrimination Act' (2004) 27 *University of New South Wales Law Journal* 892.

von Potobsky, G 'Protection of Trade Union Rights: Twenty Years Work by the Committee on Freedom of Association' (1972) 105 *International Labour Review* 69.

Vosko, Leah F 'Decent Work: The Shifting Role of the ILO and the Struggle for Global Social Justice' (2002) *Global Social Policy* 19.

Vosko, Leah F 'Gender, Precarious Work, and the International Labour Code: The Ghost in the ILO Closet' in Judy Fudge and Rosemary Owens (eds) *Precarious Work, Women and the New Economy: The Challenge to Legal Norms* (Hart Publishing, Oxford and Portland Oregon, 2006).

Vosko, Leah F 'Legitimising the Triangular Employment Relationship: Emerging International Labour Standards from a Comparative Perspective' (1997) 19 *Comparative Labour Law Journal* 43.

Vosko, Leah F *Temporary Work: The Gendered Rise of the Precarious Employment Relationship* (University of Toronto Press, Toronto, 2000).

Vranken, Martin 'Demise of the Australian Model of Labour Law in the 1990s' (1994) 16 *Comparative Labour Law Journal* 1.

Vranken, Martin 'Labour Law as an Academic Discipline: Can there be a Future?' (2003) 16 *Australian Journal of Labour Law* 381.

Waite, Matthew and Will, Lou *Self-Employed Contractors in Australia: Incidence and Characteristics* (Productivity Commission Staff Research Paper, AusInfo, Canberra, 2001).

Waring, Marilyn *Counting for Nothing: What Men Value & What Women Are Worth* (Allen & Unwin Port Nicholson Press, Wellington New Zealand, 1988).

Watson, Ian, Buchanan, John, Campbell, Iain and Briggs, Chris *Fragmented Futures: New Challenges in Working Life* (The Federation Press, Sydney, 2003).

Wedderburn, Lord 'Freedom of Association and Philosophies of Labour Law' (1989) 18 *ILJ* 1.

Wedderburn, Lord 'Freedom of Association or Right to Organise?' (1987) *Industrial Relations Journal* 244.

Wedderburn, Lord K *The Worker and the Law*, 3rd ed (Penguin, Harmondsworth, Middlesex, 1986).

Weeks, Phillipa *Trade Union Security Law* (Federation Press, Leichhardt, 1995).

Weeks, Phillipa *Trade Union Security Law: A Study of Preference and Compulsory Unionism* (Federation Press, Sydney, 1995).

Whelan, Commissioner Dominica *The Gender Pay Gap: Assessing Possible Futures in the Post-Inquiries Age* (a paper presented at the Gender Pay Gap Conference, Perth, April 2005).

Whitehouse, Gillian 'Industrial Agreements and Work/Family Provisions: Trends and Prospects under 'Enterprise Bargaining'' (2001) 12 *Labour and Industry* 109.

Whitehouse, Gillian 'Justice and Equity: Women and Indigenous Workers' in Isaac, Joe and Macintyre, Stuart (eds) *The New Province of Law and Order: 100 Years of Australian Industrial Conciliation and Arbitration* (Cambridge University Press, Australia, 2004).

Whitehouse, Gillian and Frino, Betty 'Women, Wages and Industrial Agreements' (2003) 6 *Australian Journal of Labour Economics* 579.

Williams, George 'The First Step to a National Industrial Relations Regime? Workplace Relations Amendment (Termination of Employment) Bill 2002' (2003) 16 *Australian Journal of Labour Law* 94.

Williams, George 'The Return of State Awards—Section 109 of the *Constitution and the Workplace Relations Act 1996* (Cth)' (1997) 10 *Australian Journal of Labour Law* 170.

Williams, George *Labour Law and the Constitution* (Federation Press, Sydney, 1998).

Williams, Lucy 'Beyond Labour Law's Parochialism: A Revisioning of the Discourse of Redistribution' in Joanne Conaghan, Richard M Fischl, and Karl Klare (eds) *Labour Law in an Era of Globalization: Transformative Practices and Possibilities* (Oxford University Press, Oxford and New York, 2002).

World Bank *Globalization, Growth and Poverty: Building an Inclusive World Economy* (Oxford University Press and World Bank, New York and Washington, 2002).

World Bank *World Development Report 1997: The State in a Changing World* (World Bank, Washington DC, 1997).

World Bank *World Development Report 2000/2001: Attacking Poverty* (Oxford University Press, Oxford and New York, 2000).

World Commission on the Social Dimension of Globalization *A Fair Globalization: Creating Opportunities for All* (International Labour Office, Geneva, 2004).

Zeitz, Susan J 'The Industrial Relations Taskforce Report: A Phoenix from the Ashes' (2000) 13 *Australian Journal of Labour Law* 308.

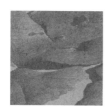

Index